# Praise for *Ours to Master a*

"Labor historians and activists will find this book always provoc.                              , _____
. . . any subsequent work on workers' control will need to take it into an account. Highly recommended."

—**Andrej Grubacic**, coauthor of *Wobblies and Zapatistas: Conversations on Anarchism, Marxism, and Radical History*

*"Ours to Master and to Own* will definitely be used in the struggle against bureaucratic and capitalist domination. We now have a text workers can understand and actually use in organizing for justice!"

—**Gerardo Dominguez**, coordinator, Mexican American Workers Association (AMAT)

"The contributors have recovered the lost . . . histories of workers' practices of participatory democracy through workers' councils in different parts of the world. They have brought alive the histories of workers' control over the network of their organizations and theoretical debates about political practices in workers' self-management."

—**Professor Rana P. Behal**, coauthor of *India's Labouring Poor: Historical Studies, c. 1600–c. 2000*

"Ness and Azzellini have done splendid work by collating a wide spectrum of historical evidence on the economic viability, political feasibility, and social acceptability of workers' cooperatives and councils. The contemporary development discourse should certainly include this paradigm in the agenda of both teaching and action-programme."

—**Debdas Banerjee**, Head of Centre for Development Studies, Central University of Bihar

"As desperation for alternatives to the neoliberal creed takes over . . . this historically grounded book on workers' movements and struggles from all corners of the world shows us that socioeconomic change is possible. "

—**Alex Julca**, editorial board, *Encyclopedia of Global Human Migration*

"Here is a remarkable tapestry of workers' struggles presented by an international array of activist-scholars. Anyone wanting to learn from the efforts of working-class brothers and sisters preceding us should make use of this inspiring and fact-filled volume."

—**Paul Le Blanc**, author of *Work and Struggle: Voices from U.S. Labor Radicalism*

"This book is very enlightening and comes at the right time. It shows us that the working class can liberate itself by its own efforts."

—**Coen Husain Pontoh**, former political prisoner in Indonesia, author, *The Catastrophe of Market Democracy*

"This book is indispensable. Against the philistines, it analyzes the revolutionary centrality of the past and present global experiences of workers' autonomous organization. For contemporary militants and activists, this book is a great resource to organize the new soviets of transnational living labor."

—**Gigi Roggero**, author of *The Production of Living Knowledge*

"A much-needed and timely book. *Ours to Master and to Own* is both historical account and theoretical reflection on experiments with workers' councils over the last hundred years."

—**Ben Trott**, global movements editor, *International Encyclopedia of Revolution and Protest*

"*Ours to Master and to Own* is a book filled with possibility and inspiration, grounded in concrete experiences of workers from around the world. . . . It is a powerful tool for transforming our world, and creating one based in self-determination and dignity."

—Marina Sitrin, author of *Horizontalism: Voices of Popular Power in Argentina*

"Long overdue, this book is the first comprehensive worldwide compilation of the struggle of workers to gain control of their work environments. It is a must-read for all who are interested in the past and future of working-class struggles and insurgencies."

—Michael Goldfield, coauthor of *Labour, Globalization, and the State*

"*Ours to Master and to Own* assembles a dazzling array of histories that document the attempts of workers to transform capitalist alienation and authoritarian control into democratic practices. The histories assembled here demonstrate that workers' councils have long been recognized as authentic expressions of the radical and democratic impulses of the working classes in all of their variety."

—Roderick Bush, author of *The End of White Supremacy: Black Internationalism and the Problem of the Color Line*

"Workers' control and direct participation in production have often been considered as key to social change and pillars of a more equally, truly democratic society. . . . This book is unique in the attempt to rehabilitate, through a blend of theoretical, historical, and contemporary accounts of workers' control, the political relevance of workers' power in building alternatives. With examples from diverse geographical, political, and economic contexts and critically informed, the book . . . is a must-read."

—Maurizio Atzeni, lecturer in Labor and Industrial Relations, Loughborough University

"Workers' councils have long beckoned as a democratic alternative to the rule of profit-driven corporations. This book brings together an extraordinary collection of case studies by leading authorities. Unprecedented in the sheer sweep of its coverage, this volume will engage and enlighten every reader from the seeker to the skeptic."

—James Gray Pope, Professor of Law, Rutgers University

"Anyone who has been involved in a plant-closing fight knows the inherent difficulties, most would say implausibility, even organized workers face trying to prevent the destruction of our jobs by corporate executives. . . . *Ours to Master and to Own* provides an important historical perspective on what workers have accomplished around the world to enable us to not only prevent further industrial bleeding but provide workers the tools and vision necessary to finally gain some control over the means of our production and provide sustainable (both environmentally and economically) meaningful jobs for our communities."

—Peter Knowlton, UE Northeast region president

"In an era of global capital's hegemonic pursuit of workplace control at all levels, the exploration of strategies and experiences that point to the potential of anticapitalist worker control and the need for new models, is essential. Important examples and threads of activism can be found in this book. Put it on your shelf! Make it a gift for colleagues in the struggle for global justice."

—Jerry Tucker, former UAW international executive board member and cofounder of the Center for Labor Renewal

# Ours to Master and to Own

### Workers' Control
### from the Commune to the Present

Immanuel Ness and Dario Azzellini
Editors

Haymarket Books
Chicago, Illinois

First published in 2011 by
Haymarket Books
P.O. Box 180165
Chicago, IL 60618
773-583-7884
info@haymarketbooks.org
www.haymarketbooks.org

Trade distribution:
In the US, Consortium Book Sales and Distribution, www.cbsd.com
In Canada, Publishers Group Canada, www.pgcbooks.ca
In the UK, Turnaround Publisher Services, www.turnaround-uk.com
In Australia, Palgrave Macmillan, www.palgravemacmillan.com.au
All other countries, Publishers Group Worldwide, www.pgw.com

ISBN 978-1-60846-119-6

Cover design by Josh On.

Special discounts are available for bulk purchases by organizations and institutions.
Please contact Haymarket Books for more information at 773-583-7884 or
info@haymarketbooks.org.

This book was published with the generous support of Lannan Foundation and
the Wallace Global Fund.

Library of Congress CIP data is available.

# Contents

*All the world that's owned by idle drones is ours and ours alone.*
*We have laid the wide foundations; built it skyward stone by stone.*
*It is ours, not to slave in, but to master and to own.*
*While the union makes us strong.*

—From "Solidarity Forever"

# Acknowledgments

This project springs from the reemergence throughout the world of theoretical and empirical curiosity about the transformative power of insurgent workers, direct action, workers' factory occupations, and the formation of workers' councils. The democratic struggles of workers are irreducible and ecumenical, but are now giving rise to an optimism that had largely been lost under a system of regulated capitalism and state domination. This volume represents the collective effort of a community of scholars who are documenting the increasing instances of workers' control in the contemporary epoch and who recognize the unbroken challenges by differentiated working classes to repression in workplaces and communities. This project is a tribute to this new revival of working-class militancy out of the institutional framework.

We thank first and foremost all those who have contributed to this work as a form of solidarity through writing, translating, and suggesting contributors. And we thank a long list of scholars and organizations who have inspired our thinking and identified this critical field of research, and who are sponsoring and conducting research on labor insurgency and workers' self-activity and direct action.

We are grateful to the many scholars, activists, and students who have helped inform and shape our knowledge and insight: Maurizio Atzeni, Au Loong Yu, Debdas Banerjee, Padmini Biswas, Joshua Board, Peter Bratsis, Sebastian Budgen, Verity Burgmann, Pedro Cazes Camarero, Carol Delgado, Ligia Consuelo Duerto, Ethan Earle, Steve Early, Bill Fletcher Jr., Ruthie Gilmore, Harris Freeman, Bernd Gehrke, Camila Piñeiro Harnecker, David Harvey, Shawn Hattingh, Rowan Jímenez, Alex Julca, Boris Kanzleiter, Tamas Krausz, Carlos Lanz, Michael Lebowitz, Staughton Lynd, Stacy Warner Maddern, Julian Massaldi, Jamie McCallum, Ichiyo

Muto, Premilla Nadasen, Andrew Newman, Silvina Pastucci, Stalin Pérez, Frances Fox Piven, Coen Hussein Pontoh, James Gray Pope, Luis Primo, Peter Ranis, Adriana Rivas, Alcides Rivero, Gigi Roggero, Pierre Rousset, Diego Rozengardt, Sari Safitri, Vittorio Sergi, Guillermina Seri, Jeff Shantz, Gregg Shotwell, Heather Squire, Russell Smith, Lars Stubbe, Hirohiko Takasu, Jerry Tucker, Lucien van der Walt, and Young-su Won. We especially thank all the workers who engaged in sit-down strikes and workers' control and agreed to be interviewed for this project.

We have benefited from financial support to fund research and translations from the following organizations and institutions: Stiftung Menschenwürde und Arbeitswelt (Berlin), Aktion Selbstbesteuerung e.V. (Stuttgart), Solifonds of the Hans Böckler Foundation (Düsseldorf), Rosa Luxemburg Foundation (Berlin), and the Professional Staff Congress and Research Foundation of the City University of New York. We thank also Loughborough University, which hosted and provided the funding to convene the Workers and Researchers Forum on Self-Management and Alternative Forms of Work Organisations in October 2009, and the Center for Place, Culture and Politics of the City University of New York. We would like to thank the Graduate Center for Worker Education, Brooklyn College/City University of New York, which provided logistical support. We are especially grateful to Caroline Luft, who has masterfully copyedited the manuscript and provided perceptive comments and suggestions, and to Leonard Rosenbaum, who compiled the very thorough index. We are thankful for the support of Anthony Arnove, Julie Fain, and the editorial collective of Haymarket Books, who recognized the fundamental significance of this book and resolutely understood that conveying the history of workers' control would require the inclusion of a diversity of scholars and activists from throughout the world.

Immanuel Ness, New York
Dario Azzellini, Caracas
January 2, 2011

# Introduction

## Immanuel Ness and Dario Azzellini

In the past one hundred years, workers have occupied factories and other workplaces and formed workers' councils and self-managed enterprises in almost all regions of the world. Under all forms of government and political rule, workers have struggled for participation in the decision-making processes of the enterprises they work for and have attempted to develop forms of co- and self-management, or workers' control; they have founded cooperatives and councils as a genuine expression and manifestation of their historical and material interests. Even without knowledge of previous council experiences, collective administration through workers' assemblies has emerged in many cases as a natural tendency of rank-and-file workers. What is clear from the work of classical and contemporary advocates is the emancipatory nature of workers' control in transforming a situation of capitalist alienation and authoritarian control into one of democratic practice. In his analysis of the Paris Commune, Marx emphasized in *The Civil War in France* that the commune "was essentially a working class government, the product of the struggle of the producing against the appropriating class, the political form at last discovered under which to work out the economical emancipation of labor."

The chapters of this book document experiences of workers' control and uncover the practices and intentions of historical and contemporary workers' movements that have been largely obscured until now. Trade unions established in the early to mid-twentieth century, operating through the institutional frameworks of governments, have held a monopoly over labor history. They had no interest in promoting workers' autonomous struggles, since the mere existence of those struggles called into question the traditional union structures and roles. In addition, most left, Socialist, and Communist parties did not promote workers' control either, since it challenged the centrality of

1

the role of the parties. Lost to historic and contemporary accounts are the creative and constructive practices undertaken by workers to bring permanence and predictability to their workplaces and to stabilize their communities through expressions of participatory democracy on the job and within society. As well as illuminating such empowering moments in labor history, we seek to reveal the important workers' struggles against forms of autocratic and inequitable command and control by capital, business, and traditional labor unions as well as by party or state bureaucracy.

Over the last century, instances of workers' control have often enlivened activists' imaginations and raised new possibilities for the democratic organization of workplaces and of communities, and for genuine innovation within unions. Rank-and-file workers' and labor networks organizing outside of established business-union structures have been crucial to the emergence of workers' control; in some cases the established mediatory mechanisms were simply displaced by workers' spontaneous, autonomous actions. This book critically examines the possibilities and problems inherent in the attempts to build workers' councils and other structures of self-management.

Almost all the historical experiences of workers' control, in particular the workers' councils, have inevitably clashed with political parties, labor unions, and state bureaucracies—from the Bolshevik Revolution to Italy in the 1970s, Poland in the 1980s, India in the 1990s, and contemporary Argentina. The dominant revolutionary left typically viewed workers' control as part of a system of dual power necessary during a transition to socialism, while contesting the power of the bourgeoisie and the capitalist-dominated state. Workers' councils were seen as an interim structure relevant only until "real power" was achieved, usually denoted by the consolidation of a revolutionary party or "revolutionary state." However, a minority current—traced from Marx's writings on the Paris Commune through council communism, Trotskyism, anarcho-syndicalism, Italian *operaismo,* and other "heretical" left currents—has always viewed workers' control and councils as the base of a self-determined socialist society.

## Historical and Geographic Arenas of Workers' Control

Workers' councils have been commonly portrayed as paralyzed by widespread difficulties and filled with acute institutional problems. But they have also confronted authentic challenges in organizing a democratic workplace. In many cases, these predicaments have been imposed by state and party officials; in others, workers have had to overcome significant hurdles in governing enterprises on their own when seeking to operate within the dominant culture of capitalist society. Unavoidable interactions with sectors of capitalist society and the potential for worker-controlled production to interact on a capitalist playing field have also resulted in complications and contradictions for workers' councils.

In the multiplicity of experiences over the past century, we can observe how workers' control usually emerges from a situation of capitalist crisis—be it political, economic, or both. This temporal and material setting of workers' control within the context of crisis contributes to several challenges, one in particular being obsolete production methods and manufacture of unnecessary products, especially in recent times and in situations without a direct revolutionary overthrow of a capitalist regime. Often, distribution markets have become so eroded that the capitalist entrepreneurs do not even wish to continue operating the firms slated for closure—even if they also oppose the firms' being controlled by workers. The problem of obsolescence of technology and market failure is a particular predicament in contemporary Latin America and increasingly in the global North as well. Even in times of capitalist crisis, among the primary difficulties arising in the supposed transition of an enterprise to workers' control is the paradox that worker-run industries must compete in the capitalist marketplace against domestic and foreign enterprises. Operating outside the logic of capitalism in a market system, the establishment of democratic working conditions and adequate wages and benefits is exceptionally difficult or nearly impossible.

This collection brings together leading historians and social scientists who have studied workers' control, factory occupation, and worker-led socialist transformation. From the origins of the Industrial Revolution to the present neoliberal capitalist era, workers' councils have been recognized as a tangible means for both expressing the radical and democratic impulses of the working class and grasping control from the ruling class through labor organizing based on solidarity and direct insurgency.

We have organized this collection in the interest of advancing academic knowledge of the history of workers' self-management by presenting chapters accessible to, and in some cases informed by, workers, labor organizers, and activists. The contributions are free of jargon and rooted in historical experience. Through its publication in translation this volume aims to accomplish the dual goals of promoting an understanding and appreciation of the historic significance and necessity of workers' councils among scholars as well as among workers throughout the world. In addition, with the help of some of the contributors and others, we have established the multilingual website www.workerscontrol.net to create a central reference and archive for inquiry and discussion around workers' control; we hope it will help spur debate and energize new efforts.

The last collection to bring together different experiences of workers' control dates back to 1971, with Ernest Mandel's publication in German of *Arbeiterkontrolle, Arbeiterräte, Arbeiterselbstverwaltung* (Worker Control,

Worker Councils, and Worker Self-Management). The legacy of workers' control is all the more relevant today during a period of global economic crisis. We were impelled to assemble a wide range of international examples to demonstrate that not only are workers' control and socialist democracy possible, as the chapters in this book suggest, but they also serve as a remedy to the human misery produced by the rapacious capitalist pursuit of profits and productivity through exploiting the working class and the poor.

This collection of historically relevant essays would be equally of use for a student in Johannesburg, Manila, or Sydney as for workers taking over or reclaiming factories in Caracas, Chicago, Glasgow, or Warsaw. These essays tell a story of the range of models and experiences of workers' control in factories and other enterprises, and illustrate the multifarious struggles that workers have endured to achieve their goals under capitalist and noncapitalist systems.

The case studies span the globe and provide international, cultural, national, and regional examinations of relevant experiences of workers' control, from the global South as well as the global North, including Russia, Germany, Italy, Spain, the United States, Great Britain, Indonesia, Poland, Portugal, India, Algeria, Canada, Argentina, Brazil, and Venezuela. Some chapters contribute a theoretical and philosophical consideration. Part I of the book provides a historical overview of workers' control and some theoretical debate on the subject. Part II focuses on experiences of workers' councils and self-administration during times of revolution in the early twentieth century. Part III offers examples of workers' control under state socialism, and Part IV shows some lesser-known examples of workers' control in anticolonial struggles and democratic revolutions. Part V presents examples of the wave of workers' takeovers against capitalist restructuring from the late 1960s to the 1980s. Part VI examines workers' control in the contemporary era.

We deliberately organized this book as a collection, drawing from a range of historical epochs, though it is by no means comprehensive. Quite a few well-known and lesser-known examples are missing, such as Hungary (1919 and 1956), China (1920s), Japan (post-WWII), Bolivia (1950s), Czechoslovakia (1968), France and Switzerland (1968–1974), Chile (under Allende), the Argentinean Cordobazo (1969), Brazil (late 1960s–1970s), and many more. This volume is the first of two book projects on the transformation to worker self-government. We believe interest is so great among workers that we have initiated a second volume covering the experiences of workers' control in a range of geographic and historical contexts.

## In Opposition to Capital, State, and Bureaucracy

We set out to distinguish clearly between workers' councils directly challenging capitalist hegemony and workers' cooperatives operating within the capitalist logic of productivity and profitability. In various cases examined in this book, especially during more recent times, workers' direct action has triggered factory occupations that have been transformed into workers' co-operatives, due to the legal structures permissible in a capitalist society. Workers continuously press for more democracy and economic and political emancipation, but the hegemonic apparatus of national and transnational capital circumscribes how far workers may go.

Although workers represent the fundamental unit of democratic control, do they have a greater right to decide on the production process than the consumers or other members of the community? Is it not a potential contradiction to assume the workers' preeminence over other constituents in society? How do workers conduct themselves as owners over the means of production in a different manner than capitalists? As enterprise owners, workers have frequently adopted a capitalist logic or turned over decisions entirely to business managers. Operating within the sphere of capitalism is a dilemma that many workers' cooperatives face. As a consequence, over the last several decades, new proposals to build an authentic democratic society have encouraged workers' control over production, with the significant inclusion and integration of subaltern sectors of society over vital decision-making processes.

New arenas for debate are emerging among socialists considering the transformative significance of workers' self-management. For instance, workers must debate not only issues of control and ownership but questions such as what to produce and how to produce for social rather than private gain. What, for example, about workers who commandeer a French factory that produces land mines or a Brazilian pesticide plant that emits toxins harmful to the community? A less obvious and more controversial area under discussion is the future of automobile production for private individual transport, which seems to have run its course and faces a temporally constrained future due to energy and ecological concerns.

Factory occupations and subsequent workers' control occurring in industries contributing to the erosion of the environment (e.g., automotive and machine parts, chemicals, electronics, energy, food commodities, furniture, livestock, and military ammunition and weapons) must address how these goods advance or detract from community needs, how they affect environmental sustainability, and that they frequently create inequality and poverty. A fundamental conundrum facing workers who seize control over enterprises is how to convert industries that produce surplus value but do not contribute to advancing health and security for surrounding communities and society as a whole.

Moreover, seizing control over enterprises does not end all problems. Self-management necessitates a struggle over how to organize the work process to improve the lives of workers and society. As the chapters in this volume will demonstrate, workers in a range of industries have frequently protested arduous, unsafe, and unhealthy working conditions, typically without the support of established trade unions. Workers' control over factories and enterprises requires ensuring the development of safe, socially beneficial environments. Workers must gain control over enterprises and democratically organize the production process within a supportive society. The designation "workers' control" is not applicable if the social division of labor and hierarchies on the job are not disposed of and replaced by direct democracy in the workplace. But more often than not, even if states articulate support for workers' control, they tend to oppose democracy as a threat to bureaucratic leadership and defer to managers who seek productivity and sometimes profitability.

Workers' councils—workers' control over the economic resources vital to their lives—have a prodigious history as one of the most dramatic forms of radical working-class action against business and corporate domination. Despite the fact that they have historically failed to maintain a lasting presence, the lessons of the past inform contemporary efforts as to the potential impediments and obstacles to building a workers' democracy.

## Direct Action and Workers' Control: Constraints and Future Prospects

The theoretical foundation of workers' control is rooted in late nineteenth-century and early twentieth-century socialism, which viewed workers themselves as the most democratic force in society. The emergence of workers' councils in Europe during the late nineteenth and early twentieth centuries coincided with a period of widespread optimism among workers and socialists, who considered these new forms as indicators of a teleological process of the collapse of capitalism and its replacement with an egalitarian society. As the chapters in this book make clear, the workers' insurgencies reinforced the view that workers' appropriation of the means of production was the emergent stage of class struggle in the eventual creation of a new state of democracy and equality.

In Western Europe, although workers did not seize state power—with the exception of the brief Paris Commune interregnum—workers' councils represented the most important weapon in their arsenal of struggle, one that was fiercely resisted by capitalists and the state. The notable early twentieth-century examples of workers' direct action in Germany, Italy, and Spain could not sweep out the capitalist societies, but did raise the possibility among a multiplicity of socialist observers that the process was inevitable. As documented in this work, the Bolshevik Revolution was stimulated by workers' factory occupations, demonstrating the initial support for the revolution among the majority of Russia's working class. The Bolshevik Revolution was supplanted by Stalinist repression and a bureaucratic-statist system, a degenerative historical process ushered in through foreign interventions and sustained by continuous internal hostility. Undoubtedly, bureaucratic centralization of a professional party played an important role in delegitimizing the socialist state.

What are the dynamics of workers' control in the neoliberal era and how do they diverge from those of the Fordist era? Does the escalating wave of workers' direct action from 2000 to 2010 foreshadow an impending, sustained shift toward labor insurgency and direct action rooted in working-class consciousness? In a context of neoliberal economic crisis, what are the prospects for challenging corporate refusal to recognize workers' self-management? The capacity of capitalism to survive and endure under crisis conditions poses a further obstacle to the construction of workers' councils, which are forced to compete for market share against privately owned enterprises supported by the enduring capitalist state.

Even if the state tolerates workers' councils, the historical accounts of this work illustrate that both capitalist and bureaucratic governments give preference to firms rooted in generating profits. As such, the capitalist focus on productivity always takes precedence over community and societal needs. And, finally, the changes in production and labor in the post-Fordist era—the end of the huge factories bringing together vast numbers of workers and homogenizing the workforce, the fragmentation of production processes, and the popularization of outsourcing and subcontracting—have rendered the classical factory councils unthinkable in many labor scenarios. Nevertheless, overcoming the rifts between the economic, the social, and the political is still a condition for emancipation and for leaving behind the bourgeois and capitalist state. We are confident that workers and communities, as history has shown, will find their answers and develop new forms of collective organizing to face the challenges of the twenty-first century.

Part

# I

# Workers' Councils

Historical Overview
and Theoretical Debate

# 1

# Workers' Control and Revolution

**Victor Wallis**

In the perpetual striving of the left to integrate long-range vision and immediate practice, the idea of workers' control occupies a special place.[1] On the one hand, its generalized application would satisfy one of the main requirements for a stateless society; on the other, the basic units and the specific measures involved are such that it can sometimes be implemented within particular enterprises in an otherwise capitalist framework. From the first of these perspectives, workers' control has always been one of the most radical possible demands, indistinguishable in effect from the communist ideal, while from the second it has been perceived as limited, innocuous, and easily co-optable.

How can a single demand appear at once so easy and so difficult, so harmless and so explosive? The contradiction lies, of course, in the system that has given rise to the demand. Prior to the development of capitalism, the concept of "workers' control of the production process" could not have been a demand; it was a simple fact of life (within the limits allowed by nature). Hence the apparent accessibility of workers' control, which on principle reflects no more than the capacity of all humans to think as well as to do. In these terms, it should not be surprising that workers on occasion take over and run productive enterprises without necessarily having an explicit socialist consciousness or political strategy. The faculties they draw upon for such initiatives are not so much new as they are long-suppressed—for the majority of the population.

1 This is a revised and updated version of an essay that first appeared in the newsletter *Self-Management* 6, no. 1 (Fall 1978). I thank Stephen M. Sachs for his initial encouragement, Dick Parker for providing me with documents on the Venezuelan experience, and George Katsiaficas for his comments during the course of revision.

It is the overcoming of this suppression, as old as capitalism itself, that constitutes the explosive side of workers' control. What workers' control points to is more than just a new way of organizing production; it is also the release of human creative energy on a vast scale. As such it is inherently revolutionary. But at the same time, because of the very weight of what it must overcome, it appears correspondingly remote from day-to-day struggles. As a political rallying point, it has two specific drawbacks. First, its urgency in many situations is not likely to be as great as that of survival demands; second, its full application will remain limited as long as there are economic forces beyond the reach of the workers—whether within a given country or outside it (Dallemagne 1976, 114). Concern with these dimensions is often seen as precluding an emphasis on workers' control and, as a result, the self-management impulse, despite its original naturalness, is consigned to utopia.

Such a dismissal is altogether unjustified. The growing interest in workers' control since the late 1960s cannot be explained merely by its timeless qualities. As in Marx's critique of capitalism, it reflects a definite historical juncture. The countries with extreme physical privation are no longer the only ones in which the system's breakdown is manifest. The advanced capitalist regimes are likewise in question, if not for the first time. A new feature of the post-1960s crisis is precisely a redefinition of the concept of basic needs. The "environment," after all, exists inside as well as outside the workplace, and the old distinction between survival needs (identified with wages) and other demands (self-determination, participation, and control) is becoming increasingly blurred. Linked to this is the fact that the fragmentation of the capitalist work process has reached a limit in the leading industrial sectors and is fast approaching it in clerical and sales operations (Bourdet and Guillerm 1975, ch. 7). As the reaction proceeds, there is no reason for it to stop halfway. Finally, with the rightward evolution of the Chinese leadership (the major international model in the third quarter of the twentieth century), new space has opened on the left to reexamine long-held assumptions about revolutionary organization.

But despite all such arguments for placing workers' control on the agenda, one may well remain skeptical as to its real promise. Consider first the potential significance of isolated self-managed or cooperative enterprises. Their usefulness as models is limited in several ways. They are generally small, and if they grow, they tend to take on traditional capitalistic incentives and administrative practices.[2] They are unlikely to emerge in core industries simply because the terms of a negotiated property transfer would

---

2 The evolution of the Mondragón cooperatives is instructive in this respect. See Huet 1997.

be beyond the financial reach of the workers. A second possibility to consider would be some of the West European reform models. These seem to have stopped short of all but the most token worker input except in the Swedish case. In Sweden, the results are more impressive, extending to major changes in the work process, flexibility in scheduling, and even the beginnings of a collective input into production decisions (Peterson 1977). However, this is still not control; it does not reflect a decisive shift of power.

As a third alternative, we might consider those post-capitalist societies that instituted some form of elective principle at the factory level. As of the late 1970s, the two major cases in point were Yugoslavia and China. But in both countries the measures were limited in their scope[3] and were subsequently offset by decisive reversions to earlier practice: market-oriented in the case of Yugoslavia; bureaucratic in the case of China. More generally, however, the regimes and leaderships of first-epoch socialism tended to view their own political rule as obviating the need for democratic restructuring of the workplace. Cuba, in more recent years, would become the first country with a broad socialist agenda to gradually implement worker-control measures following an initial transfer of class power at the level of the state.

The Cuban Revolution constitutes a kind of historical bridge between, on the one hand, the revolutions and regimes precipitated by imperialist invasions (1914–1945) and led by vanguard parties, and, on the other, the post-1989 wave of grassroots movements—most evident in Latin America—which from the outset accorded new emphasis to mechanisms of popular participation.[4] This latter development heralds a fresh chapter in the global history of workers' control. Until this most recent period, however, workers' participation in management normally fell very far short of control except in very isolated cases—even where considerable social upheaval had intervened. While workers' control thus did not appear impossible, it at least seemed to require unusual conditions for its success.

There is one type of experience, however, that transcends all boundaries: the experience of the revolutionary periods themselves. Workers' control has gone further and deeper during such periods than at any other times, whether pre- or post-revolutionary. Moreover, far from being peculiar to this or that crisis, workers' control initiatives have arisen during all such moments. Clearly, we are dealing with a phenomenon of universal force and appeal, as suggested by two immediate considerations. First is the range of settings in which the initiatives arose. Without setting any comprehensive criteria as to the depth or thrust of the crises, a listing would have to include:

---

3 On China, see Richman 1969, ch. 9; on Yugoslavia, Bourdet and Guillerm 1975, esp. 174.
4 On Cuba's place in this epochal sequence, see Raby 2006, 111–31. The historical basis for Cuba's eventual institutionalization of worker-control structures is discussed in Wallis 1985, 254–57.

Russia 1917–18, Germany 1918–19, Hungary 1919, Italy 1920, Spain 1936–39, Czechoslovakia 1945–47, Hungary and Poland 1956, Algeria 1962–65, China 1966–69, France and Czechoslovakia 1968, Chile 1970–73, and Portugal 1974–75.[5] Second and more decisive is the fact that in no case did the radical initiative die a natural death. Although there may have been natural disadvantages (inexperience, excesses, or abuses), what killed the initiative in every case was not any loss of momentum, but rather the threat or use of armed force.

If we grant, then, that workers' control has displayed a core of viability, it remains for us to ask what all these experiences imply as to its possible institutionalization under stable conditions. Focusing first on the Russian case and then on three cases (Italy, Spain, Chile) more directly pertinent to advanced capitalist democracies, we shall explore such matters as the capacities of the workers, the ripeness of surrounding conditions, and the role of political leadership. We shall then consider possible new configurations suggested by more recent developments in Cuba and Venezuela.

## Proletariat and Dictatorship in Revolutionary Russia

The Russian experience inescapably sets the terms for any comparative discussion. In its combination of hopes and disappointments, it was certainly a prototype. Its uniqueness is that—despite the immensity of the country's peasant population—it was the only revolution to have triumphed on the basis of an industrial working class.[6] This feature, combined with the forcefulness of Lenin's writings, has given the Bolshevik approach a historic influence on discussions of workers' control that far exceeds the revolution's long-term attainments in that area.

In fact, the Bolshevik leadership, from the moment it took power in October 1917, entered upon a collision course with workers' self-management initiatives. Although Lenin applauded such initiatives during the whole pre-October period,[7] his position after October is unambiguous: "large-scale machine industry—which is precisely the material source, the productive source, the foundation of socialism—calls for absolute and strict *unity of will.* . . . But how can strict unity of will be ensured? By thousands subordinating their will to the will of one" (Lenin 1971a, 424; Lenin's emphasis).

---

5 For a more comprehensive listing and discussion, not limited to revolutionary moments, see Bayat 1991. A cogent overview of the place of workers' councils in socialist revolution is E. Mandel 1973, 1: 5–54.

6 On the key role of workers in the October Revolution, see for example D. Mandel 1984, esp. 260–63.

7 See his expression of support for the factory committees, quoted in Cliff 1976, 244. For background on this issue, see Carr 1952, 62–79.

Despite the unprecedented surge of factory takeovers that occurred throughout 1917, the Bolshevik leadership looked upon such actions as at most an expression of revolt against the bourgeoisie. It did not treat them as a form to build upon in the course of a transition to socialism. Instead, going along with the emphasis on obedience, Lenin repeatedly urged a prominent managerial role for former capitalists. When the Bolsheviks adopted the slogan of "workers' control," therefore, they made clear that they understood "control" in the limited European sense of "checking" (Brinton 1970, 12). While the performance of the ex-capitalists was thus indeed to be "controlled," Lenin never spelled out what aspects of the production process the workers would be empowered to judge. What this meant in practice, however, is clearly suggested in his remarks about Taylorism, namely, that if a given method can quadruple productivity for the benefit of the capitalists, it can just as well do so for the benefit of the working class.[8]

In line with this approach, the Soviet government reacted with consistent disfavor to worker-control initiatives, even where the alternative was a factory shutdown (Voline 1974, 289ff). Lenin defended this overall position by referring to the urgency of the country's economic tasks and to the inexperience of the workers (Lenin 1971b, 451). He did not consider the possibility of using the old managers merely as consultants, but instead accepted the idea that they should retain prime authority. In defense of this stance, one can point out that many workers escaping the old discipline abused their freedom of action (Avrich 1967, 162f); however, the widespread heroism displayed by workers in the civil war suggests that if given a meaningful opportunity, they might well have acted differently. While critics of self-management are correct in stressing the need for coordination, there is no reason to view this as ruling out—particularly in periods of revolutionary mobilization—an increased reliance on rank-and-file activism.

What was at issue, in effect, was an entire approach to the transitional process. The acceptance of Taylorist methods was just one component—albeit a central one—of Lenin's larger view of the Russian economy as still requiring full development of the capitalist production process even if under (presumed) working-class leadership. Lenin referred to this contradictory stage as "state capitalism," which he saw as a necessary prerequisite to socialism (Lenin 1971b, 440). Its essence was a continuous increase of economic concentration. Lenin labeled opponents of this process petty bourgeois, even though the associated rationalization of industry might

---

8 Lenin 1970, 17. Lenin's critique of Taylorism refers to the allocation of labor and of the product rather than to the way the work is carried out. For fuller discussion of alternatives, see Sirianni 1982, 256–60.

just as well be resisted by workers. He denounced such resistance in "'Left Wing' Childishness and the Petty Bourgeois Mentality" (May 1918), in which he treats workers' self-management as being not only premature but even counterproductive to his overall strategy of reaching socialism by way of state capitalism. The either/or nature of his position is emphatic: "Our task is to study the state capitalism of the Germans, to spare *no effort* in copying it and not to shrink from adopting *dictatorial* methods to hasten the copying of it" (1971b, 444; Lenin's emphasis).

If the workers, however, are so ill-equipped for self-management, how can their party be justified in taking state power? Lenin takes up this question of prematurity in general terms in the same essay, arguing convincingly against the kind of purism that requires a perfect evenness in the development of all forces before any step forward can be taken (1971b, 448). But this properly dialectical response is offset by Lenin's decidedly undialectical exaltation of state capitalism. For while the latter approach could and did kill workers' self-management, the dialectical approach, with its recognition that people's faculties develop in conjunction with their responsibilities, prompts precisely the opposite suggestion: namely, if it was not too soon for the workers (through their parties) to seize state power, why was it too soon for them to start using it to transform production relations?[9]

What is at issue here is not in the nature of an "error" on Lenin's part. In terms of the immediate priority of defeating the counterrevolution, he was undeniably successful, although whether his approach was the only one possible remains an open question. Two things are certain, however. First, the supposedly temporary restraints upon workers' initiatives were never removed (Holubenko 1975, 23); second, the economic assumptions that seemed to justify them were not peculiar to Lenin but were widely shared in his time, even among Marxists. Briefly put, the assumptions are (1) growth is good; (2) results are more important than processes; and (3) capitalists get results. Linked to them in Lenin's thinking was a more specific belief in the neutrality of capitalist management techniques (Taylorism) and, with it, the implicit conclusion that Communists can play the capitalist game without getting drawn into it.

The irony of all this is that while Lenin's approach may have been necessary to prevent the immediate counterrevolution, it undoubtedly worked to facilitate the longer-term restoration of traditional hierarchical management practices. The negative lesson of the Soviet experience is therefore clear: socialist revolution will not lead directly to the establishment of workers' control

---

9 For firsthand testimony on the workers' commitment (based in part on archival material newly released after 1991), see Murphy 2005, esp. 63–74.

unless the appropriate measures are incorporated into the process through all its stages. What the Russian workers accomplished in 1917 was of unparalleled importance in raising this possibility. If their efforts failed, it was not due to any inherent flaw in what they were striving for, but rather to historical circumstances specific to the Russian case.

The circumstances in question all relate to Russia's position as pacesetter. First, as already suggested, the period itself was one in which the impressiveness of capitalism's productive attainments was still largely unquestioned. Second, the very economic backwardness that made Russian society so explosive also required that any revolutionary government place a premium upon growth. Third, the workers themselves operated under a series of specific disadvantages, the most decisive of which was the lack of sufficient tradition and organization to enable them to coordinate their self-management initiatives. And finally, in response to the civil war (an externally supported counterrevolution), huge numbers of the most dedicated workers—two hundred thousand by April 1918 from Moscow alone—departed for the front (Murphy 2005, 65f). For any who may have returned, the moment of their potential collective strength was lost.

## The Politics of Revolutionary Workers' Control: Three Cases

The Russian experience, although the first of its kind, was also the one in which the anticapitalist struggle came closest to success. We have seen, though, how distant it still was from a genuine victory. The capitalists were politically and militarily defeated, but their conception of workplace hierarchy survived. The subsequent trajectories of Italy, Spain, and Chile demonstrate almost the exact opposite dynamic. The capitalist class in all three cases recovered its position in the most thoroughgoing and brutal form possible, via fascism. But the workers in each case made unprecedented advances which, taken together, go far toward mapping the place of workers' control in current and future revolutions.

### Italy, 1920

The Italian factory occupations of September 1920 were in some ways more limited than their crisis counterparts elsewhere. They lasted less than a month, during which time a liberal bourgeois government remained in place, and the immediate withdrawal of the workers was based on a compromise. There was no doubt on either side, however, that class and state power were at issue throughout (Spriano 1975, 105, 131). This was the first instance of factory seizures in a capitalist democracy, and it also gave rise for the first time to the idea that the workers could make the revolution not by bringing production to a halt—the general strike—but rather by taking charge of it themselves.

If the short-run scope of the episode remained limited, it was partly because the workers lacked a strategy for going beyond the factory seizures and partly because of the reluctant patience of the capitalist class in waiting them out. The seizures themselves reflected an ad hoc decision. Although they climaxed more than a year of dramatic advances by the workers—including an election in which the Socialists emerged as the top vote-getting party—the immediate occasion for the factory seizures was a lockout (ibid., 57). The unity of the workers' direct response was not matched by thoroughness or consensus in their prior planning. As for the capitalists, their patience at that moment was prompted not only by their unwillingness to destroy the factories but also by two contingent factors: a cyclical downturn in the demand for their products (ibid., 44), and, in the person of Giovanni Giolitti, a shrewd political leadership at the national level.

These factors, however, served only to delay the more fundamental capitalist response. The full reaction began with the Fascist takeover of the government in 1922. The connection between Italy's "first" in the sphere of fascism and its "first" in the sphere of factory seizures is by no means accidental. The actual experience of the factory seizures constituted a trauma for the bourgeoisie (Salvemini 1973, 278). Giolitti's temporizing strategy had proved a sufficient palliative in only one sense: it gave short-run results simply because the workers had no way of extending their leverage beyond the factories themselves. But Giolitti had had higher hopes than just winning the immediate battle; as he admitted in his memoirs, he had assumed—in a manner doubtless common to the class he represented—that if he simply let the occupation run its course, the workers would soon realize that they were incapable of managing production (Cammett 1967, 117). This comfortable assumption was shattered once and for all. The working-class threat was clearly more profound than Giolitti had thought, and for the bourgeoisie this justified new methods of repression (ibid., 121).

Despite their brevity, the Italian factory occupations signaled a major step forward for the workers compared to the Russian experience. In Russia, the workers had displayed considerable disorganization and indiscipline, sometimes degenerating into outright corruption, all of which had provided the element of justification for Lenin's repressive approach. In the Italian factories, by contrast, "Absenteeism among workers was negligible, discipline effective, combativity widely diffused" (Spriano 1975, 84). Moreover, unlike the Russian situation, where worker-run factories had related to the market on a one-by-one basis, in Italy the workers set in motion the rudiments of a coordinated sales policy (Williams 1975, 246f). The Italian workers thus demonstrated that one-man rule in the factory is not the only alternative to chaos.

It may seem paradoxical that the workers' revolutionary self-discipline should have advanced more in a situation in which they were remote from power than in one in which they could think of themselves as a ruling class. This is not necessarily implausible, however, for the Italian workers were encouraged in their self-discipline by two practical requirements: (*a*) guarding against provocation in a setting where the factories were surrounded by hostile armed forces, and (*b*) building up support in new sectors of the population.

But one must look deeper in order to see what enabled the Italian workers to respond to these requirements in the appropriate way. Italy's political development is characterized by a unique combination of features not found together elsewhere. At the broadest level, it combines the late-industrialization traits of Germany and Russia with some of the constitutionalist traits of Northern and Western Europe. While late industrialization gave a revolutionary thrust to the working class, the possibility of incorporating democratic demands into labor struggles made the unions less "economistic" than they were in the other industrializing countries (Cammett 1967, 22). As a result, there was less of a basis in Italy than elsewhere for the radical dichotomy between trade-union consciousness and class consciousness that at certain points shaped Lenin's thinking.

As a more direct expression of Italy's uniqueness in these respects, we may note a tradition dating back to the 1860s that linked socialism very closely with anarchism (Procacci 1971, 395). Less than a year before the factory occupations, Antonio Gramsci gave a clear example of such a link when he wrote: "The proletarian dictatorship can only be embodied in a type of organization that is specific to the activity of producers, not wage-earners, the slaves of capital. The factory council is the nucleus of this organization. . . . The factory council is the model of the proletarian State" (Gramsci 1977, 100).

### Spain, 1936–1939

The Spanish Civil War provided the occasion, in certain regions of the country, for the closest approach yet made to a society fully based on workers' control. Largely hidden from world opinion at the time, the innovations in question have nonetheless been well recorded by eyewitnesses, and they constitute a vital reference point for any revolutionary strategy that looks beyond the mere seizure of state power.

The most notable aspects of the Spanish experience may be summarized as follows.[10] First, workers' control was practiced in every sector of the economy. While it went furthest in agriculture, in at least one city (Barcelona) it was introduced in all industries and services. Second, the structural changes were very radical, often entailing the elimination of certain mana-

---

10 Based on Leval 1975 and on Dolgoff 1974, especially chapters 6 and 7.

gerial positions, the equalization of wages, and, in some peasant collectives, the abolition of money. Particularly impressive is the fact that, where land expropriations took place, the peasants almost invariably preferred communal ownership to parcelization. Third, even the most radical of the changes were introduced directly and immediately, placing maximum reliance on the participation of the masses to the highest level of their abilities. Fourth, contrary to many stereotypes, the changes in question were not necessarily made at the expense of efficiency, but instead often involved advances in technology or coordination, as in the consolidation of the Barcelona bakeries and the vertical integration of the Catalan lumber industry. Finally, it was close to three years in some places before the self-managed operations were suppressed by force. There was thus ample time for them to prove themselves as practical arrangements.

The full scope of the mass initiative in Spain was so great that one hesitates to offer a schematic explanation, but we may at least sketch in some of the contours.[11]

In Spain as in Italy, we find an anarchist component to working-class culture, and we also find a constitutional political framework. But Spain was economically more backward; its constitution was newer and its anarchism stronger. Anarchist and socialist movements had already developed two rival union federations by the time the republic was established in 1931. In the sphere of government the anarchists were naturally unrepresented, but the left parties doubtless benefited from their votes. By the time of the February 1936 elections, the general polarization of Spanish society exceeded that of postwar Italy, and the Popular Front coalition won a majority in parliament. The workers and peasants could thus make their first moves under a government that, though not revolutionary, could be seen at least to some extent as their own.

The real catalyst, however, was provided by the reactionary forces. This reflected another unique aspect of the Spanish case. In Italy, as in Germany, fascism had intervened only after the high tide of the workers' movement had already passed—outlasted in the former case by a relatively unified bourgeoisie, crushed in the latter by an unholy alliance of Social Democrats and generals. In Spain of the 1930s, the bourgeoisie was still something of a rising class. An important sector of it was represented in the leadership of the Popular Front: again, an unusual circumstance in that all previous late-developing bourgeoisies had carefully avoided any political alliance with the working class. But the liberalism of the Republican bourgeoisie could not be viewed even as a temporary expedient by the rest of the Spanish ruling class. Hence

---

11 Based on Brenan 1950, part 2; Jackson 1965, ch. 1; and Payne 1970, ch. 2.

the rapidly improvised military response of Franco in July 1936—the least prepared of all Fascist risings in terms of any prior pacification of the masses.

The counterattack from below was instantaneous, massive, and revolutionary. The popular resistance far outstripped anything that could have been organized by the bourgeois republic, but by the same token it involved the immediate implementation of measures that even the most progressive of the governing parties could envisage only for a distant future. The military insurgency had hobbled the Republican power structure, and in so doing had confronted workers and peasants not only with a mortal threat, but also with an undreamed-of opportunity. They rushed to fill the vacuum. In a two-week period they collectivized industries, services, and farm villages throughout the eastern half of Spain (Broué and Témime 1972, ch. 5). With communities now authentically their own to defend, they gave themselves in full force to the military struggle against fascism.

The Republican government faced a dilemma. On the one hand, it would have fallen instantly without the popular counterattack, but on the other, it could in no way identify with the social revolution that this involved. So while it gathered some of its forces to resist Franco's Nationalist army, it mobilized others to suppress the very movement that had made such resistance possible. The government was to gain a decisive counter-revolutionary success in the Barcelona May Days of 1937 (ibid., 288).

The response from the side of the workers and peasants was ambivalent. Their dilemma was essentially the converse of that of the government: while they were tenacious about preserving their social gains, they were reluctant to aggravate divisions among the antifascist forces. At any level above that of their immediate communities, they tended to accept defeat, although this often meant that they were disarmed for the common military effort. To some extent, however, this element of resignation had shown itself even while the revolution was still at the crest of its initial upsurge. A key moment had occurred in Barcelona on July 21, 1936. The armed workers, having routed the bourgeoisie, were offered power by the Catalan president. They declined. As explained by one of their anarchist leaders: "We could have remained alone, imposed our absolute will, declared the [Catalan state] null and void, and imposed the true power of the people in its place, but we did not believe in dictatorship when it was being exercised against us, and we did not want it when we could exercise it ourselves only at the expense of others" (ibid., 131).

Considering the final outcome of the conflict, it is hard not to view such a statement as either tragic or absurd. But the tragedy/absurdity is compounded by the position of those who did think in terms of state power. For while the anarchists backed the workers but refused to accept their mandate, the Communists welcomed a role in the government but used it—with even greater insistence than their bourgeois partners—to undo the revolutionary gains of the workers (Thomas 1961, 436). Santiago Carrillo's later "Euro-communist" position had its roots at the beginning of his career; already in January 1937 he was saying, as secretary-general of the Socialist-Communist Youth, "We are not Marxist youth. We fight for a democratic, parliamentary republic" (ibid., 366). The practical meaning of such statements was revealed after May 1937, when the Republican government (with Communist participation) began the systematic restoration of private ownership in agriculture and industry.[12] This was almost two years before the final victory of fascism.

The Spanish workers and peasants thus experienced, within the lifespan of the republic, a compressed and intensified version of what the Russian workers went through after 1917. The rationales, however, were different. Lenin's reservations about self-management had rested above all on the question of expertise. In Spain, by contrast, perhaps thanks to anarchism's cultural impact, there was no lack of highly trained individuals ready to contribute their skills without demanding special privileges.

The argument for suppressing workers' control was found not in any failures of the workers themselves but rather in the international situation—a factor that became critical when Nazi and Italian Fascist forces intervened on Franco's side. The Soviet Union was the only outside power willing to aid the republic, but Stalin did not wish to jeopardize his defensive alliance with France by supporting revolution in Spain. More generally, the Communist parties argued that the only hope of additional support against Franco would come from portraying the battle strictly as one of "democracy versus fascism." For our present purposes, it is enough to make three points about this argument. First, the assumption that bourgeois governments might be swayed by such an ideological appeal proved to be totally unfounded. Second, it imposed a major limitation on the nature of foreign working-class support, for while thousands of highly politicized workers came to Spain as volunteers, the millions who stayed at home had no reason to see the issue as one of class interest, and as a result stayed aloof from the struggle. Finally, within Spain, the consequences for the workers' and peasants' fighting ability were disastrous.

### Chile, 1970–1973

Salvador Allende's Chile was a direct successor to revolutionary Spain in more ways than one: electoral stimulus, workers' initiatives, conflicts within the left, decisive foreign support to the right, and crushing defeat. In some

---

12 As the *Economist* stated in February 1938, "Intervention by the state in industry, as opposed to collectivization and workers' control, is reestablishing the principle of private property." Quoted in Broué and Témime 1972, 313.

ways, of course, Chile never reached the levels attained in Spain. Thus, the Chilean workers and peasants remained for the most part unarmed, and there were no whole regions of the country they controlled. Nevertheless, in one important sense the Chilean case carries the accumulated experience of workers' control another step forward: namely, in that the interaction between class-conscious workers and the elected government was a great deal more fluid.

The Allende government, unlike the Popular Front government in Spain, was comprised overwhelmingly of working-class parties and was committed, at least programmatically, to workers' control. The Chilean workers, for their part, did not have the same tradition of anarchism as did their Spanish counterparts, and in fact were most often identified—if only through their unions—with the very parties that made up the government. Only among the peasants had any direct takeovers been carried out prior to 1970. In effect, the autonomous workers' initiatives were, to a greater extent than in either Italy or Spain, an offshoot of the struggle being conducted at state level. While the Chilean workers never came as close to power as did their Spanish predecessors (especially in Catalonia), they certainly would not have declined the authority if it had been thrust upon them. Their problem was thus the opposite of the one that faced the Spanish workers: after a whole generation of functioning under a stable constitutional regime, and after eighteen years of steady electoral growth for the left, the Chilean workers had become accustomed to relying upon an eventual electoral success for the satisfaction of their demands. It was only after Allende's narrow electoral victory that they began to see the full extent of their own responsibility in the process.

The direct role of the workers was initially a defensive one. The first factories to be taken over were those whose owners had unilaterally cut back production (NACLA 1973). The workers did not necessarily expect to run such factories on their own; their more likely priority, at this stage, was to protect a government with which they identified. At first, it was only in the countryside that expropriations from below were undertaken on a systematic basis. But even these cases developed according to legal terms consistent with those accepted by Allende, for already on the books was an agrarian reform—passed in 1967 but previously unenforced—that set an eighty-hectare ceiling on individual holdings. In short, both workers and peasants acted in the expectation of official support for their steps.

To a greater extent than in any previous case, the official support did indeed materialize. This was not because the government's security against the right was any stronger; rather, it was because the government's dependence on the left was greater, in terms of both its original access to office and its need to confront unanimous bourgeois obstruction of economic activity.

In any case, legal norms were established through the Ministry of Labor for regulating factory organization in the "social area" (nationalized sector) of the economy, and these provided for a majority of worker-elected representatives on the administrative council of each enterprise. Within this framework, the workers again showed that their economic performance increased with the level of their participation; in turn, their participation, far from reflecting narrow sectoral interests or competitive attitudes, related directly to their identification with the overall process of change.[13]

But the Allende government was never able to free itself of its institutional moorings. The bourgeoisie, through its very obstructionism, was forcing a speedup of the transformation, but only the grassroots workers could mount an appropriate response. With the October 1972 bosses' stoppage, "business as usual" ceased completely, and expropriation became necessary not solely as a revolutionary goal but simply for the maintenance of essential services. At this point the contradiction between legally installed government and class-conscious workers became decisive. The workers overcame the stoppage and in so doing saved the government, but the government bargained away their victory by agreeing to return seized factories to their former owners in exchange for military guarantees to protect scheduled congressional elections.[14]

The available alternatives will never be fully known. Significantly, however, even a strong defender of Allende's concessions admits that the military at that moment was not yet prepared to launch a successful coup (Boorstein 1977, 212). Thus, from the workers' standpoint, the setback was total. It signaled the end of any official encouragement of workers' control, except in improvised response to the coup attempt of June 1973, when once again many plants were seized. By that time, however, the military already had the initiative, and from then on until the final coup in September 1973, workers in self-managed factories were subjected to systematic shakedowns and intimidation by the armed forces. The government said nothing, but it was powerless in any case. It had made its choice earlier. As in Spain, the workers' initiatives had been blocked *from their own side*—less wholeheartedly, but no less definitively.

Still, Chile had shown that government support for workers' control was at least a possibility. Some sectors of the governing coalition—especially the left wing of the Socialist Party—favored just such a strategy, though not to the exclusion of a coordinated approach to transition. Within the

---

13 Zimbalist and Petras 1975–76: 25, 27. For comprehensive analysis of the Chilean case, see Espinosa and Zimbalist 1978 and comments in Wallis 1983, 186–88.
14 For a narrative overview, see Smirnow 1979; for direct portrayal of worker control, Guzmán 1978.

self-managed factories, the workers with the highest level of participation had no illusions about the sufficiency of their own sphere of activity; rather, they identified precisely with these political sectors (Zimbalist and Petras 1975–76, 25) and thus with an approach that—even if belatedly—had come to see the workplace struggle and the state-level struggle as going hand in hand.

## Lessons of the Pre-1989 Experience

It should hardly be necessary to state that the struggles for workers' control and for socialism are inseparable. And yet the problem that has arisen again and again in practice is that they have found themselves organizationally in conflict. "Socialism" has been the formal monopoly of a political party (or parties), while self-management has been the direct expression of the workers and peasants themselves. Whichever one has prevailed, the result has been a setback in the movement toward a classless society. "Socialism" without self-management has revived or perpetuated rigid social strata, while self-management without a strong political direction has simply been suppressed.

One can go even further to say that the two sets of failures have reinforced each other. Thus, for every defeated workers' uprising, there are the party officials who will gain credibility by denouncing its spontaneous and undisciplined character. But at the same time, for every disappointment occasioned by a revolutionary government, there are the radical libertarians who will add a further blast to their condemnation of any strategy that doesn't emanate directly and immediately from the base. Vanguard and mass, party and class: instead of moving closer together, they move farther apart.

On what basis might this separation be overcome? Among the experiences considered here, the closest approach to a synthesis was reached in Italy. But in that case, the revolutionary party was in its earliest formative period and was quite remote from power. In Chile, there was an improvised synthesis, but it came only after the working-class parties had already taken on governmental responsibility under highly restrictive conditions. The result was that as the workers' initiatives broadened, the parties' support for them became more and more limited. What remained of such support in Allende's third year came increasingly from outside the governing coalition. In any case, it was too little and too late. Russia and Spain, for all their differences, seem in the end to display a pattern of polarization that was the trend everywhere.

An effective synthesis between the self-management impulse and a political strategy has yet to be worked out, but our four cases are not without valuable lessons. A major problem is that of technical expertise and coordination. Here we can draw several conclusions. First, a genuine movement toward self-management, far from stressing a "my firm first" attitude, leads naturally—and as a practical matter—toward efforts at mutually beneficial planning between economic units. While these efforts may initially derive only from immediately obvious requirements, the practice they entail will create a natural receptivity to the case made for more long-range or "macro" calculations. Second, workers are both able and willing to learn about technical matters. Third, where the urgency of expertise exceeds the time available to diffuse it, it is increasingly possible to find previously trained professionals (abroad if necessary) who will accept, perhaps even enthusiastically, new terms for their services.[15] Finally, looking ahead, we should recognize that technology itself is not entirely an independent factor. On the contrary, for environmental as well as political reasons, it may have to undergo a considerable number of demystifying, simplifying, and decentralizing changes, thereby undercutting pretexts for hierarchy.[16]

A second major problem area has to do with the conditions under which revolutionary workers' control can succeed. We have already noted the immediate political condition, namely, that the factory-level and state-level processes come to fruition simultaneously. This is partly a matter of conscious decisions, but it is also a matter of the economic and cultural characteristics of the society in question. Regarding this background dimension, our survey has suggested that there are many possible situations—some of them even mutually exclusive—that may prove favorable to workers' control. While the self-management impulse has always been a component of urban revolutionary movements, it has sometimes—as in Spain—appeared in even stronger form in rural settings. Within the industrial sector, it has sometimes been associated with heavy industry (Italy) and sometimes with light (Spain). Although usually associated with nondependent economies, workers' control has also become an issue in countries of the global South (Chile, Algeria, Iran). Within Europe, although the most radical thrusts have occurred in the relatively less prosperous countries (Spain, Portugal), the potential for workers' control continues to grow even in the foremost welfare state (Sweden). Related to this, if we consider the major political frameworks of military dictatorship, constitutional democracy, and people's democracy, we find self-management initiatives arising in all three (1918 Germany, 1972 Chile, 1968 Czechoslovakia). Finally, there may be considerable variation in terms of immediate circumstances such as war and peace, economic crisis, and fascist threats.

---

15 I witnessed this directly in Nicaragua in 1984. The involvement of professionals as well as workers in *autogestion* was illustrated in France in 1968 (Seale and McConville 1968: chapter "The Liberal Professions"). In some instances, managerial personnel also lent support to worker initiatives (Katsiaficas 1987, 106).

16 See Commoner's (1976) remarks on solar technology; also Wallis 2004.

All this does not add up to a theory as to where workers' control is most likely, but it does tell us that there is no single factor that automatically excludes it. The role of conscious choice must therefore be substantial. Among the objective factors, the only one that clearly facilitates such a choice is the existence of an established cooperative tradition. This was a reality in many of Spain's rural areas, and the urban workers were not yet remote from it. The challenge elsewhere, then, is to develop some equivalent to such a culture while still relating to immediate political options.

The question of leadership is the final major problem area that we must consider. What seems to be needed is a revolutionary party that would give priority to workers' control at every stage of its development. The difficulty of such a project is already clear. Being serious about workers' control means forgoing a certain type of discipline, while being seriously revolutionary means taking steps that are not limited by workplace perceptions. The possibility of meeting both requirements is suggested by some of the experiences we have surveyed, but a firm synthesis must be more systematic. It must recall Marx's emphasis on the work process, his interest in cooperative forms, and his distrust of "leaders"[17]—facets overlooked in the Leninist tradition. This new synthesis must accept the importance of what Spanish Revolution historian Gaston Leval calls "the capacity to organize the new society quickly" (Leval 1975, 354), a process that depends not only on thorough preparation but also on broad human involvement. Insofar as a party is needed, it is primarily for the movement's cohesion and self-protection; those who shape the party will have to recognize the perils of discipline as well as the risks of spontaneity.

## Toward a New Synthesis

If 1989 marks an endpoint, it also signals a new beginning. November of that year witnessed the fall of the Berlin Wall and with it, the effective collapse of first-epoch socialism. But less than nine months earlier, a sudden groundswell had come in Venezuela, which opened the way to that country's Bolivarian Revolution. The Caracazo was a spontaneous uprising of *caraqueño* slumdwellers, triggered by neoliberal economic policies, out of which emerged the transformative current that would eventually shape itself into a political force under the leadership of Hugo Chávez (Gott 2005). Chávez's election to the presidency in 1998 and his subsequent initiatives—both substantive and structural—created the setting within which workers' control would become a defining factor in the larger revolutionary process.

---

17 On the importance Marx attached to the work process, Braverman 1974, 8; on Marx's interest in cooperatives, Bourdet 1971, 102; on his view of "leaders," Marx and Engels 1942, 311.

It is important to view this development in its full international setting. Initially this points our attention toward Cuba, in terms of both that country's own institutional development and its support of the Venezuelan struggle.

The present study, in its original 1978 version, did not include Cuba. The focus was on cases of workers' control that emerged in direct conjunction with climactic revolutionary moments. This reflected an observed pattern in which most such moments included worker-control initiatives. Cuba, however, did not appear to fit this pattern. Although wageworkers, especially in big foreign-owned enterprises, were among the revolution's strongest supporters (Zeitlin 1970, 277), the direct takeover of production processes was not what defined their activism during the two-year guerrilla struggle leading up to the 1959 victory. Workplace changes following the triumph were incremental. Formal authority remained in the hands of an appointed management, although particular managers could now be rejected by the workers, who continued to be represented via existing union structures (Harnecker 1980, 26). This was part of a more general evolution, beginning in the late 1960s, toward an institutionalized practice of workplace consultation (Zeitlin 1970, xxxvii-xl). As a culture of equality supplanted hierarchical authority, it became clear that a new model of the link between state-level and factory-level transformations was emerging. The Cuban case showed, in effect, "that workers' control as a general practice does not have to be just the sudden fruit of revolutionary crisis; it is something that can be deliberately nurtured" (Wallis 1985, 261). It became equally clear, however, that revolution was integral to this process; what varied between the different national cases was only the sequence or timing of the changes implemented at distinct levels of revolutionary activity.

The development of worker-control institutions in Cuba has been continuous. Its underpinnings can be seen in the mass-participation practices—militias, voluntary labor, and the literacy campaign—that marked the early years of the revolution (Fuller 1992, 187–91). By the mid-1980s, "base-level input into planning" was routine among production workers (ibid., 116). And in the wider institutional debate that has been taking place since 2002, the goal of deepened participation in every sphere of public life has taken center stage (Duharte 2010). In the process, there is a continuous push toward decentralization of power and, at the theoretical level, a sense that the relationship of reform to revolution is, over the long term, not one of antagonism, but rather one of mutual reinforcement (Hernández 2010). Confidence that reform will not undermine revolution reflects the social consciousness developed over five decades, and most distinctively expressed in Cuba's large-scale programs of international solidarity—ranging from anti-apartheid military combat to disaster relief, and including also long-term educational and medical assistance (Akhtar 2006).

It is hard to conceive the launch of Venezuela's "twenty-first-century socialism" in the absence of Cuban solidarity. The massive presence in Venezuela of Cuban healthcare workers and teachers was a core component of the gains that could be credited to the Chávez government in its early years. This form of aid is unique in that it does not stem from any great economic or military power. Cubans in Venezuela—unlike Soviets in Cuba in the 1960s and '70s—are not trying to shape their host country's development strategy. They are not guides, but participants. Not only have they come by the thousands, but they also work directly in the popular neighborhoods (rather than as technical advisers). Their presence in the country reflects a relationship of equals. Although the power-transfer phases of the Cuban and Venezuelan revolutions had little in common, in both cases the popular protagonists became imbued with a culture of commitment and, hence, of participation.

In terms of workers' control and revolution, the Venezuelan case returns us to the earlier model of contemporaneity between factory-level and state-level struggles, with the difference that for the first time we now find a political leader who not only provides an umbrella for worker protagonism—a key Bolivarian concept—but actively encourages it, promotes a constitutional framework for legitimating it, and ratifies plant takeovers initiated by the workers themselves. The vigilance of Venezuelan workers provided a lifeline to the Chávez government in response to the attempted economic coup (via national lockout) of late 2002. That disruption gave a broad stimulus to factory occupations (Bruce 2008, 98ff), pitting the expertise of the workers—especially in the oil industry—against sabotage carried out by anti-Chavista engineers (GWS 2004). There is thus a clear sense in which a radical power shift in the workplace was dictated as a matter of economic survival, even before Chávez called the Bolivarian revolution socialist. Once the socialist agenda was explicitly articulated, it was a logical step to carry transformative measures even further, as in the case of the valve factory Inveval, whose employees took up Chávez's 2007 call for the formation of workers' councils and established a fully worker-controlled enterprise, including measures to overcome the social division of labor (Azzellini 2009, 184f).

Although the Venezuelan Revolution, like its Cuban counterpart, is far from complete, its trajectory epitomizes a new global stage of socialist awareness. Chávez's acknowledged present-day theoretical mentor is István Mészáros, whose central critique of first-epoch socialism is that it failed to establish "the socialist mode of control, through the self-management of the associated producers" (Mészáros 1995, xvii). This concern meshes fully with that of the grassroots movements that have spread throughout Latin America in recent years. Although there is a strong antistatist thrust to many of these movements (Esteva 2010), the Venezuelan process embodies at least a partial convergence between state and non-state protagonists pursuing a common goal. It is all the more significant that the Venezuelan government has advanced further than the Cuban government did in establishing an international network—encompassing banking and media as well as material aid—to support similar initiatives in other Latin American countries.

In terms of worldwide prospects for a new socialist epoch, it may be of suggestive interest to note that, faced with severe job loss in the wake of the 2008 financial meltdown, the United Steelworkers of America, the largest U.S. industrial union, signed a long-term cooperation agreement with the Spanish Mondragón cooperative (Davidson 2009). It is of course unwise to entertain illusions about the ease of progressive change within the world's most unrestrainedly capitalist social order. Nonetheless, so sharp a recognition of the need for an alternative locus of economic power cannot fail to reflect a degree of fragility in that order's popular acceptance.

## References

Akhtar, Aasim Sajjad. 2006. Cuban doctors in Pakistan: Why Cuba still inspires. *Monthly Review* 58, no. 6 (November).

Avrich, Paul. 1967. *The Russian anarchists*. Princeton, NJ: Princeton University Press.

Azzellini, Dario. 2009. Venezuela's solidarity economy: Collective ownership, expropriation, and workers' self-management. *Working USA: The Journal of Labor and Society* 12, no. 2 (June): 171–91.

Bayat, Assef. 1991. *Work, politics and power: An international perspective on workers' control and self-management.* New York: Monthly Review Press.

Boorstein, Edward. 1977. *Allende's Chile: An inside view.* New York: International Publishers.

Bourdet, Yvon. 1971. Karl Marx et l'autogestion. *Autogestion*, no. 15.

——, and Alain Guillerm. 1975. *L'Autogestion.* Paris: Seghers.

Braverman, Harry. 1974. *Labor and monopoly capital: The degradation of work in the twentieth century.* New York: Monthly Review Press.

Brenan, Gerald. 1950. *The Spanish labyrinth.* Cambridge: Cambridge University Press.

Brinton, Maurice. 1970. *The Bolsheviks and workers' control: The state and counterrevolution.* London: Solidarity.

Broué, Pierre and Emile Témime. 1972. *The revolution and the civil war in Spain.* London: Faber & Faber.

Bruce, Iain. 2008. *The real Venezuela: Making socialism in the 21ˢᵗ century.* London: Pluto.

Cammett, John M. 1967. *Antonio Gramsci and the origins of Italian communism.* Stanford: Stanford University Press.

Carr, E. H. 1952. *The Bolshevik Revolution, 1917–1923*, vol. 2. London: Penguin.

Cliff, Tony. 1976. *Lenin*, vol. 2. London: Pluto.

Commoner, Barry. 1976. *The poverty of power.* New York: Knopf.

Dallemagne, Jean-Luc. 1976. *Autogestion ou dictature du prolétariat.* Paris: Union générale d'éditions.

Davidson, Carl. 2009. Steelworkers plan job creation via worker coops. *Z* magazine, November 3, 2009. www.zmag.org/znet/viewArticle/23059.

Dolgoff, Sam (Ed.). 1974. *The anarchist collectives: Workers' self-management in the Spanish*

*Revolution, 1936–1939.* Montreal: Black Rose.

Duharte Díaz, Emilio. 2010. Cuba at the onset of the 21ˢᵗ century: Socialism, democracy, and political reforms. *Socialism and Democracy* 24, no. 1 (March): 49–69.

Espinosa, Juan and Andrew Zimbalist. 1978. *Economic democracy: Workers' participation in Chilean industry, 1970–1973.* New York: Academic Press.

Esteva, Gustavo. 2010. Another perspective, another democracy. *Socialism and Democracy* 23, no. 3 (November): 45–60.

Fuller, Linda. 1992. *Work and democracy in socialist Cuba.* Philadelphia: Temple University Press.

Gott, Richard. 2005. *Hugo Chávez and the Bolivarian Revolution.* London: Verso.

Gramsci, Antonio. 1977 [1919]. Unions and councils. In *Selections from political writings (1910–1920),* ed. Quintin Hoare. New York: International Publishers.

Guzmán, Patricio. 1978. *The battle of Chile* (film), part 3.

GWS (Global Women's Strike). 2004. *The Bolivarian Revolution: Enter the oil workers* (film).

Harnecker, Marta. 1980. *Cuba: Dictatorship or democracy?* Westport, CT: Lawrence Hill.

Hernández, Rafael. 2010. Revolution/reform and other Cuban dilemmas. *Socialism and Democracy* 24, no. 1 (March): 9–29.

Holubenko, M. 1975. The Soviet working class: Discontent and opposition. *Critique,* no. 4, 5–25.

Huet, Tim. 1997. Can coops go global? Mondragón is trying. *Dollars and Sense* (November–December).

Jackson, Gabriel. 1965. *The Spanish republic and the civil war, 1931–1939.* Princeton, NJ: Princeton University Press.

Katsiaficas, George. 1987. *The imagination of the New Left: A global analysis of 1968.* Boston: South End Press.

Lenin, V. I. 1970 [1914]. The Taylor system—man's enslavement by the machine. In *On workers' control and the nationalization of industry,* 15–17. Moscow: Progress Publishers.

———. 1971a [April 1918] The immediate tasks of the Soviet government. In *Selected works,* 401–431. 1 vol. New York: International Publishers.

———. 1971b [May 1918] 'Left-wing' childishness and the petty bourgeois mentality. In *Selected works,* 432–455. 1 vol. New York: International Publishers.

Leval, Gaston. 1975. *Collectives in the Spanish Revolution.* London: Freedom Press.

Mandel, David. 1984. *The Petrograd workers and the Soviet seizure of power.* London: Macmillan.

Mandel, Ernest. 1973. Introduction. In *Contrôle ouvrier, conseils ouvriers, autogestion,* ed. Ernest Mandel, 3 vols. Paris: Maspero.

Marx, Karl and Friedrich Engels. 1942. *Selected correspondence, 1846–1895.* New York: International Publishers.

Mészáros, István. 1995. *Beyond capital: Towards a theory of transition.* New York: Monthly Review Press.

Murphy, Kevin. 2005. *Revolution and counterrevolution: Class struggle in a Moscow metal factory.* Chicago: Haymarket Books.

NACLA. 1973. *New Chile.* New York: North American Congress on Latin America.

Payne, Stanley. 1970. *The Spanish Revolution.* New York: Norton.

Peterson, Martin, ed. 1977. Industrial democracy. *Scandinavian Review,* special issue.

Procacci, Giuliano. 1971. *Storia degli italiani.* Bari: Laterza.

Raby, D. L. 2006. *Democracy and revolution: Latin America and socialism today.* London: Pluto.

Richman, Barry M. 1969. *Industrial society in Communist China.* New York: Random House.

Salvemini, Gaetano. 1973. *The origins of fascism in Italy.* New York: Harper & Row.

Seale, Patrick and Maureen McConville. 1968. *Red flag/black flag: French revolution 1968.* New York: Ballantine Books.

Sirianni, Carmen. 1982. *Workers control and socialist democracy: The Soviet experience.* London: Verso.

Smirnow, Gabriel. 1979. *The revolution disarmed: Chile, 1970–1973.* New York: Monthly

Review Press.

Spriano, Paolo. 1975. *The occupation of the factories: Italy 1920.* London: Pluto.

Thomas, Hugh. 1961. *The Spanish Civil War.* London: Eyre & Spottiswoode.

Voline [V. M. Eichenbaum]. 1974. *The unknown revolution, 1917–1921.* New York: Free Life Editions.

Wallis, Victor. 1983. Workers' control in Latin America. *Latin American Research Review* 17 (2): 181–189.

———. 1985. Workers' control: Cases from Latin America and the Caribbean. In *Latin America and Caribbean Contemporary Record*, ed. Jack W. Hopkins, vol. 3, 254–263. New York: Holmes & Meier.

———. 2004. Technology, ecology, and socialist renewal. *Capitalism Nature Socialism* 15, no. 2 (June): 35–46.

Williams, Gwyn A. 1975. *Proletarian order: Antonio Gramsci, factory councils, and the origins of Italian communism, 1911–1921.* London: Pluto.

Zeitlin, Maurice. 1970. *Revolutionary politics and the Cuban working class.* New York: Harper & Row.

Zimbalist, Andrew and James Petras. 1975–76. Workers' control in Chile during Allende's presidency. *Comparative Urban Research* 3 (3): 21–30.

# 2

# Workers' Councils in Europe

## A Century of Experience

**Donny Gluckstein**

Recent events have called into question the much-trumpeted "inevitability" of capitalism and neutrality of the state. The smug optimism of the proponents of market forces was brutally destroyed by the credit crunch of 2008 and the deep economic crisis that has followed. If there has not (yet) been a repetition of the Great Depression of the 1930s this is due to massive intervention by the state to prop up an ailing system. It is now blatantly ridiculous to maintain that the parliamentary state stands above classes or is accountable to voters. Vast sums have been handed brazenly to a tiny minority of bankers and corporations at the direct expense of the great majority of the electorate and the public services they depend on.

Far less obvious, however, is what might be the alternative. The early utopian socialists, such as Owen and Fourier, imagined ideal societies and sought to implement them in reality, but these abstract schemes failed. Writing in the mid-nineteenth century, Marx avoided blueprints although he articulated the social and economic preconditions for socialism. An effective challenge to capitalism must be based in a numerous group of people—a class. This class must not be driven by the pursuit of private gain as are the capitalists, but by a collective, shared interest. Finally, it must possess the power to defeat capitalism. So, although the struggle against capitalism can involve a huge variety of people and take an infinite variety of forms (anti-imperialism, resistance to oppression on grounds of race, gender, and sexuality, etc.), only the working class meets these criteria. It cooperates in workplace units and produces the necessities of life.

Since Marx, a number of people have claimed to have discovered the path to socialism. In the early years of the twentieth century Kautsky and the reformist Second International believed in the inevitability of socialism through parliamentary means. The First World War shattered this illusion and ushered in a thirty-year period of barbarism that culminated with Auschwitz and Hiroshima. After 1945 Stalin asserted that Russia's centralized bureaucratic state would guarantee the victory of "actually existing socialism." This system has since been exposed as state capitalism and as fatally flawed. In recent years mass social protests have been mounted against capitalism's violence and poverty. The millions who marched on February 15, 2003, against the Iraq war were one striking example. Certain currents within this movement argue from an anarchist/autonomist position that the state itself should be ignored, suggesting spontaneous street action can suffice to transform society. However, the contemporary state not only remains powerful, but also acts, in the words of Marx's *Communist Manifesto*, as the "executive committee of the ruling class." So today there is an urgent need for a practical alternative to capitalism and its state. Not only does the combination visit economic devastation on ordinary people, but the state and economy seem incapable of effective action when our very survival on the planet is possibly at stake.

The experience of more than a century of mass struggle does offer some clues. At key moments workers' councils have emerged to provide a glimpse of an alternative to capitalism. Unlike the fanciful schemes of the utopian socialists, bourgeois parliaments, or bureaucratic state machines, these bodies have grown naturally out of class struggle and embody mass direct democracy. Workers' councils are not imposed by any party; they grow out of the grassroots conditions of working life. Part of the present, they represent a transition to the future, constituting a radically different kind of power.

The germs of the workers' council can be found wherever labor takes action on its own behalf. However, full-blown councils are very much the exception, because under the "normal" conditions of capitalism, workers' self-activity is limited in scope and time. Trade unions exist to negotiate with employers, not to overthrow them. If they conduct strikes these tend to be economic—concerning pay and working conditions—rather than escalating into a political challenge. Reformist political leaders use workers' votes to gain leverage within capitalist institutions rather than destroy them. In each case the process of radicalization is cut short and subordinated to the needs of the representatives rather than the represented.

Class struggle escapes from these confines only when the usual mechanisms of control are disrupted, such as during war. The first condition for a workers' council, therefore, is major crisis. The second condition is a high level of independent organization among workers. This chapter considers European workers' councils during the Franco-Prussian War of 1870–1871 and the First and Second World Wars. Through these events it traces the councils' origins, development, and ultimate fates.

## The Civil War in France, 1871

The revolution of 1871 is usually labeled "the Paris Commune." As we shall see, this obscures the role of the first workers' council, which was, in many ways, far more radical an innovation than the commune itself. The first condition for the emergence of workers' mass democracy—major crisis—was met when France's Emperor Napoleon III suffered catastrophic defeat at the hands of Prussia in 1870. The bulk of his army was taken into captivity and in September he was overthrown. Without the ability to wield physical force the new government found it very difficult to reestablish the authority of the French state.

The prospects for the second condition, collective organization, looked initially unpromising. Although the Parisian working class formed the majority of the capital's population (Bron 1968, 115), they labored in tiny workshops. Sixty percent of economic units consisted of just two workers, while only 7 percent had more than ten (Gaillard 1977, 55–6). All this changed when the Prussian army mounted a siege of the capital. Most of the rich fled in advance, economic life ground to a standstill, and the poor were subjected to an appalling famine during which they had to resort to eating dogs, cats, and rats. In a bid to head off mass discontent and provide a means of defending the city, the government armed the workers, who now formed the overwhelming majority of the 340,000-strong National Guard.

Thus the Parisian working class acquired a collective organization, even if by a highly peculiar route. Officers of the National Guard were elected and the rank and file could exert direct democratic control over them through daily assemblies for drill (Lucipia 1904, 222). A central committee composed of delegates from the various militia units gave direct democratic expression to this mass movement. Its constitution stated: "The National Guard has the absolute right to choose its officers and to recall them as soon as they lose the confidence of those who elected them" (EDHIS 1988). These features of direct and ongoing democracy plus the right of recall were to appear in later workers' councils.

Once the French government had made its peace with Prussia it saw these militiamen as a mortal threat. On March 18, 1871, it gathered the few soldiers it had left and attempted to disarm the guards by removing their cannon from Montmartre. Mass protests by working-class women and a soldiers' mutiny prevented this, whereupon the remnants of the state decamped to nearby Versailles and launched a civil war, which culminated in the breaching of the city walls and indiscriminate slaughter of the Parisian working class.

Nevertheless, in the form of the National Guard Central Committee, a workers' council had triumphed over the capitalist state, if only in one city and for a short time. The day after the revolution one newspaper described it as without example in history. Your revolution has a special character that distinguishes it from others. Its fundamental greatness is that it is made entirely by the people as a collective communal revolutionary undertaking, anonymous, unanimous, and for the first time without leaders . . . a massive achievement strong in its authority of the workers! This is a natural power, spontaneous, not false; born from the public conscience of the "vile multitude" which has been provoked and attacked and now legitimately defends itself (*La Commune* 1871).

In the wake of this first workers' council, between March and May 1871 popular initiatives enjoyed an extraordinary flowering, which, alas, we lack space to discuss here. Radical experiments in education, workers' control, the arts, and social justice were initiated (Gluckstein 2006, 11–54).

There were problems, however. Many activists were influenced by Pierre-Joseph Proudhon's theories on anarchism and argued against establishing a new state, even if based on collective power.[1] They hoped that creating the model of a new society would be enough to win external support and avoid destruction by the Versailles forces. Others, such as the Blanquists, were solely interested in a revolutionary dictatorship and centralized political organization. They saw mass efforts to operate democracy or create socialism as a distraction from the fight for survival.

Furthermore, the workers' council was so novel that its unique character was not properly understood. So rather than identifying in the National Guard the key institution of the March revolution, the committee declared, "Our mission is completed" (Rougerie 1971, 135) and ceded power to the commune. The latter was a town council elected on a geographical basis according to rules predating the revolution. Of course, in the environment of mass popular mobilization and civil war, this local government behaved very differently from an ordinary municipal body, but the unique features of the National Guard Central Committee that made it both accountable to its constituents and a direct emanation of collective strength, were absent from the commune.

Eventually the forces of Versailles, bolstered by soldiers hurriedly released by the Prussians to prevent the spread of subversion, drowned Paris in blood. The toll of victims in just one week, many of them noncombatant women and children, exceeded those executed in the Great French Revolution of 1789–93 several times over (Edwards 1971, 346). This was a warning of how far capitalism would go to defend its privileges and take revenge on its enemies. Nevertheless, the experience of 1871 was invaluable. It showed that collective, democratic self-organization can arise in the most unusual ways, and through the "Internationale"—the song written by a

---

1 Proudhon (1809–1865), author of the famous phrase "property is theft," stressed the idea of communes as the basis for a federal society without a central political authority.

Communard and symbolizing the revolution's aims—it remains an inspiration to this very day.

## World War I and Its Aftermath

The workers' council that appeared in Paris in 1871 was to be atypical. Capitalism's further development led to increasingly large and concentrated units of production. This meant that collective organization would develop within the workplace, which now tended to be the industrial factory. The phenomenon became evident when war broke out in 1914 generalizing conditions of crisis across the European continent. Tendencies toward workers' councils could be observed in a host of countries. In the following section we will look at four of these, each demonstrating a different characteristic of council development. During 1915 the embryo of a workers' council emerged in Glasgow. In 1918–1919 workers' councils in Berlin grew much further and momentarily challenged state power. During Italy's "two red years" that immediately followed World War I, the workers' council was given a clear theoretical expression by Gramsci, who reflected on the experience in Turin. Finally, we will look at Russia, where the workers' councils reached their highest point.

The background of all four situations was similar. Until the outbreak of war on August 4, 1914, socialist parties across Europe had denounced imperialist war and promised "to intervene for its speedy termination" (1907 resolution of the Second International, quoted in Frölich 1972, 168–9). Within days of the outbreak most had abandoned their pledge and lined up with their respective state machines. On August 2 the British Labour Party held a demonstration on the theme "Down with War!" (McNair 1955, 43–4). A few months later it entered the wartime coalition government and supported the Defence of the Realm Act (DORA) and the Munitions Act outlawing strikes. All but one of Germany's mighty Social Democratic Party (SPD) deputies voted to back the war, and the Kaiser declared a "state of siege."

Italy's Socialist Party (PSI) was verbally opposed to the conflict but declared that "for the time being class struggle is forbidden on account of the war"(*Avanti!*). In Russia the tsarist regime had its repressive machinery in place even before the war began.

With the official leadership willingly donning their patriotic blindfolds, the working class was easy prey to employers keen to become what the British called "profiteers." War imposed similar conditions on both sides of the trenches. For example, inflation soared everywhere, the wartime totals being 205 percent for Britain, 300 percent for Germany, and 400 percent for Italy (Gluckstein 1985, 50).

Munitions workers, the key industrial force for modern warfare, were a particular target for the state. In Britain the Munitions Act restricted the right to strike, and this was copied by Germany in its Auxiliary Service Law. Stoppages were already outlawed in Russia, while many of Italy's workers were conscripts who faced courts-martial if they struck. Hours in the munitions industries rose to the physical limit. Fiat workers had a seventy-five-hour week, while turners in Berlin worked a standard six-day week with compulsory Sunday working of five to twelve hours (ibid., 52). Trade union officials, following their reformist political counterparts, did nothing to oppose this. In Italy, despite verbal opposition to the war, the engineering union stated that "[they] were unable to prevent the war so it would be childish and ridiculous to think of resisting its consequences" (B. Buozzi, leader of FIOM, quoted in Abrate 1967, 168).

However, the huge expansion of employment in the munitions industries (135 percent in Russia, 34 percent in Britain, and 44 percent in Germany) (Smith 1983, 10; Gluckstein 1985, 47) offered these workers unprecedented bargaining power—if they were organized. Abandoned by the officials they had no choice but to generate their own structures. Across engineering centers like Petrograd (St. Petersburg), Berlin, Glasgow, and Turin, rank-and-file representatives were elected and committees formed. In tsarist Russia they were sheltered within the official war industry committees. In Berlin the representatives were called *Obleute*, in Glasgow shop stewards, in Turin commissars. Without consciously choosing the road to workers' councils, the first steps had been taken. Once more an ongoing electoral unit—in this case the workshop—furnished the basis for instant recall and direct democracy.

But these were not yet workers' councils. They required further development, both organizational and ideological. If a shop stewards' committee confined itself to economic demands and the individual workplace, it was no more than a temporary substitute for the trade union. However, the war also challenged an important ideological prop of capitalism—the split between economics and politics. Under "normal" conditions there is a division of labor—reformist deputies deal with politics in parliament; trade union officials handle work-related topics. Thus, struggles over pay and conditions are restricted to the economic sphere, divided by industry and enterprise. They do not threaten the state. Official politics does not deal with capitalist/worker relations, so any debates that take place do so on ruling-class terms.

These considerations were barely relevant in Russia, where tsarist repression threatened every strike and the parliamentary institution, the Duma, had little credibility. As a consequence, overtly political strikes outstripped economic ones from the start in industrial centers like Petrograd (Smith 1983, 50). In Western Europe the transition from economics to politics, from the individual workplace to citywide councils, was more protracted. The war, however, aided the process. Emergency laws brought striking workers into immediate conflict with the state. Any action to defend pay from galloping inflation or mitigate appalling working conditions was unofficial, illegal, and therefore implicitly political. In the face of government repression, stoppages dared not remain localized. They spread across entire cities through strike committees encompassing many different enterprises.

These committees solidified into permanent organizations with the following characteristics: (1) democratic representation of workers at the point of production and instant recall of delegates who, as stewards, received no special pay; and (2) embryonic workers' power—the independent self-organization of the workers across plants in a wide geographical area, creating the possibility of a challenge to capitalism that went beyond the economic to the political.

### Glasgow

While the above-mentioned features were shared internationally, each country had its own trajectory. In Britain the traditional separation of politics and economics ran deep and only the first tentative steps toward a workers' council were taken. In early 1915 workers in Glasgow struck for a pay raise—despite the war. To run the dispute a committee was formed, linking ten thousand unofficial strikers from twenty-six firms (Hinton 1973, 106).

Later that year the Clyde Workers' Committee (CWC) crystallized in the Glasgow region. Bringing together three hundred stewards weekly (Gluckstein 1985, 68), it was effectively a permanent strike committee. Its first leaflet explained the fundamental principle of rank-and-file organization: "We will support the officials just so long as they rightly represent the workers, but we will act independently immediately [if] they misrepresent them. Being composed of Delegates from every shop and untrammeled by obsolete rule or law, we claim to represent the true feelings of the workers" (Clyde Workers' Committee 1915). The formation of trade unions had been a tremendous step forward for labor, but they remained bodies to negotiate a better deal *within* capitalism. The shop stewards' movement began where trade unions left off and lit the path toward a transition *beyond* capitalism.

Despite its spontaneous appearance, however, the Clyde Workers' Committee was not the creation of newcomers. Most leading stewards were members of socialist parties, like Willie Gallacher (British Socialist Party) or Tom Clark (Socialist Labour Party). The same was true in every other WWI workers' council movement. Yet because the CWC voiced "the true feelings of the workers" the socialists among them hesitated to openly voice their more politically advanced ideas in the factories. They campaigned on economic issues, such as the threat to skilled engineers of the employment of unskilled women. On occasion they would humble the government with magnificent campaigns through which they fought the consequences of imperialist war, such as high rents. But they did not denounce the war itself. As J. T. Murphy, a leader of the Sheffield shop stewards' movement put it: "None of the strikes which took place during the course of the war were anti-war strikes. They were frequently led by men like myself who wanted to stop the war, but that was not the real motive. Had the question of stopping the war been put to any strikers' meeting it would have been overwhelmingly defeated" (Murphy 1941, 77). Murphy's account illustrates that the very strength of the workers' council—its genuine representative character—was also a potential weakness. If the majority of workers were not convinced of the need for radical politics the council would fail to challenge the capitalist state and ultimately be broken by it. In February–March 1916 the CWC was destroyed by a series of arrests and the initiative passed to shop stewards in Sheffield.

### Berlin

The German workers' council movement began under circumstances similar to those in Glasgow, but went much further. War brought runaway inflation and food shortages, but it also brought political activity, especially after the fall of tsarism in Russia. During April 1917 two hundred thousand Berlin workers struck over a cut in rations, while in Leipzig the first German workers' council was created, calling for food and peace (Flechtheim 1966, 102–3). While the war endured, however, a combination of state repression and persuasion by reformist political leaders prevented an all-out challenge to the state and the workers' council movement receded momentarily, though it remained a popular organizational concept.

Military defeat and the Kiel sailors' mutiny on November 2, 1918, broke the dam and brought a nationwide rebellion that toppled the kaiser. By November 9 industrial centers like Berlin, Bremen, and Hamburg had held workplace elections to choose delegates whose assemblies linked workers across entire cities. When these representatives joined with rebelling soldiers and sailors they constituted a radical center of mass physical force that could rival the capitalist state. This was what the Bolsheviks in Russia called "dual power."

As in Glasgow, a layer of radical engineering militants had laid the foundations for the workers' councils (*Arbeiterräte*). In Scotland the radical current stayed in control, if only by keeping quiet about its politics. In Germany, because these bodies had become truly mass organizations, they more closely represented the majority mood in the working class and thus were dominated by the reformist SPD. This was ironic, as the SPD was bitterly hostile to any form of council power as an alternative to parliament. Although the workers' and soldiers' councils effectively ran most of Germany, their Executive Committee voted 12 to 10 to accept the restoration of the Reichstag, which translated to the maintenance of capitalism (Institut für Marxismus-Leninismus 1968, 138–145).

This was not the end of the matter, however. Whatever the formal politics of the Arbeiterräte, the social crisis, which saw eight hundred Germans dying from hunger every day, impelled the councils to step in to organize rationing and requisitions, while in the factories a process of expropriating the bosses was under way. The tension between ideology and the brutality of capitalist crisis would inevitably be resolved one way or another.

On the other side the ruling class and their ally in the SPD were impatiently anticipating a counterattack. They feared the increasing self-confidence of workers who, as one example, rejected a generous pay deal on the grounds that "in a socialist state there is no longer any room for negotiations with private capitalists"(*Freiheit* 1918). In early January 1919 the government sacked Emil Eichhorn, Berlin's left-wing police chief, knowing that this would provoke the revolutionaries into action in Berlin. This posed a dilemma for the revolutionary left, which, though growing fast, still did not command a majority in the Arbeiterräte. Should they first win over the councils to the idea of challenging for state power, or should they bypass them and act immediately? A section of the Obleute and the newly formed German Communist Party (KPD) decided to follow the latter path. The result—the so-called Spartacist rising—was a disaster.

While the mass of the German working class remained largely passive, the Communist leaders, Rosa Luxemburg and Karl Liebknecht, were killed, along with two hundred others. It made little difference that a few weeks after the Spartacist rising the radical left won a majority in the Berlin workers' council (Gluckstein 1985, 156). The movement had suffered a critical setback.

If the lesson of Glasgow had been that the left should not refrain from promoting an alternative socialist vision of the state and society when the workers' council expands beyond the circle of radical militants to acquire a mass following, the bitter lesson of Berlin was that socialists dare not ignore the council, which, as a sensitive barometer of workers' opinion, was a crucial indicator of what was—and was not—politically and tactically possible.

*Turin*

Turin was the center of a powerful council movement during the "two red years" in Italy that followed World War I. It was rooted in the Fiat automobile plants and consciously sought to establish workers' control of production and to supplant the employers. In the article "Workers' Democracy" the Marxist intellectuals Antonio Gramsci and Palmiro Togliatti characterized this current, asking: "How are the immense social forces unleashed by the war to be harnessed [and] given a political form" so that "the present is welded to the future?" Unlike those who saw parliament as the only route to social transformation, or those who rejected political strategy altogether, Gramsci and Togliatti suggested that "the socialist state already exists potentially in the institutions of social life characteristic of the exploited working class . . . the workshop with its internal commissions [shop stewards' committees]" (Gramsci 1977, 65).

This represented a systematic theory to describe what the stewards in other Western European states had been groping toward. It both reflected and inspired the evolution of the workshop-based "internal commissions" into factory councils, which covered larger units. These soon spread beyond engineering to embrace Turin's industries generally. Their mobilizing potential was so great that it was claimed they were strong enough to cause a complete stoppage of sixteen thousand Fiat workers in five minutes, and "without any preparation whatsoever, the factory councils were able to mobilize 120,000 workers, called out factory by factory, in the course of just one hour" (ibid., 318).

However, the aim of amassing democratic workers' power without simultaneously consciously challenging the capitalist state and the employing class more widely proved inadequate. Workers' control and the usurpation of power at the level of the workshop or even factory was not the same as possessing the coercive physical power of a state, as had been seen in Germany or in Russia. The limitations of the movement were revealed in April 1920 when a major strike developed: it was confined to Turin and so was defeated. Gramsci realized that as important as workshop organization was, it did not go far enough. Without diminishing the importance of democratic control organized from the bottom up on a rank-and-file basis, he began to stress additionally that "power in the factory can be seen as just one element in relation to State power" (ibid., 182). This brought to the fore the issue of political leadership, and Gramsci subsequently played a key role in the establishment of the Italian Communist Party.

### Petrograd

It was in Russia that the workers' council movement attained its greatest success, for here the council (or, to use the Russian term, *soviet*) became the basis of a new state. This body had already been established in St. Petersburg in 1905, when defeat in the war against Japan triggered a revolution. Leon Trotsky, chair of the Petersburg Soviet, summed up its strengths in this way. It was

> a response to an objective need—a need born of the course of events. It was an organisation which was authoritative and yet had no traditions, which could immediately involve a scattered mass of hundreds of thousands of people while having virtually no organisational machinery; which united the revolutionary currents within the proletariat; which was capable of initiative and spontaneous self-control—and most important of all, which could be brought out from underground within twenty-four hours (Trotsky 1971, 122).

Although tsarism recovered temporarily and the soviet of 1905 was disbanded, its memory persisted. Then World War I brought intense suffering to Russia. Unlike Western Europe, where political and trade union reformists were (albeit with difficulty) able to act as safety valves to hold back council movements, in Russia government repression had closed off this channel. Therefore, when the army refused to fire upon hungry striking workers in Petrograd in February 1917, there were no obstacles to the mass re-creation of the soviets. They underwent virtually no incremental development such as was observed in the West. The Petrograd council really did appear within twenty-four hours. It was based on one factory delegate per one thousand workers and one delegate per regiment. From the start collective power in the workplace was fused with the physical power of armed men. And this system confronted a capitalist state in virtually total disarray.

Nevertheless, in its fundamentals the soviet was no different from the shop stewards' committee or factory council, in terms of both its strengths and weaknesses. Despite the lack of well-established reformist politics the majority of the soviet delegates did not comprehend the potential of the institution they embodied. Tsarism might have been abolished, but most expected the next step to be a capitalist state along Western parliamentary lines. A more radical outcome was not widely envisaged, and this belief was reflected in the council majority—the Mensheviks, representing the less radical workers, and their Social Revolutionary allies, based among the numerous peasantry. Thus the Bolsheviks, who argued for "All power to the soviets," could muster only 65 deputies out of 2,800.

However, the successive political crises of April, July, and September reflected a constant, democratic evolution in the soviet's political complexion. As the continuing war and deepening social collapse took their toll, so did the soviet march in step with workers' radicalization. In April 1917 Vladimir Lenin had argued that the Bolshevik Party he led must "struggle for influence within the Soviets . . ." (Lenin 1964, 49), and as time passed this approach paid off. Instant recall meant that popular disappointment with Menshevik and Social Revolutionary government policy led to their delegates being progressively withdrawn, with revolutionaries taking their places. By October 1917 the Bolsheviks had a majority in the Petrograd council, and in an almost bloodless insurrection the Military Revolutionary Committee of the Petrograd Soviet took power, seizing control of the Winter Palace and toppling the Kerensky government with a minimum of casualties. The revolutionary committee then declared that the soviet system would form the basis of the new socialist state.

This evolution demonstrated the essential difference between Russia and other examples. Russia's workers' councils were strong enough to constitute a real state power in their own right. This had been the case in Germany as well. But Russia, uniquely, had a mass revolutionary party committed to the idea of workers' council power. The Bolshevik Party was strong enough to withstand the pressures within workers' councils to accommodate to the majority still wedded to reformism. Such pressure had prevented the socialists in Glasgow from airing their radical views. Nor did the Bolsheviks' desire for socialism—combined with their initial lack of controlling influence within the soviet—impel them to try to bypass the councils, as had transpired in Berlin. Lenin's party had the confidence to foresee the victory of its arguments in the long term. It understood the need to win over the soviets to revolutionary change. The experience of 1917 was summed up by Trotsky who, once again, had been elected as the chair in Petrograd:

> The organisation by means of which the proletarian can both overthrow the old power and replace it, is the soviets . . . . However, the soviets by themselves do not settle the question. They may serve different goals according to the programme and leadership . . . . Whereas the soviets in revolutionary conditions—and apart from revolution they are impossible—comprise the whole class with the exception of its altogether backward, inert or demoralised strata, the revolutionary party represents the brain of the class. The problem of conquering the power can be solved only by a definite combination of party with soviets (Trotsky 1977, 1021).

Tragically, Russia's soviet state was short-lived, even though the name was retained. The numerical weakness of the working class in a largely peasant country, and its physical destruction in civil war and foreign wars of intervention, led to the hollowing out of the councils as meaningful democratic bodies. This was linked with the simultaneous degeneration of the Bolshevik party under Stalin. The two organizations had relied on each other to succeed and neither could survive long in power if the other were absent. This dynamic would prove to have profound consequences when the next major war began.

## World War II and the Missing Councils

At first glance World War II had all the ingredients for a reemergence of workers' councils on a grand scale. This was an event that, in terms of sheer human suffering, social and economic upheaval, and the destruction of conventional state structures, far surpassed the 1914–1918 conflict. However, in some countries we have already considered, conditions prior to the war made the development of councils unlikely. During the 1930s repression in Stalinist Russia and Nazi Germany was so thorough and intense that very little independent working-class activity could be expected.

Parallels with World War I were closer in other settings. The political/economic truce offered by reformist politicians and trade union leaders to their governments once more left workers in Western Europe vulnerable to an enormous increase in exploitation. In Britain the Labour Party had joined Churchill's coalition government and prominent trade unionists such as Ernest Bevin threw their efforts into maximizing production. In France the process followed a different path. It took just six weeks for Germany's Wehrmacht to overrun the country in 1940. This unexpected collapse was widely attributed to the readiness of the French political and military establishment to collaborate with Nazism rather than rouse the population to fight back. In both England and France the hold of traditional labor movement organizations was weakened, making a workers' council movement feasible.

As in World War I Britain experienced a number of strikes during World War II, but none of them produced permanent independent rank-and-file bodies such as the Clyde Workers' Committee. France, under Nazi occupation and the Vichy regime, did give birth to a powerful resistance movement, and Paris was once again the center of action. During 1944 there were mass strikes in the capital involving police, postal, and metro workers. Despite General de Gaulle's begging them "to return to work immediately and maintain order until the Allies arrive" (quoted in Tillon 1962, 318), a general insurrection erupted. Yet there was very little challenge to de Gaulle's aim of reestablishing a capitalist France. Therefore, just three days after the liberation of Paris he was able to start dissolving the popular militias, and the process met with minimal resistance (de Gaulle 1998, 661).

Despite its years of fascist rule, Northern Italy saw the greatest level of workers' activity of the entire Second World War. In March 1943, with Turin once again its epicenter, every factory in Piedmont was on strike (Battaglia 1957, 32). This movement played a significant role in the decision of the Fascist Grand Council and king to eject Mussolini as ruler a few months later. In the years that followed immense general strikes swept through the entire north of the country. In some areas the resistance even established liberated zones. The largest of these was the Republic of Domodossola, which was located near industrial Milan. It was "the only substantial part of Hitler's occupied Europe to achieve independence, and obtain recognition" (Lamb 1993, 220).

Yet no institution resembling a workers' council appeared in Britain, France, or Italy during this time. Why was this? The crucial factor was the opposition of the various Communist parties. They might have originated in the 1917 revolution and with the establishment of a soviet state, but by World War II that was long forgotten. These parties enjoyed huge influence in their respective labor movements, but from 1941 onward each one strove to deliver maximum support to Moscow in its desperate battle for survival against Hitler, sustained by collaborating with whichever capitalist state offered help. Stalin therefore downplayed the imperialist motives of Britain,

France, and the United States, muted the criticism of their capitalist governments, and presented the war as a pure, unadulterated battle against fascism. Thus the revolt against the conditions of war that was a defining feature of the World War I workers' councils was absent during World War II.

In Britain, for example, the Communist Party campaigned to maximize wartime production and denounced any stoppage as sabotage (see, for example, Croucher 1982). In France the Communist Party tamely accepted the postwar dissolution of the resistance because that suited Moscow's foreign policy aims.

By mid-1945 the Italian partisans effectively controlled much of the north. However, when Togliatti, the Italian Communist leader who had written the seminal article "Workers' Democracy" with Gramsci in 1919, returned from Russian exile he astounded his supporters by declaring, "The working class must abandon the position of opposition and criticism which it occupied in the past"(quoted in Sassoon 1981, 22). Instead of encouraging workers' councils, the partisan newspaper for antifascist resistance fighters, in a piece entitled "Hail the Government of National Unity," insisted that "every disagreement about the regime we want in our country, every legitimate reform, if it is not urgent, must take second place, be set aside, be delayed until after the victory" (*Il Combattente*, May 1944, in Longo 1971, 180).

## Conclusion

The developments of World War II reinforced, in a negative sense, the hard-won lessons of the Paris Commune and World War I. In the earlier cases workers' councils could not succeed when they lacked the self-consciousness and revolutionary purpose that could only be injected into them by a radical socialist party. During World War II workers' councils failed even to get off the ground when the Communist parties, which once might have been expected to promote them, refused to play that positive role and actively discouraged their formation.

The lesson of the European experience has been that workers' councils are the basis for a different kind of state. Through instant recall, and the fact that shop-floor delegates receive no special pay while being directly and immediately responsible to their electors, they offer a kind of democracy undreamt of by any conventional institution. As the collective expression of the working class they provide a means of overcoming the sham democracy of parliamentary elections under capitalism. In capitalism real power is held by the bosses, not the disparate mass of individuals grouped together by an accident of geography, who do little more than put an "x" on a sheet of paper before abandoning the field to power and privilege for the next several years.

However, the formation of workers' councils cannot be undertaken in isolation, but only in a symbiotic relationship with organized radical ideas. Without a self-conscious understanding of the revolutionary potential of the council, its very strength—grassroots democracy—will tend to reflect reformism and stay within the bounds of capitalist society. Equally, without workers' self-organization and democracy—without the workers' council—there can be no socialism.

## References

Abrate, Mario. 1967. *La lotta sindicale nella industrializzazione in Italia, 1906–1926,* 2nd rev. ed. Milan: Angeli.

*Avanti!* 1918. Turin edition, October 17.

Battaglia, Roberto. 1957. *The story of the Italian resistance.* Trans. P. D. Cummins. London: Odhams Press Limited.

Bron, Jean. 1968. *Histoire du mouvement ouvrier français.* 2 vols. Paris: Les Éditions Ouvrières.

Clyde Workers' Committee. 1915. Leaflet, November 1915, Glasgow. Beveridge Collection, St. Andrews University.

Croucher, Richard. 1982. *Engineers at war.* London: Merlin Press.

De Gaulle, Charles. 1998. *The complete war memoirs.* New York: Carroll & Graf Publishers.

EDHIS [Editions d'histoire sociale], eds. 1988. Federation Republicaine de la Garde Nationale. Comite Central. Status Declaration prealable, 26 September 1870. In *Les Révolutions du XIXe siècle, 1852–1872.* Paris: EDHIS.

Edwards, Stewart. 1971. *The Paris Commune, 1871.* London: Eyre and Spottiswoode.

Flechtheim, O. K. 1966. *Die KPD in der Weimarer Republik.* Frankfurt: Europäische Verlagsanstalt.

*Freiheit.* 1918. December 30.

Frölich, Paul. 1972. *Rosa Luxemburg: Ideas in action.* Trans. Joanna Hoornweg. London: Pluto Press.

Gaillard, Jeanne. 1977. *Paris, la ville 1852–1870.* Lille-Paris: Honoré Champion.

Gluckstein, Donny. 1985. *The Western soviets: Workers' councils versus parliament 1915–20.* London: Bookmarks.

———. 2006. *The Paris Commune: A revolution in democracy.* London: Bookmarks.

Gramsci, Antonio. 1977. *Selections from political writings, 1910–20.* London: Lawrence and Wishart.

Hinton, James. 1973. *The first shop stewards' movement.* London: Allen & Unwin.

Institut für Marxismus-Leninismus. 1968. Protokoll der Sitzung des Vollzugsrate der Arbeiter- und Soldatenraete am 16 November 1918. In *Beitrag zur Geschichte der Arbeiterbewegung,* 138–145. Berlin: Institut für Marxismus-Leninismus.

*La Commune,* 1871. March 19.

Lamb, Richard. 1993. *War in Italy, 1943–1945: A brutal story.* London: Da Capo Press.

Lenin, V. I. 1964. Letters on tactics. In *Collected works,* vol. 24. Moscow: Progress Publishers.

Longo, Luigi. 1971. *Sulla via dell'insurrezione nazionale.* Rome: Editori Riuniti.

Lucipia, Louis. 1904. The Paris Commune of 1871. *International Quarterly* no. 8 (September 1903–March 1904).

McNair, John. 1955. *James Maxton: The beloved rebel.* London: Allen & Unwin.

Murphy, J. T. 1941. *New horizons.* London: John Lane/The Bodley Head.

Rougerie, Jaques. 1971. *Paris libre, 1871*. Paris: Editions du Seuil.

Sassoon, Donald. 1981. *The strategy of the Italian Communist Party: From the resistance to the historic compromise*. London: Frances Pinter.

Smith, Steve. 1983. *Red Petrograd: Revolution in the factories, 1917–18*. London and New York: Cambridge University Press.

Tillon, C. 1962. *Les FT*. Paris: Julliard.

Trotsky, Leon. 1971. *1905*. London: Penguin Books.

_____. 1977. *The history of the Russian revolution*. London: Pluto Press.

# 3

# The Red Mole

## Workers' Councils as a Means of Revolutionary Transformation

**Sheila Cohen**

*The red mole may weave unexpected patterns and assume strange disguises; it
is digging, digging fast, and moving in roughly the right direction . . .*
—Daniel Singer, *The Road to Gdansk*

The term "workers' councils" can be seen as a catchall term for a form of organization renewed at different times and across different countries by groups
of workers often unaware of this kind of structure or of previous historical
precedents. Its highest expression the soviet, its "lowest" the workplace representatives' committee, this form of organization springs up again and again
in situations of major class struggle and even everyday industrial conflict.

Why do workers independently adopt this identical committee-based,
delegate-led, directly democratic structure for their most powerful expressions
of resistance? The answer is simple, because the form is simple, created by the
requirements of the situation, not plucked from thin air. Workers swept up in
struggle have no time, need, or inclination to consider a range of possible alternatives: the workers' council structure is "spontaneously" generated because
it immediately answers the organizational needs of grassroots struggle.

Full-fledged workers' councils exist, almost by definition, at times of
heightened class conflict, which also tend to feature all the other typical expressions of major class struggle: mass strikes, occupations, sometimes riots.
A full exploration of the nature of workers' councils also requires an examination of other aspects of such periods and their common features: dual
power, direct democracy, self-activity from below, unofficial and cross-union
types of worker organization, solidarity and class unity, and above all,
heightened class consciousness.

Accounts by Marx and Lenin of the 1871 Paris Commune and 1905
Petersburg Soviet, in which workers' councils took over cities and factories

in a potentially revolutionary process, point to a key dynamic in which these worker-generated structures simultaneously challenge the capitalist state and create the potential template for a new, worker-run society organized along the same directly democratic, accountable lines. In this sense the "everyday" form of the workers' council provides a crucial link between organizational form and fundamental political transition, pointing to the key historical and political significance of this structure.

This chapter offers examples throughout the history of capitalism to show how the workers' council structure is continuously regenerated, from the struggles of 1840s Chartism to those of twenty-first-century Argentina. A relevance of the workers' council model to today's political and economic situation is beyond doubt: first, because the unpredictable and "spontaneous" nature of workers' council formation suggests that such structures can resurface even in the unlikely context of twenty-first-century neoliberalism; and second, because the power, poetry, and inspiration of these fundamentally working-class organizations stand as an important reminder to the left of the continued relevance of class.

## "The ability. . .to recall any delegate immediately"

As mentioned, a fundamental feature of the formation of workers' councils is the instinctive adoption of direct democracy. This, unlike the "representative" type of democracy purveyed by conventional political and trade union electoral processes, is a form of democratic decision-making that directly voices the will of the majority, as expressed through workplace-based delegates who are immediately held to account if they fail to hold to the decisions of the workforce. Direct democracy is demonstrated in mass meetings, delegate structures, and accountable, revocable "local leaders" typical of many workplace situations (Fosh and Cohen 1990).

These directly democratic features have been identified in the earliest working-class upsurges under capitalism, such as Chartism, the British workers' fight in the 1830s and 1840s for the six-point "Charter," which included the demand for universal suffrage. This mass movement developed a rank-and-file leadership that came into its own during the historic General Strike of 1842, when a series of delegate-based conferences reflected an even earlier tradition of "cross-trade conferences," held as early as 1810 (Charlton 1997).

The same direct, participative forms of democracy have arisen during rapid upsurges of rank-and-file resistance. In the "Great Upheaval" of the late 1870s in the United States, railroad workers taking mass strike action against wage cuts "chose . . . delegates to a joint grievance committee, ignoring the leadership of their national unions; as the strike sped on to St. Louis, workers at a strike meeting 'set up a committee of one man from each railroad, and occupied the Relay Depot as their headquarters'" (Brecher 1997, 17, 32).

Almost identical structures were generated twenty years later in a series of massive battles with U.S. railroad companies during the 1890s. Workers on strike against Pullman in 1894 established a central strike committee with representatives from each local. The newly launched American Railway Union, led by Eugene Debs, lent strong support, but control of the strike remained in the workers' committees. Rather than running the strike itself, the union, in Debs' words, "authorize[d] that committee to act for that yard or that road" (ibid., 101–102). This degree of backing for rank-and-file action by established unions is of course unusual; even Debs, later an avowed socialist, eventually held back the "mass direct action" in the Pullman strike for fear of "insurrection" (ibid., 114).

The nineteenth-century strike waves documented by Brecher clearly showed an almost insurrectionary character. Yet workers' struggles during World War I posed a far more alarming level of revolutionary potential to a nervous ruling class. Leaving aside the Russian soviets and their crucial role in the 1917 revolution, the heart of the workers' council movement was found in Germany, where the potential for a revolution to build on and support the Soviet example was as strong as its failure was tragic. One participating sailor documented a mutiny in November 1918 in which the sailors "elected delegates who, ship by ship, formed a Council" (Appel 2008). During the 1914–18 war, "similar organisations had made their appearance in the factories. They were formed in the course of strikes, by elected representatives." Appel comments further that "the independent activity of the workers and soldiers adopted the organisational form of councils as a matter of expediency; these were the new forms of class organisation." While factory councils, according to this account, were seen by the KPD (the early German Communist Party) as "a mere form of organisation, nothing more," the workers saw it as "a vastly different matter—a means of control from the bottom up" (ibid.).

In Italy during 1919–20, a factory council movement that reached its high point in Turin unmistakably demonstrated, once again, the possibility—though not the reality—of workers' power. This movement, originally based in the shop-floor "internal commissions" established by the official union federation, FIOM (Federazione Italiana Operai Metallurgici), was overtaken by insurgent workers, showing the same patterns of direct democracy. According to one participant of the first-ever factory council, established in August 1919: "The key characteristic of the councils was the ability of the rank and file to recall any delegate immediately." By October 1919 the factory council movement was able to call a conference of delegates from thirty factories representing fifty thousand workers (Mason 2007, 246–7). As Italian revolutionary

Antonio Gramsci argued, "Trapped in the pincers of capitalist conflicts . . . the masses break away from the forms of bourgeois democracy" (Williams 1975, 163; see also chapter 7 in this volume).

Even in "moderate" Britain, soldiers' mutinies in 1919 to protest delayed demobilization displayed identical features of direct democracy. One of the highly organized mutinies took place in Calais, where strike committees were established in all the camps of soldiers waiting to be sent home. These soldiers elected a council, called the "Calais Area Soldiers' and Sailors' Association," with four or more delegates from the larger camps and two each from the smaller. British government officials recognized the revolutionary danger of such structures, warning the prime minister that he "should not confer with soldiers' delegates . . . . The soldiers' delegation bore a dangerous resemblance to a *Soviet*" (quoted in Rosenberg 1987, 12, emphasis in original).

But the widespread use by different groups of workers of these directly democratic and accountable organizational structures was not confined to the openly revolutionary World War I period. Almost identical patterns of rank-and-file organization arose in various worker upsurges that erupted against Stalinist governments in Eastern Europe during the 1950s, 1960s, and beyond. Moving accounts of the 1956 Hungarian Revolution and up-risings in Czechoslovakia, Poland, and elsewhere provide vivid examples of grassroots democracy as part of the workers' council structure.

As one historian of the workers' council organization during the Hungarian Revolution observed, the council delegates "were merely those with the responsibility of carrying out the will of the working class;" workers' councils "arose quite naturally out of direct workers' democracy" (Nagy 2006). The essential element of accountability is confirmed in another writer's comment that "No one ever questioned the principle that delegates to the Central Councils should be revocable, at all times. The principle became an immediate reality" (Anderson 1964).

Similar patterns are found in the 1970s and 1980s worker revolts in Poland, which eventually led to the founding of the once "revolutionary" union, Solidarnosc (Solidarity). Daniel Singer's vivid history recounts the formation of workers' councils in shipyards paralyzed by strike action: "Each section had five delegates but also elected directly one member of the strike committee . . . . Surrounded by troops, threatened, the Warski Shipyards paralyzed by the strike was a school for democracy" (1982, 173).

Yet examples of direct democracy and workplace-based committee structures can also be found during "ordinary" periods of worker organization and resistance, which, even if seriously challenging the ruling class and union bureaucracy, did not directly threaten the system. The 1968–1974 upsurge in the United States, UK, and parts of Western Europe gave rise to rank-and-file organizational structures that, although not classical workers' councils, displayed parallel types of democracy and accountability. Multi-union shop steward committees in manufacturing plants, cross-company combine committees, and industry committees gave rise to forms of direct democracy rooted in members' concrete interests. Their delegate-based committee structure "ensured a closeness and accountability to the membership lacking in 'representative' democracy" (Cohen 2006, 166).

During this same period a number of oppositional rank-and-file trade union "reform caucuses" emerged in the United States, rooted in concrete issues of pay and workplace conditions while also challenging the bureaucracy. Such workplace groups, which adopted the same committee-based structure, were described by an activist as "the power base for the insurgencies from below that in the last three years have ended or threatened official careers of long standing . . . . Almost without exception the revolts were conducted primarily to improve the conditions of life-on-the-job" (Weir 1967).

More dramatically, the "revolutionary year" of 1968 saw French workers involved in the "May events," in which extended strikes nearly brought down the de Gaulle government; workers formed *comites d'action* based on the same processes of direct democracy (Singer 2002, 314f). In Italy's "Hot Autumn" strike wave of 1969, which created factory councils and cross-union Comitati Unitari di Base (united rank-and-file committees), the workers' slogan was "We are all delegates" (Wright 2002; see also chapter 17 in this volume). The *empresas* (factory councils) that sprang up within days of the 1974 coup against Portuguese dictator Salazar were "highly democratic," not to mention participative—at the Plessey factory, for example, "The commission . . . included 118 workers—all of whom insisted on going to the first meeting with the management" (Robinson 1987, 91). The twenty-first-century upsurge in Argentina generated by the effects of the financial crisis on ordinary people saw "new movements . . . outside the old traditional trade union organisations, with direct democracy from below and new leaders" (Harman 2002, 31; see also chapter 20 in this volume).

## "The only thing between us and anarchy. . ."

A related and equally important characteristic of these delegate-based, accountable workers' organizations was their freedom from official and institutional structures—in particular from the established trade unions. Evidence of independence and autonomy crops up repeatedly in historical descriptions of workers' councils.

The 1910–14 Great Unrest, during which, as Trotsky (1925) put it, "The vague shadow of revolution hovered over Britain," was an entirely unofficial strike wave in which workers across England staged solidarity actions "clearly unofficial in character, conducted by local strike committees acting entirely independently of union officials" (Holton 1976, 191). Strike committees among Welsh miners across different South Wales pits "had no specific grievance in common—they simply shared a distrust of the Miners' Federation of Great Britain and a scorn for their own Executive" (Dangerfield 1961, 242). The strikes of the Great Unrest "all showed the same curious irritation, the same disposition to disregard Union authority" (ibid., 237).

Although the revolutionary potential of the Great Unrest was stalled by the outbreak of war in 1914, within one year unofficial and equally subversive workplace committees were forming as part of the World War I shop stewards' movement. Hinton's study of the movement notes that "because of their delegatory character these committees were capable of initiating and carrying through strike action independent of the trade union officials. It is this independence that primarily defines the rank-and-file movement" (1972, 296).

Workers' independence from official trade unionism proved highly disturbing to the ruling class. In the British strike wave of 1919, Churchill remarked that "The curse of trade unionism was that there was not enough of it . . ." while the Chancellor of the Exchequer, Bonar Law, went further: " . . . the Trade Union organisation was the only thing between us and anarchy" (Rosenberg 1987, 68).

Along the same lines, the German workers' council movement was preceded in 1917 by "a flood of unofficial strikes [which] suddenly swept over the country. No official organisation led it" (Appel 2008). The workers' councils that sprang up a year later were "the front line in a workers' offensive which the traditional forces of labour were unwilling to lead" (Gluckstein 1985, 106–7). This independence was central to the success of such mobilizations: "Free from experience of the 'usual and right way' of conducting class struggle under normal circumstances, it was the sailors who were to act boldly and nudge the vanguard workers into action" (Gluckstein 1985, 112).

The independence that worried the ruling class was equally disturbing to union officials and even, following the Russian revolution, for the leaders of the Communist parties in Europe. In Italy, the Turin workers' council movement was viewed with suspicion by both the Italian trade union federation and the main left parties, including the Communists, as being "anarchist."

Yet this "anarchism"—workers' self-activity rooted in the democratic structure of workers' councils—defines the fundamental nature of effective working-class struggle. The independent, class-based nature of workers' council organization is confirmed in the solemn pledge of Balazs Nagy, writing of the Hungarian workers' councils: "We shall not forget that it was the workers themselves, without any organisation, party, group, trade union or whatever, who as it were re-learned the experiences of the whole history of the workers' movement, enriching it as they did so" (2006).

## Spontaneity and Self-Activity

Similar issues of working-class independence and self-activity are clear when we look at how workers' councils tend to arise "spontaneously," without conscious preparation. Many have criticized the notion of spontaneity, arguing that leadership always is crucial in even the most grassroots of struggles (see, for example, Les Leopold's biography of U.S. oil worker activist Tony Mazzochi). British observers of union organization like Kelly (1998), Darlington (2009), and Gall (2009), have examined workplace leadership as part of a discussion of worker mobilization.

Yet it seems clear when looking across the wide historical and geographical sweep of workers' council organization that spontaneity is inescapable when describing the movement's roots and motion. All accounts of workers' councils and similar structures describe them as having been "sparked" in an unpremeditated fashion out of the concrete needs of workers, whether in the workplace or broader workplace-based movements.

The Chartist movement of the 1830s and 1840s saw "spontaneous crowd alliances in which trade boundaries and unskilled/skilled boundaries melted into the air" (Charlton 1997, 6). Writing on the Paris Commune, in which workers staged a brief but historic seizure of state power, Lenin remarked, "The Commune sprang up spontaneously. No one consciously prepared it in an organised way" (Marx and Lenin 1968, 100). Even the 1905 Russian Revolution, which saw the first appearance of soviets, was "far more spontaneous than Lenin had thought possible" (Lynd 2003).

The workers' councils created in revolutionary Germany appeared and reappeared spontaneously even after being crushed by forces on both the right and left. Appel (2008) comments that "no party or organisation had proposed this form of struggle. It was an entirely spontaneous movement" (5). In Italy, the workers' council movement can be traced to "spontaneous" workers' movements in the summer of 1917, "when the factories exploded into an anti-war demonstration . . . . The immediate uprising seems to have been entirely spontaneous" (Williams 1975, 63).

In the many struggles that have given rise to workers' councils in the last century, this element of spontaneity continually resurfaces, showing that workers independently and repeatedly learn and put into practice class-based lessons. In recounting the May 1968 events in France, Singer writes: "Spontaneous is the recurring adjective in all the descriptions of the movement . . . . The May Movement was visibly spontaneous in the sense that the official parties and unions never took the initiative" (2002, 315). The political crisis in Chile in the early 1970s saw "spontaneous and unorganized acts of resistance by the working class" (Gonzalez 1987, 64), and the workers' uprising of 2000–2001 in Argentina was not centrally planned.

## "Fused by their common adversity":
## Class Unity within Workers' Councils

In spite of their spontaneity of action, the main features of workers' councils defined thus far—delegate-based structures of direct democracy, self-activity, and class independence—do not arise out of thin air. Workers' continual re-creation of the specific council structure arises from a shared experience of the capitalist labor process, which, even during relatively "quiet" periods, shapes a unity and solidarity within the fundamentally collective nature of work. In his account of the Italian factory councils movement, Williams suggests that in the workplace, "Unity is inherent in the very process of production, the creative activity which creates a common and fraternal will" (1975, 115).

This production-based class unity shapes the collective and participative nature of workers' council activity, even in less revolutionary times. During the Great Upheaval, a local Ohio newspaper reported that at strike committee meetings, workers "proceeded with notable coherence, as though fused by their common adversity" (Brecher 1997, 33; quoted from *Columbus Dispatch*, July 20, 1877). Similarly, Hungarian workers' council delegate Ferenc Toke noted how during the key central meeting of the councils on November 14, 1956, "Everybody, although they came from different factories, wanted exactly the same thing, just as if they had agreed their views in advance." Nagy comments that "in this way the councils really put the unity of the working class into practice" (2006, 31).

Thus workplace solidarity finds expression in revolutionary periods of crisis as well as in everyday working-class experience. Describing the strengthening work-group organization of the 1950s and 1960s, Brecher commented, "It is largely in these groups that the invisible, underlying process of the mass strike develops. They are communities within which workers come into opposition to the boss . . . and discover the collective power they develop in doing so" (1997, 277). For Brecher, this process highlights "the two elements of labor struggles that carry the seeds of social transformation: self-directed action and solidarity" (ibid., 298).

## The Issue Is Not the Issue . . .

These examples show how the seeds and structures of potentially revolutionary episodes are contained in "everyday" levels of rank-and-file worker response and resistance. The type of consciousness that develops during workers' council organization is tied, even at its most revolutionary levels, to workers' response to the "ordinary" experience of the capitalist labor process, with all its everyday aggravations.

In this way, disputes sparked by everyday material issues and demands in "normal times" represent the tip of an iceberg of underlying class conflict, which becomes clearer as the struggle gains momentum. In this sense, as Brecher writes, it may be said that "the issue is not the issue" (Brecher 1997, 282). Workers' experience of exploitation and oppression creates an ongoing resentment and class anger that may not itself spark resistance but rises to the surface and becomes explicit in situations of open conflict. This "dual" or hidden consciousness was evoked by Gramsci in arguing that worker resistance "signifies that the social group in question may indeed have its own conception of the world, even if only embryonic; a conception which manifests itself in action, but occasionally and in flashes—when, that is, the group is acting as an organic totality" (ibid., 327). Describing the dockers' struggle during the 1910–1914 Great Unrest, Dangerfield argues: "It would be very difficult to state exactly what they wanted . . . . But at the very heart of their grievances there stirred a rising anger at being indifferently paid . . . . A strike about money is not at all the same as a strike about wages; [it] comes from a sense of injustice . . . . It is a voice in the wilderness, crying for recognition, for solidarity, for power" (1961, 249). This dual consciousness, in turn, can lead to a situation in which workers' demands become "transitional"—that is, raising the possibility but also the necessity of an entirely new type of society: "In periods of mass strike, workers think, speak, and act. . .as oppressed and exploited human beings in revolt. Their agenda is based on what they need, not on 'what the market will bear'" (Brecher 1997, 286).

The history of workers' councils reveals that these processes and their linked changes in consciousness are almost always rooted in basic material issues, which can spark insurrectionary levels of revolt from an apparently trivial or "economistic" base. One historic example is the Petrograd typographers' strike of 1905, which, in Trotsky's words, "started over punctuation marks and ended by felling absolutism" (Trotsky 1971, 85). Thus, this "ordinary" strike sparked the 1905 revolution, resulting in the first (very weak) form of parliamentary democracy in Russia—as well as the first-ever soviet in Petrograd. Although even Russian revolutionaries failed to note the significance at the time, it was this soviet structure—a workers' council—that later helped bring the working class to power in 1917.

The revolution of February 1917 was sparked by women textile workers' strikes and protests over bread shortages, and a very "ordinary" strike against victimization at the giant Putilov engineering works (Trotsky 1967, 110). That same year in Italy, working-class women laboring up to twelve hours a day in the factories and forced to stand in line for hours for meager rations eventually launched a hunger riot, which "reached insurrectionary proportions when the women made [a] crucial link with workers' industrial power" (Gluckstein 1985, 169–70).

History provides many other examples of movements rooted in everyday grievances that result in challenges to the capitalist system. The Chilean, Portuguese, and Iranian upsurges of the mid- to late 1970s all produced independent yet similar forms of workers' council organization with an emphasis on basic material needs. In Chile, where workers created "a new form of organisation . . . the 'industrial belt' or *cordon*, one Chilean agricultural worker commented, 'We've people to feed and families to keep. And we've had it up to here'" (Gonzalez 1987). Although revolutionary councils of soldiers, sailors, and workers were established in the factories of Portugal after the 1974 coup, "Those who set [them] up saw the workers' commissions as being merely economic" (Robinson 1987). In Iran, the movement leading up to the 1979 revolution developed through "strikes, sit-ins and other industrial protests [most of which] were confined to economic demands" (Poya 1987).

This focus on basic material issues has been shown repeatedly not to impede the explosions of rapidly expanding class and political awareness in a process not dependent on any preexisting "socialist" politics. As one U.S. organizer in the 1930s noted, "The so much bewailed absence of a socialist ideology on the part of the workers, really does not prevent [them] from acting quite anti-capitalistically" (Brecher 1997, 165).

Once made, however, the "leap" to class independence and consciousness is often experienced as transformational; workers involved in the twenty-first-century uprising in Argentina claimed, "We have done things which we never even thought of and we still don't know what else we'll have to do" (Harman 2002, 23). Similarly, as the economically oriented workers' councils were developing in Portugal, "Workers and soldiers were hungry for ideas . . . Lenin's *State and Revolution* was a best-seller in the shops" (Robinson 1987, 97). Commenting on French workers' activity in May 1968, Singer observes, "The general strike can be a school of class consciousness . . . attended by eager millions who in normal times are not within reach" (2000, 161–2).

## "The stilled soul of a whole industry . . ."

Along with the explosion of political consciousness that so often marks workers' uprisings and the creation of workers' councils, the issue of class power is posed regardless of the experience and awareness of those involved. This is certainly clear to the ruling class and "reformist" labor leaders. As Appel contends, during the revolutionary movement in Germany, the workers' council "showed itself to be the only form of organisation that allowed the outline of workers' power, and therefore . . . it alarmed the bourgeoisie and the Social Democrats" (2008, 5).

The key issues of the "dual power"—indeed state power—posed by the workers' council organization are discussed further below. The examples above also demonstrate the enormous economic power workers wield through the withdrawal of labor. As Dangerfield explains, describing miners' strikes during the Great Unrest, "a spontaneous and impulsive strike, begun by a handful of Welshmen against the advice of leaders . . . ultimately sounded its alarum in the stilled soul of a whole industry" (1961, 247).

During the Hungarian Revolution, intellectuals and nonindustrial workers who initially had not understood the importance of the workers' councils soon "recognised that *here* was the heart of real power in the country. Kadar [the Stalinist leader] knew it too" (Anderson 1964, 87). Writing on the Polish workers' revolt in 1981, Singer (1982) sums up the point: "Whatever some experts might have thought or hoped, the power of Solidarity ultimately rested on . . . the capacity of the working class to bring industry to a standstill and to paralyze the country" (255).

Even in today's less dramatic examples of worker resistance, the forces of both the state and trade unions are immediately marshaled in determined opposition to any potential stranglehold by workers on ownership and profitability. Workers' stories of occupations in 2008 and 2009 at Vestas and Visteon in Britain (Smith 2009, Wilson 2009) are testament to this process.

## "Are you ready?" Dual Power and the Soviet

It is on the historic occasions when workers' councils emerge in their full revolutionary or quasi-revolutionary character that the nature and meaning of workers' dual power and the full-fledged soviet are clearest; in fact "the soviet can arise only during a situation of dual power," according to Gluckstein (1985, 218).

What do we mean by "dual power"? The previous section placed the nature and importance of workers' power, whether potential or actual, firmly at the center of the argument. Such power is intrinsically tied up with the role of workers in production and the impact, always threatening to capital, of the withdrawal of labor. The concept of dual power is linked to this central production-related dynamic, but involves another, crucial dimension: worker-led domination over the organization of capital and the economic system. The workers' council or general strike committee in a situation of widespread conflict often shares power with a reluctant and alarmed bourgeois state. The usual power relations in society are fundamentally upended, with major political and often revolutionary implications.

History provides numerous examples of dual-power situations with a clearly revolutionary direction if not always end result. In the strikes that raged across Liverpool during the Great Unrest, a cross-city strike committee operated a transport permit system that "clearly challenged, and was perceived to challenge, the legitimacy of civil power" (Holton 1976, 102). In 1919, a mass strike in Seattle based its organization in a general strike committee, which "form[ed] virtually a counter-government for the city" (Brecher 1997, 122).

In the same year, the ever-cunning Lloyd George left British trade union leaders to be hoist on their own petard by spelling out the political implications of threatened cross-union action: "The strike . . . will precipitate a constitutional crisis of the first importance. For, if a force arises in the State which is stronger than the State itself, then it must be ready to take on the functions of the State . . . . Gentlemen, have you considered, and . . . are you ready?" Needless to say, union leaders immediately flunked the challenge (Rosenberg 1987, 74). The last major British upsurge of the period, the 1926 General Strike, saw the establishment of "Councils of Action" and some experience of dual power for the strikers; as one put it, "Employers of labour were coming, cap in hand, begging for permission . . . to allow their workers to perform certain operations" (Postgate et al. 1927, 35).

By that time, the revolutionary wave across the industrialized world had crested. Mass confrontations with capital were not seen again until the strikes and sit-downs of American workers fighting for union organization in the 1930s. But the balancing act with the capitalist state embodied in the term "dual power" had not disappeared. In the postwar turmoil of 1945, when "all that really stood between the French workers and effective power were a few shaky bayonets," French Communist Party leader Thorez inadvertently invoked the potential power of workers' local Committees of Liberation when he condemned them for "substituting themselves for the local governments" (Anderson 1964, 9).

In the wave of Eastern European workers' protests after the war, the workers' council in one Hungarian town "formed workers' militias . . . and organised itself as a local government independent of the central power." By November, almost all the radio stations were controlled by revolutionary councils; "a classical situation of 'dual power' existed" (Anderson 1964, 69, 78–9). In the insurgent Poland of the early 1970s, the Warsaw government "began to perceive the nightmarish vision of Lenin's 'dual power'" and when similar workers' council–based struggles again erupted in 1980, "[t]he interfactory committees acted and appeared as an organ of parallel power" (Singer 1982, 221).

As already noted, these quasi-revolutionary patterns of struggle can also surface in nonrevolutionary times. During the 1978–9 "Winter of Discontent" strike wave in Britain, often criticized as "economistic" and "sectional" (Kelly 1988), elements of dual power soon surfaced. As one activist writer described the dispute: "Within a short time strike committees were deciding what moved in and out of many of the ports and factories. Passes were issued for essential materials . . . In some cases strike committees controlled the public services of whole cities" (Thornett 1998). One government minister himself described the local strike committees of truck drivers, train drivers, and other groups organizing the transport of essential supplies as "little Soviets," while, echoing the "dual power" theme, Tory prime minister-to-be Thatcher wrote that "the Labour government had handed over the running of the country to local committees of trade unionists" (Thatcher 1995, 420; Cohen 2006, 50).

Also in Britain, a twenty-first-century episode of conflict took place that earned the unexpected description "Seven Days That Shook New Labour" from the press. During the course of one surreal week in September 2000, a "leaderless revolt" against massive fuel taxes catapulted road haulage workers into the headlines when they blockaded oil depots and refineries in a desperate protest. Within a few days supermarkets were running out of food, ambulance services had imposed speed limits, and funeral directors were reporting that they had enough petrol to pick up bodies, but not to bury them.

However, the desperate workers conducted the dispute on clear "dual power" terms; newspapers described pickets as "voting on a case-by-case basis whether to let the tankers out of the refinery . . . the driver presents his case to the picket-line and awaits their decision." The parallels with the Winter of Discontent were clear, and were spelled out by government leaders with "deep fears . . . about the political implications of this crisis" (Cohen 2006, 133–4).

As shown in this case, "dual power situations" have occurred in many nonrevolutionary situations; despite the politician's ironic reference to "little Soviets" during the British Winter of Discontent, the defining feature of potentially revolutionary situations is the formation of workers' councils. History shows that many situations and structures can give rise to the form shared with the unmistakably revolutionary Russian soviets without, in the end, a revolutionary outcome. It is the soviet form of organization that poses, more than any other, a fundamental challenge to the capitalist economic and political order. This topic is fully explored in our concluding sections.

## "A peculiar sort of state . . ."

What *were* the soviets?

Trotsky's description of the 1905 revolution, in which soviets played the initial and pivotal role, makes it overwhelmingly clear that these were organizations created by workers, rather than by the "social-democratic organization" (the revolutionary party). As he wrote of the Petersburg Soviet:

"This purely class-founded, proletarian organization was the organization of the revolution as such." Describing the soviet, Trotsky refers directly to the production-based logic of the workers' council structure: "Since the production process was the sole link between the proletarian masses . . . representation had to be adapted to the factories and plants . . . . One delegate was elected for every 500 workers . . . [although] in some cases delegates represented only a hundred . . . workers, or even fewer" (Trotsky 1971, 104).

From this description we can see that it was not the organizational structure of the soviet that distinguished it from its historical predecessors—quite the opposite. Nor, of course, were its origins in workers' own independent organization, rather than any "political" leadership, unique. What was truly exceptional about the Russian soviets was their role, however brief, as organizations of actual, rather than potential, working-class power. In this sense the soviets, in their revolutionary moment, expressed the unity described by both Marx and Lenin between this form of organization and the structure of what is, potentially, both workers' government and workers' state.

It was the crucial connection between the soviet form of worker organization and the structure of a potential workers' state, in which all top-down institutions would necessarily "wither away," to which Lenin drew attention in his writings on the Paris Commune. As he put it in *The State and Revolution,*

> The Commune would appear to have replaced the shattered state machinery "only" by fuller democracy: [for example] all officials to be fully elective and subject to recall. But . . . the "only" signifies a gigantic replacement of one type of institution by others of a fundamentally different order. Here we observe a case of "transformation of quantity into quality": democracy . . . is transformed from capitalist democracy into proletarian democracy: from the state (i.e., a special force for the oppression of a particular class) into something which is no longer really the state in the accepted form of the word (Marx and Lenin 1968, 110–11).

In the same way, the soviets backed by Lenin and Trotsky in the 1917 Russian Revolution took on the political meaning of a transitional structure, both embodying the features of a potential workers' state and possessing the potential to lead to the conquest of power in order to achieve that type of state—and thus, eventually, the "withering away" of the state altogether. Hammering home the point, Lenin argued in his April *Theses*, written six months before the October Revolution, that the Soviets were "not understood . . . in the sense that they constitute a new form or, rather, a new *type of state.*" This was "the type of state which the Russian revolution *began* to create in 1905 and 1917," and that, in certain respects, as Engels argues . . . is "no longer a state in the proper sense of the word" (Marx and Lenin 1968, 127, emphasis in original). In this sense the "withering away of the state" under socialism and communism is enabled by the very form—the soviet—that workers spontaneously adopt as the vehicle to fight for their own class demands.

As Singer suggests, the "workers' state" was always "going to be a peculiar sort of state, transitional by definition, since it was designed from the very start to carry out its own destruction—to build a stateless society" (2002).

That this is a hard-fought, contested process is clearly demonstrated in John Reed's historic *Ten Days That Shook the World,* which vividly describes the fanatical resistance of the ruling class—and indeed of the "soft left" as well—to any real, rather than symbolic, seizure of power by the "shabby soldiers [and] grimy workmen . . . poor men, bent and scarred in the brute struggle for existence" who had seized and made their own the now bureaucratized Soviets"[1] (Reed 1977, 123). It was the Bolsheviks' unceasing backing of the workers' own soviet form of organization and revolutionary power, which the Bolsheviks alone adopted, that gained them—at least for this brief and magical period—the passionate loyalty of the Russian working class.

It was not to last; as implied above, there is nothing sustainable about working-class democracy of the soviet structure outside the context of international working-class rule, and thereby the eventual "withering away" of the state. Even the soviets of 1905, revived and reestablished in the run-up to the February 1917 revolution, were not beyond corruption; as Lenin noted bitterly, "Such heroes of rotten philistinism as the Skobelovs and the Tseretelis[2] . . . have managed to pollute even the Soviets, after the model of the most despicable petty-bourgeois parliamentarianism, by turning them into hollow talking shops" (Marx and Lenin 1968, 114–5). Singer drives the point home: "It was . . . difficult to conceive that in [the] distant future the soviets would be a fiction, the . . . dictatorship a parody of socialist democracy, and the so-called workers' state a mighty organ of coercion" (2002, 339). This final irony was evident when, during the Solidarnosc uprising in Poland, leading CP bureaucrat Ruwelski "vituperated against the workers' councils, the soviets [as] a diabolical invention of the Bolsheviks" (Singer 1982, 270).

This bureaucratization of once dynamically revolutionary workers' organizations points to a crucial lesson indicated by the nature and structure of workers' councils. The features of direct democracy, independence from officialdom, spontaneity, and self-activity examined above are essential to their potential success in achieving and sustaining fundamental social

---

1 See Reed 1977, e.g., 32: "At that time [ July 1917] the majority of the Soviets was 'moderate' Socialist . . . ." See also Koenker 1981 for an account of institutionalized soviets "between the revolutions" in Moscow.
2 Mensheviks then in control of the Petrograd Soviet.

change. Rather than being "anarchistic," the criticism leveled against the factory councils by the suspicious Communist and Socialist parties of Italy, their characteristics of spontaneity, self-activity, and class antagonism were what could, under different political leadership, have carried them to the political barricades and thus to the aid—across Western Europe—of the increasingly fragile Soviet regime in Russia.

## "I was, I am, I will always be . . ."

The argument presented here has not centered on the historic failure of workers' council organization to achieve a lasting regime of workers' power and ownership, participative democracy, and freedom from the oppression and exploitation under which the world currently labors. While this failure is crucial to any analysis of the future of such organizations, this chapter aims to emphasize the continually renewed and extraordinary potential of these "fresh, young, powerful, organizations," to paraphrase Luxemburg in *The Mass Strike* (1925, 35).[3] The same workplace-based, directly demo-cratic, "spontaneous" formation repeatedly surfaces and resurfaces, often in entirely unpredictable surges of working-class struggle. It is this resilience that provides us with the only hope available in a "new world order" dom-inated by the greed, immorality, and violence of neoliberalism.

Much current (and indeed past) socialist analysis would question whether working-class activity is the "only hope available." Many left per-spectives place considerable weight on new social movements involving youth, radicalized women, oppressed ethnic minorities, and other identity-based groups as the main forces for reviving an anticapitalist movement. Again, causes not directly based at the point of production, such as the en-vironmental crisis, seem to have more credibility than the labor struggles discussed here for a left urgently seeking to chime in with twenty-first-cen-tury culture.

The present argument in no way denies the importance of these issues. What is argued here is the continued relevance of working-class struggle, in all its diverse twenty-first-century manifestations. The economic crisis once again calling into question the viability of the capitalist system has al-ready manifested the predictable strategy of an attack on working-class liv-ing standards—and, repeatedly, on the class response of those so victimized.

The history set out above points beyond a doubt to the political potential of grassroots workplace-based resistance, which, from the earliest stages of

---

3 Luxemburg's description in *The Mass Strike* of newly formed workers' organizations during the 1917 Russian Revolution.

industrial organization to today's globalized waves of unionization and strike action, has challenged the existing order in ways that its rulers, at least, regard with the utmost seriousness (Moody 1997, Mason 2007). Looking at political transformation from this point of view, workers' councils continue to offer the organizational form most relevant and effective even for twenty-first-century struggles. Workers swept up in the super-exploitation imposed by globalization in the newly industrializing countries are no less likely to adopt this form than their "developed" counterparts, just as they have increasingly adopted similar forms of trade union organization.

On all these grounds, the current contribution is a plea to today's left—and, even more importantly, to the layer of politicized working-class activists who, despite everything, still wage the anticapitalist fight in the workplace—to recognize the radical potential of the grassroots, directly democratic, resurgent organizations chronicled above. On the basis of the historical probability of the reemergence of such organizations, we conclude on the note of revolutionary optimism sounded by Rosa Luxemburg in her last defiant shout to the bourgeoisie: "Your order is built on sand. Tomorrow the revolution will raise its head again and proclaim to your horror, amid a brass of trumpets: I was, I am, I will always be."

## References

Anderson, Andy. 1964. *Hungary '56,* London: Phoenix Press.

Appel, Jan. 2008. Origins of the movement for workers' councils in Germany. *Commune,* no. 5.

Barker, Chris, ed. 1987. *Revolutionary rehearsals.* London: Bookmarks.

Birchall, Ian. 1974. *Workers against the monolith: The Communist parties since 1943.* London: Pluto Press.

Brecher, Jeremy. 1997. *Strike!* Boston: South End Press.

Charlton, John. 1997. *The Chartists: The first national workers' movement.* London: Pluto Press.

Cohen, Sheila. 2006. *Ramparts of resistance: Why workers lost their power, and how to get it back.* London: Pluto Press.

Dangerfield, George. 1961. *The strange death of liberal England.* New York: Capricorn.

Darlington, Ralph. 2009. Organising, militancy and revitalisation: The case of the RMT union. In *Union revitalisation in advanced economies: Assessing the contribution of union organising,* ed. Gregor Gall, 83–106. Basingstoke; New York: Palgrave Macmillan.

Fosh, Patricia and Sheila Cohen. 1990. Local trade unionists in action: Patterns of union democracy. In *Trade unions and their members,* ed. Patricia Fosh and Edmund Heery. London: Macmillan.

Gall, Gregor. 2009a. *Union revitalisation in advanced economies: Assessing the contribution of union organising.* Basingstoke; New York: Palgrave Macmillan.

———, ed. 2009b. *The future of union organising: Building for tomorrow.* Basingstoke; New York: Palgrave Macmillan.

Gluckstein, Donny. 1985. *The Western soviets: workers' councils versus Parliament 1915–20.*

London: Bookmarks.

Gonzalez, Mike. 1987. Chile 1972–3: The workers united. In *Revolutionary rehearsals*, ed. Chris Barker. London: Bookmarks.

Gramsci, Antonio. 1971. *Prison notebooks.* London: Lawrence and Wishart Harman.

Harman, Chris. 1974. *Bureaucracy and revolution in Eastern Europe.* London: Pluto Press.

_____. 2002. Argentina: Rebellion at the sharp end of the world crisis. *International Socialism* 94 (Spring 2002).

Hinton, James. 1972. *The first shop stewards' movement.* London: George Allen and Unwin.

Holton, Bob. 1976. *British syndicalism 1900–1914.* London: Pluto Press.

Kelly, John. 1988. *Trade unions and socialist politics.* London: Verso.

_____. 1998. *Rethinking industrial relations: Mobilisation, collectivism and long waves.* London: Routledge.

Koenker, Diane. 1981. *Moscow workers and the 1917 revolution.* Princeton, NJ: Princeton University Press.

Leopold, Les. 2007. *The man who hated work and loved labor.* Vermont: Chelsea Green.

Luxemburg, Rosa. 1925. *The mass strike.* London: Merlin Press.

Lynd, Staughton. 2003. Students and workers in the transition to socialism: The Singer model. *Monthly Review* 54, no. 10.

Marx, Karl and V. I. Lenin. 1968. *Civil war in France: The Paris Commune.* New York: International Publishers.

Mason, Paul. 2007. *Live working or die fighting: How the working class went global.* London: Harvill Secker.

Moody, Kim. 1997. *Workers in a lean world: Unions in the international economy.* New York: Verso.

Nagy, Balazs. 2006. *How the Budapest central workers' council was set up.* Liverpool: Living History Library.

Postgate, R.W., Ellen Wilkinson, and J. F. Horrabin. 1927. *A workers' history of the Great Strike.* London: The Plebs League.

Poya, Maryam. 1987. Iran 1979: Long live revolution! Long live Islam? In *Revolutionary rehearsals*, ed. Chris Barker. London: Bookmarks.

Reed, John. 1977. *Ten days that shook the world.* London: Penguin Books.

Robinson, Peter. 1987. Portugal, 1974–5: Popular power. In *Revolutionary rehearsals*, ed. Chris Barker. London: Bookmarks.

Rosenberg, Cheni. 1987. *1919: Britain on the brink of revolution.* London: Bookmarks.

Singer, Daniel. 1982. *The road to Gdansk: Poland and the USSR.* New York: Monthly Review Press.

_____. 2002. *Prelude to revolution: France in May 1968.* Cambridge: South End Press.

Smith, Mark. 2009. Vestas occupation. *Solidarity* 25.

Thatcher, Margaret. 1995. *The path to power,* New York: HarperCollins Press.

Thornett, Alan. 1998. *Inside Cowley.* London: Porcupine Press.

Trotsky, Leon. 1926. *Where is Britain going?* London; Allen & Unwin.

_____. 1967. *The history of the Russian Revolution.* London: Sphere Books.

_____. 1971. *1905.* New York: Vintage Books.

Weir, Stan. 1967. *U.S.A.—the labor revolt.* Boston: New England Free Press.

Williams, Gwyn A. 1975. *Proletarian order: Antonio Gramsci, factory councils and the origins of communism in Italy 1911–1921.* London: Pluto Press.

Wilson, Phil. 2009. We knew we had nothing to lose. *Solidarity* 25.

Wright, Steve. 2002. *Storming heaven: Class composition and struggle in the Italian autonomist Marxism.* London: Pluto Press.

# 4

# The Political Form
# at Last Discovered
## Workers' Councils against the Capitalist State

**Alberto R. Bonnet**

> *It was essentially a working class government, the product of the struggle of the producing against the appropriating class, the political form at last discovered under which to work out the economical emancipation of labor.*
> —Marx, *The Civil War in France*

These were Marx's words, written during the Franco-Prussian War applauding the innovation of the Parisian Communards. Half a century later, at the end of World War I, a new generation of intellectuals committed to workers' struggle again welcomed the creation of a modern political form for the emancipation of labor, represented by workers' councils. This chapter discusses analyses of the World War I workers' councils in order to better understand the truly innovative nature and capacity of this revolutionary structure. The main argument of this essay is that the workers' council showed an inherent potential to overcome the division between the economic and the political spheres. Considering that this division underpins the capitalist state, overcoming it means in fact overcoming the capitalist state itself.

With the Paris Commune as background, the first part of this chapter takes a close look at how a group of brilliant theoreticians, witnesses to the councils' creation, viewed their formation. The second section focuses specifically on these intellectuals' recognition of the potential of the workers' council to overcome the separation of the political and the economic, and the conclusions they drew regarding the political position to take toward the state. The third part analyzes the range and limitations of their reflections.

## The Creation of Workers' Councils

The creation of workers' councils at the end of World War I validated the position of intellectuals whose ideas prior to the war had been regarded as the left wing of social democracy. These theoreticians (also known as councilists) believed in the ability of the working class to autonomously create its own version of revolutionary struggle and organization. This was especially true for the Dutch Tribunists and, in particular, for Anton Pannekoek.[1] In fact, the positions defended by Pannekoek during the controversies over the strategy of the political mass strike, which arose after the political strike in Belgium in 1902, the first Russian Revolution in 1905, and the Prussian political crisis in 1909 (see Parvus et al. 1975–1976), anticipated his later positions toward workers' councils. Pannekoek recognized in these mass strikes a *"particular and new form of activity of the organized workers"* (1912, italics in original), which indicated a new political practice, different from the traditional parliamentarian and unionist approaches typical of the Social Democrats.

This new practice was born out of the transformations that had occurred in the capitalist productive system and the corresponding composition of the working class. While the leaders of parliamentary and, especially, unionist social democracy supported the conservative argument, repeated by Karl Kautsky in the socialist debates inside the German Social Democratic Party, that a premature mass strike could lead to the destruction of the existing workers' organizations—an argument rooted in the strategy of party-managed ascension to state power—Pannekoek defended the capacity of the working class to create its own forms of revolutionary struggle and organization, within the development of an insurrectionist strategy.

Even if Pannekoek suspected before the war that the product of this working-class self-organization process would be different from the existing party or trade unions, it was only after the war that he would identify it as the workers' council. Until that moment, Pannekoek, like Rosa Luxemburg, was limited to believing in the action of the mass strike and the organizational consciousness it could rouse among workers, but without articulating the political form it would adopt:

> The organization of the proletariat, which we identify as its most important means of power, must not be confused with present forms of organization

---

1 The Dutch were among the earliest and most radical in turning toward the left of the social democracy. Pannekoek, Gorter, and Roland-Holst joined the Social Democratic Workers' Party (SDAP, the Dutch version of Second International socialism) at the end of the nineteenth century, and fought against the party leadership of Pieter Troesltra during the first decade of the next. In 1907 they formed the left wing of the party and associated around the newspaper *De Tribune* (hence the name Tribunists). In 1909 they split off as the Social Democratic Party (SDP). The SDP, which would later transform itself into the Communist Party of Holland, was the only instance of a Communist Party being founded from a party preexisting the October Revolution in Russia (see Hansen 1976).

and association, which are expressions of that proletarian organization within the framework, still firm, of the bourgeois order. *The essence of that organization is something mental, the total transformation of the proletarians' character*" (Pannekoek 1912, italics in original).[2]

The creation of workers' councils during the surge of class struggle at the end of World War I filled the gap. And the councilists recalled Marx's words, quoted earlier, recognizing in those workers' councils "the political form at last discovered." Even though the Paris Commune was crushed quickly and brutally by the armies of the bourgeoisie, it was universally recognized as the most advanced experience of workers' emancipation struggles until World War I.

A *new* form? In his first reflections on the recent German Revolution, in a short note composed in late November 1918, Pannekoek wrote that, to destroy the capitalist rule concentrated in the state,

> It is necessary to break the old government's organisation, the old bureaucracy, and to strengthen the temporary organisation of the masses into lasting power. This happened in Paris in 1871 by the Commune and in Russia in November by the Soviets. In Germany the workers have created such an organisation, the same as took place in Russia, in the formation of Workers' and Soldiers' Councils (1919a).

Pannekoek identified in the workers' councils a new form of mass organization opposed to the capitalist state, and he attributed to them a revolutionary character due to their very existence—not due to their program, which during the German Revolution was still merely democratic, not revolutionary.

In his subsequent writings Pannekoek turned his attention back to this concept with much more precision. Thus, in his critique of social democracy, Pannekoek referred to the conclusion drawn by Marx from the experience of the Paris Commune concerning the need to destroy the capitalist state and replace it with a new form of organization, but he also noted an interesting detail that made the commune different from the workers' council.[3]

---

2 This stand was analogous to the revolutionary syndicalists—and this parallel was stressed by Kautsky, who attacked Pannekoek and Luxemburg as supposed anarchists. But this similarity was inevitable: Those oriented politically to the left of social democracy before the war shared the same political space with revolutionary unionism, because the revolutionary character that the social democracy was losing in its political practice seemed to be transferred more and more to the political practice of revolutionary syndicalism. See for example, concerning Pannekoek and the Tribunists, the influence of Domela Nieuwenhuis, the father of Dutch socialism, who later joined the anarcho-syndicalist movement. He questioned the parliamentarianism of the SDAP and became one of the main advocates of the mass strike strategy against the menace of war threatening Europe.

3 Pannekoek didn't explicitly quote Marx, but we can certainly refer to his famous phrase, "the working class cannot simply lay hold of the ready-made state machinery, and wield it for its own

In the Commune, the citizens and workers of Paris elected a parliament after the old model, but this parliament was immediately transformed into something quite unlike our parliament. Its purpose was not to entertain the people with fine words while allowing a small clique of businessmen and capitalists to preserve their private property; the men who met in the new parliament had to publicly regulate and administer everything on behalf of the people. What had been a parliamentary corporation was transformed into a corporation of labor; it formed committees that were responsible for framing new legislation. In this manner, the bureaucracy as a special class, independent of and ruling over the people, disappeared, thereby abolishing the separation of legislative and executive powers. Those persons who occupied the highest posts over the people were at the same time elected by and representatives of the people themselves who put them in office, and could at any time be removed from office by their electors (Pannekoek 1927, 10).

The commune was elected as "a parliament after the old model"—thus the commune was still a bourgeois political form, although it went through a metamorphosis, and "was transformed into a corporation of labor," an incipient proletarian form. But the workers' councils were inherently different, as Pannekoek noticed:

A new and important step was taken in 1905 in Russia, with the establishment of councils, or soviets, as organs of expression of the fighting proletariat. These organs did not conquer political power, although the Saint Petersburg central workers council assumed the leadership of the struggle, and exercised considerable power. When the new revolution broke out in 1917, the soviets were once again constructed, this time as organs of proletarian power. With the German November Revolution the proletariat took political control of the country and provided the second historical example of proletarian State power (Ibid.).

But the new councils were different from the old commune, in particular because they had a much stronger potential to overcome the division between the political and economic:

In the council system, political organization is built upon the economic process of labor. Parliamentarism rests upon the individual in his quality as a citizen of the State. This had its historical justification, since bourgeois society was originally composed of producers who were equal in respect to one another, each one of whom produced his commodities himself and together formed, through the sum of all their little transactions, the production process as a whole. But in modern society, with its giant industrial complexes and its class antagonisms, this basis is becoming increasingly obsolete. . . .

---

purposes" (1871). This is the main teaching of the Paris Commune, as Marx and Engels stated in their 1872 preface to a German revised edition of *The Communist Manifesto* (1848).

Parliamentary theory views each man primarily as a citizen of the State, and as such, individuals thereby come to be abstract entities, all of them equal. But in practice, the real, concrete man is a worker. . . . In order to unite men in groups, parliamentary political practice divides the State into electoral districts; but the men who are assigned to these districts, workers, landlords, street peddlers, manufacturers, landowners, members of every class and every trade, haphazardly lumped together due to the purely accidental fact of their place of residence, can by no means arrive at a communitarian representation of their common interest and will, because they have nothing in common. The natural groups are production groups, the workers of a factory, who take part in the same activity, the peasants in a village, and, on a larger scale, the classes (Ibid.).

Had a superior form been discovered at last? To deepen our analysis let us take a look at Karl Korsch's reception of this novel form. Korsch pointed out that if the working class had been successful with the revolutionary upsurge at the end of World War I, it would have constituted its government as a councils' republic. But, he added, after defeat and facing new historical challenges,

We, the revolutionary proletarian class-fighters of the whole world, cannot any more hold subjectively onto our old belief, quite unchanged and unexamined, in the revolutionary significance of the council concept and the revolutionary character of *council government* as a direct development of that *political form of the proletarian dictatorship* "discovered" half a century ago by the Paris Communards (Korsch 1929, italics in original).

In other words, as a theorist of the constitution of political forms, Korsch affirmed that the revolutionary working class had tried, at the end of the war, to constitute its government as a councils' republic. However, once the counterrevolution had succeeded, as a theorist of historical specificity, he warned about the hypostatization of this or any other political form.[4] There is a "historical dialectic," he argued, which exists as follows:

Every historical form turns at a certain point of its development from a *developing form* of revolutionary forces of production, revolutionary action, and developing consciousness into the *shackles* of that developing form. And as this dialectical *antithesis* of revolutionary development applies to all other historical ideas and formations, it equally applies also to those *philosophical and organizational results of a certain historical phase of revolutionary class struggle*, which is exemplified by the Paris communards of almost 60 years ago in the "finally discovered" political form of government of the working class in the shape of a *revolutionary commune*. The same is applicable to the fol-

---

4 I refer to two main aspects of Korsch's theories, which due to space constraints I am unable to explain in detail here: his conceptualization of the *constitution* of political forms (see Negt 1973) and his principle of *historical specification* (see Kellner 1977).

lowing new historical phase of struggle in the revolutionary movement of the Russian workers and peasants, and the international working class, which brought forth the new form of the *"revolutionary councils' power."*

Instead of bewailing the "betrayal" of the council concept and the "degeneration" of the council power we must gather by illusion-free, sober, and historically objective observation the beginning, middle, and end of this whole development within a *total historical panorama* and we must pose this *critical question:* What is—after this total historical experience—*the real historical and class-oriented significance of this new political form of government,* which brought about in the first place the *revolutionary Commune* of 1871, although its development was forcefully interrupted after 72 days duration, and then the *Russian Revolution of 1917* in concrete, more final, shape? (Ibid., italics in original).

Korsch, along with Pannekoek, argued that the commune, as a political form, wasn't any different from the bourgeois parliament. It was in fact a more ancient bourgeois form, one that dated to the eleventh century, and in the character of its organization was even truer to the struggle of the revolutionary bourgeoisie than was the parliament. When Marx welcomed the commune as a new political form, Korsch understood that

> He was far removed from expecting any wondrous effects for the proletarian class struggle from the political *form* of the communal constitution per se— detached from the definite proletarian class-oriented content, with which the Paris workers, according to his concept, had for one historical moment filled this political form, achieved through struggle and put into the service of their economic self-liberation (Ibid., italics in original).

The Communards could use the medieval commune effectively, argued Korsch, because it was a *"relatively undeveloped and indeterminate"* form, in contrast to the institutions of the more centralized, modern representative bourgeois state. It was not at all Marx's "desire—as some of his followers later claimed and still do so to this day—to designate or brand *a definite form of political organization,* whether it is called a *revolutionary commune* or a *revolutionary council system,* as a singularly appropriate and potential form of the revolutionary proletarian class dictatorship" (Ibid., italics in original).

Korsch obviously was not affirming any neutrality of the political form in relation to its class content, rather he was warning about the fetishization of the council form as deduced from a dialectic between form and content. The contradiction between this political form and its class content transformed the political form into a process:

> The *revolutionary communal constitution* thus becomes under certain historical conditions the political form of a *process of development,* or to put it more clearly, of a *revolutionary action* where the basic essential goal is no longer

to *preserve any one form of state rule,* or *even to create a newer "higher state-type,"* but rather to create at last the material conditions for the "withering away of the state altogether" (Ibid., italics in original).

## Workers' Councils and the Capitalist State

A *political* form? Let us have a detailed look at the potential of the workers' councils to overcome the division between the political and the economic and, because this separation is a fundamental constituent of the capitalist state, finally at their potential to overcome the capitalist state. All the councilists under discussion identified, in some fashion, this potential but not all drew the same conclusions concerning the political position to be adopted regarding the state. We will begin the analysis with the complex relationships Korsch saw between workers' councils and the state within the organization of production.[5]

Korsch (1920) affirms that at the end of the war, the revolutionary process itself presented the problem of socialization, which had been neglected or considered utopian by the Social Democratic leadership, on the German political agenda. What was the relationship between the workers' councils and the state in the socialization process? In his first extensive writing on the subject, the 1919 pamphlet *What Is Socialization?*, Korsch proposed a system that combined a unionist form of organization (from the producer's point of view) with a political form of organization (from the consumer's point of view). The socialization could either take place through the state (as an indirect socialization from the producer's perspective and a direct one from the consumer's point of view), or follow the union's logic (as a direct socialization from the producer's perspective and an indirect one from the consumers' perspective) (Korsch 1919a). In another work from 1919 Korsch distinguished clearly between the socialization of the product (indirect when the worker is still a wage earner but now paid by the state, a cooperative, or a community; direct when the worker is the owner of the means of production), and the socialization of the production process (the worker decides what, how, and under which conditions to produce). He

---

5 Korsch was one of the main theorists of postwar socialization. His interest in the topic had its origins in his relationship with the Fabian Society during his residence in London (1912–1914: see his writings of those years in Korsch 1980) but reached its peak at the end of the war, when he—while still a member of the USPD (Independent German Social Democratic Party)— temporarily served on the commission created after the German November Revolution (1918) to prepare the socialization of German industries. The somewhat artificial tone of his writings of those years is probably a result of the no less "artificial" character of the commission, which Pannekoek (see Bricianer 1975) and others denounced as a move by the social democratic leadership to avoid any real socialization.

tried to outline a socialization modality that responded to the conflicting interests of the community of producers and the community of consumers (Korsch 1919b). In these writings, Korsch still considered the main challenge of socialization to be the contradiction between the interests of producers and consumers, and he looked for a synthesis that could reconcile them.

By that time, however, Korsch had already declared, in the first pages he wrote about the German Revolution, that "the convenient *form* of socialization is not, generally speaking, the centralization but the *autonomy*" (1919c, italics in original). In the pamphlet mentioned earlier, he revealed his preference for socialization as a direct action and his concerns regarding socialization as statization (nationalization under state control), for example, in his insistence on the educational nature of direct action (1919a) or the distinction he drew between socialization and mere statization (1919a). Korsch accepted openly, but without the "revolutionary gymnastics," the program of the Spartacists, which affirmed that the economic transformation could only take place as a process implemented by the proletarian masses. Socializing decrees by revolutionary authorities were just empty words, which only a mass of workers could transform into reality. The workers' control of production would be achieved through the tenacious struggle against capital in every enterprise through the direct pressure of the masses, strikes, and the creation of enduring representational organs (Korsch 1919a).

Concerning the second point Korsch criticized the orthodox Social Democratic understanding of socialization as statization: "Most of them [the Social Democrats that were in charge of socialization], identified the 'socialization' with 'statization,' thinking, with more or less clarity, that, as 'it is obvious,' the 'state' of the socialist era, which has to regulate production and consumption in an integral and unified way, would be a totally different state from the previous 'class state'" (1919d).[6] Such a "conception of a state socialism" had to be rejected. The statization implied a "simple change of employer" that, moreover, would lead to a "paralysis of the productive forces."

---

6 As Korsch does here, Pannekoek also warned about the similarities between the statizations intended by the Social Democrats (Rathenau, Bauer) in the postwar period and the nationalizations carried out by the bourgeoisie (Neurath, Wissel) during the war. And he pointed out that nationalizations under state control were not socialism; socialism was the power of the proletariat. But since in the ideal world of social democracy socialism and state economy were not far away from each other, the Social Democrats would not entertain any arguments against the state socialism policies, which tended to reduce the proletariat to slavery (in "Wenn der Krieg zu Ende geht," *Vorbote* 1, no. 2 [April 2, 1916], quoted in Bricianer 1975). After the war Pannekoek wrote: "Just as the 'socialist' government is only the continuation of the old bourgeois domination under the socialist banner, 'socialization' is only the continuation of the old bourgeois exploitation under the socialist banner" (1919b).

Korsch was clear: "The worker as such doesn't win more freedom; his way of life and work won't be more humanized because the manager appointed by the owners of private capital is replaced by an official appointed by the state government or the municipal administration" (Ibid.).

Nevertheless, the statization continued to be necessary because a "general economic plan" had to go along with the "industrial democracy." The tension was inevitable; however, Korsch solved it simply by identifying the totality with a system of councils: "Today the way to make these *two* requirements contained in the slogan of socialization, on one hand the control from above (by the collective) and on the other the control from the bottom up (by the ones directly involved in the process of production), come through quickly and safe, is no other than the one represented by the frequently mentioned and so often misunderstood '*system of councils*'" (Ibid., italics in original).

In *Labour Law for Factory Councils* (1922), he proposed his most advanced version of a "labor constitution"; a constitution for democracy in the economic sphere, as industrial or productive democracy, which would complement the democracy in the political sphere achieved in the November Revolution. Korsch wrote: "With the election of its 'revolutionary councils,' the workers expressed their determination to take into account every company, as well as the totality of the national capitalist economy—composed by a number of individual companies and trusts in mutual competition—as a real 'labor community,' and the workers employed by it, as 'citizens' with full rights" (Ibid.).

Nevertheless the relationship between the two democracies, or in other words between the councils and the state, was still a conflictive matter in Korsch's argumentation. He defined the totality as an "economic system of councils, controlled by the proletarian state" (Ibid.) and he conceded that the state could in the interim even limit the power of councils. Korsch had no doubt that the introduction of the proletarian democracy instead of the bourgeois democracy would accelerate considerably the development of more direct forms of industrial democracy, but only in the long term. For the short term he considered the possibility of limiting, temporarily, to a certain degree the cooperative rights of workers or even the autonomy of the unions. But in the proletarian state, per Korsch, these limitations were not carried out in favor of the exploiting capitalist class, but in favor of the working class organized as the state (Ibid.).

At that time, Korsch was still a member of the KPD (German Communist Party), and his model for the relationship between the state and workers' councils was the supposed relationship between the state and soviets in the Soviet Union. Meanwhile, between 1918 and 1921, the new, alleged "workers' state" led by the Bolsheviks in the USSR had already aborted the instances of workers' control of production—which had never become generalized as an experience of real workers' management.[7] By 1922 the oppression had been carried out completely, and Korsch was not indifferent to this authoritarian deviation of the USSR. For him, the main challenge of socialization was no longer the contradiction between the interests of producers and consumers but the contradiction between those producers and consumers altogether, with the working class as a whole on one side, and a new bureaucratic establishment on the other.[8] This didn't mean that he didn't consider the other challenge as well, but Korsch's emphasis from that moment on lay in maintaining the autonomy of the workers' councils and other organizations of the working class.

Some years later, after the defeat of the German workers' councils but before the emergence of the Spanish revolutionary commune, Korsch defended without hesitation collectivizations by the masses, organized autonomously in unions, and argued against nationalizations and the state interventions advocated by Social Democrats and Communists: "The energy of the anti-state attitude of the revolutionary Spanish proletariat, unhampered by self-created organizational or ideological obstacles, explains all their surprising successes in the face of overwhelming difficulties" (1939, 181). And Korsch notes that, contrary to what was common in other revolutionary processes in Europe, in Spain revolutionary collectivization was implemented right from the beginning and extended to private as well as to state- or city-owned companies.[9]

We have examined the path followed by Korsch because it reveals, in a heightened fashion, the type of problems encountered in any systematic exploration of the relationship between workers' councils—or other forms of workers' self-organization—and the state. But Korsch's is not, and was not, the only possible course. Two contrasting cases are examined below.

Otto Rühle traveled to Moscow in June 1920 to assist at the Second Congress of the Comintern as a delegate of the dissident KAPD (German Communist Workers' Party). He informed himself of the politics the Bolsheviks were developing in the USSR—as well as what they were developing toward

---

7 The factory committees that had emerged together with the so-called soviets in February 1917 had lived those experiences of workers' control. But their institutionalization, after October 1917, with the November decree, marked the beginning of their suppression: first, by subordinating the committees to mainly party-guided trade unions, and then by replacing them with managers appointed by the state without any other procedure (see Brinton 1972).

8  As Gerlach points out correctly in his introduction to Korsch (1974).

9  Korsch travelled to Spain in 1931 with the German anarcho-syndicalist Augustin Souchy (although he was a militant of the CNT-FAI), and his closest collaborator, the Hungarian Paul Partos, who collaborated as of 1933 with the Spanish Revolution, also joining the CNT-FAI (Kellner 1977).

Europe, because Lenin apprised Rühle in advance of the content of *"Left-Wing" Communism, an Infantile Disorder*. Rühle left Moscow, returning to Germany even before the Congress had begun. In his report as a delegate, he wrote:

> The Russian tactic is the tactic of authoritarian organisation. It has been so consistently developed and in the end carried to extremes by the Bolsheviks as to the fundamental principle of centralism, that it has led to over-centralism. The Bolsheviks didn't do that out of wantonness or desire to experiment. The revolution forced them to it. . . . Centralism is the organisational principle of the bourgeois-capitalist age. With it the bourgeois state and the capitalist economy can be built up. Not however the proletarian state and the socialist economy. They demand the council system. For the KAPD—contrary to Moscow—the revolution is no party matter, the party no authoritarian organisation from the top down, the leader no military chief, the masses no army condemned to blind obedience, the dictatorship no despotism of a ruling clique; communism no springboard for the rise of a new Soviet bourgeoisie. For the KAPD the revolution is the business of the whole proletarian class within which the communist party forms only the most mature and determined vanguard (1920).

Consequently Rühle was active in the creation of unitary organizations (*Einheitsorganizationen*) to bridge the division between the political and the economic, inherent to the classical distinction between the party and the union; as such the aim was for these organizations to promote the creation of workers' councils (Ibid.).[10]

Young Antonio Gramsci, in contrast, traveled to Moscow to the Fourth Congress of the Comintern during November and December 1922, as a delegate of the recently founded PCI (Italian Communist Party). The PCI, led by Amadeo Bordiga, was almost as dissident concerning the directives from Moscow as the KAPD of Hermann Gorter, the Dutch socialist poet and theoretician. But Gramsci, who in the pages of *L'Ordine Nuovo* in 1919–1920 had promoted the conversion of the factory commissions of the huge Turin companies into workers' councils, and had identified with precision the potential of those workers' councils to overcome the separation between the political and economic, held on and stepped back. Gramsci himself became one of the main agents of the subordination of the PCI to directives from Moscow, including the Bolshevik policy toward Europe: united front, workers' and peasants' government, participation in unions and parliament, Bolshevization of the Communist parties, and so on.[11]

---

10 About the unitary organization experience (in particular, the Allgemeine Arbeiter Union—Einheitsorganisation led by Rühle) see Barrot and Authier 1978.
11 About Gramsci's role in this political alignment of the PCI with Moscow, see the short but accurate analysis of Bates 1976.

From the defeat of the factory councils during the *Biennio Rosso*, Gramsci had drawn the dubious conclusion that, in order to avoid new defeats, the revolutionary political practice of forming workers' councils needed to be placed in the vanguard party's hands. And when the subordination of the PCI to Moscow directives reached its peak, in 1926 at the party's Third Congress of Lyon, Gramsci and Togliatti declared in the "Lyons Theses" that organizing the proletarian vanguard in the Communist Party had to be an essential part of the organizational activity. Their conclusion from the Italian workers' experience of 1919–20 was that without the leadership of the Communist Party, built as the party of the working class and as the party of the revolution, victory in the struggle to tear down the capitalist regime would not be possible (Gramsci and Togliatti 1990).

The development of Korsch's line of thinking was much more complex and nuanced than either of these two, and thus reveals much more clearly the challenges inherent in considering the relationship between workers' councils and the state. In summation, we can say that, as Korsch himself was to recognize later, he moved little by little toward the more radical councilists' positions.[12]

Pannekoek had affirmed already before the war that

> the struggle of the proletarians is not just a struggle against the bourgeoisie *for* state power as an object, but a struggle *against* state power. The problem of the social revolution can be resumed as follows: Raise the power of the proletariat to the point it is superior to the state power. And *the content of that revolution is the destruction and the dissolution of the means of power of the state by the means of power of the proletariat*" (1912, italics in original).

The means of power of the proletariat was endowed with a truly new form by the creation of workers' councils at the end of World War I. And a new modality for overcoming state power by the power of the proletariat would be a system of such councils. Pannekoek wrote later in 1946: "The workers' councils are the form of self-government which in the times to come will replace the forms of government of the old world. . . . Workers' Councils are the form of organisation during the transition period in which the working class is fighting for dominance, is destroying capitalism and is organizing social production" (1946).

As a result the transitional "dictatorship of the proletariat" no longer represented the Jacobinic reaffirmation of the division between the political and economic of the French Revolution, as it did for Lenin; in contrast, it

---

12 After he broke definitively with the KPD in early 1926, Korsch recognized that the critique of the Bolsheviks by Luxemburg and Liebknecht in 1917–18 and the later critique by the Tribunists Pannekoek and Gorter in 1920–21 had paved the way for his split (Korsch 1930a).

was suited to the process of overcoming the division. Pannekoek then reiterated Engels's statement: "Do you want to know what this dictatorship looks like? Look at the Paris Commune. That was the Dictatorship of the Proletariat" (Engels 1974, 242). Although, naturally, under the contemporary circumstances, he directed the reader to look at the workers' councils:

> Seventy years ago Marx pointed out that between the rule of capitalism and the final organisation of a free humanity there will be a time of transition in which the working class is master of society but in which the bourgeoisie has not yet disappeared. He called this state of things the *dictatorship of the proletariat*. At that time this word had not yet the ominous sound of modern systems of despotism, nor could it be misused for the dictatorship of a ruling party, as in later Russia. It meant simply that the dominant power over society was transferred from the capitalist to the working class. . . . We see now that council organisation puts into practice what Marx theoretically anticipated but for what at that time the practical form could not yet be imagined. When production is regulated by the producers themselves, the formerly exploiting class automatically is excluded from taking part in the decisions, without any artificial stipulation. Marx's conception of the dictatorship of the proletariat now appears to be identical with the labor democracy of council organisation (1946).

## Conclusion

As part of our conclusion it might be illuminating to identify some of the limitations of these reflections on workers' councils. For reasons of space we will focus on two problems related to the council as form. The first problem is strictly a conceptual one. The rigorous analysis of the tendency of the workers' councils to overcome the division between the political and economic and, in so doing, to overcome the compartmentalization of the capitalist state itself, requires a conceptualization no less rigorous of the state as a form of capitalist social relations. Such a conceptualization does not appear among the writings of our councilists. It was the so-called state derivation debate in mid-1970s West Germany that eventually provided the basis for the conceptualization used in this essay.[13] But this is not to deny that the councilists employed a similar concept of form. Pannekoek emphasized its importance with regard to the council form:

> The idea that a particular organisational form is revolutionary has been held up to scorn in the party disputes in Germany on the grounds that what

---

13 See the classical compilation of Holloway and Picciotto 1978 and, for a summary of the debate, see Bonnet 2007.

counts is the revolutionary mentality of the members. But if the most important element of the revolution consists in the masses taking their own affairs—the management of society and production—in hand themselves, then any form of organisation which does not permit control and direction by the masses themselves is counterrevolutionary and harmful; and it should therefore be replaced by another form that is revolutionary in that it enables the workers themselves to determine everything actively. This is not to say that this form is to be set up within a still passive work-force in readiness for the revolutionary feeling of the workers to function within it in time to come: this new form of organisation can itself only be set up in the process of revolution, by workers making a revolutionary intervention. But recognition of the role played by the current form of organisation determines the attitude which the communists have to take with regard to the attempts already being made to weaken or burst this form (1920).

Korsch also stated the need for a rigorous approach to the concept of form. In his discussion of Evgeny Pashukanis's contributions to the critique of the juridical form, for example, Korsch lamented the fact that, until that moment, among Marxists there was "not even one, who beyond the critique of the changing law contents would have approached also the task of the materialist critique of the juridical form in itself" (1930b). He traced a parallel between the critique of the fetishization of the commodity form expressed by Marx and the critique of the fetishization of the legal form by Pashukanis. He attributed Karl Renner's dismissal of this critique to "his absolutely fetishist faith in the state" and his "parliamentary imbecility," concluding that "no 'change of norm' neither of the abstract written "law" nor of the *jus quod est* [the state of law] really existent in society, will abolish that main social function of law that isn't connected to any special historical legal content, but is given with the juridical form itself" (Ibid.).

In short, our councilists did not develop a systematic analysis of the concept of form, which is necessary for a theoretical and practical approach to analyzing the problem of the relationship between workers' councils and the state.

The second problem is more historical in nature and refers specifically to the workers' council as a form of workers' self-organization. The conviction of the councilists that the workers' council was the organizational form par excellence was completely justified. Although the council movement was aborted, the experience of their formation at the end of World War I was sufficient proof of their potential to overcome the division between the political and the economic. The councilists' conviction that this was central to workers' emancipation was also correct. But whether workers' councils remain the ideal organizational form to face the challenges of today is less certain.

Of course, the formation of workers' councils was not a phenomenon restricted to the end of World War I—other chapters in this volume examine subsequent experiences, such as Spain in 1936, Poland in 1956, and many more. But, as Pannekoek stated, the viability of the council form must be assessed in light of the current characteristics of the capitalist productive system and the composition of the working class; or, in other words, in the context of the achievements in socialization and the accompanying intellectualization of that social work. In this sense, the final word on this subject has not been spoken. Whether it is a workers' council or a different kind of organization that will be, to quote Pannekoek, "the political form at last discovered under which to work out the economical emancipation of labor," the final word will be spoken by the workers themselves, through their revolutionary practice.

## References

Barrot, Jean and Denis Authier. 1978. *La izquierda comunista en Alemania 1918–1921,* Madrid: Zero zyx.

Bates, Thomas R. 1976. Antonio Gramsci and the Bolshevization of the PCI. *Journal of Contemporary History* 11.

Bonnet, Alberto. 2007. Estado y capital. Los debates sobre la *derivación* y la *reformulación* del estado en Alemania y Gran Bretaña. In *Marxismo y Estado. Un siglo y medio de debates,* ed. Mabel Thwaites Rey. Buenos Aires: Prometeo.

Bricianer, Serge. 1978. *Pannekoek and the workers' councils.* Introd. by John Gerber. St. Louis, Missouri: Telos Press.

Brinton, Maurice. 1970. *The Bolsheviks and workers' control 1917–1921.* London: Solidarity.

Engels, Frederick. 1974. Introd. to *The civil war in France* by Karl Marx [1891]. In *Marx/Engels/Lenin on historical materialism.* New York: International Publishers.

Gerber, John. 1988. From left radicalism to council communism: Anton Pannekoek and German revolutionary Marxism. *Journal of Contemporary History* 23.

Gramsci, Antonio and Palmiro Togliatti. 1990. The Italian situation and the tasks of the PCI. In *Selections from political writings 1921–1926* by A. Gramsci, 340–378. Minneapolis: University of Minnesota Press.

Hansen, Eric. 1976. Crisis in the party: 'De Tribune' faction and the origins of the Dutch Communist Party 1907–9. *Journal of Contemporary History* 11.

Holloway, John and Sol Picciotto, eds. 1978. *State and capital: A Marxist debate.* London: E. Arnold.

Kellner, Douglas. 1976. Korsch's revolutionary historicism. *Telos* 26:70-93.

———. 1977. Revolutionary Marxism. Introd. to *Karl Korsch: Revolutionary Theory,* ed. Douglas Kellner. Austin and London: University of Texas Press.

Korsch, Karl. 1919a. What is socialization? A program of practical socialism. *New German Critique,* no. 6 (Autumn 1975): 60–81.

———. 1919b. Sozialisierung und Arbeiterbewegung. *Freies Deutschland* Jahre 1, no. 4 (March 22, 1919).

———. 1919c/1980b. Die Politik im neuen Deutschland. Repr. in Korsch 1980b.

———. 1919d/1980. Die Sozialisierungsfrage vor und nach der Revolution. *Der Arbeiterrat,* no. 19: 15. Repr. in Korsch, 1980.

———. 1920/1980b. Grundsätzliches über Sozialisierung. Repr. in Korsch, 1980b.

_____. 1922/1968. *Arbeitsrecht für Betriebsräte*. Repr. Frankfurt: Europäische Verlagsanstalt.

_____. 1929. Revolutionary Commune. *Die Aktion*, no. 19. Trans. Andrew Giles-Peters and Karl-Heinz Otto. www.marxists.org/archive/korsch/1929/commune.htm.

_____. 1930a. The present state of the problem of "Marxism and philosophy"—an anti-critique. In *Marxism and philosophy* by K. Korsch. Trans. Fred Halliday. Repr. New York: Monthly Review Press, 1970; 2008.

_____. 1930b. Rezension von Eugen Paschukanis: Allgemeine Rechtslehre und Marxismus, sowie Karl Renner: Die Rechtsinstitute des Privatrechts und ihre soziale Funktion. *Archiv für die Geschichte des Sozialismus und der Arbeiterbewegung*, Jahre 15. www.mxks.de/files/other/KorschPakuRECHT.html.

_____. 1939. Collectivization in Spain. *Living Marxism* 4, no. 6 (April 1939).

———. 1974. *Politische Texte*. Introd. and ed. by Erich Gerlach and Jürgen Seifert. Frankfurt am Main: Europaische Verlagsanstalt.

———. 1980a. *Gesamtausgabe*, vol. 1, *Recht, Geist und Kultur: Schriften 1908–1918*. Frankfurt: Offizin Verlag.

———. 1980b. *Gesamtausgabe*, vol. 2, *Rätebewegung und Klassenkampf*. Frankfurt: Offizin Verlag.

Marx, Karl. 1934/1971. *The civil war in France*. Repr. Chicago: Charles H. Kerr.

Marx, Karl and Frederick Engels. 1848/1967. *Manifesto of the Communist Party*. Repr. London: Penguin.

Negt, Oskar. 1973. Theorie, Empirie und Klassenkampf. Zur Konstitutionsproblematik bei Karl Korsch. *Jahrbuch Arbeiterbewegung* 1:107–138. Frankfurt: Fischer Verlag.

Pannekoek, Anton. 1912. Massenaktion und Revolution. *Die Neue Zeit*, Jahre 30, vol. 2. www.marxists.org/deutsch/archiv/pannekoek/1912/xx/massenaktion.htm.

_____. 1919a. The German Revolution—first stage. *Workers Dreadnought*, May 24. Written 1918. www.marxists.org/archive/pannekoe/1918/germany.htm.

_____. 1919b. Socialization. Originally published as Die Sozialisierung. *Die Internationale* 1, no. 13–14 (September 1919). www.marxists.org/archive/pannekoe/1919/socialisation.htm.

_____. 1920/1978. World revolution and communist tactics. In *Pannekoek and Gorter's Marxism*, ed. and trans. D. A. Smart. London: Pluto. www.marxists.org/archive/pannekoek/tactics/index.htm.

_____. 1927. Social democracy and communism. *Kommunistische Arbeiterzeitung*. First published as a pamphlet under the pseudonym K. Horner in Hamburg, 1919. This translation is based on the later version. www.marxists.org/archive/pannekoe/1927/sdc.htm.

_____. 1946/2003. *Workers' councils*. Ed. and introd. by Robert F. Barsky. Repr. Oakland, CA: AK Press.

Parvus, Alexander, Franz Mehring, Rosa Luxemburg, Karl Kautsky, Emile Vandervelde, 1975–1976. Debate sobre la huelga de masas. 2 vols. Córdoba: Cuadernos de pasado y presente, no. 62.

Rühle, Otto. 1920. Report from Moscow. www.marxists.org/archive/ruhle/1920/ruhle01.htm.

Part

# II

# Workers' Councils and Self-Administration in Revolution

Early Twentieth Century

# 5

# From Unionism to Workers' Councils
## The Revolutionary Shop Stewards in Germany, 1914–1918

**Ralf Hoffrogge**

When World War I broke out in the summer of 1914, the labor movements of most European countries abandoned their internationalist principles and turned their support toward the war efforts of their respective governments.[1] This rapid and unforeseen change did not go without protest. Within the German labor movement, by then the leading Socialist group in the Second International, two parallel movements against the war developed. The first formed inside the Social Democratic Party (SPD); another opposition emerged out of the strong union movement. Both movements fought to bring organized labor back to the idea of peace and international solidarity. The protests within the SPD eventually led to the splintering of the party— first into Social Democrats and Independent Socialists, later into Social Democrats and Communists.

While the split between Communists and Social Democrats developed into a longstanding and worldwide rivalry, the split within the German unionist movement did not form any new organization that survived the postwar period. This is the main reason that today it is largely overlooked. Nevertheless, it can be said that this unionist antiwar movement was historically as important as its counterpart in the Reichstag, the German parliament. Starting as small groups of dissenting unionists, it evolved into a large mass-strike

---

1 This essay is the result of my research on Richard Müller, one of the leaders of the Revolutionary Stewards, published as Ralf Hoffrogge, Richard Müller—*Der Mann hinter der Novemberrevolution*, Berlin 2008. Special thanks goes to Tavi Meraud for assisting me with this English translation based on the essay "Räteaktivisten in der USPD—Richard Müller und die Revolutionären Obleute," in Ulla Plener, ed., *Die Novemberrevolution 1918/1919 in Deutschland*, Berlin, 2009.

movement that later transformed itself into a movement of workers' councils, directed against both the government and the union bureaucracy.

During the German Revolution of November 1918, this workers' movement, along with rebellious soldiers and naval conscripts, brought down the monarchy in Germany and ultimately ended the Great War, which had already cost millions of lives. The movement also inspired a completely new idea of socialism, one that focused not on state power and centralization but instead on grassroots democracy and workers' control: the idea of council communism.

This bottom-up model took all the major socialist theoreticians by surprise. Whether they were centrists like Karl Kautsky or left-wing radicals like Lenin or Rosa Luxemburg, for decades all of them had imagined socialism as the end point of a gradual centralization of both economic and state power. Now, in the middle of one of the greatest crises that capitalism had ever seen, workers themselves generated a model of socialism that was not built upon the idea of central economic planning but instead was focused on the self-governance of the working class.

## The Revolutionary Shop Stewards

This essay will describe the history of the Revolutionary Shop Stewards, who were the main organizers of the German mass-strike movement between 1916 and 1918. The Revolutionary Stewards were the only antiwar organization in Germany that actually had a network of activists within the factories, organizing the working class from the very bottom. In Berlin, fifty to eighty Revolutionary Stewards coordinated a network of several hundred spokesmen, which, in turn, represented several thousand workers in the factories. Only experienced union veterans were ushered into the inner circle of this group. The Revolutionary Stewards and their political leader, Richard Müller, followed a radical pragmatism: they intended to mobilize and radicalize the masses, but never called for actions that might lack the support of the majority. Between 1916 and 1918 they managed to become a synthesis of an avant-garde group and a grassroots organization, pushing the masses forward but never failing to represent them. In November 1918, the Revolutionary Stewards were one of the main organizing forces behind the German Revolution; afterward, they became a driving force within the movement of workers' councils.

Despite its strength and momentum this movement was very short-lived. By the end of 1920, the working class was represented once again by political parties and unions alone. What happened? The revolution and its councils were stopped both by counterrevolutionary violence and their own failure to disarm the economic and political elites of imperial Germany. After an unsuccessful general strike in March 1919, the workers' councils were dissolved by state legislation and transformed into subordinate organs, which still exist as *Betriebsräte* (work councils) in contemporary German labor legislation.

The Revolutionary Shop Stewards disintegrated and one faction joined the Communist Party, as did many other groups and individual protagonists of the councils' movement. Unlike the Social Democrats or the Communists, grassroots radicals like the Revolutionary Stewards never established their own historiographic tradition. Very few scholarly works about their history exist; almost none of this has been published in any language other than German.[2]

## Richard Müller and the German Metalworkers Union

The Revolutionary Stewards evolved out of the lathe operators' section within the Berlin branch of the German Metalworkers Union, DMV (Deutscher Metallarbeiter-Verband). The head of the DMV lathe workers section was Richard Müller, who had resisted the collaborationist policies of the union leadership since 1914. The Berlin lathe operators were a highly skilled workforce and, as such, enjoyed a good bargaining position. They used this not only to pursue their own demands, but also to protect more vulnerable groups of employees—for example, the many female workers who were drawn into the production sphere during the war (Müller 1924, 94).[3]

Richard Müller was not a radical from the beginning. Back in 1913, he presented himself as a rather typical unionist of his time. In the preface of a pamphlet on his work he declared that his personal goal was to "educate the last one among our colleagues to be a fighter—fighter for the idea of socialism (Müller 1913).[4] In order to realize this goal Müller used rather peculiar methods. He invented a system of six different kinds of matching forms and questionnaires. This bulk of paperwork was used to control and secure the participation of the members of his union, who were scattered around the city in many small-scale shops that often had poor internal communication.

His questionnaires enabled Müller to gather information and develop statistics about the size of the workforce in every enterprise, the working condi-

---

2 The complete history of the Revolutionary Stewards' movement has yet to be written; neither West nor East German historiography has produced a monograph covering the movement as such. Essays on the topic are rare. For an overview of the available literature see the publications mentioned in footnote 1.

3 The weaker position of women in collective bargaining derived not only from the attitude of the employers, but also from biases of the unionists themselves, who in their majority saw working women as an exception while the male breadwinner was the norm.

4 Translation of this and other quotes from German sources by the author.

tions, the average wage, and the degree of organization in every single shop. This system professionalized the work of the union and especially the system of collective bargaining. With the information from Müller's questionnaires, the workers' representatives possessed their own in-depth knowledge about the production experience and used this knowledge to push for their demands.

Considering all these advantages, however, the professionalization and specialization of German unionism also meant bureaucratization. On the one hand there was a fierce revolutionary rhetoric of socialism and class struggle; on the other hand, the actual class struggle became more and more piecemeal and full of paperwork, organized by professionals and semipro-fessionals like Müller. At the time, however, as an organizer Müller did not see any contradiction between the ideals and the practices of his union. It was the shock of the war that eventually made him and others reconsider their former activities.

The outbreak of World War I was not a total surprise to the European labor movement. Since the turn of the century there had been growing in-ternational tensions among the European powers—a development that had prompted the Socialist parties of Europe to discuss taking measures against a potential war. Peace conferences were organized, like the one held in Basel in 1912, and resolutions were made, but in the end such measures were symbolic more than anything else. No concrete strategies of resistance in the case of war were formed.

Due to the strong symbolism of the peace conferences, however, it came as a surprise—indeed, to many as a shock—when the German Social De-mocrats, along with all the other major socialist parties of Europe, decided not to resist the war but instead to support their national governments. In Germany, the decision of the unions to drop all strikes during wartime even preceded the Social Democrats' parliamentary support of war bonds on Au-gust 4, 1914. It was argued that in Germany's case, the war was a war of defense and therefore justified—furthermore, the working class would suffer most from a military defeat. Therefore the war had to be supported from the beginning.

The lathe operators and other branches of the Berlin metalworkers re-sisted this nationalist turn within their union. It is interesting to note that they were not driven by pacifist or internationalist principles from the be-ginning. Until 1916 they resisted the prohibition of strikes during the war mainly because they did not want to give up their only means of putting pressure on the employers. Only later did Müller and his circle become rad-icals. The name "Revolutionary Shop Stewards" itself was chosen relatively late, in November 1918.

The Revolutionary Stewards acted as a parallel structure within the met-alworkers union, DMV. They started in Berlin, where the lathe operators organized allegedly apolitical pub evenings or met privately after the official union sessions—sessions that were often infiltrated by the police or at least dominated by patriotic unionists. Paul Blumenthal, the leader of the welders' section of the Berlin DMV, later made this comment regarding how the Revolutionary Stewards first formed: "In the conferences unionist questions were discussed. But soon the oppositional comrades began to recognize each other, and later we met over a glass of beer. We exchanged our experiences and this became the beginning of the Revolutionary Stewards in Berlin!"[5] Before long the informal drinking events became clandestine meetings and soon Müller and his fellow workers began the systematic organization of a resistance group.[6]

## From Opposition to Resistance: The Union Goes Underground

The Revolutionary Stewards could build upon systems of workers' representatives that were already in place. Like Müller and Blumenthal, who led the sections of the lathe operators and welders, there were representatives for every profession within the industry. Every section had a system of shop stewards in the big enterprises and each steward had sub-stewards and confidants in the departments and workshops of the enterprise. These representatives were informal positions approved by the union—unpaid, not protected by law, and often not recognized by the employers. They were the connection between the rank-and-file unionists and the union leadership. What happened between 1916 and 1918 was essentially a rebellion against the union leadership by the members and the lower representatives of the DMV.

Müller and his comrades began to organize the Revolutionary Stewards apart from the official channels. Due to the fact that one steward represented an entire enterprise or at least a factory, the Revolutionary Stewards could, after a time, directly influence and represent thousands of workers, even though their organization had only fifty to eighty members at any given time. Because of this structure the Revolutionary Stewards were not "mass organizations to which everybody had access. They were an exclusive circle of people who had a certain education and experience in the political as well as the unionist struggles of the day." They also needed to have a certain influence among the workers. As Müller put it, the Stewards literally were a "vanguard of the proletariat" (Müller 1924, 161f).

---

5  Unpublished recollections of Paul Blumenthal, Bundesarchiv Berlin (Federal Archives Berlin), SG Y 30/0079, 10.

6 On the origins of the Revolutionary Stewards see also the unpublished recollections of Paul Eckert, Bundesarchiv Berlin (Federal Archives Berlin), DY 30 IV 2/2.01.

Richard Müller's words should not be mistaken for some kind of top-down, Leninist concept of the vanguard: despite their restricted membership the Revolutionary Stewards were the most authentic representatives of the German working class at the time. Because they were so deeply rooted in the shops and factories, their demands came directly from the workers and the Stewards never forced the masses to take action against their will. In the event of a strike there were often walkouts in factories that were not even part of the Stewards' network. In 1918, the fourth year of the war, the group was able to totally paralyze the entire war industry of Berlin as well as that of some other cities (Müller 1924, 161).

Because of their unique combination of grassroots organizing and small membership the Stewards were not only very efficient, but also well protected against agents provocateurs and infiltration by the police. In the aftermath of the larger strikes many of the Stewards were drafted into the military as punishment—but the police never once managed to immobilize or infiltrate the network.[7]

*Independent Socialism*

In April 1917, conflicts about the further support of the war led to a split within the Social Democratic Party (SPD). Conflicts had arisen back in late 1914, but similar to the unions the party opposition took almost two years to organize. The final break came when those Social Democratic members of the Reichstag who refused to vote for another series of war bonds were expelled from the party. In reaction to this provocation, the opposition members of the Reichstag and the state parliaments formed, along with some rank-and-file opposition, the Independent Social Democratic Party. The Independents, or USPD, served as a kind of collecting pool for the formerly scattered opposition. The new party was therefore very heterogeneous. It included both left-wing radicals like Karl Liebknecht, Rosa Luxemburg, and their Spartacist League, as well as leading revisionists like Eduard Bernstein, who openly argued for a "revision" of Marxism and the transformation of the SPD into a reform-oriented party. Bernstein and his followers were as opposed to revolution as they were to the war.

The Stewards became members of the new independent party, but also remained independent unto themselves. They never subordinated their network to the party leadership and rather used the USPD as a platform for their grassroots activism (Müller 1924, 161f).

---

7  In 1917 and 1918 the Stewards made connections with other cities and regions; in the DMV sections of Düsseldorf and Braunschweig in particular there were strong subgroups of the organization. See Morgan 1975, 211. Richard Müller himself stated that the Stewards eventually became a nationwide organization.

*Mass Strikes against the War*

In the event of a political strike, the Stewards were the ones who gave out the orders. This utterly confused the German labor movement, with its well-established division of responsibility. According to custom, the party was responsible for the political sphere, while the unions were to deal only with economic issues. The Revolutionary Shop Stewards were the first to introduce political mass strikes into German politics. Before that they had existed only in theory, advocated by leftists like Luxemburg but rejected by the center. Now the Stewards organized these strikes from below without the permission of party or union officials.

The Stewards independently decided on the timing. Only when the plans were suspended did they ask the leadership of the USPD for support, but not for permission. For example, in January 1918, the Stewards invited USPD deputies from the Reichstag and several state parliaments to a meeting and demanded support for a revolutionary strike. The party leaders were hesitant, fearing repression or a complete ban of the newly formed party. Eventually they agreed to a leaflet that called for "protests" but did not directly mention strikes or uprisings (Muller 1924, 139).[8]

The Stewards were always a workers' organization; the only intellectuals admitted into their ranks where Ernst Däumig and Georg Ledebour. Däumig was the former editor of the main social democratic newspaper, *Vorwärts*, who had lost his position due to his oppositional stance.[9] Ledebour was a well-known member of the Reichstag from the SPD's left wing and subsequently a founding member of USPD.

Däumig became a member of the Stewards late, in the summer of 1918, after Richard Müller had been drafted into the military following the January 1918 strike. Together with Emil Barth, head of the plumbers' section of the metalworkers union, Däumig quickly became a leading figure in the organization.

The general political route the Stewards took during the war can be described as both pragmatic and radical. They were leftists compared to the rest of the USPD and its leadership, who strongly resisted extra-parliamentary actions. But the Stewards also were opposed to the Spartacus League, led by Karl Liebknecht and Rosa Luxemburg. The Spartacists demanded ongoing actions, strikes, and demonstrations. They did not fear confrontations with the police but rather embraced them, hoping that street fights would escalate the tension and bring about a revolutionary situation. The Stewards ridiculed

---

8 On the strike of January 1918 see Boebel and Wentzel 2008.
9 On the biography of Ernst Däumig see Morgan 1983; see also Naumann 1986.

these tactics as "revolutionary gymnastics"; Richard Müller condemned them as idealistic voluntarism that the working masses would not accept (ibid., 165ff). Because of these disagreements the Stewards did not allow the Spartacists to join their regular meetings and met separately with Liebknecht and his followers. But despite their differences both groups cooperated when it came to decisive actions.

The Stewards organized three major mass strikes. The first, which took place in June 1916, was intended to express solidarity with Karl Liebknecht, who had been arrested in the course of an illegal May Day demonstration. The second was organized in April 1917 and became a massive protest against the food shortages of that year. The third political strike took place in January 1918. In this last mobilization, involving about half a million workers in Berlin, the strike committee called itself a "workers' council" (*Arbeiterrat*), and became a model for the councils that emerged during the German Revolution (Schneider and Kuda 1968, 21).

The strike committees consisted mostly of the Stewards themselves, but in the January strike they co-opted representatives from the USPD and even the SPD to widen the strike's influence. To the military authorities and the government these wildcat mass strikes, especially in the arms industry, were the most alarming manifestations of resistance against the war. Neither the alliance of state military and union leadership nor the mass repression and drafting of revolutionary workers in the aftermath of each strike could bring the movement to a permanent stop. The initiative for these strikes always came from the Stewards, because both the USPD and Spartacus League lacked the network of active workers that the Stewards had built within the factories. The Spartacists were able to organize only some local strikes; the USPD confined itself to parliamentary action. Therefore the Stewards—especially after 1917, when they expanded their contact with activists in other cities—were the strongest oppositional group in Germany during the First World War.

Being an illegal and secret organization, the Stewards did not advertise their successes. They did not issue flyers nor did they leave behind protocols of their meetings. They acted in secrecy, and only in the weeks following the November Revolution of 1918 did they issue the first press release with their name on it. This lack of paper trail is a main reason that later historians, for the most part, have underestimated the influence of the Stewards.

The public actions against the war were undertaken by Spartacus and the USPD. Both groups agitated against the war and the covert establishment of a military dictatorship in the homeland. The illegal literature of the Spartacists and the parliamentary speeches by the Independents definitely had more influence on public opinion than did the secret organizational work of the Stewards, and were fundamentally important not only for affecting public opinion, but also for radicalizing the Stewards themselves. Without the continuous discussions with the other groups and consequent mutual influences, the Stewards might have remained ordinary unionists not opposed to the war as such, only to its negative influence on wages and working conditions.[10]

It is a fact that the three mass strikes organized by the Stewards failed. All three broke down after several days with none of the demands having been met. But each of these strikes was bigger than the one before. Starting with fifty thousand workers in Berlin in 1916, they followed with four hundred thousand strikers in several cities in April 1917 and, in January 1918, an estimated seven hundred fifty thousand people were on strike. After this last strike was suppressed without yielding results, the Stewards changed their tactics. In 1918, they began stockpiling weapons in order to make the next strike an armed uprising. These plans were, by and large, inspired by the October Revolution in Russia.

*From Strike to Revolution*

Both Germany and Russia prior to 1917 were authoritarian monarchies; both rulers claimed to be fighting a war of self-defense. But in 1917 the Bolshevik Revolution changed everything when Lenin made clear that the Bolsheviks were willing to stop the war immediately and start negotiations.

Peace talks began, but the German government insisted on taking over Ukraine, parts of Poland, and the Baltic states—their aim was to exploit Russia's weakness in order to realize the dream of a German colonial empire in Eastern Europe. Peace negotiations slowed to a complete halt when these demands were presented. At this point in history, it was clear that in Germany's case the World War had never been one of self-defense. Even Social Democratic workers or members of influential Christian unions now knew that there would be no peace unless a political revolution were to overthrow the monarchy and break its military backbone. Radicalization was on its way. Tensions mounted even after Germany and Russia made a separate peace in March 1918: the war continued on the Western Front, and the large annexations in the Brest-Litovsk peace treaty stood as a sign for the ongoing aggression of German imperialism.

The strike of January 1918, which took place just weeks after the Bol-

---

10 Fritz Opel is correct when he states that the Stewards did not have a political concept of their own for quite a long time and were ideologically dependent on the writings of the Spartacus League and the USPD. Nevertheless they always remained totally independent when planning political actions. See Opel 1957, 55. On the radicalization of the Stewards between 1914 and 1918 see also Hoffrogge 2008, 25–63.

shevik Revolution, was directly caused by the breakdown of the peace process. It was the first attempt at going beyond the act of protesting to try to stop the war by means of a civil uprising. It failed because the German army was still intact and willing to defend the monarchy, but the Stewards knew this situation could change so they prepared for that future day.

Unexpectedly, however, the German Revolution did not start in Berlin. Although the Stewards were the only group prepared for an armed uprising, it was sailors from the coast who started the movement toward revolution.

The revolt within the navy had begun at the end of October 1918. An order of the admiralty had called for the fleet to seek a decisive battle with Britain. The sailors, already radicalized by a suppressed revolt the year before, refused this order, which they saw as a suicide mission, and staged a mutiny on their ships. They succeeded: the German fleet was totally immobilized. On November 4, 1918, the revolt moved from the sea to the land: the navy men took over the northern port city of Kiel and established a soldiers' council controlling the city. They knew from their previous revolt that if they did not move further and enforce peace, heavy repression, culminating with the death penalty, would hit them all. Most of the sailors were former workers, some of them even union members or socialists. The giant battleships of World War I, sometimes called "floating factories" by contemporary commentators, became the starting point for the revolution.

In Berlin, things did not move as quickly. In a secret meeting on November 2, the Revolutionary Stewards, the Spartacus League, and some members from the left wing of the USPD had decided to postpone an uprising planned for November 4. Instead, they wanted to mobilize for an armed general strike on the 11th. The reason was that no one could provide detailed information about the political atmosphere beyond Berlin and, more importantly, about the loyalty of the troops. The Stewards knew they could never win a civil war against a functioning and loyal German army. Especially in Berlin, where the military presence was concentrated to protect government buildings and other institutions, a victory would only be possible if the troops sided with the uprising or stayed neutral. Müller feared that premature action might lead to a failure of the uprising and result in an unprecedented bloodbath (Müller 1924, 173).

Karl Liebknecht and the Spartacus League, in particular, were unhappy with Müller's hesitation. Liebknecht, who had been released from jail on an amnesty intended to appease the situation, called for instant action. But Müller, Emil Barth, and the Stewards refused. They did not want to take the risk; Liebknecht and the Spartacus radicals would have to wait.

But when rumors about the revolt in the north spread to Berlin, the plans had to be changed. After Ernst Däumig was arrested on treason charges on November 8, the Revolutionary Stewards decided in favor of instant action, since they feared that otherwise their plans would be revealed to the police. All three groups called for a general strike the next day.

The response was overwhelming. Everywhere, the working masses took to the streets, and the plan succeeded in taking the police and troops by surprise. There was almost no resistance; the vast majority of the exhausted troops sided with the revolutionaries in the hope for instant peace.

The rule of the Hohenzollern Dynasty, which had ruled Prussia and Germany for centuries, fell within one day.

## The Socialist Republic of Germany

On the afternoon of November 9, 1918, the Revolutionary Shop Stewards met at the Reichstag, where a motley congregation of soldiers' councils was debating. The Stewards took over the meeting and convinced the participants to issue a call for a central vote the next day of workers' and soldiers' councils throughout Berlin with the purpose of electing a revolutionary government.

The election took place, but the Stewards failed to dominate this new government. Due to the chaotic and sudden course of the revolutionary events, but even more so due to the immediate reaction of the SPD, the Stewards had to accept parity between the USPD and the SPD in the revolutionary government.

Two revolutionary governmental bodies were elected: the Berlin Executive Council and the Council of the Peoples' Deputies. The Executive Council was elected by the Berlin workers' councils and would serve as the highest revolutionary authority until a national convention of workers' and soldiers' councils could congregate. Richard Müller became one of the two chairmen of this council, and all the USPD seats were filled by the Revolutionary Stewards. Since the Executive Council was the highest organ of the revolutionary regime, Müller technically was head of state of the newly declared Socialist Republic of Germany.

But the real power was exercised elsewhere, by the Council of the People's Deputies. This organ served as an interim government and became increasingly dominant.[11] The plumber Emil Barth represented the Stewards on this council—but he was the only radical among the six deputies. When decisions were urgently required, Barth's two USPD colleagues, members of the moderate wing of the party, collaborated with the SPD deputies and often voted against him.

---

11 On the Executive Council see Materna 1978; on the Council of the People's Deputies see Miller 1969.

Therefore Friedrich Ebert, the leader of the three SPD deputies, gradually came to dominate the Council of the People's Deputies, specifically because he and his party had the support of the military elite, the liberal press, and the state apparatus—an apparatus that had been briefly disempowered by the revolution but was never destroyed. The old elite of the German Empire hoped that their support for the Social Democrats would decrease the influence of the Independents and other radicals—a move that was successful.

In the Executive Council, Müller and the USPD members had constant fights not only with the Social Democrats, but also with the soldiers' delegates. Many of the latter had only recently been drawn into politics; almost none of them had a clear political conviction. When in doubt they tended to side with the Social Democrats because they mistrusted the radicals. The Executive Council therefore quickly became paralyzed. The intention to establish a "red guard" to defend the revolutionary achievements was vetoed by soldiers and Social Democrats—a fatal turn of events, which not only prevented the revolutionaries from consolidating the process within the critical first weeks, but also left both Social Democrats and leftist radicals defenseless when the counterrevolution made its moves in 1919. Since the Executive Council had blocked itself, it was easy for Ebert and the SPD to gain control of the political process via the Council of the People's Deputies. At the end of December 1918, the USPD left the Council of the People's Deputies in protest after an attack by government troops on revolutionary soldiers in Berlin. From that point on, the Social Democrats were in control of the main revolutionary institutions.

Moreover, the revolution was blocked from below as well as from above. The national convention of workers' councils, which met on December 16, 1918, voted against the consolidation of the council system and instead decided to elect a national parliament. Richard Müller, who had held the inaugural address for the national convention of councils, was shocked that the councils had voted themselves out of power and called the convention a "suicide club" (Engel 1997, 16).[12] In December 1918 the Social Democrats had a strong majority even within the council movement, although the party itself rejected the very idea of workers' councils. But the USPD and the radicals failed to convince the majority of the German workers to follow their ideas. Many workers did not see any reason to draw support away from the SPD. When the war that had split the party was over, they demanded a joint action of their representatives in both parties, overlooking the fact that behind the question of war lay other deep splits within the labor movement.

---

12  Speech by Müller given before the general assembly of the Berlin workers' and soldiers' councils on December 23, 1918.

The crisis of December 1918 regarding the future of the revolution also led to a split between the Stewards and the USPD leadership, which left the Stewards isolated within the USPD. Nevertheless, they did not align with the Spartacists, who formed their own party on January 1, 1919, the German Communist Party (KPD). The Stewards were invited to the founding congress, but the meeting was disrupted when the negotiations between the Stewards and Spartacists took longer than expected. In the end no compromise was reached. It is interesting that Müller and the Stewards were alienated by the dominance of syndicalism in the newly formed KPD, which later would become a model Leninist party. In particular, the Stewards were strongly opposed to the idea of boycotting the election of the national assembly (Hoffrogge 2008, 96ff).

### The Workers' Council Movement

The Stewards remained a part of the USPD but continued to act independent from official party leadership. Their new field of action was the workers' council movement. In the early days of 1919, this movement evolved out of the diverse collection of councils, which by this time were very heterogeneous and did not share a common program. Although there had been councils during the mutinies and mass strikes since 1917, there was no unifying theory of council communism, nor had there been debates about this form of organization among the German socialists before or during the war. As was the case in Russia in 1917, the councils had developed spontaneously out of the political struggles.[13] The historical precedents and theoretical analyses were present to facilitate moving forward—for example, the Paris Commune of 1871 and Marx's reflections on those events. But those writings of Marx were not prominent among the ideas of Germany's prewar Social Democrats—they held a rather statist if not authoritarian idea of politics, largely informed by the realities of the authoritarian imperial regime, which explains their astonishing hostility toward any attempts to further the German Revolution (see Hoffrogge 2009b).

Richard Müller and Ernst Däumig founded a newspaper called *Der Arbeiter-Rat* (The Workers' Council) and outlined a theory of council communism—the "pure council system" (*reines Rätesystem*). This was one of the first theories of council democracy, which ranged from single-factory councils to regional-industry councils all the way to a national economic council.[14] Critics at the time as well as afterward described their ideas as

---

13  When searching for historical predecessors of the German councils of 1918, Dirk H. Müller suggests looking at the political culture at the grass roots of the unionist movement; see Müller 1985.
14  Some of Müller's and Däumig's writings on council communism were reprinted in Schneider and Kuda 1968. For an in-depth analysis of their ideas see Hottmann 1980; for council theory see also Hoffrogge 2008, 108–116.

schematic; nevertheless, this was the first attempt by the revolutionaries to offer a coherent vision of what a society governed by the producers could look like.

In spring 1919, it became obvious that the Council of People's Deputies was not doing much to further the socialization of the main industries. The idea of socializing the heavy industries and other highly concentrated and monopolized sectors of the German economy was supported by all three Socialist parties and was even popular among unorganized workers and other parts of the population. Accordingly, the national convention of workers' councils in December had assigned the government to implement these plans. Nothing happened, however, and the Peoples' Deputies did not take any serious steps toward socialization.

This lack of action, coupled with the repressive politics of the government—which, in January had suppressed an uprising in Berlin with military force—caused major unrest among the workers. The January uprising had started as a general strike and culminated in shootouts between government troops and armed workers. Karl Liebknecht and Rosa Luxemburg, the leaders of the young KPD, were murdered in the aftermath of the fights.[15] The Revolutionary Stewards themselves were divided on this issue. While Müller was opposed to the insurgency as being premature, other members of the group were leading figures in the revolutionary committee that cooordinated the uprising.

Although the revolutionaries were defeated, the government lost much of its legitimacy after these events, and the unrest among the working masses grew. Out of this atmosphere a wave of strikes erupted in the spring of 1919, with centers in Berlin, the Ruhr area, and the industrial regions around Halle and Merseburg. This strike wave was the most powerful action put forth by the followers of the council system and helped create national momentum. Ideas that had been confined to the small circle of the Stewards and popularized in the *Arbeiter-Rat* newspaper now proliferated to become popular demands of a national movement. By surrounding the city of Weimar and blocking the proceedings of the national assembly, the strikes seemed to re-open the question, "workers' councils or parliamentary democracy?"

But these strikes suffered the same fate as the uprising in January 1919 and all other efforts to drive forward the revolutionary process: they remained local and uncoordinated events that could easily be isolated and

---

15 The "Spartacist rising" was sparked by the refusal of the Berlin chief of police, Emil Eichhorn, a member of the USPD, to give up his position. In defense of Eichhorn, Berlin workers called a general strike, which evolved into a revolutionary uprising. Unfortunately the uprising was defeated by the military in a matter of days; this was due not only to the army's brutality but also to a lack of public support. Although the majority of workers supported the general strike, only a minority supported the armed uprising; after the devastation of World War I, violence in political struggles was unpopular, even among the most radical workers.

suppressed by the military.[16] Richard Müller and the communist Wilhelm Koenen anticipated this problem and tried to establish a nationwide coordination for the ongoing strikes in order to concentrate their power—but this attempt failed. While in one region the strikes had just started, they had already begun to fade elsewhere. And if they had not, brute force would make them fade: in Berlin the end of the strikes in March 1919 closely resembled a civil war. Government troops, formed mostly of right-wing units, used heavy artillery and machine guns in the working-class districts of Berlin-Lichtenberg and Berlin-Friedrichshain. Many uninvolved civilians were killed and the casualties numbered more than one thousand (Müller 1925b, 124–163; Morgan 1975, 230ff).[17]

*End of the Revolution: Integration of the Councils*
The brutal crushing of the strike movements in 1919 destroyed all hopes that another armed revolution could topple the Social Democratic government. Following the USPD's departure from the Council of People's Deputies at the end of December 1918, the Social Democrats had ruled alone. And they had done everything to transform the revolutionary regime into a liberal but capitalist democracy. The national assembly was the final triumph in this process. In response to this situation Müller, Däumig, and most of the Stewards changed their course.

After realizing that the full installation of a workers' council republic was impossible, they tried to integrate the councils into the new constitution as secondary institutions (Morgan 1983, 252). By this time, the Revolutionary Shop Stewards had lost its unique, exclusive character and had more or less merged with the USPD faction of the general council movement. A split had developed in the organization back in January at the time of the uprising. A faction of the Stewards had supported the action, but Müller and Däumig had vetoed this decision, seeing no chance for success—the strike was based only in Berlin, and although a majority of Berliner workers supported it, they were strictly opposed to armed fighting. These differences surrounding the uprising seem to have weakened the Stewards as a group, but it is unclear whether they actually dissolved at this point or not. Regardless, many of the Stewards continued to work together in the Executive Council, in the council movement in general, and later within the KPD.

---

16 Richard Müller later blamed the shock of the disastrous January uprising for the subsequent failure of the strikes in March 1919. See Müller 1925b, 154.
17  On the fighting in March there is an unpublished eyewitness account by Franz Beiersdorf, Bundesarchiv Berlin (Federal Archives Berlin), DY 30 IV 2/2.01.

After the defeats of the year 1919, the workers' council movement was transformed into a movement of shop councils or factory councils, since the regional councils had fallen apart. These shop councils (*Betriebsräte*) were intended to represent the workers of a singular enterprise. The new German Constitution of 1919, legislated by the national assembly, included a paragraph on workers' councils that was open to interpretation. It had been drafted under pressure from the strikes in March, and a special law was supposed to concretize what role the councils would eventually play. Müller, Däumig, and their comrades aimed to secure as much influence for these councils as possible, campaigning for the shop councils to be autonomous from the entrepreneurs and permitted to associate on a regional and national level. They also proposed a national council to exercise a strong influence over the general economic decisions of the government. But all these plans failed. The final law on industrial relations only legalized the existing councils on the shop level. They were allowed to represent workers' demands, but exercised no control over the production. A national economic council was put in place as well, but it also included factory owners and thus was intended as an instrument of class collaboration rather than class struggle. In practice, the national economic council rarely met and exercised almost no influence.

Protests against this legislation failed; during the parliamentary debate on the subject, a huge demonstration in Berlin demanding more rights for workers was shot upon. Forty-two people were killed, yet the legislation was not changed. As a result, the shop councils of the newborn German Republic became subaltern and powerless organs, reduced to basically the same rights as the Betriebsräte of Germany today.

The last fight on this field was a battle over the actual politics of the newly legalized shop councils. Would they act autonomously as a movement, or would they be subordinated to the unions—unions still dominated by the SDP? Richard Müller was the most prominent figure to argue for autonomous councils. When the Executive Council was dissolved by force in the summer of 1919, he and some of the Stewards created an independent center of shop councils in Berlin. The idea was to bundle the forces of these councils for further revolutionary movements. At the first national congress of shop councils, held in Berlin in October 1920, Müller and the communist Heinrich Brandler defended the Berlin model but failed to convince the delegates. The councils were subordinated to the unions. The council movement in Germany was over.[18]

---

18 The protocols of this assembly were published as *Protokoll der Verhandlungen des ersten Reichskongresses der Betriebsräte Deutschlands—Abgehalten vom 5.–7. Oktober 1920 zu Berlin*, Berlin 1920.

## The Revolutionary Stewards Become Leninists

During these crucial confrontations, it became evident that Müller and some of the former Stewards were drifting toward the KPD. When the USPD split in late 1920, the Stewards were part of the left wing, which supported Lenin's "Twenty-one Conditions" for membership in the newly founded Third International. Although the majority accepted these conditions, there was a large faction opposed. This faction split from the majority and merged with the Social Democrats in 1922, while the left-wing majority joined the KPD in December 1920.

In 1920, for some months Richard Müller was part of the Central Committee of the left USPD and after the merger he became chairman of the Center on Union Affairs within the KPD. Formed out of the failed Berlin center of shop councils, most of its members were former Revolutionary Stewards.

The merger was a giant leap for the young KPD. Beforehand it had been nothing more than a radical splinter party, organizing a small minority of the German workers. The merger not only brought three hundred thousand members to a party that previously numbered only seventy thousand members, but it also brought the experience of people like the Stewards and existing infrastructure, such as newspapers, to the Communist Party. It was only after this merger that communism in Germany truly became a mass movement (Krause 1975, 132–216).

Müller, Däumig, and many other members of the Stewards now worked within the KPD—Däumig even became chairman of the party. But just weeks after starting, Däumig was forced to resign due to internal fighting. In March 1921, Müller was forced to give up his position as chairman for union affairs as well because he criticized the "March Action," a failed uprising in the industrial region around the cities of Halle and Leuna. In a parallel to the failed January 1919 uprising, Müller refused to call strikes for Berlin—but the party officials did not want to hear his criticism.

Thanks to an intervention by Clara Zetkin, a founding member of the KPD, Müller and other former Stewards such as Heinrich Malzahn were invited to the Third Worldwide Congress of the Communist International, which took place in Moscow in the summer of 1921. Zetkin organized a personal meeting between Müller, Malzahn, and Lenin.

Lenin was enthusiastic about this meeting with Müller and the Stewards and very critical of the failed uprising of March, which he condemned in front of the congress. The delegates sided with Lenin, and the divided KPD was forced to accept this judgment.

But back in Germany the conflict resumed—and this time Müller and other opposition members did not get support from Moscow. In order to preserve the integrity of the party both Trotsky and Lenin switched sides and supported the KPD leadership against the growing number of critics. Müller and many others were forced to leave the Communist Party (Tosstorff 2004, 392–395).

Despite this ugly affair, Müller continued to support Lenin, even praising him in the foreword of the three-volume history of the German Revolution he wrote between 1924 and 1925 (Müller 1924, 9; see also Müller 1925a; 1925b). These works by Müller remain noteworthy today, as they offer a fascinating narrative of the war, the rise of the labor opposition, and the revolution and its eventual failure. Because he drew upon many unpublished records of meetings from his private collection, his writings are histories, not merely memoirs. Although Müller's works are not completely free of apologetics, they are interesting to read. He sides with neither the Social Democrats nor with the Spartacists, subverting the two interpretations that became canonized during the Cold War and still dominate the historiography of the German Revolution (Hoffrogge 2008, 171–183).

Müller's activities endeavors as a historian marked the end of his political career. It is difficult to trace his activities or those of the Stewards beyond 1921. The informal core group of Stewards that had coordinated the unionist activities of the KPD was dissolved with Müller's and Däumig's dismissal from the party.

## The Disappearance of the Revolutionary Shop Stewards

By 1920, the council movement was over and the political concept of the Stewards seemed to have no place in the postrevolutionary era. The political parties once again became the main agents of socialist politics and the unions were reduced to dealing with purely economic issues. Although Germany now had more than one political party, two rather dubious patterns of prewar socialist politics were reinstated: the leading role of the party within the labor movement and the separation of the economic and political spheres.

The Stewards themselves had long ago lost their political homeland. Within the USPD they had managed to maintain a very productive symbiosis of party politics and grassroots activism, but this was impossible within a Communist Party that had become more and more centralized. There were some later attempts to launch a new network of Revolutionary Shop Stewards as an autonomous structure, but these efforts failed (Koch-Baumgarten 1986, 418ff). By the 1920s, only a few Stewards remained within the KPD. Others participated in smaller splinter groups; many abandoned politics completely. Richard Müller did so and became a business-man. Little is known about his life after 1925. He died in 1943.[20] The vanishing of Richard Müller—from a prominent position as a head of state into oblivion—parallels the history of the Stewards as an organization. Although they completely revolutionized not only the patterns of Socialist politics but also the idea of socialism itself, the Stewards failed to create a legacy for their movement. While the Spartacists were immortalized by generations of historians from the KPD and East Germany, the history of the Revolutionary Shop Stewards has disappeared among the footnotes.

## References

Boebel, Chaja and Lothar Wentzel, eds. 2008. *Streiken gegen den Krieg—Die Bedeutung der Massenstreiks in der Metallindustrie vom Januar 1918*. Hamburg: VSA Verlag.

Engel, Gerhard; Gaby Huch, Bärbel Holtz, Ingo Materna, eds. 1993–2002. *Groß-Berliner Arbeiter und Soldatenräte in der Revolution 1918/19*, 3 vol. Berlin: Akademie-Verlag.

Hoffrogge, Ralf. 2008. *Richard Müller—Der Mann hinter der Novemberrevolution*. Berlin: Karl Dietz Verlag.

_____. 2009a. Räteaktivisten in der USPD—Richard Müller und die Revolutionären Obleute. In *Die Novemberrevolution 1918/1919 in Deutschland*, ed. Ulla Plener. Berlin: Karl Dietz Verlag.

_____. 2009b. Die wirkliche Bewegung, welche den jetzigen Zustand aufhebt—Sozialismuskonzepte und deutsche Arbeiterbewegung 1848–1920, *PROKLA—Zeitschrift für kritische Sozialwissenschaft*, no. 155, Münster: Westfälisches Dampfboot.

Hottmann, Günter. 1980. Die Rätekonzeptionen der Revolutionären Obleute und der Links- (bzw. Räte-) Kommunisten in der Novemberrevolution: Ein Vergleich. Thesis, Göttingen.

Koch-Baumgarten, Sigrid. 1986. *Aufstand der Avantgarde*. Frankfurt and New York: Campus Verlag.

Krause, Hartfrid. 1975. *USPD—Zur Geschichte der Unabhängigen Sozialdemokratischen Partei Deutschlands*. Frankfurt: Europäische Verlags-Anstalt.

Materna, Ingo. 1978. *Der Vollzugsrat der Berliner Arbeiter und Soldatenräte 1918/19*. Berlin: Karl Dietz Verlag.

Miller, Susanne. 1969. *Die Regierung der Volksbeauftragten 1918/1919*. Düsseldorf: Droste.

Morgan, David W. 1975. *The socialist left and the German Revolution—a history of the German Independent Social Democratic Party—1917–1922*. Ithaca and London: Cornell University Press.

_____. 1983. Ernst Däumig and the German Revolution of 1918. In *Central European History* 15(4):303–331. Cambridge: Cambridge University Press.

Müller, Dirk H. 1985. *Gewerkschaftliche Versammlungsdemokratie und Arbeiterdelegierte vor 1918*. Berlin: Colloquium Verlag.

Müller, Richard. 1913. *Die Agitation in der Dreherbranche*. Berlin.

_____. 1924. *Vom Kaiserreich zur Republik*. Vienna: Malik-Verlag.

_____. 1925a. *Die Novemberrevolution.* Vienna: Malik-Verlag.

20 For the information I could find about his later career see Hoffrogge 2008, 198–216.

————. 1925b. *Der Bürgerkrieg in Deutschland.* Berlin: Phöbus-Verlag.

Naumann, Horst. 1986. Ein treuer Vorkämpfer des Proletariats. Ernst Däumig, *Beiträge zur Geschichte der Arbeiterbewegung* 6, no. 28 (1986): 801–813, Berlin.

Opel, Fritz. 1957. *Der deutsche Metallarbeiter-Verband während des ersten Weltkrieges und der Revolution.* Hannover: Goedel.

Reichskongress der Betriebsräte Deutschlands. 1920. *Protokoll der Verhandlungen des ersten Reichskongresses der Betriebsräte Deutschlands—Abgehalten vom 5.–7. Oktober 1920 zu Berlin*, Berlin.

Schneider, Dieter and Rudolf Kuda. 1968. *Arbeiterräte in der Novemberrevolution.* Frankfurt: Suhrkamp Verlag.

Tosstorff, Reiner. 2004. *Profintern—Die Rote Gewerkschaftsinternationale 1921–1937.* Paderborn: Schöningh Verlag.

# 6

# The Factory Committee Movement in the Russian Revolution

**David Mandel**

This chapter traces the evolution of the factory committee movement in Russia through 1917 and the first part of 1918, with particular focus on Petrograd, the militant center of the labor movement. It argues that the radicalization of the committees—while fundamentally a defensive response to the threat to jobs, and so to the revolution itself—was made possible, and to some degree stimulated, by the committees' view of the managerial prerogatives of the owners as conditional and thus temporary, pending the transition to socialism. The chapter concludes with a brief discussion of the fate of the committees in the civil war.

Workers' control had not figured in the programs of any of Russia's Socialist parties before 1917. The goal of the anticipated revolution was to overthrow the autocracy and establish a democratic republic. Although all Socialist parties considered land reform and the eight-hour workday integral to this revolution, lending it a definite social dimension, the revolution itself was originally bourgeois-democratic, not socialist.

The Bolsheviks reoriented their program following Lenin's return from exile in April 1917, a few weeks after the overthrow of the monarchy. They called now for the transfer of power from the liberal-dominated provisional government to the soviets of workers', soldiers', and peasants' deputies. But they remained vague on the social program of soviet power. Lenin wrote that "it is not our *immediate* task to 'introduce' socialism, but only to bring social production and the distribution of products at once under the *control* of the Soviets of Workers' Deputies" (Lenin 1962, 116). In Russian *kontrol* implies oversight, as distinct from administration. Sukhanov, the left Menshevik chronicler, commented that this was far from socialism. "True, control was a cardinal point at all workers' meetings. But this 'socialism' was still very timid and modest." It pointed in a different direction but in essence did not go beyond what the moderate Socialists in the coalition government were proposing (Sukhanov 1923, 24–26).

In September, Y. Sverdlov, a member of the Bolshevik Central Committee, told the party's Petrograd Committee that "there is insufficient clarification of the economic question." He explained that current work was absorbing all the party leadership's energies. In fact, however, the Bolsheviks had not yet decided on their program. At a national conference of factory committees on the eve of the October Revolution, a Menshevik delegate argued that one could not discuss workers' control without first deciding the nature of the revolution, which "we say . . . is not social but political but with a social leavening" (*Oktyabr'skaya revolyutsiya i fabzavkomy* 1927–29, 2:182; henceforth cited as FZK). An anarchist delegate was equally definite: "We are living through a social revolution" (ibid., 183). But N. Skrypnik, a Bolshevik, would not be pinned down: "Workers' control is not socialism. It is only one of the transitional measures that bring us nearer to socialism" (ibid., 184).

As Marxists, the Bolsheviks could not be specific in their analysis of Russia's capitalist economic development. In their analysis Russia, a poor, mainly peasant society, albeit with a militant working class, lacked the conditions for socialism. But the war had created the need as well as the political conditions for the overthrow of capitalism not only in the developed West, but in Russia as well. And the generalized crisis meant that Russia could realistically count on the support of revolutions in the West. The social nature of Russia's revolution, indeed its very survival, thus depended on events abroad.

Such was the analysis. But in the immediate reality the revolution was driven forward by practical need. The economic program implied a sort of dual power: the soviet government, supported by the committees, would "control" the capitalists, who would continue to manage their enterprises. But just as dual power would soon prove untenable in the political sphere— the bourgeoisie refusing to be "controlled" by the soviets and, in fact, determined to crush them—so too it would prove illusory in the economic. After all, the bourgeoisie's last line of defense was its economic power.

Contemporary commentators and later Western historians often portrayed workers' control as an anarchist-inspired, "instinctual" revolt aimed at taking over the factories (see, for example, Sukhanov 1923, 192–93; Carr 1966, 63–64). Even more sympathetic historians have viewed, and continue to view, the factory committees as essentially a libertarian movement for industrial democracy and, as such, opposed to central planning and regulation (see, for example, Lewin 1975, 7; Churakov 2005, 255–57). But the reality was more complex. If anarchists naturally gravitated to the committees, the committees were, in fact, dominated by Bolsheviks almost everywhere from the start. Anarchist positions at factory committee conferences evoked little support, while Bolshevik resolutions calling for soviet power and state economic regulation garnered large majorities.

When the committees were first elected after the February Revolution, in the private enterprises they did not set goals that went beyond the aspirations of militant trade unions. But they did differ from most trade unions in that membership was not voluntary—the committees represented the entire nonmanagerial workforce. But more important was their implicit ideological orientation: they did not accept capital's managerial prerogatives as legitimate or inevitable. If they were tolerated, it was because the balance of forces, linked to Russia's level of development and thus to the workers' own managerial capacities as well, did not yet allow for them to be rejected.

## The February Revolution and the Factory Committees

The general strike in Petrograd that eventually drew in the capital's garrison to become the February Revolution was at once a political mobilization against the autocracy and also an economic strike against capital. As such, it was in direct continuity of the prewar labor movement, in which economic and political demands had been inextricably intertwined.[1] After the tsar's abdication, the workers returned to their factories only long enough to adopt economic demands and to vote to continue the strike until their demands were won. Most factories ignored the appeal of the Petrograd Soviet, then led by moderate Socialists (Mensheviks and Socialist Revolutionaries), to resume work on March 7, since the workers had not yet won the eight-hour day or wages "befitting a worker and free citizen" (from the textile workers' union paper, cited in Volobuev 1964, 64). Those who did resume work had already introduced the eight-hour day without consulting management.

Besides better wages and shorter hours, the workers expected the democratic revolution to usher in a "constitutional regime" in the factories (Maevski 1918, 43). This meant an end to autocratic managerial despotism. A 1912 convention of the St. Petersburg Society of Factory and Mill Owners had ruled out even the minimal shop-level representation permitted by law and rejected any interference of workers' organizations in the spheres of wages, work conditions, hiring and firing, and the internal regime (Kruze 1961, 99–100). The war had added repressive measures, including the loss of military deferral.

---

1 The most striking manifestation of this interweaving of the economic and political was the ubiquitous demand for "polite address" (second person plural) from management. The minister of trade and industry, himself an entrepreneur, declared this a political demand (Kleinbort 1923, 11).

When work did resume, one of the workers' first actions was to purge management of its most oppressive members, sometimes carting them out of the gates in wheelbarrows with sacks over their heads, a mark of particular opprobrium. In this, as well as in the unilateral introduction of the eight-hour day (limited mostly to Petrograd), one could already discern a certain conditional attitude toward capital's managerial powers, an attitude bolstered by the workers' justified feeling that they had made the revolution, not the bourgeoisie, which had been paralyzed by its fear of the masses.

But at the core of the "constitutional regime" was the workers' collective representation in the form of elected factory committees to "supervise" (*vedat'*) the "internal order." At the Radiotelegraph Factory, the general assembly instructed the committee to draw up rules and norms for the length of the workday, the minimum wage, the organization of medical care, management of the sick fund (based on a 1912 law), establishment of a mutual-aid fund, hiring and firing of workers,[2] conflict resolution, labor discipline, rest time, factory security, food provision,[3] and the establishment of a permanent, elected factory committee (Gaponenko 1958, 491–492). The spectrum of activities was thus broad and some elements were obviously meant to be negotiated with management. But there was no intention of challenging the administration's basic prerogatives in managing the technical and economic side of production. The demand for "workers' control," let alone workers' management, was not raised in the private factories.

Nevertheless, the inclusion among the committees' responsibilities of the physical security of the factories, as well as a reference to technical incompetence as grounds (although never sole grounds) for the purging of certain managers, indicates a new sense of workers' responsibility with regard to production. Still embryonic, it would evolve into more radical positions, as workers came to see their jobs and the revolution come under threat from capital. N. Kutler, a prominent industrialist and a leading Kadet (liberal) was not alone in observing a new "enthusiasm for work" following the February Revolution (Volobuev 1964, 157). Related was a changed attitude toward the war: most workers now felt they had something to defend—their revolution. (This "revolutionary defensism" would, however, prove very short-lived, as the provisional government made clear it was not interested in seeking peace.)

In state-owned plants however, workers did adopt more radical positions, based on the view that in a democratic state, workers should participate in

---

2 Like the other measures, this was aimed at preventing managerial abuses and ensuring justice. Of particular concern to workers was the presence of well-to-do elements hiding in factory employment from the draft.

3 Mainly through consumer cooperatives.

the management of public enterprises (*Rabochii kontrol' i natsionalizatsiya promyshlennykh predpriyatii Petrograda v 1917–19 gg* 1949, 179). Moreover, the top administrators in these plants were military officers and thus part of the autocratic state apparatus; many of them had fled during the revolution. But the desire to take over management did not last long. A conference of committees of state plants on April 15, 1917, claimed broad rights of control (i.e., monitoring), including access to information and documents and the right to dismiss administrators who proved "unable to ensure normal relations with the workers." But, continued the conference resolution, "not wishing to assume responsibility for the technical and administrative organization of production in the given circumstances until the full socialization of the economy, the representatives of the general factory committee have only a consultative voice in management" (Gaponenko 1958, 383–386). The chairman of the committee of the Admiralty shipbuilding factory attributed this retreat to the workers' concern not to undermine efficiency, given the complexity of running a factory and the workers' inexperience at doing so. But his committee did claim the right to control, including the right to demand the removal of staff through arbitration (Central State Archive of St. Petersburg, hereafter abbreviated as TsGASPb, f. 9391, op. 1, d. 11, l. 4).

Between February and October 1917, the committees in state factories wielded considerably more power than in private enterprises, where management stubbornly resisted incursions into its prerogatives (FZK, 2:100).[4] In state plants, too, there were reports of increased productivity after the February Revolution. At a conference in March of factories of the Artillery Authority the workers even accused the Authority of mismanagement and called for its abolition (TsGASPb, f. 4601, op. 1, d. 10, l. 33).

## Fear of Sabotage and Emergence of the Demand for Workers' Control

The balance of political forces after February made it difficult for the industrialists to resist the workers' economic demands. However, they considered these concessions, in particular the eight-hour day and the restrictions on their power to hire and fire at will, to be only temporary. Only a few weeks after the revolution, the bourgeois press began a campaign directed at the workers' "selfish demands" that were allegedly undermining military production. The aim was to drive a wedge between the soldiers and the workers and in so doing to undermine the popular alliance that had

---

4 For a view of the range of the committees' activities in state enterprises, see *Fabrichno-zavodskie komitety Petrograda v 1917g. protokoly,* Moscow: Nauka, 1979.

made the revolution possible. The campaign failed—the workers invited the soldiers to visit the factories and see for themselves. But it did put an end to the illusions of national unity that had appeared in February, when the bourgeoisie seemed to have finally rallied to the side of the democratic revolution. This negative campaign served to remind workers of the industrialists' longstanding hostility to their aspirations.

Workers began to question the explanations offered by management—mainly supply difficulties—for productive capacity that was standing idle. On March 20, a workers' deputy to the Petrograd Soviet proposed to elect a commission made up of delegates from the factories to conduct inspections "with a view to control," in order to "make sure there are no abuses" (TsGASPb, f. 1000, op. 73, d. 16, l. 6).

In early May, the left Menshevik paper observed "cutbacks in production in a whole series of plants. So far these have been limited to medium and small enterprises. But all the same, it is beginning to worry workers" (*Novaya zhizn'*, May 10, 1917). Nor did the bourgeois press try to calm the fears: "Two or three weeks will pass," wrote the Kadet paper, "and the factories will start closing one after the other" (*Rech'*, May 13, 1917). Even the paper of the moderate Mensheviks, who were by now participating in the provisional government, warned of an "Italian" (i.e., go-slow) strike by the industrialists, a flanking movement in preparation for an offensive. "We have before us a different means of struggle—the hidden lockout. In the Soviet's Labor Department . . . we encounter facts every day that confirm the existence of a definite plan among the industrialists" (*Rabochaya gazeta*, May 20, 1917). The term *lokaut* carried with it bitter memories. In just the six months preceding the outbreak of war, Petrograd's workers had been treated to three coordinated lockouts, in the course of which three hundred thousand had been fired (Kruze 1961, 328). And mass lockouts in November and December 1905 had dealt a fatal blow to Russia's first revolution.

Meanwhile, the industrialists adamantly rejected state economic regulation, something they had been promoting before the revolution to shore up the economy, which was cracking under the strain of war and government mismanagement. Now it was all the fault of the workers' "inordinate demands." In mid-May, the liberal minister of trade and industry, himself an industrialist, resigned from the government, citing the soviet's in fact quite timid plan of economic regulation and other "excessive demands." He warned that "if in the near future there is not a sobering of minds, we will witness the closing of tens and hundreds of enterprises" (*Novaya zhizn'*, May 19–20, 1917). Opposition to state regulation was the leitmotif of the Congress of Representatives of Trade and Industry in June (ibid., June 2, 1917; Chugaev 1959, 197). P. Ryabushinskii, another liberal capitalist, explained that regulation was acceptable in the West but not in Russia, where the government was itself "under control" of the soviets (*Izvestiya moskovskogo voenno-promyshlennogo komiteta*, no. 13, 1917:15).

On May 19 the Bolsheviks' Petrograd Committee for the first time issued an appeal to set up control commissions in the factories (*Pravda*, May 21, 1917). The appeal made clear it was responding to actions that the workers were already taking of their own initiative. The movement for workers' control thus arose "from below." "When our factory committee arose," explained the committee of the giant Putilov works, "it was handed neither a program of action nor a charter to guide its activity. As the functions of the committee developed, its own practical measures became the basis for its guiding principles. In this way, the factory committee had the best teacher—life itself" (Gaza 1933, 431).

The conflict at the Langezipen machine-building factory[5] illustrates the motives behind the movement for control. On April 27, the committee posted guards at the gates, refusing to allow the administration, including the director, to leave before the end of the workday. According to the government's factory inspector, the workers suspected management of holding up production (Gaponenko 1958, 444). A joint commission of the Petrograd Soviet and the employers' association was unable to resolve the dispute. Then, on June 2, the director announced he was closing the factory. He cited losses incurred from defense contracts due to rising costs; a decline in output, which he attributed to the eight-hour day; a decline in labor productivity; and shortages of fuel and materials. The committee turned for help to the Central Council of factory committees, elected just at the start of June. Its inquiry uncovered a long chain of suspicious stock transfers, at which point the director announced he had "by chance" come across 450,000 roubles, loaned by an acquaintance, which would allow production to resume (FZK, 1:182; *Izvestiya*, June 17, 1917; *Novaya zhizn'*, June 19, 1917). Meanwhile, the workers set up control: nothing was to leave the plant without the committee's authorization; its orders were binding on all personnel; management's orders required its validation; no documents could be destroyed before the committee had reviewed them (*Rabochii kontrol' i natsionalizatsiya*, 1:104).

In claiming the power to issue binding orders, the committee went beyond the initial conception of workers' control that excluded direct participation in management. (It is not clear how successful the committee actually was in exercising its claimed powers.) But the basically defensive motives of the committee are evident in its declaration that the workers had been "placed before the necessity" of adopting these measures in view of management's decision

---

5 This plant had seen thirty-one strikes in 1912–14, for a total of 103,970 lost worker-days. It had 1,200 workers in 1917 (Kruze 1961, 73, 323).

to close, its violation of an earlier arbitration decision on the salaries of office personnel, and its refusal to recognize the workers' control commission.

*Izvestiya,* the soviets' daily, still controlled by the moderate Socialists, described the conflict as characteristic of a whole series of cases of announced closures that were reaching the Central Council of factory committees. Most often the owners cited financial losses and a lack of funds. "But at the first attempt of the workers' organizations to verify the reasons . . . , they very often uncover the most complex and crafty machinations aimed at a lockout" (*Izvestiya,* June 17, 1917). Nor was this phenomenon limited to the capital. In the textile center of Ivanovo-Voznesensk, when several mills failed to reopen after the Easter holiday, with the owners claiming supply problems, the local soviet announced that idled workers were to receive full wages and that it was setting up a control commission. The mills reopened immediately (*Utro Rossii,* April 27, 1917).

## Workers' Control and Political Power

The idea for a citywide conference of committees arose out of the realization that the balance of power in isolated plants, as well as the workers' lack of experience, made effective control impossible. Meanwhile, the specter of industrial collapse loomed ever larger. A member of the organizing committee opened the conference with the following words:

> Whether they want to or not, the factory committees have to intervene in the economic life of their factories—otherwise they will close. All the factories in Petrograd are in crisis. But management has not been active in ensuring the supply of materials and fuel. The workers must become active where the industrialists are not. . . . This is an entirely new task that the revolution has placed before us. The theoretical task of the conference is to define how to accomplish that. The practical task is to create a powerful center of factory committees to lead and develop the maximum working-class influence in an economy that has been completely ruined by the imperialist war and the rapacious banditry of the big bourgeoisie (FZK, 1:81).

On the other hand, the Menshevik minister of labor, ignoring the industrialists' opposition to state regulation, told the conference that the revolution was bourgeois and so regulation was not the affair of any single class but of the state (ibid., 84). To this a delegate replied:

> To us workers it is clear that the bourgeoisie, by undermining production, is . . . skillfully, at first glance imperceptibly, organizing a counterrevolution. . . . Sabotage in the Donbass, in the textile industry, in a whole series of Petrograd factories, requires the organized intervention of the working class in the form of the immediate establishment of workers' control. . . . Otherwise,

all the workers' organizations will be destroyed. Unemployed, hungry workers won't think about organization; it is naive to think the Provisional Government will set up control over its own capitalists. . . . Life itself has put
forth the demand for workers' control but it will be fully realized [only . . .]
under a government of revolutionary democracy [that is, of workers and
peasants]. Until then, the factory committees will have a great role to play
in carrying out workers' control and saving the country (ibid., 105).

Two resolutions were adopted by overwhelming majorities. The first
called for giving workers two-thirds representation in all state economic institutions and for the factory committees, soviets, and trade unions to have
the right to participate in the control of the factories. Such control should
"gradually and carefully, but without undue delay" develop into full regulation of production and distribution by workers (ibid., 86). The other resolution demanded soviet power—a first for any major citywide workers'
assembly (ibid., 114).

Where was all this leading? V. Levin, of the newly elected Central Council, replied: "No one knows how this revolution will end up. At the least, it
will deprive capital of some of its rights; at the most, who can say whether
from a Russian revolution it will not become a world revolution" (ibid., 113).
Some anarchists called for the takeover of factories. But a Bolshevik delegate
replied: "Control is not yet socialism, nor even taking of production into our
hands. But it already goes beyond the bourgeois framework. . . .Having taken
power into our hands, we should direct capitalism along a path such that it
will outlive itself. . . .Having taken control into our hands, we will learn in a
practical way to work actively in production and we will direct it toward socialist production in an organized manner" (ibid., 126).

## Capital's Response

This gradualist approach rested on the assumption that the industrialists
would continue to manage under the "control" of the workers. But this was
far from evident. Following the July Days, when the moderate Socialists tacitly
sanctioned repressions against workers, soldiers, and the political left, who
had been demonstrating to demand that the Central Executive Committees
of Soviets take power, the balance of forces momentarily shifted. Sensing the
shift, the industrialists became more aggressive. With the government's support, they prohibited the factory committees from meeting during working
hours and from interfering in hiring and firing; they stopped paying wages to
the committee members; and they blocked any access to the factories for representatives of the committees' Central Council (ibid., 193).

On August 3, the liberal banker Ryabushinskii reaffirmed the bourgeoisie's outright rejection of state regulation to the Congress of Commerce

and Industry. The revolution was "bourgeois," he declared, and those at the helm of the state must act accordingly. "Unfortunately, the long bony hand of hunger and national impoverishment will have to grab the false friends of the people by the throat, the members of the various soviets and committees, before they come to their senses" (*Eknomicheskoe polozhenie Rossii nakanune Velikoi oktyabr'skoi sotsialisticheskoi revolyutsii* 1957, 196, 200–201). This evoked a "thunder of applause" from the assembled captains of industry. But by the workers this was taken as an open admission that a creeping lockout was under way, a view supported by the growing number of announcements, now also coming from the larger factories, of impending closures and cutbacks in production (Stepanov 1965, 140–41; *Izvestiya* August 18, 1917).

Meanwhile, the newly appointed chief of staff of the armed forces, Cossack general Kornilov, was being widely touted in bourgeois circles as Russia's new savior. In accepting the command, he demanded the extension of the death penalty to the rear (it had been abolished by the February Revolution but had been reinstated in June for the front) and complete freedom of action. He would be responsible only to his "conscience and to the entire people" (Sukhanov 1923, 8:110). With the tacit support of the liberals, he marched on Petrograd at the end of August with the avowed aim of crushing the workers' organizations. But his forces melted away en route under the influence of worker-agitators who had rushed out from the capital to meet the troops.

The coup's failure only increased the industrialists' aggressiveness in the factories, as they were the last line of defense. The Committee of United Industry now demanded guarantees from the government of the owners' exclusive rights over hiring and firing, the right to discipline workers up to and including dismissal, the complete exclusion of workers' organizations from interference in management, an end to any obligations on management's part to workers' organizations, and the dismissal of workers whose productivity fell below their level of the previous year. "Without these measures to influence the worker masses, industry is threatened with complete shutdown," the committee declared (*Rech'*, September 10, 1917).

The essentially defensive motivation of workers' control, on the one hand, and the employers' resistance, on the other, meant that sustained struggles over control in private plants were limited mostly to situations presenting an imminent threat of mass layoffs or closure. Thus, it was only as of September that the committee of the very militant Rozenkrantz copper-rolling factory took decisive action on control, in response to "attempts of sabotage by the administration, with the acting minister of trade and industry himself threatening to come and shut down the plant" (Gaponenko 1962, 286–87). But effective control, at least in private factories, largely eluded the workers. On the eve of the October Revolution, a delegate from the Putilov shipyard told a factory committee conference that

> We are aware of how often the factory committees turn out to be helpless, knowing how to prevent the stoppage of production but without the possibility of intervening . . . . Both private and state administrations are sabotaging, while citing [decisions of] the Society of Factory and Mill Owners. They are still strong. The conference must first of all point out the obstacles that prevent people of action from saving the country. These obstacles are being placed before us by the bourgeois government. Only a reorganization of state power can make it possible to develop our activity (FZK, 2:121).

## Moving Beyond "Control" and the Question of Class Collaboration

The committees' most frequent incursion into managerial prerogatives was not, in fact, to assert "control" but to obtain fuel and materials for their plants, sometimes orders and finances as well. Even before the first citywide conference, held at the end of May, the factory committees had met to discuss the supply situation. They sent delegations as far as eastern Ukraine in search of fuel (Gaza 1933, 337; *Rabochii kontrol' i natsionalizatsiya*, 1:70, 75, 80). "Strangely, after the first weeks of the Revolution," observed a delegate to the conference, "in one plant after the other there was no fuel, no raw materials, no money. More important, management took no steps to find what was needed. Everyone saw this as an Italian [slowdown] strike. The factory committees sent representatives all over in search of fuel—to other factory committees, to railroad junctions, warehouses, etc. . . .[and ] as a result of their activity, oil, coal, money, orders were found" (FZK, 2:121).

Some committees went even further. At the Vulkan machine-building factory, the committee responded to an announced cutback in production and possible closure by proposing measures to reduce defective output, strengthen discipline, and make technical improvements. The workers' general assembly endorsed these measures and in addition decided to allow overtime provided it could be justified. Management accepted all the proposals except for the technical measures, which it considered an incursion on its rights. It then went ahead and announced 640 layoffs, warning that more were to come. At the same time, it cut the wages of the committee members in half and prohibited office personnel from giving out information. In response, against the advice of their committee, the workers' general assembly then gave the director forty-eight hours to clear out, declaring that they were absolving the committee of any responsibility for actions they might take. The Central Council of factory committees was able to convince the government to establish control over the Vulkan management.

But Vulkan's committee reported that the workers had little confidence in control by a government that was not "democratic" (that is, representative of the popular classes), given that there was no workers' control on the national level (Stepanov 1965, 216; *Rabochii put'*, October 8, 1917; *Znamya truda*, September 30, 1917; Chugaev 1962, 326–27; see also Reed 1960, 8). The committee of the New Parviainen machine-building factory committee averted 1,630 layoffs by proposing measures to reduce fuel consumption by 30 percent. Even so management only adopted them under pressure (*Rabochii put'*, September 8, 1917; FZK, 2:17). At the state-owned Sestroretsk rifle factory, when fuel began to run out, the committee decided to dig a canal to a source of water power on a nearby estate (ignoring the landowner's protests). The left Socialist Revolutionary paper reported this under the headline: "What Would Happen to the Factories without the Factory Committees?" (*Znamya truda*, October 1, 1917).

These examples show that the workers were moving beyond "control," itself often elusive, to active participation in management. As one worker explained, "They tell us to control. But what will we control when we have nothing left but walls, bare walls?" (FZK, 1:269). Formally, the goal remained "control." The rapporteur on workers' control at the national factory committee conference in October observed that "many comrades pointed out that the reports [to the conference] did not make clear the executive functions of the factory committees. This was done purposely, since economic functions are only an inevitable evil that should not be built into a system" (FZK, 2:184).

Incursion into managerial prerogatives within the framework of a capitalist economy raised the thorny issue of class collaboration. Class independence, both in the factories and in the political arena, had long been a defining principle of the prewar Russian labor movement. Mensheviks and moderate Bolsheviks, who often had links to the unions, used this issue to argue against the factory committees. D. Ryazanov, a moderate Bolshevik with union connections, told the national conference that "the trade-union movement does not bear the stain of the entrepreneur. But it is the misfortune of the committees that they are an integral part of the administration. The trade union opposes itself directly to capital, but a member of a factory committee involuntary turns into an agent of the entrepreneur" (ibid., 192). Gast'ev, a member of the executive committee of the Petrograd Metalworkers Union, remarked on the "touching solidarity [of the committees] with management." He told of representatives of committees arriving from the provinces to praise their factories in support of their owners' requests for contracts and subsidies from the government (*Pervaya vserossiiskaya tarifnaya konferentsiya rabochikh metallistov* 1918, 7). These Menshevik and moderate Bolshevik critics also accused the committees of anarchism, of pursuing the narrow group interests of their respective plants at the expense of the common interest, and of aiming at the group seizure of the plants. But underlying this criticism, itself largely unfounded, was the fundamental opposition to workers' incursion into managerial prerogatives in the context of a bourgeois-democratic revolution—which to the critics' minds was all they could achieve in backward Russia.

Lenin also criticized the factory committees for acting as "errand boys for the capitalists." But he was coming from a very different angle than the moderate Socialists, emphasizing that only soviet power and worker majorities in state regulatory bodies could ensure that the committees served the workers' interests, not those of capital. But as noted, the vast majority of the delegates also called for the transfer of power to the soviets. Meanwhile, however, they had to act to save their jobs. One responded: "The factory committees had to obtain raw materials. This is not 'running errands.' If we didn't support the factories in this way, who knows what would happen?" (FZK, 1:91–92, 100).

Workers were, in fact, prepared to cooperate with management to save jobs, but they insisted on guarantees of good faith in return. That was the role of control. At the Baltic wagon factory, management announced that it was closing the loss-incurring automobile department. When the committee questioned management's figures, the director agreed to keep the factory open on the condition that the workers maintain productivity and keep the department profitable. The committee accepted these terms but insisted on obtaining control, a demand management rejected as "having no precedent" (*Izvestiya*, June 17, 1917).[6]

Incursions into managerial prerogatives were often made reluctantly by the committees under pressure from their rank and file. N. Skrypnik, a Bolshevik member of the Central Council of factory committees, reported to his party on the eve of the October insurrection that "everywhere one observes the desire for practical results. Resolutions no longer satisfy. It is felt that the leaders do not entirely express the mood of the masses. The former are more conservative. One notices an increase in the influence of anarchists in the Moscow and Narva Districts" (*Oktyabr'skoe vooruzhennoe vosstanie* 1957, 52).

This "conservatism" arose out of a reluctance to assume responsibility for management. The committees were not at all sure they could handle the task, especially in conditions of economic dislocation. The rank-and-file workers, more removed from these problems, were more tempted by anarchist calls to direct action. But more than that, the committee activists feared being compromised if they took on managerial responsibility without having

---

6 It is not clear how this conflict ended.

the commensurate power to take effective measures to save the factories.

As the economic situation continued to deteriorate, management in the state factories, as well as in some private ones, offered the committees minority participation in the administration. In October the national conference of factory committees overwhelmingly rejected this, insisting on control through commissions separate from management (FZK, 2:192). A member of the Central Council explained: "The members of the factory committee would turn into pushers, whom management would use as extra help, themselves remaining inactive. Such phenomena are already being observed in state factories. Besides, … in a critical moment … the workers will direct all their discontent at the factory committee" (FZK, 2:174). The state factories took the same position, while affirming their right to be present at managerial meetings and to have access to all information (*Oktyabr'skoe vooruzhennoe vosstanie* 1957, 110, 127).

In early October, facing the layoff of ten thousand workers—a third of the workforce—due to the fuel shortage, the Putilov factory committee discussed the offer by the minister of trade and industry of a minority voice in a joint commission with management. No one doubted that the intention was to shift responsibility for the dismissals to the committee without giving it any real power. "The entrepreneurs are at present seeking by all means a way to make the workers whip themselves. . . . When it turned out that the government could not do without us and things were in a bad way, it came to us for help." After a long and painful discussion, the committee decided that it could not pass up any opportunity to defend workers' jobs and accepted the offer, but solely with a view to gaining control and explicitly rejecting responsibility for management (Gaza 1933, 386–91; *Rabochii kontrol' i natsionalizatsiya*, 1:205; *Fabrichno-zavodskie komitety Petrograda v 1917g*, 483–87, 494–97).[7]

## All Political Power to the Soviets! But How Much Economic Power?

The factory committees were not blind to these contradictions. Everyone, except some of the anarchists, considered the transfer of state power to the soviets as the only possible solution. "Our conference said from the start that under a bourgeois government we would not be able to establish consistent control," explained Skrypnik to the national conference of factory committees in October. "To speak of a [national] controlling body under a

---

7 The Putilov factory had been placed under state management in 1915 but remained privately owned, with the stockholders on the board of directors keeping a close watch over its affairs.

bourgeois government makes no sense. Therefore, the working class cannot bypass the question of state power, as [anarchist] comrade Renev recommends" (FZK, 2:121). For the workers, the economic crisis was the most immediate and potent argument for an insurrection. At a meeting of union and factory committee leaders in mid-October to discuss the food and employment situations it was agreed that the economic dam was about to burst. The government was doing nothing except making things worse. Soviet power was the "indispensable condition for the successful struggle against economic dislocation and the food crisis." Among other things, it would establish workers' control on a national scale, demobilize industry, and organize public works (Gaponenko 1962, 119–25).

Where would soviet power take the factory committees? The answer remained unchanged. At the October 1917 conference of Petrograd's factory committees, Evdokymov, a Bolshevik member of the Central Council, told the anarchists that "to demand the transfer of all factories to the workers is premature. That means the transition to a socialist system. But the time for socialism in Russia has not yet arrived. Our revolution is not socialist but transitional. The most numerous class in Russia is the peasantry, and the peasantry, a petty bourgeoisie, is individualistic" (FZK, 2:43). Yet earlier, in August, another member of the Central Council had warned: "It is possible that we stand before a general strike of capitalists and industrialists. We have to be ready to take the enterprises into our hands to render harmless the hunger upon which the bourgeoisie is counting so much as a counterrevolutionary force" (FZK, 1:269).

Once the soviets had taken power, the factory committees shifted from their refusal to assume responsibility for management—a position that, in any case, had been more formal than real. The Central Council's draft guidelines on workers' control read:

> Workers' control of industry, as an integral part of control of the entire productive life of the country, must not be conceived in the narrow sense of inspection [*reviziya*] but, on the contrary, in the broadest sense of *intervention* into the disposition by the entrepreneur of capital, inventory, raw materials and finished goods belonging to the enterprise; as the *active* monitoring of the correct and rational fulfillment of contracts, the utilization of energy and the labor force, and as *participation in the organization of production itself* on a rational basis, etc., etc.

This included the right to issue orders to management, which would have three days to appeal to higher organs of workers' control before the orders became obligatory (*Izvestiya*, December 7, 1917; FZK, 3:167–79; 4:416; *Natsionalizatsiya promyshlennosti SSSR* 1954, 78).

"This is not socialism," insisted the Bolshevik Skrypnik at a conference of Petrograd's factory committees in November.

It is a first step. . . .We are linked to other countries. . . .The torch that our revolution has raised will ignite the proletariat of Western Europe. . . .Socialism is not created at once but by the gradual restructuring of all economic and political life. We have entered the first period of that restructuring. . . . Our foundation is all power in the hands of the soviets of workers' and soldiers' deputies. Not all power to the soviet but to the soviets, including the soviets in the factories and the villages. (FZK, 3:36).

The "active" approach to control supported by the factory committees met with opposition from "comrades on the right" (designated as such by the factory committees), who received the backing of the All-Russian Trade Union Council and the Trade Union Congress. They insisted on "passive" control (for attitudes of various unions and union leaders to control, see FZK, 3:115–31). Their own draft guidelines for the committees read: "The control commission does not participate in management of the enterprise and does not bear responsibility for its work and activity, which remains that of the owner." Only government and higher trade union bodies could countermand management's orders. The guidelines provided for up to two years' imprisonment and confiscation of property for violation of these instructions or for plant seizures (FZK, 3:93–95; *Izvestiya* December 17, 1917; *Rabochii kontrol' i natsionalizatsiya*, 1:341). The argument was that giving the factory committees power to intervene actively in management would encourage their allegedly anarchist tendencies, since each committee would defend the group interests of its workers at the expense of the common good.

But this argument was to a large degree disingenuous, since committee conferences consistently emphasized that workers' control could be effective only within a framework of national economic regulation. Indeed, the urgency of centralism—to combat the growing economic chaos, to distribute scarce supplies and contracts, to convert industry to peacetime production— was the central leitmotif of the sixth Petrograd conference of factory committees in January 1918. The proposal of the Central Council to create regional *sovnarkhozy* (economic councils) was met with enthusiasm (*Rabochii put'*, nos. 6–8, 1918).[8] The decisions of regional sovnarkhozy were to be binding on all local institutions, including factory committees (FZK, 4:439). (Petrograd's Central Council eventually fused into the sovnarkhoz of the Northern Region [FZK, 3:128, 286; 4:26, 34; for the council's efforts to organize the supply and distribution of fuel and materials, see FZK, 3:253–77].) The guidelines on workers' control stated that factory committees would execute the will of the plants' general assemblies but "at the same time they carry out all instructions, guidelines . . . and measures of higher state

---

8 The full protocols are published in FZK, 4.

economic organs and are responsible to the state authority for the strictest order and rational management of the enterprise, in accordance with the needs of the entire toiling people, as well as for the integrity of the enterprise's property" (FZK, 4:417). Other resolutions called for centralized distribution of fuel and contracts (ibid., 443–44).

These decisions made clear that in the case of conflict the decisions of the higher bodies would take precedence over local interests (ibid., 158). To the argument made by an anarchist delegate that centralization would inevitably lead to "some kind of autocracy," another replied: "The factories have to coordinate their activity. Who can do that? Only a higher organization that...has all the information, which distributes the contracts, and knows what each plant is doing. We control directly in the factory; we...inform of what we need. But distribution has to be centralized....We need organization, centralization, like oxygen....Otherwise we will be lost and never get out of the present mess" (ibid., 180). Another delegate observed that, for all their criticism, the anarchists could not explain how they would organize the economy. To be consistent, they would have to be opposed to the factory committees themselves, since the committees too limited the freedom of individual workers (ibid., 187). Fears of bureaucratic despotism were undoubtedly allayed by the provision for election from below of higher economic organs, which were to function on principles of democratic centralism (ibid., 421).

From the workers' viewpoint, the "comrades on the right" were ignoring reality by asking that they limit themselves to passive control. It was fine to call for centralized regulation but immediate action was needed. At the start of 1918, the employed industrial workforce in Petrograd had shrunk to 339,641 from 406,312 the year before, and most of that decline had occurred after October 1917; by May 1918 there would remain only 142,915 employed industrial workers in the capital (*Materialy po statistike truda severnoi oblasti* 1918, 33). According to the paper of the Central Council, "[The factory committees] view themselves as the basic units of the higher regulating institutions of the economy and are doing everything in their power to follow the path laid out by these organs and institutions. And it is not their fault that all these institutions do not yet exist....It is not their fault that, faced with total uncertainty in this or that matter, circumstances and lack of time force them sometimes to act at their own risk and responsibility" (Katyn 1918).

Not surprisingly, the owners preferred the position of the "comrades on the right." A report to the All-Russian Society of Leather Manufacturers in January noted the existence "an anarchist current, represented by the factory committees" as well as a "thought-out system of gradual transition to state socialism on the basis of the existing capitalist system..., supported by...the union movement. The union people are the only allies of industry." The report also approvingly cited an article in the Menshevik press arguing that the revolution was bourgeois and that private property had to be respected. The leather manufacturers unanimously endorsed the "passive" guidelines as "something we can live with" (*Novaya zhizn'*, December 5, 1917; see also FZK, 3:106; *Natsionalizatsiya promyshlennosti SSSR*, 82–86; *Rabochii kontrol' i natsionalizatsiya*, 1:345–47). The Petrograd Society of Factory and Mill Owners called on its members to abandon their factories if faced with "active" control (*Rabochii kontrol' i natsionalizatsiya*, 1:346–47).

The more left-wing unions, like the Petrograd metalworkers, did, however, support "active control" (*Metallist*, no. 1, 1918, 13). In contrast, the Mensheviks, opposed to soviet power, argued that "active" control would "rivet the workers' horizon to *their own* enterprise." Ignoring the earlier reports by their own press about a hidden lockout aimed at crushing the workers' movement, they now declared talk of sabotage to be "demagogic fantasy" (*Rabochaya gazeta*, November 12, 1917).

In reality, the factory committees themselves demonstrated concern not to needlessly alienate the industrialists by insisting on "active" control when a plant was functioning well. In January 1918 the Putilov committee reported:

> In defending the workers' interests, the committee not only adhered to the principle of resolving conflicts between capital and labor but tirelessly pursued the tendency of intervening in the economic life of the factory, doing that, as far as possible, by assuming only control, not executive functions. All the results in that area, all the control positions achieved by the committee were won without open conflict with the representatives of capital, without summoning the masses to defend these positions, exclusively through verbal negotiation and similar measures (FZK, 3:216–17).

The Erikson telephone factory, long a Bolshevik stronghold, reported that management had agreed to cooperate with the committee in securing fuel and materials, as those activities were not perceived as a threat to its prerogatives. But management refused to allow control over finances and access to information, threatening to resign over the demands. The committee, therefore, decided not to press the issue in order "to avoid premature complications that could lead to a temporary stoppage" (*Rabochii kontrol' i natsionalizatsiya*, 1:325–26). At the Tenteleevskii chemical factory the administration agreed to "passive" control in return for the committee's pledge to respect management's executive powers (ibid., 285). When the head of the control commission at the Novaya Bumagopryadil'naya cotton mill insisted on checking for unnecessary expenses before countersigning a check, thus provoking the owner's departure, she was called to order by her committee and replaced. "Don't you know we can't manage without a specialist!" she was told (Perazich 1927, 142).

These examples argue against the "anarchist" interpretation of workers' control. It is true that the Central Council's guidelines for regional sovnarkhozy initially called for their election solely by the factory committees, a syndicalist position. However, the council did not oppose the Supreme Sovnarkhoz's proposal to include representatives from the soviets, cooperatives, and technical-managerial personnel (FZK, 3:437–79).

## Calls for Nationalization

In both versions, however, control was a form of dual power, a compromise between opposing interests and thus unstable by nature. As noted earlier, workers' control was predicated on the industrialists' being willing to continue managing their factories. But the demand for control had initially arisen precisely because this could not be taken for granted. The Petrograd Society of Factory and Mill Owners, ignoring its official position, did advise its members not to abandon their plants as long as they represented any value. But this stance was less and less prevalent. Even those entrepreneurs who did not engage in sabotage or fear worker takeover could not be very optimistic about their prospects for making money in the foreseeable future, in light of the termination of military contracts, the expense and complexity of conversion to peacetime production, and the transport crisis that made supply a huge problem.

It was this unwillingness or inability of the owners to maintain production that drove the workers beyond the demand for control, passive or active, to press for complete takeover of management and nationalization. This logic emerges clearly in a letter from the committee of the Vulkan machine-building factory 1918 to the sovnarkhoz of the Northern Region in March:

> The entire policy of management...has been conducted with a definite view toward closing, ...[and] if the factory has not already been shut, the credit belongs to the factory committee, whose entire policy, in face of unending and insurmountable obstacles, was aimed at maintaining the life of the factory.... The kind of control that management is willing to accept is only a palliative, since it will continue to be the master of the enterprise, while responsibility...will lie entirely with the control commission, and, consequently, dual power will not be eliminated. . . .The only way out is nationalization and we once again affirm this with this present petition (*Natsionalizatsiya promyshlennosti SSSR*, 351).

Even the "comrades on the right" had to admit this. Yu. Larin, a former Menshevik and coauthor of the instructions on "passive" control, told a congress of the Metalworkers Union in January 1918:

> We tried in many cases to put off the moment of full management of the enterprises and to restrict ourselves to control. But all our efforts came to

naught. In the present situation none of the existing forces can—and sometimes they do not even want to—manage the economy. Example: the Volga merchant fleet, where the industrialists have stopped repairing the ships and have ceased activity in general. . . .Either we move forward or we go down. Like it or not, we have to abandon the idea of workers' control and shift to a system of full management of the enterprises and direction of the country's economy (*Novaya zhizn'*, January 21, 1918).

Nationalization was the main point on the agenda of the sixth Petrograd conference of factory committees in late January 1918. The only issue in dispute was the speed, with anarchists demanding immediate and complete takeover of the factories. The resolution, adopted unanimously, recognized that immediate nationalization of all industry was impossible without first creating an "organized technical apparatus, corresponding to the interests of the proletariat," working under the direction of the Supreme Sovnarkhoz. But it called for immediate nationalization in cases in which management refused to recognize workers' control, openly or secretly sabotaged production, or refused to pursue it.

The conference did, however, sound a new note in calling also for the immediate nationalization of factories that were in good physical and financial shape and suited for peacetime production, "since the proletarian Republic takes from the hands of the predators not only the ruined economy that will be a burden on the people's finances, but also enterprises that can function intensively, providing the people with economic resources and so helping to restore the health of the people's property" (*Novyi put'*, nos. 4–5 [8–9], 1918:13–14; nos. 6–8 [10–12]:22–24). This indicated a break with the hitherto predominantly defensive view of workers' control.

But it would be wrong to see in this shift a sudden naively optimistic upsurge. All those who spoke at the conference painted a deeply somber picture of the situation: "We have heard here reports of such ruin, of such a horrible reality, which, in fact, we ourselves have already been experiencing" (FZK, 3:241). Nor did they spare their own class organizations from criticism. But the task had changed. "Every one of us knows that our industrial life is coming to a standstill and that the moment is fast approaching when it will die. We are now living through its death spasms. Here the question of control is no longer relevant. You can control only when you have something to control. . . .Everyone, from the left to the right wing, agrees on one thing: we have to rebuild economic life itself on a new basis." This analysis was echoed in the resolution on demobilization, described as "a tremendously difficult task. . .that only the proletariat can realize on a national scale and in a planned, organized way" (ibid., 241, 446).

But if the mood was somber, it was also determined. Some invoked 1905, a revolution defeated by mass lockouts. They were not going to let that happen

again (FZK, 4:241, 174–77). In explaining the decision to call for nationalization, the Central Council noted that committees were increasingly coming
to it with demands for the state to take over their factories. "Thus, unexpectedly arises the practical question of nationalizing production" (ibid., 5, 290;
*Novyi put'*, nos. 6–8 [10–12], 24).

Over the next months nationalization proceeded slowly and on an individual basis in the metal sector, either as a punitive measure or to prevent
closure (*Trudy I Vserossiiskogo s'ezda sovetov narodnogo khozyaistva* 1918, 53,
91–92). After the merchant fleet, which workers repaired over several
months without receiving pay, the first sector to be nationalized was sugar
in May 1918, followed by oil, and then the rest of the metal sector (Carr
1966, 189). The decree on general nationalization was issued in June 1918.
As with workers' control, nationalization was viewed primarily as a policy
imposed by circumstances, not as an ideological imperative, as it has so often
been portrayed by historians. A prominent Bolshevik wrote in 1918: "Yes,
'socialist experiments,' as our opponents mock. . . .[But] this is no 'fantastic
theory' or 'free will.' *We have no choice.* And since it is done by the working
class and in since the capitalists are removed in the course of the revolutionary struggle, it has to be socialist regulation. . . .Will this be another Paris
Commune or will it lead to world socialism? That depends on international
circumstances. But we have absolutely no choice" (Stepanov 1918, 13–14).

## After Nationalization

The January 1918 factory committee conference called for the committees
to manage the nationalized enterprises, since "a government of workers, soldiers and peasants is strong insofar as it rests on the confidence of the toilers
and their organizations. . . .The workers' committees should be at the head
of these enterprises locally, working under the leadership of the sovnarkhozy"
(FZK, 3:443). To the suggestion that the committees limit themselves to a
few representatives in management and to only a consultative voice, a member of the Central Council retorted: "That is extremism, some kind of de-
formed Bolshevism. . . .The factory committees must absolutely stand at the
head of the factories, . . .subordinated, of course, to the state regulating organization, the sovnarkhoz, . . .[since] the committees know best the situation at their factory and the workers have confidence in them." If they lacked
expertise, they could invite technical staff (ibid., 293–94; 255–56).

But a March decree of the Supreme Sovnarkhoz fell far short of the committees' position. It called for the directorate of each industrial branch
(*glavky*) to appoint a commissar to each factory under its supervision, as well
as technical and administrative directors. The technical director could be
overruled only by the commissar or by the branch directorate. The adminis-

trative director, on the other hand, would work under the supervision of an economic administrative council, consisting of representatives of the workers, white-collar and technical staff, the trade union, and the local soviet. But workers and white-collar employees would constitute no more than half of its members. As for the factory committees, they could not issue orders but had to go through the economic administrative councils (Carr 1966, 92).

The emphasis on centralism at the expense of meaningful worker participation in management would grow stronger with the outbreak of full-scale civil war and the deepening economic crisis that forced the Soviet state into a desperate survival mode for the next several years. These conditions strengthened the hand of supporters of authoritarian management, with people like Lenin and Trotsky, formerly on the left, rallying to their side. (The Mensheviks continued to limit themselves to demanding trade union autonomy.) Within the Bolshevik Party the cause of the factory committees was taken up by the Left Opposition and, later by the Workers' Opposition, the latter unsuccessfully defending a syndicalist position.

There is an obvious contradiction between centralism, an essential element of socialist planning, and self-management, also essential to socialism, since the more power the center wields the less is left for workers in the enterprises. But this contradiction can be managed and even become a positive factor if certain conditions are present: objective circumstances must allow for a significant limitation of central control, and the economy must be able to provide workers with economic security and a decent standard of living. Without the first, self-management is not meaningful; without the second, workers cannot be expected to sacrifice local group interests for the general good. Both conditions were absent in Russia.

Yet another important condition is a working class capable of defending self-management against the spontaneous centralizing tendencies of the state apparatus. At the January conference, an anarchist proposed to amend the guidelines requiring the factory committees to obey orders from the higher organs. He proposed a proviso: when these orders did "not violate the interests of the proletariat." The speaker for the Central Council replied that it had in fact considered such a reservation but decided against it, since

> The sovnarkhoz, that we are ourselves organizing, will not turn against us, as it is not a bureaucratically constructed organ but one elected by us and composed of people whom we can recall. . . . Don't forget that the sovnarkhoz is a class organ. If we adopt an attitude of mistrust from the outset, then these organs will scarcely be able to function correctly. . . . Only an anarchist who in general rejects and mistrusts any leadership [*verkhy*] could propose such an amendment. But we, the proletariat, . . . build leadership on the principle of complete democratism. . . . If these organs really do turn away from the masses, then, of course we will have to introduce that amendment. Indeed,

we will have to overthrow those organs, and perhaps make a new revolution. But so far we feel that the Soviet of People's Commissars is our soviet and the institutions it creates are fully in accord with us (FZK, 4:316, 323–34).

This response reflected the confidence of workers who had led three revolutions. But conditions were fast undermining the independent power of the Russian working class, whose members were being dispersed by unemployment and absorption into the new state apparatus and the army. Those who remained in industry were quickly being demoralized by hunger, cold, and disease. At the same conference, another delegate proposed a converse amendment: the committees should not be responsible to their general assemblies when the latter adopted decisions that contradicted the general interest. A member of the Central Council replied that "it would be out of place for us, who base ourselves on the support of these proletarian masses, to introduce such a condition that places them beneath any criticism....For as long as I have observed workers in the factories, I can say, comrades, that we can consider them...conscious enough not to adopt decisions that their factory committee cannot carry out because they contradict the interests of the country" (ibid., 318–320).

Yet the conference heard examples that cast doubt on this. One delegate observed:

> Some factories are not needed and have to be shut. Here you need a state apparatus that can sort this out....Comrade Bleikhman says: "Take [the plants] into our hands, and basta!".... I'd like to ask these comrade anarchists... how they presently conduct themselves in the factories among their unconscious masses. Do they speak openly to them? I don't know how to talk to masses that are demanding money. I came late...because things aren't very good at my plant: we are laying off a hundred people. There you have anarchy, ...and not the kind...about which comrade Bakunin wrote. That would be heaven on earth. But until then we have to live through all these disputes,.. .when each worker only wants to get not merely a month and a half [of severance pay], but to grab two or three months' worth (ibid., 284).

Others replied that such conflicts arose mainly among workers still fresh from the countryside. But the dispute between the committees of the Treugol'nik rubber factory and the Putilov works indicated that the problem went deeper. Treugol'nik had fuel reserves beyond the three-month limit established by the Central Council. Meanwhile, Putilov, facing mass layoffs, was preparing for conversion and lacked fuel. Treugol'nik would sell its excess only at an exorbitant price, arguing that it had to cover amortization of newly purchased fuel tanks that would be standing empty. "'You have to fend for yourselves; but we won't give.' This might be patriotic and very good for the workers of Treugol'nik. ... .But it is not good for the country and not for the working class that is desperately struggling to revive industry" (ibid., 338–39;

354–56; *Novaya zhizn'*, January 28, 1918). The conference decided to put all fuel beyond a two-month supply under the sole control of the regional sovnarkhoz (*Novyi put'*, nos. 4–5 [8–9], 1918:14).

The contradiction between centralism and self-management would only become more acute with time. In June, the metal section of the northern sovnarkhoz reported:

> The committees, ignoring everything, defend the interests of their own parish in an effort to obtain subsidies and advances. . . . [They] try to revive the operation of closed enterprises even when there is no objective basis. . . . The data we receive from them. . . are always one-sided. . . . [They] very often besieged the authorities, snatched up contracts, obtained advances, . . . and without the approval of the sovnarkhoz, reopened their factories. Unfortunately, the majority of such contracts objectively could not be fulfilled, not to mention that they very much disorganize the work of our section . . . [which] will have to take control of all orders and reorganize them in the interests of the general state mechanism. This will not happen without a struggle of the workers' government against the workers' organizations (*Natsionalizatsiya prommyshlennosti i organizatsiya sotsialisticheskogo proizvodstva v Petrograde* 1958, 99).

At the First Congress of Sovnarkhozy in May, N. Osinskii, a member of the Left Opposition in the Bolshevik Party, defended the factory committees. But he began by lamenting that the "absolute decline of the productive forces [that] is reaching the extreme point when an economy starts to die." It was necessary, he argued, to shift to a minimalist survival mode, to a "miserly" economic policy, under which the state would monopolize existing productive forces and enforce the strictest accounting and use of scarce resources. And yet, he went on to oppose centrally appointed commissars to run the factories. He called for at least two-thirds worker representation in management. "It is all a question of the general conditions . . . . If there is no bread and money, then production proceeds badly even under commissars, who are themselves forced to trade in monopolized goods or factory property" (*Trudy I Vserossiiskogo s'ezda sovetov narodnogo khozyaistva*, 57–66).

A. Rykov, chairperson of the Supreme Sovnarkhoz, replied by citing an article written by Osinskii himself: "The preservation of existing productive forces . . . is possible only by means of their most systematic concentration; the most effective utilization of the available technical forces makes completely inevitable the nationalized management of these forces from a single center" (ibid., 98).

G. Lomov, also of the Left Opposition, was caught in the same contradiction. "The use of commissars of all kinds not only does not summon forth local energies to increase production and strengthen productive forces, but, on the contrary, decreases and destroys local energy." But only minutes later he observed that "workers and peasants are presently becoming enveloped, like worms, in their domestic shells and show signs of life only insofar as it is necessary to satisfy their own personal needs. Everything is broken. We have totally suppressed the vital, creative forces in the country. Everything is going underground and existing only for itself" (ibid., 74–75).

The argument could be, and was, made both ways. But with the survival of the revolution at stake and the social base of the advocates of democratic management increasingly dispersed and demoralized, the situation favored the proponents of centralized, authoritarian management. All agreed that there was no hope without revolution in the West. But while the Left Opposition used that as an argument against sacrificing socialist principles for the sake of survival, others drew the opposite conclusion: defeat of the Russian Revolution would be a major blow to the revolutionary movements in the West, and so it was better—temporarily—to sacrifice principle.

The actual evolution of factory management during the civil war awaits further study. Recent research based on archival materials has shown workers' continued attachment to participation in management and has also found that the committees in some of Petrgorad's largest plants continued to participate in management despite official policy throughout the civil war, and in some cases they wielded full power. The same was true of collegial management (which normally meant a strong factory committee presence), which was in violation of the official policy of one-person management (Gogolevskii 2005, 216; ch. 6).[9]

Even after suppression of the limited trade union rights in the second half of the 1920s, Soviet authorities never ceased to pay lip service to workers' participation in management. When Gorbachev launched his perestroika program, initially portraying it as a socialist renewal, he tried to breathe some life into the ideology, though in a limited, contradictory manner. But it was only after he embraced the restoration of capitalism in 1989 and retracted the self-management measures that a genuine movement for self-management finally arose (see Mandel 1991). It was, however, cut short by the ensuing "revolution from above" before it could develop a militant base and a clear program.

## References

Carr, E. H. 1966. *The Bolshevik revolution 1917–23*, vol. 2. Baltimore: Penguin.
Central State Archive of St. Petersburg [TsGASPb, formerly LGAORSS].

9 This does not necessarily mean that the committees were still under the control of their general assemblies, another area of question that requires further research.

Chugaev, D. A., ed. 1959. *Revolyutsionnoe dvizhenie v Rossii v mae-iyune 1917g.* Moscow.
———, ed. 1962. *Revolyutsionnoe dvizhenie v Rossii v sentyabre 1917g.* 1962. Moscow.
Churakov, D. O. 2005. *Fabzavkomy v bor'be za proizvodstvennuyu demokratiyu,* Moscow: Prometei.
*Eknomicheskoe polozhenie Rossii nakanune Velikoi oktyabr'skoi sotsialisticheskoii revolyutsii.* 1957. Moscow and Leningrad: Akademiya Nauk.
*Fabrichno-zavodskie komitety Petrograda v 1917g., protokoly.* 1979. Moscow: Nauka.
Gaponenko, L. S., ed. 1957. *Revolyutsionnoe dvizhenie v Rossii posle sverzheniya samoderzha-viya.* Moscow: Akademiya Nauk SSSR.
———, ed. 1958. *Revolyutsionnoe dvizhenie v Rossii v aprele 1917g.* 1958. Moscow: Akademiya Nauk SSSR.
———, ed. 1962. *Revolyutsionnoe dvizhenie v Rossii nakanune Oktyabr'skogo vooruzhen-nogo vosstaniya v Petrograde.* Moscow and Leningrad: Akademiya Nauk.
Gaza, I. I. ed. 1933. *Putilovtsy v trekh revolyutiyakh.* Leningrad: Iztoriya zavodov.
Gogolevskii, A. V. 2005. *Revolyutsiya i psikhologiya: politicheskie nastroeniya rabochikh Petrograda v usloviyakh bol'shevistskoi monopolii na vlast' 1918–1920.* St. Petersburg: University of St. Petersburg.
Katyn', N. 1918. Ot rabochego kontrolya k organizatsii i regulirovaniyu proizvodstva. *Novyi put',* no. 1–2 (5–6). January 14.
Kleinbort, L. M. 1923. *Ocherki rabochei intelligentsii, 1906–16,* vol. 1. Petrograd: Petropechat'.
Kruze, E. 1961. *Peterburgskie rabochie v 1912–14gg.,* Moscow and Leningrad: Nauka.
Lenin, V. I. 1962. *Polnoe sobranie sochinenii,* vol. 31, 5th ed. Moscow: Izdatel'stvo politich-eskoi literatury.
Lewin, M. 1975. *Lenin's last struggle,* London: Pluto Press.
Maevski, E. 1918. *Kanun revolyutsii.* Petrograd.
Mandel, David. 1918. "Destatization" and the struggle for power in the Soviet economy. *The Socialist Register 1991,* ed. by R. Miliband and Leo Panitch. London: Merlin Press.
*Materialy po statistike truda severnoi oblasti.* 1918. vyp. V. Petrograd.
*Natsionalizatsiya prommyshlennosti i organizatsiya sotsialisticheskogo proizvodstva v Petrograde.* 1958. vol. I. Leningrad: Leningradskii universitet.
*Natsionalizatsiya promyshlennosti SSSR.* 1954. Moscow: Izdatel'stvo politicheskoi literatury.
*Oktyabr'skaya revolyutsiya i fabzavkomy* [FZK]. 1927–29. vol. 1–3. Moscow: VTsSPS.
*Oktyabr'skaya revolyutsiya i fabzavkomy* [FZK]. 2002. vol. 4. St. Petersburg: St. Petersburg University.
*Oktyabr'skoe vooruzhennoe vosstanie v Petrograde.* 1957. Moscow: Akademiya Nauk.
Perazich, V. *Tekstili Leningrada v 1917g.* 1927. Leningrad.
*Pervaya vserossiiskaya tarifnaya konferentsiya rabochikh metallistov.* 1918. Petrograd.
*Rabochii kontrol' i natsionalizatsiya promyshlennykh predpriyatii Petrograda v 1917–19 gg.* 1949. vol. 1. Leningrad: Nauka.
Reed, J. 1960. *Ten days that shook the world.* New York: Vintage.
Stepanov, I. 1918. *Ot rabochego kontrolya k rabochemu upravleniyu v promyshlennosti i zemledelii,* Moscow.
Stepanov, Z. V. *Rabochie Petrograda v period podgotovki i provedeniya Oktyabr'skogo vooruzhennogo vosstaniya, avgust-sentyabr' 1917g.* 1965. Leningrad: Nauka.
Sukhanov, N. 1923. *Zapiski o revolyutsii,* vols. 6–8. Moscow, Berlin, and Petrograd: Z. I. Grzhebina.
*Trudy I Vserossiiskogo s'ezda sovetov narodnogo khozyaistva.* 1918. Moscow.
Volobuev, P. V. 1964. *Proletariat i burzhuaziya v 1917g.* Moscow: Mysl'.

Newspapers and Journals

*Izvestiya; Izvestiya moskovskogo voenno-promyshlennogo komiteta; Metallist; Novaya put'; Novaya zhizn'; Novyi put'; Pravda; Rabochaya gazeta; Rech'; Rabochii put'; Utro Rossii; Znamya truda*

# 7

# Factory Councils in Turin, 1919–1920

"The Sole and Authentic Social Representatives of the Proletarian Class"[1]

**Pietro Di Paola**

> *The factory council, a different approach, I mean for really uniting the work-ing class. When all the factory councils met together in Turin, they were the highest authority. Higher than the party and higher than the union. And that united us; in fact, anarchist trade unionists agreed with us, some from the Catholic trade unions agreed with us. . .*
>
> —Battista Santhià, oral testimony
> (Bermani, Gramsci, *gli intellettuali e la cultura proletaria*)

The emergence and rapid spread of factory councils in Turin in 1919 and 1920 demonstrated the innovation and revolutionary potential of this form of workers' organization. Conversely, the movement's eventual failure re-vealed the inherent flaws of workers' councils and the complexity of their contradictions.

The factory councils were the outcome of a high point of widespread mil-itancy, independent local action, and confrontation that erupted immediately after World War I among industrial workers in Turin and in the rest of Italy. This new form of organization created an important shift in workers' self-perception: from "wage earner" to "producer" (Masini 1951, 9). The nature of industrial conflict addressed by factory councils shifted. It widened from the economic to include the political field, moving from bargaining and the management of industrial relations to attempting to achieve complete control over production. However, this approach not only encountered fierce oppo-sition from industrialists but also encroached on the sphere of activity of the

---

1 Quote in chapter title is from Bordiga 1920.

traditional labor organizations: the national union federation Confederazione Generale Italiana del Lavoro (CGIL) and the Italian Socialist Party (PSI). An area of further conflict, particularly within the CGIL, concerned the role and degree of participation in decision-making that would be given to nonunionized workers. For the organizers of factory councils, all workers were considered "producers," and therefore all were theoretically entitled to take an active part in the new organization and its governing body.

If militancy and spontaneity were key factors in the emergence of factory councils, their rapid spread and consolidation in Turin and the surrounding area were due to the vigor of the editorial crew of the newspaper *L'Ordine Nuovo* (New Order) and of the anarchist militants within the local section of the iron and steel industrial union, the Federazione Italiana Operai Metallurgici (FIOM). The young intellectuals—Antonio Gramsci, Palmiro Togliatti, Umberto Terracini, and Angelo Tasca—who helped organize *L'Ordine Nuovo* beginning in the spring of 1919 made a crucial contribution to both the theoretical framework and the practical constitution of the factory councils.

They committed time to practice-based research, studying "the capitalist factory as a necessary form of the working class, as a political organ, as the 'national territory' of workers' self government" (Gramsci 1920). The newspaper *L'Ordine Nuovo* became an organ of analysis and investigation based "not on abstraction . . . but on the real experience of the masses" (Montagnana, 1952, 111). Gramsci and Togliatti interviewed workers about every aspect of the system of production and about their lives within the factories:

> In the Chamber of Labour, at party headquarters, even on the tram . . . we did not understand why they pressed so hard with their questions.[2] They wanted to know . . . the manufacturing processes in use, how the factories were equipped, the organization of production, what skills the engineers had, their relationships with the manual workers, and the reasons for fines. And the worker being questioned had to make a big effort. He would have preferred, at least when not at work, not to think about the things that drove him mad six days a week (Santhià 1956, 60).

At the same time, the libertarian group in Turin and anarchist workers— particularly Pietro Ferrero, secretary of the local branch of FIOM, and Maurizio Garino—played equally important roles in the promotion of factory councils. This group, in contrast to the position of anarchist militants in the Unione Sindacale Italiana, argued for the need to participate in reformist trade union organizations in order to fight the reformists from within and build contacts with a greater mass of workers (Masini 1951, 12).

---

2 The Chamber of Labour (Camera del Lavoro) was (and still is) an umbrella body that brought the different unions together within a specific geographical area.

One of the cardinal reasons for the success of this form of organization was rooted in the "aspirations already latent in the conscience of the working masses" (*L'Ordine Nuovo*, 1919b) as "the traditional institutions of the movement have become incapable of containing such a flowering of revolutionary activity" (*L'Ordine Nuovo*, 1919a). After the war, social and industrial protests of unprecedented intensity and scale broke out all over Italy. Membership in trade unions, the Socialist Party, and the anarchist movement increased dramatically; however, most social conflicts of the period were characterized by an unparalleled level of autonomy from party and trade union organization. Popular discontent burst out spontaneously and unexpectedly in the shape of cost-of-living and bread riots, occupations and seizures of land, mutinies, and strikes (Bianchi 2006). Trade unions strove to channel this combative energy. This was a vital issue within the factories: employers were ready to grant considerable concessions at a time that they were investing heavily to convert their systems of industrial production to meet peacetime rather than military needs. For both the industrialists and the unions, the presence of a representative body within the factory was essential.

During the war this function had been performed by union representatives that comprised the Commissioni Interne (internal commissions), most of which remained in place after the conflict (Clark 1977, 36–45). On the one hand, the internal commissions guaranteed the factory managers that the implementation of national or local agreements as well as the resolution of shop-floor disciplinary disputes would be carried out. On the other, the union representatives could wield complete control over the development of industrial relations and labor disputes. A national agreement, signed in February 1919, gave formal recognition to the internal commissions; most importantly, it established the eight-hour workday for metalworkers. This agreement also established a long and complicated system of negotiations before a strike could be called, ruling out unofficial strikes and implicitly committing the trade unions to a period of "social peace" that would prove, however, to be illusory (Castronovo 2005, 83; Maione 1975, 7–12).

The representatives on the internal commissions were union members elected from a list drawn up by union officials, without debate or interaction between the candidates. Moreover, the nomination of these candidates was based largely on personality and charisma. As a consequence, the internal commissions were "trade union organs" rather than representative of the workers as a whole (Terracini 1920; Magri 1947, 184–187). The trade unions saw "the whole workforce as one close-knit, uniform body, almost as if thousands of workers made the same movement and performed the same task. This was due to the fact that . . . the Trade Union only considered the worker in his capacity as wage earner" (Terracini 1920).

These features rendered the internal commissions incapable of effectively marshaling the growing unrest of the mass of the workers. At Fiat, for example, the internal commissions were systematically bypassed by groups of workers who were able to exert pressure on the management (Castronovo 2005, 86). In spite of this, "a tendency to subvert official procedures emerged within the internal commissions themselves, as their attitudes became more contentious than those of the unions" (Soave 1964, 13).

In addition, the exponential growth in membership of local organizations (FIOM had more than twenty thousand members, the Chamber of Labour more than ninety thousand) challenged the effectiveness of the representative structures of the labor movement and their relationship to the growing numbers of recently unionized and nonunionized workers.

## Toward the Factory Councils

> *How are the immense social forces unleashed by the war to be harnessed?*
> *How are they to be disciplined and given a political form [ . . . ]? How can*
> *the present be welded to the future?*
> —Gramsci and Togliatti, unsigned, "Democrazia Operaia,"
> *L'Ordine Nuovo*, June 21, 1919

In the spring of 1919 a debate about transforming the internal commissions developed in several labor movement publications and in heated discussions in the rooms of Socialist clubs in Turin. The debate focused on several issues: the system of representation and its function, relationships between unionized and nonunionized workers, and the role of skilled and white-collar workers in the labor movement. The debate also incorporated the analysis of experiences of factory councils in other countries, including Britain, Germany, Hungary, Russia, and the United States. The search for an alternative system of shop-floor organization had begun.

That March, in an article published in the newspaper *L'Avanguardia*, Alfonso Leonetti proposed the creation of "Italian Soviets from the industrial organizations existing in Italian Factories" (Levy 1999, 142). *L'Ordine Nuovo* reopened the issue toward the end of June. Gramsci and Togliatti saw the internal commissions—freed from the limitations imposed on them by employers—"as a germ of workers' Soviet style government" (Gramsci 1920). Instead of organs of workers' democracy dealing with arbitration and discipline, they envisaged the internal commissions as "organs of proletarian power, replacing the capitalist in all his useful functions of management and administration" (Gramsci and Togliatti,

1919).[3] In August, Ottavio Pastore launched the idea of a different procedure for the election of the internal commissars. While stating firmly that the internal commissions were the creations of the trade unions and not oppositional bodies, he proposed that the workers of each unit in the factory, whether union members or not, should elect their own "workshop commissars."

The members of the internal commission would then be selected from these commissars. This proposal, however, still allocated a traditional role to the internal commission and tried to minimize the impact of nonunionized workers (Pastore 1919). Pastore reported that some workers were already trying out the new form of organization. Indeed, the system had recently been adopted at the Fiat Centro plant. The internal commission had resigned and it was decided to appoint a temporary commission with a mandate to organize new elections based on each work unit. The new commission, however, was elected only by unionized workers (Magri 1947, 187).

In fact, the structure of factory councils was determined not only by theoretical debates and discussions, but also through "the practical experience that suggested the definitive forms of these organisms" (Montagnana 1952, 116). The Turin workers established factory councils without a predetermined plan: "They entered, in a chaotic way perhaps, but spontaneously, a new route" (Togliatti 1919).

The first factory council was established in early September 1919 at the Fiat Brevetti plant. More than two thousand workers, unionized and nonunionized, participated in the voting. Each shop floor and each work unit elected their commissars. Thirty-two commissars were nominated: all were union members except one, who promptly resigned (L'Ordine Nuovo, 1919d).

In the following weeks, workshop commissars were elected and factory councils were constituted in almost all the metalworking factories in Turin, as well as in the chemical and other industries, representing more than fifty thousand workers (Spriano 1971, 54).

L'Ordine Nuovo hailed these developments and encouraged future courses of action for these delegates (L'Ordine Nuovo 1919c). On October 17, the first assembly of workshop commissars was held in Turin, with representatives of more than thirty thousand workers. The formation of factory councils was considered a "point of no return": with the new system, the executive commission—the descriptor adopted by the assembly to replace "internal commission"—was the direct expression of the workers and their ideas. The assembly emphasized that the two most urgent problems, "that of the vote for non-unionized workers, and the relationship with the Trade

---

3 Levy underlines that Gramsci's emphasis was not only on geographical ward committees but also on industrial organizations (Levy 1999, 144–145).

Unions, must be resolved in a general and systematic way in order to facilitate these mass organizations" (*Avanti!* 1920). Three days later a Study Committee for Factory Councils was formed; in the following months this committee would help coordinate theory with practice.

The relationship between factory councils and trade unions and the question of the voting rights of nonunionized employees were closely linked. The resulting debate illustrated contrasting conceptions of workers' organizations not only in industrial and political relations, but also in the development of a revolutionary movement. As the anarchist Garino reflected:

> As regards the relationships with union organizations, three ideas were supported. The first wanted the councils to be inside the unions, in such a way as to cancel out their autonomy. The second, supported by Antonio Gramsci and the socialists of *L'Ordine Nuovo*, was opposed to this assimilation and considered the councils as revolutionary bodies preparing to take political power. And finally, the third, defended by us, the anarchists, saw the councils as revolutionary bodies outside the unions, capable not of assuming power, but of destroying it (Lattarulo and Ambrosoli 1971/2009).

The presence of the anarchists within the council movement in Turin was significant: anarchist militants were "chosen as workshop commissars in disproportionate numbers." The anarchists also exerted an influence on the local branch of FIOM: one hundred militants were associated with FIOM, and three of the nine members of the executive committee established in November 1920 were anarchists (Levy 1999, 150). Moreover, both the Unione Anarchica Italiana (UAI) and the Unione Sindacale Italiana (USI) supported the factory council movement.[4]

As means of revolutionary struggle, the councils were considered by the anarchists to be excellent instruments for immediate action and for guaranteeing the continuation of production both during and after the revolution. The factory council, by developing among the workers the consciousness of their role as producers, heightened the tendency toward expropriation, taking "the class struggle on to its natural terrain" (Garino 1920). However, for the anarchists, factory councils could be effective only in a revolutionary period; under different circumstances they could easily become organs of class collaboration. Another problem was that factory councils reduced the control of the state apparatus without actually destroying it. They would therefore be ineffective without the intervention

---

4 A motion in favor of the factory councils was approved at the first congress of the UAI, a national federation of anarchist groups established in Bologna in July 1920. The USI was founded in 1912 by the revolutionary wing of the Socialist trade union movement. After the war, the anarchists and direct action syndicalists were the dominant force of the USI, led by the anarchist Armando Borghi.

of an organized political force to overthrow the state, an issue that was not addressed by *L'Ordine Nuovo*.

Furthermore, for the anarchists, factory councils were not to be confused with the soviet: "While the Council is the coalition of all productive labor, the Soviet is the political organ through which the authoritarian communists intend to exercise their power" (Garino 1920). Opposing political views about the future of factory councils were underlined by Garino:

> [Gramsci's] agreement with our proposal for the Factory Councils stopped precisely at the issue of the State, of the dictatorship of the proletariat . . . .He told me: "Not only are we working together now, but we must do so until the overthrow of capitalism. At that point, if there are different assessments by us communists, and by you, the libertarian communists, we'll each go our own way." . . . Until then we had worked together in practical action, union action, preparation for the revolution, even armed preparation.

In his discussion with Gramsci, Garino clearly indicated his fear that the revolution would devolve into a one-party state dictatorship:

> I said: "Look, Gramsci, I think that the dictatorship of the proletariat will eventually mutate and degenerate into the dictatorship of a party or, even worse, of an individual." Gramsci replied, "No, no, Garino! That can't happen, the party will not allow one man to take the reins of power and do whatever he likes." "I'm not convinced," I said, "and I'll tell you what I believe: when you take power, we'll be the first to be shot." Gramsci jumped to his feet, with that big bushy head: "Garino, Garino, no! Don't say that! That will never happen!" Yes, with Gramsci there was an incredibly close relationship (Garino, oral testimony in Bermani 2007, 298).

Gramsci's search for an organizational form to replace the parliamentary system and "his conception of an industrially based socialism developed over a long period" (Levy 1999, 138). However, in the spring of 1919 Gramsci and the editors of *L'Ordine Nuovo* focused specifically on the internal commission as a possible form of self-government for the working classes, something that "could be compared to the Soviet, which shared some of its characteristics" (Gramsci 1920).

One of the theoretical bases for the creation of factory councils lay in the idea of the conquest of the state. *L'Ordine Nuovo* made clear that:

> In the light of the revolutionary experiences of Russia, Hungary and Germany . . . the Socialist State cannot be embodied in the institutions of the capitalist State. We remain convinced that with respect to these institutions . . . the Socialist State must be a completely new creation. . . . The formula "conquest of the State" should be understood in the following sense: replacement of the democratic-parliamentary State by a new State, one that is generated by the associative experiences of the proletarian class . . . .New

State-orientated institutions must arise and develop—the very institutions which will replace the person of the capitalist in his administrative functions and his industrial power, and so achieve the autonomy of the producer in the factory (*L'Ordine Nuovo* 1919a).

Factory councils, "arising from the condition created for the working class in the present historical period by the structure of capitalism," were the nucleus of this new organization. They represented the model of the proletarian state because the unity of the working class was realized in practice within factory councils. "On the shop floor the workers are divided into teams and every team constitutes a work unit (a craft unit). The Council itself is made up of the delegates the workers elect on a craft basis in each shop floor. . . . The Council is based on the concrete, organic unity of the craft as it is forged by the discipline of the industrial process" (*L'Ordine Nuovo* 1919e).

Factory councils were seen as the product of a historical development that was making traditional labor organizations obsolete: "The craft unions, the Chambers of Labour, the industrial federations and the General Confederation of Labour are all types of proletarian organization specific to the period of history dominated by capital. It can be argued that they are in a sense an integral part of capitalist society, and have a function that is inherent in a regime of private property" (ibid.)

In the capitalist system the workers could rely only on the sale of their labor power and professional skills; trade unions were the organizations "expert in this kind of transaction, capable of controlling market conditions, of drawing up contracts, assessing commercial risks and initiating economically profitable operations." As unions organized workers not as producers, but as wage earners, they were "nothing other than a form of capitalist society, not a potential successor to that society" (ibid.) Indeed, all the achievements and the victories of the unions were based on the same foundation: the principle of private property and the exploitation of man by man. Thus trade union action, within its own sphere and using its customary methods, stands revealed as utterly incapable of overthrowing capitalist society or embodying the proletarian dictatorship (ibid.). According to the theorists of *L'Ordine Nuovo*, because factory councils were based on "producers" and not "wage-earners," they could not be coordinated or subordinated to the union. On the contrary, their emergence would cause radical structural changes for the trade unions (*L'Ordine Nuovo* 1920c). Nonetheless, while the capitalist system was in place, trade unions were still an indispensable form of organization for improving workers' living conditions.

Both the anarchists and *L'Ordine Nuovo* pressed for the inclusion of nonunionized workers in the election of workshop commissars. Their exclusion would have meant "reducing the factory councils to bureaucratic organs, emptied of their class and unifying functions, making them just a mechanism for connecting union officials with the factory" (Santhià 1956, 66).

By the summer of 1919, Andrea Viglongo had already pointed out that allowing only unionized members to vote placed the internal commission under the influence of the trade unions, seriously damaging it. To exercise its full influence, the internal commission needed to be elected by all the workers, even if that necessitated a radical transformation of the unions. The role of the internal commission was not only to maintain discipline in the workshop, but also to prepare the working class to replace the capitalists in management of the factories: all the workers, not just union members, were to take part in the soviet republic (Viglongo 1919).

The proposal to allow nonunionized members to participate in the election of the internal commissions met with fierce opposition from FIOM and CGIL. Indeed, the system of election was vital in determining the relationship between the new bodies and the trade unions. Two interrelated issues were under discussion: who, among the workers, had the right to elect the workshop commissars; and to what extent the commissars should determine who was elected onto trade union committees and other bodies.

For Emilio Colombino, a member of the national secretariat of FIOM, giving the vote to nonunionized workers meant that the workshops, not the working class, would lead the trade union according to their corporative interests, in this way undermining its very existence. Factory councils needed to be subsidiary organisms: unions were the expression of the working class, not of the workshop. The members of union executive bodies needed to be the most able and experienced union activists, and not selected on the basis of their role in the production process (Colombino 1920, 26–29).

The first discussion in a formal setting about the relationship between factory councils and the unions was held at the annual meeting of the local branch of FIOM in Turin on November 1, 1919. Before the meeting, the assembly of the workshop commissars drew up a *Program of the Workshop Commissars*, which included a declaration of principles and regulations of the factory councils (Comitato di Studio dei Consigli di Fabbrica 1920).

The first principle stated that "Factory commissars are the sole, true social (economic and political) representatives of the proletarian class, because they are elected, in universal suffrage, by all workers at their workplace." As a consequence, "the commissars. . .represent a social power, and because they are union men elected by all proletarians can represent the will of the union men themselves within the organizations."

With some contradictions, the document underlined the different functions of the craft and industrial unions and factory councils. It recognized that trade unions were an indispensable form of organization and that craft and industrial unions needed to "continue in their function of organising individual categories of workers to obtain improvements in wages and working hours." However, the *Program of the Workshop Commissars* made it clear that the trade unions had to act according to the will of the mass of the workers represented by the commissars, and not vice versa:

> The union workers in the councils accept without question that discipline and order in industrial action, partial or collective, be decided by the trade unions, provided, however, that directions to the unions are given by factory commissars as representatives of the working mass. They reject as artificial, ineffective and false every other system that the trade unions want to use to discern the will of the organized masses (Comitato di Studio dei Consigli di Fabbrica 1920).

At the meeting, Giovanni Boero and Garino, representing the workshop commissars, presented a motion stating that trade unions should be the direct manifestation of the will of their members, as expressed by bodies emerging from the workplace. The FIOM officials opposed this approach. Their secretary, Uberti, rejected the proposal that the management committee of the unions' local branches should take its lead from the factory councils. He also condemned the practice of allowing nonunionized workers to vote, a principle that in his opinion clashed with the raison d'être of trade union federations and Chambers of Labour. The only point they conceded was the establishment of the workshop commissars, but only under the control of the unions and as an instrument to increase the democratic participation of the growing numbers of workers.

The motion presented by Boero and Garino obtained the majority of votes and the advocates for factory councils gained control of the local section of FIOM. A few days later, the leader of the Socialist Party, Serrati, commented on this victory in the newspaper *Avanti!* He wondered with dismay how it could be thought that the organs of unity of the working class could be created by the "non-united" workers—those "that up to now have stood on the sidelines watching, with the scepticism of the conservative or the individualism of the anarchist? . . . To claim that the trade unions are outdated bodies is proof of great superficiality, and extremely dangerous for the future of the proletariat" (Serrati 1919).

Despite the passage of the motion in favor of the factory councils, FIOM's official line was promptly reaffirmed at a national meeting in Florence few days later. A motion was passed stating that:

> The metalworking congress . . . declares that the union organization must have total responsibility for the movement and activity of the class both within and outside the factory. . . .It draws the attention of all unionized workers to the danger and the consequences for the union caused by the establishment of new organizations, which could be considered as overriding

the union, which in this way could be placed under the dominant influence of non-unionised masses (Antonioli and Bezza 1978, 121–124).

With this motion, the factory council experiment was allowed only as a continuation of the work of the internal commissions and under the co-ordination of the trade union.

A similar confrontation took place in December at the congress of the Chamber of Labour in Turin, the difference being that in this case all industries were involved. The motion in support of factory councils and for giving the vote to nonunionized workers was passed: "By this time the factory council movement was branded as anti-union by the reformist leadership of FIOM and CGIL, as well as the maximalist directorate of the PSI" (Levy 1999, 146).

The new institution also met with strong opposition from the majority of industrialists. At a national congress of the Industrialist League, Gino Olivetti warned of the more dangerous nature of the Italian system of councils as compared to the Russian or German experiences. Tolerating an institution that undermined management's power in the factory was out of the question: "It is not possible to establish the existence of a dualism of power in a firm . . . .Until a communist system is established by a legislative act, the introduction of factory councils is unacceptable" (*L'Ordine Nuovo* 1920a). In the beginning of March 1920, the General Confederation of Industry expressed its firm opposition to the establishment of factory councils.

## The April Strike

*April 1920—It was called the "clock hand strike" because the industrialists wanted to return to daylight savings time and they put the clock back without consultation with the factory councils, with the internal commission. . . .It was a question of power, of deciding . . . who was to organize the rhythm of work within the factory . . . it was a conflict of power.*
                                —Leonetti, oral testimony in Bermani,
                                *Gramsci, gli intellettuali e la cultura proletaria*

On March 20, 1920, the president of the Industrial League, De Benedetti, Olivetti, and the Fiat company owner Giovanni Agnelli visited the prefect of Turin to complain about the widespread indiscipline in the factories and the persistent and unreasonable demands of the workers. The three made clear that they intended to resort to a general lockout to put a stop to this situation. The prefect warned them about the damaging consequences of a lockout and suggested they oppose all unjustified requests and punish any breach of the internal regulations (Taddei, 1920a). Four days later he informed the minister of the interior that the industrialists had followed his suggestions.

At the Fiat Acciaierie steelworks plant, the management closed a workshop because the workers had walked out in protest at not having received an answer to their request for compensatory payment for the members of the internal commissions. At the Industrie Metallurgiche factory, also owned by Fiat, the workers halted production because members of the internal commission had been dismissed for insubordination—they had readjusted the hands of the official factory clock from summer time to standard time without permission.[5]

About a thousand workers rejected a first agreement reached between the unions and management to resolve this issue, and refused to leave the factory (Taddei, 1920b). They were subsequently forced to leave by the police. The minister of the Interior sent clear instructions to the prefect to act without hesitation, to use the army in defense of the factories, to ban all meetings, to keep dangerous characters under surveillance, and to arrest troublemakers (Taddei, 1920b). In the following days the army took control of the factories to forestall potential occupation by the workers; the offensive against the factory councils had been launched.

The following day, the employers agreed to rescind the dismissal of the members of the internal commission at the Industrie Metallurgiche factory, but with the proviso that those individuals would not be reelected for a year. This condition was regarded as an unacceptable interference in the selection of workers' representatives. Moreover, the employers stressed that in the future the internal commissions should act in strict observance of the regulations of the national agreement.

On March 26, the workshop commissars of all the metalworking factories elected an action committee and an internal strike was called for the following day. The strike was supported by thirty thousand metalworkers.

> The best meetings that I can remember took place within the plants. Public and speakers, all in their work clothes, made for an unforgettable sight. Everybody was there: from skilled workers to white-collar staff, and then unskilled workers and apprentices. Everybody, at that point, understood that the game being played was an extremely serious one, and that to lose this battle would mean, for everybody, the loss of a great, great deal (Montagnana 1952, 120).

The two disputes were regarded as matters of principle. However, as reported by the prefect, the focus of the confrontation was the industrialists'

---

5 The Socialists and the trade unions opposed the introduction of daylight savings time, considered a return to wartime practices.

intention to introduce norms and regulations for the internal commissions that represented a "repudiation of the status quo, either agreed or implicitly accepted, in some of the factories" (Taddei, 1920d)

After several meetings, an initial agreement was reached. As regards the Industrie Metallurgiche factory, the workers' representatives agreed that the internal commission should not have moved the clock hands, that the workshop commissars should resign, that workers should not receive any payment for the hours of stoppage time, and that the local branch of FIOM should have been consulted before striking. More importantly, they agreed that "the local branch of FIOM should pledge itself to recall the Internal Commissions to their specific functions of safeguarding the workers' interests in matters concerning wage agreement and factory regulations" (Clark 1977, 102).

At the Acciaierie plant the managers not only intended to fine the workers for their unofficial strike, but they claimed that, before work was resumed, it was necessary to reach an agreement about the role of the internal commission and "with regard to the clarifications needed in certain cases, where concessions have been made in certain factories based on a wider interpretation of regulations, it is absolutely essential that such important details should be cleared up" (Clark 1977, 102).

Then, in an attempt to elevate the dispute to a national footing, the Chamber of Labour and the National Committee of FIOM were asked to join the negotiations. The national secretary of FIOM, the reformist Bruno Buozzi, led the discussions. An agreement was reached on April 8. The workers at the Acciaierie works were to be fined a symbolic one hour of pay, and the money would go into their unemployment fund. Discussions about factory regulations were to be postponed. The prefect considered it "a great victory for the industrialism," as the pact implied limitations on the scope of the internal commission. The terms of the agreement, however, were rejected by the local branch of FIOM and also by the assembly of workshop commissars. Consequently, a ballot of the metalworkers of Turin was organized, but out of the 50,000 workers entitled to vote only 11,579 actually voted. The result was a majority of 794 in favor of the settlement. After two stormy meetings it was decided to return to work on April 12.

When the workers' representatives went to sign the agreement, the real issue of the dispute emerged. Claiming that the issue of the regulation of the internal commission had not been resolved, the industrialists presented a proposal depriving it of most of its functions and capacities to take action (Taddei, 1920c). At this point, the dispute had become focused on the very existence of factory councils. On April 13 the workshop commissars rejected this proposal, and the following day the Chamber of Labour and the local and provincial sections of the PSI formed an action committee. On April 17 a general strike was called in the Piedmont region.

The authorities forbade all public meetings. The prefect requested four thousand more troops in support of the three thousand already present in the city (Taddei, 1920e).

> Turin was under siege. From the first days the arrests were continuous, especially of our comrades; and the first was of our friend Garino, one of the most active anarchists among the metalworkers in Turin. . . .In Turin all the public buildings were transformed into barracks, armoured vehicles patrolled the streets incessantly, machine guns nests were mounted on the palaces and churches (*Volontà* 1920).

During the negotiations, Buozzi and the workers' representatives put forward alternative proposals for regulation of the internal commissions. For the industrialists, however, the main issue was the factory councils, which had not been addressed in any previous agreement. They requested that the trade unions repudiate factory councils. There was no attempt by Buozzi and the union representatives to steer the negotiations toward recognition of this form of organization. This would have required the full support of the CGIL and the PSI at a national level.

The executive committee of the workshop commissars had already identified, at the beginning of the confrontation, the political problem of the recognition of factory councils:

> The form of the Factory Council depends on the political and economic strength of the working class . . . .It is beyond any doubt that the industrialists will never recognize nor allow the peaceful functioning of the Factory Councils, which aim at destruction of the capitalist system . . . .Recognition would only be given to the Councils if their proponents promised to restrict themselves to action concerning work contracts, and to conform . . . .To obtain recognition for the Factory Council it would be necessary to sign agreements and to accept all the legal limitations that the industrialists may wish to introduce. This would mean the death of the new workers' institution, which can establish itself and develop only if it retains the freedom to manoeuvre and change its approach in response to the changing needs of the revolutionary process and the psychology of the working class (*L'Ordine Nuovo* 1920b).

At the same time, the national conference of the PSI was being held in Milan. The leader of the CGIL, Ludovico D'Aragona, arrived in Turin. The action committee argued for extending the action to the whole country: a national general strike was now the only way that a successful outcome could be achieved by the protest. On April 21 the Committee of the Study of the Workers' Council launched a national manifesto exhorting the working class and the peasantry to join the struggle in defense of the workshop commissars and factory councils (*Umanità Nova* 1920).

The manifesto was published in the anarchist newspaper *Umanità Nova* and the Turin edition of *Avanti!* However, the Rome and Milan editions of *Avanti!* refused to print it. Indeed, the national leaders rejected any widening of the conflict and requested instead a full mandate for the negotiations. On the same day, D'Aragona met with Olivetti. After twenty days of action in the metalworking factories and ten days of general strike—the longest strike in Piedmont history—D'Aragona accepted all the conditions that the industrialists had put forward earlier. On the evening of April 22 the strike was called off. Union officials spent two more days overcoming the resistance of the workshop commissars, who wanted to resume work without signing any agreement: a clear rejection of the union's role as mediator.

We very much doubt that the leaders of the Italian Socialist Party will dare to confess—openly, clearly, without euphemisms—that the metalworking and general strike in Turin and Piedmont ended with the greatest defeat that can be remembered in the history of the Italian proletariat (Mussolini 1920).

## Conclusions

Although Gramsci and Togliatti emphasized the importance of a protest focused on political rather than economic aims, the defeat of "the longest and most fully supported strike that had ever taken place in Piedmont" (see Gramsci 1921) had remarkably negative consequences for the labor movement. Italian workers witnessed the inconsistent, contradictory nature of the Italian Socialist Party: the extent of the gap between its revolutionary claims and its political action, and the profound divisions within its leadership. Moreover, the feeling of having been betrayed by the officials of FIOM and the CGIL, and the consequent resentment, spread quickly outside the region and helped prejudice the labor movement against trusting in officialdom. In another area, the failure of the factory councils undermined the authority of *L'Ordine Nuovo*, which had shown itself unable to lead the movement. Despite its central role within the Turin working class, *L'Ordine Nuovo*'s lack of impact in the national context was evident, particularly within the executive hierarchies of the Socialist Party and the trade unions.

The leader of the more radical, "maximalist" faction of the PSI, Amadeo Bordiga, considered the defeat a corroboration of his previous criticism of the council form. In his newspaper *Il Soviet*, he had repeatedly criticized *L'Ordine Nuovo* and the factory council movement. For Bordiga, the party—the Socialist Party purged of its reformist faction—was the revolutionary organ and the driving force for the assumption of political power. Without a soviet revolution, factory councils could only be reformist and collaborationist institutions; after a successful revolution they could exist as expert bodies focusing on the management of production, but without any political function. The stark differences between Bordiga's faction and the *L'Ordine Nuovo* group created the impression for workers that there was no effective central leadership able to expand the factory council movement (Pepe 1970, 121). Indeed, outside Piedmont factory councils proliferated only to a very limited extent.

The failure highlighted the unresolved contradictions of the relationship between factory councils and national union organizations. Despite Gramsci's attempt to keep the two bodies separate, it was clear that for much of the movement factory councils stood in opposition to the reformist trade unions. At the national congress of FIOM in May 1920, the factory council experiment was an object of bitter criticism and attacks by most union officials (Antonioli and Bezza 1978, 571–72). The question of the relationship between this form of workers' representation and the unions also led to the debate between Gramsci and Tasca in the spring of 1920 (Spriano 1971, 89–92). At the congress of Turin's Chamber of Labour at the end of May 1920, Tasca proposed a motion that reestablished the union leaders' position locally: internal commissions would continue to exist, but without the capacity to decide policy; local union representatives would not be elected by the workshop commissars. Political decisions would rest with the union leadership. Tasca's motion "proved acceptable to local union leaders and won easily" (Levy 1999, 163).

Equally unresolved was the relationship between the councils and the Socialist Party, and the question of the genuine potential of factory councils as revolutionary organs when operating only within the factories and without the support of external political reference points.

Disputes emerged between the Socialists and the anarchists. The anarchists were "depressed and angered by the strike's failure." They accused the socialists of betrayal and condemned "what they believed was a false sense of discipline that had bound Socialists to their cowardly leadership" (ibid., 161). In August, when elections for the PSI executive were held in Turin, *Avanti!* had already engaged in a six-week campaign against the anarchist contagion in the Torinese labor movement (ibid., 163). All these problems flared yet again, and with even more dramatic consequences, during and after the occupation of the factories in the autumn of 1920. The subsequent Fascist offensive would soon destroy the labor movement and its organizations.

Only after several decades did the struggle to introduce factory councils reemerge in Italy: in the 1970s, once more a time of heightened militancy and creative action by the working class.

# References

Antonioli, M. and Bezza, B. 1978. *La FIOM dalle origini al fascismo. 1901–1924*. Bari: De Donato.

*Avanti!* 1920. Cronache. La prima assemblea dei Consigli di fabbrica. Turin ed. October 20.

Bermani, Cesare. 2007. *Gramsci, gli intellettuali e la cultura proletaria*. Milan: Cooperativa Colibrì.

Bianchi, Roberto. 2006. *Pane, pace, terra, il 1919 in Italia*. Rome: Odradek Edizioni.

Bordiga, Amadeo. 1920. Towards the establishment of workers' councils in Italy. *Il Soviet* 3, nos. 1, 2, 4, 5, 7; January 1, 11, February 1, 8, 22.

Castronovo, Valerio. 2005. *Fiat. Una storia del capitalismo italiano. 1899–2005*. Milan: Rizzoli.

Clark, Martin. 1977. *Gramsci and the revolution that failed*. New Haven and London: Yale University Press.

Colombino, Emilio. 1920. *I Consigli di fabbrica nel Movimento Sindacale*. Varese: Tipografia Varesina.

Comitato di Studio dei Consigli di Fabbrica Torino. 1920. *Regolamento dei Commissari di reparto*. Turin: Tipografia Alleanza.

Garino, M. 1920. Relazione sui consigli di fabbrica e di azienda presentata da M. Garino al congresso della Unione Anarchica Italiana, Bologna 1–4 luglio 1920. *Umanità Nova*, July.

Gramsci, A. and Togliatti, P. [Unsigned] 1919. Democrazia operaia. *L'Ordine Nuovo* I, no. 7. June 21.

Gramsci, Antonio. 1920. Il programma dell'Ordine Nuovo. *L'Ordine Nuovo*. August 14.

———. 1921. Il movimento torinese dei consigli di fabbrica. Rapporto inviato nel luglio 1920 al Comitato esecutivo dell'Internazionale comunista. *L'Ordine Nuovo*. March 14.

———. 1977. *Selections from the political writings 1910–1920*. Ed. Q. Hoare. London: Lawrence and Wishart.

Lattarulo G. and R. Ambrosoli. 1971/2009. I consigli operai. Un'intervista con il compagno Maurizio Garino. *A*, April 1971. Trans. in *The Italian Factory Councils and the Anarchists*, ed. by Anarchist Federation London, 17–18. London: Stormy Petrel.

Levy, Carl. 1999. *Gramsci and the anarchists*. Oxford: Berg.

*L'Ordine Nuovo.* 1919a. La conquista dello stato. July 12.

———. 1919b. Ai Commissari di reparto delle officine Fiat-centro e brevetti. September 13.

———. 1919c. Cronache. September 13.

———. 1919d. Sindacati e consigli. October 11.

———. 1920a. L'opinione degli industriali sui consigli di fabbrica. March 25.

———. 1920b. Il parere del C. E. sui consigli di officina. March 27.

———. 1920c. La relazione Tasca e il congresso camerale di Torino. June 5.

Magri, Francesco. 1947. *Controllo operaio e consigli di azienda in Italia e all'estero*. Milan: Editrice Accademia.

Maione, Giuseppe. 1975. *Il biennio rosso. Autonomia e spontaneità operaia nel 1919–1920*. Bologna: Il Mulino.

Masini, Pier Carlo. 1951. *Anarchici e comunisti nel movimento dei Consigli a Torino. Primo dopoguerra rosso 1919–1920*. Turin: Gruppo Barriera di Milano.

Montagnana, Mario. 1952. *Ricordi di un operaio torinese*. Rome: Edizioni Rinascita.

Mussolini, B. 1920. Dura lezione. *Il Popolo d'Italia*. April 25.

Pastore, O. 1919. Il problema delle commissioni interne. *L'Ordine Nuovo*. August 16.

Pepe, Antonio. 1970. Introduction. In *Lotta di classe e democrazia operaia. I metalmeccanici ed i consigli di fabbrica*, vol. 1 by FIOM. Rome: La tipografica.

Santhià, Battista. 1956. *Con Gramsci all'Ordine Nuovo*. Rome: Editori Riuniti.

Serrati, G. 1919. Perché non si equivochi. *Avanti!* November 4.

Soave, E. 1964. Appunti sulle origini teoriche e pratiche dei Consigli di fabbrica a Torino. *Rivista Storica del Socialismo* 7(21): 14.

Spriano, Paolo. 1971. *L'Ordine Nuovo e i Consigli di fabbrica.* Turin: Einaudi.

———. 1975. *The occupation of the factories.* London: Pluto Press.

Taddei, Paolino. 1920a. Correspondence with minister of the interior. Archivio Centrale dello Stato Divisione Generale Pubblica Sicurezza, 102. March 20.

———. 1920b. Correspondence with minister of the interior. Archivio Centrale dello Stato Divisione Generale Pubblica Sicurezza, 102. March 24.

———. 1920c. Correspondence with minister of the interior. Archivio Centrale dello Stato Divisione Generale Pubblica Sicurezza, 22. April 11.

———. 1920d. Correspondence with minister of the interior. Archivio Centrale dello Stato Divisione Generale Pubblica Sicurezza, 102. April 13.

———. 1920e. Correspondence with minister of the interior. Archivio Centrale dello Stato Divisione Generale Pubblica Sicurezza, 22. April 14.

Terracini, Umberto. 1920. I Consigli di fabbrica: vicende e problemi, dall'Inghilterra alla Russia, dalla Germania a Torino. *L'Almanacco Socialista.* Milan.

Togliatti, P. 1919. L'Assemblea della sezione metallurgica Torinese. *L'Ordine Nuovo.* November 8.

*Umanità Nova.* 1920. April 21.

Viglongo, A. 1919. Verso nuove istituzioni. *L'Ordine Nuovo.* August 30.

*Volontà.* 1920. May 1.

Williams, Gwyn, A. 1975. *Proletarian order.* London: Pluto Press.

# 8

# Workers' Democracy in the Spanish Revolution, 1936–1937

**Andy Durgan**

In terms of socioeconomic experiments the revolutionary movement in Spain during the summer of 1936 went further than most similar movements in Europe in the twentieth century. But unlike in Russia in 1917 or Germany in 1918, rather than workers' councils a myriad of committees emerged to provide the basis of a new and highly fragmented revolutionary democracy. These bodies were both an inspiration of Spain's powerful libertarian[1] movement and a result of the practical needs of workers and peasants faced with a Fascist military uprising and the temporary collapse of the state.[2]

## Precedents

The idea that working-class people should run society was common among organized workers in Spain by the first decades of the twentieth century. The libertarian movement in particular had propagated this concept through a variety of forms of popular education and propaganda.

Spanish anarchism did not have a uniform vision for a future society, but it lacked for neither ideologues nor ideas when it came to drawing up plans or schemes for such an eventuality. Anarchist strategies for social revolution ranged from the mass revolutionary general strike to different forms of direct action and armed insurrection. All currents saw prefigurative forms of organization—whether the union or the municipal commune—as central

---

[1] Please note that "libertarian" and "anarcho-syndicalist" are used interchangeably in this chapter, as both were terms used to describe the nature of the revolutionary committees.

[2] On the revolution and civil war see Broué and Témine 2008; Bolloten 1991; for an outline of the main historiographical debates and further reading, Durgan 2007.

to the revolutionary project. In contrast to the libertarians, Spain's would-be Marxists were far less prolific when it came to posing alternatives to bourgeois democracy. The Socialist Workers' Party's (PSOE) deterministic brand of Marxism saw socialism as inevitable and amounting to little more than state control; although the immediate task was the completion of the bourgeois revolution, not socialism.

With the establishment of the republic in April 1931, the small Spanish Communist Party's (PCE) call for the overthrow of the "bourgeois Republic" and "all power" to the (nonexistent) "soviets" was met with indifference if not hostility. However, the general enthusiasm for the new parliamentary democracy would not last long. In a context of deepening economic crisis, strikes led by the anarcho-syndicalist union, the CNT, were repressed and social reform was systematically blocked by the right. As a result both the powerful anarchist and Socialist movements underwent a process of radicalization during the first two years of the republic.

Inside the CNT the radical anarchist groups, in particular those organized inside the Federación Anarquista Ibérica (FAI), were increasingly influential. Sections of the CNT now launched a series of armed insurrections—in January 1932 and January–December 1933—which saw the emergence of various forms of "revolutionary committees," anticipating the similar bodies that would play an important role in 1936. Meanwhile, inside the Socialist movement a "revolutionary" left wing emerged under the leadership of veteran trade unionist Francisco Largo Caballero. By the elections of November 1933, the Socialists had broken with their petit bourgeois Republican allies in favor of an "all Socialist" government. The leadership of the CNT urged workers to boycott the elections altogether, thus contributing to a rightist victory.

It was widely perceived that the new, rightist government would be merely a staging post on the road to a quasi-fascist regime under the clerical reactionary party, Confederación Española de Derechas Autónomas (CEDA). The violent repression of the workers' movement in Germany and Austria heightened the belief on the left that only armed insurrection and social revolution would avoid the Spanish workers' movement suffering a similar fate. In response, "Workers' Alliances against Fascism" were formed, first in Catalonia in December 1933 and over the coming months in many other parts of the country. These alliances were based on delegates from existing workers' organizations: Socialists, dissident Communists (the real inspirers of the alliances), CNT "moderates" (*Treintistas*), and non-aligned unions (Durgan 1996, 240–266).

There was little consensus among the component organizations as to the alliances' exact role in any revolutionary process. Only the dissident communist Bloque Obrero y Campesino (BOC—workers' and peasants' bloc) and the Trotskyists defended the centrality of workers' councils to the creation of a future socialist society. This meant the alliances would need to be "democratized" by being elected from below rather than comprised of representatives of existing organizations.

Events would soon reveal both the limitations and potential of the alliances as organs of power. With the entrance of the reactionary CEDA into government in October 1934, the Socialist Party called a general strike to block the path to "fascism." Without clear leadership or organization the strike soon faltered, except in Asturias. The region's context as a mining community threatened with economic crisis—combined with local traditions of solidarity and the fact that the whole workers' movement, including the CNT, supported the alliances—kept the strike going. Communications, economic activity, and military defense were coordinated through the alliances, which rapidly became the only authority in the region and the basis of a revolutionary government. Crushed by the army after two weeks of heroic resistance, the Asturian Commune would prove an important milestone on the road to war and revolution.

With elections approaching in early 1936, encouraged by the Social Democratic wing of the PSOE and the PCE, a Popular Front coalition of the whole left was formed, spanning from the petit bourgeois Republican parties to the POUM (Workers' Party of Marxist Unification).[3] The general context of growing radicalization in the months to follow belied any claim that the Popular Front's electoral victory in the 1936 elections reflected support for liberal democracy. Organized workers had voted en masse to obtain an amnesty for the thousands imprisoned after the October 1934 strike and to avoid a victory for the right. The lack of any unity initiative from left Socialists and anarcho-syndicalists alike had meant there had been no electoral alternative to the Popular Front.

With the Republican parties in government the left Socialists still advocated "revolution" as the only road open to the working class. What this revolution would entail was less than clear. Rather than through democratically elected soviets, they saw socialism being introduced through a party dictatorship, which, in turn, was confused with the dictatorship of the proletariat per se. The left Socialists' passivity—they somehow believed the Republican project would fall apart of its own accord—combined with their ideological ambiguities explains, to some degree, their lack of any independent role in the coming revolution.

---

[3] The Partido Obrero de Unificación Marxista was founded in September 1935 on the basis of the BOC and the Trotskyists. The new party opposed the Popular Front as "class collaboration" but decided to sign the electoral pact once it had failed to persuade the other workers' organizations to set up a "Workers' Front"; see Durgan 2006, 35–38.

The CNT for its part, having suffered greatly from repression, opted at its congress in May 1936 to abandon its insurrectional strategy in favor of a "revolutionary alliance" with the Socialist trade union federation, the UGT. Nevertheless most of the congress was dedicated to elaborating its vision of a future libertarian society. In the resulting documents—based on some one hundred and fifty proposals from different unions—the municipal commune gave way to the union as the basic organism of daily life. Despite the intensity of this debate the CNT, according to Xavier Paniagua, would enter the revolution two months later "without having clarified the most basic economic concepts" (1982, 265–272).

## The Committees

The military uprising of July 18, 1936, divided Spain into two antagonistic zones. The presence of thousands of armed—albeit poorly—workers in the streets assured in many areas the loyalty of the Assault Guards (the Republican police force) and even the paramilitary Civil Guards. Where the workers' movement waited for the authorities to take the initiative, the rebels were usually victorious given the Republican parties' reluctance to distribute arms to the civilian population. The immediate territorial division of the country left about 60 percent of the population and most of the main industrial areas in the hands of the Republic. The rebels controlled some of the more important agricultural areas and managed to divide the loyalist zone in two, the north being isolated from the center and east.

With the collapse of much of the Republican state's infrastructure, the facilitation of everyday life, soon profoundly affected by the stringencies of war, passed directly to the working class and its organizations. Participation in the unfolding revolutionary movement was not confined to the most active sectors of the organized working class: local studies show a high level of involvement of the masses in general. In particular, many women now entered into political life for the first time and played a leading role in the rearguard mobilization (Pozo 2002, 28; Durgan 2007, 79–87).

Barcelona, the epicenter of the revolution, saw what Chris Ealham has described as the "biggest revolutionary fiesta in twentieth-century Europe." Workers' control extended to the expropriation of property and its reallocation for social needs. In some of the city's poorest neighborhoods there was an existing prewar culture of resistance and occupation of urban space, and this provided the basis for an embryonic process of social transformation. Not only did parties and unions occupy premises on a massive scale, but churches, the houses of the wealthy, and other buildings were also transformed into hospitals, schools, popular restaurants, warehouses, and garages (2005, 113, 122–127).

Once the working-class armed resistance had defeated the military uprising in over half of Spain, a military coup now became a civil war. One of the most immediate consequences of the workers' victory was the near disintegration of the Republican state in those areas not under Fascist control. Instead, power resided in a myriad of local and regional committees. Most of these committees consisted of representatives of existing organizations and in this sense were similar to the workers' alliances of 1934.

In many localities the committees took over the functions of municipal government, which often proceeded to disappear altogether. Where local town councils continued to exist, they were generally subordinate to or controlled by the revolutionary committee. One of the first acts of the committees in each town was to burn property titles, convert the church (if it had not been burnt down) into a warehouse or garage and collectivize the land. The procedure was similar in larger towns and cities. Barcelona served as an example:

> The (CNT) defense committees, transformed into revolutionary neighborhood committees, in the absence of any slogan from any organization and without any more coordination than the revolutionary initiatives that each moment demanded, organized hospitals (and) popular dining halls, confiscated cars, lorries, arms, factories and buildings, searched private homes and carried out arrests of suspicious individuals and created a network of Supply Committees (Guillamón 2007, 80).

Most set up subcommittees to carry out these various tasks. They often financed themselves by expropriations or by charging local businesses a "war tax." Some committees had their own press, invariably having taken over the local conservative newspaper.

The committees soon established their own security forces—"control patrols" or "rearguard militia"—as much to end arbitrary killings as to repress counterrevolutionaries. The victims of repression were usually members of rightist organizations, landowners, industrialists, and the clergy. The widespread nature of this repression in the first weeks of the war in the Republican rearguard was a reflection, albeit an unpalatable one, of mass radicalization; it contrasted starkly with the bourgeois-democratic pretensions of the Popular Front.

The committees also immediately set themselves the task of recruiting and equipping militia columns to be sent to the front. These militias soon numbered around one hundred fifty thousand combatants, including former army troops. They were usually organized along democratic lines, especially those controlled by the CNT. The equivalents of officers were either elected by the troops or appointed by the left organizations; section and company leaders (the equivalents of sergeants and corporals) were nearly always elected. The civilian commanders of militia columns and units had often been leaders of prewar labor defense groups. Professional officers acted as military advisers. There were no differences in pay or treatment among ranks. Political discussion was common but orders were usually accepted without question once action had to be taken.

The most extensive system of committees was in Catalonia.[4] Hundreds of these bodies controlled local political, social, and economic life, adopting a variety of denominations: "revolutionary committee," "antifascist committee," "defense" or "militia committee," and, in a minority of cases, "Popular Front committee" (more common in the rest of Spain). As elsewhere, most were established by the workers' organizations "from above"; only in small villages where these organizations hardly existed were there direct elections. In a few localities the representatives were elected by assemblies of the members of the workers' organizations, or by the militia, or by armed civilians.

The CNT dominated the majority of committees in Catalonia. Represented to a lesser extent, depending on local circumstances, were the peasants' union, Unió de Rabassaires, the POUM, the UGT, and the newly formed PSUC.[5] The petit bourgeois parties were sometimes excluded in the first weeks from the committees as being "not sufficiently antifascist." But in contrast with the left Republican organizations in the rest of Spain, the principal Catalan Republican party, Esquerra Republicana de Catalunya (ERC), was a genuine mass party. Many of its members were in the CNT and in some towns outside Barcelona were active in resisting the military uprising in July 1936. The peculiarities of the ERC explain its resilience in the weeks to come and its ability to reassert its influence.

One of the clearest examples of the rupture with institutional authority in Catalonia was the city of Lleida—soon to be of strategic importance, given its position as a stopover for the Aragonese front. Here the ERC and other "bourgeois" parties were excluded from the Popular Committee that now ran the city; the influence of the POUM determined that only the working-class organizations were represented. A general assembly of union committees—effectively a "workers' parliament"—debated and ratified the decisions of the committee. The first people's tribunal in Catalonia, set up to judge the republic's enemies, was established in Lleida in August; the Workers' Social Brigade controlled the streets and hunted down counterrevolutionaries. Agrarian and supply subcommittees were also established and a municipal committee replaced the town council (Sagués 2005, 71–76).

---

[4] The only complete study of the revolutionary committees concerns Catalonia; see Pozo 2002.
[5] The Partit Socialista Unificat de Catalunya was founded in July 1936 by the Catalan Communist Party, the Catalan Federation of the PSOE; the Social Democratic Unió Socialista de Catalunya, and the left Nationalist Partit Català Proletari.

In fact, in nearly all the most important committees in Catalonia, in spite of the inclusion of the Republicans the working-class organizations were in the majority. But if the distinction is made between revolutionary and Popular Front organizations, the majority usually tipped in favor of the latter. For example, in the important Sabadell Defense Committee, the workers' organizations in general accounted for nine of the eleven representatives; specifically the CNT-POUM, only four.

Apart from the local committees, regional and provincial bodies were also established in the first days of the war. Some, like the Catalan Comité Central de Milicies Antifeixistes (CCMA), the Junta of Vizcaya, or the Council of Aragon, functioned as "truly autonomous governments." These regional committees were of basically three types. At one extreme were regional Popular Fronts grouped around the civil governor, and at the other the anarchist-run Council of Aragon. Between these two extremes were those committees in which the most powerful organization in the region wielded the most influence (Broué 1982, 38, 42–3).

Often presented as an embryonic proletarian government, the CCMA was set up under the auspices of the Catalan government, the Generalitat, on July 21 with representatives from all the left and workers' organizations. The Catalan president, Lluis Companys, hoped to channel resistance to the military uprising by creating a unitary body outside his government and hence acceptable to the anarcho-syndicalists. Earlier the same day an extraordinary plenum of the CNT had voted to accept the formation of the CCMA and to reject any possibility of taking power ("going for all"), as this would mean the establishment of a "libertarian dictatorship." The Popular Front majority in the CCMA was not regarded as a problem by the anarcho-syndicalists, who believed the revolution was safe given their armed strength.[6]

The declared intention of the CCMA was not to replace the Generalitat but in practice it soon did. As the anarchist leader Adad de Santillán put it, the CCMA was at the same time "the [Catalan] war ministry, the interior and foreign ministry and directed the activities of similar economic and cultural organisms. [It was] the most legitimate expression of the people's power" (cited in Bernecker 1982, 390). Apart from helping to coordinate the organizing, provisioning, and sending of militia columns to the front, the CCMA established transport, health, education, and, most importantly, civilian supplies and security subcommittees.

---

[6] The CCMA was made up of three representatives each from the ERC, CNT, and UGT, two from the FAI, and one each from the PSUC, POUM, Acció Catalana Republicana, and the Unio de Rabassaires.

Its first decree was for the maintenance of "revolutionary order" and it immediately established the "control patrols," composed of members of all the left organizations but principally from the CNT, to impose order.[7] The patrols became one of the most lasting symbols of proletarian revolution in Barcelona. For the more moderate sections of the population the patrols stood as an uncomfortable example of revolutionary power, a power enhanced by their semi-autonomous status. Without the consent of any organization, they established their own tribunal to mete out justice to suspected counterrevolutionaries. Apart from the patrols, the CNT and other organizations and neighborhood committees had their own armed security units.

Parallel to the CCMA the Generalitat established the Consell d'Economia de Catalunya to "co-ordinate the revolution [and] the collectivization of the economy." In practice the economic council acted independently of the Catalan government and was dominated by the CNT (Cendra 2006).

The CCMA also attempted to impose its authority on the local committees outside Barcelona, insisting they should serve as no more than recruiting bodies for the militia and even refusing to recognize those committees that did not include all the antifascist organizations. Its success in this regard was limited; most local bodies continued to enjoy a large degree of autonomy even when they were based on representatives of the very same organizations as were in the CCMA.

Elsewhere in the Republican zone the various regional and provincial committees exercised varying degrees of political, economic, and military control. In Valencia the Popular Executive Committee (CEP) was based on the parties that had signed onto the Popular Front program along with the anarcho-syndicalists; the workers' organizations had nine representatives and the Republican and regionalist parties four. The central government in Madrid appointed a rival junta in the city, which demanded the CEP's dissolution. But it was the junta that was soon forced to step down when the CEP forces stormed the remaining barracks in rebel hands at the end of July. The CEP was now the only authority in the city, and it established commissions to carry out the most urgent tasks: supplies, transport, health, justice, banking and taxes, militias and war, propaganda, press and communications, agriculture, commerce, and industry. In early November 1936 the CEP established an economic council with representatives from the unions to plan production and extend collectivization to all workplaces in which the owner had supported the rebels or that had more than fifty workers. In reality each local union took over the running of expropriated businesses

---

[7] By the end of October the control patrols were made up of 931 militants, around 400 from the CNT (Guillamón 2007, 89).

without considering the number of workers or the political affiliation of the owner. Like its Catalan counterpart, the CEP's attempts to coordinate the extremely diverse local committees in the region were not particularly successful (Girona 1986, 32–73; Bosch 1983, 21, 67, 385).

In some areas competing committees both tried to impose their authority. This was the case in Murcia, with two principal committees: one in the administrative and agricultural center, the provincial capital, led by the Socialists; and the other in the industrial and commercial center of Cartegena, led by the anarcho-syndicalists (González Martinez 1999). Likewise in Asturias there were two rival committees: the Provincial Committee in Sama, controlled by the Socialists; and the War Committee in Gijon, which, although including Socialists and Republicans, was "dominated by the anarchists." The Gijon committee controlled the coast and surrounding area, setting up numerous intermediate committees at a neighborhood and factory level that ran security, services, and industry (González Muñiz et al. 1986, 37, 88; Radcliff 2005, 134).

In Andalucía localist traditions impeded the unification of the different committees (Bernecker 1996, 489). The most powerful committee in the region was Malaga's Committee of Public Safety, despite its authority hardly extending beyond the city. As on most other committees, the workers' organizations were hegemonic. The CNT played a decisive role, given that it provided the majority of fighters, had mass support, and controlled economic life. Although Malaga's municipal government continued to exist, and had been purged of rightists, the CNT—unlike in many places in the Republican zone—refused to participate, rendering it ineffective (Lorenzo 1969, 161; Nadal 1988, 138–145).

The Council of Aragon was quite exceptional in that it was initially in the hands of the anarchists alone. It was set up at a plenum of unions in Bujaraloz in early October with the clear intention to put an end to the "excesses" of the militia columns in the region and to "direct economic, social and political activities"; to this end it created seven departments. The council organized its own police, carried out requisitions, imposed rigid mechanisms on the administration of the economy, directed the export of important quantities of oil, almonds, and saffron and the import of other products, and above all used its apparatus to consolidate the power of the CNT (Bernecker 1982, 133–170; 418–430).

## Collectivization

In June 1937 the newspaper of the Socialist Land Workers Federation in Valencia stated: "Each revolution has it original characteristic: in England it was Parliament, in France the Rights of Man, in Russia the Soviet; [in

ours] . . . the collectives" (Casanova 1988, 79). The widespread collectivization of agriculture, industry, and services was the clearest example of workers'
control and direct democracy during the Spanish Revolution. The nature of
this process differed from region to region and had few precedents prior to
the war. Most collectives had an extremely practical aim: to keep production
and services functioning, to adapt to the specific conditions of war, and to
collect the harvest in order to feed both the front and the rearguard.

Services and industry were subject to different forms of intervention by
workers or the Republican authorities: socialization, collectivization, workers' control, cooperativization, municipalization, and nationalization. Employers affected were principally those who had supported the military
uprising, although some enterprises were taken over regardless of the
owner's political leanings. Where employers and managers stayed on they
usually worked as technicians or advisors.

Collectivization was most common where the CNT was strongest: Catalonia, Valencia, and cities such as Malaga and Cartagena. In Catalonia
40 percent of all industry and services were expropriated; in Barcelona this
rose to nearly 80 percent. Most firms were taken over spontaneously in the
first days of the military uprising even before the CNT issued instructions
to its members to do so. Evidence points to the great majority of workers
in industry and services in Barcelona supporting collectivization. The petit
bourgeoisie, state functionaries, and technical staff, while opposing the military uprising, tended to favor private property or state control. Parallel to
collectivization an arms industry was organized by the Catalan government
and the unions but was under the control of the former.

For the CNT collectivization was a means to an end: the socialization
of economic production. Over the coming months, both locally and region-
ally the anarcho-syndicalists drew up plans for establishing the basis of the
new economy. At a regional and citywide level many industries were formed
into associations to coordinate production. The aim of such associations
was the socialization of any given industry, whereby production and profits
would be subordinated to the common good.

Collectivized firms were run by factory councils, involving both blue-
and white-collar representatives and in a few cases the former employer.
These councils were elected through mass meetings or were based on existing union bodies. Even when elected they tended to consist of established
union leaders and activists. There were also subcommittees dealing with
different aspects of running the collective. Although independent union
committees were supposed to ensure working conditions did not deteriorate, in practice they did not always carry out this role given the extent of
union involvement in the management of the collectives. The level of participation of the workforce in making decisions on running the collective

differed from workplace to workplace. In general, decision-making was simplified; most members of the factory council continued working on the shop floor and received wages according to their professional status, with the intention of avoiding the emergence of an internal bureaucracy.

A majority of collectives made moves toward reducing wage differentials. Medical services were established, as were pension schemes. Nurseries were sometimes organized, reflecting the integration of women into industry. Training and education were also promoted and work was occasionally given to those previously involved in "pernicious activities," such as "prostitutes, gamblers and boxers" (Castells 2002, 136).

The collectivization of industry and services took place under extremely unfavorable circumstances—industrial production had fallen by half by the end of 1937. The war led to shortages in raw materials, the loss of markets, the disruption of trade and transport, and a lack of men of working age (partly compensated by the incorporation of women into the labor process). Late or nonpayment by state bodies further exacerbated financial difficulties. There was also the need to adjust production to address military needs. Further difficulties were caused by technical and white-collar staff opposing collectivization or at least certain measures, such as a more egalitarian wage structure. There were also problems of discipline and lack of effort and the fact that many workers were ill equipped for administrative tasks (Castells 2002, 135).

Despite all these obstacles many urban collectives proved surprisingly efficient, especially when grouped together in associations. In addition to generally improving working conditions, they introduced administrative and structural reforms: for instance, accountancy was centralized, which facilitated bookkeeping and statistics. There was also a drastic reduction of intermediaries: producers and consumers were in closer contact. Developmental research was encouraged, as was import substitution to overcome the war's disruption of trade. In some cases, the industrial plant and stock were in a better condition when they were returned to the owners at the end of the war than when they had been taken over.

Where the collectivization process went furthest was on the land. By 1937, there were more than 1,500 different rural collectives involving one and half million people. Although Eastern Aragon and the Levante were the principal centers of agricultural collectivization, there were also hundreds of collectives in Andalucía and New Castile. Most of the collectivized land had belonged to large landowners or Fascist sympathizers, or was taken over on the basis of the voluntary merging of existing smallholdings. While in some cases collectivization was enforced from outside, in most cases the peasants and farm laborers took the initiative themselves (Bosch 1983; Casanova 1985, 1988).

Agrarian collectives were usually run by an elected committee and brought under common use fundamentals such as fertilizers, seeds, and machinery. In many, artisans and traders also participated. Frequently schools and cultural centers were established and literacy campaigns launched. Most collectives did not confine themselves to economic issues but often took responsibility for the economic, social, and political life of the village as a whole.

Formally the CNT recognized the rights of small property owners to continue cultivating on an individual basis but in practice some were obliged to work collectively (Bernecker 1996, 541–542). Peasants tended to reject or support collectivization depending on their class interests, the poor and landless understandably being the most enthusiastic. In Valencia, for instance, collectivization was backed by poorer peasants, sharecroppers, and laborers but fiercely opposed by conservative smallholders. Catalonia was a case apart; most peasants were reluctant to give up individual cultivation and collectivization took place mainly where sharecroppers or tenants were poorer. The province of Jaen was unusual in that small and mid-sized landowners joined the collectives alongside sharecroppers and tenant farmers (Garrido González 1979).

In Valencia there were no precedents for collectivization or land occupations. During the anarchist uprising of January 1933, few examples of libertarian communism were put into practice. So the wave of collectivization in 1936 can only be understood in the specific context of the war. Moreover, the 343 Valencia collectives differed greatly, ranging from libertarian experiments to straightforward cooperatives. Yet, despite problems of coordination, insufficient transport, the loss of markets, and a lack of fertilizers, the most efficient collectives, according to the unions, were to be found in this region (Lorenzo 1969, 151).

Agrarian collectivization involving both the CNT and UGT also occurred in Andalucía, Castile, and Murcia. In Andalucía, the Socialist Land Workers' Federation had included collectivization as part of its program; there had been examples in latifundio (large estates) areas before the war.

Collectivization had also been previously carried out in Castile. When the civil war began the practice spread throughout the region. Initially spontaneous, the collectivization process was soon taken over by the unions, especially the predominant UGT. The CNT, in contrast, hardly existed in Castile at the beginning of the war but grew from three thousand to one hundred thousand members during the first ten months of the war, especially among smallholders. Eventually the anarcho-syndicalists ran 186 of the 455 collectives in the region. According to César Lorenzo, "collectives were . . . so general and spontaneous" in Andalucía and Castile "that no one dared to argue against them." As a result even members of the PCE and the Republican parties were sometimes involved (Rodrigo González 1985; Lorenzo 1969, 160).

In Eastern Aragon there were an estimated 450 collectives involving 300,000 people by February 1937. Here the collectivization differed in various ways. For instance, unlike in many other areas, prewar inter-union rivalries led local Socialists to be opposed to the process. It has also been claimed frequently that the Catalan anarchist militia initiated the collectivization of land instead of the local peasants themselves. According to Julian Casanova, collectivization in Aragon was inspired by urban revolutionaries whose theories were designed more for landless farmhands than for the smallholding peasantry of Aragon. Available evidence points to different levels of acceptance of the process; whether collectivization was "imposed" or "spontaneous" depended on factors such as class structure and types of land ownership. In general, Casanova concludes that the demise of Republican legality in the region was more important than the armed presence of the CNT militias. Outside pressure to collectivize was greatest near the front and in areas where the CNT had not existed before the war (Bernecker 1996, 521; Casanova 1985, 119–129).

It was in Aragon that the most radical experiments in collectivization took place, reflecting both the poverty of most villages and the fact that in this region the state had collapsed altogether. Hence in many localities a system of vouchers often replaced money. This was not primarily for ideological reasons, as has often been assumed, but because the absence of the state and the subsistence nature of the local economy made the use of currency unnecessary. Goods and food were distributed on the basis of villagers' needs.

Any surplus produced was reinvested in the collective. For those embracing libertarian ideals there was a strong ethical undercurrent to the collectivization process in the "sharing of poverty," which was as important ideologically as it was practical economically. Women, however, participated little in the running of the collectives and often received a lower minimum wage than men, illustrating the limitations placed on egalitarianism, even in revolutionary Aragon.

The coordination of agrarian collectives at a regional level, especially during the first year of the war, was usually undertaken by the rural unions, which developed plans to improve and organize production. Valencia was the center of the most ambitious of these regional organizations, exporting citrus fruit on a massive scale.[8] The Council of Aragon controlled consumption and production, channeling exports and imports through the port of Tarragona.

---

[8] The Consejo Levantino Unificado de la Exportación Agrícola was set up by the CNT and UGT in September 1936 and eventually had 270 branches and 1,500 warehouses. It managed to export 750,000 tons of oranges—a figure unmatched until 1951.

Due to lack of surviving primary sources it has been difficult to ascertain to what degree the agrarian collectives were effective; taking into account the adverse objective circumstances, most evidence suggests that agricultural output was more or less sustained but there simply was not enough time for these revolutionary experiments to take root.

## Rebuilding the State

The revolution under way in much of the Republican zone was shaped by both the military situation and the divisions within the left. By the autumn of 1936, the Fascist army threatened to overwhelm the republic. The lack of a strong centralized authority and the shortcomings of the republic's military organization had to be solved if defeat were to be averted. For the Popular Front parties[9] this meant finishing with a revolution they saw as alienating the middle classes and, in particular, the foreign democracies from which they hoped to obtain arms. The Soviet government, given its aim of forming an alliance with the democracies against the Fascist powers, made the adoption of such a nonrevolutionary policy a condition for the provision of arms to the republic.

The first step toward pushing back the revolution was the formation of a new government, headed by Largo Caballero, on September 4, 1936. Its most immediate aim was to secure a monopoly over armed force. The creation of a regular army, the Popular Army, was counterposed to the claimed ineffectiveness of the revolutionary militias. The militias' limitations had been demonstrated in facing the better-trained troops under Fascist command, especially on open ground. To overcome such weaknesses the CNT and the POUM also called for a centralized command, but for one controlled by the workers' organizations rather than under control of the Popular Front government.

In Catalonia the anarcho-syndicalists hoped, by accepting a more direct relationship with the Popular Front parties, to get reciprocal treatment elsewhere in terms of representation as well as supplies and arms for their militias. Consequently the Catalan CNT decided to disband the CCMA and participate in the Generalitat, albeit on the premise that this would be a form of "defense council" and not a "government." Inside the CCMA no one opposed its dissolution. The POUM argued in its press for the CCMA to "take power" but, fearing isolation from the CNT, it accepted the creation of the new government provided it carried out the "socialist program" of the Consell d'Economia de Catalunya.

---

[9] Refers to those parties that continued to support the liberal democratic program of the Popular Front: (moderate) Socialists, Communists, and Republicans (liberals).

Established in late September, the new Catalan government, like the CCMA before it, had a Popular Front majority but the CNT maintained, at least for the time being, a powerful influence.[10] The most important initiative taken by the Generalitat Council was the introduction of a collectivization decree, which sanctioned and systematized the process under way since July. Under the decree management councils were set up in each company, unions being represented proportionally along with a representative named by the Generalitat. The decree represented a compromise among the different factions in the government. It put an end to spontaneous collectivization and opened the way to increasing state intervention in the economy.

Other measures introduced by the new Catalan government included the expansion and municipalization of public services, a system of people's tribunals to try suspected supporters of the rebels, legislation regulating civil marriage, a very liberal divorce law, access to birth control, legalized abortion, the promotion of progressive methods in education, and an ambitious program of school building.

Despite these progressive policies—a clear reflection of the balance of forces in autumn 1936—the majority in the Catalan government sought to undermine the revolution. The conversion of the local antifascist committees into municipal councils would prove an important first step toward this aim, allowing the Republican ERC to return to power at a local level, accompanied by the PSUC. The CNT, and to a lesser extent the POUM, presented the municipal councils as a step toward the unity needed to win the war and even as a continuation of the revolution. Opposition to the forming of the new local governments was usually in response to their composition rather than their existence as such. For instance, in Lleida a joint assembly of CNT and POUM members stated that "under no circumstances" should members of Republican parties be allowed representation in the municipal government (Pozo 2002, 307). In many cases the revolutionary committees continued to exist alongside the restored municipal authorities, maintaining control over collectivization and internal security. It usually took the intervention of the CNT leadership to put an end to this parallel situation. Even then, in a third of the new municipal councils, the distribution of representatives stipulated by the Generalitat was not followed (Pozo 2002, 294).[11]

Events in Catalonia proved a precedent for CNT participation in the central government. Military setbacks had reinforced the belief among

---

[10] The Generalitat Council was made up of three representatives each from the ERC and the CNT/FAI, and one each from the UGT, PSUC, POUM, ACR, and the Unió de Rabassaires, plus a military adviser.
[11] In theory the new councils had the same proportional representation as the Generalitat Council; see note 10.

many anarcho-syndicalist leaders that some form of statewide authority was essential. But a proposal by the CNT in mid-September to set up a "National Defense Council" comprised of itself, the UGT, and the Republicans came to nothing once the Socialist union refused to contemplate taking this step without including the workers' parties.

In early November, with Madrid threatened by Franco, the CNT, claiming that circumstances had changed the nature of the Spanish state, agreed to enter the government as necessary to win the war and protect the conquests of the revolution. With the authority gained by the participation of the CNT and through its control of the armed forces, credit, trade, and communications sectors, the central government could begin to reestablish its authority. The decision to participate in government appears to have been accepted by most CNT activists. The "tragic reality" of the war had "imposed itself over ideology" (Peirats 2001, 172–184; Bolloten and Esenwein 1990).

With the new central government installed, and following the experience of Catalonia, the remaining antifascist and revolutionary committees were gradually disbanded or absorbed into reconstituted regional, provincial, and municipal authorities. In Andalucía the antifascist committees were dissolved during November and replaced with new municipal committees with CNT participation. In Asturias the Council of Asturias and Leon was formed in December 1936 with a clear majority of representatives from the workers' movement. In Valencia the CEP continued to meet until January but its authority was undermined by the arrival in early November of the central government. Although new municipal councils were established concurrently throughout the Levante, in an echo of the Catalan process, many committees, especially those controlled by the CNT, initially refused to disband.

Such resistance did not last, however. Even the anarchist-run Council of Aragon sought to incorporate itself within Republican legality, and in January 1937 it was reorganized with the participation of all the Popular Front organizations, albeit still under libertarian hegemony.

The underlying tension between those that advocated continuing with the revolution and those that saw it as an impediment to winning the war was most dramatically reflected in the campaign by the PSUC and the Soviet government against the dissident Communist POUM. The campaign against "Trotskyism" was now exported beyond the borders of the USSR. The PSUC and PCE, like Communist parties elsewhere at the time, were completely subordinate to Moscow and soon launched a massive campaign of slander against the "Trotskyist-Fascist" POUM. Inevitably, given the strength of both the revolution and the POUM in the region, this campaign centered on Catalonia.

Much of the Catalan Communists' newfound strength was in the UGT, whose ranks had swelled once the obligatory unionization of all workers was introduced in August 1936. This growth was particularly marked among the white-collar and technical sectors, which provided a counterweight to the anarchists in the collectives. The PSUC, like the PCE in other regions, also received support from sections of the lower middle classes and peasants frightened by the revolution.[12]

By the spring of 1937 civilians began to feel the full impact of the war. In the Republican rearguard there were increasing shortages of basic goods. Thousands of refugees had arrived in the already overextended cities, soon to be subjected to unprecedented air raids. It was in this context that the PSUC stepped up its campaign against the "excesses" of the revolution, which it blamed for the calamities befalling the civilian population. In particular, it agitated around the growing food shortages with the slogan "more food, less committee."

Moves by the Republican authorities to gain control in the economic sphere were accompanied by measures to create a state monopoly over security. By spring 1937, violent clashes in Catalonia between rival factions and between the police and radicalized workers had become increasingly frequent. Continual accusations in the Communist press that the POUM and other "uncontrollables" were "fascist agents" provided further justification for attacks on the extreme left. Bloody clashes in the countryside between collectivists and their opponents were used by the Generalitat—now more firmly in the hands of the ERC and PSUC—to justify the creation in February 1937 of a unified police force under its control and permitting no political or trade union affiliation.

Attempts to reassert Republican authority solely by administrative means and propaganda were not sufficient. Apart from the POUM, many anarcho-syndicalists still believed that they were fighting not to defend the Republic but to advance the social revolution. This unsustainable situation came to a head on May 3, when Republican Assault Guards tried to seize the Barcelona telephone exchange, a symbol of workers' control in the city. The resultant street fighting proved a watershed for the revolution. Resistance was organized by the CNT defense committees, rooted in the poorer neighborhoods, and the radical anarchist group, the Friends of Durruti.[13] The latter stood apart from other anarchist groupings, having called for the creation of revolutionary juntas based on the CNT, FAI, and POUM that should "take power."

---

[12] The clearest example of this was the establishment in October 1936 of the small business and traders' association, the Federació Catalalan de Gremis i Entitats de Petits Comerciants i Industrials (GEPCI), which became part of the UGT.

[13] Benaventura Durruti had been one of the most prominent anarchist military leaders and prewar advocates of direct action.

The CNT and FAI leaderships, nevertheless, balked at a POUM proposal to completely take over Barcelona, fearing such an initiative might further aggravate the situation. Calls by the libertarian leaders for a cease-fire led to both the dismantling of the barricades and the deepening of opposition inside the CNT to collaboration with the Popular Front parties. The aftermath of the fighting saw widespread repression of the radical left—the control patrols were disbanded, hundreds of CNT militants imprisoned, the POUM declared illegal, and its leader Andreu Nin murdered.

With the defeat of the revolutionaries in Catalonia, the new government—headed by moderate Social Democrat Juan Negrín and lacking CNT participation—turned its attentions to the last stronghold of the revolution, eastern Aragon. In August 1937 the Council of Aragon was dissolved by the government, its leaders arrested, and many of the region's collectives dismantled. Meanwhile in Catalonia, as the political situation swung harder against the revolution, there was also an increase in the harassment of collectives, with police raids, confiscations, and support for returning property to the former owners (Castells 2002, 135). Parallel to this, collectivized industries were increasingly dependent on the Catalan government. Goods exported by collectives were sometimes confiscated at their port of entry, so they had to trade through the Generalitat and thus had no direct access to foreign currency. The Catalan government's control of credit further undermined collectivization.

The strengthening of the central government's hold over the military and political situation was combined with attempts to at least regulate, if not eliminate, workers' control in the economy throughout Republican Spain. State control replaced collectivization. In those industries taken over by the central government all worker participation in the decision-making process was abolished and a new elite of state functionaries was imposed. As in Catalonia, control of credit was also used to bring the remaining collectives under state tutelage.

According to Antoni Castells, state control proved inefficient because it was opposed by wide sectors of the working class and led to demoralization and a subsequent decline in productivity. In many cases state intervention dismantled programs aimed at increasing the economic efficiency of collectivized firms. The increasing number of bureaucrats hampered production and stoked further discontent among the workers. The state also lacked competent personnel and often acted on the basis of political bias rather than on criteria of economic efficiency. Evidently state intervention was not part of a socialist plan but carried out by a government with a thoroughly liberal-democratic orientation (1996).

Earlier, in October 1936, the Agricultural Ministry, in Communist hands, had introduced a decree that allowed for the return of land to former owners, obliged the revision of expropriations carried out by unions, and ensured that peasants could choose between individual or collective exploitation of land. Attempts at enforcing the decree led to increasing tension between the collectivists—who generally refused to observe its regulations—and their opponents. This was particularly the case in Valencia, where the PCE organized conservative peasants into the Federación Provincial Campesino (FPC). Aided by the police, the FPC used the decree to arrest collectivists and destroy property. By January 1938 the Valencian CNT could report that the "counter revolution was active in every village" (Casanova 1988 38–9).

The offensive against the agrarian collectives had a deleterious effect on the harvest. The head of the Agrarian Reform Institute, the Communist José Silva, admitted later that the arbitrary dissolution of collectives, including prosperous and voluntary ones, had wreaked havoc on the countryside. As a result many collectives had to be reestablished—including in Aragon—and most of those remaining were left untouched. In August 1938, the Agrarian Reform Institute reported that 40 percent of fertile land in fifteen provinces was still under collective cultivation. There were now 2,213 collectives involving 156,822 families—considerably more than in 1936. Of these only 54 percent had been collectivized legally—a clear sign that many collectivists continued to resist government encroachment despite the radical change in the political situation inside the Republican zone (Bernecker 1996, 522, 539).

## The Unfinished Revolution

For the revolution to have triumphed a viable form of alternative power structure would have needed to be established, not just to centralize economic production but, above all, to win the war against fascism. Whether or not the complex network of committees that emerged at all levels in July 1936 could have developed into such an alternative is debatable. There were clearly differences between the committees in Spain and the Russian soviets or German workers' councils: the former were not, in most cases, elected directly by the masses or set up in opposition to the government; they included representatives of "bourgeois" parties, and were prevented by their fragmented nature from becoming an alternative to the existing state.

Agustin Guillamón, for example, argues that the CCMA was merely an "organ of class collaboration" through which the Generalitat regained control over public order and military force. Rather than a relationship of "dual power" between the Generalitat and the CCMA there was a "duplicity of powers." "Embryonic organs of working class power" existed instead among the diverse defense, supplies, neighborhood, and factory committees (2007, 63–68).

Yet whatever the perceptions of the protagonists, the committees were indisputably an alternative power base to a discredited and paralyzed state apparatus. Even committees that collaborated with the local authorities, or were nominally formed by them, differed from them fundamentally. Especially at a regional and provincial level, the committees that emerged—without seeking to confront the state—substituted for many of its functions.

Thus the combination of committees, armed patrols, and collectives represented a revolutionary power in a global sense. The dominant classes "had lost control of an important part of the state" to the benefit of the working class (Pozo 2002, 506–509). What existed in most of the Republican zone during the first weeks of the war can best be described, as by Carlos M. Rama, as a situation of de facto dual power (González Muñiz et al. 1986, 87).

In the end, according to Pierre Broué:

> All the elements for the return of a bourgeois state were already found in the new organs of revolutionary power in Spain, the same as in Germany, as in Russia, and, from this point of view, constituted a *form of transition* towards the return to what the program of the Popular Front and the parties that [supported it] considered as "normal" . . . .Did this mean that in the situation in which the new organs of revolutionary power [found themselves] in Spain, in the summer of 1936, there did not exist elements that would have allowed the transition in an opposite direction? Not at all. . . . [Fundamentally] . . . there was no difference in nature between the Spanish situation in 1936 and the Russian situation in February 1917.

What determined the absence of a new revolutionary power based on the working class and peasantry, Broué concludes, was the compromise by the workers' organizations with the Popular Front (1982, 44–46).

For the CNT and the POUM, winning the war would have been possible only by harnessing the popular enthusiasm generated by the revolution. The problem was that the anarcho-syndicalists had no strategy for pursuing the revolution beyond their practical, day-to-day involvement in the militias, the collectives, different forms of expropriation, or the creation of general propaganda. For most of the CNT's cadres the revolution had already been won. It was not only unnecessary to conquer power but also unwise; trying to do so would only have led to the establishment of a dictatorship. The CNT neither considered the committees as an alternative power base nor did they see the need to create one.

The committees were seen by the CNT leadership as a means for controlling the Republican authorities or, at least, as a way of channeling "collaboration," and even as a way to maintain the union's independence, but never as an alternative to the state. In reality, as in the case of the CCMA, specialization and the creation of bodies with both workers' and Generalitat representatives opened the way to the complete restoration of legal powers. It was only later, when the logic of collaboration with a revitalized Republican state became clear, that some CNT and FAI activists began to pose what was effectively the "taking of power"; as was most clearly illustrated by the Amigos de Durruti's call for the formation of "revolutionary juntas."

In the economic sphere, while the anarcho-syndicalists were extremely active in the day-to-day running of the collectives, they lacked, according to Walther Bernecker, any "coherent plan" to adapt the economy to the needs of war (1996, 556). The creation of agrarian and industrial federations and associations, along with increasingly ambitious schemes for streamlining the collectivized economy, had only a limited impact on some of the difficulties facing the revolution. Large swathes of industry in particular suffered from what Castells describes as "working class neo-capitalism," whereby workers treated collectivized firms as their own "property," competing with other collectivized firms and sharing out any profits rather than pooling them for the common good (Castells 1993, 49–64).

These problems would never be overcome: the logic of collaboration with the bourgeois state led elsewhere. By the summer of 1937 the CNT and FAI had explicitly abandoned their antistatist principles and, declaring themselves the "enemies of dictators" and of "totalitarian forms of government," called on their members to collaborate with existing state institutions. Parallel to this the FAI adopted a structure that abandoned affinity groups in favor of a form of centralization closer to that of a political party. With the crushing military defeat in Aragon in March 1938, the CNT returned to a Republican government now firmly in the hands of the moderate and most antirevolutionary sectors. The CNT's abandonment of libertarian principles was epitomized by the manifesto it signed with the UGT, which recognized the role of the state in economic issues and the need to subordinate everything to winning the war (Bernecker 1996, 495–6).

In contrast to the CNT, the POUM insisted on the need for a new proletarian state if the revolution were to survive and fascism be defeated. The party called for a workers' government to be elected from an assembly of representatives from workers', peasants', and combatants' committees. These would be committees elected by the rank and file and would thus differ from many existing revolutionary committees (Tosstorff 2009, 108).

The POUM's relative lack of strength was an obvious impediment to its influencing events. But this did not mean it was not presented with alternative lines of action. Inside the party, both during and after the civil war, there was considerable criticism of its decision to participate in the Catalan government. In particular, the potential of the committees to have represented the basis of a new power was later recognized. One POUM leader wrote after the war that the Generalitat Council had had "one historical mission. . .to liquidate the committees" and that the POUM had been "entrusted to convince the revolutionary forces" of the necessity of doing so; it was then expelled from the government (December 1936) once this "invaluable service" had been carried out. The central problem for the POUM was how to influence the anarcho-syndicalists. Its inability to break even a part of the CNT's mass base from its political subordination to the Popular Front condemned the POUM to isolation and, it can be argued, the revolution to defeat (Durgan 2006, 44, 64).

The Spanish Revolution was replete with examples of working people taking the initiative to run society in their own interests. But without presenting a clear political alternative and in the context of a rapidly deteriorating military situation, these great social and economic experiments were soon undermined. The libertarian movement chose not to "go for all," as the Catalan anarchists phrased it, yet this choice was coherent with their ideals and principles. Nevertheless the dichotomy of "dictatorship" versus "collaboration" was a false one. Collaboration was indeed necessary in the form of united action with the rest of the working-class movement to defeat fascism. The alternative, rather than a dictatorship, was a new, centralized structure based on grassroots committees and direct democracy—but its success was predicated on the CNT's having a strategy to ally with the other tendencies in the workers' movement, in particular the left Socialists and the POUM. Not prepared to build a new power, Spain's anarcho-syndicalists helped rebuild the old one.

## References

Bernecker, W. L. 1982. *Colectividades y revolución social. El anarquismo en la guerra civil española 1936–1939,* Barcelona: Editorial Crítica.
———. 1996. La revolución social. In *La guerra civil. Una nueva visión del conflicto que dividió España,* ed. S. Payne and J. Tusell. Madrid: Temas de hoy.
Bolloten, Burnett. 1991. *The Spanish civil war: Revolution and counterrevolution.* Hemel Hempstead: Harvester Wheatsheaf.
Bolloten, Burnett and George R. Esenwein. 1990. Anarchists in government: A paradox of the Spanish civil war 1936–1939. In *Elites and power in twentieth-century Spain. Essays in honour of Sir Raymond Carr,* ed. Frances Lannon and Paul Preston. Oxford: Clarendon Press.
Bosch Sánchez, Aurora. 1983. *Ugetistas y libertarios. Guerra civil y revolución en el País Valenciano 1936–1939.* Valencia: Institució Alfons el Magnànim.
Broué, Pierre, and Emile Témime. 2008. *The revolution and civil war in Spain.* Chicago: Haymarket Books.
Broué, Pierre. 1982. Los órganos de poder revolucionario: ensayo metodológico. In *Metología histórica de la guerra y la revolución españolas* by P. Broué, et al. Barcelona: Fontamara.
Casanova, Julián. 1985. *Anarquismo y revolución en la sociedad rural aragonesa 1936–1938* Madrid: Siglo ventiuno.

_____, ed. 1993. *El sueño igualitario*. Saragossa: Institución Fernando el Católico.

Castells, Antoni. 1993. *Les collectivitizacions a Barcelona 1936–1939*. Barcelona: Hacer.

_____. 1996. *Desarollo y significado del proceso estatizador en la experiencia colectivista catalana 1936–1939*. Madrid: Nossa y Jara.

_____. 2002. Revolution and collectivization in civil war Barcelona 1936–9. In *Red Barcelona. social protest and labor mobilization in the twentieth century*, ed. Angel Smith. London: Routledge.

Cendra i Bertran, Ignasi. 2006. *El Consell d'Economia de Catalunya 1936–1939. Revolució i contrarevolució en una economia collectivitzada*. Barcelona: Publicacions de l'Abadia de Monserrat.

Durgan, Andy. 1996. *B.O.C. El Bloque Obrero y Campesino 1930–1936*. Barcelona: Laertes.

_____. 2006. Marxism, war and revolution: Trotsky and the POUM. In *Stalinism, revolution and counter-revolution. Revolutionary History 9*, no. 2. London: Socialist Platform.

_____. 2007. *The Spanish civil war*. Basingstoke: Palgrave.

Ealham, Chris. 2005. The myth of the maddened crowd: class, culture and space in the revolutionary urbanist project in Barcelona 1936–1937. In *The splintering of Spain, 1936–1945: New historical perspectives on the Spanish civil war*, ed. Chris Ealham and Michael Richards. Cambridge: Cambridge University Press.

Garrido González, Luis. 1979. *Colectividades agrarias en Andalucia: Jaen 1931–1939*. Madrid: Siglo ventiuno.

Girona i Albuixec, Albert. 1986. *Guerra y revolución al País Valencià*. Valencia: Biblioteca d'Estudis i Investigacions.

González Martinez, Carmen. 1999. *Guerra Civil en Murcia: un anàlisis sobre el poder y los comportamientos colectivos*. Murcia: Universidad de Murcia.

González Muñiz, Martin. A. et al. 1986. *La Guerra Civil en Asturias*, 2 vols. Madrid: Ediciones Jucar.

Guillamón, Augustín. 2007. *Barricadas en Barcelona*. Barcelona: Ediciones Espartaco Internacional.

Lorenzo, C. M. 1969. *Los anarquistas españoles y el poder*. Paris: Ruedo Ibérico.

Nadal, Antonio Sánchez. 1988. *Guerra Civil en Málaga*. Malaga: Editorial Arguval.

Paniagua, Xavier. 1982. *La sociedad libertaria. Agrarianismo e industrialización en el anarquismo español 1930–1939*. Barcelona: Editorial Crítica.

Peirats, José. 2001/2006. *The CNT in the Spanish Revolution*, 3 vols. Hastings: The Meltzer Press.

Pozo González, J. A. 2002. El poder revolucionari a Catalunya durant els mesos de julol a octubre 1936. Crisi i recomposició de l'estat. Doctoral thesis, Universitat Autònoma de Barcelona.

Radcliff, Pamela. 2005. The culture of empowerment in Gijón 1936–1937. In *The splintering of Spain, 1936–1945: New historical perspectives on the Spanish civil war*, ed. Chris Ealham and Michael Richards. Cambridge: Cambridge University Press.

Rodrigo González, Natividad. 1985. *Colectividades agrarias en Castilla-La Mancha*. Toledo: Servicio de Publicaciones de la Junta de Comunicaciones.

Sagués San José, Joan. 2005. *Una ciutat en guerra. Lleida en la guerra civil espanyola*. Barcelona: Publicacions de l'Abadia de Monserrat.

Tosstorff, Reiner. 2009. *El POUM en la revolució espanyola*. Barcelona: Editorial Base.

# Workers' Control
# under State Socialism

# 9

# Yugoslavia

## Workers' Self-Management as State Paradigm

**Goran Music**

Struggles for workers' control in the twentieth century have usually been linked to ruptures of state power and the ruling paradigm, whether of the capitalist or state socialist variety. As a rule, creative initiatives for direct participation arrive at their pinnacle in the relatively short periods of dual power—the time spans between the rapid decay of the old order and the stabilization of the new regime. These initiatives are therefore connected with the broader emancipative movements from below and possess the ability to preserve their autonomy from the state.

The experience of Yugoslav self-management is somewhat exceptional as it is closely identified with the official state ideology of social organization spanning across four decades. A successful modernization effort and rising living standards opened up political space for the socialist authorities to experiment with a system of self-management inside Yugoslavia, a country encompassing extensive cultural diversity[1] and uneven degrees of economic development.[2] Due to these historical circumstances, the most appropriate context for examinination of the different phases of Yugoslav workers' self-management would be the continuity of state institutions rather than the labor movement itself. Of course, recognizing the primary role of ruling structures in the shaping of the Yugoslav self-management system should

---

1 The six republics comprising post–World War II Yugoslavia were Slovenia, Croatia, Bosnia and Herzegovina, Serbia, Montenegro, and Macedonia. In addition to the six main nationalities, the federation also recognized a number of national minorities. In 1974, Vojvodina and Kosovo were granted the status of autonomous provinces inside Serbia.
2 The economic profile of the country was as heterogeneous as its demographics. By the 1980s the per capita income of Kosovo was only 72 percent of that of Slovenia, with similar regional disparities in the levels of unemployment.

not lead us to overlook another major factor in the process: the reactions—whether acceptance or resistance—of the working class to governmental policy shifts, especially at crucial historical turning points on the "Yugoslav road to socialism."

The Yugoslav self-management project is inseparable from the insistence of the Titoist revolutionary leadership on the rights of the socialist states, following World War II, to seek their own paths of development, independent from the model endorsed by the Soviet Union. The popular character of the antifascist Partisan movement[3] and its successes in liberating the majority of the country without the help of the Red Army had set the Yugoslav and Soviet Communist parties on a collision course early on. Several factors contributed to serious strains in Yugoslavia's relationship with Moscow, among them the territorial claims of the postwar Yugoslav government in parts of Italy and Austria, attempts at regional alliances with Albania and Bulgaria, Yugoslav support for the leftist guerrillas during the Greek civil war, and the perception that the arrangements the Soviet Union was making with the newly established "people's democracies" in Eastern Europe were unfair. All these, combined with what David A. Dyker describes as the "general tendency of the Yugoslavs to keep doing things off their own bat" (1990, 18), culminated in the expulsion of Yugoslavia from the Cominform in 1948.

## In Search of the "Yugoslav Path"

The unexpected purge from the official international Communist movement forced the Yugoslav leadership to differentiate itself and to legitimize the Partisan revolution through a critique of the dominant Stalinist concept of state and economic organization. Former Partisans took the time to carefully reread the Marxist classics and found inspiration, particularly in Marx's writings on the Paris Commune and Lenin's *The State and Revolution,* for an answer to the basic question, simplistically formulated by Milovan Ðilas,[4] as to "why Stalinism was bad and Yugoslavia was good" (Rusinow 1977, 50). The Yugoslav Communists came to the conclusion that state ownership of

---

3 During the World War II Nazi occupation of Yugoslavia, the resistance movement, organized by the Communist Party, emerged as the strongest antifascist force on the ground by skilfully combining popular appeal for national liberation with calls for social reform. As the only political and military faction that effectively crossed ethnic lines within the population, the Communist guerrillas, popularly known as the Partisans, had by the end of the war evolved into a conventional army, with eight hundred thousand men and women under arms.

4 Milovan Ðilas was a member of the Politburo and the minister of propaganda. In the mid-1950s Ðilas turned into a dissident and started to develop the critique of what he saw as the "new class" inside Yugoslavia, comprised of the Titoist leadership.

the means of production was simply the lowest form of social ownership, which, if not transcended soon after the revolution, would lead inevitably to centralized control by the state bureaucracy of the produced surplus value and thus to the establishment of state capitalism. Decentralization of state power on the macro level and the abolition of hierarchical organization inside the single enterprises were identified as two main measures for preventing the Soviet mistakes and reviving the process of the "withering away of the state," as had been envisioned by Marxists prior to Stalinist revisionism.

Apart from vague references to the Paris Commune, the Yugoslav Communists were nevertheless reluctant to connect their new course overtly with historical instances of grassroots democracy in other countries or the associated alternative socialist traditions. The experience of workers' council movements during the Russian Revolution or the Spanish Civil War continued to be interpreted in the glorified orthodox manner of the country's Communist historiography, reflecting the origins of the Yugoslav leadership in the Stalinist purges of the 1930s as well as the attendant need to justify the initial statist course of the revolution. The official line was that the model of administrative planning utilized up to that point was a necessary first step in the channeling of resources and raising the rate of accumulation, which prepared the ground for the new phase. The self-management ideology was thus interpreted within a national framework—as an application of Marxist ideas to the given stage of development and specific conditions of Yugoslavia, not as a universal alternative to Stalinism or as a continuation of the initiatives of worker democracy seen in the previous decades.

However, in the years to come, the official Yugoslav interpretations would be keen to establish continuity between this radical shift of the ruling paradigm and the democratic forms of organization established during the revolution. Even though the wider political mobilizations and self-initiative of the masses in World War II certainly opened the space for the independent course taken by the Yugoslav leadership, there are few traces of the demand for workers' control developing out of the war of liberation itself. Before World War II, Yugoslavia was predominantly an agrarian country; the Partisan movement took the form of a guerrilla army, consisting mostly of peasant youth and operating far from the urban centers. It is true that the party took great pride in the layer of the prewar proletariat joining the Partisan forces and tried to raise their profile despite criticism from Moscow[5]; however, a great number of these pioneer working-class cadres

---

5 The establishment of the so-called Proletarian Brigades as the shock troops during the war was severely criticized by Stalin at the time, as Moscow was careful not to scare away the Allies with the overtly revolutionary character of the Communist organized resistance.

lost their lives in the war while those that survived quickly became absorbed into the new state apparatus.

Regardless of the historical accuracy of Milovan Đilas's anecdote claiming that the car parked in front of his villa was the birthplace of the idea of workers' self-management, it nevertheless provides a good depiction of the nature of decision-making in the early postwar years—as an affair of a closed group of comrades-in-arms with little or no input from the broader layers of the party or organized labor:

> One day—it must have been in the spring of 1950—it occurred to me that we Yugoslav communists were now in a position to start creating Marx's free association of producers. The factories would be left in their hands, with the sole proviso that they should pay a tax for military and other state needs "still remaining essential". . . . I soon explained my idea to Kardelj and Kidrič while we sat in a car parked in front of the villa where I lived. They felt no reservations and I was soon able to convince them of the indisputable harmony between my ideas and Marx's teaching. Without leaving the car, we thrashed it out for a little more than half an hour . . . . A couple of days later Kidrič telephoned me to say that we were ready to go ahead at once with the first steps (Đilas 1969, 157).

The new doctrine of "workers' self-management" was publicly announced and legislated in June 1950 when Josip Broz Tito presented a draft of the new bill as the "most significant historic act of the Federal Assembly next to the Law of Nationalization of the Means of Production" (Tito 1950). The legislation rendered the workers' collective of a single enterprise a sovereign body, able to debate and vote upon fundamental factory matters through the workers' council, elected among its members. The workers' council met once a month and elected a management board—a professional administration, headed by an enterprise director concerned with day-to-day management. To prevent the alienation of the management from the work collective, three-quarters of this board had to consist of manual workers; the members were reelected on a yearly basis and could serve a maximum of two terms in that position. The enterprise director was nominated by the party for a four-year term but had to be approved by the workers' council as well.

Reviewing Tito's address to the Federal Assembly, the desire to position self-management as the "most definitive and convincing answer to all calumniators" (Tito 1950) becomes plainly apparent. Against the backdrop of Cominform accusations, the young Yugoslav state was eager to reclaim its revolutionary credentials in the eyes of the socialist world and improve its image in the West in the wake of opening to foreign aid and trade agreements. A closer reading, however, hints at other motives related to the country's growing internal economic hardships and not only to its international image. Passing references to the stabilization of work discipline and rational distribution of labor (Tito 1950) reveal a possibly more important, practical rationale for the introduction of workers' councils.

Contending with the Cominform economic blockade and potential military intervention, and faced with the imperative of consensus among all social layers, the Yugoslav leadership had to be innovative in finding noncoercive and nonconfrontational ways for raising labor output. Andrew Pienkos mentions the self-serving and manipulative functions of self-management (1984, 59), while Sharon Zukin sees the workers' councils as a tool for breaking the growing militancy of the trade unions in the midst of chronic labor shortage (1981, 291–294). Such critical appraisals are best summarized by Susan Woodward:

> In fact, a primary goal of the introduction of workers' councils in 1949–50 was to deprive the unions of their bargaining power . . . . Elected representatives of skilled production workers were to be consulted by managers on how to cut labor costs. The aim was to have workers accept limits on wages and benefits within enterprise net revenue, approve capital investment even if they cut into incomes and sanction dismissals of workers when required by budgets or modernization programs. The essence of self-management. . .was this attempt to enforce incomes policies and financial discipline without state involvement or central regulation (1995a, 261).

## The Formative Years

Regardless of the particular motivations or original, narrow objectives of the new enterprise regime, once the changes were implemented, they had wide-reaching and often unpredictable implications for the Yugoslav socioeconomic system as a whole. If these new measures were to stimulate maximal growth, the leadership had to open up macroeconomic space for the grassroots initiatives of the workers' councils. In their eyes, the best way to do this was to introduce the finished-goods market and consumer demand as the guiding principles for day-to-day enterprise decisions and as stimulation for labor productivity.

The development of a socialist economy through market incentives was soon turned into one of the defining concepts of Yugoslav socialism with the theory of "socialist commodity production." According to this doctrine, the law of value was an "objective economic law," influencing socialist societies as equally as the capitalist ones. Any administrative move against it would prove counterproductive and lead to bureaucratization. Self-management units should be free from the arbitrary exercise of power by the "outside factors" that could distort distribution to their own ends (Pašić 1975, 60). Therefore, exchange through the market, grounded in the law of value, together with collective ownership, supposedly provided the only objective criterion for socialist distribution.

As self-management became linked to the autonomy of the single enterprise in order to maximize its gain in the market of final products, democratic participation of the working class suddenly appeared to stand in conflict with the state's economic planning and the social goals of the society as a whole. The introduction of "social property" as an additional distinguishing characteristic of Yugoslav society had deep consequences for the self-perception of the working class. With enterprises transformed into self-managed units and the concept of state property abandoned, a single worker was no longer defined structurally as a wage earner in relation to capital or to the state, but as a property-owning producer receiving a share of the company's income. This tendency to view workers' councils as "collective entrepreneurs" rather than as organs of workers' control over management led Sharon Zukin to compare them to the stockholder meetings of capitalist corporations, with the difference being that "participation is founded on employment rather than equity" (1981, 287). Other authors were more prone to seek continuities with the preindustrial forms of moral economy and the peasant, small-property consciousness associated with the traditional *zadruga* (communal associations) found in the Balkan countryside (Pienkos 1984, 59).

The government failed to balance the focus on single enterprises as the source of political and economic rights with a broader, nationwide political space that could potentially coordinate various grassroots interests and grievances. The Council of Producers, introduced to the legislative bodies at all levels in 1953, was an attempt to base political representation on the awakened power of the producers; however, it never managed to recalibrate or substitute for the dominant legislative system, based on geographical representation (Comisso 1979, 47). The system thus discouraged the formation of an all-Yugoslav working class with a sense of common interest, as social tensions were channeled into bargaining between collective units of property owners and regional authorities instead of being directed at the aggregate dividing line between the workers and employers.

In this situation, organized labor focused its interest on the extension of the scope of market reforms. During the 1950s, increased decentralization, reduction in government investment, and the autonomy to seek profit in the market were perceived as victories of "workers' control" over "political forces." Solidarity with the technical and managerial cadres, who were close to the producers inside the enterprise and contributed to the total income of the work collective, seemed to make more sense than political alliances with the distant and unaccountable government bureaucracy (ibid., 54). It is therefore no surprise that in the initial two decades of the development of self-management, the trade unions were an "essential, if seldom recognized" (Rusinow 1977, 115) ally of the liberal pro-market faction of the Yugoslav leadership. Likewise, the first attempt on the federal level to provide an independent political forum for direct producers, the Congress of Workers' Councils in 1957, resulted in loud demands for further removal of state regulations, lower taxes, and greater autonomy of single enterprises in investment decisions.

The younger generation of party cadres was not bound by the same revolutionary experience and ideological orthodoxy as had been established during World War II, and was eager to embrace more liberal policies of free-market reform as the means of catching up with the more advanced Western societies. Yet it would be in error to conclude that the tactical alliance between the working class and liberals on the macro level, or even the identification of common interests within a single enterprise, managed to free workers' councils from antagonisms and provide smooth co-optation of the working class into the arena of collective entrepreneurialism. Along with the ever-increasing reliance on profitability criteria and the loosening of the budgetary character of investments, the workers' councils came under pressure to abandon the egalitarian ethos of the initial years and, instead, to allow the professional and managerial layer the upper hand inside the self-management structures. Surveys at the time showed the actual practice of self-management lagged far behind the normative standards, with low participation from the shop-floor workers and a high degree of influence by technical staff and the director (Prout 1985, 53). The workers did not feel they had the necessary time, competence, or information to make increasingly complex market decisions, so they let management formulate the options and present them to the workers' council.

In reality, management was the only body capable of making sound business evaluations, but formally any major decisions had to go through the blue-collar-dominated workers' councils. This process opened the door for client-patron practices, corruption, passivity, and cynicism toward self-management in general. Realizing that the workers' councils could not be used as a vehicle for the emancipation of wage labor, the workers quickly adapted and started using their votes as a bargaining tool with management. The workers' participation was often trivialized to the degree that a council could go on for hours discussing whether the night guard had the right to free coffee, whereas the major investment, marketing, and production proposals were simply rubber-stamped (Pienkos 1984, 63). The workers were therefore prepared to cede the initiative and responsibility to specialists as long as they felt the latter's measures were contributing positively to the company's total income. This, however, only increased the sense of alienation and suspicion inside the work collectives. One executive, from a factory observed by Ellen Turkish Comisso, stated that in order to move forward the workers would have to "get rid of the wage-earning mentality" (1979, 179). Yet the day-to-day experiences of workers did not encourage the idea of moving beyond wage labor, but instead reinforced the feeling that, within the structure of formal rights, the workers had little real influence over decisions within a given enterprise or society in general.

Despite the abandonment of administratively set production targets and the introduction of markets for final products, the operational freedom of the Yugoslav firm in the 1950s was still far from that of the capitalist economies. The limits to freedom of investment through heavy taxation, federally imposed accounting regulations, and strictly prescribed rules for distribution of profits between different funds, as well as the tight political control over the banking sector and foreign exchange, made the companies sensitive to government policies at least as much as to the market demand. The "social property" rights over land and capital also implied that a company's right to pursue self-interest was severely limited, due to its duty to serve broader social goals beyond merely private ones. The Yugoslav state spent the next four decades trying to balance the conflicting objectives at the core of its system. The practical task of harmonizing the two poles was made additionally difficult and contentious by the absence of clear, democratically controlled institutions responsible for the social interests at large.

Rapid decentralization of the state apparatus left the Communist Party as the sole institution with mass support and the authority to influence the structure of investments at the federal level. However, its clandestine existence before the war and the military command structure forged in the revolution had left its internal structure rigid and unable to open up to democratic impulses. As Dennison Rusinow observed, there were only four Central Committee plenums held during the ideologically crucial years between 1948 and 1952, and the only plenum that took place at the time of the constitution of the first experimental workers' councils in 1949 did not even touch upon the matter (1977, 49). Moreover, the policy of enterprise autonomy and the separation of the party and the state left Tito without an efficient nomenklatura, as found in other socialist countries, at his disposal. The party's ability to steer the overall direction of development therefore became contingent on recruiting professionals and managers into its ranks (Woodward 1995a, 322). This practice made the industrial workers additionally skeptical about accepting the Communist Party as their own organization. By the mid-1960s about half the party membership consisted of people employed in administrative jobs while workers comprised only about a third (Arsic and Markovic 1984, 20).

The former party leadership was cautious in their experiments with the market. The system was a mixture of liberal and socialist understandings of economic behavior, with the majority of productive factors and accumulation policy remaining cut off from market influence. These safeguards ensured that neither the law of value nor planned production for use-value gained hegemony within the national economy. Nevertheless, the relation of forces inside the country coupled with the global processes at the time made the overall trajectory of development clear. The rapid development in the 1950s gave momentum to organizational structures that drew connections between economic growth and liberalization measures. The liberal coalition, pushing for greater autonomy, decentralization, and market incentives, consisted of forces organized along production principles, such as firms, economic institutions, professional associations, and trade unions, as well as the political leadership of the more economically developed regions. Again, the ideological premises of the rights of "productive labor" against "bureaucratic statism" gave these forces moral high ground as representatives of working-class interests (Comisso 1979, 70).

The country was also aiming its developmental policy increasingly toward integration into the international division of labor and agreements with Western financial institutions. The dependence of domestic industrialization on the acquisition of foreign capital and intermediate goods made greater penetration into Western markets and access to hard currency a necessity. But in order to reach the protected Western markets, Yugoslavia was in turn forced to enter international trade agreements and expose itself to the influence of the global market through reduction of its own state control over foreign trade. The International Monetary Fund strongly supported decentralization in the first two decades of Yugoslavia's development, as it hoped this would spur "non-institutional economic laws" (Pienkos 1984, 61). The resulting deficit in the balance of payments was counteracted with increasing financial discipline. Susan Woodward notes how, instead of government expenditures being cut, entire categories were removed from the federal budget and "handed to authorities closer to producers or to independent agencies with autonomous self-management funds, as in the case of social services" (Woodward 1995a, 234). By the late 1950s, self-management in Yugoslavia was thus devoid of its emancipative potential not only inside the factories but also in the context of macro-economic policy; it also became the primary pretext for the structural adjustments required by the country's international position.

## Market Socialism

Maintaining the illusion of equality among the nationalities of socialist Yugoslavia became increasingly difficult. The policy of balanced regional growth—made possible by the central government's dominant role in the allocation of capital investments—had become a point of contention as of the late 1950s, as it frequently contradicted individual republican interests. Painfully aware of the many long-standing ethnic and republican rivalries, which had nearly torn apart the first Yugoslavia before World War II, the Titoist leadership sought to shift the burden from the central state and the party by emphasizing the influence of the market, which would allegedly transcend regional borders with a profit stimulus.

However, the results did not match the desired outcome. Industrialization proceeded in an autarchic fashion, spurred by connections between the managerial and political elites, with each region supporting local employment through a range of production facilities without regard to duplications on the national level or to the long-term economic viability of the projects. In support of these enterprises the local authorities pushed for further decentralization, aiming at exclusive access to regional markets and direct access to foreign credit.

This decentralized, profit-driven, and export-oriented industrialization strategy created bottlenecks in the production chain and regional disparities: there was overdevelopment of processing factories, concentrated in the northern republics, which enjoyed developed transportation and communication links with Western Europe; the subordinated basic industries, dependent on federal subsidies, were located mostly in the southern republics. This division further strengthened the popular belief that the "political factories," financed by the federal budget, were wasteful investments, whereas those projects on the lower levels, more in tune with market signals, were the successful parts of the economy leading the country forward. The main counterweight to the splintering tendencies of "socialist commodity production" was the policy of centralized national accumulation, made possible by the Federal Investment Fund, which obligated individual companies to maintain the value of social capital through prescribed rates of depreciation and a minimum rate of savings.

The middle-ground solution between the plan and the market was impossible to maintain in the long run. The structural imbalances in the Yugoslav economy offered new opportunities for the liberal faction inside the party. They argued that political influence contributed to an irrational distribution of investments between and within different sectors and that the only solution would be to follow the lead of the final product markets, bringing investment decisions under the discipline of the domestic and global market signals. Apart from that, they believed that forced high levels of accumulation restricted working-class consumption and impaired the growth of productivity (Prout 1985, 33–34). The fact that workers did not have full control over the surplus value produced in their enterprise seemed to prove that statist and bureaucratic elements were still blocking the full development of self-management relations in production. Labor, for its part, was also pushing for reforms in the hope of higher wages as well as the fulfillment of the original revolutionary ethos of distribution, "to each according to his work."

The localization of economic interests made a national consensus on fundamental economic issues almost unattainable. It seemed that any significant breakthrough in political decisions was made possible only through the direct interference of Josip Broz Tito as the ultimate intermediary and undisputed symbol of the revolution. With rising antagonisms threatening to tear the party apart, the liberal solution of substituting endless bickering with an impersonal arbiter was a tempting choice. The market was suitable and viable inasmuch as it was invisible and apparently reasonable. The Titoist experimentation with market incentives had brought about record growth rates, while Western markets appeared to offer space for further integration. Besides, the leadership's understanding of socialism offered no serious alternative. The only option besides the market was centralization, but a return to the system of administrative control and ideological rigor was out of question by that point. As the 1950s drew to a close, it had become time for a qualitative change in the interpretation and practice of Yugoslav self-management.

Nineteen sixty-five marked the watershed moment when the implicit tendencies of the preceding years were finally rolled out as an official party line popularly known as "market socialism." As Christopher Prout states, the mid-1960s reform measures were significant "not for what they created but for what they removed" (1985, 47). The multitude of smaller reforms accreted into a qualitatively new concept of the state as the leadership embraced the liberal assumptions. The enterprises' autonomy was increased significantly, with government taxation decreasing from 60 percent to just 30 percent of the work collective's income, thus leaving it up to the workers' councils to decide freely between consumption and accumulation (Comisso 1979, 73). The state withdrew further from the economic sphere, giving companies the freedom to enter independently into contract with each other and their foreign partners. The aggregate results determined the level of macro-industrial output and the structure of investments. A complex system of multiple exchange rates was replaced with a unified exchange rate and general liberalization of foreign trade (Schrenk et al. 1979, 26–27). The federal government's share of total investment finance had fallen to 22.5 percent by 1963, leaving the decision of macroinvestment proportions up to specialized banks and competitive capital markets (Dyker 1990, 63). The federal annual and five-year plans continued to exist only in a purely informational sense as there was no institutional level left to enforce these goals.

The workers' councils responded accordingly. After a constitutional amendment was enacted in 1968 that granted collectives almost complete freedom, they took this opportunity to formulate their own structures, re-draft individual statutes, transfer power to a number of specialized executive boards, and abandon the compulsory quota of blue-collar workers on the councils, thus bracing the enterprises for market competition (Prout 1985, 57). The old idea of integrating the workers' councils into the state appara-tus via the Council of Producers was abandoned; the legislative bodies of the government were divided into four separate chambers more in tune with the territorial principle within Yugoslavia.

Perhaps the most significant among this wave of reforms was the dis-mantling of the Federal Investment Fund and the establishment of the Fed-eral Fund for the transfer of financial resources to the less developed republics. This act stood as a clear abandonment of the concept of organi-cally integrated development of the country as a whole. The logic of profit prevailed, recognizing that the areas offering higher return on investments should be relied upon as the poles of economic growth, while the less de-veloped regions should be compensated through the mechanism of soli-darity transfers. The republics were therefore recognized as the prime units of economic life, whereas the role of the federation was reduced to a mere redistributive function. This mechanism of solidarity transfer between re-publics proved a controversial issue, suitable for political manipulation by the republican leaders, as the "plus" for one region inevitably appeared as a "minus" for another during the years of economic stagnation.

By the end of the 1960s the economic reforms were widely perceived as having been a failure. Between 1964 and 1967, at the height of the reforms, the average yearly growth amounted to 2.9 percent compared to almost 10 percent between 1961 and 1964 and 12.7 percent between 1957 and 1960 (Rusinow 1977, 202). In 1965, the unemployment rate stood at 8.8 percent, some 326,800 unemployed people in total, despite the encouragement of massive immigration policy toward Western Europe. In the early years of the planned economy, wage differentials were maintained at a ratio of 1: 3.5. By 1967, they had reached a disparity of up to 1: 20, depending on the industry or the particular enterprise. The inequality among enterprises was even greater if one took into account the various social services and fringe benefits that self-management transferred to the company level, such as housing, transportation subsidies, meals, individual education, and consumer credits.

The withdrawal of the state from the economic arena allowed high-wage industries to develop intensive capital formation, while the companies in basic industries were under pressure to raise wages and relied increasingly on the banks for investment. Large trading enterprises used the opportunity to merge with financially troubled firms and integrate their suppliers into conglomerates, restricting the sales of raw materials and forbidding local firms to buy elsewhere. This development was associated with the surfacing of "technocratic managerialism"—a term used to describe the bonds between the directors and the republican political authorities (Prout 1985, 30).

## The Last Revolution from Above

The reforms of the 1960s created an atmosphere in which each group felt exploited by the others, with no clear divisions. Agriculture felt threatened by industry, industry by the banks, basic industry by processing, small companies by larger ones, the less developed areas by the richer republics, and the more developed republics by the trade monopolies concentrated in Belgrade. The rising insecurity did not lead to political solidarity networks from below, able to overcome the atomization of self-management, but to splintering. By the late 1960s the Yugoslav version of socialism was experiencing a serious identity crisis. Beyond the vague commitments to self-management and "brotherhood and unity," there seemed to be no clear concept or direction (Pienkos 1984, 62).

The regime, which had once been able to deal confidently with instances of dissent behind closed doors, now seemed incapable of resolving the internal contradictions it had created, or of preventing the frustration from spilling over into the streets. Between 1968 and 1972, political challenges to the Titoist leadership came from all sides, revealing the complicated extent of the vertical and horizontal cleavages created by the reforms. The student protests in the summer of 1968 were followed in the fall by a movement in the province of Kosovo, demanding more rights for ethnic Albanians, as well as nationalist protests in Croatia in the early 1970s calling for further liberalization and autonomy for the republics.

While the protests in Kosovo and Croatia reflected general trends within the party and utilized the official interpretations of self-management in an attempt to further decentralization as well as regional, economic, democratic, and national rights, the student protests proved much more dynamic on a political level. They were able to formulate an alternative discourse of self-management, oriented exclusively toward the working class, independent of the regional divides. Drawing on the ideas of the Praxis group[6] of socialist-humanist intellectuals in the universities and the global 1968 movement, the students insisted that the emergence of a technocratic elite in the enterprises and the resurrection of nationalism were processes connected to and inseparable from the introduction of autonomous market competition. Ac-

---

6 A journal launched in 1964, *Praxis* was the focal point for critically inclined left-wing scholars who sought to advance New Left politics internationally. Among other activities, *Praxis* organized summer schools on the Adriatic island of Korčula, bringing the leading Marxist intellectuals of the time to Yugoslavia, and initiated translations of their works.

cording to Nebojša Popov, the regime, in response to the students' position, took careful steps to prevent communication between students and workers by making sure that the party remained the only official link between the enterprises and the rest of society. They also used organized guards and action committees from within the enterprises to physically prevent the students from reaching the factories (2008, 87).

Only when viewed in light of the developments inside organized labor at the time are these extreme "safety" measures fully comprehensible. During the previous decade, workers had handed over control of the factory councils to management in exchange for greater total income and higher wages. The growing reliance on the marketplace as a parameter for determining individual compensation in exchange for work, however, had brought down the living standard of blue-collar workers and created workplace insecurity. The key tenet of Yugoslav socialism, invoked to gather support for economic liberalization, among other things, was the distribution slogan, "to each according to his work." The spread of reform measures revealed just how differently this principle was interpreted by shop-floor workers as opposed to management. Ellen Turkish Comisso's lucid account of occupational values inside the Yugoslav enterprise shows that workers tended to interpret the credo in its most literal sense, taking it to mean that one should receive back the value of labor power invested during the production process.

Management, on the other hand, upheld the principle of distribution according to the "results of work," and thus wages should not depend on the quality or quantity of individual labor, but on the capability of the firm to realize its products and attain a favorable position for them on the market (Comisso 1979, 159–171). The close of the second decade of Yugoslav self-management therefore marked the end of an uneasy coalition between the workers and the liberal faction of the party. Workers' disillusionment with the bureaucratization of Yugoslavia's economy expanded. With the intensification of strikes[7] during the 1960s and pressure at the 1968 trade union congress for more resolute representation by the union functionaries, workers exhibited a shift toward the politicization of their demands and an exit from the stage of individual, self-managed enterprises (Carter 1982, 159–207).

In an effort to regain control over the economy and discipline in the party ranks, the Yugoslav leadership launched the final and most ambitious reconstruction of the self-management project on all levels. After crushing the demonstrations in Kosovo and pacifying of the student movement, the

---

7 Industrial strike actions by workers were becoming commonplace during the 1960s, despite being labeled as an absurdity within a self-managed economy and denied legal status. Increasingly tolerated by the authorities, more than two thousand strikes were recorded between 1958 and 1969.

Titoist leadership seized upon the more radical wing of the Croatian national movement as the impetus to start a sweeping purge of nationalist and liberal elements in the party apparatuses of all the republics, followed by a clampdown on left-wing professors and opposition at the University of Belgrade. The political space was cleared for a departure from a decade of market socialism.

The goal was to eliminate the harmful monopolies without upsetting useful market incentives, as well as to reintegrate the party into the social and economic processes without reinstating the hierarchic state apparatus. The enterprises were broken down into "basic organizations of associated labor" (BOALs)—the smallest units whose product or service could be expressed in terms of market value. Each of these smaller entities was equipped with its own set of self-management organs and joined the larger work organizations voluntarily on the basis of a contract and delegate representation in the central workers' councils. Each enterprise was transformed into a federation of BOALs with full legal and political sovereignty.

Relations between the enterprises and the state and among the enterprises themselves were constructed on a similar principle. Instead of regulations imposed from above, the new economic planning was to be accomplished through a series of agreed-upon "social compacts" aggregated on the national, regional, or industry-specific level (Prout 1985, 73–77). Each enterprise would take the initiative to form a number of "social compacts" with the local communities and "self-management agreements" with other BOALs and work organizations. The aim was that through this complex web of compacts and agreements the associated labor would gain control over the blind forces of commodity production and bypass the technocratic elements in self-management relations. The self-management bodies were expected to work in close collaboration with the local branches of national mass organizations and workers were encouraged to participate in both structures simultaneously. The idea was that these activities would help bind the enterprises more closely to the greater social interests.

Concurrently, in another attempt at the autonomous representation of industry within the political apparatus, a reconfigured chamber structure was introduced. Each legislative assembly, from the communal assembly level up to the republican government, now consisted of three separate chambers with delegates from the communities, work organizations, and sociopolitical organizations (Schrenk et al. 1979, 45). However, it is revealing that the Chamber of Associated Labor, representing work organizations, was never introduced to the Federal Assembly, the highest legislative body in the country. Far from helping to open up political space to enable the development of alternatives to the prevailing regional and ethnic allegiances, these steps toward more direct workers' democracy proved to be merely a minor adjustment to the Constitution of 1974, which, ironically, had integrated many demands of the various national movements and thus entrenched the republics as the primary vehicles for political negotiation inside the country.

It seems that with each subsequent reform the capability of the leadership to mobilize the masses behind it decreased. This new "revolution from above" remained largely formalistic, engulfed in a stream of legislation written in highly bureaucratic language. Positioned as the route to peak power for direct producers, it never managed to animate the workers, who saw it either as an irrational and problematic deconstruction of previously integrated production processes, or as a multiplication of bureaucracy and what they considered "empty talk." While management made sure the enterprise structure conformed to the new laws, the new organizations operated in a perfunctory manner, keeping the authorities satisfied so that, at the end of the day, everybody could go on with their business as usual. The practical impact of the changes was disappointing:

> It is revealing to note that the analysis by the 1976–1980 Social Plan of the major economic weaknesses in Yugoslavia, written in the mid-1970s, is almost identical to that contained in the mid-1960s. Both refer to imbalances of sectoral growth between the manufacturing, raw materials and infrastructure sectors as the basic source of instability in the economy . . . .It is almost as if time had stood still (Prout 1985, 70).

## Giving In

Josip Broz Tito's death in 1980 coincided with the trend of rising oil prices on the world market and deteriorating terms of trade for developing countries. For decades, the country had based its development on the integration into the international division of labor. The global recession of the late 1970s hit Yugoslavia harder than any other socialist country; the increasing prices of raw materials, spare parts, and components—all needed for the exporting industries—resulted in the increase of production costs and loss of competitiveness. In addition, the interest on loans was rising steeply and, by 1981, the Yugoslav government found itself on the edge of bankruptcy with over $20 billion in foreign debt (Sörensen 2009, 77). The prolonged economic crisis gave rise to the feeling that further reforms were necessary. Once the source of great pride, the system of self-management was no longer regarded as a unique, worthy pursuit but viewed increasingly by government officials as an obstacle to further modernization.

A series of "stabilization programs" were introduced at the advent of the 1980s with the aim of improving international competitiveness and reining in galloping inflation. They consisted mainly of decreases in collective consumption and stricter market parameters for company performance. The austerity measures placed the primary burden of the reforms on the shoulders of the industrial workforce in the socialized sector of the economy. In the first three years of the decade average incomes had fallen by 33 percent in real terms. By 1988 the standard of living for workers in the socialized sector had been pushed back to the levels of the 1960s (Schierup 1992, 86). If efficiency-oriented economic reform were to be implemented, it was estimated that out of a workforce of approximately eight million, roughly two million workers would have to be thrown out of work. Combined with one million workers already unemployed and the increasing number of former "guest workers" returning home from recession-hit Western Europe, the Yugoslav government was finding it increasingly hard to maintain social peace.

Indeed, these types of policies soon provoked movements from below and stirrings at the top of society. Workers' mobilizations, tacitly accepted and positively perceived by the public, were the most prominent grassroots initiatives at the time. The number of strikes recorded nationwide went from 247 in 1980 with 13,507 workers involved, to 1,851 strikes involving 386,123 workers in 1988 (Marinkovic 1995, 83). These statistics place Yugoslavia among the European countries with the highest level of strike activity at that time. Unlike the strikes of previous decades, focused mainly against company management and limited to the factory premises, workers were now eager to connect their demands to wider political issues and to present their grievances to the authorities by staging marches, street demonstrations, and gatherings in front of government buildings. Although opposed to the austerity policies and the individual politicians who advanced them, the workers supported the Titoist heritage more generally by holding strikes and protests under the party iconography. Their demands ranged from insistence on higher wages to multiparty elections and the inclusion of organized labor delegates in the political debates of the Federal Assembly.

Once the workers had started to move en masse, it became clear how ineffectual the self-management bodies had become over the years—most of the strikes and grassroots actions were organized outside of these structures. Nevertheless, even though the workers might have had negative experiences with the self-management in their particular surroundings, all sources indicate that as a group they were still attached to the general values and interpretations of Yugoslav socialism, and they projected their ideas for change within this framing. As Susan Woodward points out, the demands for multiparty elections did not originate from popular pressure but from politicians aspiring to more regional power and nationalist intelligentsia seeking more influence in political affairs (Woodward 1995b, 45).

The mounting popular discontent gradually spilled over into the ruling party. Lower-rank officials and local state enterprise managers attempted to join forces with various protest groups inside the republics. The tipping point was reached in the autumn of 1988, when the Serbian branch of the League of Communists of Yugoslavia, under the leadership of Slobodan Milošević, openly broke with the unified line of the federal government against the street protests and extended political support to handpicked demonstrations. By reinterpreting the hitherto dominant notion of the dichotomy between the "exploiter and exploited" in nationalist terms, this group of the Serbian political elite organized a wave of rallies in Serbia and the surrounding republics, co-opting the movement previously based on class issues. These top-down, nationalist mobilizations, which came to be known as the "antibureaucratic revolution," opened the door for the violent disintegration of the country.

By 1989, the new Enterprise Law and Foreign Investment Law effectively ended self-management as the dominant form of enterprise organizing, allowing for full foreign ownership and repatriation of profits, and legalizing market allocation of labor and capital (Warner 1990, 216–219). The trade unions did not oppose the dismantling of self-management, as they hoped the labor market would finally end atomization and grant labor greater influence within society through the practice of collective bargaining. Once the Wars of Yugoslav Secession started in 1991, however, "national interests" took precedence over labor grievances, effectively narrowing the space for any attempts at a formulation of class politics.

The Yugoslav working class never managed to capture the institutional opportunities presented by self-management that could have transformed worker-managed enterprises from instruments of the ruling bureaucracy into authentic vehicles for democratic control from below. Despite—or perhaps precisely because of—the multifarious institutions established over several decades by the self-management system, the workers lacked a clear channel for voicing their grievances. The self-management councils, as the principal structures, could not serve as democratic organs for exercising dissent, since their primary purpose was to play a managerial function in the operation of firms, not to serve as political organs of the working class. Sociopolitical organizations operating on the shop-floor level remained too ensconced in the bureaucracy to accommodate dissenting voices.

On a larger scale, the apparent contradiction between the self-interest of a single factory or a given region and the interests of society as a whole was not resolved through centralized democratic control of the overall economy by the working class. In the absence of such a control mechanism, the consensus of the republican elites remained the prerequisite for any unified policy. Until the very last day of the Yugoslav Federation the dominant reading of self-management in society remained that of increased autonomy and local control. Once the country disintegrated, however, the elites had no more interest in its maintenance. The labor movement, for its part, was not strong enough to endow the concept with fresh, relevant meaning and use it as a guide for action in the new socioeconomic surroundings. Two decades after its abandonment, the experience of Yugoslav self-management thus leaves an ambivalent legacy waiting to be reclaimed by the social movements and reappraised by the social sciences.

## References

Arsic, Mirko and Dragan R. Markovic. 1984. *68. Studentski bunt i društvo*. Belgrade: Prosvetni Pregled.

Carter, April. 1982. *Democratic reform in Yugoslavia: The changing role of the party*. London: Frances Pinter.

Comisso, Ellen Turkish. 1979. *Workers' control under plan and market: Implications of Yugoslav self-management*. New Haven, CT: Yale University Press, 1979.

Đilas, Milovan. 1969. *The unperfect society: Beyond the new class*. London: Methuen & Co.

Dyker, David A. 1990. *Yugoslavia: Socialism, development and debt*. London: Routledge.

Johnson, A. Ross. 1972. *The transformation of communist ideology: The Yugoslav case, 1945–1953*. Cambridge, MA: MIT Press.

Marinkovic, Darko. 1995. *Štrajkovi i društvena kriza*. Belgrade: Institut za politi ke studije.

Pašic, Najdan. 1975. Self-management in Yugoslavia: Some impending problems. In *Self-management: New dimensions to democracy*, ed. Ichak Adizes and Elizabeth Mann Borgese. Santa Barbara, CA: Clio Press.

Pienkos, Andrew. 1984. Socialist transition in the capitalist world-economy: The Yugoslav experience. *Insurgent Sociology* 12 (1/2): 57–69.

Popov, Nebojša. 2008. *Društveni Sukobi—Izazov Sociologiji: Beogradski Jun 1968*. Belgrade: Službeni Glasnik.

Prout, Christopher. 1985. *Market socialism in Yugoslavia*. London: Oxford University Press.

Rusinow, Dennison. 1977. *The Yugoslav experiment: 1948–1974*. London: Royal Institute of International Affairs.

Schierup, Carl-Ulrik. 1992. Quasi-proletarians and a patriarchal bureaucracy: Aspects of Yugoslavia's re-peripherialization. *Soviet Studies* 44 (1): 86.

Schrenk, Martin, Cyrus Ardalan, and Nawal A. El Tatawy. 1979. *Yugoslavia: Self-management socialism and the challenges of development*. Baltimore, MA: Johns Hopkins University Press.

Sörensen, Jens Stilhoff. 2009. *State collapse and reconstruction in the periphery: Political economy, ethnicity and development in Yugoslavia, Serbia and Kosovo*. New York: Berghahn Books.

Tito, Josip Broz. 1950. *Workers manage factories in Yugoslavia*. Pamphlet, Belgrade, June 26. www.marxists.org/archive/tito/1950/06/26/htm.

Warner, Malcolm. 1990. Yugoslav "self-management" and industrial relations in transition. *Industrial Relations Journal* 21 (3): 209–220.

Woodward, Susan L. 1995a. *Socialist unemployment: The political economy of Yugoslavia. 1945–1990*. Princeton, NJ: Princeton University Press.

———. 1995b. *Balkan tragedy: Chaos and dissolution after the cold war*. Washington, DC: Brookings Institution Press.

Zukin, Sharon. 1981. The representation of working-class interest in socialist society: Yugoslav labor unions. *Politics & Society* 10 (3): 281–316.

# 10

# Give Us Back Our Factories!
## Between Resisting Exploitation and the Struggle for Workers' Power in Poland, 1944–1981

**Zbigniew Marcin Kowalewski**

*Translated from the Spanish by Marco Gomez*

## Mode of Exploitation and Workers' Resistance

The Soviet-dominated People's Republic of Poland,[1] which existed from 1944 to 1989, was one of the transitional social formations between capitalism and socialism to emerge on the periphery of the world capitalist system. This periphery lagged behind the Western center in the historical process of industrial revolution (Aldcroft 2006). Poland's dependent capitalist system between the wars had hindered the nation's industrial development; consequently, its overthrow by the Red Army after World War II allowed this delayed revolution to occur. In the newly industrialized People's Poland, the commodities exchange ceased to be the general form of social relations, but bureaucratic domination blocked the transition to the new planned relations. This domination was based on a double set of contradictions: between the overthrow of capitalist domination on a national and regional scale and its prevalence in the world system; and between the suppression of capitalist relations of exploitation and the persistence of the productive forces fused in the crucible of these relations. The more the productive forces had adapted to capitalism, the more they hampered the development of relations of nonexploitation (Rey 1977, 130; Rey 1985, 131; Turchetto 1995 and 2007).

The bureaucracy was not a genuine dominant class but a parasitic stratum (Post 2000); its political domination was not rooted in a specific mode of production, yet it was able to extract surplus labor from the workers. The

---

1 This was the official name from 1952–1989.

exploitation to which the workers were exposed was but a pale reflection of the dominant relations of production in the world capitalist system. The inability of the bureaucracy to develop new productive forces, or to "really subsume" those that it disposed of, generated strong tendencies toward the overexploitation of labor power (the extraction of absolute surplus labor) and desocialization of productive forces (see Marx 1982, 1021, 1024).

The use of pallets that produced a technical revolution in construction transport is a good illustration of this desocializing tendency inherent to bureaucratic domination. At the end of the 1970s, after fifteen years of efforts by six government commissions in charge of introducing pallets into the economy, the transportation of bricks continued as follows: instead of being placed on pallets in the brickyard at the beginning of the whole chain, they were loaded by hand into train wagons, unloaded by hand at the station of destination, then loaded by hand into trucks, unloaded by hand from the trucks at the building site, and only at the end—when the manual process ran into an insurmountable technical obstacle—were the bricks finally placed on pallets so that a crane could lift them to the eighteenth floor of a skyscraper under construction (Kusmierek 1980).

Ticktin has stated, ironically, that to sector I (producing the means of production) and sector II (producing the means of consumption) the political economy of "actually existing socialism" added an ever-expanding sector III: the repair of the means of production. When a reduction in the number of workers operating the machines occurs simultaneously with an increase in the number of workers repairing them, the contradiction between the requirements for socializing the productive forces and the atomization prevailing in the labor process becomes practically insurmountable (1973). One of the manifestations of this contradiction was the low or null-use value of the massive production of the means of consumption and production in which the social nature of labor did not materialize. Another, during the final phases of production plans, was the global scarcity of the forces, means, and objects of labor on the one hand, and on the other, the overabundance of the same in the enterprises that had stocked, underutilized, or kept them in reserve during "dead times," awaiting "strong times." The over-demand of labor power in the enterprises guaranteed full employment, which in turn was the decisive factor legitimizing "actually existing socialism" (Pravda 1981, 46).

The forms of the labor process, inherited from capitalism and subsumed under neither the bureaucracy nor the working class, were strained by the contradiction between the permanent tendency to overexploit labor power and the likewise permanent tendency to resist this exploitation. Workers' resistance took the forms of a high labor turnover, absenteeism, and a wide-ranging although partial workers' control of the labor process. Filtzer (1986) has shown how extraordinary was the speed and range with which the new working class, having recently arisen from the Stalinist industrial revolution, assumed what Arnot (1981, 1988) has called "negative workers' control." Although atomized, it was a way for an individual worker or a small workers' collective to appropriate a certain amount of the labor time, to determine the work pace, to avoid complying with tasks and norms or applying rationalizations and innovations, to enforce being paid on a time basis while working on a piece basis, and so forth. When confronted by this "negative workers' control" over the labor process, the Tayloristic form of work organization that the bureaucracy had borrowed from capitalism produced what could be described—resorting to a blatant *contradictio in adjecto*—as an "arrhythmic taylorism" (URGENSE 1982).

Workers resorted to the weapon of the strike only when the increase in the overexploitation of labor was so strong that the conventional methods of "negative workers' control" were unable to neutralize or counter that increase. Mass strike movements were the principal means for accumulating forces, fighting capacities, and experiences. A qualitative leap in the process of "class accumulation" occurred in the event that workers occupied factories. Independent of the demands of the strikers, every sit-down strike went beyond the limits of the bureaucratic regime by posing in a practical manner the question of who was to run the factories: the bureaucrats or the workers? If the sit-down strike raised this question episodically, workers' councils elected by all the workers of a given enterprise raised it permanently, by instituting a counterpower opposed to bureaucratic management and constituting an organ of struggle for workers' self-management (cf. Trotsky 1977, 146). The historical experience of the workers' movement in People's Poland has confirmed that "class struggle is a process producing the working class" (Lebowitz 2003, 179–184), and that the struggle for and the exercise of workers' control "must be seen as a preparation for situations of 'dual power,' in connection with the conquest of the whole political power" (Panzieri 1976, 23).

## The First Political Expropriation
## of the Working Class: 1945

In 1944–1945, the liberation of Poland by the Red Army and the assumption of power by a Stalinized workers' party led to the overthrow of the capitalist political and economic regime. Already during the Nazi occupation, German imperialism had generally expropriated the Polish industrial bourgeoisie. The defeat of this imperialism coincided with the generalized demand for the nationalization of the main means of production. The widespread practice by workers, begun in the wake of liberation, of taking over abandoned enterprises and reopening them under the direction of ad hoc "works councils" (*rada zakladowa*), garnered the support of the new state power in gestation. Still very weak, the new state had no choice but to count on the organizational and productive initiative of the workers as a decisive factor in the industrial and economic reconstruction of the country.

Nonetheless, for numerous Communist and left-wing Socialist cadres, this was not a pragmatic but rather a programmatic issue: they wanted all industrial power to be handed over not just to the new state, but to the working class itself. However, the February 1945 government decree on works councils barely gave them limited rights to participate in the management of enterprises. When the decree came into force in May, eleven days later it was annulled by an instruction from the Ministry of Industry enforcing the full and exclusive singular power of the chief manager over an enterprise. This illicit act represented a huge blow by the bureaucracy that was quickly consolidating itself inside the economic state apparatus. The works councils, deprived not only of any capacity to manage the enterprises but also of any right to co-management, were incorporated into the labor unions, which were soon transformed into "transmission belts" for the governing party and, in fact, for the state apparatus (Golebiowski 1961; Kowalewski 2007). The defeat of this first self-management movement of the working class was soon followed by strike movements against food shortages, low wages, the rise of production quotas, and the lengthening of the workday (Kaminski 1999).

Eventually, by overcoming the large obstacles that dependent capitalism had placed in the way of the development of the productive forces, it was possible to achieve an extensive industrialization of the country. Between 1950 and 1956, the number of industrial workers increased by 70 percent. Between 1938 and 1958, the proportion of the industrial labor force with respect to the total active population more than quadrupled. The new working class diluted within its ranks the "older" working class that was the bearer of the class practices, experiences, and memories of struggle. The new working class lent itself rather easily to the increases of exploitation through Stakhanovism[2] and "socialist emulation," but it also learned to resist through "negative control" over the labor process, and to use, in a rudimentary fashion, the weapon of the strike. Between 1951 and 1953, during the

2 Named for Alexey Stakhanov, a Soviet coal miner in the Donets Basin whose team in 1935 increased its daily output sevenfold, Stakhanovism was officially aimed at increasing industrial production by the use of more efficient division of labor and working techniques. In actuality it was aimed at drastically speeding up and intensifying human effort, analogous to demands placed on workers in capitalist enterprises. Stakhanovism resulted in low-quality products and disorganized production processes and was massively resisted by workers as a means of brutal overexploitation. Its use lapsed gradually after Stalin's death.

most intense phase of industrialization, a new wave of strikes took place. The power of the bureaucracy, which was politically organized in the framework of the Polish Unified Workers' Party (PZPR)—the backbone of the state machinery—revealed itself to be much more fragile than it appeared.

## The Workers' Council Movement: 1956

In June 1956, the city of Poznan witnessed Poland's first use of the mass inter-enterprise strike combined with street demonstrations. One hundred thousand workers held a rally in the public square. There were also attempts at armed insurrection by the new working-class elements, but they were not supported by the older class. The bureaucracy responded with the occupation of the city by ten thousand troops and three hundred sixty tanks. There were fifty-eight deaths. However, the onset of a serious political crisis of the bureaucratic regime prevented even those who took up arms from being condemned to prison (Jastrzab 2006).

Barely four months later, the working class erupted again, with its more advanced sectors organizing democratically elected workers' councils (*rada robotnicza*). This time, during the dramatic days of October, these councils actively and decisively intervened in a new regime crisis. Armored columns of the Soviet Army were marching toward Warsaw from their bases in the western part of Poland. Under the direction of Lechoslaw Gozdzik, a young Communist leader of the Warsaw auto works, the workers' councils acted in alliance with the student movement, the reform anti-Stalinist sectors of the PZPR, and the troop commanders of the Ministry of the Interior, ready to resist a possible Soviet military intervention.

The main objective of these workers' councils was to establish self-management as the basis for workers' and socialist democracy. A general point of reference was the Yugoslav "self-management socialism." For the radical left—the so-called October left—that headed the movement, the key issue to be resolved was: who should control the means of production, the bureaucracy or the working class? "Within the ideological systems of the radical left the concept of the working class was fundamental. The working class was the most important sector of society, the vanguard and the driving force of the transformations that could lead to an exploitationless and classless society. The 'October left' was convinced that only the workers that took into their hands the means of production could achieve political democracy" (Friszke 2010, 29, 32). "If workers' councils emerged that could take power within the enterprises, then a real revolution could take place and power . . . would shift from the bureaucracy to the organized workers" (Kuron 2002, 31).

The Law on Workers' Councils, which was passed in the Diet (parliament) in November 1956 under pressure from the October left and the working-class movement, established that "the workers' council manages the enterprise in the name of all the workforce." Many other articles of the same law limited its reach when not overtly contradicting it; regardless, its passage was a great victory. However, the new leadership of the PZPR, headed by Wladyslaw Gomulka, prevented any coordination of the workers' councils or the establishment of a Workers' Diet or a Chamber of Self-Management that could take over the democratic management and planning of the national economy. Gomulka also repressed a strike by streetcar workers in Lodz and shut down the weekly *Po Prostu*, the organ of the October left, when it was about to launch the slogan "All power to the workers' councils" (Lopienska and Szymanska 1986).

These councils were active in more than 3,300 enterprises. In December 1958, the Diet passed a new law on workers' self-management that not only diminished the councils' role to the level of "organs of co-participation of the workforce in the management of enterprises," but also forced the councils to share the "co-participation" with the committees of the party organization and the bureaucratized labor union. Thus, by disempowering them, the law condemned the workers' councils to a slow but sure extinction (Sowa 1979).

During the so-called "small stabilization" of the Gomulka regime, based on price-wage stability, the standard of living of the workers and of the population in general improved. Between 1957 and 1960, real wages increased by 20 percent and strike activity diminished to a quarter or a fifth of what it had been in the period before 1956: from around eighty or a hundred strikes down to about twenty strikes a year.

## Blood Wedding on the Baltic Coast: 1970

During the first years of the 1970s, at the University of Warsaw, student groups of left opposition began to emerge, led by two former militants of the October left, Jacek Kuron and Karol Modzelewski. In 1965, the circulation of their "Open Letter to the Party"—a critique of the bureaucratic regime, a call for an antibureaucratic revolution, and a program for the institutionalization of a workers' democracy organized through a national system of workers' councils—was the cause for the first imprisonment of Kuron and Modzelewski (Friszke 2010, 81–353). Fifteen years later, the "Open Letter," little known outside the immediate political circles of the authors, would serve as a political and programmatic reference for some of the militants and leaders of the Solidarity labor union, even though the authors themselves had by that time renounced its contents. For this reason, Barker (1982) was correct in seeing in this letter the "missing link" of the prehistory of Solidarity.

In March 1968, the political group headed by Kuron and Modzelewski unleashed a student rebellion for socialist democracy at the University of Warsaw that spread to all the universities in the country. It was the only mass movement in People's Poland that did not arise within the working class (Eisler 2006; Oseka 2008; Kowalewski 2008a; Friszke 2010, 472–883). Although the student movement called for their support, the workers remained largely quiet until their own uprising in December 1970.

As a protest against rising prices of consumer basics—increases of between 16 and 31 percent—mass strikes combined with demonstrations and street fighting were detonated in the industrial cities of the Baltic Coast, mainly in Gdansk and Szczecin. The police and the army intervened and killed forty-four people. In Gdansk, where the building of the provincial committee of the PZPR was besieged and set on fire, the main instigators of direct actions during the struggles against the repressive forces were the youngest workers. Their lack of experience in mass struggles was a deciding factor in the unfolding of the uprising in the city. In some places, a semi-insurrection took place, and a local dynamic of "dual power" was created. In Gdynia, where the uprising was better organized and articulated by workers than in neighboring Gdansk, the municipal authorities were forced to reach an agreement with the city strike committee and essentially handed over the local government. The immediate response by a regime that perceived the danger of the establishment of local workers' power was the massacre of eighteen workers by armored army troops (Domanski 1991; Eisler 2000a).

In Szczecin, during the street fights, crowds of workers set fire to the buildings of the party's provincial committees and labor unions and took the police headquarters by assault; thirteen workers were killed and twenty-eight armored vehicles destroyed. Street fighting ceased with the outbreak of a general strike, combined with factory occupations. This was the first mass sit-down strike in People's Poland and the first time that the right to freely organize in labor unions was demanded. The city strike committee, with its headquarters in the Warski shipyard representing worker forces from more than 120 enterprises, established a veritable workers' power in Szczecin. Despite an army siege and strong repression, the "dual power" dynamic in the city was able to prevail for five days (Glowacki 1989; Paziewski 2000, 2008; Wegielnik 2010a).

As a result of the uprisings, Gomulka was forced to resign, discredited as he was for having authorized the intervention of the army and the use of firearms against the working masses. He was replaced as the head of the PZPR by Edward Gierek, the powerful party boss of Upper Silesia, the largest industrial center of the country. Gierek recognized the working-class nature of the uprisings on the Baltic Coast; he also acknowledged the need to reestablish the party's ties with the workers and to reform "actually existing socialism."

The rebellion came to an end, but when new strikes were organized in Szczecin a month later, in an unprecedented gesture Gierek went to the Warski shipyard and personally participated in long debates with the delegates of the strike committee. He also met with the workers' delegates in Gdansk, promising to "develop the country, strengthen socialism, and improve the workers' standard of living." He also promised that the people would never again be fired upon (Wacowska 1971; Wegielnik 2010b). However, it wasn't until the great strike of February 1971 by fifty-five thousand women workers of the textile industry in Lodz that Gierek was forced to revoke the price increases decreed by Gomulka (Mianowska and Tylski 2008).

Barely a month after the rebellion of the Gdansk workers, democratic elections were held at the Lenin shipyard to revive all three bodies of the tripartite Conference of Workers' Self-Management, established by the 1958 legislation: the workers' council, the enterprise council of the labor union organization, and the enterprise committee of the party organization. In the Northern shipyard, also in Gdansk, forms of workers' self-management emerged at the level of brigades. In the Warski shipyard in Szczecin, the strike committee became an independent democratic representative body called the "Workers' Commission."

The Workers' Commission's main task, which Gierek approved, was to monitor the elections to the bodies of the Conference of Workers' Self-Management to ensure that they were held in a democratic manner. Elections to the conference bodies were also held in many other Szczecin enterprises. After three weeks, the Workers' Commission was formally dissolved, but it continued to function informally and some of its leaders were also active in the shipyard union council. During the official celebration of May Day in Szczecin, the former Workers' Commission organized a "black march" to protest the impunity of the perpetrators of the bloody repression of December, but afterward the informal commission slowly disintegrated due to severe blows struck by the political police, including murder and attempted murder (Baluka and Barker 1977; Krasucki 2007; Wegielnik 2009, 2010c).

The first half of Gierek's decade witnessed an explosive economic expansion. Real wages and salaries increased by 42 percent, but at the same time there was an unprecedented growth in social inequality: 30 percent of the population now lived below the poverty line. The central political power—composed, in this regime, of the state political bureau, the Central Committee of the ruling party, the government, key ministries, and bureaucratic economic agents—lost its control, already precarious, over the balance of forces among the different "branch and territorial pressure groups" within the bureaucracy. The powerful groups in control of heavy industry exercised immense pressure on the accumulation fund, greatly strengthened by Western loans; consequently the consumption fund was reduced and bureaucratic planning disrupted. The foreign debt to capitalist countries increased twenty-five-fold and stifled the economy, while chaotic investment drove it into disarray and the massive reorientation toward exports strangled internal consumption.

The potentiality for extensive industrial development was clearly declining, as it was based on the extraction of absolute surplus labor. Bureaucratic domination, increasingly holding back the development and socialization of the productive forces, prevented intensive development based on the growth of labor productivity. The effect was to systematically wear down the labor force through the extension of the workday and the intensification of work. As one example, the workday of the miners was extended to eleven hours with a six-day week, and forty-two Sundays a year. During the second half of the decade, an acute socioeconomic crisis broke out, eventually provoking a revolution at the end of the decade. Its motor was the contradiction—exacerbated by the accumulation of other contradictions that fused together into an explosion—between the increasing tendency toward the social appropriation of the means of production and its management by a parasitic stratum. Strike activity rose again, approaching the levels of the 1940s and '50s.

The most important movements were the strike actions and demonstrations in June 1976 against price increases, which took place simultaneously in the industrial cities of Radom (where a general strike broke out, the party's provincial committee building was set on fire, and street fights against police forces occurred); Ursus (a suburb of Warsaw, where the workers blocked the main national and international railways); and Plock. This time, the government immediately revoked the price increases, the army did not intervene, nor did the police fire on the multitudes, but the detained workers were savagely beaten and dozens of workers were condemned to several years of imprisonment (Pawlowicz and Sasanka 2003; Sasanka 2006; Sasanka and Stepien 2006). The antiworker repression reactivated the former left-wing opposition that, crushed during 1968, had renounced its Marxist inspiration and antibureaucratic revolutionary program. On a purely democratic basis, the revived opposition formed the Workers' Defense Committee (KOR). The underground newspaper *Robotnik* (worker), published by one of its sectors, helped prepare the ground for the emergence of an independent workers' movement.

## A Workers' Revolution: 1980–1981

On July 1, 1980, the government decided that all meat products provided in the cafeterias and kiosks of the enterprises—very scarce due to the economic crisis—were to be sold according to "commercial" prices, much higher than regulated prices. This was the proverbial "spark that ignites the prairie fire." It incited a huge wave of strikes in July in Lublin and in August in Gdansk and Szczecin. In Gdansk, the slogan hung on the gate of the Lenin shipyard read: "Workers of all enterprises, unite!" Meanwhile, in Szczecin the slogan in the meeting hall of the Warski shipyard strike committee stated: "Yes to socialism, no to its distortions." The strikes spread to the other industrial centers of the country.

Accumulated historical experiences of repression translated into significant changes in the behavior of the strikers. This time the workers, having learned from the bloody repressions and chaotic developments of the uprisings in 1970 and 1976, decided not to take to the streets. Instead, they revived what the Szczecin workers had done years before: they occupied the factories, where they were able to self-organize, exercise control over the struggle, and discuss and decide democratically how to fight. The first of the twenty-one demands put forth by the inter-enterprise strike committee of Gdansk was to legalize the labor unions independent of the party and of the employers, and the second was to guarantee the right to strike.

Paralyzed by its own internal crisis, the regime refrained from using force. First it accepted negotiations, under strict monitoring by the striking workers, with three inter-enterprise strike committees: the Gdansk and Szczecin shipyards and the coal mine in Jastrzebie-Zdroj. Then, in the agreements reached with these committees (August 30–31 and September 3), as well as with the inter-enterprise workers' committee based at the Katowice steelworks (on September 11), the government accepted all demands, including the more radical ones. The agreements stated: "The necessity is acknowledged of creating new, self-managed labor unions, genuinely representing the working class," and "the new law on labor unions will guarantee workers the right to strike" (Paczkowski and Byrne 2007, 66–80). Almost immediately, based on these inter-enterprise strike committees, all over the country workers organized inter-enterprise constituent committees or inter-enterprise workers' commissions of a new, independent, self-managed labor union, Solidarity (Solidarnœc). These regional committees and commissions supported the buildup of the new union in all workplaces.

Solidarity went beyond the traditional limits of industrial unionism by prioritizing the unity of the working class, over and above its sectoral interests. It was not a confederation of branch federations but a national federation of regional union organizations; the regional organizations, in turn, federated the workplace union organizations. This unique form of organization gave the Polish workers' movement an impressive capacity for mobilization, struggle, and exercise of a counterpower.

The new union intended to rediscover and reproduce internally the classical principles of workers' democracy. The regional general assemblies of delegates were sovereign bodies: they freely made all the fundamental decisions on the regional level and elected the regional leaderships, which were charged with putting these decisions into practice. In turn, the regional leaderships responded to and were subordinated exclusively to the regional assemblies, rather than to the national leadership. The regional assemblies also ratified the decisions made by the national commission of Solidarity, composed of the regional delegates, in order to confirm the validity, timeliness, and regional feasibility of these decisions. At all organizational levels the union leaders were democratically elected; they were accountable to the electorate and were revocable at all times (Garton Ash 1983; Barker 1986; Kowalewski 2008b). In the course of its formidable and sudden rise and expansion, Solidarity would organize more than nine million wageworkers, around 55 percent of the total, marginalizing the former bureaucratic unions.

The possibility, sought by "moderates" on both sides, of a conflicting but lasting coexistence with the bureaucracy revealed itself to be mere illusion, as tensions and confrontations multiplied and became more severe. It was necessary to launch warning strikes and threaten longer-lasting ones in order to achieve a number of basic demands: wage increases that had been promised, the legal recognition of Solidarity without needing to mention "the leading role of the PZPR" in its bylaws, Saturday as a day off, free access to the mass media, and more. In October 1980 and again in March 1981 an indefinite general strike with factory occupation was almost declared. If one of these two strikes had taken place, the consequences would have been difficult to predict; most likely it would have led directly to a revolutionary crisis. The bureaucratic regime, profoundly destabilized and afflicted with internal contradictions and sectoral disputes, had gone off course. The PZPR lost control of its constituency: half its members had joined Solidarity, while many of its grassroots organizations became autonomous, coordinating with one other to form horizontal structures, and frequently allying with the independent union.

Once again, Poland was threatened with the possibility of Soviet military intervention. "In the history of socialist societies this was the most serious crisis in which labor relations . . . became the focus of a struggle for solutions to the economic crisis and for political power" (Petkov and Thirkell 1991, 183).

## The Struggle for Workers' Self-Management: 1981

In many enterprises, the workers expelled chief executives, blocked new bureaucratic appointments, and questioned the bureaucratic management of the industries. Among the union militants and workers unionized within Solidarity, the conviction was widespread that in People's Poland the legitimate collective owner of the means of production was the working class, and that it was necessary to wrench those means away from the bureaucracy. A new refrain emerged: "A union is to defend; we also need a workers' council to manage."

In January 1981, the Lodz regional leadership of Solidarity declared its refusal of any attempt to reanimate the defunct Conference of Workers' Self-Management, and in general of any idea that the workers "co-participate" in the management together with the bureaucracy. The Lodz leadership became the first to call for the struggle for a "true workers' self-management," which it defined as "the transfer of all power in the enterprises to the workers' councils" (Kowalewski 1981a; Phelps 2008). The stand taken by this regional union leadership, which included a reference to the workers' council experience of 1956, was to have a very strong influence on the organization and development of the movement for workers' self-management throughout the country. In the factories of Lodz and many other regions, the workers, relying on the support of the Solidarity union organizations, began to organize "constituent committees of workers' self-management" and to elect workers' councils.

By July 1981, the growing movement for workers' self-management on the national scale began to group itself around two different tendencies. One, the Network of Solidarity Union Organizations of the Leading Enterprises, was headquartered in Gdansk. It demanded that "workers be given back their factories" and proposed a legislative act called the "Law of the Social Enterprise." The legislation supported transferring the management of public enterprises to the workers' councils; it did not propose that they undertake the management of the entire national economy, but suggested substituting the imperative central planning with an indicative model, and broadening the commodity relations. The other tendency, the Interregional Initiative for the Cooperation of Workers' Councils, met in Lublin. This tendency encouraged the establishment of regional coordinations of workers' councils and then of a national coordination in order to build, from the bottom up, an integrated system of councils that would take into its hands the management and planning of the development of the entire economy and society. It also demanded the institution of a second chamber in the Diet, the Chamber of Self-Management, conceived as a workers' parliament. If this goal were attained, it would have meant taking "dual power" to the highest level, and posing the question of not only who was to run the enterprises, but also who was to run the state.

At the outset, the balance of forces between these two tendencies was more or less even; however, the balance began to tip toward the second tendency as it gained more and more support from the grassroot militants of the movement for workers' self-management. As of the autumn of 1981, this tendency held the leading role in the movement (Kowalewski 1985, 1988; Jakubowicz 1988).

The First National Congress of delegates of Solidarity, which took place in Gdansk over two sessions in September–October 1981, was the most representative and democratic assembly in the history of the Polish workers' movement. It also served as a grand arena for the struggles between the tendencies within the movement. The question of workers' self-management became the main issue of the debates in the congress, as well as the main theme of confrontation between the congress and the regime. At the time, workers' councils were active in about 20 percent of public enterprises, particularly the largest ones, located in the greatest concentrations of the industrial proletariat. The more radical of the two tendencies was moving full speed ahead. Its standpoint provided the basis for the historical programmatic resolutions adopted by the congress.

In these resolutions, Solidarity demanded a democratic socioeconomic reform at all levels "associating planning, self-management, and the market," which could be "put in practice solely as a result of the mass workers' movement."

> The fundamental unit of organization of the economy is to be the social enterprise, managed by the workers' council and operationally led by the director appointed by the council on the basis of a contest and revocable by the former. . . .The reform must socialize planning. The central plan should reflect the wishes of society and be accepted by it. For this reason, the debates on central planning should be made public. . . .The true workers' self-management must be the fundament of the Self-Managed Republic" (Solidarnosc 1981).

The path being opened was quite clear. The self-managed republic should be built according to the "model of the 'workers' councils' inherited from one of the most fruitful currents of European socialism"; and "in order to guarantee better allocation of the collective benefits in favor of wageworkers, as well as a true social democracy in the enterprises. . . .The workers should constitute the fundament and the summit of all future political edifications" (Bafoil 2000, 81). It was the highest point ever reached under "actually existing socialism" by the working-class "moral economy" (Rossman 2005).

The first session of the Solidarity congress ended with a vote on a resolution that triggered a panicked reaction from the regime. In this resolution, denounced by the regime as unconstitutional, the congress warned that if the Diet adopted the laws on workers' self-management and enterprise as proposed by the PZPR, Solidarity would call to boycott them. Frightened by this challenge, an important sector of parliamentary deputies opted not to vote on two bureaucratic projects unless a compromise could be reached with Solidarity and its approval be guaranteed. For the first time, the regime ran the risk of losing the majority vote in parliament, which had always been assured by a landslide. Its disintegration was accelerating.

To the astonishment of the majority of the delegates, the president of Solidarity, Lech Walesa, took advantage of the intermission between the sessions of the congress to come to the aid of the regime. In violation of the principles of union democracy that governed Solidarity, and in violation of the sovereignty of its congress, Walesa negotiated an agreement with the Diet that portended an enormous setback for the movement for workers' self-management. The day before the inauguration of the second session of the union congress, the Diet passed the laws under dispute, in order to place before Solidarity a fait accompli. The second round began in a storm: many of the delegates denounced the agreement reached by Walesa, subjecting him to relentless criticism that undermined his leadership—which, until then, had been unquestioned. The legislative action was considered a declaration of war. In response, by a great majority of votes, the Solidarity congress adopted a new resolution proposed by the radical sectors. It declared that the union would unconditionally support the struggle for true workers' self-management, according to the will and aspirations of the workers. It also proposed to organize of its own accord a national referendum, so that the workers could democratically choose between the laws enacted by the Diet and the project supported by Solidarity.

At the same time, Solidarity's regional office in Lodz decided to activate and radicalize the struggle for workers' self-management by applying the tactics of the active strike (also known as the "work-in strike"). The tactics consisted of launching a large strike movement with factory occupation, led by the union. The movement would advance from a passive occupation to an active one, from a "sit-down" to a "work-in." This meant that during the strike production would be retaken by the workers, initially under the direction of the strike committees, then the power over the enterprises—conquered through direct action—would be handed over to the workers' councils (Kowalewski 1981b). The idea found a favorable response in many sectors of the union. The Lodz regional organization was relying on the Solidarity organizations in other regions to follow the same course, and prepared to launch the strike. For Kennedy (1991, 101) there is no doubt that "Kowalewski is right to argue that a regional active strike in Lodz would have brought other provinces into the struggle," and that "the active strike was, as Kowalewski acknowledges, a *revolutionary* strategy" that "effectively abandoned Solidarity's self-limitation." The regime denounced the idea as an open attempt to seize political power; it was also strongly criticized by Walesa's moderate followers, who defended the strategy of the so-called "self-limited revolution," which should not pose the question of power. Yet the relation of forces in the "civil" battlefield was increasingly moving in favor of the independent workers' movement, which was becoming more and more radicalized (Kowalewski 1982).

But the active strike was never launched, because the regime acted faster by declaring martial law. Without the leadership of a workers' party that could guarantee political guidance in accordance with the dynamics and aspirations of the working class, and in an unfavorable relation of forces on the international level, the movement was incapable of resolving the question of power. The bureaucracy proved capable of doing so, but only by shifting the confrontation from the civil arena to the military battlefield, where it held overwhelming supremacy, and where the mass movement found itself defenseless.

On December 13, 1981, the Military Council of National Salvation was formed ad hoc, completely outside the constitutional order, under the direction of the first secretary of the PZPR and prime minister, General Wojciech Jaruzelski. The military council decreed a "state of war" or martial law, confined nearly ten thousand Solidarity activists in internment camps, surrounded all the occupied enterprises with tanks, and crushed the working-class movement. The workers were unable to recover from this defeat, which nine years later resulted in the restoration of capitalism in Poland.

As Marx would have put it, "by deed instead of by argument" the struggles for workers' self-management in Poland "have shown that production on a large scale, and in accord with the behests of modern science, may be carried on without the existence of a class of masters employing a class of hands," and that, for a time, "in broad daylight the political economy of the middle class succumbed to the political economy of the working class" (Marx 1985, 10–11; cf. Lebowitz 2003).

## References

Aldcroft, Derek H. 2006. *Europe's third world: The European periphery in the interwar years*, Aldershot: Ashgate.

Arnot, Bob. 1981. Soviet labour productivity and the failure of the Shchekino experiment. *Critique*, no. 15.

———. 1988. *Controlling Soviet labour: Experimental change from Brezhnev to Gorbachev*, Armonk, NY: M.E. Sharpe.

Bafoil, François. 2000. La classe ouvrière post-communiste: Des "héros au pouvoir" à l'exclusion des "petites gens." *Genèses* 31, no. 1.

Baluka, Edmund and Ewa Barker. 1977. Workers' struggles in Poland. *International Socialism*, no. 94.

Barker, Colin, ed. 1982. *Solidarnosc: The missing link? A new edition of Poland's classic revolution-*

*ary socialist manifesto: Kuron & Modzelewski's open letter to the party.* London: Bookmarks.

_____. 1986. *Festival of the oppressed: Solidarity, reform, and revolution in Poland, 1980–81.* London: Bookmarks.

Domanski, Pawel, ed. 1991. *Tajne dokumenty Biura Politycznego: Grudzien 1970.* London: Aneks.

Eisler, Jerzy. 2000a. *Grudzien 1970 w dokumentach MSW.* Warsaw: Bellona.

_____. 2000b. Grudzien 1970: Geneza—przebieg—konsekwencje. *Sensacje XX Wieku* [Sensations of the Twentieth Century, television series], Warsaw.

_____. 2006. *Polski rok 1968.* Warsaw: IPN.

Filtzer, Donald. 1986. *Soviet workers and Stalinist industrialization: The formation of modern Soviet production relations, 1928–1941.* London: Pluto Press.

Friszke, Andrzej. 2010. *Anatomia buntu: Kuron, Modzelewski i komandosi.* Krakow: Znak.

Garton Ash, Timothy. 1983. *The Polish revolution: Solidarity, 1980–82.* London: Jonathan Cape.

Glowacki, Andrzej, ed. 1989. *Robotnicze wystapienia w Szczecinie 1970/1971: Wybor dokumentow i materialow.* Szczecin: Uniwersytet Syczecinski.

Golebiowski, Janusz W. 1961. *Walka PPR o nacjonalizacje przemyslu.* Warsaw: KiW.

Jakubowicz, Szymon. 1988. *Bitwa o samorzad 1980–1981.* London: Aneks.

Jastrzab, Lukasz. 2006. *Rozstrzelano moje serce w Poznaniu: Poznanski Czerwiec 1956 r.— straty osobowe i ich analiza.* Warsaw: Comandor.

Kaminski, Lukasz. 1999. *Strajki robotnicze w Polsce w latach 1945–1948.* Wroclaw: Gajt.

Kennedy, Michael D. 1991. *Professionals, power, and solidarity in Poland: A critical sociology of Soviet-type society.* New York: Cambridge University Press.

Kowalewski, Zbigniew Marcin. 1981a. *"Solidarnosc" i walka o samorzad zalogi.* Lodz: Ziemi Lodzkiej, Zarzad Regionalny NSZZ "Solidarnosc."

_____. 1981b. *O taktyce strajku czynnego.* Lodz: Ziemi Lodzkiej, Zarzad Regionalny NSZZ "Solidarnosc."

_____. 1982. Solidarnosc on the Eve. *Labour Focus on Eastern Europe* 5, no. 1–2.

_____. 1985. *Rendez-nous nos usines! Solidarnosc dans le combat pour l'autogestionouvrière.* Paris: La Brèche.

_____. 1988. *Poland: The fight for workers' democracy.* San Francisco: Walnut.

_____. 2008a. Marzo 1968 in Polonia: Un interludio studentesco tra le lotte operaie. In *Cosa vogliamo? Vogliamo tutto. Il '68 quarant'anni dopo,* ed. C. Arruzza. Rome: Alegre.

_____. 2008b. Solidarnosc. In *La France des années 1968: Une encyclopédie de la contestation,* ed. A. Artous, D. Epsztajn, and P. Silberstein. Paris: Syllepse.

Krasucki, Eryk. 2007. Antypochod 1 maja 1971 r. w Szczecinie. *Biuletyn Instytutu Pamieci Narodowej,* no. 7.

Kuron, Jacek. 2002. Lechoslaw Gozdzik i jego czas historyczny. In *Wasz Gozdzik naszym Gozdzikiem: Droga zyciowa i aktywnosc polityczna Lechoslawa Gozdzika,* ed. K. Kozlowski. Szczecin: Archiwum Panstwowe.

Kusmierek, Jozef. 1980. O czym wiedzialem. In *Raport o stanie narodu i PRL.* Paris: Institut Littéraire.

Lebowitz, Michael. 2003. *Beyond Capital: Marx's political economy of the working class.* New York: Palgrave Macmillan.

Lopienska, Barbara and Ewa Szymanska. 1986. *Stare Numery.* London: Aneks.

Marx, Karl. 1982. *Capital,* vol. 1. Harmondsworth: Penguin/NLR.

_____. 1985. Inaugural Address of the Working Men's International Association. In *Collected works of Marx and Engels,* vol. 20. New York: International Publishers.

Mianowska, Ewa and Krzysztof Tylski, eds., 2008. *Strajki lodzkie w lutym 1971: Geneza, przebieg i reakcje wladz.* Warsaw and Lodz: IPN.

Oseka, Piotr. 2008. *Marzec '68.* Krakow: Znak.

Paczkowski Andrzej and Malcolm Byrne, eds. 1987. *From Solidarity to martial law: The Polish crisis of 1980–1981. A documentary history.* Budapest: Central European University Press.

Panzieri, Raniero. 1976. *Lotte operaie nello sviluppo capitalistico.* Torino: Einaudi.

Pawlowicz, Jacek and Pawel Sasanka. 2003. *Czerwiec 1976 w Plocku i wojewodztwie plockim.* Torun: Wyd. Adam Marszalek.

Paziewski, Michal. 2000. Rewolta uliczna 17–18 grudnia '70 w Szczecinie. In *Pomorze Zachodnie w Tysiacleciu,* ed. P. Bartnik and K. Kozlowski. Szczecin: PTH.

_____ . 2008. Dramatyczny tydzien—opis wydarzen, ofiary, pytania badawcze—Szczecin. In *Konferencja Grudzien '70—Pamietamy,* ed. A. Friszke and H. Sikora. Gdansk: Fundacja Centrum Solidarnosci.

Petkov, Krastya and John E. M. Thirkell. 1991. *Labour relations in Eastern Europe: Organisational design and dynamics.* London and New York: Routledge.

Phelps, Christopher. 2008. Solidarnosc in Lodz: An interview with Zbigniew Marcin Kowalewski. *International Labor and Working-Class History* 73, no. 1.

Post, Charles. 2000. Ernest Mandel and the Marxian theory of bureaucracy. In *The Legacy of Ernest Mandel,* ed. G. Achcar. London: Verso.

Pravda, Alex. 1981. Political attitudes and activity. In *Blue-collar workers in Eastern Europe,* ed. F. Triska and C. Gati. London: Allen & Unwin.

Rey, Pierre-Philippe. 1977. Contradictions de classe dans les sociétés lignagères. *Dialectiques,* no. 21.

_____. 1985. Production et contre-révolution. *Canadian Journal of African Studies / Revue Canadienne des Études Africaines* 19, no. 1.

Rossman, Jeffrey J. 2005. *Worker resistance under Stalin: Class and revolution on the shop floor.* Cambridge, MA: Harvard University Press.

Sasanka, Pawel. 2006. *Czerwiec Geneza—przebiega—konsekwencje.* Warsaw: IPN.

Sasanka, Pawel and Slawomir Stepien, eds. 1976. *Czerwiec 1976.* Warsaw: IPN.

Smuga, Cyryl [ Jan Malewski]. 1985. Ni plan, ni loi de la valeur: Sur la logique de l'accumulation et la crise économique en Pologne. *Quatrième Internationale,* no. 19.

Solidarnosc. 1981. Program NSZZ "Solidarnosc" uchwalony przez I Krajowy Zjazd Delegatow. *Tygodnik Solidarnosc,* no. 29.

Sowa, Ewa. 1979. Historia rad robotniczych po 1956 r. Manuscript in possession of the author, Katowice.

Ticktin, Hillel. 1973. Toward a political economy of the USSR. *Critique,* no. 1.

Trotsky, Leon. 1977. *The transitional program for socialist revolution,* New York: Pathfinder Press.

Turchetto, Maria. 1995. Ripensamento della nozione di "rapporti di produzione in Panzieri." In *Ripensando Panzieri trent'anni dopo.* Pisa: Biblioteca Franco Serantini.

_____ . 2007. I "due Marx" e l'althusserismo. In *Da Marx a Marx? Un bilancio dei marxismi italiani del Novecento,* ed. R. Bellofiore. Rome: Manifestolibri.

URGENSE. 1982. Un taylorisme arythmique dans les économies planifiées du centre. *Critiques de l'Économie Politique,* no. 19.

Wacowska, Ewa, ed. 1972. *Rewolta szczecinska i jej znaczenie.* Paris: Institut Littéraire.

Wegielnik, Tomasz. 2009. Szczecinska Komisja Robotnicza: Grudzien geneza Sierpnia. www.sedinum.stetinum.pl.

_____ . 2010a. Pierwszy strajk generalny w PRL. www.sedinum.stetinum.pl.

_____ . 2010b. Strajk styczniowy roku 1971. www.sedinum.stetinum.pl.

_____ . 2010c. Po wielkich strajkach 1970/1971. www.sedinum.stetinum.pl.

Anticolonial Struggle,
Democratic
Revolution, and
Workers' Control

# 11

## Workers' Control in Java, Indonesia, 1945–1946

**Jafar Suryomenggolo**

After the Second World War, as the colonized nations of Asia and Africa still endeavored to gain national independence, other newly independent countries were hailed for realizing their native populations' aspirations to end the colonial regimes, bringing profound changes in the geopolitical situation of the day. Since the 1950s there have been numerous studies examining the sociopolitical implications of these changes at the level of the state-society relationship. In particular, political scientists have analyzed the interaction between the postcolonial state and the labor movement, in the hope of illuminating the nature of the political structure of the new state. A common technique of this analysis is to use the labor movement as an important lens for viewing how the independent states were grafted upon the newly free society—in terms of the differences from their colonial predecessors—and how that interaction might have shaped domestic policies regarding civil society.

Over the past five decades we have gained important insights from various in-depth country studies (as well as some others with a comparative approach), which have shown that the interaction between the postcolonial state and the labor movement is indeed too complex to be reduced to a one-dimensional perspective. Some studies, especially of the African continent, have made a significant contribution to the literature by documenting the nation's extensive timeline of experiences, thereby solidifying the connection of the labor movement to the postcolonial state in the struggle for independence. In this regard, the analysis of the origins of the state-labor relationship is enriched with the historical background of the nation.

Studies of colonial societies have demonstrated that in the complex spatial system of exploitation under the colonial state, native labor was the main requirement for the continued production of commodities to be consumed in the mother state. Native peasants were hurled off their lands and transformed into dependent workers in order to provide a supply of manpower to the economic system of the colony. Disciplined under the "modern" technologies of the industrial framework brought into the colony, native workers served the interests of the colonial state. Thus, when labor unions were introduced into the urban cities of the colony, their main organizing force was the accumulation of natives' experiences against colonialism, garnered under nationalism. In French and British Africa, as noted by Frederick Cooper (1996), the formation of labor unions was actually meant as a challenge to colonial policy. The colonial state, with its repressive apparatus and exploitative structure toward African resources, was viewed by the native workers with rage; this created a yearning for national liberation. In many parts of colonized Asia, labor unions exposed the native workers to a common experience of equality in brotherhood that transcended the local-cultural boundaries among them—providing both an antidote to the hierarchical system of colonial racism and the necessary modern organizing power with which they could stand against the corrupt bureaucracy of the colonial state.

In this regard, the history of labor unions in the colonial landscape is a history of colonial repression and the resistance of native workers against the state as the manifestation of the abusive system. In terms of its historical militancy against colonialism, the labor movement in Asia and Africa proved a potential ally in terms of popular mobilization. Thus, it has been commonly noted that native labor leaders were an integral part—in some countries, the dominant actors—of the nationalist movement in the colony whose main objective was to seize (colonial) power in order to take control of national resources.

Once these leaders succeeded in expelling their colonial rulers from the land, they began building a state that could formally accommodate their nationalist aspirations. In these newly independent countries, the state was no longer considered a threat, as it had been under the colonial system, but instead was envisaged as embodying the natives' struggle for their own nation—including labor's expectations of freedom from the colonial capitalist system. By virtue of its nationalist ideological links, the labor movement provided support in the formation of the new state, hoping that in exchange the new state would institutionalize protections for native workers that they had never enjoyed under the colonial state. Meanwhile, the institutions of the new state were still fragile under the sociopolitical circumstances left by the colonial state, so the support of the labor movement was of substantial importance.

It was necessary for these newly independent states to develop a labor constituency in order to support and strengthen the nationalist government in its early formation. Thus labor issues were accorded significant attention;

it was crucial for the new state to delineate those issues as a legacy of the colonial times, and to present a promising path to enable the labor movement to reach its objectives under the new regime. The main reason for this, as Kassalow (1963, 258) concludes in his comparative study of the labor movement across postwar countries, was that "although this working class is relatively small, the very nature of what is going on in these countries tends to make it important politically."

However, many studies have demonstrated that the labor movement was later easily drawn—sometimes entrapped or lured—into the postcolonial state's projects for a variety of reasons that had little to do with labor. In Vietnam, the development of independent labor unions was curbed with no trouble once the Communist Party of Vietnam—the major resistance group fighting against the colonial French—took power over the course of the revolution and designated the "unions [as] one of the mass organizations that carried out party policy" (Nørlund 2004, 108). The party seized the moment and claimed to represent the voices of the working class, thus dissolving the autonomy of the labor movement and co-opting it into their state-building programs. In Botswana, the postcolonial state leaders were quick to restructure and take control of the labor movement, declaring that "the trade unions should develop a role which meets the needs of the country and should not adopt . . . an imported trade union philosophy with its folk history and perceptions built up over years of strife in Europe" (Mogalakwe 1997, 77). This illustrates that most nationalist leaders in Asia and Africa, in order to serve their political purposes, were motivated to neutralize the labor movement upon capturing the political space in their newly independent states. To varying degrees, under the rhetoric of rejecting class conflict as a "European" or "Western" perspective, they have succeeded in subordinating the labor movement to the postcolonial state.

This chapter suggests that this political space (however limited) could have been granted by the postcolonial state for the labor movement to pursue its own objectives; it could also be rescinded in particular sociopolitical circumstances whereby the state was faced with the issue of its own development. In the case of Indonesia, the labor movement and the nationalist leaders might have complemented each other in the struggle for the independence of the nation, but they were also pursuing their own agendas, and this often led to tension following the dissolution of the colonial regime.

This is precisely what happened in Java, Indonesia, during the first few months of independence in 1945–1946. After the defeat of both the Japanese occupation army and the incoming Dutch troops attempting to recolonize the by then independent Indonesia, workers began to seize control of factories, railway stations, and plantations. In those early months of August 1945 to January 1946, as the new Indonesian state was just coalescing and developing its institutions, workers started their organizing drive by setting up workers' committees to manage those public facilities themselves. This chapter further suggests that workers' control is not merely a historical accident, but has the capacity to give workers a taste of power and autonomy. Indeed, in the case of Indonesia, workers' control laid the keystone for the formation of an independent labor movement in the development of a postcolonial state, in spite of its emergence during the time of social instability that marked the political shift from colonial to postcolonial order.

## Labor and the New Indonesian State in Revolution

August 17, 1945, the day the Proclamation of Indonesian Independence was signed, allowed for little preparation time in bringing forth a new state, as there was a rush to fill the power vacuum under the global circumstances, foremost the catastrophic events in Japan. Kahin (1952, 138) notes, "The establishment of a government for the newly proclaimed Republic proceeded rapidly," and within a week the first constitution was drafted. Although the new government had to face the Dutch, who were eager to return with their troops under the sponsorship of the Netherlands Indies Civil Administration (NICA), it continued efforts to establish the necessary institutions and extend state functions to various fields. From the very beginning the republic was eager to operate as a normal state. It had a formal set of basic principles that encompassed the necessary sociopolitical structure of a sovereign state and an orderly framework of offices and decrees from the central government in Jakarta—which later moved to Yogyakarta—to administer functions and develop military units. These components of the state's institutions were well designed, at least on paper.

The republican cabinets, however, changed every few months and were replaced one after the other. In reality, the scope of the government's aims was limited and restricted due to budget constraints, as even members of the cabinet did not receive their monthly wages regularly. In these early days of independence, many of the state institutions were just starting to gear up, trying to penetrate society by imposing rules and regulations. The state's scope, institutions, and instruments were only beginning to take form—as was the case with the Djawatan Kereta Api (railway bureau), described below.[1] Thus, the revolutionary period may be regarded as an early phase in the Indonesian state's formation. In the midst of revolu-

---

1 It is only with caution that we can regard the newly proclaimed republic as a normal state with a fully functioning administration. Within the government, elites and politicians were competing for ideological influence, thus the image of the strong state as a leviathan was hardly apparent in daily life.

tionary zeal, the Indonesian state was taking shape through a process of trial and error.

While the state was busy getting organized, labor activists at the national level arranged a general meeting. On September 15, 1945, in Jakarta, the Barisan Buruh Indonesia (BBI—Indonesian Labor Front) was formed with the purpose of uniting and coordinating workers from the various industries (Sandra 1961). This meeting and the BBI itself enjoyed active support from Iwa Kusumasumantri, minister of social affairs. There was a strong possibility that he might provide further unofficial backing by promoting the BBI's resolutions in the government.[2] His long-standing personal interest in the labor movement aside, Kusumasumantri's involvement in this arrangement clearly indicated the state's active role in the promotion of unionism.

The labor movement proved to be a critical ally in popular mobilizations due to its historical militancy against colonialism, establishing its political importance to the new Indonesian state (see Ingleson 1981; Shiraishi 1990). As a source of civilian defense when the army had not yet been formed, BBI was perceived as channeling and mobilizing the movement in the struggle for independence. Hence, the labor movement at the national level was viewed as part of the arm of the state.

## Spontaneous Acts of Workers' Control

While at the national level labor activists were forming an alliance to strengthen the independence struggle, workers at the local level had already begun organizing weeks earlier for the same purpose. These workers would do what was necessary to defend the proclamation of independence (which they had learned of via the radio), with or without the support of the state; they came together in regional groups and were ready to protect it. It was under this "pure" nationalist orientation that workers began to wrest control of factories, plantations, and railway stations from the Japanese occupation army.

Railway workers were the first to engage in such an act by taking over their stations. They were daring, young in spirit, and determined to transform their nationalist convictions into real action. This led them to initiate the takeover of the central office of the railway bureau, as described in one account:

> In Jakarta, the spirit to take over power from the Japanese occupation army was so overwhelming, that on the night of September 3, a meeting was held

---

2 Anderson (1972, 213) notes that Iwa Kusumasumantri not only unofficially promoted BBI's demands but also "officially recognized the BBI as the sole representative of federated labor on Java."

in Bro. Bandero's house just to discuss the steps in taking over power from the Japanese army. The next morning, without even waiting for any news from last night's meeting, the take-over was carried out in the Jakarta office of the West Exploration area. Since September 4, 1945, the management of the Railway Bureau in Jakarta has been taken over from the Japanese army (Panitia Penjusun Buku 1970, 29).

On that same day, their fellow manual workers at a different railway station, the Manggarai railway center, proceeded with a similar action:

> At the Manggarai railway center in Djakarta, railway workers passed a resolution in the name of all railway employees in Indonesia, which declared the railway systems in Indonesia to be milik negara Republik Indonesia (state property) as of that day. Indonesian personnel were urged to consider themselves state employees, and a committee headed by Soegandi was set up to facilitate their take-over of the railways (Sutter 1959, 293).

Although not in a coordinated fashion, the news from Jakarta spread to other areas in Java. By the end of September, the initiatives of these young Indonesian workers had intensified to the point that all the railway stations throughout Java had been declared state property. Due to the stations' vital function as public space as well as means of transport, the railway workers had a crucial security task during the revolution: to guard the stations and keep them under republican control. In stations throughout Java's main cities, these workers formed groups to complete the takeover process. By October 5, the takeover process had been completed rather smoothly, and subsequently it was formally announced that all railway stations in Java were no longer under the control of the Japanese army; not a single Japanese soldier was allowed to enter any railway station, office, or workshop (Prarwitokoesoemo 1946).

In taking over the stations, the groups of railway workers were acting with an intention that served the nationalist purpose. Similar accounts were recorded among the plantation workers in Java[3]; this same nationalist motive provided the initial impetus for their actions, as well as for the later groupings to ensure that the takeover process remained under their control. The railway workers formed a unit at each station in order to execute this task accordingly, and the station at which they worked became their main point of reference. This territorial forming of groups was similar to that of manual workers in many other industries.

---

3 Unlike their counterparts in Java's plantation areas, who were active in taking over plantation estates, plantation workers in North Sumatra did not undertake such actions as "they were unlikely candidates for revolutionary militancy" because of the "little room for labor activism on the estates and little opportunity for contact with the nationalist underground outside their borders" (Stoler 1983, 163).

These initiatives did not conclude with physical control of the stations. Due to the unstable political situation, the railway workers realized it was their obligation to administer and manage the railway system, despite their often limited knowledge and skills—inevitably without any support from the government. Seizing control proceeded quite easily, as reported in many accounts, but once the workers got their hands on the station operations, they began to organize in a new direction. The task of managing the railway's operation made it immediately necessary to set up an accountable, workable system of self-organization.

Adam Malik (1950, 71), a *pemuda* (youth) leader at that time who witnessed the phenomenon, recalled that upon the takeover of Central Station in Jakarta, the workers selected heads for each department from among their group, and these individuals "swore their oath and promise in the upper open hall of the Jakarta station before the lower-level workers, youths and general public." Later, within each exploration area office,[4] they formed a group known as *dewan pimpinan* (council of leaders)—their original form of primus inter pares. This council of leaders supervised, managed, coordinated, and ultimately held authority over the railway system.

Selo Soemardjan, based on his personal observations and experiences as "a member of the country's civil service during the time," also noted a similar episode among the sugar plantation workers in Yogyakarta:

> A meeting of all the native factory and field workers was called to decide upon the status of the factory and to determine the way in which the open positions should be filled. The meeting unanimously decided not to recognize the foreign company as owner of the factory, but no decision was reached as to its future ownership. A second decision was made that the workers then present should run the factory and the cane plantation. Use of the profits was to be determined by a board, its composition reflecting the former technical staff and its head to be the director. In overwhelming majority, a man who had been the assistant of a former European sugar analyst and who had chaired the meeting was elected director; he was the only one who had any specialized education in sugar production (actually only a one-year training period). The other open positions were to be occupied by the highest-ranking and oldest native worker in each branch (1957, 194).

---

4 Since the Dutch colonial period, in early 1900s, the railway system in Java—similar to Java's administrative matters—has been divided into three "exploration areas": West, Central, and East. Each was administered by one office in the respective area. They were coordinated and supervised under the Balai Besar (Central Office) located in Bandung, West Java. In the end of March 1946, the central office was moved to Cisurupan (in the West Java area). For a year, until May 1947, it was moved again to Gombong and Kebumen (in Central Java). Later, after the first Dutch military attack in July 1947, it was moved to Yogyakarta.

Here we can see how the plantation workers followed the same path as the railway workers, first moving to manage the operations of the plantation by organizing a meeting to consolidate their group, then later electing a representative to supervise the directions given by the management.

This initial control of operations by the workers themselves created a situation in which, for example, authority over the plantation was placed with one of their own colleagues who had more skills and experience. The elected councils of leaders took on the tasks of management and made themselves accountable to the workers, as they understood the control of production was in their hands. The leaders' skills were acknowledged as the grounds for letting them have the last word on how things should be arranged—as such, the railway workers accepted that their leaders would impose order and discipline in the operation of the railways.[5]

There is no record of outside instigators trying to implement workers' control from above or to influence the workers' consciousness with propaganda. Instead the instances of workers' control all seem to have emerged organically during the revolutionary period, the workers framing their as a nationalist duty in the best interest of the young nation. Workers' self-management emerged as a suitable response to the unstable socioeconomic environment of the day, and the workers eventually established independent paths to controlling the facilities.

After electing members to positions of authority, workers began to resume their designated jobs. In the case of the railway workers, following the seizure of control, they operated, managed, and coordinated the railway system based on their respective areas under the direction of the council of leaders, dewan pimpinan. The organization of work was still based on the hierarchy constructed during the Japanese occupation, which differentiated workers into three levels—high, middle, and lower—but this time the workers weren't required to report to any Japanese military officials or white colonial Dutch master. Most railway workers remained in their previous positions, except the few who were selected as members of the dewan pimpinan, and performed their routine duties to secure the railway operation as usual. For months the workers maintained service, and the operation of the railways during this time was noted by Sutter (1959, 359) as being "reasonably smooth . . . [although] with the occurrence of fighting and incidents connected with the expansion of British (and Dutch) bridgeheads," as it

---

5 I found no document describing an account of discontent among the workers under their council of leaders, or how power within the council of leaders could be checked and revoked in the case of abuse of power. Such discontent might have occurred; however, there was a general understanding that the workers accepted that the elected council would be the decision-making body in the railway operation, and the council seems to have performed its responsibilities well.

connected Java's major cities regardless of the occupying forces. With skills acquired during the period of Japanese occupation, these young workers proved capable of operating and coordinating the railway system, successfully serving the public for the first several months of independence under the management and coordination of their own council of leaders.[6]

Now that the management and operation of these public industries were under workers' control, at this point the railway and plantation workers were inspired to improve their livelihood—to cater to their own needs as workers—by extending the organizational capacities of their groups. Lingering memories of the poor working conditions during the Dutch colonial times and especially under the Japanese occupation prompted the desire for improvements. In the case of the railway workers, the stations had become their centers of organizational activity directly after being seized from the Japanese authorities. Not only were the working conditions at the stations substandard, but also the workers were not receiving their regular wages to be able to provide for their basic daily needs. In the meantime the workers came to a common understanding that by performing their usual duties, they as a group were accountable and, as such, earned a sort of collective entitlement—they were aware it was informal and provisional in nature— to maintain the railway operation.[7] A similar situation also occurred in the case of the plantation workers, as witnessed by Selo Soemardjan:

> The director and the board, not knowing to whom they owed responsibility, communicated every important decision to their fellow workers by written announcement upon the communication boards. As an additional incentive for the workers, the board decided to distribute a part of the sugar product to them, everyone receiving an amount of sugar according to the position he held in the hierarchy. Another part of the sugar product was put aside to support the guerilla troops. Relations with others outside the factory were carried out by the director, assisted by the members of the board. In this way the factory for several months acted as an autonomous organization, resisting any interference from outside (1957, 195).

---

6 There are records as to how the railway workers had to deal with a lack of equipment and the operation of old trains with inefficient engines. Due to a lack of coal, workers had to collect at least twenty-five thousand tons of teakwood daily to keep the track running. It was a common situation railway workers faced daily, even until late 1947. See AMK 1947.

7 After the government had successfully taken over some of the major factories and plantations held previously under workers' control (around March 1946), the issue of salary became a serious concern among the workers, who were considered civil servants. In May 1946 the government drafted a salary composition for civil servants, which soon caused deep resentment in the labor movement as it favored the higher-ranking workers (the officials). Unions filed protests and negotiations lasted for two years. With some revisions, the government finally drafted a new salary composition for civil servants in 1948.

What had once been the property of the Dutch capitalists or the colonial state had been expropriated by the hands of the workers—including production. Workers came to perceive that they had the right to the products of their own labor on the plantation. Under their own management, they ran and administered the workplace so as to continue production, eventually contextualizing the situation in such a way as to defend their own economic interests. This system of self-management allowed them to retain their jobs and survive the hardships of this time.

This form of organization and production was therefore of major significance to a newly independent country on the edge of economic chaos, in which workers had to protect their economic interests in the face of shortages of basic life necessities. Instead of using conventional tactics such as strikes, sabotage, or the abandonment of the factories that they had worked during colonial times, they had coordinated operations among themselves. As they organized this self-management system, the workers pushed to create a structure in which a division of labor was based not on one's social status but instead simply on the functions that one performed. This was in stark contrast to the hierarchal and racially discriminatory working conditions to which the workers had earlier been made accustomed under the colonial system.

The self-management system also empowered the workers by allowing them to gain control, make decisions, implement what they decided, and (re)distribute the results of their own efforts—all of this being carried out by the workers themselves, without the oversight of an entity above them. The council of leaders, although equipped with managerial authority, acted as the workers' representative in putting together all their collective work. Under the Dutch colonial system, the production of goods (especially in the case of the sugar plantations) was determined by the demand of the world market, and under the Japanese occupation army, workers' manpower was channeled solely to support the war campaign (Brown 1994).

In this new system of mutual coordination and self-management, the line of industrial command was horizontal, in contrast to the vertical structure of industrial organization common under the capitalist system. Self-management was thus a phenomenon that defied the colonial capitalist system of production and its pillars: the racial division of labor, market-based production targets, uncontested prerogatives of the colonial employers, and the liberal legal-based conception of private property. Furthermore, with its successful operation—as manifested in the smooth operation of the railway and the fine workings of the plantations—it called into question the need for the commanding orders of a patron, whether economic (the employers) or political (the state). It is precisely because of this implication that the Indonesian workers' experiment with self-management was ultimately short-lived.

## The Political Discourse on "Self-Management" versus "Syndicalism"

By the end of 1945, the state had gradually become more politically stable and the central government better established, and its attentions turned to the self-management of the railways stations and plantations. This the state viewed with deep concern. Since the plantations were the main means of production in Java, and the railway stations the means of transporting those products, their strategic functions made state control desirable—if not imperative—in the government's view. With a growing number of industrial factories and estate plantations under workers' self-management, the government surmised that the spread of this social phenomenon would not be conducive to general economic stability or a sound investment climate, as some enterprises, legally speaking, still belonged to the Dutch.[8] As workers had de facto control of the establishments but not legal ownership, self-management created an economic dilemma for the new state. By early 1946 the state was trying to regain control over Java's railway stations and plantations.

The state also feared workers' self-management as a potential source of political instability. In November 1945 a parliamentary cabinet was introduced as the form of governance of the new Indonesian state. This form was chosen partly because the state leaders, Soekarno and Hatta (president and vice president, respectively), recognized that the previous political instruments were inadequate to stave off the mushrooming of party formation among their political rivals. They also wanted to show the outside world that the new Indonesia was not a puppet of the Japanese army, but instead a democratic state with real legislative power under the newly transformed Komite Nasional Indonesia Poesat (KNIP—Central Indonesian National Committee) as the transitional parliament. Indeed, many political parties, either based on leftist ideas or with a religious bent, were formed during this time of political change.

While the government was dominated by Socialists or leftists of various kinds, they did not have a strong hold over the parliament, whose members represented various groups in the society. In the meantime, Tan Malaka, a respected Communist leader who was in exile during the time of Dutch colonial rule and returned shortly after the Japanese occupation of Java in July 1942, entered the national scene and soon gained enough political power through popular support to oppose the government. In particular he advocated the seizure of all foreign establishments without any compensation, although he did not explicitly say they ought to be under workers' con-

---

8 Soemardjan (1957, 196) notes that workers' control "prevailed in almost every foreign-owned factory in the province."

trol.[9] Tan Malaka formed the umbrella organization Persatuan Perdjuangan (the Fighting Front) to lead the course of the revolution he was espousing.

Following this development, labor activists on the national scene began to separate themselves from the state. Under the seemingly democratic political climate for the new state, labor leader Sjamsu Harja Udaja—despite dissent within the BBI—saw the chance for the labor movement to pursue its own political agenda. He mobilized the movement to establish the Partai Buruh Indonesia (PBI—Indonesian Labor Party); it soon held its first congress on December 15, 1945. With this new form of labor organizing, activists at the national level pushed the labor movement into the political arena in search of power.

A political party formed by the labor movement itself was a clear sign of its discontent with the state. This development was viewed by the governing elites as a move away from labor's previous loyalty; they believed that labor activism should be kept to a minimum, under the control of the state, and moreover should support the nascent government at all costs. Thus, the governing Socialist cabinet under Sjahrir (November 1945–March 1946) was suspicious of labor's loyalty and further support, fearing that perhaps it would pursue its own goals or be mobilized by opposition groups. The PBI had been in close contact with Tan Malaka's group Persatuan Perdjuangan, which had been outspoken in opposing Sjahrir's negotiation with the Dutch; the resulting political accord, the Linggadjati Agreement, stated as one of its provisions, "the recognition by the Republic of all claims by foreign nationals for the restitution and maintenance of their rights and properties within the areas controlled by the Republic."[10]

In light of these developments, the new Indonesian state began to reconsider the idea of labor as an ally in the revolution. Labor's industrial activities in organizing self-management were now cast as "political" activism. In contrast to what the minister Kusumasumantri had done earlier by supporting and in fact promoting pro-labor policies, the state now feared the labor movement's potential control over the national economy and its ambitions in the political arena. From this time on, labor was perceived as a separate entity from the state that needed to be monitored and whose political maneuvers had to be rendered predictable.

---

9 Kahin (1952, 172) mentioned three sources of support for Tan Malaka: his personal charisma as a leader with outstanding vision, some political and military leaders who were discontented with Sjahrir's policies, and the "surging tide of nationalism which made it difficult for many people to countenance any negotiations whatsoever with the Dutch." For Tan Malaka and his organization, Persatuan Perdjuangan, see: Anderson 1972, ch. 12, 269–295. For the life of Tan Malaka, see Mrázek 1972.

10 See Wolf (1948, 43–44) for an analysis of this agreement.

Starting under the Sjahrir cabinet, labor was viewed warily, as an opponent whose power could challenge or even take over the state. Labor was constantly reminded of its duty to defend the nation and to bind itself to the struggle for independence. At the local level, the governing elites labeled the self-management of workers as "anarcho-syndicalism"—a term borrowed from Marxist literature to describe the danger and risks of workers being beyond the state's control[11]; however, the label was not intended to describe the actual process of workers' control, rather to reject and condemn the phenomenon.

Using the term "syndicalism" brought the political discourse regarding workers' control onto new terrain. In contrast to the actual self-management practices of the workers, it implied that their industrial actions had always had a political end, and that workers' control in particular was a challenge to the state's authority. In the context of the Indonesian revolution, the term "syndicalism" itself was double-edged; the labor movement was acknowledged to have the power to supply mass mobilization for the state, as well as the power to topple the existing government, still in its infancy. That is, the "proletarian power" of the labor movement was celebrated, admired, and deemed functional, but also feared for its potential backlash.

Far from suppressing or taming the labor movement, Sjahrir was more concerned with incorporating labor under the state's arm so as to uphold the image of a democratic government. He realized that suppressing labor would only increase its militancy. In a short manuscript published in 1933 (republished in 1947), Sjahrir wrote that "labour should not give all of its power to the independence struggle at the expense of fulfilling its own objectives" (25). From this we can construe that he must have calculated that labor might have its own program to pursue, and thus the state could not expect its full support. The best course of action for the state then, would be to channel the labor movement toward the interest of the state. To this purpose, incorporation was the moderate way to handle the labor movement.[12]

It was Vice President Hatta who named and criticized publicly the workers' self-management practices as "syndicalism" at the Yogyakarta economic conference in February 1946 (Sutter 1950, 377). The conference was organized with the goal of creating a blueprint for the national economy; thus Hatta, speaking more as an economist than as a politican, warned the labor

---

11 Reid (1974, 125) notes that "Abdulmadjid and his colleagues had brought (the term) from Holland."

12 NEFIS Publicatie no. 11, dated June 27, 1946 (061300), notes that "the whole trend of regime policy is to make unions corporatively orged [*sic*] than syndicalist." This document was kindly provided by Professor Benedict Anderson.

groups not to "misconstrue syndicalism as economic democracy or arbitrarily replace their managers without the knowledge or approval of the Government" (Sutter 1959, 393). There is little doubt that Hatta must have heard reports from several local governments on how difficult it was to keep the labor groups under their control. His reading of the political situation might have unsettled the labor groups, who at that time saw no organizational alternative, as they were still searching for a suitable format to accommodate their nationalist aspirations while also protecting their interests as workers.

Although the PBI under Sjamsu tried to radicalize the workers involved in the widespread self-management practices in the belief that workers' discontent with economic matters could be exploited to topple the government (Anderson 1972, 251–6), other parties of the left—although they did not support Sjahrir's cabinet program—shared the ruling Socialist Party's suspicions of political labor activism. It seemed there was a kind of consensual outlook among the political elites, especially on the left, in viewing the phenomenon as a potential danger for the national economy. In addition, many prominent national leaders, based on their interpretation of Marx, did not support the practice of workers' control and simply condemned it as "syndicalism"—an attitude dominant among the urban intellectuals.[13] In the absence of employers (or any group representing the capitalist class), they believed the national economy ought to be administered by the state's authority; labor was just one component under its command. Furthermore, they all held the same opinion that self-management should not be allowed to become a permanent institution. Since it was strongest in the often foreign-owned industrial production sectors, they encouraged the workers to hand over control of the enterprises to the central government.

From the workers' perspective, there was not any political objective to be gained by having permanent control over the plantations and railways other than to maintain the operation of public facilities. Railway workers understood the importance of transportation during this challenging and dangerous period, and by managing and maintaining the railway operation well, just as they had during "normal" times, they believed they were doing their part to defend the nation's independence. Although labor groups were depicted as difficult to control under the local government, no accounts ever reported that workers at the local level had transformed the self-management practices into specific political objectives. It is apparent that workers' self-management was a new phenomenon to comprehend, and with this

---

13 Many Socialist leaders were setting up "labor courses" in their attempt to educate the masses on Marxist-Socialist ideas. These trainings later on led to the establishment of the "Marx House" in Madiun.

the national political elites sought to encapsulate it or channel it along the lines most advantageous to their own political objectives—instead of listening directly to the workers themselves and appreciating what they had achieved and sacrificed in order to support the nation's independence. By ignoring the voice of labor, the elites managed to confine self-management within the limits of their own political vocabulary and goals.

After Hatta's speech in Yogyakarta the government directed its attention toward overcoming the situation. As there was no solid plan, their general objectives were simply to gain control over the self-managed workplaces and to tame the potential threat of the labor movement at the local level.

Labor activists at the national level also supported the objective of taming the workers' self-management practices and gaining control of the situation. This was evident from the BBI's official statement on the matter (BBI 1946). In this statement the blame was put on workers at the local level, who were described as having "a misconception of the real meaning of socialism," and self-management was dismissed as nothing more than a "*Kinderziekte*" (childhood disease)—again, a political label borrowed from the Dutch vocabulary—"[that] does not have roots in the history of the Indonesian labor movement." The BBI recommended that the government "pursue immediate and correct actions" in order to accomplish the following:

1. Expand and deepen information and education for labor that would guide the workers to the true labor struggle, as well as undertake efforts to consolidate the still unsteady labor organizations.
2. Coordinate all the still abandoned establishments, plantations, and factories by enlisting the cooperation of the production leaders, and also take a firmer stand toward the status of some foreign-owned vital enterprises that were still under workers' control.
3. Cleanse the labor movement of the influences of damaging persons or groups, as it was also part of the labor leaders' responsibilities to operate with restraint.

It was understood that the BBI's official statement was meant to support the government under any given circumstances. Although claiming to be labor's representative, labor activists at the national level, nevertheless, were not truly aware of what was at stake. Indeed, by calling for the state's arm to take control of self-management and "cleanse the labor movement," the national-level activists had given the government a blank check to interfere in the labor movement's course. Events later demonstrated that the BBI did not in fact have a strong grip at the local level where workers were struggling on their own. By dismissing self-management simply as a "childhood disease," the BBI played down the real progress of labor's self-organization, instead binding the movement to the direction of the state.

The government, however, realized that its institutional capacities were still too limited to abolish the self-management practices in total. Initially, the government took action based on each specific situation. The railway was centralized from the top down by means of government directives (*makloemats*). The administration and management of the railways was centralized under a new governmental body, the Djawatan Kereta Api (railway bureau), which created a management board representing twenty-seven divisions and sub-areas. Membership on the board was by exclusive appointment by the central government; its establishment formally dissolved the workers' dewan pimpinan.

Afterward, knowing that it would be difficult—if not theoretically impossible—for the state to bring the widespread self-management practices in other industries solely under the control of the central government, it was announced on March 20, 1946, that "all enterprises formerly controlled by the Japanese government would now be managed by the regional governments of the Republic" (Reid 1974, 125). Subsequently, self-management was transformed as the workers remodeled their dewan pimpinan to organize an independent union. Under the state's direct policy to put an end to self-management, workers were quick to divert their activities to form new organizations that could retain and channel their nationalist orientation while also defending their interests as workers.

## The Historical Significance of Workers' Control to Indonesia

As we have seen in the case of Indonesia's labor-state relationship from 1945–1950, to understand the nature of organized labor at that time requires bringing into perspective the revolutionary situation that Indonesians were facing. This was a crucial period during which the Indonesian state was working desperately to consolidate its resources and establish power. As the revolution in Indonesia was spontaneous and the resulting economic conditions devastating, the Indonesian labor movement had an unprecedented opportunity to pursue its own interests, rather than focusing its struggle solely on defending the nation's independence.

The Indonesian labor movement was also seeking a possible role within the juncture of political events and was thus not easily confined to the postcolonial state's arrangement. This situation provided the material context for workers in Java to assert authority over the means of production, under the relative absence of state power. It created a space for the labor movement to gain self-control and to decide its own route, well beyond the workers' prior skills and knowledge. During the period of state formation, workers' control boosted the bargaining position of the labor movement so that the postcolonial state had much more to consider than simply absorbing the labor movement into its sphere of control.

It is evident that the experience of self-management made the Indonesian workers self-reliant within their own organizations. Although workers' control and the self-management of railway stations and plantations exercised by the dewan pimpinan lasted only a few months, the experience prepared the labor movement to muster a strong defense against the postcolonial state's eventual normalization drive to tame it.

Since the Indonesian labor movement had discovered that it could transmute nationalist determination into the advancement of its members' interests under the self-management operation of the railway stations and plantations, this in turn served as a building block for the movement's political capacity and, in time, for its political strength to stand before the postcolonial state. This gave rise to Indonesia's postcolonial labor movement of the 1950s, which could maneuver and organize its interests for the protection of its members, allowing it to take its own initiatives and affording it a means for evading, if not resisting, the roles designed by the state. Thus the state-labor relationship in Indonesia had more of a dialectical character, rather than the monolectical kind, in which the state could immediately impose certain limitations on the development of an independent labor movement through actions of coercion and violence, as was the case in Egypt (see Beinin and Lockman, 1998) or through co-optation via the promotion of national labor law, as in the case of French Africa (Cooper 1996) and the Philippines (Kerkvliet 1999).

## References

AMK [Young Railway Workers]. 1947. The Republican railways. *Voice of Free Indonesia*, no. 61 (1947): 319–320.

Anderson, Benedict. 1972. *Java in a time of revolution: Occupation and resistance, 1944–1946.* Ithaca, NY: Cornell University Press.

Barisan Buruh Indonesia [BBI]. 1946. *Merdeka*, May 11.

Beinin, Joel and Zachary Lockman. 1998. *Workers on the Nile: Nationalism, communism, Islam and the Egyptian working class, 1882–1954.* Cairo: American University in Cairo Press.

Brown, Colin. 1994. The politics of trade union formation in the Java sugar industry, 1945–1949. *Modern Asian Studies* 28 (1): 77–98.

Cooper, Frederick. 1996. *Decolonization and African society: The labor question in French and British Africa.* Cambridge: Cambridge University Press.

Ingleson, John. 1981. Bound hand and foot: Railway workers and the 1923 strike in Java.

*Indonesia* (April 31, 1981): 53–87.

Kahin, George. 1952. *Nationalism and revolution in Indonesia.* Ithaca, NY: Cornell University Press.

Kassalow, Everett. 1963. Unions in the new and developing countries. In *National labour movement in the postwar world*, ed. Everett Kassalow. Chicago: Northwestern University Press.

Kerkvliet, Melinda Tria. 1999. Manila workers' union, 1900–1950. PhD dissertation, University of Hawaii.

Malik, Adam. 1950. *Riwajat proklamasi 17 Agustus 1945.* Jakarta: Widjaja.

Millen, Bruce. 1963. *The political role of labor in developing countries.* Washington DC: The Brookings Institution.

Mogalakwe, Monageng. 1997. *The state and organised labour in Botswana: "Liberal democracy" in emergent capitalism.* Aldershot, UK: Ashgate Publishing.

Mrázek, Rudolf. 1972. Tan Malaka: A political personality's structure of experience. *Indonesia* 14 (October): 1–48.

NEFIS. 1946. Publicatie no. 11 (061300). June 27. From the personal collection of Professor Benedict Anderson.

Nørlund, Irene. 2004. Trade unions in Vietnam in historical perspective. In *Labour in Southeast Asia: Local processes in a globalised world*, ed. Rebecca Elmhirst and Ratna Saptari. London: Routledge Curzon and International Institute of Social History.

Panitia Penjusun Buku, ed., 1970. *Sekilas lintas 25 tahun perkereta-apian, 1945–1970.* Bandung: PNKA.

Prarwitokoesoemo. 1946. Kereta Api didalam perdjoeangan kemerdekaan satoe tahoen, *Kereta Api* 24, 18–20.

Reid, Anthony. 1974. *The Indonesian Revolution, 1945–1950.* Hawthorn, UK: Longman.

Sandra. 1961. *Sedjarah perkembangan buruh Indonesia.* Jakarta: Pustaka Rakjat.

Shiraishi, Takashi. 1990. *An age in motion: Popular radicalism in Java, 1912–1926.* Ithaca, NY: Cornell University Press.

Sjahrir. 1947. *Pergerakan Sekerdja.* Yogyakarta: Sarekat Buruh Pertjetakan Indonesia.

Soemardjan, Selo. 1957. Bureaucratic organization in a time of revolution. *Administrative Science Quarterly* 2 (2): 182–199.

Stoler, Ann Laura. 1983. In the company's shadow: Labor control and confrontation in Sumatra's plantation history, 1870–1979. PhD thesis, Columbia University.

Sutter, John. 1959. Indonesianisasi: Politics in a changing economy, 1940–1955. Vol. 2: The Indonesian economy during the revolution. Data paper no. 36-II, Cornell University.

Wolf, Charles Jr. 1948. *The Indonesian story: The birth, growth and structure of the Indonesian republic.* New York: John Day Co.

# 12

# From Workers' Self-Management to State Bureaucratic Control

*Autogestion* in Algeria

**Samuel J. Southgate**

In the Algerian context self-management refers to a popular movement that arose in the immediate aftermath of independence in 1962. This movement was primarily constituted of the rural working class, which seized control of colonial estates abandoned by the *pied-noir* (settler) population that had departed the country en masse as terms were reached between the French government and the Front de Libération Nationale (FLN). Workers in the cities also seized small businesses and factories in the chaotic aftermath of liberation. These actions represented a fait accompli for the new government, which emerged following a fratricidal conflict within the nationalist movement. Never envisaged by FLN leaders as a form of economic organization appropriate to post-independence Algeria, self-management offered both a practical solution to immediate economic problems and, later, a powerful ideological totem that purported to embody the country's embrace of socialism.

In reality self-management, or *autogestion,* represented something of a founding myth for the Algerian state. Though formalized and then theorized by Ahmed Ben Bella's FLN government, self-management was soon circumscribed in practice—to a significant degree through the legislation that supposedly institutionalized workers' control. However, while the laws outlining autogestion contained inherent contradictions, the underlying reasons for the neutralization of self-management are to be found in the dynamics of Algerian society at the economic, social, and political levels. This chapter will attempt to understand these dynamics by surveying the history of autogestion and examining the factors that rendered its initial promise a dead letter.

Given the set of extreme circumstances prevailing at the time of independence—a massive economic crisis, the departure of close to a million *colons* (colonials), the destruction wreaked by eight years of war and the displacement of three million people—we may feel entitled to ask whether the Algerian example is useful for comparative purposes. Yet not only does this case share substantial similarities with other examples of workers' control, many of which were likewise born in moments of social crisis, it also offers to illuminate a number of theoretical questions, especially regarding the role of the state bureaucracy, the relationship between self-management and the state, the logics of "economic" and "political" power under workers' control, and the nature of class struggle in such circumstances. These questions should be kept in mind as we consider the history of autogestion.

## Algeria at Independence: Crisis and Conflict

As the French government and the nationalist leaders of the FLN were negotiating Algeria's independence at Evian in the spring of 1962, an exodus was beginning. Thousands of colons of French and other European origins—many of whose families had been in Algeria for generations—were leaving the country. Even though the accords guaranteed the status and property of these settlers, most preferred to depart for France as the colonial order was overturned. A trickle of tens of thousands became a flood as independence was established. In all some nine hundred thousand settlers—almost the entire colon population—fled the country, leaving a devastating hole in the Algerian economy (Ruedy 2005, 185; Stora 2001, 124). As settlers left they scrambled to sell their assets, often to Algerian speculators at rock-bottom prices. Elsewhere properties were left in the care of Algerian managers or closed "temporarily." In many cases properties were simply abandoned. Ultimately one million hectares of land and seven hundred industrial enterprises were deserted (Lazreg 1976, 49).

Since the colonial economy had privileged the pied-noir population, their exodus presented the nascent Algerian state with an enormous problem. Not only did the colons' departure deprive the country of the vast majority of its managerial class, it was accompanied by the mass flight of capital, which—coming at the end of almost eight years of war—had a severe impact on the economy.[1] In addition, as the war reached its denouement, settlers and especially those grouped in the terrorist Organisation Armée Secrète smashed much of the country's social capital, destroying government buildings, factories, hospitals, and other infrastructure. After the stampede for France, not more than thirty thousand colons remained (Ruedy 2005, 185–186).

---

1 For figures on the economic situation pertaining at this time, see Ruedy 2005, 195; Bennoune 1988, 89–90; Amin 1970, 129–134; Stora 2001, 124.

The destruction inflicted on the country's infrastructure was matched by the destitution of its population. Apart from the dead, numbering at least in the hundreds of thousands, more than two million Algerians were released from "imitation concentration camps" where villagers had been interned as part of the French *regroupement* policy (Amin 1970, 127). Several hundred thousand refugees began to return from Tunisia and Morocco; in total, three million rural Algerians had been displaced during the war (Ruedy 2005, 190). Finally the various "clans" of the heterogeneous FLN were engaged in a fratricidal battle as the Armée de Libération Nationale (ALN), based outside the country, raced to Algiers to defeat its opponents in the Gouvernement Provisoire de la République Algérienne (GPRA) and their guerrilla fighters of the interior. This conflict was an expression of long-standing strategic and ideological differences within the FLN (Stora 2001, 180–185).

It is worth considering the structure of Algerian society at the moment of independence, since the experience of 132 years of French colonial rule had substantially altered indigenous social formations.[2] In rural areas, expropriation by colonists led to the pauperization of the Algerian peasantry, which was forced from the most fertile lands. Peasants were compelled to choose among struggling to continue their previous way of life, selling their labor to the French landowners, or migrating to the cities, including Paris (Bourdieu 1961, 134–192). The vast majority of peasants remained on what land they could, but significant numbers opted for the latter options.

The colonial economy has frequently been characterized as a "dual economy," with a "modern" technical European sector set alongside a "traditional" Algerian economy. While this formulation is unhelpful in some respects, there was certainly a duality in the case of agriculture, where large colonial estates were worked by an Algerian rural working class that, by independence, numbered 130,000 permanent and 450,000 seasonal agricultural workers. As rural–urban migration and urban populations increased dramatically during the war, there developed a small urban working class in colon factories and other enterprises. However, this class remained small—about 110,000 workers, owing largely to the character of the economy.

Oriented toward the colonial *métropole*, the colonial economy was geared to the export of primary products and used as a dumping ground for consumer products manufactured in France. Thus Algeria had a small manufacturing sector and negligible large-scale industry. The Algerian working class based in France, composed of four hundred thousand émigrés, was of lesser significance than a native, two million–strong urban "sub-proletariat,"

---

2 For more on class formation in colonial Algeria, see Lazreg 1976; Bennoune 1975.

a result of the expropriation of the peasantry and the high rate of rural population growth (Bennoune 1988).

While colonialism had assisted in the creation of these classes, it had hindered the development of other social strata. Since Algerians were systematically excluded from political and economic power and the economy's structure hindered the development of a native industrial sector, an indigenous bourgeoisie did not properly develop. There existed the remnants of a large landowning class in the countryside and the embryo of an entrepreneurial bourgeois class in the cities, but both were stifled by colonialism. However, there was a limited degree of social mobility for Algerians, and a petit bourgeois class had emerged. Often French-educated, francophone, and occupying positions in the liberal professions, this class took advantage at various points of the small concessions offered by the French for Algerian political representation. It had benefited from French reforms that brought more Algerians into low-level positions in the colonial administration but at the same time provided the cadres for the early nationalist movement, which demanded assimilation with France (Bennoune 1988, 93–94).[3]

It was the rural working class that, in the chaos before and immediately after Algeria's formal independence on July 5, 1962, seized control of many colonial estates. Upon the farms that were taken over, workers established management committees to continue production. There are numerous cases of such takeovers, although—owing to the situation at the time—the documentary accounts are not substantial. One example cited by Blair comes from a large agricultural estate composed of vineyards and wheat fields on the Atlas Plateau near Médéa. When the French patron and his family went "on vacation" in June 1962 and did not return for the wine harvest, "[t]he Algerian foreman and 150 workers continued to operate the farm as they had in the past." After a provisional government decree in August, "the farm was declared vacant and taken over by an elected committee. On the door of the mansion next to the inscription 'Domaine Malevalle 1914,' there appeared another one scrawled in black crayon, 'Ferme Collective Malevalle Bien Vacant 1962'" (1970, 47).

A similar phenomenon took place in urban areas, where factories and small businesses were commandeered. The Union Générale du Travailleurs Algérien (UGTA), established in 1956 and autonomous of the FLN, played a role in these occupations, especially in Grand Alger and Oran, where its leadership "had decided on the forced occupation of factories and commercial enterprises." The union had called as early as February 1962 for socialization rather than just nationalization of property, stating: "Independence

---

3 On the early national movement, see Ruedy 2005, 131–133.

is inseparable from the Revolution, but the Revolution is more important than independence" (Clegg 1971, 49). Once colons started leaving the country, the union appealed for workers to restart production, demanding they "direct and control the economy of our country." UGTA militants also attempted to spread autogestion by setting up workers' committees in the larger towns and on farms in the Mitidja and Cheliff valleys (Ottaway and Ottaway 1970, 50–53). The autogestion movement was strongest in the rich coastal belts where agriculture was organized in large estates with concentrated, proletarianized workforces (Ruedy 2005, 198–199). Around 1.2 million hectares of land and one thousand industrial and commercial enterprises were seized by workers and placed under self-management in the summer of 1962 (Tlemcani 1986, 97).

The extent to which these "spontaneous" takeovers represented the expression of the workers' "class consciousness" is a question that has been extensively debated in studies of the period (Clegg 1971, 48–56; Lazreg 1976, 89). Without entering the debate here, it may be useful to recognize that material interests played a part in their actions, but that the formation of workers' councils—a recurrent revolutionary form—overturned the preexisting relations of production and posed fundamental questions over the wider organization of society.

An important consideration is that workers were not the only ones to stake a claim to the former colonial economy. Individual Algerian speculators, guerrilla fighters, army officers, and bureaucrats all enriched themselves by acquiring colons' interests, sometimes expelling "illegal workers' councils" (Tlemcani 1986, 97). The colons' departure "paved the way for the quick enrichment as well as for the upward social mobility of the privileged social strata" (Bennoune 1988, 96). Furthermore, it was conceivable that the colons would return; many had left claiming they were merely taking a "vacation." There was nothing in the Evian Accord to suggest colons' property would be forcibly expropriated and, in fact, the provisional executive reassured settlers that their property would be guaranteed in an independent Algeria. In the August decree the executive demanded that departmental prefects protect abandoned properties, known as *biens-vacants*. There was no threat of nationalization, but if French owners did not return within thirty days the prefects were empowered to appoint managers. This set off a "wild stampede" by property-owning classes to register and claim biens-vacants (Ottaway and Ottaway 1970, 51; Clegg 1971, 47; Blair 1970, 46).

Even once autogestion was legalized by Ben Bella's government in the fall, it was explicitly stated that the colons' rights would be respected and settlers could return and be integrated into the new management structures. Yet the pace of workers' occupations accelerated after both the August government decree and Ben Bella's endorsement. Amid the rush to claim deserted properties and set against the legal context, the working class's seizure of the means of production can been interpreted as an attempt to guard against either the expropriation by the Algerian propertied classes or the establishment of neocolonialism. Indeed, there were many instances of confrontation between workers and prefects or Algerian bourgeois over abandoned property. Clegg provides two examples: in Céligny, crops and buildings bought by Algerians were burned by "irate peasants who felt they had not benefited from this transaction," while at Meloug the sub-prefect supported by local army units had put a private Algerian owner in charge of the estate, but he was driven off by agricultural workers who had already occupied it (1971, 48). Whereas the nationalist movement had attained political independence by overturning the colonial order, Algeria's working class demonstrated the effects in the economic arena. The nascent conflicts over self-management at this stage foreshadowed a coming battle over the country's economic future.

## Formalizing and Neutralizing Workers' Control

As mentioned, none within the FLN's senior ranks had envisaged workers' self-management as an appropriate model by which to structure the economy of an independent Algeria; in fact, the nationalist movement had been unable to outline a coherent vision of its plans for the country. The closest it came was with the Tripoli Program, written in May 1962 for the party's congress in the Libyan capital. The document—reflecting the political fault lines within the movement—denounced the FLN leaders' "petit bourgeois" and "paternalistic" instincts and called for a popular democratic revolution led by the rural masses. Its prescriptions revolved around three main areas: agrarian reform with land redistribution and the formation of state farms, state planning with workers' participation, and nationalization and state-led industrialization. Despite its analysis of Algerian society, the Tripoli Program did not "transcend the various statements made by the FLN throughout the war," and clearly favored *étatism* over workers' control (Lazreg 1976, 125).

By September 1962 Ben Bella was in power, supported by the army, and he faced a very different political landscape from that outlined in the Tripoli Program. Economic activity had plummeted, the government hemorrhaged tax revenues, its deficit swelled, and it faced the burden of stabilizing both the economy and a society in turmoil due to the effects of war and manifold socioeconomic crises. To make matters worse, the administration itself was in shambles. The bulk of the state's employees had departed—including three hundred thousand workers responsible for the administrative and economic management of the country—meaning the government was rendered unable even to achieve many of its basic functions (Stora 2001, 124).

In this context, the government had little choice but to endorse autogestion, especially since self-management was keeping in motion vital sectors of the economy. Self-management also fit with the populist rhetoric of the FLN in which all factions talked of building an "Algerian socialism." Moreover, autogestion was the most popular grassroots movement in the country and had "captivated the national imagination"; thus Ben Bella unhesitatingly put himself at its head (Ruedy 2005, 199). Within a month of taking power, he had set up the Bureau National Pour la Protection et Gestion des Biens-Vacants (BNBV) to oversee the running of abandoned properties and to examine ways of regularizing autogestion. In a series of decrees issued in fall 1962, Ben Bella provided for the creation of management committees on vacant agricultural estates, industrial enterprises, mines, and artisans shops. Decrees also forbade transactions in abandoned French property and established a national marketing and trade agency for self-managed agriculture (Blair 1970, 49–50).

This official endorsement of autogestion had an immediate effect upon rural workers, who wasted no time in installing self-management on thousands more estates. For example, workers on the Bluchette domaine in Saïda, near Oran, met at their 690,000-hectare estate's headquarters and elected a management committee: "In the next week, twenty thousand people went to work." Local FLN militants also played a substantial role in establishing workers' control on abandoned farms, for example in Saint Eugène, where seventy-four farms were reactivated with each enterprise managed by a committee of nine members, including five workers' delegates. Blair quotes a local FLN member explaining the party's role: "For three months we were in charge of everything; we went out and mobilized the people and explained our tasks to them and helped them start *comités de gestion*" (Blair 1970, 50). It should be stressed that far from representing an innovation based on Ben Bella's government's legislation, these takeovers were an amplification of an ad hoc process that had been under way since independence.

In the fluid political situation that emerged around the time of Ben Bella's endorsement of autogestion, there materialized some remarkable examples of ingenuity that hinted at the possibilities of the creative forces that could be mobilized through workers' control. An outstanding case comes from estates around the town of Cherchell, a coastal town west of Algiers. There, before the fall, some 2,400 workers assisted in reactivating 90 farms and vineyards and set up committees for maintaining agricultural machinery, as well as for health and social welfare. Most interestingly, from an economic point of view, the workers stressed the interdependence of industry and agriculture and reopened a local olive oil factory that had been abandoned during the war:

> A hundred factory workers organized a committee, cleaned up the débris, repaired the machines, and began production with tons of raw materials diverted from settler companies. At one all-night meeting they decided that the first annual profits would be shared equally for four purposes: taxes, repairs and purchase of machinery, loans to local agricultural comités de gestion, and the remainder as bonuses for themselves. They declared their solidarity with their "brother workers on the farms" and planned to provide new jobs for seasonally unemployed farm workers by processing other crops during the off-season (Blair 1970, 51–52).

Such independent initiatives, which had sustained the autogestion movement from its inception, were gradually to be stifled by government moves, beginning with the takeover of the UGTA at its January 1963 congress. The leadership of the three hundred thousand–member union had expressed its wish to remain autonomous and had signed an agreement to this effect with the government in December. However, it was already apparent that Ben Bella was unwilling to tolerate the existence of rival centers of political power within a system over which he had gained a precarious ascendancy. Furthermore, the union had significant ideological differences with the government. At its congress the UGTA's demands for autonomy and the right to strike were criticized by FLN leaders, and the UGTA was brought under government control (Clegg 1971, 117–118).

That the suppression of the UGTA was followed by the promulgation in March of decrees formalizing the structure and organization of the self-managed sector demonstrated no contradiction on the part of the government. Rather, it showed the Ben Bella regime's desire to delimit any alternative form of power. The March decrees were drawn up by a small coterie of advisers to Ben Bella within the BNBV and set out the basic structure and functions of the whole self-managed sector, attempting to formalize and regularize the ad hoc and heterogeneous creations of workers. The group that drew up the decrees included the former leader of the Fourth International, Michalis Raptis (aka Michel Pablo), who had assisted the FLN during the war, Mohamed Harbi, and other Trotskyists. The decrees also brought into existence a number of national agencies including the Office National de la Réforme Agraire (ONRA), which was given responsibility for supervising the self-managed sector. In all about 22,000 colonial farms covering 1 million hectares of Algeria's finest agricultural land, 450 factories, and thousands of shops and artisanal enterprises were put under autogestion. The decrees did not extend to the whole economy, only to the biens-vacants and properties of "national importance." Especially for the industrial sector, the retention of a mixed economy and competition from private firms would assist in the gradual degradation of the sector (Clegg 1971, 59; Ottaway and Ottaway, 39).

It is worth taking a moment to outline the structure of self-management set out in the March decrees, although in reality the sector rarely functioned along these lines. In theory, the sovereign entity of self-management was an assembly composed entirely of full-time workers, and was supposed to meet at least once every three months. The assembly elected a workers' council from among its membership, with a minimum of ten members plus one for every fifteen workers above a basic level of thirty, up to a maximum of one hundred. The council members were elected for terms of one to three years, and were supposed to meet at least once a month. At the next level, the council or in its absence the assembly elected a management committee of between three and eleven people, which met at least once a month and elected a president from among its ranks. Both the council and the committee were supposed to be composed of at least two-thirds production workers. The committee members were elected for three years while the president's term was one year. At the apex of this pyramidal structure was a director who represented the interests of the state. According to the decrees, the council was to make long-term decisions over the purchase of machinery, the procurement of loans, and the like. The committee was to be the body, that is, much more active in day-to-day management, including drawing up development plans, organizing short-term loans, buying raw materials and plants, and keeping accounts. The president was charged with watching over all the organs of self-management, signing all financial documents, and representing the enterprise in law. The powers of the director were more extensive. He was responsible for checking the legality of all the enterprise's transactions, holding its accounts, signing all documents, and maintaining minutes for all the management bodies. The final of four decrees promulgated in March allowed for profit-sharing among workers, the enterprise, and the state, each of which was due to receive a one-third share (Ministry of Information 1963, 54–66).

We can see a number of contradictions built into the structure of autogestion. For one, the decrees established a divide between full-time and seasonal workers by preventing the latter from participating in self-management based on their "lack of long-term interest," thus de facto excluding this larger set of workers—some 450,000 as compared to 130,000 full-time rural workers—from having any stake in autogestion. Furthermore, the structure lent itself to the creation of a duality of personnel within individual enterprises (Bennoune 1976, 94; Hermassi 1972, 198). The roles of the council, which was intended as an intermediary between the workers' assembly and the committee, were not clearly demarcated from those of the committee, while the functions of the assembly itself—theoretically the sovereign body—amounted merely to that of a rubber stamp. Then there was the director, whose responsibilities overlapped greatly with those of the president, thus containing "the seeds of an almost inevitable jurisdictional conflict" (Clegg 1971, 65). The state-appointed director, with his considerable responsibilities, was frequently the only literate member of an agricultural enterprise, allowing plentiful opportunity for abuse of the role. The decrees failed to spell out the relationship between the enterprises and ONRA and, furthermore, no allowance was made for workers' representation either within this agency or at the national level. Ruedy describes the decrees as "a compromise package of overlapping jurisdictions and confusing institutional directions," which were almost incapable of being implemented "by the largely illiterate rural workers" (2005, 199).

All these structural deficiencies would eventually find their expression in various ways as the potential of autogestion was strangled almost at birth. The inbuilt weaknesses in this bureaucratic apparatus would be a source of dysfunction and a means for the administration and its agencies to smother the self-managed sector. They not only hindered its efficiency at an economic level, but stifled the democratic and participatory promise of autogestion as it had emerged in practice.

Yet autogestion retained a central place in the official ideology of Ben Bella's government and it had significantly increased his popularity. The question of Ben Bella's own orientation toward self-management is a difficult one and riddled with contradictions. So in a speech announcing the March decrees he could produce a statement such as "The abandoned property will from today be administered by the State" while also maintaining its opposite, pronouncing, "Algeria belongs to you and it is for you alone to prove to the world that the Algerian revolution can and will be at the vanguard of Socialist experiences in this generation" (Hollingworth 1963). Similarly, in terms of his allies, he was able to embrace the Trotskyists Pablo and Harbi alongside those such as minister of agriculture Ali Mahsas and finance minister Bachir Boumaza, who were unequivocally opposed to the autonomy of the autogestion sector. Such inconsistency reflects not only the unstable political equilibrium of post-independence Algeria, but also the contradictions of the nationalist movement: anticolonialist and regarding itself as revolutionary, reifying the imagined role of the peasant masses in the independence struggle, while simultaneously prioritizing national development over radical social change. These contradictions would eventually work themselves out in the straightforward state capitalism of the Boumedienne years, with the notion of workers' control definitively shelved. In the meantime, however, Ben Bella was to extend autogestion to wider sections of the economy while workers voiced complaints about growing bureaucratization, state control, and the removal of vital managerial responsibilities from workers' control.

## The Neutralization of Self-Management

Once the March decrees were passed it became apparent that self-management was not operating in accordance with the government's prescriptions. In many cases elections for councils and committees were not taking place or directors and presidents were behaving akin to new owners. Elsewhere former guerrilla fighters were running farms as personal fiefs, and within the autogestion sector there was a chronic shortage of qualified technicians and accountants, which led in 1963 to farms being consolidated into larger units, mainly for the purpose of sharing qualified staff. There was also the problem of growing bureaucratization by ONRA, the agency of the agriculture ministry set up to supervise the self-management sector, which assumed increasing responsibility for farm-level management functions. Within a month of the March decrees it had taken control of both farms' credit and marketing, thus controlling enterprises' most crucial inputs and outputs; in effect the self-managed estates became "state farms in all but name" (Ruedy 2005, 200).

Just two months after issuing the decrees, on May 15, Ben Bella launched a nationwide "democratic reorganization" to secure their proper implementation, although its results were not impressive.[4] Rather than tackling the formalized structure's obvious deficiencies, Ben Bella pressed ahead with extending self-management throughout 1963. The first major nationalizations of European property took place around this time, totalling around six hundred thousand hectares and including the estates of the wealthiest and most prominent settlers, seizures that were extremely popular among Algerians (Griffin 1973, 398; Coryell 1964, 7–8; Joesten 1964). In July the national assembly passed a law nationalizing illegally acquired property, and a month later approved a new constitution that "proclaimed autogestion as a major arm of the fight against poverty and economic dependency" (Ruedy 2005, 200). There was a further expansion of autogestion in October when Ben Bella dramatically announced the nationalization of all remaining settler land, meaning self-management now covered 2.3 million hectares—or one-quarter of the country's farmland—and, by late 1964, was organized in 2,284 units employing 200,000 workers.

Ben Bella's decision to nationalize all French-owned land was certainly politically expedient: while dominating the power structure as head of state, head of government, and secretary-general of the FLN, and with the backing of the army, he was increasingly isolated in terms of any popular base. Thus he relied more heavily on the "politics of gestures" to garner support from the beneficiaries of his policies (Ruedy 2005, 199–202). Nevertheless, the nationalizations were certainly popular: some two hundred thousand Algerians gath-

---

4 For a good account of this period, see Blair 1970, 54–61.

ered in the capital to hear the announcement, which was "decisive and wildly applauded" by banner-carrying crowds that welcomed what seemed to be the fulfillment of the promise of decolonization (Blair 1970, 65).

To tackle his political problems and to deflect anger from the malfunctioning self-managed sector, Ben Bella called two congresses of workers within autogestion; the first, for agricultural workers, was in October 1963 and the second, for the industrial sector, was held in March the following year. These congresses proved that the autogestion sector was deeply dysfunctional; workers gave voice to all the complaints that had emerged since the decrees of the previous March. Moreover, although the congresses succeeded to some extent in bolstering support for the regime and Ben Bella hailed their example of "real democracy," the agreed-to resolutions were tightly controlled by his government, demonstrating once again the regime's reluctance to allow genuine democratic participation by workers (Ottaway and Ottaway 1970, 106–115).

The 2,500 delegates at the farm workers' congress laid out a long list of grievances over the operations of the sector, including insufficient funds to run farms, bottlenecks in the state marketing agencies, a lack of farm machinery, and a shortage of trained personnel. They also complained that the March decrees were still not being implemented correctly, saying ONRA did not respect the autonomy of farms under autogestion, but equally did not provide technical assistance. In numerous instances, power had concentrated in the hands of a few members of the management committee and on "many farms the president or the director took over the vacant house and with it the way of life of the French *colon.*" Workers also complained about problems of embezzlement, corruption, and salary payment, which was overseen by ONRA and frequently delayed for months. The conference agreed on resolutions that proposed remedies to some of the workers' complaints, such as creating marketing cooperatives for farms, establishing a state-run bank for the agricultural self-management sector, and distributing farm profits to workers, as promised in the March decrees. Drafted by FLN-controlled commissions and approved by conference delegates, the proposals were applied only haphazardly. Some minor demands, such as wage increases, were implemented but profits were never distributed, and, while a marketing cooperative was set up, it was controlled by ONRA. The state bank wasn't operative until mid-1967 (Ottaway and Ottaway 1970, 65–66, 109–110).

The industrial workers' congress again saw the government under fire for its handling of the self-managed sector. The appointment of qualified technicians was also a problem in this sector; by the end of 1963 only 25 directors had been appointed in 450 firms. These firms were further hindered because the administration did not favor self-managed enterprises in awarding contracts and often did not pay its bills on time. The government also, incredibly, held these enterprises liable for taxes and debts incurred by their former French owners, shackling them from the start. Besides these problems, the self-managed industrial enterprises were forced to turn to private banks for funding because of difficulty in obtaining loans from the government and its central bank. It is worth remembering that autogestion was situated within a mixed economy and faced competition from a private sector that outnumbered it fivefold; this competition was heaviest for industrial enterprises, since autogestion was even less extensive in that area. Once again, the impact of resolutions agreed to at the congress was slight and their implementation was uneven (Ottaway and Ottaway 1970, 64–66, 110–114).

Despite these problems self-management continued to be emphasized by Ben Bella and his government. According to the Algiers Charter, adopted in April 1964 at the first FLN congress since independence, autogestion was identified as the route to socioeconomic development and socialism; it was declared that self-management would gradually be extended to the entire economy and local government institutions. In the meantime it was to be enhanced through agrarian reform and the establishment of cooperatives in the private farm sector, along with nationalization and central economic planning (Ottaway and Ottaway 1970, 119–122). The FLN was portrayed in the charter as an avant-garde revolutionary party that expressed the will of the masses and could temper the threat from a "bureaucratic bourgeoisie." Yet this presentation was wholly inaccurate, as Ruedy notes: "by 1964, the FLN had itself become a major vehicle of upward mobility for Algerians anxious to improve their material and community standing" (Ruedy 2005, 205).

If self-management was crippled during the Ben Bella era, it was finally killed off after his regime's overthrow in June 1965. Shortly before the coup d'état led by Ben Bella's former ally Houari Boumedienne, the head of the military, a change in the regime's direction had seemed possible. This was especially the case because the leadership of the state-controlled UGTA was being challenged by an emergent layer of militants. There had been a wave of strikes after the takeover of the union in January 1963 and throughout 1964, many of which were directly political: workers were either challenging the false promise of the autogestion sector or attempting to compel the government to nationalize private firms by forcing French owners to abandon their enterprises. These strikes demonstrated that despite the growing bureaucratization of self-management, UGTA members were still engaged in a battle over the direction of the economy and were still enthusiastic about the idea of autogestion. The UGTA's weekly periodical, *Revolution et Travail*, replicated the demands of a half dozen striking unions in June 1964 by calling for "the institution of worker control over the management of enterprises in the private sector by the application of laws conforming to our [socialist] option." An earlier, ten-day strike at the French oil company Compagnie Générale de Geophysique had ended in an agreement to share its management with workers (Braestrup 1964). Yet despite the vocal support for the extension and reinforcement of self-management—a cause with which Ben Bella closely identified himself—there was scarcely any protest when he was overthrown, so poorly mobilized behind him was any popular constituency.

Boumedienne aimed to take the country in a completely different direction: he was surrounded by a layer of technocrats who had been increasingly alarmed at Ben Bella's embrace of self-management. Although he utilized the populist rhetoric of autogestion, Boumedienne subjected the sector to an economistic logic by arguing that individual enterprises must be profitable, and most were not (Singh 1966, 455). He also held workers responsible for the failings in their firms, as opposed to the bureaucrats who wielded the most power over them. In any case, the new regime quickly set about a wave of denationalizations, dismantling self-managed enterprises in the retail and tourism sectors. Boumedienne's larger economic policy consisted of the formation of national corporations to take control of strategic sectors of the economy. His advisers viewed the establishment of heavy "industrializing" industries and the nationalization of foreign firms as the basis for development and economic independence. However, the autogestion model was essentially abandoned in the expanding "socialist sector," and "consultation" with workers was the new paradigm within the ever-increasing number of *sociétés nationales,* which had a management body appointed directly by a government ministry.[5] When ONRA was abolished by Boumedienne in 1967, control of self-managed farms was merely transferred to the agriculture ministry, further centralizing control of the sector.

Boumedienne's takeover brought to an end the stalled three-year experiment in autogestion, but his leadership constituted as much continuity as change. The direction he set for Algeria's future—toward an increasingly consolidated state capitalism, bureaucratic control, and the logic of profit within the self-managed sector; away from the notion of workers' control as a model to be extended throughout the economy—was already being charted during Ben Bella's administration (Helie 1973, 473). Both leaders utilized the language of populism and the national myth of autogestion to their benefit even as the sector itself was critically weakened.

Thus far we have observed some of the structural and operational problems of self-management and examined briefly some of their immediate

---

5 For a discussion of "socialist management," see Branine 1994. For more on the development of state capitalism in Algeria, see Farsoun 1975.

causes. To gain a deeper understanding of the reasons for the failure of workers' self-management in the Algerian context, we must proceed to an analysis of the more fundamental dynamics at play during this period and how they impacted the development of autogestion.

## Self-Management and Class Struggle

While the issue of "class consciousness" was earlier set aside, one has to consider the attitudes and level of political education among the working class and how these affected the role it played in defending autogestion. In a 1960 study, Bourdieu found that a large number of workers appeared to lack what he termed "trade union consciousness," favoring individual solutions to achieving higher wage levels (Clegg 1971, 106). Furthermore, in many instances old workplace hierarchies were maintained after independence: autogestion merely represented a change of personnel from *patron* to director (Lazreg 1976, 94). Those who devised the structure of autogestion viewed profit-sharing as a crucial mechanism that would permit workers to view enterprises as their own—although, of course, ownership remained with the state. While it is doubtful such a system would have achieved its objectives, it was never put into practice; profits were never shared with workers.

Political organization among the working class was also minimal at the time autogestion was established. The UGTA possessed only a small membership among rural laborers—the majority of workers—and the union was neutralized early in 1963. Although Ben Bella's government frequently called on the union to mobilize workers behind autogestion, it was of course unable to play this role. Furthermore, the FLN never fulfilled any kind of organizational role among the Algerian masses; despite debates in 1962 over whether it should be structured along the lines of a mass party or should play a more "avant-garde" role, it had essentially been hollowed out during the war for independence due to France's effective counterinsurgency effort and the shift of the struggle's center of gravity to the "exterior"—away from the rank and file of the FLN inside Algeria and toward the political leadership and the upper echelons of the ALN, based in neighboring Tunisia and Morocco. Once Ben Bella's hastily created political bureau had seized control of the party in the summer of 1962, it was merely filled with his acolytes.

Nevertheless, it is worth reflecting that even without such political organization, Algerian workers had, in the summer of 1962, created almost spontaneously a new form of economic organization that succeeded in keeping the economy going. The autogestion movement was ad hoc and its structures variable: sometimes enterprises were managed by an elected workers' council, at other times they were run along hierarchical lines similar to those pertaining under the colonial system. In adopting autogestion as a core part of its official ideology, Ben Bella's government gave encouragement to this movement, and the March decrees replicated schematically many facets of the workers' own democratic inventions while also incorporating aspects of Yugoslav self-management. Yet inherent weaknesses were built into this system that permitted its bureaucratization. The decrees created the cleft by which autogestion could be broken apart; the social forces at play provided the leverage.

What were these social forces? One can analyze the battle over self-management as a struggle between competing classes in the new Algerian state that began in the summer of 1962 and persisted as a partially disguised ideological battle. It is clear that there were divisions within the FLN over how the organization of the economy should proceed, with some favoring a statist approach to development while others were more committed to a semblance of workers' control. Even in the latter case, however, what predominated was a pedagogical approach, with workers not trusted to take their own initiative without the assistance of an "*avant-garde*" (Bennoune 1988, 104; Ottaway and Ottaway 1970, 68; Singh 1966, 449; Hermassi 1972, 198–199).

It is crucial to note that even after the extension of self-management through nationalization, the sector still formed a minority of the Algerian economy and existed alongside private as well as wholly state-operated sectors. In addition, the state inherited and then reactivated the capitalistic legal system of the French colonial state; even the regressive labor code was maintained. Thus self-management existed in an economic, legalistic, and political environment that was profoundly hostile. Throughout the experience of autogestion, workers raised concerns about the rise of a "bureaucratic bourgeoisie" operating through ONRA, its local directors, and the Ministry of Agriculture. Such concerns, as we have noted, were also expressed in the Tripoli Program and the FLN's Algiers Charter. They were borne out in the actions of the postindependence administration, which was responsible for overseeing the self-management sector and enacting the legislation that was supposed to consolidate and extend it (Helie 1973, 468; Tlemcani 1986, 88, 90–91).[6]

The greater part of this administration consisted of Algerians of petit bourgeois origins who had occupied lower-level positions in the colonial bureaucracy (Stora 2001, 129). There was a startling degree of mobility for such administrators, who swiftly filled the vacuum at the top of the hierarchy, as former guerrillas and political appointees began to take up the lower-level positions. There were also many thousands of French administrative assistants

---

6 For an excellent account of class struggle in postindependence Algeria, see Bennoune 1976.

who played a guiding role in the new state bureaucracy. This administration grew in size enormously after independence (Ottaway and Ottaway 1970, 83–84; Tlemcani 1986, 91). Therefore, it should come as little surprise that the growing bureaucracy did not implement autogestion with enthusiasm and in many instances scuppered self-management; drawn from the same class as those individual speculators attempting to buy and seize colon land, most were intractably opposed to the extension of workers' control.

Some have explained the struggle for power in the new Algeria in terms of ideology, personal power, and competing "clans" (Quandt 1969; Zartman 1975; Entelis 1986). Yet while these notions all inform our understanding of the context, the dynamics of the struggle over autogestion are best illuminated through an account of class conflict. It is crucial to note that the nationalist movement was engaged not in a social revolution but a war of independence in which class distinctions were elided for the sake of the national struggle. As noted by Bourdieu during the independence struggle: "While the conflicts between classes are not consciously felt or explicitly expressed, and while they remain hidden or attenuated because the general feeling of the dominated society was one of opposition to the dominant European society, these conflicts nevertheless potentially exist" (1961, 191). If anything can be described as a revolution, it was the working class's takeover of the means of production via autogestion. That such a takeover was vigorously opposed by other classes is amply demonstrated by the documented struggle with elements of the petite bourgeoisie and rural bourgeoisie for control of abandoned properties. What ensued, following the establishment by the workers of a sort of "dual power" in the summer of 1962, was a protracted conflict over autogestion that lasted throughout Ben Bella's rule and into Boumedienne's regime. This conflict found expression in political and economic policy, in legal decrees and, most of all, in bureaucratic maneuvers that rendered self-management defective even on the terms set out by the Ben Bella regime. This bureaucratization created the conditions in which autogestion could be attacked for being uneconomic.

The role of this bureaucracy has been a focus of debate in general theoretical terms and also regarding Algeria specifically. In the case at hand, Tlemcani argues that the state bureaucracy constituted a "new class," suggesting it was sharply differentiated from other classes and identifying its existence as a "real social structure" controlling the process of labor, organizing the distribution of surplus value, and mediating between other class interests (1986, 6–10).[7] Accordingly, this "oligarchy," formed of the military,

---

7 Clegg (1971) also discusses this notion of a "new class" (185–186). See also the discussion in Tlemcani and Hansen 1989.

colonial administration, and the petit bourgeois leadership of the nationalist movement, utilized its political power (in the form of the state) to conquer economic power through nationalization, the centralization of autogestion, and the creation of national corporations. Lazreg's account (1976) is more nuanced in that she considers the state bureaucracy as an arena of struggle in which different classes and class fractions meet.[8] Identifying the state as both a producer and reproducer of classes, she describes technocratic and military factions of the petite bourgeoisie as having assumed political power after independence in opposition to the bourgeoisie. The goals of this petite bourgeoisie, the leadership of which was drawn from the radical nationalist wing of the FLN, happily coincided with those of the state: national development, economic independence, and the construction of state capitalism. Paradoxically, although this path necessitated the neutralization of workers' control of industry, it also assisted in generating a capitalist industrial class in Algeria.

However we analyze the state bureaucracy, it is clear that this was the crucial instrument in undermining and destroying autogestion as created by the working class. Once self-management was formalized and the ad hoc inventions of workers disbanded, the relations of production remained the same as far as an individual worker was concerned: the state owned the enterprise, workers received a wage, democratic participation was at a low level, and vital areas of decision-making were beyond the workers' grasp. Crucially, while the working class had seized control of the means of production in some of the most important sectors of the economy, it had neither set about extending workers' control on its own nor consolidated individual units into greater organizational bodies. Thus by the fall of 1962, the process had effectively stalled and the government was in a position to assume responsibility for the movement.

Weaknesses in organization and political education permitted this takeover, with the UGTA unable to play a significant role after January 1963 and the FLN neither the mass party nor the avant-garde its various factions claimed. These weaknesses were also a product of the nationalist movement per se: while eventually successful in overthrowing the colonial order, the practical absence of any class analysis of Algerian society by the FLN left the mass of that society unprepared for the incipient class conflict that was visible in the summer of 1962 (Pfeifer 1985, 4). The extant social conditions must also be identified: the Algerian working class was a tiny minority in a predominantly rural, peasant-based society convulsed by social dislocation in the aftermath of independence. Finally, autogestion could be

---

8 See also Pfeifer's claim for the "relative autonomy" of the Algerian state (1985).

paired conceptually with a radical nationalist discourse of economic independence that, through a "process of both reification and interpretation," eventually allowed self-management to be subjected to an economic logic that undermined its very foundation. Such a discourse, heavily deployed by Boumedienne, demonstrates the way in which ideology becomes a field of struggle in itself (Lazreg 1976, 131), for autogestion retained an enduring power as a founding myth of the Algerian state long after it had been emptied of its content.

## References

Amin, Samir. 1970. *The Maghreb in the modern world: Algeria, Tunisia, Morocco.* Trans. Michael Perl. Harmondsworth: Penguin, 1970.

Bennoune, Mahfoud. 1976. Algerian peasants and national politics. *MERIP Reports* 48, 3–24.

_____. 1988. *The making of contemporary Algeria, 1830–1987.* Cambridge: Cambridge University Press.

_____. 1975. The origins of the Algerian proletariat. *Dialectical Anthropology* 1 (1–4): 201–224. .

Blair, Thomas Lucien Vincent. 1970. *The land to those who work it: Algeria's experiment in workers' management.* Garden City, NY: Anchor Books.

Bourdieu, Pierre. 1961. *The Algerians.* Boston: Beacon Press.

Braestrup, Peter. 1964. "Worker control" sought in Algeria. *New York Times.* June 11, 10.

_____. 1965. Ben Bella Plans Reform in Labor. *New York Times.* January 17, 8.

Branine, Mohamed. 1994. The rise and demise of participative management in Algeria. *Economic and Industrial Democracy* 15 (4): 595–630.

Clegg, Ian. 1971. *Workers' self-management in Algeria.* London: Allen Lane.

Coryell, Schofield. 1964. Algeria's self-managing institutions. *Africa Today* 11 (2): 7–8.

Entelis, John P. 1986. *Algeria: The revolution institutionalized.* Boulder, CO: Westview Press.

Farsoun, Karen. 1975. State capitalism in Algeria. *MERIP Reports* 35, 3–30.

Griffin, Keith B. 1973. Algerian agriculture in transition. In *Man, state and society in the contemporary Maghrib*, ed. I. William Zartman. London: Pall Mall Press.

Helie, Damien. 1973. Industrial self-management in Algeria. In *Man, state and society in the contemporary Maghrib*, ed. I. William Zartman. London: Pall Mall Press.

Hermassi, Elbaki. 1972. *Leadership and national development in North Africa: A comparative study.* Berkeley: University of California Press, 1972.

Hollingworth, Clare. Takeover in Algeria: Abandoned property goes to workers. *Guardian.* March 30, 1.

Joesten, Joachim. 1964. *New Algeria.* Chicago: Follett Publishing Company.

Lazreg, Marnia. 1976. *The emergence of classes in Algeria: A study of colonialism and socio-political change.* Boulder, CO: Westview Press.

Ministry of Information. 1963. *Documents on self-management (auto-gestion).* Bone, Algeria: Documentation and Publications Department.

Ottaway, David, and Marina Ottaway. 1970. *Algeria: The politics of a socialist revolution.* Berkeley: University of California Press.

Pfeifer, Karen. 1985. *Agrarian reform under state capitalism in Algeria.* Boulder, CO: Westview Press, 1985.

Quandt, William B. 1969. *Revolution and political leadership, Algeria, 1954–1968.* Cambridge, MA: MIT Press.

Ruedy, John. 2005. *Modern Algeria: The origins and development of a nation.* 2nd ed. Bloomington, IN: Indiana University Press.

Singh, K. R. 1966. The Algerian experiment in socialism. *International Studies* 8 (4): 444–456.

Stora, Benjamin. 2001. *Algeria 1830–2000: A short history.* Ithaca, NY: Cornell University Press..

Tlemcani, Rachid. 1986. *State and revolution in Algeria.* London: Zed Books.

Tlemcani, Rachid, and William W. Hansen. 1989. Development and the state in post-colonial Algeria. *Journal of Asian and African Studies* 24 (1/2): 114–133.

Zartman, I. William. 1975. Algeria: A post-revolutionary elite. In *Political elites and Political development in the Middle East*, ed. Frank Tachau. Cambridge, MA: Schenkman.

# 13

## The Limits and Possibilities of Workers' Control within the State
### Mendoza, Argentina, 1973

**Gabriela Scodeller**

During 1973 Argentina was rocked by an intense period of workplace occupations. This chapter describes the experiences that developed in the midwest province of Mendoza, where state-owned enterprises and institutions were the main battleground. The takeovers of state branches of government enterprises were driven by workers who subsequently conceived, elaborated, and implemented models of self-management and self-organization that represented exercises of workers' control within the state.

Argentina's extensive history of military dictatorships and the repression since 1955 of the Perónist party prompted the workers' struggle to follow noninstitutionalized paths. With the return of democracy in May 1973, many workers recognized the necessity of taking into the political-institutional realm the organizational tools developed during nearly two decades of conflict. Workers' democracy and power were formed and sustained through a class-conscious and mobilized rank and file, regarded as a means of transforming the state from below.

Given the contradictions and complexities during a time of increasing class struggle the experiences in Argentina in 1973 present intriguing material for analysis. The unfolding of events demonstrates that contesting for power in the workplace did not always translate into challenging the government or the employers. This case study also allows us to reflect on the limitations and practical difficulties that workers faced during these attempts at workers' control within the state.

## Social Struggle in Argentina in the 1970s

Since the military coup of 1955, the Perónists—Argentina's leading party— had managed to survive despite eighteen years of proscription, mostly through the support of workers and the lower classes. During those years the broad Perónist movement had developed a range of tactics for its struggles—including military insurrection, electoral boycott, and industrial sabotage—and formed alliances with other political and social forces to engage in factory takeovers, urban and rural guerrilla warfare, and mass rebellions. Throughout this course of struggle and organization, Argentinean society in general was moved to question its major institutions. But inside the Perónist movement there were differing goals. While some fought against the military government and for the return of their exiled leader Perón without questioning capitalist social relations, others fought against the regime itself, thus exceeding the limits of the system and turning their struggle into one for revolutionary change (Bonavena et al. 1998).

In this context, the armed struggle that surfaced during this era should be considered as the expression of a specific stage in political-military class struggle. However, the practice of direct physical violence was not restricted to armed guerrilla organizations—the radicalized masses also exercised forms of popular armed struggle to prevent the closure of state enterprises. The process of political radicalization within certain sectors of society was accelerated in reaction to the military dictatorship of the "Argentine Revolution" (1966–73) and the question of class power was placed firmly on the agenda. With each day the people became more fearless of the regime.

As a response to this social and political crisis, the government of General Alejandro Agustín Lanusse (1971–73) implemented the Great National Agreement (GAN), calling for democratic elections in order to regulate the transition from dictatorship to democracy. The goal was to institutionalize the social conflict and disarm the masses politically, and then return to the traditional Argentinean paradigm of domination under parliamentary democracy. The elections of March 1973 were won by the Perónists, although Juan Perón himself was not allowed to run; in May of the same year, Perónism, in alliance with smaller parties and represented by the new president Hector Cámpora, assumed power after eighteen years of repression. As some researchers observe, "From a strategic point of view it was a bourgeois victory, due to the strategic defense that was accomplished through the implementation of elections. The mere fact of voting meant, in that context, a political disarmament for the masses; however, from a tactical point of view, victory corresponds to the popular sectors, which rise with the success of the polls" (Bonavena et al. 1998, 106).

Contrary to the goals of the GAN, the social mobilization of the working class did not subside, but instead was advanced. The social climate of euphoria that characterized President Cámpora's short-lived government expressed itself in spontaneous takeovers of public and private workplaces throughout the country. Even though this phenomenon lasted only a short time, it had high intensity and was therefore significant. Under the newly changed circumstances the common enemy, represented by the dictatorship, had vanished; consequently, the social force antagonistic to the regime started to split up in the face of intensified internal differences.

With the assumption of Perónist governor Alberto Martínez Baca in the province of Mendoza, many of the practices of rank-and-file organizations were transformed into state policies. During the initial months several government posts were assigned to leaders of the Revolutionary Tendency[1]: especially after the Mendozazo,[2] the capacity of mobilization and organization of the revolutionary groups had expanded. But quickly the most reactionary right-wing factions within the government recognized the challenge to state power and instigated a process to obstruct popular power in order to regain influence and control.

From 1973 on, three major contesting sociopolitical forces can be distinguished: Peronism in government; the revolutionary movements; and the traditional system of domination (Marín 1984). While the revolutionary movements were increasingly isolated from the popular sectors and traditional elites sought to create a consensus for "order," the split of the Perónists enriched the other two (Izaguirre 2009). This conflict between antagonistic factions encompassed the whole of society, splitting Peronism into what became known as the right wing (the orthodox or historical sectors of the party plus the union bureaucracy) and the left wing (sectors linked to the Revolutionary Tendency). While the right wing identified with the slogan "Perónist homeland" (*patria perónista*), the left supported the notion of creating a socialist homeland (*patria socialista*).

Once the government of Martínez Baca assumed power, the tension between the two disputing Perónist factions became more apparent: Martinez Baca was supported by the Revolutionary Tendency, while the vice governor Carlos Mendoza, leader of the Metal Workers' Union (UOM), was the head of the Perónist right wing. After several conflicts, the right wing succeeded in June 1974 in suspending the governor from his duties through political impeachment. Perón, who by that time had assumed the presidency, em-

---

[1] The Revolutionary Tendency consolidated Perónist groups that identified with socialist transformation, such as armed organizations (Montoneros and Fuerzas Armadas Revolucionarias), militant youth groups in universities (Juventud Universitaria Perónista), secondary schools (Union de Estudiantes Secundarios), trade unions (Juventud Trabajadora Perónista), and organizations from poor neighborhoods (Movimiento Villero Perónista).

[2] Popular uprising in Mendoza on April 4, 1972, provoked by ongoing police repression against labor unions and demonstrators, which culminated in the killing of protesters by the police. In the ensuing days, the protests spread throughout the city and turned into a rebellion, marking a break with the prevailing social order despite police use of live ammunition and lethal violence against the workers' insurrection.

barked on a nationwide campaign aimed at overthrowing the governors linked to the Revolutionary Tendency. When the vice governor assumed provincial executive power, repressive measures and censorship increased in all sectors, from the university to the poor neighborhoods. The most reactionary factions had retaken the initiative in the class struggle.

In Mendoza, as throughout Argentina, the relation of forces became increasingly unfavorable to mass movements. While the pro-revolutionary forces were still in formation, the counterrevolutionary forces had already consolidated.

### The Nationwide Occupations

One of the last actions carried out by the regime of the "Argentine Revolution" to maintain its influence over the administration of the Perónist government was the appointment of officials who would ensure the political continuity of the military dictatorship. Supporters of the government elected in March 1973 opposed the military as an obstruction, and denounced these political maneuvers. This triggered a series of workers' occupations in an attempt to prevent those who supported dictatorship from participating in a popular government.

During Cámpora's government (May 25–July 14, 1973), workers' struggles acquired a particular character. Most conflicts assumed the modality of takeovers, whether in workplaces or in trade unions. The takeovers were the most significant advance of workers on employer's terrain, since the workplace is "socially and legally alien, but they feel it practically and morally as their own" (Izaguirre and Aristizábal 2002, 51).

Most occupations were declared as being "against the continuity" of the military government and its officials, but a closer look reveals a huge variety of motivations, expressing the differences in the struggle for the reappropriation of the social and political system. The Argentine sociologist Flabián Nievas argues that the primary conflict motivating the takeovers was "more concerning the social order than the political order, which the different social forces tried to signify from the inside, more in a sense of appropriating it than confronting it" (Nievas 1999, 359).

In his research on takeovers in Argentina, Nievas identifies four distinct periods. The first runs from the beginning of Cámpora's government until June 3 (1999, 351–393). The second extends from June 4, when the huge wave of takeovers began, until June 14, when Abal Medina, secretary-general of the Perónist party Partido Justicialista (PJ), urged an end to the occupations. During this period more than five hundred occupations took place nationwide. More than three hundred fifty were carried out between June 11 and June 15 alone. The effect of Abal Medina's call was immediate: the number of takeovers dropped dramatically, although they resumed shortly thereafter with even greater intensity in factories and union sites. In addition, Abal Medina's call demobilized the less politicized groups of workers that rallied behind the slogan "against the continuity," reducing the confrontation to the more organized groups. The third period ranges from June 15 to June 20, the date of the "Ezeiza massacre."[3] The fourth period began June 21 and lasted until the fall of Cámpora's government on July 13. During these days the province of Mendoza saw significant activity, together with the province of Tucuman; it was the fourth jurisdiction nationally in number of takeovers (Bonavena and Nievas 1999, 1).[4] As we will see, many of these occurred during the second and third periods.

As noted, a large variety of social groups, often with opposed interests, gathered under the banner "against the continuity." Nievas distinguishes two different types of takeovers: first, the "occupations for the socialist homeland," referring to the takeovers of the "New Left," including those they did not directly organize but with which they maintained a certain affinity (1999, 364–372).[5] These activities had an anticapitalist bent, although with different degrees of consciousness informing their actions. In this category he includes the occupations performed by the leftist armed organizations, by the Perónist left-wing armed or political organizations, and by rank-and-file workers.

The second category is called "occupations for the Perónist homeland," which Nievas describes as reactionary due to their content or because they were initiated in response to the left-wing takeovers. The nationalist-oriented occupations were commonly carried out by much smaller groups. In this category we find takeovers organized by the Perónist right and "preventive takeovers" initiated to avert leftist takeovers, motivated by the goal of maintaining the status quo (ibid., 373–381). Nievas found that occupations favoring the "socialist homeland" had massive participation but the majority of Perónist occupations were conducted by small groups not exceeding forty people, who typically carried firearms.

Of all the takeovers, 54 percent nationwide were aligned with the "socialist homeland," while those associated with defending the "Perónist homeland" represented 46 percent. However, although the socialist occu-

---

[3] One of the biggest mass demonstration in those years, motivated by the return of Perón to Argentina; the different political factions of Peronism clashed violently with each other.
[4] Another characteristic of the movement in Mendoza, comparable only to that of Rosario, was that in contrast to the rest of the country, two-thirds of the occupations were accomplished by students (Bonavena and Nievas 1999, 1).
[5] "New Left" stands for a heterogeneous variety of political, social, and cultural groups that expressed their rejection of the dominant order in different ways. They shared a common language and the horizon of social change, and were perceived as being part of a whole despite their differences (Tortti 1999, 207).

pations were significantly more active, the latter focused on key sectors—media, health centers, and public enterprises.

### The Mendoza Occupations

Considering the different elements addressed by Nievas, we can see that in the province of Mendoza the dynamic of occupations presented a series of peculiarities.[6] As Table 1 shows, unlike in the national process, more than half the occupations in Mendoza occurred after the official government call on June 14, 1973, to suspend takeovers. Additionally, those who remained active were rank-and-file workers neither armed nor affiliated with political organizations.

#### Table 1 Enterprise Occupations: 1973

| TOTAL: | | 18 | (100 percent) |
|---|---|---|---|
| Phase 1: | May 25–June 3 | 0 | |
| Phase 2: | June 4–June 14 | 8 | (44.4 percent) |
| Phase 3: | June 15–June 20 | 9 | (50.0 percent) |
| Phase 4: | June 21–July 13 | 1 | (5.5 percent) |

As shown in Table 2, only 16.6 percent of the occupations were staged by groups linked to conservative forces, all in state dependencies—provincial roads, the General Irrigation Department, and radio station LV4 of San Rafael. In contrast, 83.3 percent of the takeovers were carried out by social forces in formation, which combined support for the newly elected government and a policy of "national and social liberation" with a simultaneous questioning of the organization of the different working sectors. Moreover, they demanded workers' participation in decision-making arenas as the only way to ensure the response to the interests of the working class.

Among all occupations, 77.7 percent were carried out by rank and filers in their workplaces without the explicit mediation of political or armed organizations, although they were supported by their respective trade unions. However, after the initial outbreak of takeovers, organizing and planning became less significant.

These rank-and-file occupations occurred in twelve different state dependencies[7]: the Social Welfare Bank, the National Roads Department, the Provincial Transport Company (EPTM), the bus terminal, the Direction

---

[6] The following presents the results of doctoral research based on contemporary newspaper sources and oral interviews (Scodeller 2009).
[7] The analysis of this kind of takeover will be deepened by looking at two cases: that of the Provincial Transport Company (EPTM) and the Infrastructure and Water Services Dependency (DOSS).

of Traffic and Transportation, the Infrastructure and Water Services Dependency (DOSS), the Construction Department, the Service of Adult Education, the Railway Polyclinic Hospital, the Revenue Department, the Fellow Students Institute, and the Department of Geodesy and Cadastre.

The same dynamics and characteristics developed in takeovers at some private enterprises, such as the occupation of the Argentine Telephone Company and the center of the Argentine Construction Workers' Union (UOCRA). Just one of the occupations—radio station LV8, Libertador— was carried out by the Perónist left and none by leftist armed organizations.

### Table 2: Political Character of Occupations

|  | # | Percentage |
|---|---|---|
| Total Occupations: | 18 | 100.0 |
| Socialist homeland: Subtotal | 15 | 83.3 |
| Leftist armed organizations | 0 | 0 |
| Perónist left-wing groups | 1 | 5.5 |
| Rank-and-file: subtotal | 14 | 77.7 |
| Public dependencies | 12 | 66.6 |
| Private enterprises | 1 | 5.5 |
| Trade union sites | 1 | 5.5 |
| Perónist homeland: Subtotal | 3 | 16.6 |
| Perónist right-wing groups | 2 | 11.1 |
| Preventive | 1 | 5.5 |

In Mendoza, 56 percent of the occupations were considered "effective" and 44 percent "symbolic"—of very short duration or because, despite the protest, employees continued to work and provide services.

All takeovers oriented toward a "socialist homeland" were decided in workplace assemblies. This marks a clear difference from the occupations of the "Perónist homeland" tendency, which were carried out by small groups without broader support. The right-wing tendency was also opposed by other groups of workers, revealing the development of an important political intra-class struggle.

All takeovers took place in spaces that workers considered as their own. Only one of them was a local union headquarters (of the UOCRA); all others occurred in workplaces. The state apparatus represented the main area of conflict; 88.8 percent of takeovers were carried out in state companies and institutions. The differentiation between the political natures of the takeovers occurred unmistakably in the context of the struggle between antagonistic social forces, expressed through the local structures of Peronism. The conflict between the internal tendencies of Peronism became even more visible when some of the provincial ministers were accused of "Marxist infiltration" by regional leaders of the union General Confederation of Labor (CGT).[8] Significantly "it did not only matter who was removed, but, and especially, who was left in charge" (Nievas 1999, 353). Behind the problem concerning the continuity of officers in the dictatorship, a new axis of confrontation emerged, revealing the still forming, antagonistic sociopolitical forces in favor of working-class democracy and against state and capitalist repression.

The declaration of the workers of the Social Welfare Bank lays out their demands, decided within workers' assemblies during takeovers. The workers listed as their goals: "a) to demonstrate the real vocation of workers in the guidance of the institution; b) to appoint comrades able to implement policies to achieve national liberation and reconstruction" (*Diario Mendoza* June 29, 1973, 8).

In the Railway Hospital workers demanded participation of the personnel in decision-making areas in order to "intervene in health and employment policy" (*Diario Mendoza* June 17, 1973, 6). Similarly, in the Revenue Department and in the Fellow Students Institute occupations, workers' assemblies defined themselves as "instruments for change of the system" (*Diario Mendoza* June 19, 1973, 6).

According to a participant, the takeovers "were . . . a way of expression, to participate in the seizure of power. . . . When the comrades, the construction workers, occupied the Distribution Department, they sent the guy in charge to hell. They suddenly felt that finally some power was in their hands, even if it was just a small quota of power" (Vázquez 2005). However, it should be noted that while these activities objectively questioned private property and a particular form of social organization, the fact that workers pronounced support of the new (bourgeois) government demonstrates that they intended not to transform the sociopolitical system but to reappropriate and resignify it more favorably toward their class interests.

So, what was the content and form of the new state sought by workers?

### Limits and Possibilities of Workers' Control within the State: Two Case Studies

The takeovers were relatively ephemeral actions, with varying degrees of success in each case. The most interesting factor is not so much the actions themselves, but the developments in the workplaces afterward. The most

---

[8] The CGT had given Martínez Baca, even before he assumed government office, a list of persons who should not be assigned to government positions because of their ideological inclinations. Both the governor and the CGT general-secretary Fiorentini received support.

important experiences in the province of Mendoza took place in the Provincial Transport Company (EPTM) and in the Infrastructure and Water Services Dependency (DOSS).

Both, as with all takeovers in the sphere of the state, had the support of the trade union, the Workers and Public Employees Union (SOEP). Formed a year earlier—after the Mendozazo—the organization adopted the militant unionism of the era. During those years, a large number of new unions emerged with characteristics rooted in the centrality of shop stewards, who persistently called on rank and filers to participate in assemblies, strikes, and demonstrations. The strong militancy was accompanied by profound internal democracy. These workers' groups defined themselves as antibureaucratic, anti-employer and anti-imperialist.

In statements to the press regarding the occupations, the SOEP leaders declared:

> The occupations . . . respond clearly to the line drawn by our organization. This means the mobilization of the rank and file, in support of the revolutionary administration of the comrade governor . . . .The unions, as key sectors in the construction of the workers' fatherland, must guarantee the activities of the comrades elected by the people, with the massive support of the working class, so that our leaders can keep an honest and militant orientation, which can assure the way to national and social liberation (*Diario Mendoza* June 15, 1973, 9).

On Thursday June 14, 1973, an assembly of the personnel of the Provincial Transport Company of Mendoza (EPTM) decided to occupy the company due to doubts as to its economic stability and ability to pay its workers their next wages. The workers challenged the inactivity of the authorities in making future investments and the failure to resolve growing labor disputes. Workers announced that the occupation would last until the government appointed new authorities "in favor of a real national and social liberation and a greater participation of the employees in the company's management" (*Diario Mendoza* June 15, 1973, 5).

The takeover of the EPTM—carried out with the participation of the SOEP—dissolved the company board and decreed the abolition of all hierarchical levels, including manager, accountants, and legal advisors. In their place, the workers appointed an interim executive board, formed by four employees, until the government assigned new officials. The SOEP reported that "the decision made by the workers and employees of this state company follows the urgent need for the power of decision making and management of the company to be assumed by the true representatives of the people" (*Los Andes* June 15, 1973, 6). As general supervisor they proposed a shop steward who had been working at the company for more than fifteen years.

According to the union activists, "The company is under perfect self-management since it was taken over by its workers three days ago" (*Diario Mendoza* June 16, 1973, 6). During the occupation, the trolleybus service continued to operate. Large signs were placed on the buses, announcing: "Trolleybus taken by its personnel for a real and effective national and social liberation" (*Los Andes* June 15, 1973, 6).

Regarding this experience, the SOEP union secretary recalls:

> The department was taken over, the guy in charge was kicked out and workers took control of the administration. And a new administration was named among the comrades . . . they gathered in an assembly in which we the union participated . . . . One comrade was appointed on behalf of the garages, one on behalf of the drivers, and another comrade on behalf of the administration employees . . . . They built the new authority, appointed by the assembly, and started to manage the trolley company . . . and they made it work exceptionally! It was a public company under workers' control (Vázquez 2005).

According to the union secretary, workers operated the factory efficiently during the occupation that lasted from one to two months.[9]

The recollections of a shop steward regarding this experience are somewhat different: "In those years we occupied everything. We took over the trolleybuses because we wanted a self-managed company . . . under workers' control. The schools were occupied. . . . So in this context we felt encouraged to take over the trolley company." The shop steward continued, describing the takeover's impending end:

> We achieved some of our demands, but not what we proposed . . . .We gained control of the accountancy, but not workers' control over production. We achieved the participation of the shop stewards, the control of entries and exits, while previously we didn't have access to anything. But the company was returned, because as I said, the ax . . . [at which point the shop steward made a cutting gesture symbolizing the approaching counterrevolutionary process]" (Moyano 2005).

The Infrastructure and Water Services Dependency (DOSS) was occupied on June 15 for three hours, after a workers' assembly. They demanded that the governor implement a series of legal instruments to improve services and guarantee the company's solvency and continuous operation. Once again, an interim board was appointed by the workers' assembly and previous authorities were replaced. The assembly demanded that the new

---

[9] Participants do not recall precisely the duration of the takeover, nor were published newspaper accounts or other news sources found that documented the exact time frame of the events.

administrators be chosen from a list of names proposed by the workers and that they have the authority to transform the DOSS according to the new "Law of Autarky," which had been approved by the government but not yet applied. They also requested an amendment to one article of the law concerning the composition of the board, so that it would be integrated by workers' and users' representatives.

The process that took place after the occupation reveals the creative content that accompanied the direct action. The SOEP financial secretary recalls: "Seven groups were formed and each one had to formulate a plan how to restructure the DOSS. Then, these seven papers merged to form one proposal. This proposal was introduced as a bill to the local parliament. . . . We incorporated some very, very important aspects for us . . . but finally it wasn't approved" (Berro 2005).[10]

The draft of the bill proposed that two out of nine members of the board of directors should be workers' representatives. This was justified with the following:

> . . . the need for this sector, being the one that develops the plans and programs, to participate in decision making, since it is this sector as a whole that has profound knowledge of the problems and complexity facing the department. On the other hand, it enables the working class, the action and motor nerve center of national life, to mature in the practice of leading through regular and organic participation (Lilloy 1973, 10).

According to the draft, the other sector to be represented on the board of directors was the users of the service. The workers intended for the utility to be operated for cooperatives or neighborhood units of public services, due to the "need to integrate and make effective the participation of service receivers in decision-making" (Ibid., 9). In both cases the board members were to be appointed by the provincial executive power from a list of nominations by each sector.

The bill proposal emphasized the benefits of placing the drinking water service in the hands of the provincial state through a decentralized body because as part of the "collective needs it cannot be left with liberal criteria to the private initiative" (Ibid., 1). The workers argued for the necessity of creating an organ of control, coordination, and execution throughout the province due to "the need for a direct contact between the official body and the workers or beneficiaries of this public service" (Ibid., 2).

---

[10] The bill, "Proposal creating the Department of Infrastructure and Water Services as an autonomous body" was introduced by the left-wing Perónist deputy Rubén R. Lilloy in Mendoza, October 10, 1973.

What were the real-time obstacles to the development of these plans? The financial secretary of SOEP states that the difficulties were due to the low level of technical and political preparation, not only of rank-and-file workers, but also of activists and union leaders.

> Our great concern was to gather information about self-management experiences.... Our experience ... of self-management mechanisms was very limited ... workers of the different departments weren't prepared enough to assume a responsibility of that nature. We wanted all state services and companies to be self-managed. In some of them we had more success than in others.
>
> For example, in the Infrastructure and Water Services Dependency, where I was working, we appointed an experienced sanitary engineer. Well, that administration had a stronger technical guarantee than other places where that didn't happen . . . . Following the union's initiative an internal discussion with all workers was organized.
>
> All the personnel were divided into seven working groups, where all concerns could be expressed; especially of workers with fewer resources and the most marginalized . . . . We wanted the professionals to share their knowledge through discussions with all the workers. In many cases, as you can imagine, the level of knowledge was very low, very low" (Berro 2006).

This reflection by a union leader enables us to recognize that, beyond the unfavorable context from 1974 onward, workers frequently lacked the theoretical, technical, and political capacity to advance the struggle for a state in workers' hands even when the banner of self-management and workers' control had been unfurled and workers actually directed state enterprises. One major difficulty was that most rank-and-file workers and activists were predisposed to direct action and mobilization and not fully conscious of the longer-term significance of their acts. At the time, political education and instances of reflection on practical experience were not understood within the union culture to be part of the same dynamics as struggle. As such, the secretary of SOEP stated, "We were born and started to fight ... we had no time to stop and reflect about anything" (Vázquez 2005).

According to Italian theorist Antonio Gramsci, this emphasis on the practical moment of the struggle indicates that society was experiencing a historical point in time when "the new" had not yet formed organically—although it was in the process of emerging (Gramsci 1997, 17–18). Instances of theoretical and political education, and reflection on practical experiences, usually arise when class struggle increases. This awareness develops because the learning experience is considered more valuable when obtained on the battlefield, where—as Marx, Lenin, and Luxemburg argued—one learns in a few days what otherwise would take years. But these moments of reflection are crucial if the goal is to have the knowledge necessary to analyze any situation and organize struggle strategically, especially during times—examined herein—when counterrevolutionary forces are on the advance at a national and global level.

## Struggle for the Reappropriation of the State

Throughout this chapter we have seen forms of struggle that did not follow institutionalized patterns. Workplace takeovers questioned the existing social order in a process that developed based on different levels of consciousness. Within the framework of a bourgeois state, the workplaces were territories expropriated by workers from their employers. Most of the occupations were carried out not against but in defense of the Perónist polity, seen as a "people's and workers'" government, against another faction cohabitating within the same administration. Thus the analysis suggests, on the one hand, that the class struggle manifested itself within the working class through political disputes. On the other hand, the early 1970s were a complex historical period for Argentina, exacerbating the still unresolved contradictions of a social force under construction.

Occupations expressed a challenge to the established hierarchical order. They were a result of the course of direct action that workers had developed since 1955, during which power was rethought and constructed. The occupations represented higher grades of autonomy by asserting the need for direct and majoritarian workers' participation in the exercise of power as the only way to guarantee the construction of a political project expressing working-class interests. The problem was that these interests were understood in very different ways.

Once a new battlefield had opened with the return of parliamentary democracy in 1973, workers collectively recognized the importance of forging their own paths in order to contest for political power. The radical actions adopted through factory occupations and the takeover of state services aimed to elevate workers to positions of power; in this way they tried to transfer to the political level what was already unfolding through militant union practices. But the struggle for workers' democracy exceeded the sphere of the unions.[11] The workers attempted to install the experience accumulated in terms of union struggle—a power built and sustained on workers' democracy and mobilization—into the state apparatus, endowing it with democratic content and form by redefining workers' control over the workplace.

Yet the relationship between form and content is neither immediate nor linear. Why were these workers looking for participation in decision making?

---

[11] In his analysis of the nationwide takeovers, Nun pointed out the close relationship between the struggle for union democracy and the demands for workers' control (1973, 223–232).

What were their goals? While the social activist assumes that everyone was pursuing revolutionary change, in reality a diversity of perspectives and interests, some conflicting, were involved. These contradictions went unacknowledged in Argentina during 1973 because the emphasis was on the practical moment, a major obstacle to the movement's success.

Additionally, the pro-revolutionary faction of workers was a social force in its infancy, and did not recognize the looming and growing offensive of another, already constituted, counterrevolutionary social force. In view of the complexities of the era, a valid question is whether it would have been possible to move solidly toward a revolutionary transformation, conscious of its construction and accumulation of power. The more comprehensive, strategic goals for workers' power were not sufficiently accompanied by instances of reflection and elaboration regarding their collective practices.

From the narrative of the Mendoza occupations during June 1973, it is evident that the extremely high level of mobilization did not necessarily correspond to a development of working-class consciousness. As Nievas contends, the workers fought for heterogeneous objectives—as evinced by the fact that not all "occupations for the socialist homeland" actually identifed as anticapitalist.

The workers combined their support for certain government policies with the demand for participation in decision-making arenas with the goal of securing their class interests within the state. However, differences emerged over the definition of those interests—for some it meant overcoming capitalist social relations; for others, gaining workers' participation in the production process or management sphere was enough, and questioning the capital-labor relationship was off the table. One of the interviewees summarizes what workers as a whole were looking for with the takeovers: "People wanted to decide about their lives, and their rights, and achieve what they did not yet have" (Moyano 2005). After years of repression and censorship, the occupations of 1973 demonstrated the general desire of the working class to bring an end to political oppression, yet only a minority sought to bring an end to the exploitation inherent in a capitalist society supported by the state.

## References

Bonavena, Pablo and Flabián Nievas. 1999. Las tomas estudiantiles en la Provincia de Mendoza durante el camporismo. In *Actas de las VII Jornadas Interescuelas/Departamentos de Historia.* Bariloche, Argentina: Universidad Nacional del Comahue.

Bonavena, Pablo Augusto, et al. 1998. *Orígenes y desarrollo de la guerra civil en Argentina. 1966–1976.* Buenos Aires: Eudeba.

*CLAVES para interpretar los hechos.* 1973. Mendoza, June–July.

*Diario Mendoza.* 1973. Mendoza, June.

Gramsci, Antonio. 1990. *Escritos políticos 1917–1933.* Mexico City: Siglo XXI.

_____. 1997. *El materialismo histórico y la filosofía de Benedetto Croce.* Buenos Aires: Nueva Visión.

Izaguirre, Inés and Zulema Aristizábal. 2002. *Las luchas obreras. 1973–1976.* Buenos Aires: IIGG, FSOC-UBA.

Izaguirre, Inés, ed. 2009. *Lucha de clases, guerra civil y genocidio en la Argentina. 1973–1983: Antecedentes. desarrollo. complicidades.* Buenos Aires: Eudeba.

Lilloy, Rubén R. 1973. *Proyecto de ley creando la Dirección de Obras y Servicios Sanitarios como ente autárquico* [Bill project creating the Department of Infrastructure and Water Services as an autonomous body]. Mendoza, October 10.

*Los Andes.* 1973. Mendoza, June.

Marín, J. C. 1984. *Los hechos armados. Un ejercicio posible.* Buenos Aires: CICSO.

Nievas, Flabián. 1995. Hacia una aproximación crítica a la noción de "territorio." *Nuevo Espacio. Revista de Sociología,* no. 1, 75–92. Buenos Aires: University of Buenos Aires.

_____. 1999. Cámpora: primavera-otoño. Las tomas. In *La primacía de la política. Lanusse, Perón y la Nueva Izquierda en tiempos del GAN,* ed. Alfredo Pucciarelli, 351–393. Buenos Aires: Eudeba.

Nun, José. 1973. El control obrero y el problema de la organización. *Revista Pasado y Presente* no. 2/3, nueva serie, año 4 (July/December): 205–232.

Scodeller, Gabriela. 2009. Conflictos obreros en Mendoza (1969–1974): Cambios en las formas de organización y de lucha producto del Mendozazo. PhD thesis, La Plata.

Tortti, María Christina. 1999. Protesta social y "Nueva Izquierda" en la Argentina del GAN. In *La primacía de la política. Lanusse, Perón y la Nueva Izquierda en tiempos del GAN,* ed. Alfredo Pucciarelli, 205–234. Buenos Aires: Eudeba.

**Interviews**

Berro, Marcos. 2005–2006. Interview by author. [Berro was an employee of the Infrastructure and Water Services Dependency and financial secretary of SOEP (1972–1974). Activist in the Peronism of the Bases (PB). Interviews conducted in June 2005 and July 2006.]

Vázquez, Luis María. 2005. Interview by author. [Vázquez was an employee of the Provincial General Account and union secretary of SOEP (1972–1974). Interview conducted in July 2005.]

Moyano, Nora. 2005. Interview by author. [Moyano was an employee of the General Schools Department, shop steward, and a member of SOEP (1972–1974). Activist in the Independent Group of the Bases and Agrupacion Clasista 1° de Mayo. Interview conducted in July 2005.]

# 14

# Workers' Councils in Portugal, 1974–1975

**Peter Robinson**

By the late 1960s, Portugal, under the Fascist regime of Salazar, was the least developed country in Western Europe. It had a large peasantry in the north, landed estates in the south, and relatively small, concentrated industrial centers around Lisbon and along the north coast in the Porto region. Foreign capital and the multinationals were attracted to the cheap labor and advantageous conditions it offered, setting up large, modern plants mostly in the Lisbon industrial belt. But they were frustrated by the country's inadequate banking and financial network and by labor shortages. Workers also grew impatient. It was estimated that from October 1973 to March 1974 more than one hundred thousand workers from about two hundred firms put in for wage increases and about sixty thousand resorted to strike action. Other forms of action included go-slows, street demonstrations, factory gate meetings, overtime bans, and the presentation of lists of grievances.

Having acquired the first of the European colonial empires, Portugal clung to it long after other nations had relinquished theirs. Though there was no prospect of beating the liberation movements in Portuguese Africa, nearly half of Portugal's central budget expenditure went to the armed forces, and the army was being blamed for these imperial failures. Within the middle ranks of the army, a clandestine network—the Movimento das Forças Armadas (MFA; Armed Forces Movement)—was organizing, and by April 1974 it had built a network of three hundred supporting officers from all three services and drafted its first program, calling for "Democracy, Development and Decolonization."

The MFA masterminded the coup of April 25, 1974, with remarkable ease; the regime that had lasted nearly fifty years crumbled in less than a day. Red carnations were famously adopted as the symbol of the revolution. Soldiers stuck carnations in their rifle barrels. The MFA had mutinied but sought a social base to legitimize its position and give it the mass support it needed. Their slogan, "The MFA is with the people, the people are with the MFA," soon gained enormous popularity.

The overthrow of fascism in Portugal on April 25 led to a social crisis that lasted twenty months, during which time the population took part in a remarkable democratic upsurge from below. Celebrations were quickly translated into workplace battles that raised both economic and political demands, though they were rarely coordinated. Some strikes lasted a few hours and others months. Wage claims sprouted haphazardly. In the big companies, especially the multinationals, economic demands accompanied demands for *Saneamento*, the purging of all members of the management with Fascist connections; this process was carried through in more than half the firms employing more than five hundred people. In May, at least 158 workforces were involved in fierce confrontations, including 35 occupations. In four of these, members of management were held prisoner (Santos et al. 1976).

Before April 25, clandestine workers' committees had existed under various names very briefly at moments of conflict. The high level of struggle forced them to meet and consult frequently. By the end of May 1974, workers' commissions, councils, and committees had been formed at almost all the workplaces in the Lisbon region. They usually assumed the name Comissões de Trabalhadores—CTs. It has been estimated that between May and October, four thousand CTs were established, one in virtually every workplace, almost always following mass meetings (*plenários*) of the workers (ibid., ch. 1). The meetings were controlled collectively through the core principle of temporary and instantly recallable delegates. Not only were factories taken over, but empty houses and apartments were requisitioned as well. The organization of tenants and residents was incomparably larger than anything else seen in Europe. Popular clinics and cultural centers mushroomed. This study focuses on some of the many instances of CTs coming together, not only with other CTs, but also with residents' organizations, with land workers, and especially with members of the armed forces.

## Workers' Soviets

*Soviet* is the Russian word for "council." Typically in revolutionary periods, when faced with particular issues requiring practical solutions, people have coordinated their struggles by establishing bodies of elected delegates. One can point to the Paris Commune of 1871 when, after military defeat by Prussia, the working people of Paris resisted government troops who tried to seize their artillery, and established an independent state. Marx, defending the Paris Commune, argued: "But the working class cannot simply lay hold of the ready-made state machinery, and wield it for its own purposes.

. . . Its true secret was this. It was essentially a working class government, the product of the struggle of the producing against the appropriating class, the political form at last discovered under which to work out the economical emancipation of labor" (Marx and Engels 1975–2005, 328, 334).

As Marx described, the members of the 1871 commune were elected, could be recalled at any time, and were paid workmen's wages. The commune lasted only a few weeks, but it carried through measures that would have taken a parliamentary body far longer to resolve—it canceled rent payments, abolished night work in bakeries, and allowed pawned goods to be reclaimed freely. There were few large workplaces in Paris, and the commune was based on constituency elections. The next time workers' democracy emerged it was based much more firmly in the workplace.

This study is drawn from other research[1] and highlights, chronologically, four examples from Portugal of "workers' councils," organizations that linked workers from different enterprises, namely:

1) Inter-Empresas; May 1974–March 1975
2) CRTSMs (Revolutionary Councils of Workers, Soldiers, and Sailors); April 1975–June 1975
3) Popular Assemblies: June 1975–November 1975
4) Comité de Luta de Setúbal; October 1975–November 1975

Within Portugal there were many other examples of popular power and council-type formations; however, little has been published in English.[2] My study focuses upon those councils that linked various workplaces, recognizing that military barracks are also places of work. When examining these incidents I try to look at the following features:

- Depth of representation in workplaces
- Breadth of representation, reaching beyond workplaces
- Accountability and the right to recall
- Self-activity, direct power of the workers, and potentially an alternative power

---

1 I worked in Portugal as a political organizer for nine months in 1975–76 and returned a number of times to do further research and, in particular, to interview activists. Details of the interviews can be found in my M Phil thesis, "Workers' Councils in Portugal in 1974–75"; this study draws heavily upon interviews, so in those instances all I have cited here is the interviewee's name and date.

2 The Centro de Documentação 25 de Abril, which is part of the University of Coimbra, has collected many important documents and bibliographical materials from this period. It has published an annotated bibliography; see Chilcote 1987. Academics attached to the Gabinete de Investigações Sociais have written extensively on the workplace struggles and a number of case studies can be found in their journal, *Análise Social*. Volume 1 of *O 25 de Abril e as lutas sociais nas empresas* (Santos et al. 1976) provides a useful overview of the workplace struggles.

## On the Side of the Workers

Before discussing the developments in the workers' councils, it is important to mention some of the forces that had been active in the workers' movement. The PCP (Portuguese Communist Party) had a respected tradition of opposition to fascism, and by April 25, 1974, the party had developed a cadre of perhaps five thousand members, with a substantial base and some influence in the working class. As a partner in the provisional government, the PCP immediately played its main card, that of influence over the workers' movement. It distanced itself from the wildcat strikes and the accompanying workers' commissions (over which it had little influence), and within a fortnight it was organizing a demonstration against strikes, accusing the workers' commissions of being "ultra-left," of "playing the game of the right" and of being "lackeys of the bosses."

While working alongside the MFA, the PCP was putting its resources not into the workplaces but into an alternative power base—the Intersindical. The Intersindical emerged in 1970 as a loose conglomeration of relatively independent unions. Within weeks of the coup the number of affiliations to the Intersindical rose from twenty-two to about two hundred unions, dramatically transforming it into the national trade union umbrella organization. A smaller rival also emerged, allied to the Socialist Party.

The takeover of unions by the Intersindical was often achieved in collaboration with the Ministry of Labor. In some cases, but by no means always, the unions were empty shells. Despite their presence, they were not the "natural" way that workers related to one another. Very occasionally, for example in some textile factories, workers belonged to a single union, and the union committee was in effect the workers' commission.

Workers' commissions arose spontaneously. Many of the leading activists in the workers' commissions were in the PCP and were dismayed by the PCP's attacks on the commissions. These activists left or were expelled by the PCP and as result a great many Marxist-Leninist (often labeled Maoist) sects emerged. Revolutionaries from other traditions were also present, albeit in small numbers. One such group was the PRP/BR (Revolutionary Proletarian Party/Revolutionary Brigades—the two organizations combined in 1972), who had carried out various attacks upon military installations before April 25, 1974. The Movement of Left Socialists (MES) originated around 1970 as a network of Socialist forums, including trade unionists, Catholics, and students. The workers' movement also attracted anarcho-syndicalists, who were attracted to the notion of a movement above parties—some would even say they were "antiparty."

*The Inter-Empresas*

Immediately after April 25, links among workplaces were rapidly established. The key workforce, employing ten thousand people, was the Lisnave ship repair yards, the most modern and second-largest in Europe. Artur Palácio worked at Lisnave for many years and had been a member of the Lisnave Workers' Commission since its inception. He recollected the inter-workplace meetings:

> I attended some fifteen or twenty meetings but cannot recall how often they met. They were not regular meetings but occurred whenever the need arose. I believe that the initiative to form the Inter-Empresas came from Lisnave itself but am not sure. . . . The first meeting had more than two hundred people; it was held at Lisnave during the period of the May strike . . . . That first meeting in May had the character of support for strikers. Twenty-five *contos* (twenty-five thousand *escudos*—approximately £500 in 1974) was collected for the workers of Sorefame.
>
> . . . There were many people experienced in workers' struggles, including some from CUF, Parry & Son, S.R.N., Olho de Boi (a naval base shipyard), Cergal, Applied Magnetics, and Sogantal. Some of the factories had not even a workers' commission then, just workers who came from the factories (Palácio 1982).

The meetings were informal, "a place for people to meet and discuss." In the early days the network was known by a variety of names; Palácio used the term inter-comissões. In addition to organizing collections, the inter-empresas helped organize demonstrations in defense of workers who were under attack by the government, sometimes by the armed forces, and always by the PCP and the Intersindical.

For example, on June 19 the government called in the army against one thousand postal workers (the CTT) who had gone on strike. Two army cadets refused to participate and were imprisoned. Activists in the inter-empresas were involved in organizing a demonstration in support of the cadets.[3]

A dispute at the Lisbon airport led to a military occupation of the administrative offices, the imprisonment of 15 militants, and the sacking of 280 workers. A protest demonstration of 4,000 TAP (the national airline) workers, including the entire maintenance section, forced the government to release the 15 militants, but the 280 workers were sacked the following day. Several thousand TAP employees went on strike on September 27 and organized a demonstration; the inter-empresas network played a major role in organizing the support of delegations from other workplaces and planning a bigger demonstration for Saturday, September 29. The industrial sociolo-

---

3 By contrast with the Communist Party, the Socialist Party had conspicuously supported the strike and stressed the democratic (i.e., non-PCP) nature of the strike organization. By doing so it enhanced its reputation as "democratic" and "left wing"—which proved important later.

gist Fátima Patriarca recalled the meeting of September 27:

> Every organization was having meetings. Their messengers were running from one meeting to another to keep contact. All the key activists were at the Inter-Empresas meeting. It was the intervention from the Lisnave delegate, a member of the PRP, which settled the issue of the demonstration. He wasn't a delegate in the fullest sense. . . . The Intersindical neither supported nor condemned it. Also there were practical reasons for refraining from demonstrating (Patriarca 1980).

In the end there was a demonstration of about forty thousand people on September 28, certainly not large by the standards of the time. But there was a distraction; hence Fátima's reference to "practical reasons." President Spínola urged the so-called silent majority to mobilize, culminating in a three hundred thousand–strong march that very day. Leading industrialists had met with him and a few generals, and their conclusion was that the use of armed force was becoming necessary to attack the left and reestablish "order"; they claimed they had a mandate from the population to organize a coup. On the 28th many workers preferred not to come into Lisbon. Since the night before, soldiers and civilians had been mounting barricades and searching cars heading into Lisbon. The government was forced to ban the march of the silent majority; the debacle led to Spínola's resignation and the strengthening of the left, as well as the bond between the MFA and the popular movement.

After September 28, the CTs consolidated their power and the Inter-Empresas started capitalizing their name. The meetings were very open; more people were being delegated by their commissions. An official bulletin was published, and the meetings settled down into a once-a-week pattern.

By January 1975, battles against layoffs were coming to the forefront; one example concerns the thousand workers in the Lisbon branches of an electrical engineering group, Efacec/Inel, who called upon the Inter-Empresas to organize a demonstration (see Efacec/Inel 1976, 39–42). A TAP worker recalled the Inter-Empresas planning meeting of February 2, 1975: "The biggest meeting I can remember was in the 'Voz do Operário' . . . there were about a thousand people. It was the meeting to plan the demonstration. The support of Lisnave workers was decisive" (May 8, 1982).

About thirty-seven or thirty-eight CTs (accounts vary) were involved at the time and the demonstration called for February 7. The lead banner was to read "Unemployment is an inevitable consequence of capitalism. That is why workers want to destroy it and build a new world."

But it wasn't the call for a new world that jeopardized the alliance between the government and the MFA. At the last minute, another slogan was added: "NATO out, national independence!" This was because part of the American fleet was in Lisbon, undertaking NATO exercises. All the political parties in the coalition government opposed the demonstration and it was prohibited. The PCP concluded that any "clash with NATO troops would favor the interests of reaction"; Octávio Pato from the PCP even went on television and advised people to give flowers to the marines of the NATO fleet. But the MFA still had to consider its position. The French newspaper *Libération* commented at the time: "By coincidence, the monthly delegate assembly of the MFA was taking place on the Thursday. It was expected that it would ban the demo . . . . On the Friday morning members of the Commissions [i.e., the Inter-Empresas] went to see COPCON [the newly created internal security force]. At the end of this meeting it was announced that MFA did not object to the demo" (Big Flame 1975, 15–16).

Eighty thousand people demonstrated. Palácio from Lisnave tells his part of the story:

> The demonstration met police and military officers all along the way. They wanted to discourage or divert us. The demonstration never stopped in spite of different attempts to stop it. The army blocked the streets leading to the American Embassy . . . I asked the people through the megaphone whether or not they should advance . . . the people would not let themselves be fooled or impeded. So I went to talk to an officer and told him "the people of the demonstration want to pass." And so we moved on. . . . . As the demonstrators went past, the commandos turned their backs on the demonstration, turned their weapons on the building, and joined the people in the chanting (Palácio 1982).

*Libération* reported that "people were crying with joy" and that "such a scene helps you understand Portugal today." The demonstration eroded the PCP/MFA bond and opened the way to future MFA/People Power developments.[4] The majority of the MFA had disagreed with the PCP and favored the expression of autonomous workers' power.

The demonstration was the most significant single action organized by the Inter-Empresas, in addition to its role in linking the most militant workplaces. It was also its last major initiative. Behind the scenes the Inter-Empresas had been losing ground due to several related factors. The PCP had developed a strategy of fighting from within and attempting to win over the workers' commissions: "In this period the PCP took control of the CTs in various enterprises such as Lisnave, Setenave, Siderurgia, Efacec (but this took a long time), and Sorefame. It had the majority of factories.

---

4 Contending forces offered two models for building a socialist society: centralism and popular power. The centralized model, supported by the PCP, argued for a socialist transformation from above and for abolishing private ownership, thereby ending exploitation. The popular power ("People Power") model, which the MFA helped to articulate much more clearly in the early summer of 1975, rejected this notion of socialism "from above," insisting on direct participation by all.

When it took control it allied the CTs with the Intersindical" (Lisnave workers 1982).

Carlos Nunes, a PRP militant and a delegate to the ad hoc CT of Lisnave in May–June 1974, told me how the PCP gained control at Lisnave:

> The PCP had stepped up its level of aggression and repression in factories, even resorting to physical means . . . meetings being manipulated so that only PCP members or people on their side were permitted to speak. They went around with lists of those to be supported, nudging people which way to vote.
>
> So a new secretariat was elected comprising six members of the PCP, four from the Socialist Party and one or two of the revolutionary left (Nuñez 1984).

The PCP, now in favor of CTs, organized an ostensibly "nonparty" conference on February 2, which was attended by 191 CTs from throughout the country.

The Inter-Empresas were viciously attacked by the PCP and the unions; many of the revolutionaries of the far left were vigorous in their counterattacks, and political sectarianism was an endemic and negative feature. The Marxist-Leninists were extremely hostile to the existing union leadership; those unions that had not responded sufficiently to the April 25 coup were considered relics of fascism, while those under the PCP were branded as social-fascist. It was not clear whether the intention was to replace the unions, bypass them, or complement them. But in practice the unions were also making headway, addressing "bread and butter" demands.

### March 11, 1975

The Inter-Empresas were weakening dramatically, so much so that they came to be perceived as little more than a Marxist-Leninist front, with a much diminished base in the workplaces. Above all, the Inter-Empresas would be dwarfed by the shift of events and the radicalization of the MFA. This shift was catalyzed by a bungled coup by Spínola and his supporters on March 11, 1975. Although March 11 was an amateurish and a rather desperate affair, it succeeded brilliantly in cementing the alliance between soldiers and workers. Within hours of the attack, barricades were set up along the main roads, sometimes using expropriated bulldozers, trucks, and cement mixers. Soldiers fraternized openly with workers manning the barricades and handed over arms. Armed workers searched cars and the strikers at Rádio Renascença went back to work, occupying the Catholic radio station in order to "defend the revolution."

The MFA made decisions at a dizzying speed, institutionalizing its own organization and setting up a new supreme governing body, the Council of Revolution. The first act of the Council of Revolution after March 11 was to nationalize the Portuguese-owned banks and insurance companies. After the failure of the March coup, land occupations increased dramatically. The importance of the struggle of the land workers cannot be overemphasized, and for the first time in living memory the drift of workers from the land to the city was reversed.

## The CRTSMs Project

In the wake of March 11 the PRP/BR, which had by now pulled out of the Inter-Empresas, decided that it was time to formally launch the CRTSMs (Revolutionary Councils of Workers, Soldiers, and Sailors). This was the first effort to unite workers with soldiers in a nonparty organization. Representation was to include delegates from barracks on the grounds that soldiers were workers in uniform. The PRP/BR came from a guerrilla warfare tradition that accentuated the role of the few in seizing power by means of armed insurrection, acting in the name of the workers.

The anniversary of the overthrow of the old regime, April 25, 1975, was chosen for Portugal's first ever elections based on universal suffrage. The weekend before, hundreds of thousands of people attended election meetings; however, 660 people attended a rather different type of meeting: the founding conference of the CRTSMs. This included representatives (not delegates) from 161 workplaces such as Lisnave, Setenave, TAP, and also, most significantly, 21 military units. The press and the organizers were quick to note that a number of the soldiers were in uniform. This event was the only one at the time that was not devoted to whom and what to vote for; instead it posed an alternative power system. The headline of that week's edition of the PRP/BR paper, *Revolução*, was "VOTE FOR REVOLUTIONARY COUNCILS— for the Dictatorship of the Proletariat." Christopher Reed of the *Guardian* reported that "Workers plan control Soviet style" (1975).

More than five and a half million people voted in the elections, 91.73 percent of the electorate. The Socialist Party, led by Mario Soares, emerged as the victors with 37 percent of the vote. Soares had a strong antifascist record and the victory of the Socialist Party brought credibility to an alternative, antifascist, democratic route outside that of the Communists and the far left. The newly elected Constituent Assembly was not a supreme body but merely an advisory body to the MFA, which still appointed the president. The subordination of the victors of the elections to the armed forces was to be a source of increasing tension. Within twenty-four hours there was chanting at a Socialist Party victory demonstration of "Down with the MFA," signifying for the first time open conflict between a major political party and the MFA.

After the elections, the MFA found it increasingly difficult to preserve its fragile unity. There was some talk of refusing to hand over power, as well as talk of a benevolent dictatorship. Another idea was that the MFA should become an actual political party. Given the options that presented themselves, the game of balancing—of making concessions to both sides—became more and more risky to play. There was a shuffling of schemes.

The CRTSMs project was resuscitated by elements of the internal security force, COPCON, including its commander, Otelo Saraiva de Carvalho. The architect behind the April 25 coup, Carvalho needed a base outside the army, such as a national network of these councils. The CRTSMs called a demonstration for June 17. This demonstration of some thirty thousand people was politically one of the most radical since April 25, as it challenged all the political parties and their associated institution, the Constituent Assembly. Slogans in support of the MFA were conspicuously absent. The main slogans were "For a revolutionary nonparty government" and "For a Socialist revolution." On the day of the demonstration, a third slogan was added: "Immediate dissolution of the Constituent Assembly!" The demonstration itself was preceded by a streetwide banner, proclaiming "*Fora com a canalha: O poder a quem trabalha!*" (Out with the scum: Power to those who work!)

The CRTSMs were superficially very political, claiming to be "the first soviet of revolutionary Portugal," but they were antiparty and called for "a revolutionary government without political parties." The CRTSMs' disdain for party politics resonated alongside the military tradition of the MFA and its role in reflecting and mediating the different classes. Accordingly, this somewhat slight organization, with relatively few roots in the workplaces, had a significant influence with some officers and helped shape events.

## The Popular Assemblies

"People Power" wasn't just rhetoric. Every day workers were taking over their factories at an unprecedented rate. The scale of factory occupations recalled Turin in 1920, Catalonia in 1936, and France in 1936 and 1968. The takeovers of the land, of workplaces, and of houses and apartments in the cities drew in many people who would otherwise have been excluded from self-organization, since they did not work in factories.[5] A golf course in the Algarve declared that it was now open to everyone except the members. Rádio Renascença hung a live microphone in the street so that whenever there was a demonstration passing by or a deputation outside, there would be a live broadcast of street politics.

Following an industrial dispute, the workers at *República* took control and

---

5 A slight note of caution. Many of the takeovers were driven by necessity, the owners and landlords having abandoned the enterprises. In general the workplaces under workers' control were the smaller enterprises, and not necessarily those of the most militant workers.

ran the paper in the name of the Poder Popular (popular power) movement. The workers' statement of aims on May 24 declared that "*República* will not henceforth belong to any party. All the progressive parties will be given identical treatment, depending only on the importance of events" (República Workers 1975). However, this also deprived the Socialist Party of its main newspaper and led to many heated arguments around the right to publish and freedom of speech—very significant, given that the Socialist Party had been prohibited before April 25.

Twenty-four hours after the CRTSMs demonstration, the Revolutionary Council of the MFA declared that the "MFA rejects the dictatorship of the proletariat supported by its armed militia since it does not fit into its pluralistic concept, already defined, of the Portuguese revolution." Within days, the general assembly of the MFA narrowly approved the "guidelines for the alliance between the people and the MFA," otherwise known as the MFA/Povo pact, which managed to unify momentarily the PCP, the Fifth Division officers around MES, COPCON, and some of the supporters of the CRTSMs. Its aim was to set up a parallel authority to the state and parliamentary system. The organizations of Poder Popular would be integrated, as popular assemblies, in the form of a pyramid under the protection of the MFA.

The adoption of the MFA/Povo pact, together with the continued incapability of the government to ensure the return of *República* and Radio Renascença (as for which mass demonstrations had forced the MFA to veto a government decision to return the station to the church, allowing the workers to retain control), prompted the resignation of Soares and the Socialist Party from the government. This resignation—on July 10, the day *República* was reopened—led to the formation of yet another provisional government: the fifth provisional, headed by General Vasco Goncalves (who was close to the PCP) and consisting predominantly of Communists and fellow travelers. This was the first government that did not include the Socialist Party or the conservative PPD (Partido Popular Democrático).

The Pontinha Popular Assembly was cited as a living example of Poder Popular. The Pontinha regiment of engineers had been the command headquarters for the April 25 coup. Most of the soldiers were trained mechanics and workers by background, and their regimental assembly became a model for other units. The soldiers and officers formed direct links with the local population, building roads and bridges with military equipment. After the failed countercoup of March 11, meetings between workers and soldiers became much more organized. The first joint assembly was held just before the MFA/Povo pact, with seventeen factories and about thirty local tenants' commissions present. At its peak the assembly had some two hundred delegates from its constituent associations.

There was much talk of popular assemblies—throughout that summer and autumn *República* mentions at least thirty-eight—and planning meetings for a great many others. Although they may have been formally established, few in fact ever got off the ground. Usually the more stable were those that in effect assumed the functions of local government. The assemblies were dominated by representatives from residents' commissions, swamping those from workplaces. Members of these assemblies spent hundreds and hundreds of hours planning and sometimes even implementing actions. Given the circumstances the assemblies were never able to realize their potential and their critics claimed they were just "talking shop."

## The Comité de Luta de Setúbal

This was a period of rapid radicalization and polarization. Over the "Hot Summer" of 1975 and into the autumn, a number of forces, such as the peasants in the north, the *retornardos* from the colonies, the Socialist Party, and the Catholic Church, were becoming bolder and gathering momentum. On July 13 in Rio Major, north of Lisbon, the PCP offices were burned down, followed by the destruction of the PCFP and MDP offices and homes of local leaders throughout northern and central Portugal. The Socialist Party provided cover for large and sometimes violent popular demonstrations against the fifth provisional government, in which a parody of the MFA's popular slogan—"The people are *not* with the MFA"— was chanted on the streets. All this was accompanied by developments within in the military coalition formed around Melo Antunes and his "Group of Nine" officers, who had been from the beginning important members of the MFA. Antunes and the Group of Nine enjoyed the credibility of being opponents of the Fascist regime and, despite ultraleft polarization, could not easily be dismissed as "fascists." The fifth provisional government was forced out of office on August 19 and the ensuing sixth brought back the Socialists, Popular Democrats, and some original members of the MFA; the Communists were given the Public Works Ministry. In effect the PCP had been sidelined, for the first time since April 25. The crisis split the MFA and "the specter of civil strife was real" (see Maxwell 1995, 152).

The Comité de Luta de Setúbal (Committee of Struggle) was formed in reaction to the attempt on September 29 by the sixth provisional government to close down all the radio stations including, in particular, Rádio Renascença. At this moment a number of the popular assemblies were attempting to reconstitute their organizations, placing less reliance on the leadership of the now hopelessly divided MFA. It was no accident that the Comité de Luta named itself a committee of struggle, not a popular assembly. Representatives from the barracks met the night of September 30 with others from workers' and residents' commissions, and set up what was to become the most advanced example of a workers' council to emerge in Western Europe since the end of World War II.

The city of Setúbal had, in addition to the four thousand workers at the Setenave shipyards, a number of factories from newly established and more militant industries. Compared to other Portuguese towns and cities, in Setúbal there was a high concentration of manual workers.

The first proper meeting of the Comité de Luta was on October 6, 1975, and five hundred people came. This was the first of eight meetings. The structure, maintained until November 25, consisted of a weekly plenary session of workers' and residents' commissions—unions and other popular organizations could join the debates but had no right to vote. Meetings started at 9 or 9:30 p.m. and lasted until 1:00 in the morning. At each session the members drew up the agenda for the next meeting. Attendance usually ranged from three hundred to five hundred people, but there were smaller meetings and also joint meetings with other groups such as the city council (Dows et al. 1978, Downs 1980).

"From the beginning emphasis was given to the need to carry out work orientated to the real problems of the city and factories, enabling unity of the workers in practice" (Downs 1980, 319).

Along with debating the national issues of the day, the Comité set out to organize and coordinate a number of practical actions. The list is impressive. The first major action was to organize "the most important demonstration in Setúbal since that of the First of May, of soldiers and people," which eventually took place on October 16.

In a meeting on October 13, the Comité agreed to support a takeover of the local paper, *O Setubalense*, by the workers. With moral support of the committee the workers sacked the proprietor and took over the paper on October 21.

The following day the regional agrarian reform center in Alcácer do Sal (the nearest town south of Setúbal) was destroyed by a bomb, so land workers occupied a house in Alcácer do Sal and made it the new center. Support was coordinated by the Comité: soldiers went to help, giving away guns to citizens, and civilian reinforcements were also sent in.

For many, the most striking achievement was the distribution of agricultural products, which was undertaken by the Committee of Consumption, comprised of elected delegates from the Comité.

The vitality of the residents' commissions proved an important contribution to the life of the Comité. They were already organizing the occupation of all vacant housing, new or old; establishing criteria to tie rent to income; taking into consideration the age of the building, its location and size, family size, and other factors; and arranging for rent to be paid to the committee, not the landlord (Downs 1980).

The residents' commissions initially represented were Bairro do Liceu, 4 Caminhos, Matalhidos, and São Gabriel. The following workers' commissions were represented on the secretariat (the number employed is shown in parentheses): Setenave shipyards (4,000); Entreposto—car assembly firm (731); Secil—cement firm (1,000); SAPEC chemical products (949); Conservas Unitas–fish canning factory (98); Bronzes Cetobriga—bronze metal workshop (24) (Dows et al. 1978).

One of the leading participants, Isabel Guerra, told me that although the CTs were welcomed in the popular assemblies, in practice their voices were drowned by the noisier immediate problems of the populace. This happened even in the Comité de Luta de Setúbal; however, at its best the committee transcended divisions:

> The Comité was a front united in common activities, despite political differences.
>
> I learned that people can organize and discuss together even when they have political differences. I remember one political discussion, prior to a demonstration organized by the PCP, MES, UDP, LCI, PRP and MRPP. It was decided that the slogans would be by consensus. They would never be voted on. They would talk until agreement was reached. And they did. (Guerra 1984a).

## November 25, 1975, and the Response in Setúbal

The subsequent twists and turns of events are complicated and difficult to parse. The so-called ruling government couldn't rule, fundamentally because it couldn't rely upon the armed forces. Many of the units, perhaps the majority, had sworn allegiance to the "revolution" and couldn't be "trusted."

The revolutionary process was rudely punctured on November 25 by the relatively small forces of two hundred commandos, who were sent in to suppress a revolt by paratroopers at four airbases. During the day all the left-wing units within the military collapsed, likely surprising the commandos with the ease with which the maneuver had succeeded. In real terms the level of physical repression was slight.

This military action was masterminded by the "moderates" from the Socialist Party and the Group of Nine officers around Melo Antunes, and was not a right-wing coup, despite the many rumors that followed. These officers had nothing to do with the conservative right. The popular movement was looking for an external enemy, not one within the MFA, and not on the left of the political spectrum. Socialism or barbarism seemed to be the only options. The vast majority of the left thought "that there would be sharp armed clashes between the classes within a few months." Carvalho, the commander of COPCON, commented, "What worries me is the possible Chileanisation of Portugal . . . they are building machines to kill. Machines for repression. With them they can set off a new Chile. I am haunted by that fear" (Faye 1976, 49–50).

The neofascists were not real contenders for power. The Portuguese ruling class itself had already suffered the inconvenience of a right-wing authoritarian regime. Nor was the murder of Allende in Chile in 1973, followed by the Pinochet dictatorship, as inspiring to big business and the CIA as the left feared.

Rumors of impending coups were an endemic and exhausting feature of political life—in Barreiro, across the Tagus estuary from Lisbon, the *bombeiros voluntários* (voluntary firemen) would sound the fire bells at any perceived sign of a putsch; the population, often awakened in the early hours of the morning, would rush into the streets only to discover the alarm was false. It is also probable that workers and soldiers could have physically resisted any conservative putsch. The moderates around the Group of Nine claimed that an insurrection was being prepared. Thus, the November 25 move against the left was justified on the grounds that the left itself was preparing a coup. Such preparations were much less advanced than the moderates and the right liked to imagine.

Yet it is certainly true that elements of the left had been dallying with the notion. Those around Carvalho wanted shortcuts to power. Often sections of the left saw the military as its own shortcut. The downside of the interest in the military was that it became a diversion, one that played into the hands of the moderates. Events in Setúbal were described as follows: "A related weakness was that the problems of the soldiers were not openly discussed in the meetings. The PRP was more interested in discussing these in a more conspiratorial manner. . . . On November 25 construction workers collected bulldozers and blocked the roads into Setúbal so that the Pagnards, the army cars, could not go into the city. They made the first move" (Guerra 1984b).

Building workers contacted the Comité de Luta and asked them to set up blockades around the city. The Comité set up an underground radio station that operated for a few days. The town hall was occupied. Isabel Guerra recalled:

> We tried to contact all the organizations including the unions and cultural organizations. We called a rally outside the barracks . . . . The problem of November 25 was that neither the unions nor the CTs controlled by the PCP were interested . . . so they did not mobilize . . . people. In the regiment the soldiers took arms from a captain and controlled the situation as long as they could. . . . November 25 showed that the Comité de Luta could function in time of crisis. But the problem . . . of the Comité and even the CTs was . . . that most of the time these activists were a militant minority. This weakness

is very important to the understanding of the success of the November 25 offensive. The kind of discussion that took place in the Comité could not be held in the place of work. It was [a] . . . political . . . discussion of a minority—the intelligentsia within the workers' movement. Even in the CTs the delegates to the Comité were those who, although sincere and honest, were already open to the ideas of the Comité de Luta (1984a).

The activists in the Comité decided not to organize an insurrection, not because they couldn't, but because they would have been isolated as there was no national network of like-minded organizations. November 25 was the turning point, and the revolutionary process petered out.

## Reflections

The stress from the overthrow of fascism and rise of counterrevolution blurred the distinction between fascism and capitalism. Many on the left argued that there was only one solution—socialism—and that the alternative was barbarism. There was an underestimation of the capacity of capitalism to modernize and reform, using the tools of social democracy.

The Socialist Party played an enormous part in the reform process; its arguments around free speech and workers' control, for "progress, democracy, and socialism" enabled it to appeal to broad sectors of the population (Birchall 1979). Such promises of reform, commonplace elsewhere, were unknown in Portugal.

Kenneth Maxwell argues convincingly that ferment was central to the transition to democracy: "The strength flows from the fact that it was a democracy born of struggle" (1995, 1). Indeed, the relatively peaceful resolution contributed to the development of Portuguese democracy. Maxwell suggests "the Portuguese upheaval was more like the European revolutions of the 1820s and 1848 than the great revolutions of 1789 in France or 1917 in Russia." But this is not to suggest, and Maxwell does not, that the movement for change was superficial (1995, 4). The fact is that the revolution failed and has left very little evidence. In 1974 and 1975 the walls of buildings were covered with revolutionary murals. There is no sign of them now. It suits the victors to accentuate how they came to power peacefully and with legitimacy. The danger is the tendency to homogenize the story into a model of capitalist development, and to marginalize the upheavals and revolts of the time as having been figments of the imagination.

At the time, Western capitalism was extremely worried by what was happening in Portugal. The Spanish regime was still Fascist and looked as if it might collapse. The conservative figures put out by the Spanish government showed that in 1974, 1,196 industrial disputes were registered, involving 669,861 workers. Troops in other European countries were becoming restless. In Italy more than a thousand soldiers, wearing uniforms and handkerchief masks, took part in a demonstration in support of Portuguese workers and soldiers. The events in Portugal did not occur in isolation, but rather the events occurred because Portugal could not continue to exist in isolation.

The first task is that of the historian—to record and capture the events. When faced with particular issues requiring collective solutions, workplace organizations coordinated their struggles with other workers' committees, with residents' organizations, with land workers, and, especially, with members of the armed forces by establishing higher-level bodies of elected and recallable delegates.

Of the four organizations described, the Inter-Empresas potentially had the deepest roots in the workplaces, but the militants at the Inter-Empresas meetings could not always claim to represent their workplaces. They lost ground at the expense of the PCP, which began to focus on the CTs more systematically, and also to the development of the trade union movement. The political sectarianism, of the Marxist-Leninist type in particular, did not help.

The Inter-Empresas helped prize rank-and-file solders away from the authorities. This happened with increasing frequency, but the Inter-Empresas took the lead almost from the outset. The three examples above from the Inter-Empresas show how workers formally collaborated with soldiers—a potentially powerful combination.

Unlike the other examples in this study the CRTSMs project was a national organization. The other groups couldn't claim representation from 161 organizations, let alone 21 military units. However there was some disconnection between day-to-day struggles and this grand political "project"; in practice the Revolutionary Council did not grow deep roots in the workplaces.

The popular assemblies also involved tenants and other community organizations. This account has not been able to focus in depth on their many manifestations. However, the assemblies often got bogged down while attempting to be extensions of the local government and their positions were at times incoherent given their ambivalence toward the government as well as the officers who helped inspire them.

The achievements of the Comité de Luta de Setúbal were among the most inspiring. The Comité was potentially able to coordinate the resistance to November 25 but unwilling to organize an insurrection, partly because there was no national infrastructure but also because many of the people in Setúbal did not see November 25 as the return of the extreme right.

During those twenty months of social upheaval in 1974–75 hundreds of thousands of workers took over their workplaces, the land, and abandoned houses, and tens of thousands of soldiers rebelled. Nobody had predicted that so many would try quickly to learn and put into practice the ideas that explode forth from the exploited when they try to take control of their own destiny. I would suggest that the extent and depth of the workers' council movement is an important indicator, indeed the most fundamental, of the profundity of a revolutionary process.

Perhaps the councils could have been stronger, but "the feeble and reflected light of the moon makes possible important conclusions about the sunlight" (Trotsky 1934/1977, 208).

It was an extraordinary period, one that needs to be further studied and celebrated.

## References

Barker, Colin, ed. 1979. *Revolutionary rehearsals.* London: Bookmarks.

Bermão, Nancy. 1986. *The revolution within the revolution: Workers control in rural Portugal,* Princeton, NJ: Princeton University Press.

Big Flame. 1975. *Portugal: A blaze of freedom.* Birmingham, UK: Big Flame Publications.

Birchall, Ian. 1979. Social democracy and the Portuguese revolution. *International Socialism,* second series, no. 6, Autumn.

Chilcote, Ronald H. 1987. *The Portuguese revolution of 25 April 1974.* Coimbra: Universidade Coimbra.

Cliff, Tony. 1975. Portugal at the crossroads. *International Socialism* 1, nos. 81–82, special edition. London.

Downs, Charles. 1979. *Revolution at the grassroots: community organizations in the Portuguese Revolution.* Albany, NY: State University of New York Press.

———. 1980. Community organization, political change and urban policy: Portugal 1974–1976. PhD thesis, University of California at Berkeley.

Dows C., F. N. da Silva, H. Gonçalves, and I. Seabra. 1978. *Os Moradores e a Conquista da Cidade.* Lisbon: O Armazén das Letra.

Efacec/Inel Workers. 1976. *Jornal da greve (suspensa) dos trablhadores da Efacec/Inel Lisboa.* Efacec/Inel: Lisbon.

Faye, Jean-Pierre. 1976. *Portugal: The revolution in the labyrinth.* Nottingham: Spokesman Books.

Hammond, John. 1988. *Building popular power: Workers' and neighborhood movements in the Portuguese revolution.* New York: Monthly Review Press.

Harman, Chris. 1975. Portugal, the latest phase. *International Socialism, no. 83 (November).* London.

Mailer, Phil. 1977. *Portugal: The impossible revolution?* London: Solidarity.

Marx, Karl and Frederick Engels. 1975–2005. *Collected works,* vol. 22. London and Moscow: Lawrence & Wishart.

Maxwell, Kenneth. 1995. *The making of Portuguese democracy.* Cambridge: Cambridge University Press.

Patriarca, Fátima. 1978. Operários da Lisnave de 12 Sept. 1974. *Análise Social,* no. 56.

Porch, Douglas. 1977. *The Portuguese armed forces and the revolution.* London: Croom Helm.

Reed, Christopher. 1975. Workers plan control Soviet style. *Guardian* (UK). April 25.

República Workers. 1975. Statement, May 24.

Robinson, Peter. 1999. *Portugal 1974–1975: The forgotten dream.* London: Socialist History Society.

_____. 1989. *Workers' councils in Portugal 1974–1975.* M Phil thesis, Centre for Sociology & Social University, Open University, 1989.

Santos, Maria de Lourdes Lima, Marinús Pires de Lima, and Vitor Matias Ferreira. 1976. *O 25 de Abril e as lutas sociais nas empresas.* 3 vols. Porto: Afromento.

Sunday Times Insight Team. 1975. *Portugal: The year of the captains.* London: Sunday Times.

Trotsky, Leon. 1934/1977. *The history of the Russian revolution.* Trans. Max Eastman. Repr. London: Pluto Press.

Interviews:

Guerra, Isabel. 1984a. Interview by author. March 6.

———. 1984b. Interview by author. April 6.

Lisnave workers. 1982. Interview by author. February 8.

Nuñez, Carlos. 1984. Interview by author. March 6.

Palácio, Artur. 1982. Interview by author. February 8.

Patriarca, Fátima. 1980. Interview by author. January 9.

# Workers' Control against Capitalist Restructuring in the Twentieth Century

# 15

## Workers' Control and the Politics of Factory Occupation

### Britain, 1970s

**Alan Tuckman**

On July 30, 1971, members of the press waiting at the gates of the Upper Clyde Shipbuilders (UCS) heard Jimmy Reid, chair of the shop stewards committee at the yards in Glasgow, announce

> the first campaign of its kind in trade unionism. [The yard workers] . . . are not going on strike. We are not even having a sit-in strike. We are taking over the yards because we refuse to accept that faceless men can make these decisions. We are not strikers. We are responsible people and we will conduct ourselves with dignity and discipline. We want to work. We are not wildcats (BBC 1971).[1]

The reason for this announcement was the ending of financial support from the government, putting the yards formally into bankruptcy and into the hands of a receiver whose role was to realize any assets for creditors. The very presence of the press at the gates indicates their anticipation that the shop stewards were to stage some opposition to the closure. However, since Reid had distanced the action from a sit-in and, for the following eighteen months, the shop stewards organizing the "work-in" essentially maintained a system of dual power with the receiver's office, the action proved the focal inspiration for more than 260 worker occupations in Britain during the following decade.[2]

---

1 See also McGill 1972; Foster and Woolfson 1986.
2 This figure for the number of occupations in Britain in the decade following the UCS work-in was taken from an examination of newspaper reports covering the period. Searches were carried out among UK daily papers that gave coverage of industrial relations, principally the *Financial Times*, the *Times* (London), the *Guardian*, and some weekly and monthly publications such as *Socialist Worker* and *Labour Research*. For some specific occupations local newspapers were also searched,

# The Logic of Workplace Occupation under Capitalism

Reid was also distancing the work-in from strikes, the traditional weapon in the arsenal of industrial action. A strike, as the withdrawal of labor, means workers abandoning the workplace, perhaps a counterproductive tactic in the circumstances of possible closure. The UCS work-in meant those dismissed by the receiver still turned up to work each day, although not as paid labor. However, while this remained the defining action of the period, other occupations went further in their command of the workplace. Workplace occupation inherently challenges the fundamental principles of the control of private property, involving workers claiming control through their labor and excluding those with ownership rights.

Occupation also challenges the limits of the sale of labor power to capital, posing an extension of access rights beyond the temporal limits of the employment contract. While a recent commentator argues that the "occupation of a factory is a tactic of class struggle—not an experience in workers' control," there are inherent issues of control raised by the action (Sherry 2010, 126). Not only were workers appropriating, however temporarily, the means of production, they were also maintaining organizational capacity to sustain the plant while promoting their justification of the action. If the occupation involves a continuance of production, a work-in, then this will also involve the organization of production and therefore some element and an anticipation of workers' self-management. It raises questions of alternative futures for the organization and role of the workforce as well as of formal ownership of the plant.

The occupation tactic clearly raises further questions. Why should this particular tactic be adopted at a particular time? And why should such a tactic then almost disappear for the next quarter century? Even in its disappearance, what heritage has the tactic and the period of conflict left behind for later generations of struggle? This essay might shed some light on the reappearance of the workplace occupation in reaction to crisis through examining the explosion of creativity that accompanied the tactic (Gall 2010).

## The End of Britain's Political Consensus

By the early 1960s the postwar political consensus in Britain, based around industrial expansion and economic growth, underpinning greater consumer affluence, was beginning to appear frail. While the economy had

---

such as *Manchester Evening News* for the engineering disputes and the *Hull Daily Mail* and the *Leicester Mercury* for Imperial Typewriters. Cross-referencing of these results was conducted against a number of studies covering shorter periods carried out by the TUSIU (1976), by Metra Consulting (1972), and Hemingway and Keyser (1975). See Tuckman 1985 for details.

been expanding it had been doing so at a far slower rate than its industrial competitors. The consensus had also been built on state ownership of key industries and services, health and welfare provision, and strong organization by the trade unions, which were becoming contentious in the growing economic crisis. The Wilson Labour government, taking office in 1964, launched its own more explicit modernization, attempting links with the explosion of popular culture in the wake of the Beatles.

The program included the extension of industrial and economic planning—launching Britain into "the white heat of technological revolution"—by attempting to meet international competition through the merging of companies in particular industrial sectors, a process also known as rationalization. One of these mergers, of five shipyards, resulted in the creation of UCS in the 1960s. Principally this was to be attempted through the Industrial Reorganisation Corporation (IRC), whose purpose was "to promote structural change which will improve the efficiency and profitability of British industry" (Hansard 1974). The IRC had a significant impact in its attempt to rationalize British industrial capital, bringing together large conglomerates that sought to streamline multisite operations to achieve their promised economies of scale, which itself led to confrontations with organized workers championing "the right to work." Conservative opposition formulated a "quiet revolution," arguing that the market ought to operate to allow for failing companies—the "lame ducks" of the economy—which were not to be given state support, and so allowed to collapse.

Unemployment was growing and approaching one million, a number considered politically unsustainable. Trade unions were growing in membership as well as influence in the new corporate state, with a significant shift in influence to the shop-floor organization (see Panitch 1976 and Crouch 1977). The Wilson government also made the first attempt at a legislative reform of industrial relations of the period, "In Place of Strife," a bill that sought to regulate the actions of trade unions. While basic terms and conditions may have been subject to national bargaining between employers' organizations and full-time officers of the trade unions, these were now enhanced or superseded by local bargaining by shop stewards. With the growing significance of multiplant conglomerates, shop stewards were increasingly establishing cross-site combine committees for communication and coordination of strategy.

Although portrayed in popular imagery as the promoters of conflict within the workplace, the shop steward system had in reality minimized open dispute through bargaining disputes down into a plethora of "plus payments." An important corollary to the rise of shop stewards was the development of training courses, which emerged principally in the extramural departments of universities. These courses existed haphazardly, largely dependent on sympathetic instructors, and while considering the role of stewards in recruitment, organizing, and bargaining skills, the curriculum was often renegotiated annually to address broader industrial and economic issues and policy.

It was not only Labour and Conservative Party support that fractured in the 1960s. The Communist Party, which had sustained a strong base in the postwar trade unions, had been hit first by the Khrushchev denunciation of Stalin and then by the 1956 invasion of Hungary, which saw the revival of workers' councils as a focus for the organization of popular revolt (see, e.g., Anderson 1964, Lomax 1976, and Lomax 1980).

A "New Left" began to emerge, exploring alternative models of socialism. Some examined the potential of the "self-management" of the postwar Yugoslav regime. Drawing on this experience, as well as on past experience of workplace organizations, some New Left commentators argued for the need to return to a concern with "workers' control." In an article published in *New Left Review* in 1964, Tony Topham argued that:

> the quantitative growth of the shop stewards' strength in industry, the causes and numbers of strikes (particularly local, spontaneous strikes) are significant factors, and that the whole area of conflict surrounding the role of the shop steward is likely to intensify in the near future...whilst the Left's main task should be to assist at the birth of articulate and explicit demands for control at shop-floor level, we must insist upon the need to generalize these outwards to embrace the whole framework of social, economic and political decision-making (Topham 1964, 4).

A series of conferences were organized involving trade union officers, shop stewards and other activists, and academics, leading to the founding in 1968 of the Institute for Workers' Control (IWC). While it is a mistake to generalize about a specific IWC position or line (Barratt Brown, Coates, and Topham 1975), as their publications covered an eclectic range of areas and perspectives (Hyman 1974), the central academic figures presented a view of workers' control as "encroachment" by organized labor into managerial prerogative. Promoting the slogan of "open the books," they advocated the development of control bargaining by trade unions, and particularly shop stewards, in nonremunerator areas around working conditions and work rate. By the late 1960s they had initiated a number of industrial working groups around the docks, the steel industry, and other industries (Coates 1968; see also Topham 1967). Key figures in the movement were engaged in trade union education; plans and discussion often emerged from classes run for shop stewards in these industries.

With massive unemployment blamed largely on factory closures, there was speculation about an escalation of industrial action to challenge closures. Increasing insecurity in the labor market drew inspiration from the recent experience of student sit-ins and the occupations in France. In February

1969 the BBC broadcast a television play, *The Big Flame*, directed by Ken Loach, which depicted an occupation of the Liverpool docks.

*The Occupation in Britain*

In the context of strongly organized and potentially militant workplaces, as well as the increased currency of the idea of "workers' control," there was anticipation that some major resistance to large-scale redundancy was imminent. However, while the occupations have been principally associated with the large-scale closures of the period, and most of the protracted occupations were indeed contesting closure, many others involved more limited challenges to layoffs, redundancies, dismissals, or the threat of lockout. In this context it is also necessary to establish an accepted definition of "occupation" since, it could be argued, the normal state of the workplace is when the workforce is in occupation; a traditional image of dispute—of strike action—is the workforce withdrawing from the workplace. However, many tactics in industrial disputes, such as a work-to-rule or an overtime ban—often presented as "short of strike action"—involve workers remaining in occupation. The very progression of a spontaneous dispute may mean some period of uncertainty with the workforce withdrawing from work but not from the workplace. While the eviction of management is a sure indicator of worker occupation, this is not a requisite: at UCS the receiver remained at the yard.

## The Big Flame and UCS

One of the key targets of IRC support was the electronics and electrical power conglomerate GEC-AEI. Formed from the merger of three companies— GEC, AEI, and EE—in order to achieve economies of scale, it hoped to achieve competitiveness in an increasingly global market. At the time of the merger the company operated on 135 sites in Britain with 228,000 employees, making it the largest private-sector employer at the time in the UK (see Anti Report 1972 and IWC 1969). Rationalization following the merger precipitated large numbers of redundancies (see, e.g., Newens 1969 and Schubert 1970).

When workers at three Merseyside plants were faced with closure, the shop stewards agreed to resist with an occupation. The proposal was abandoned due to concerns over the loss of redundancy pay or the possibility of criminal prosecution (see IWC 1969 and Chadwick 1970). This indicates the main tension within a workforce facing closure: on the one hand, collective resistance; on the other, acceptance of redundancy pay or the chance of alternative employment. Trade unions have a strategic choice between the mobilization of resistance and bargaining the terms of redundancy for those losing jobs.

It was not until 1971, after the election of Heath's Conservative government, that the "big flame" was lit by the occupation at UCS. The "lame ducks" policy meant a government rejection when the company approached it for continuing financial support, leading to threats of redundancies to the workforce. Shop stewards had discussed some form of occupation and, when redundancies were announced, they informed the gatekeepers at the yards that they had taken over control.

As with other occupations of the period, the work-in built on the trade unionism at the yards. The usual divisions between different craft unions in the yards were transcended with the transformation of the Joint Shop Stewards Committee into the Work-in Coordinating Committee, following its extension into representing managers also under threat of redundancy. "Dual power" existed for the next eighteen months, shared between the shop stewards trying to maintain employment and the receiver appointed to realize the capital assets. Shipyard workers made redundant were encouraged by the stewards to continue coming to work in the yards. While the action can only tenuously be defined as an occupation, the UCS work-in mobilized considerable support.

### Labor's Movement and Labour Politics

Mass demonstrations were held through the streets of Glasgow, which attracted senior Labour politicians, most notably their Industry spokesperson Tony Benn, along with trade union leaders. The government worried about possible social unrest if they attempted to evict the work-in or bar access to the yards. Merging the yards had created a key tension between the navy yards required by the government and the civil yards, which were under severe competition from the shift to cheaper bulk shipping containers. Little argument challenged the yards' military role, so arguments began to emerge concerning the social cost of closure (see IWC 1971 and Murray 1972). Lasting for eighteen months, the UCS dispute was the very act of resistance to have an impact on the UK labor movement, particularly in mobilizing occupation and raising new questions concerning closure and redundancy.

UCS, however, was not typical of the occupations to follow. Perhaps the first incident typical of the UK occupations in the 1970s was at a Plessey armaments plant, just a short distance from Glasgow on the River Clyde, which started about a month after the work-in at UCS. The workforce at the plant had been downsized and when the last 250 workers were told to report to collect their remaining wages rather than attend for work, they jumped the locked gate.

The Plessey occupation was to last four months until a deal was reached for a takeover that protected seventy of the jobs (see *Labour Research* 1972;

*Times* 1972; Coates 1981, 55–56). After such a protracted occupation, seventy was likely the approximate expected number of remaining participants: this highlights two significant factors concerning the development and outcome of occupations. First, numbers were subject to decline as participants found alternative employment or simply became disillusioned or pessimistic about prospects. Second, when solutions did emerge, the number offered reemployment and the qualifications for it seemed to equate to the number and qualifications of those remaining in occupation. As with most occupations, resistance was sustained in support of employment, for "the right to work," but with little clear strategy for achieving this.

## Escalation of Worker Factory Occupations

By the end of 1971 occupations had spread further south to the steel and engineering works around South Yorkshire and into Wales, all resisting redundancies. Most of the reflection on occupation and property rights initially revolved around property rights in the sale of labor, the idea being that in some way employment vested property rights in the job similar to those of a shareholder. This was the very ethos—never explicit—that developed around redundancy pay. Initially introduced, reflecting Keynesian views on labor mobility, to assist the flow of industrial change and enhance the ability of workers in declining sectors and regions of the economy to move to developing areas, its practice was to commodify jobs by putting cash payment in place to buy out any job "possession" by workers (see Fryer 1973; 1981).

Thus divisions among workers occurred around whether to resist or accept redundancy terms, as they did in terms of support for public or private ownership; little debate occurred, except pragmatically, concerning any form of self-management or how things might operate under workers' control. While occupation was sometimes suggested as resistance in advance of impending closures, the action itself tended to be spontaneous. The occupations also tended to be acts of relative desperation in the face of job loss with no real plan beyond the hope that another owner might be found. However, some occupying workers began to drift into establishing worker cooperatives—out of pragmatism rather than any deeper commitment—when an alternative buyer did not materialize.

In February 1972 the shoe manufacturer Sexton, Son and Everard declared bankruptcy and announced that their factories in East Anglia would be closed and the seven hundred workers made redundant. A meeting of the employees voted almost unanimously to contest the closure by means of occupation and controlling machinery and stock (Wajcman 1983; *Socialist Worker* 1972). Before the resolution was implemented the firm was bought by a local developer, who guaranteed five hundred of the jobs. But among those still to lose their jobs were forty-five women workers at a satellite factory in Fakenham, which machined leather uppers for the main factory. Feeling ignored they decided to go ahead with occupation when the first round of the women lost their jobs. They had machinery and scraps of leather from which they produced bags and other goods for sale locally, bearing the label "Fakenham Occupation Workers." The women began to contemplate the prospect of working for themselves in a workers' cooperative.

At Briant Colour Printing, workers occupied to resist the closure of their East London plant. This became a work-in when the occupying workers obtained printing contracts, often for left-wing or labor movement organizations. Members of this work-in also seemed to have addressed the possibility of establishing a workers' cooperative but rejected the idea (*Inside Story* 1973). Mass pickets were held when the plant workers were threatened with eviction and, eventually, a new owner was found. However, only fourteen weeks after the new ownership took over, the plant was again closed. This time the workforce could not respond with an occupation: having received redundancy notices through the post they arrived at the plant to find it already shuttered and guarded by a security firm (*Labour Research* 1973a).

Workers at Leadgate Engineering in Durham also began an occupation against closure. The date of closure had been strategically chosen and would have allowed for the removal of machinery without the repayment of government grants; it also meant the minimum redundancy pay to the workforce. However, one hundred members of the three hundred–strong workforce occupied the site, prohibiting any movement of plant and machinery. Ultimately, after a six-month occupation, the owners came to an agreement with the remaining thirty workers for a plan to establish a workers' cooperative. In exchange for the machinery still held in the plant, the workers could lease one of the factory buildings, supported by a loan to the cooperative and guaranteed against subcontract work for the previous owner (see Mooney 1973; *Labour Research* 1973b).

The Leadgate workforce seemed no less cynical about a workers' cooperative than those at Briant Colour but occupation on its own did not constitute a solution. The cooperative repaid the loan by the end of the year, even taking on extra workers, and gained additional contracts although it collapsed in late 1975 and work ceased (Coates 1981, 137; see also *Labour Research* 1973b).

Fisher-Bendix, a motor components plant near Liverpool, had diversified into a range of other products following changes in ownership. In early 1972 there was talk of redundancies and the shop stewards made contact with UCS and Plessey as well as the stewards at the nearby Merseyside plant of GEC-AEI, which had considered occupation in 1969 (see Clarke 1974; Eccles 1981; Solidarity 1972). Although there had been prior discussion, the occupation of Fisher-Bendix was spontaneous and unplanned: a meeting was stormed and management evicted, with the gates subsequently welded shut. With the intervention of Harold Wilson, local Member of Parliament and—at that time—Leader of the Opposition, a new owner was found although without offering any long-term security for the plant or workforce.

These occupations built on the influence of workplace organization, formally represented through the shop steward system. This was sometimes at odds with the formal trade union structure, which was more inclined to come to terms on redundancy and suspicious of unofficial shop-floor organization. These roots in the shop steward movement, and tension with trade unions, were to become more evident in the events around the national dispute in the engineering industry.

### The Manchester Engineers

Shortly before the occupation in Fakenham, in early 1972, workers at Bredbury Steelworks took over the plant near Manchester, setting a pattern for about fifty further occupations in the engineering industry. Basic pay and conditions in the industry were determined in long-term agreements between the Engineering Employers Federation (EEF) and the Confederation of Shipbuilding and Engineering Unions, constituted of the thirty-one trade unions with members in the industry. However, workplace bargaining had become increasingly important, with shop stewards negotiating local deals that could mean double the basic pay in some plants. The union had presented a claim for £25 a week for skilled workers, a thirty-five-hour week, and an extra week of vacation with the latter two items part of a strategy to counter rising unemployment. When the claim was rejected by the employer's side, the unions moved the campaign to the regions.

The Manchester region, with perhaps the best-organized and most militant shop steward organization, put forward national demands on a plant-by-plant basis. Submission of the claim was often accompanied by the imposition of sanctions—an overtime ban, work-to-rule, etc., to which some employers responded with threat of lockout (Chadwick 1973). Commentators have tended to see the escalation of the dispute into occupation in about thirty plants in the region as being promoted by the integration of the left, predominantly Communist as well as a few Socialist Worker shop stewards and union officials (Mills 1974; Darlington and Lyddon 2001). However, it was the EEF that targeted a challenge at particular plants where there were, as they saw it, "communist stewards."[3] The president of the EEF

---

3 Comment from author interview with EEF regional secretary in April 1976.

stressed to employers "the importance of standing firm in this situation. There's little doubt that a policy of militant plant bargaining . . . [was] intended to expose the industry to a free-for-all in wages and conditions claims. If the unions are out to test the fibre of our unity, we should leave them in no doubt as to its durability" (EEF 1972).

In plants with shop-floor representatives more amenable to compromise with the EEF position, the workforce was rewarded with offers of pay increases beyond the national claim but without any other benefits. At Mather & Platts, with a moderate union organization, the offer accepted was for a £5.50-a-week increase, significantly more than the claim that amounted to a £4.00 increase without any concessions on holidays or hours.

The EEF took a page out of the trade union book and maintained unity and discipline among its membership, holding the federation line that plant settlements should only be reached on pay. Most of the settlements claimed by the union had been made with companies outside of the EEF. The few members of the EEF who made agreements also covering holiday and working hours faced expulsion. Not only was this an attack on militant shop stewards and support for the more acceptable face of workplace representation, it also highlighted what was to become the initial neoliberal position on bargaining: collective bargaining should be premised on what a company could afford—the relative market situation of the company—rather than extraneous subsistence concerns of workers, such as considerations of the cost of living.

By April 1972 workplace occupations had spread to the Sheffield region, where unions also put in the "carbon copy claim"; employers at two plants threatened to withhold pay in retaliation against trade union sanctions. Elsewhere, at for instance Stanmore Engineering in London, long-standing grievances coalesced with the presentation of the national claim, and conflict between employers and workers escalated into occupation. The occupations continued into August. However, the Manchester shop stewards dropped opposition to cash-only settlements and gradually the national unions imposed discipline over disputes that had not had explicit union sanction. The EEF loosened its opposition to settlements, including some concession on hours and holidays.

### Changes

The UCS work-in and the occupation movement began to have an impact. The Heath government, which had entered office with a neoliberal policy, was moved to make a U-turn. A new Industry Act was introduced in 1972, allowing intervention to support industry in deprived areas or where it was considered in the national interest.

Powers were assigned to the secretary of state for Industry to give up to £5 million to an enterprise before it needed to be put to a parliamentary vote. To avoid the bankruptcy of Rolls-Royce, the flagship company would be nationalized; assistance could be given as well to UCS to implement a survival plan. One of the shipyards was sold to Marathon Oil for the construction of rigs for the expanding North Sea oil field. To this sale the government contributed grants worth £6 million, and declared that the company was not a "lame duck." The remaining yards were reorganized, receiving £35 million in government aid, a sum considerably more than they had previously been refused.

The economic situation was deteriorating, with unemployment continuing its rise while inflation was moving into double figures. The government introduced pay restraint, holding down wages across the economic sectors. The oil crisis hit the economy in 1973 and, at the same time, the miners threatened their second national strike in two years. Further emergency measures were introduced to save power, including a three-day workweek. Finally, in 1974, Heath called an election around the issue of "who governs Britain?" The obvious inference was that power was slipping toward organized labor.

In March 1974 Labour took office as a minority government with policies of establishing a National Enterprise Board to manage and expand public enterprise, and of extending industrial democracy. The architect of the industrial policy was to be Tony Benn, who had played an active role within the IWC as well as in the campaign around UCS; he sought a new model of state enterprise alongside greater involvement of workers in "bottom up" decision-making (see Benn 1979). For a short period while he was in office, causing antagonism from other ministers, trade unions, and his own officials, Benn offered direct access to problems brought to him by shop stewards' committees in threatened plants and companies.

The Conservative administration had left a number of open applications under the 1972 Industry Act, some with a long heritage of state intervention and worker occupation. One concern was the decline of the motorcycle industry. Consolidation of the remaining manufacturers (into NVT, Norton Villiers Triumph), meant the proposal of factory closure and created conflict between workforces over the allocation of work. Initial proposals from NVT, supported by the government, were for the closure of the Meriden plant with work transferred to the two remaining plants. When the closure was announced, Meriden workers evicted management and occupied, initially around a work-in during which they produced motorcycles from existing components.

## The Heyday of Occupation

In the limbo of the election period, as a means of freeing up machines, spares, company records, and "the contents of the engineering department,"

NVT had come to an agreement with the Meriden occupation. This plan would allow the prospective workers' cooperative assets of between £2 million and £7 million, to be selected from a list compiled by the company, as long as evidence of their ability to pay was provided before the end of March (NVT 1974). When Benn arrived at the Department of Industry this plan was on his desk. Previously the government assistance to the motorcycle industry had been directed at NVT itself but Benn now encouraged the Meriden workforce to formalize their plans for a workers' cooperative into an application to the Department of Industry for assistance under the 1972 Industry Act.

Benn facilitated rapid assistance to the Meriden workforce. It incorporated as a separate entity so that it could qualify for £4.96 million in aid awarded separately from the assistance that NVT had already received. This allowed not only the establishment of the cooperative but also for NVT to get the release of the machine tools and plans they had been waiting for. It also gave them a ready buyer for the factory and excess plant capacity. It also meant the creation of, essentially, a subcontractor to produce the Triumph Bonneville motorcycle.

The Meriden experience had a profound effect on Benn's perspective. Through his identification of the workers' cooperative—reminiscent of the roots of Labour radicalism—he had resolved the paradox between extending "socialization" of the economy with the commitment to extending industrial democracy. The workers' cooperative that the Meriden workers had proposed seemed to be the solution, especially when similar plans were forwarded from workers at Beaverbrook newspapers in Glasgow, occupying over closure. Their plan was to allow the establishment of a newspaper, the *Scottish Daily News*, which they were to run for a few months as a workers' cooperative. Other groups of workers approached Benn directly. The workers at Fisher-Bendix, by then renamed IPC, were again facing closure and sought assistance. Benn encouraged them to put forward their own business plan to support their request and advised them to consider establishing a cooperative.

Lucas Aerospace, which had assistance through the IRC to facilitate mergers and rationalization, was also proposing plant closures. Some of these were resisted by occupation. To challenge the proposed restructuring, shop stewards across different plants had established a combine committee that met regularly. With concern about these job losses, and how this might be alleviated by inclusion in the government-proposed nationalization of the aerospace industry, the combine met with Benn at the Department of Industry. There he asked them to produce their own plans for preserving jobs (Wainwright and Elliott 1982). This followed the logic emerging in the resistance to closures and occupations, efforts that had been reflected in the "social audit" at UCS but going much farther. Consideration was increasingly given to the "use" of products and of production itself, with the Lucas Combine challenging the dependence on armament production, initiating a wider debate on arms conversion, as well as addressing the alienating character of work under capitalism (see Cooley 1980).

Benn was picking up on some of the IWC strategy. Workers were directed to put forward their own proposals for how to save their industries. This was integral to a realization by these workers that the minister favored the cooperative form rather than "old style" nationalization. When, in January 1975, Litton Industries announced plans to close its Imperial Typewriter factories in Hull and Leicester, workers produced a plan arguing for support from Benn's department (TGWU 1975; IWC 1975).[4] When Benn addressed a lobby of workers from the Hull plant he advised that they "stay together."[5] When the Hull factory was closed on February 20, a day earlier than announced, members of the workforce climbed the gate and started an occupation. A sign was erected outside the plant announcing "Tony is with us." However, by the following month Benn was to write to Tony Topham, "The whole official machine is 100% against you as you probably realise, and I am doing my best to prevent disastrous recommendations from going in so as to give you time to reorganise. It is going to be very hard, but I will do my very best" (Benn 1975).

While Benn was instrumental in mobilizing action among groups of workers, his openness to delegations, especially from workforces staging what appeared to be militant industrial action, was isolating if not demonizing him elsewhere.

When the Lucas Combine Committee produced their plan, which was to pioneer and symbolize "socially useful production" (Lucas 1978; Wainwright and Elliott 1982), they found their path blocked by a bureaucratic web (Lucas 1979; 1982). Trade union officials also objected to ministerial access being given to shop stewards and combines, both of which they considered unofficial bodies. A crucial factor in the state assistance for the workers' cooperatives in the short period Benn was at the Department of Industry was that not only was the aid minimal compared to the overall assistance given by government to private industry, but also most of it went to compensate previous owners for what was already an obsolete plant. Hence while all three cooperatives were short-lived, their eventual closure

---

4 The plan was principally authored by Tony Topham of the IWC, who was also a local university tutor in trade union studies. Topham worked with the Hull TGWU during the Imperial Typewriters occupation. The plan was published as a pamphlet by the IWC (1975).

5 I am grateful to Tony Benn for a taped copy of his address and discussion at the Hull Imperial workers lobby at the House of Commons, February 18, 1975.

was inevitable, as even with assistance they were still drastically undercap-italized and therefore unable to resolve problems or to establish an inde-pendent existence through research and development.

## Toward Thatcherism and Declining Workplace Occupations

With the exception of early 1972, which saw the Manchester engineering dispute, the period of late 1974 to mid-1975 saw more occupations than any other. The period brought together workers facing closures and redun-dancies, the conditions that generate occupation, and the apparent possi-bility of support from the very center of government. The three workers' cooperatives—the "Benn cooperatives"—have become totemic of the period and cooperative development became associated with economic policies, formulated by some UK local authorities, that challenged the emergent ne-oliberalism of the Thatcher government.

The idea of socially useful production, associated with the Lucas Com-bine shop stewards, is another important outcome from the period; its pro-posals, including hybrid engines and alternative power sources, have a significant resonance with growing environmentalism.

This is not to argue that workplace occupation disappeared altogether. Several significant occupations, including at Meccano, Lee Jeans, Lawrence Scott, and the magazine *Time Out*, occurred toward the end of the 1970s. However there was a noticeable decline in number. Occupation had always been a minority activity; even earlier in the 1970s only a small minority of workers facing closure or large-scale redundancy considered the tactic and even fewer deployed it. And this deployment was usually the relatively spon-taneous action of a small minority of the workforce involved.

Far more commonly, when closure or redundancies were announced, the union saw its role not as mobilizing opposition but as negotiating the most advantageous redundancy terms. The 1975 Employment Protection Act, enacted by the Wilson government, introduced the formal requirement for employers to give ninety days' notice of redundancies, and to consult with recognized trade unions over these redundancies. This consolidated the role of the trade union as negotiating terms and conditions of redun-dancy and allowed collective resistance to fragment and dissipate.

The Labour government, faced with a monetary crisis, approached the IMF for a $3.9 billion loan in 1976. Conditional of the loan was a 20 per-cent cut in the budget deficit. Almost three years before the election of Thatcher's Conservative government Britain witnessed the initiation of the rolling back of the Keynesian welfare state. One significant area of ration-alization was in the National Health Service (NHS), with moves toward consolidation in larger units and the closure of smaller, specialist, or local hospitals and some hospital wards. This often meant redeployment of staff rather than redundancy, but it still led to opposition. A number of occupations occurred to try to keep hospitals open. The first, at Elisabeth Garret Anderson, a specialist women's hospital in central London, lasted for more than two years. In some cases these occupations involved continued care; however, at Hounslow, despite a "raid" staged by the management to remove hospital patients, occupation continued based around ex-staff, usually redeployed within the health service, and local supporters (see Hounslow Hospital Occupation Committee 1978). As such the hospital occupations developed in a rather different way than the factory occupations.

## A Future for Worker Resurgence?

We might see the foundation of the occupations in Britain in the 1970s as being rooted in the strong and confident workplace trade unionism that had developed within the full employment of the postwar consensus. Through the 1960s and 1970s we can see signs of this form of organized resistance coming under threat, for example, in the escalation of the engineering industry dispute in 1972, caused by management's attempt to control shop stewards. By the early 1980s this threat had become a full assault. Signs were evident earlier that employers were becoming more willing to challenge and attempt legal action to evict occupying workers, but in the early 1980s the legal framework for trade unions and employment relations in Britain was itself transformed, making workers' direct action more difficult.

In a detailed study of the occupation of Caterpillar in Uddingston, Scotland, in 1987, perhaps the last of this wave of actions in Britain, Woolfson and Foster note that while the work-in at UCS had been dependent on strong organization by politically active shop stewards, the action at Caterpillar lacked these "organisational advantages" (1988). The motive for mobilizing the occupation was that the workers at Caterpillar saw no alternative: they literally had nothing to lose. The Caterpillar occupation, paradoxically, may represent not the tail end of the '70s wave of occupations but a precursor of a new wave, sparking occupations at the wind turbine plant Vestas and the Ford component plants of Visteon in the UK (Gall 2010), or at Republic Windows and Doors in the United States, during the very different climate of 2008 (Lydersen 2009).

# References

Anderson, Andy. 1964. *Hungary 56*. London: Solidarity.

Anti Report. 1972. *The General Electric Company Limited*. London: Counter Information Services.

Barratt Brown, Michael, and Ken Coates. nd. *The "big flame" and what is the IWC?* Nottingham: Institute for Workers' Control.

Barratt Brown, Michael, Ken Coates, and Tony Topham. 1975. Workers' control versus "revolutionary" theory. In *Socialist Register 1975*, ed. Ralph Miliband and John Saville, 293–307. London: Merlin Press.

BBC News. 1971. July 30.

Benn, Tony. 1975. Letter to Tony Topham. March 17.

———. 1979. Labours industrial programme. In *Arguments for Socialism*, ed. Chris Mullin. Harmondsworth: Penguin.

Chadwick, Graham. 1970. The big flame—an account of the events at the Liverpool factory of GEC-EE. *Trade Union Register*, ed. Ken Coates, Tony Topham, and Michael Barratt Brown. London: Merlin Press.

———. 1973. The Manchester engineering sit ins 1972. In *Trade Union Register*, ed. Ken Coates, Tony Topham, and Michael Barratt Brown. London: Merlin Press.

Clarke, Tom. 1974. *Sit-in at Fisher-Bendix*, IWC pamphlet no. 42. Nottingham: Institute for Workers' Control.

Coates, K. 1968. *Can the workers run industry?* Sphere in association with the Institute for Workers' Control.

———. 1981. *Work-ins, sit-ins and industrial democracy*. Nottingham: Spokesman.

Cooley, Mike. 1980. *Architect or bee? The human/technology relationship*. Slough: Langley Technical Services/Hand and Brain.

Coventry, Liverpool, Newcastle, N. Tyneside Trades Councils. 1982. *State intervention in industry: A workers inquiry*. Nottingham: Spokesman.

Crouch, Colin. 1977. *Class conflict and the industrial relations crisis*. London: Heinemann Educational Books.

Darlington, Ralph, and Dave Lyddon. 2001. *Glorious summer: Class struggle in Britain, 1972*. London: Bookmarks.

Eccles, Tony. 1981. *Under new management: The story of Britain's largest worker co-operative— its successes and failures*. London: Pan Books.

Engineering Employers Federation [EEF]. 1972. Presidential address. February 24.

Foster, John, and Charles Woolfson. 1986. *The politics of the UCS work-in: Class alliances and the right to work*. London: Lawrence & Wishart.

Frayn, Michael. 1967. The perfect strike. In *The incompatibles: trade union militancy and the consensus*, ed. R. Blackburn and A. Cockburn, 160–68. London: Penguin in association with New Left Review.

Fryer, R. H. 1973. Redundancy, values and public policy. *Industrial Relations Journal* 4 (2): 2–19.

Fryer, R. H. [Bob]. 1981. State, redundancy and the law. In *Law, state and society*, ed. Bob Fryer, A. Hunt, D. McBarnet, and Bert Moorehouse, 136–59. London: Croom Helm.

Gall, Gregor. 2010. Resisting recession and redundancy: Contemporary worker occupation in Britain. In *WorkingUSA: The Journal of Labor and Society* 13 (1): 107–32.

Hansard. 1974. Industrial policy. *House of Commons, Debate 12 July 1974*, vol. 876, Cc1745–846 1974/07/12. http://hansard.millbanksystems.com/commons/1974/jul/12/industrial-policy#S5CV0876P0_19740712_HOC_147.

Hemingway, J., and W. Keyser. 1975. *Who's in charge? Workers sit-ins in Britain today*. London: Metra Consulting Group.

Hounslow Hospital Occupation Committee, EGA Joint Shop Stewards Committee, Plaistow Maternity Action Committee, Save St. Nicholas Hospital Campaign. 1978. *Keeping hospitals open: work-ins at E.G.A. Hounslow and Plaistow hospitals.* London.

Hyman, Richard. 1974. Workers' control and revolutionary theory. *Socialist Register* 11, no. 11.

*Inside Story.* 1973. How red was Briants Colour? *Inside Story,* no. 10.

Institute for Workers' Control [IWC]. 1969. *GEC-EE workers' takeover.* Nottingham: Institute for Workers' Control.

———.1971. *UCS: The social audit,* IWC pamphlet no. 26. Nottingham: Institute for Workers' Control.

———. 1975. *Why Imperial Typewriters must not close: A preliminary social audit by the union action committee.* Nottingham: Institute for Workers' Control.

*Labour Research.* 1972. March.

———. 1973a. January.

———. 1973b. February.

Lomax, Bill, ed. 1980. *Eyewitnesses in Hungary: The Soviet invasion of 1956.* Nottingham: Spokesman.

———. 1976. *Hungary 1956.* London: Allison & Busby.

Lucas Aerospace Combine Shop Stewards Committee. 1978. *Lucas: An alternative plan.* Nottingham: Institute for Workers' Control.

———. 1979. *Democracy versus the circumlocution office,* IWC pamphlet no. 65. Nottingham: Institute for Workers' Control.

———. 1982. *Diary of betrayal: A detailed account of the combine's efforts to get the alternative plan implemented.* London: Centre for Alternative Industrial and Technological Systems.

Lydersen, Kari. 2009. *Revolt on Goose Island: The Chicago factory takeover, and what it says about the economic crisis.* New York: Melville House Publishing.

McGill, Jack. 1972. *Crisis on the Clyde.* London: Davis-Poynter.

Metra. 1972. *An analysis of sit-ins.* London: Metra Consulting Group.

Mills, A. J. 1974. Factory work-ins. *New Society,* August 22.

Mooney, Bel. 1973. The lessons of Leadgate. *New Statesman.*

Murray, Robin. 1972. *UCS: The anatomy of bankruptcy.* Nottingham: Spokesman Books.

Newens, Stan. 1969. The GEC/AEI takeover and the fight against redundancy at Harlow. *Trade Union Register,* ed. Ken Coates, Tony Topham, and Michael Barratt Brown. London: Merlin Press.

Norton Villiers Triumph [NVT]. 1974. *Meriden: Historical summary 1972–1974.* Coventry: Norton Villiers Triumph.

Panitch, Leo. 1976. *Social democracy & industrial militancy: The Labour Party, the trade unions and income policy 1945–1974.* Cambridge: Cambridge University Press.

Schubert, J. 1970. Big flame flickers. *Anarchy* 10 (2): 41–42.

Sherry, Dave. 2010. *Occupy! A short history of workers' occupations.* London: Bookmarks.

Smith, B. 1981. *The history of the British motorcycle industry 1945–1975.* Birmingham: Centre for Urban and Regional Studies, University of Birmingham.

*Socialist Worker.* 1972. March 11.

Solidarity. 1972. *Under new management? The Fisher Bendix occupation,* pamphlet no. 39. London: Solidarity.

TGWU. 1975. Threatened closure of Imperial Typewriters, Hull: The case for government aid to maintain production, and/or to establish a co-operative to assume ownership and management of the plant: A preliminary statement. Brynmore Jones Library, University of Hull, DTO unclassified papers donated by Tony Topham.

*Times* [London]. 1972. January 29.

Topham, Tony. 1964. Shop stewards and workers' control. *New Left Review,* no. 25, 3–15.

———. ed. 1967. *Report of the 5th national conference on workers' control and industrial democracy.* Hull: Centre for Socialist Education.

Tuckman, Alan. 1985. Industrial action and hegemony: Workplace occupation in Britain

1971 to 1981. PhD thesis, University of Hull.

TUSIU. 1976. *Worker occupations and the north-east experience.* Newcastle-upon-Tyne: North-East Trade Union Studies Information Unit.

Wainwright, H., and D. Elliott. 1982. *The Lucas plan: A new trade unionism in the making?* London: Allison & Busby.

Wajcman, J. 1983. *Women in control: Dilemmas of a workers' co-operative:* Open University Press.

Woolfson, Charles, and John Foster. 1988. *Track record: The story of the Caterpillar occupation.* London and New York: Verso Books.

# 16

# Workers' Direct Action and Factory Control in the United States

**Immanuel Ness**

This chapter examines decisive historical moments of workers' control and self-management in the United States—the model capitalist state that, as demonstrated over the past century, supports predatory forms of labor exploitation. While workers repeatedly struggle to advance their rights, the apparatus of the capitalist state reflexively supports management efforts to gain absolute dominance through the suppression of direct mass action. The legal supremacy of capital is presupposed by management and labor unions.

The United States is the epitome of a capitalist paradise where, almost always, employers are assured full support of the state juridical and martial apparatus to repress those workers who break established rules of the labor-management engagement, unless businesses themselves abrogate agreements. In almost every historical example since the advent of mass production, workers have secured power only through breaking rules, striking, and occupying factories (Pope 2006). As a consequence, worker dissent is historically manifested through rank-and-file action surfacing in the workplace against the decrees of capital, the state, and, quite often, collaborationist trade unions.

In the last century, U.S. workers have almost always opposed management efforts to extract surplus value—reducing wages, imposing speedup, exposing the workforce to safety and health hazards, layoffs, implementing mandatory overtime, and more—through an array of strategies. Most workers are keenly aware that capital rejects living-wage standards and relentlessly reinvests surplus value, derived from the toil of workers of the past and present, into new enterprises employing lower-wage labor and modern labor-saving technology.

The history of militant workers' resistance to these tactics of industrial capitalism provides evidence that U.S. workers have engaged in fierce struggles to defend their rights through a repertoire of collective action. The aspiration to workers' self-management in the interest of democracy punctuates most mass labor insurgencies. Jerry Tucker, the legendary United Auto Workers (UAW) worker and organizer, asserts that we must move from a defensive posture of preventing corporate abuse to an offensive strategy of advancing worker power. To do so, "Workers must commandeer social space, both on the shop floor and in the community." As such, Tucker considers the imperative driving workers' struggles to be the quest for the social appropriation of privately owned economic and social resources (Tucker 2010b). Ultimately, worker dissent arises out of unsatisfactory wages and job conditions. But worker resistance against management can also challenge the corporate model of domination, and, in so doing, advance communal participation in the democratization of workplace decisions and the production of goods and services for collective needs rather than private interests.

The fundamental revolutionary nature of workers is established in workplaces and communities, as socialists from Marx and Lenin to Luxemburg and Gramsci have argued. Lenin recognized the centrality of workers in particular, as opposed to Karl Kautsky and the evolutionary socialists, maintaining in *The State and Revolution* that the formation of the soviet is not to "shift the balance of forces, but to overthrow the bourgeoisie, to destroy bourgeois parliamentarism, for a democratic republic after the type of the Commune or a republic of soviets of workers" (Lenin 1917/1998, 100). In the U.S. context, despite the intermittent and ephemeral nature of workers' councils, the very act of commandeering the workplace is rooted in the self-activity of workers, against capital and labor bureaucracies that conform to or are unable to resist capital's logic of the reckless domination of society.

## Activism at the Point of Production

The prodigious history in the United States of organizing at the "point of production," or on the shop floor, is what socialist labor unionists consider the "purest form of unionism." In 1905, the anarcho-syndicalist Industrial Workers of the World (IWW) was founded to resist capitalist efforts to introduce new technology and low-wage labor, with the faithful support of the state. Today, as a century ago, workers remain under assault from the same efforts to impose new technology and lower wages, which increase labor competition and intra-class conflict by creating divisions that give rise to nativism and xenophobia toward immigrant laborers. The IWW Manifesto (1905) declared: "These divisions, far from representing differences in skill or interests among the laborers, are imposed by the employer that workers may be pitted against one another and spurred to greater exertion in the shop, and that all resistance to capitalist tyranny may be weakened by artificial distinctions."

As this chapter on U.S. workers' control demonstrates, workers have opposed labor union bureaucracies, supposed managerial benevolence, and employer domination through direct action—rather than relying on traditional employer- and trade union–based grievance systems and dispute resolution, which now prove less effective than at any time since the 1930s (Lynd 1992). While success is never certain, new forms of democratic unionism grounded in class solidarity are essential for breaking the absolute control of capitalists over workers. Yet concurrently, since the 1950s, organized labor has remained quiescent—as compared to European social democracies—failing to defend the organized working class, due to a justified fear that capital will migrate to lower-cost regions where greater profits can be reaped through extracting surplus value from cheap labor and advanced technology (Arrighi and Silver 1984).

## U.S. Sit-Downs, Workers' Control, Unionization: 1935–1939

We start with the assumption that labor seeks democratic control over its work, and factory takeovers are just one step in the process of workers' control and self-management. From the 1930s to 2010, factory occupations have been contingent on four main factors:

1. Development of working-class consciousness, rooted in collective needs
2. Calculations of the economics of workers' capacity to confront capitalists
3. Institutional arrangements in capitalist society regulating workers through the state. The state always privileges business over workers, except in crisis conditions, when modest concessions are provided to insurgent workers who demand control over social and economic resources
4. Capacity and support of workers' efforts to self-organize and mobilize under repressive conditions

### Toledo Auto-Lite Direct Action

The U.S. Midwest became the epicenter of the mass wave of workers' factory occupations in mass-production industries to compel recalcitrant employers to recognize the newly founded labor unions. Following the success of militant rank-and-file insurgencies during the 1930s, which included mass pickets, sit-down strikes, and resistance to corporate and government violence, industrial workers achieved greater control over their workplaces. Militancy and insistence on democratic control became the norm among mass-production workers—so much so that employers were forced to back off from their relentless determination to dominate and repress workers in these industries.

In 1934, Toledo, Ohio, found itself the site of an epic class struggle as management and state police launched the first salvo against a resurgent workers' solidarity movement demanding union recognition through strikes to improve wages and working conditions. The government, firmly in support of the Electric Auto-Lite Company of Toledo, waged a hot war against the workers, who stopped production with mass picket lines numbering up to ten thousand striking and unemployed workers. In this particular case, the striking workers and the unemployed prevented some 1,500 strikebreakers from entering or leaving the factory. On May 24, 1934, after the Ohio National Guard hurled gas bombs to disperse an assembly of six thousand workers, an intense battle was waged, killing two strikers and leaving more than two hundred injured. It is worth noting that the strike against Auto-Lite, launched by workers who were members of AFL Federal Union 18384 (an unaffiliated labor union), benefited from the active participation of unemployed workers organized by the Trotskyist-inspired Socialist Party and the National Unemployed League, led by A. J. Muste (Bernstein 1969, 221–229). The strike was won on June 2, 1934, when Auto-Lite agreed to a 5 percent wage increase and union recognition—an accord achieved only through worker solidarity at the factory gates. The strike inaugurated a five-year insurgency in mass production through direct action within the factories.

### Akron Tire Worker Sit-Down Strikes

By most accounts, the surge of major sit-down strikes in the United States began in Akron, Ohio—an industrial center that produced tires for motor vehicles. In January 1936 workers seized control over the three largest tire companies—Firestone Tire & Rubber Company, Goodyear, and B. F. Goodrich—all of which refused to recognize the United Rubber Workers of America, the workers' fledgling union, and ignored demands for fair work rules. In the tire production sector, the major rubber companies disciplined workers who challenged the company's tyrannical control: in 1935 and 1936, when workers opposed management's efforts to speed up production by extending the workday, 1,500 workers were sacked (Green 1998, 153). On January 29, 1936, after Firestone Tire & Rubber arbitrarily suspended a worker and refused to hold a trial, workers staged a fifty-five-hour occupation of the plant. The Firestone occupation sparked parallel sit-down direct actions at B. F. Goodrich and Goodyear by workers seeking a democratic workplace (Pope 2006, 6–11).

At the peak of the wave of factory occupations, some ten thousand tire workers in Akron resisted court injunctions to end the sit-downs, even opposing the United Rubber Workers Union's efforts at conciliation, until they prevailed through a recognition agreement and establishment of fair work rules. Historian James Green asserts: "To the workers, the sit-down offered a new way to control their own strikes, ensure speedy negotiations, and prevent the sellouts they had experienced in the past" (1998, 153). Workers' resistance to management supremacy in mass production represented a formidable challenge both to employers and to capital, which considered mass production as a means to exercise complete control through ownership of the means of production. Unlike with skilled craft workers, who could demand that employers abide by union wages and working conditions, management believed it could unilaterally impose wages and conditions on manufacturing workers, who did not own the means of production.

### Flint Autoworker Sit-Down Strike

In 1936, an unambiguous labor insurgency had begun to form among industrial workers committed to the self-management of manufacturing enterprises, in opposition to the capitalists who had dominated production since the disappearance of a modicum of control by craft workers in the late nineteenth century. The sit-down movement, forged in factories, exemplified the democratic potential of workers' control among millions of workers to establish rules and labor unions, challenge corporate despotism, and even advocate workers' self-management of factories.

Certainly the economic depression of the 1930s degraded workers' bargaining power through widespread unemployment and the vast industrial reserve army of labor, which drove down labor costs and weakened the embryonic labor unions. Concomitantly, expressions of syndicalism and demands for worker autonomy reached an apogee in the early twentieth century, dominating the consciousness of workers who recognized that management tactics such as speeding up production and raising piecework requirements were undermining their collective bargaining power. The ideology of individualism through hard work metamorphosed into a collective IWW ideology of "an injury to one is an injury to all."

In December 1936, following the wave of sit-down strikes among tire producers and motor-vehicle parts plants, autoworkers in Michigan staged the most significant sit-down strikes in U.S. history to gain greater control of the workplace. In Flint, Michigan, on December 30, 1936, automobile workers initiated a forty-four-day occupation of General Motors' Fisher Body Plants no. 1 and no. 2 in a showdown in which workers and UAW organizers resisted government injunctions and threats to call in the National Guard to crush the insurgency. Workers prevailed in an initial police assault on the Flint plants, sustaining the occupation with coordinated mass pickets outside the factory gates and preventing federal and state government officials from ending the sit-downs. The inside-outside strategy served to successfully stop automobile production and garner legitimacy and support among the majority of U.S. workers.

The Flint sit-down strike, which lasted more than six weeks, became the focal point of a class war against GM, the largest manufacturing company in the world. The UAW benefited from a mobilized and disciplined workforce motivated to take direct action through a major insurgency, despite police efforts to paralyze the strike through violence. Unquestionably, the workers' occupation had the advantage of sympathetic picketers and ordinary residents in the city, who engaged in a struggle against police seeking to scatter them from the plant. In an ongoing battle that lasted into the early morning of December 31, police fired gas bombs to drive away the protesters, who in turn hurled rocks back at the police.

On January 11, the first day of the riot dubbed "The Battle of the Running Bulls," Flint police attempted to disperse picketers and workers by commandeering a bridge and firing long-range tear gas shells. Despite their use of force, the police could not end the plant occupation; the mass picketers were firmly entrenched and refused to be dislodged until an agreement was reached to recognize their union (Fine 1969, 6–7).

Worker solidarity was unbroken, and due to political pressure, Michigan governor Frank Murphy rejected calling on the National Guard to stage a major confrontation, which would have further inflamed the conflict and contributed to popular militancy and outrage (ibid.). The workers' occupation demonstrated that the conventional strike was not sufficient to gain unionization, given the implacable opposition of GM and other major manufacturers. To unionize the U.S. auto industry, workers had to occupy the plants and stand firm against compromise. The plant seizure ended on February 11, 1937; a month later GM negotiated a contract with the UAW governing workers—conceding only after the lone unionization campaign that genuinely succeeded in the automobile industry. According to Nora Faires, some 80 percent of Flint's workers participated in the pickets and sit-downs that besieged GM and finally led to its surrender (1989).

Following the workers' occupation in Flint, an unrelenting wave of sit-down occupations was sustained in mass production industries around the country. According to James Green, in the next year, some 400,000 workers participated in 477 workplace occupations (1998, 157) and the United States became the front lines of worker militancy worldwide. But worker power in manufacturing enterprises proved fleeting, in the short term due to GM's persistent campaign against workers.

While the Flint sit-down strikes inaugurated a twenty-five-year period of tranquility in most plants, Sidney Fine argues the experience activated worker militancy that remained in many plants:

UAW members ... were reluctant to accept the customary discipline exercised by management, and they "ran wild in many plants for months." Union committeemen aggressively pressed the grievances of union members upon oftentimes unyielding foremen, and as some UAW member later conceded, "every time a dispute came up the fellows would have a tendency to sit down and just stop working (Fine 1969, 321).

At the same time, some GM managers antagonistic to the union disregarded the accord following the sit-down strike that paved the way for UAW representation. In the immediate aftermath of the Flint workers' occupation, Fine notes that plant managers actively discriminated against workers who supported the union. Arthur Lenz, manager of the Flint Chevrolet plant, "had armed about one thousand nonunion workers with specially manufactured clubs and was marching them through the plant as to intimidate union and potential union members" (ibid.).

But beyond the threats and bullying, the workers' democratic governance was also undermined by federal legal constraints and the emergence of labor union bureaucracy in the UAW.

The triumph of the workers' plant occupations was considered a severe defeat for the U.S. capitalist class. Yet for more than seventy years, the strategy of the sit-down, despite its proven success, was replaced by collaboration between labor unions and employers, severely eroding workers' solidarity and eviscerating the improved conditions won by workers. Subsequent UAW-sponsored actions were predominantly conventional strikes, which failed to increase or maintain membership and worker power in the auto industry as the union evolved into a centralized command structure that utilized collective bargaining and the relatively anemic strike weapon to win contracts.

Over the long term, the workers would be defeated by capital's predictable response of undermining gains achieved only through worker militancy. GM found new ways to control and repress workers—without appreciable opposition from the UAW—through strict work rules, automation, restructuring, and the ultimate weapon of threatening plant closures: securing concessionary agreements and moving production when advantageous to the company. Nonetheless, worker militants have always sought innovative direct actions against the imposition of speedup of the assembly through automation, most notably the twenty-two-day strike of workers in Lordstown, Ohio, in March 1972, without the authorization of the UAW leadership. Though defeated, the workers demonstrated the resilience of the rank and file to oppose the management—as well as the bureaucratic national union (Garson 1994).

### Emerson Electric Sit-Downs and Radical Unionism
The Flint sit-down strike is remembered as the culmination of the insurgent workers' movement in the United States. The autoworker strike was a decisive

development that spread to manufacturing plants throughout the Midwest. In most instances, the dramatic upsurge in labor militancy was rooted in the growing conviction among workers that self-organization was essential to improving their oppressive work lives and their communities. The militant movement for union democracy was organized by activists in UE (United Electrical, Radio and Machine Workers of America) District 8, unique in the United States for its promotion of an insurrectionary brand of unionism, rooted in the principles of workers' control over their organizations, workers' occupation of factories, and even democratic community planning. The sitdown movement among UE locals in the Midwest was inspired by William Sentner, a syndicalist and also a member of the Communist Party, with a firm commitment to democracy, antiracism, and rejection of hierarchical labor organizations. In 1933, Sentner identified the CP's Trade Union Unity League's (TUUL) Food Workers Industrial Union, an organization of both employed and unemployed workers, as exemplary of a steadfast commitment to militant, antiracist union organizing (Feurer 2006, 36–40). The Food Workers Industrial Union called a strike for wage racial parity among black and white women workers employed at Funsten, a nut processing company in East St. Louis, Illinois, where some 40 percent of the workers were on relief. For ten days in May 1933, five hundred black women and two hundred white women staged a strike that doubled wages and provided for equal pay for black workers, even if failing to gain union recognition (ibid., 37–38).

The successful strike, waged through mass picketing, spurred organizing drives throughout the region, including the campaign to organize Emerson Electric in St. Louis, a plant with some two thousand employees, which culminated in the workers' occupation of the entire factory, demanding union recognition, higher wages, and standardized work rules. Socialists were drawn to District 8 of the UE as it was categorically in favor of supporting workers' direct action, unlike most CIO (Congress of Industrial Organizations) unions—which had, of course, benefited from worker insurrection to achieve union recognition and collective bargaining agreements with employers. Emerson Electric, a rapidly expanding producer of electric motors and fans, had installed a company-dominated union to prevent workers from forming their own organization.

By 1936, Emerson Electric workers were systematically joining UE Local 1102 and, in March 1937, UE Local 1102 declared it had obtained the support of all the workers in every department of the plant. Sentner, originally assigned by the CIO to organize steelworkers, turned all his energy and attention to UE's Emerson Electric organizing drive (ibid., 50–56). The union had unqualified support among workers for the sit-down strike that began promptly at noon on March 8, 1937. Consequently, the workers' occupation occurred in an orderly manner, as some two hundred of the youngest employees "went floor-by-floor escorting foremen out the door" (ibid., 56). As management was told to leave the facilities, hundreds of workers jubilantly encircled the plant.

Sentner and UE organizers emphasized that the sit-down was directed at building working-class power in the plant and community through direct action. Throughout the strike, Sentner stressed the connection between workers' immediate demands and the issue of community and power, both for the strikers and the public. He linked the struggle to the city's welfare: "Our organization, which is primarily interested in the economic welfare of the working people, is however also interested in the effects of their economic status on our community" (ibid., 57).

Sentner and UE Local 1102 organizers and workers sought higher wages for women; they ended the sit-down on April 29, after the company granted recognition of the union and agreed to collective bargaining. On May 14, workers gained modest wage increases, seniority rights, grievance procedures, and other boilerplate union language that later, unfortunately, would be used to hinder their power—including the no-strike/no-lockout clause.

The UE was at the forefront of CIO struggles, reaching 750,000 members at its peak through promoting direct action, racial and gender equality, worker militancy, and democratic unionism. However, by the late 1940s, the UE had fallen victim to the Red Scare and perception of Communist Party influence. By 1949, the UE was forced out of the CIO and replaced by the rival International Union of Electrical Workers (IUE), a union not rooted in worker democracy (ibid., 225–238). As an independent, unaffiliated union, the UE remained viable and effective in organizing workers through appealing to worker democracy, class solidarity, and militancy. Although it lost members to factory closures like other unions, the UE did not engage in mass concessions to employers. The union's rich legacy of workers' control made famous by the Emerson Electric Strike was to foreshadow the Republic Windows and Doors sit-down seventy-one years later in December 2008.

## Trade Unions and Worker Power on the Job

In the United States, as a result of the flight of manufacturing industry to more profitable destinations, workers' demands from 1980 to 2010 have not even approached those of the time when heavy manufacturing industries were growing dramatically. Due to corporate disinvestment and the relocation of facilities to low-wage areas of production, workers employed in manufacturing throughout the United States and a growing number of European countries lost the political power of the 1930s–1950s. During that time significant power was brought to bear, forcing capitalists to recognize and bargain with the incipient mass-production unions. Worker militancy paved the way for the organization of unions and then for their recognition by the U.S. federal government through the landmark 1935 National Labor Relations Act (NLRA). Between 1936 and 1939 alone, U.S. workers occupied 583 plants, threatening employer hegemony over the workplace and sowing fear among a growing number of corporations. Mass sit-down actions in factories led to the U.S. Supreme Court opinion in *National Labor Relations Board v. Fansteel Metallurgical Corporation* in 1939, which circumscribed workers' rights gained legislatively by effectively banning the sit-down occupation of factories (Galenson 1960, 145–148).

The 1930s sit-down strikes represented the apogee of working-class power in the United States. That trade unions did not oppose *Fansteel* revealed their own fear that sit-downs would erode their external bureaucratic influence as representatives who delivered labor peace and cordial industrial relations to management. Subsequently, unions went further to eviscerate member power through the World War II no-strike pledge and the purging of left-led unions that ensued after the passage of the 1949 Taft-Hartley Act. Devoid of militancy and ideology, labor unions grew increasingly irrelevant in the private sector due to worker cynicism and distrust of labor leaders, and by the early twenty-first century had been rendered almost inconsequential.

From 1940 onward, the vast majority of workers had few alternatives but to conform to repressive laws and embrace the propaganda of capitalist logic.

## Neoliberalism, Deindustrialization, and Decline in Worker Power

The 1970s to 2010 saw periodic work actions and wildcat strikes among some fierce union locals, and militant autoworker in-plant strategies frequently slowed or averted concessions. Largely without the support of national union officials, workers challenged the major auto companies even as divestment from manufacturing and the relocation of production industries overseas reduced their leverage (Brenner, Brenner, and Winslow 2010). As an institutional force organized labor in the United States, as in Europe and beyond, devolved into a partner with capital. Detached from the rank-and-file members, organized labor manifested as an interest group seeking modest legislative reforms to permit growth within the labor market, but without the will or capacity to wage offensive actions as a class. For István Mészáros, labor union struggles for real working-class participation through democratic, fully autonomous self-management are doomed to failure within parliamentary representative systems, which invariably subordinate labor to the interest of capital:

For the ironical and in many ways tragic result of long decades of political struggle within the confines of capital's self-serving political institutions turned out to be that under the now prevailing conditions the working class has been totally disenfranchised in all of the capitalistically advanced and not so advanced countries. This condition is marked by the full conformity of the various organised working class representatives to the "rules of the parliamentary game"…massively prejudiced against the organised force of labour and by the long established and constantly renewed power relations of capital's materially and ideologically most effective rule over the social order in its entirety (2010, 11).

The sit-down strike and factory occupation remain the fundamental sources of worker power under capitalism; however sparingly used, they elicit fear throughout the capitalist class. Occupations of factories prevent and delay businesses from redeploying production to worksites in lower-cost regions and writing off the facilities for tax breaks.

Even more significantly, workers' occupations are an ideological threat to capital and business, paving the way for an alternative to capitalist domination. Prohibition of the sit-down weakens workers and degrades their capacity to physically prevent capital from directing production and extracting further surplus value through labor savings, technological innovation, and relocation.

### Concessionary Bargaining and Contained Worker Resistance

From 1940 to 2000, workers engaged in the sit-down strike sporadically, almost always against union advice. However, in part due to *NLRB v. Fansteel*, workers did not engage in mass sit-down factory occupations after the steel plant closures of the 1970s and 1980s, or amid the economic crises of the era. As an alternative to sit-downs, militant workers subjected to mass layoffs or surviving a severe economic crisis formed "unemployed committees," also without palpable union support (Ness 1998). By the 1980s, efforts to control the workplace survived in the United States through "inside strategies" adopted by insurgent leaders in opposition to the prevailing pattern of concessionary bargaining that had abandoned even the pretense of oppositional class-struggle unionism.

By the 1980s, collective bargaining had shifted its pattern to bargaining for mediocre wage gains based on extraction of productivity gains (LaBotz 1991, 117). The preceding decade's economic recessions and capitalist restructuring had augured a new era of bargaining through surrendering to employer demands for wage cuts, harsh work rules, speedup, and tiered workforces. If unions refused to concede at the bargaining table, corporations threatened to relocate production to low-wage regions with poor working conditions.

Most labor unions acceded to corporate absolutism, but some engaged in resistance campaigns through "inside" or "in-plant" strategies to regain a semblance of control over their jobs. Jerry Tucker, former director of UAW Region 5 in St. Louis, and later a candidate for the national union presidency in 1992, organized effective inside strategies in the early 1980s to counter concessionary contracts. Rather than striking, Tucker believed that worker resistance to concessionary agreements was best advanced by returning to work under expired contracts and engaging in an escalating strategy of direct action against repressive work rules. If workers struck, they risked permanent replacement under the provisions of the Taft-Hartley Act. Since President Reagan could fire air-traffic controllers occupying strategic positions, manufacturing workers constantly threatened by plant closures learned an important object lesson: to stay on the job.

From 1981 to 1983, Tucker orchestrated in-house strategies at the Moog Automotive Plant and Schwitzer Manufacturing and in 1984 at Bell Helicopter and LTV in North Texas, thwarting employer efforts to push through concessionary bargaining. Non-strike direct action, for a time, averted replacement.

Tucker and the workers embraced in-plant solidarity that mobilized workers collectively, undermining management by learning production and distribution schedules, implementing work-to-rule, periodic slowdowns, sickouts, and industrial sabotage. For Tucker, work-to-rule meant simply obeying the management's rules. Inasmuch as management constantly seeks to accelerate production flows, it depends on workers to bend the official work rules and cut corners to increase output. But if workers abide by the company handbooks, production always falls short of management's projections (Tucker 2010a; 2010b). The strategy of worker resistance challenged employer demands for concessions with solidarity drawn from the IWW adage: "An injury to one is an injury to all."

The effectiveness of in-house strategies was countered by capital's initiatives to ban its practice in the courts and on the job, with carte blanche from government labor regulators. But UAW officials in Detroit also felt threatened by the in-house strategy's success, which threatened bureaucratic union dominance and friendly relations with employers.

## Financial Collapse and Workers' Control

From 2008–2010, under the pretext of the financial crisis, capitalists have been determined to unload the debt burden from their books by closing factories and abrogating agreements with unions. In response, a growing number of workers vulnerable to layoffs across North America and Europe, both within and outside of unions, have resisted closures through sit-down strikes and other forms of direct action. Where unions are unwilling to resist the corporate assault on labor, militant workers are engaging in direct action through factory occupations and mass insurrections demanding that plants be reopened or layoff benefits improved.

*Stirrings of a New Workers' Control Movement*

The traditional path of labor-management collective bargaining has taken a dramatic turn in the early twenty-first century. The current crisis in manufacturing has rendered nearly helpless a growing number of officially recognized unions with government-sanctioned collective bargaining agreements and could lay the basis for escalating direct actions by workers, possibly ushering in a more militant workers' movement. As plants close and layoffs grow—and as workers recognize they can no longer interrupt the workflow with a strike when there is no flow to be interrupted—they increasingly engage in militant action to save their jobs and communities.

Over the last decade sit-down strikes were largely confined to Latin America and elsewhere in the global South, with workers occupying factories in response to economic collapse. But these same dynamics are moving to the global North, where throughout 2009 into 2010 workers occupied factories and engaged in other militant actions. Many of these actions have been in the syndicalist tradition of workers taking power directly; in some cases the workers have acted on their own, in others they have pressed lackadaisical unions for support.

In the United States, worker radicalism was in check for decades as unions offered up concessions to managers, ostensibly to save their factories. Although workers have been viewed by corporate managers as docile and weak-willed, "When workers are threatened by management they seriously consider breaking the rules and fighting back," according to autoworker and activist Gregg Shotwell, a militant worker who helped form an insurgency in 2005 in the automotive parts industry (Shotwell 2008).

Shotwell, a worker at the Delphi auto parts plant in Flint, helped found Soldiers of Solidarity (SOS), a rank-and-file association that resists UAW policies of concessionary bargaining. SOS formed as a workers' insurgency in November 2005 following Delphi's dubious bankruptcy filing and the union leadership's lackluster response. Workers at Delphi plants throughout the Midwest feared the worst—plant closures and abrogation of health and pension benefit agreements that were guaranteed after the auto parts unit was spun off by GM in 1999. Independent of the UAW, rank-and-file workers waged a mass "work-to-rule" campaign to sabotage the company's plans for mass layoffs.

The 2005–2006 insurgency at Delphi was not a reprise of the Flint sit-down strike. Still, through direct action on the shop floor, including deftly organized slowdowns and work-to-rule—for instance, fixing machines only according to company guidelines—the production process was slowed at this firm seeking to break worker power. Lacking functioning equipment, Delphi workers were "putting machines down" without the support of the UAW, and ultimately saved their own health benefits and pensions. Says Shotwell, "A sit-down strike will not come out of a political philosophy, but will occur when workers feel they will lose everything if they stay complacent and take no action" (ibid.).

The global capitalist economic crisis is leading to the devaluation of labor-management contracts that had exchanged decent wage and benefit standards and a modicum of job security for labor peace. The closure of manufacturing plants in North America swelled the ranks of distressed, often older workers seeking to preserve the economic security they had once taken for granted. However, from 2007 to 2010, the crisis has exposed the failure of neoliberal capitalism to ensure economic security through either public or private means.

While we have yet to witness the recurrence of factory takeovers on a scale of the 1936–1939 sit-downs, today a resurgence of rank-and-file militancy is palpable. In just the last few years a growing number of workers, until recently viewed as conservative and quiescent, have taken matters into their own hands and engaged in the most militant of activities: forcing their unions to concede to their demands. As one example, Ford workers voted down a company plan—initially accepted by the UAW—to implement the same concessions as GM and Chrysler.

## The UE and the Republic Windows and Doors Sit-Down Strike

By the 1990s, almost all U.S. trade union leaders were content with or re-signed to concessionary bargaining, without workers' participation, as a means of surviving and staying in power. In recent years national unions have organized workers in the rapidly growing healthcare, building services, distribution, and hospitality industries, but with few exceptions most of these unions were devoted to recognition and collective bargaining, founded on amicable relations with management. The Service Employees International Union (SEIU), whose membership had grown most rapidly, often secured collective-bargaining agreements promising to halt worker mobilization against other divisions of companies where workers had organized. From 1990 to 2010, most workers were organized into U.S. unions through mergers, without direct participation or mobilization, and, as a rule, they were excluded from bargaining with management.

In manufacturing, worker power has been circumscribed by labor law, which forbids most forms of collective action and permits employers to replace striking workers. In 1995, in the first contested election for the presidency of the sclerotic AFL-CIO, the established U.S. labor federation whose leadership was unable to staunch the decline in union power, John Sweeney was elected on the "New Voice" platform, which campaigned on the need to commit the union movement to energizing itself and increasing membership by organizing nonmembers. Under Sweeney's leadership the AFL-CIO espoused a new organizing rhetoric of economic fairness. Most trade unions appealed to the public for justice and equity through sloganeering and spent hundreds of millions on campaign contributions to elect sympathetic politicians in the Democratic Party, to fund jobs directly or indirectly dependent on public funding, and to reduce the legal impediments to organizing workers (a largely failed effort).

From 1970 to 2010, the number of unionized workers plummeted to record lows, particularly among those employed in the sacrosanct private sector. By 2008, unionization in the private sector had sunk to 7.5 percent; few workers were swayed by the advantage of membership, with the exception of immigrant workers often working at or below minimum wage. U.S. workers had largely become indifferent to unions, especially in manufacturing.

Thus the December 2008 sit-down strike at Republic Windows and Doors in Chicago is punctuated by its context of industrial and economic crisis, in contrast to the 1936–1939 sit-downs, which occurred at a time of dramatic expansion of the U.S. manufacturing sector. The Republic sit-down strike is more akin to the factory occupations in Argentina of December 2001, another situation of economic crisis, during which workers commandeered failing factories slated for closure; this paved the way for the formation of hundreds of workers' cooperatives (Sitrin 2006).

The major significance of the Republic factory occupation from December 4–9, 2008, lies in the replacement of the union in the years preceding the sit-down strike. In 2004, rank-and-file workers ousted the Central States Joint Board (CSJB), which ostensibly represented workers at the plant but excluded them from bargaining. CSJB had negotiated a concessionary three-year agreement in late 2001 that provided no wage increases, forced workers to pay for health insurance coverage, and included mandatory overtime. In an interview Armando Robles, a Mexican immigrant instrumental in organizing the strike, told journalist Kari Lydersen that in 2001 he was unaware that workers at the company were represented by a union. "Robles didn't even know that the Republic workers had a union until a co-worker showed him how dues were deducted from his paycheck. He had never seen representatives of the union, and he was never informed of any meetings or ways he could have a say in union business. The CSJB rarely filed grievances on behalf of workers" (2009, 38).

Notably, Lydersen reveals that the workers, primarily Latino immigrants, had already taken direct action without union support prior to the

December 2008 sit-down. In January 2002, workers went on a two-week wildcat strike, ending January 17, that was opposed by CSJB and was first breached by a shop steward who crossed the picket line. While the workers failed to gain a wage increase, they demonstrated crucial solidarity against their employer and corrupt union. Nearly three years later, on November 10, 2004, the workers organized themselves and voted to affiliate with the UE. Among some 450 workers employed at Republic, only 8 or 9 voted for CSJB (Lydersen 2009, 38–42). The new UE Local 1110 opposed concessionary bargaining and had a record of membership involvement and in-plant organizing strategies.

The valuable experience of the rank-and-file self-activity that ushered in the UE was put into action when, four years later, the Republic workers faced down the largest U.S. bank in order to defend their rights, force the company to abide by the law, and prevent the closure of the factory. The 250 to 280 remaining workers were prepared for resistance when Tim Widner, Republic's plant manager, told them suddenly on Tuesday, December 2, 2008, that the plant would permanently close three days later, on Friday December 5.

Under the WARN Act (Worker Adjustment and Retraining Notification), passed in 1988, mass layoffs require employers to inform workers sixty days in advance or to pay sixty days' severance pay and health benefits; no pay for unused vacation. Republic blamed the economic crisis and the end of the housing bubble for sales that had dropped from $4 million a month to $2.9 million. In addition, workers were informed that Bank of America had withdrawn a line of credit essential to keeping the company open. At that time, the bank was a beneficiary of $45 billion in federal loans and $118 billion in federal loan guarantees as part of the U.S. government's $700 billion bailout of ailing financial companies.

Weeks earlier, Robles and other workers had observed the removal of essential production machinery from the factory and informed UE organizer Mark Meinster. In advance of the closure announcement, the workers and union together planned to occupy the plant to prevent the closure and relocation of the facility.

On Tuesday, December 2, the workers assembled in the cafeteria for the official announcement were told that they would not receive severance pay, health benefits, or pay for accrued vacation time. Upon receiving official notice of the plant's scheduled closure, the workers initiated a campaign of resistance against Bank of America and Republic. Beyond the workers' demands for back wages, the sit-down strike drew national attention to the depravity of finance capital, blatantly exposing what everyone already knew or suspected: government is eager to protect capital and indifferent to workers victimized by banks and financial institutions. As well, the workers had discovered that Richard Gillman, Republic's CEO, had plans to relocate the facility to Red Oak, Iowa. In addition to demanding severance, vacation pay, and health benefits, the workers also wanted the plant—where they had developed a collective class consciousness—to stay open in Chicago.

In response to an outpouring of public support for the striking workers, local and national politicians came out in support of the factory occupation, which violated the Supreme Court's *Fansteel* decision sanctifying private-property rights. The workers had support from progressive Democratic Party elected officials, especially U.S. Representative Luis Gutierrez, a supporter of the Republic workers since their 2003 wildcat strike. Even president-elect Barack Obama responded positively to the workers' demands: "When it comes to the situation here in Chicago with the workers who are asking for their benefits and payments they have earned, I think they are absolutely right" (Pollasch 2008).

The Republic sit-down strike was turning into a colossal embarrassment for the government and corporate America, which recognized that if the workers' occupation were not ended soon, public opposition to the financial bailout would grow to a fever pitch. On December 10, under growing scrutiny, a settlement was brokered between Bank of America and J. P. Morgan Chase to provide funds to Republic to pay each worker six thousand dollars and two months' health coverage (as required under the WARN Act). But the workers wanted the factory to remain open. Two months later, in February 2009, the company was sold to Serious Materials, a Sunnyvale, California–based, private, green-energy firm seeking to expand its production of windows and glass (see Seriousmaterials.com). The company agreed to rehire all the former Republic workers, with union recognition, at the wage rate prior to the plant's closure.

How relevant is the Republic case to union and nonunion workers in manufacturing and other industries? Certainly the workers succeeded in gaining all their demands as well as the reopening of the factory during a period of mass layoffs across North America and Europe that accompanied the global financial crisis. The fact that during this same period autoworkers granted major concessions to GM and Chrysler without resistance reflects a failure to recognize that workers are capable of independently resisting and interfering with closures. Republic's attempts to circumvent labor law governing mass layoffs may reflect a lack of savvy among mid-sized businesses in defusing worker anger. However, considering that many companies subcontract production, the hemorrhaging of jobs could trigger a wave of firms that close without providing adequate notice or compensation to workers. In this vein, from 2008 to 2010 in France, Ireland, Korea, China, and the UK workers responded to corporate deception in closing factories with a wave of sit-down strikes, including at Visteon, the auto parts firm spun off from Ford. In a globalized capitalist environment, economic crisis disproportionately destabilizes those workers employed or contracted by major corporations.

Although workers' occupations are disparaged by labor unions and corporations alike as obsolete and ineffective means of defending workers' rights, the argument fails to acknowledge the direct challenge workers' control poses to corporate hegemony. The Republic sit-down strike of 2008 was the most highly publicized recent example of workers' demands for controlling their economic destiny.

## Conclusions

Worker direct action, which has manifested in U.S. history through sit-down strikes and factory occupations, is opposed by both capital and labor union representatives. Entrenched traditional trade unions oppose workers' control or self-activity that transfers power from union headquarters to the workplace. To ensure orderly relations, union leaders require hierarchical control and organizational loyalty rather than worker solidarity within the workplace and among workplaces. Most established unions appear to many workers as obsolete—ill-prepared for challenging corporate autocratic hegemony, with a sluggish, bureaucratic leadership and a structure antithetical to many workers' interests. The concept of workers' control as envisioned by the workers themselves is now being co-opted by management to suggest, outlandishly and subversively, that corporations themselves can be embodiments of freedom: As Slavoj Žižek observes:

> Instead of a hierarchical-centralized chain of command, we now see networks with a multitude of participants, with work organized in the form of teams or projects. . . . In such ways, capitalism is transformed and legitimized as an egalitarian project: accentuating auto-poetic interaction and spontaneous self-organization, it has even usurped the far Left's rhetoric of workers' self-management, turning it from an anti-capitalist slogan into a capitalist one (2009, 52).

Since the dominant model of business unionism has been failing workers, new models of workplace democracy are emerging. In contrast to organized labor's ineffectual and desperate efforts to preserve the past, some corporations purport to recognize workers' wishes for emancipation from oppressive bureaucratic structures.

However, the past lessons of workers' control indicate the need for a future of mass collective action, not the cultivation of a "horizontal workplace." Most labor unions and progressives disparage the sit-down strike or the self-organization of manufacturing and service enterprises as old-fashioned tactics that workers today are reluctant to understand and practice. These critics overlook the fact that worker-control strikes and direct action are vital expressions of opposition to employer repression in the workplace. As the factory increasingly becomes a relic of the past, the organizations of workers' control in emerging sectors of the economy will assume new forms, reflecting the transformation of economic activities and the increasing importance of service and public workplaces. With the reconstitution of capital and ongoing changes to the work process, workers will engage in new arenas of struggle that may involve the formation of socially useful forms of labor.

To advance a democratic and socialist future, workers will need to engage in resistance and insurgency against the established forces. As democracy erodes and corporate autocratic practices expand in both manufacturing and service sectors of the economy, workers' desire for emancipation from employer oppression will increase—and the struggles of the past will stand as enduring examples of the actuality of workers' self-management and control over enterprises and communities. Missing are the social agencies that could offer workers practical alternatives to capitalist domination, but as the hypocrisy of the "horizontal workplace" is self-evident across an economy increasingly dominated by service sectors, in time workers will no doubt demand self-management and control over their economic future. As in the natural environment, while most sparks or thunderbolts do not catch fire, the embers flicker on, waiting for the next combustible moment.

## References

Arrighi, Giovanni and Beverly J. Silver. 1994. Labor movements and capital migration: The United States in world-historical perspective. In *Labor in the capitalist world economy*, ed. Charles W. Bergquist, 183–216. Beverly Hills, CA: Sage.

Bernstein, Irving. 1969. *The turbulent years: A history of the American worker 1933–1941*. Boston: Houghton Mifflin.

Brenner, Aaron, Robert Brenner, and Cal Winslow. 2010. *Rebel rank and file: labor militancy and revolt from below during the long 1970s*. London: Verso Books.

Bybee, Roger. 2009. Sit-down at Republic: Will it give labor new legs? *Dissent* (Summer): 9–12.

Faires, Nora. 1989. The great Flint sit-down strike as theatre. *Radical History Review* 43, 121–135.

Feurer, Rosemary. 2006. *Radical unionism in the Midwest, 1900–1950*. Urbana and Chicago: University of Illinois Press.

Fine, Sidney. 1969. *Sit-down: The General Motors strike of 1936–1937*. Ann Arbor: University of Michigan Press.

Galenson, Walter. 1960. *The CIO challenge to the AFL: A history of the American labor movement*. Cambridge, MA: Harvard University Press.

Garson, Barbara. 1994. *All the livelong day: The meaning and demeaning of routine work*. New York: Penguin.

Green, James R. 1998. *The world of the worker: Labor in twentieth-century America*. Champaign: University of Illinois Press.

Groom, B. 2009. Why sit-ins are so 1970s. *Financial Times*. April 7.

LaBotz, Dan. 1991. *A troublemaker's handbook: How to fight back where you work—and win!* Detroit: Labor Notes.

Lenin, V. I. 1917/1998. *The State and Revolution.* Repr. Broadway, Australia: Resistance Books.

Lydersen, Kari. 2009. *Revolt on Goose Island: The Chicago factory takeover and what it says about the economic crisis.* Brooklyn, NY: Melville House.

Lynd, Staughton. 1992. *Solidarity unionism: Rebuilding the labor movement from below.* Chicago: Charles H. Kerr Publishing Company.

Mészáros, István. 2010. *Historical actuality of the socialist offensive: Alternative to parliamentarism.* London: Bookmarks.

Ness, Immanuel. 1998. *Trade unions and the betrayal of the unemployed: Labor conflicts during the 1990s.* New York: Routledge/Garland.

Pollasch, Abdon. 2008. Obama: Laid-off workers occupying factory in Chicago are "absolutely right." *Chicago-Sun Times.* December 8.

Pope, James. 2006. Worker lawmaking, sit-down strikes, and the shaping of American industrial relations, 1935–1958. *Law and History Review*, 45–113.

Sitrin, Marina. 2006. *Horizontalism: Popular power in Argentina.* Oakland, CA: AK Press.

Serious Materials. 2010. www.seriousmaterials.com. Accessed August 28, 2010.

Žižek, Slavoj. 2009. *First as tragedy, then as farce.* London and New York: Verso Books.

Interviews:

Shotwell, Gregg. 2008. Interview by author. September 18–19.

Tucker, Jerry. 2010a. Interview by author. March 8.

———. 2010b. Interview by author. August 14.

# 17

# "Hot Autumn"

## Italy's Factory Councils and Autonomous Workers' Assemblies, 1970s

**Patrick Cuninghame**

This chapter examines and analyzes the historical development of workers' councils within the Italian factory system during the "Long 1968," based on two rival models: the factory councils and the autonomous workers' assemblies. Following the 1969 "Hot Autumn" wildcat strike wave, the autonomous workers' movement aimed to topple the unions from their hegemonic position, while the three Italian union confederations—CGIL,[1] CISL,[2] and UIL[3]—attempted to recover their representative power. Conflicts over wage bargaining were used to destabilize the factory system and the capitalist division of labor, thus creating the conditions for workers' counterpower in the factory. The factory councils integrated often radically different political positions, but with the shared ultimate objective of restoring the hegemony of the unions as a unitary organizational form while still expressing the will of at least part of the rank and file.

The autonomous workers' assemblies opposed both the unions and the factory councils in an attempt to propagate workers' autonomy and the refusal of work as the predominant means of organizing workers in factory struggles. This chapter concludes that both models were too weak to displace union hegemony or to prevent the historical defeat of the Italian factory workers' movements after the loss of the 1980 Fiat strike, which marked the end of Italy's "Long 1968"[4] and coincided with the global rise

---

1 Confederazione Generale Italiana del Lavoro (General Italian Confederation of Labor).
2 Confederazione Italiana dei Sindacati Lavoratori (Italian Confederation of Workers Trade Unions).
3 Unione Italiana di Lavoro (Italian Union of Labor).
4 Italy experienced a "Long 1968," as levels of social mobilization and conflict remained significantly high until 1980, compared to France, West Germany, and the United States, which saw perhaps more intense but briefer periods of political antagonism during and immediately after 1968.

of post-Fordism and neoliberalism. The chapter also considers the March 1973 militant strike and occupation of Turin's giant Fiat plant by the Red Bandanas (Fazzoletti Rossi), the militants most representative of the autonomous workers' movement, dubbed by Antonio Negri (1979) the "Workers' Party of Mirafiori."

## Italy's Autonomist Movement

The new social movement Autonomia Operaia (Workers' Autonomy), through its practice between 1973 and 1980 of workers' autonomy and the refusal of work, can be seen as an ultimately post-workerist evolution of *operaismo* (Italian workerism). The journals *Quaderni Rossi*[5] and *Classe Operaia* were the first to research the autonomous workers' movement as it developed in the early to mid-1960s and was consolidated during the Hot Autumn of 1969. The struggles of the autonomous workers' assemblies (*assemblee autonome operaie*) and their conflictual relationship with the factory councils were at the center of Autonomia's political project. The autonomist workers saw themselves as a resistance movement against industrial and technological restructuring and its political basis—the "Historic Compromise" between the Italian Communist Party (PCI)[6] and the Christian Democrats (DC).[7] Various forms of the refusal of work, wildcat strikes, and industrial sabotage were the autonomous workers' movement's main "weapons" in this struggle.

---

5 *Quaderni Rossi* (QR) began publication in 1959 in Turin and was edited by Raniero Panzieri, a senior member of the Socialist Party and by 1960 an Einaudi editor, and Romano Alquati, a Marxist academic, with notable contributors such as Asor Rosa (later the PCI's main critic of the '77 Movement), Sergio Bologna, Mario Tronti, Vittorio Foa, Vittorio Reiser, and Goffredo Fofi from Milan and Rome and Toni Negri from Padua. However, Negri, Bologna, Tronti, and Alquati advocated a more direct intervention in factory struggles, splitting from QR in 1964 after the Piazza Statuto Fiat workers' uprising of 1962 in Turin (which they supported) led to major differences with Panzieri (who condemned Piazza Statuto) to found *Classe Operaia, Contropiano,* and finally *La Classe.* QR continued publication until 1966, having produced six issues, now considered to be classics of both neo-Marxist theory and industrial sociology.

6 Partito Comunista Italiana: 1921–1991, center-left Eurocommunist party whose electoral support peaked in 1984 at 34 percent (more than the DC for the only time), but then declined to its present 20–25 percent. It reconstituted itself for the third time in 2007 as the postcommunist Partito Democratico, having previously been the Partito Democratico di Sinistra (1991–1998) and then the Democratici di Sinistra, each time moving further to the right until reaching its present centrist position. As the largest party after the 1996 elections, it formed the first center-left coalition in Italian history, *L'Ulivo* (olive), which lasted until 2001, and was in power again under the premiership of Romano Prodi (ex-DC) in 2006–2008.

7 Democrazia Cristiana: populist center-right party that maintained its postwar political dominance until the Mani Pulite (clean hands) corruption crisis of 1993–1994, after which it became the Partito Popolare and quickly lost electoral support to Silvio Berlusconi's Forza Italia (rebranded as Il Popolo della Libertà in 2009).

A key aspect of Autonomia was its close relationship with nonindustrial workers, particularly service-sector and radicalized professional workers, as well as with unpaid labor, such as the "houseworkers" (*operaie di casa*) of the *operaist*[8] section of the women's movement, the movements of the unemployed in the South, and the university and high school students' movements.

As the autonomist workers' movement of the "mass worker" (Pozzi and Tommasini 1979)[9] began to lose ground in large-scale industrial conflicts, Autonomia became more involved in the conflicts of the "socialized worker"[10] in the post-Fordist, "diffused" or "social factory" (Cleaver 2000) that had resulted from the decentralization of the industrial economy. Such socialized workers were diffused throughout a network of mid-sized and small factories, including "black economy"[11] sweatshops and "put out" family work—forms that permitted the gradual creation of a nonunionized, precarious, and flexible workforce.

The increasingly hostile relationship in the late 1970s between the autonomous workers' movement and the PCI (including its associated trade union confederation, CGIL, which has historically adopted a consensual position with the other union confederations connected to the DC and the center-right Republican Party) led to Autonomia's isolation and criminalization—as suspected terrorist fellow travelers—and finally, repression. This internecine struggle resulted in the disintegration of working-class solidarity within the factories and the expulsion, by management and some unions, of New Left and autonomist activists. Political repression combined with the growing tensions caused by post-Fordist automation, the decentralization of production, and its resultant mass redundancies, culminated in the debacle of the "March of the Forty Thousand" and the defeat of the October 1980 Fiat strike—the event widely accepted as signifying the end of the Italian "Long 1968."

---

8 In agreement with Lumley (1989), I prefer the term operaist to workerist, as it avoids the stigmatization related to British workerism, a movement entirely different from and much less radical than Italian workerism (operaismo).

9 An operaist concept describing the new class composition in the factories of Northern Italy from the mid-1950s, made up principally of young, unskilled, and semi-skilled migrant assembly line workers from Southern Italy who did not identify with the unions and the PCI and became the backbone of the autonomous workers' struggles of the Hot Autumn of 1969. They contrasted with a previous generation of skilled craft workers (*operaio artigiano*) who were mainly Northern Italian and were the mainstay of the trade unions and the PCI.

10 A category first used by Karl Marx in *Grundrisse* in 1858, this further development of the concept of the "mass worker" by Negri (1979; Pozzi and Tommasini 1979) was an attempt to theorize the new class composition of the "diffused factory"; the product of the new social movements, industrial restructuring, "marginalization," and the "refusal of work become movement." It remains a more controversial and less well-defined social figure than the "mass worker."

11 *Lavoro nero:* the post-Fordist sector of precarious, short-term, low-paid, deregulated, and illegal sweatshop labor now performed by the *extra-communitari* (non-EU) immigrants.

## The Hot Autumn and the Factory Councils

"Hot Autumn" was the name given to the period of wildcat, "checkerboard," and "hiccup" strikes, internal factory demonstrations and marches, and industrial sabotage carried out during the autumn of 1969 by more than five and a half million workers (25 percent of the labor force), almost exclusively self-organized autonomously of the unions and the PCI (Katsiaficas 1997). With initial stirrings in the autonomously organized strikes in Milan and Porto Marghera in 1967–68, this unprecedented period of industrial unrest and civil insurrection began with the Revolt of Corso Traiano in Turin in July 1969. During the three-day battle, most of the southern part of the city, built up in the 1950s and '60s as a workers' dormitory around the giant Fiat Mirafiori plant, erupted following a police attack on a march of workers and students.[12]

This huge wave of working-class unrest continued unabated into autumn 1969 and beyond, reaching its peak with the violent occupation of the Mirafiori plant in March 1973 by a new generation of still more militant workers, the Fazzoletti Rossi, who organized autonomously even of the New Left. From then on the effects of technological restructuring and its concomitant spread of worker redundancy, as well as the unions' recuperation of consensus and control through the factory councils (*consigli di fabrica*), began to dampen the autonomous workers' revolt—which nevertheless continued at an exceptionally high level compared to the rest of the industrialized world until the 1980s.

The most important aspect of the Hot Autumn, from the perspective of operaist class composition theory (Cleaver 1991), was the leading role played by mainly nonunionized internal migrant workers from the South, who had once been stigmatized as *crumiri* (scabs) in the 1950s by the largely PCI- and PSI-affiliated Northern Italian workers.[13] In addition, the "new working class" of white-collar technicians, scientists, professionals, and office and service personnel, previously excluded from blue-collar union-management deals and also formerly considered scabs by blue-collar workers, played an important part. The operaist theoretician and historian Sergio Bologna, who worked as a technician at Olivetti in the early 1960s, focused much of his research on the struggles of the techno-scientific working-class composition in the 1970s (Cuninghame 2001).

The recently formed New Left groups, based on the 1967–68 student movement, were heavily involved in the Hot Autumn and even more so in its aftermath, particularly Lotta Continua (LC—Continuous Struggle) in Turin and Rome; Potere Operaio (PO—Workers' Power) in Rome, Milan,

---

12 See the final chapter of Nanni Balestrini's *Vogliamo Tutto* (1971/2004) for a moving description.
13 PSI is the acronym for the Italian Socialist Party.

and Porto Marghera (part of greater Venice); Avanguardia Operaia (AO—Workers' Vanguard) in Milan; and PdUP per Il Comunismo, a fragile alliance between the Partido di Unitá Proletaria (PdUP—Proletarian Unity Party) and Il Manifesto, in Rome.[14] The autonomous workers broke from the PCI's "economistic realism" and the unions' corporatist demands by chanting "We want everything!" to demand major wage increases—this time delinked from productivity deals—decreases in work rhythms, and the end of piecework and wage differentials between the various grades of blue-collar and white-collar workers. The strikes were organized locally by factory assemblies over which the unions had no control and were coordinated at a city or regional level. Thirteen thousand workers were arrested and thirty-five thousand were dismissed or suspended, but by December 1969 the employers had conceded to their demands (Brodhead 1984).

The 1970 Workers' Charter (Statuto di Lavoro), as legislated by the Italian government, conceded significant gains and formally recognized workers' self-organization within the factories by instituting the factory councils and the *scala mobile* (sliding scale).[15] Nonetheless, the largest outbreak of industrial unrest since the Biennio Rosso[16] of 1919–20 soon spread from the factories to working-class neighborhoods, where the emerging women's movement as well as student groups (many of whose members came from working-class families) and the New Left organizations became active in the self-organized neighborhood committees (*comitati di quartiere*).

These committees organized rent and bill strikes, self-reduction (*autoriduzione*) of transportation costs, and housing occupations in order to obtain material improvements in working-class living standards autonomously (i.e., independent of union-based, party-based, or any other delegated or mediated form of negotiation with the state or the market). These actions were not carried out in the spirit of reformism or corporativism, as the operaists were accused (somewhat hypocritically) by the

---

14 LC, AO, PdUP, and Il Manifesto each had their own daily newspaper in the early 1970s. Only *Il Manifesto* still continues, with a daily circulation of about twenty-five thousand.

15 A sliding-scale system that was supposed to protect wages against inflation through automatic annual pay rises. It was considered one of the main gains made by the post-1968 workers' movement but was gradually dismantled, with the acquiescence of the CGIL–CISL–UIL, under the austerity policies of the late 1970s. Seen by neoliberal economists as a principal cause of inflation, it was abolished by a decree of the Craxi government in 1984, a decision ratified by a referendum in 1985. Its abolition represented a major defeat for the workers' movement and deepened the PCI's internal crisis.

16 A revolutionary wave of strikes, occupations, and the establishment of workers' and peasants' councils on the soviet model, in which Gramsci and Bordiga played prominent roles, similar to workers' uprisings in Germany, Hungary, and elsewhere following the First World War. It led to the constitution of the PCI in 1921 as a split from the PSI. However, its defeat opened the way for the Fascist counterrevolution in 1922.

unions, but as an attack on capitalism's capacity to extract surplus value through the monetary and social wage forms (Sacchetto and Sbrogio 2009).

The autonomous workers' movement aimed to transform the triennial negotiations over national industrial wages and conditions into a major political conflict, and in so doing, remove the unions from their hegemonic position. The Hot Autumn became a struggle against the institutionalized bargaining structures inherent to the postwar Keynesian–Fordist pact and the "golden age of capitalism": top-down negotiation between unions and management of the price of labor and its use—wages and working conditions—in return for increased productivity and accelerated line speeds (Hobsbawm 1994). The basis for negotiation and compromise was replaced by constant mobilization and uninterrupted contestation. Conflicts over bargaining were used to destabilize the factory system, the capitalist division of labor, and management despotism, thus creating the conditions for workers' counterpower in the factory (Balestrini and Moroni 1997).

The Hot Autumn created the conditions for the generalized spread of the factory councils throughout the factory system, but it was to be a problematic experience from the start. As stated, the union bureaucracy took umbrage at these directly elected organisms. Furthermore, the councils in the factories where the autonomous workers' movement was weaker were the object of constant attacks by management, who feared their capacity to coordinate disruptive initiatives.

Although these same workers participated in them, the councils were also criticized by the left wing of the workers' movement, particularly by the factory militants of Potere Operaio (PO) and Lotta Continua (LC), as well as by the broader autonomous workers' movement. First, the reintroduction of the delegate principle had the power to weaken the emerging practice of self-organization from below on the shop floor. LC responded to the councils' first election of delegates with the slogan "We are all delegates!" Second, the councils' essential subordination to the mediatory role of the unions was noted. The principle on which the autonomous workers' movement had relaunched its struggles after 1967 was the rigid separation of the autonomous struggle from union negotiation (Lumley 1989; Wright 2002). This permitted the maximum room for the maneuver of actions and the constitution of new organizational and productive forms, without linking the outcomes of workers' organization to agreements with management or allowing unsatisfactory deals negotiated by the unions to pass.

However, the factory councils reintroduced the link between struggle and negotiation, presenting the right conditions for the restoration of union control over workers' self-organization. The union bureaucracy provided official recognition and protection for the councils, as well as responsibilities for their delegates "in obvious hopes that the councils will become absorbed by the union apparatus" (Cantarow 1973, 24). Wherever the autonomous workers' movement seemed to be weakening, the unions attempted to impose their functionaries as delegates on the councils to neutralize their autonomy, as happened at Pirelli in Milan in 1972 (ibid.).

The debate over the factory councils was bitter but inconclusive. The majority of the New Left–linked "vanguard workers" groups participated, considering the councils an important site not only for self-organization but also for gaining a dominant position *within* the unions (ibid.). In contrast, a section of the autonomous workers' movement participated from a critical standpoint, hoping to convert the councils into the basis for an "alternative political program":

> The task of the workers' vanguards during the present time is … not only to struggle to transfer real decision-making power to the delegates' councils, it is also, and above all, the task of beginning to construct with, and within, the councils the first foundations of a new political economy that will inform future demands by the rank-and-file; the first elements of an alternative political program to the one imposed by the bureaucracy. (See Turin Co-ordinamento Politico Operaio [Workers' Political Coordinating Committee]; cited in Cantarow 1973, 24.)

However, a radical minority remained implacably opposed, determined to build alternative forms of organization in opposition to the unions. An extract from a 1973 document of the Milanese autonomous workers' movement in the Alfa Romeo, Pirelli, and Sit-Siemens companies stated:

> The hypothesis that the [councils] are the instrument for grassroots organization, which the working class has been able to impose as an expression of the growth of its autonomy, is not exact. … Weighing up things since [their] constitution … we cannot but observe that the unions have always controlled them. They let them function when [the councils] sanction what has been established according to their line and they block them as soon as grassroots' needs prevail (Assemblea Autonoma della Pirelli-Alfa Romeo and Comitato di Lotta della Sit Siemens 1973).[17]

Autonomia Operaia's relationship with council delegates and "factory vanguards" linked to different political cultures and projects was symptomatic of its internal contradiction between movement and political organization:

> While the New Left groups oscillated between the refusal of the delegates as union functionaries or even new leaders, and acritical exultation of the factory councils exactly when they were being emptied and enclosed, *Autonomia* formed collectives, coordinations, etc., which oscillated between the nature of the representative organisms of the struggles (and were there-

---

17 All translations from Italian to English are by the author, unless otherwise stated.

fore in competition with the councils) and that of organisms linked to a particular project (that of *Autonomia*) (Borgogno 1997, 44).

Ultimately, the factory councils, while maintaining a structural autonomy from the unions, were absorbed into their decision-making process during the 1970s. They did not become "the embryo of a new, revolutionary union democracy in Italy," nor the basis for "a single industrial union over which the rank and file will maintain firm control via the councils," nor a "future working class party," as Cantarow (1973, 24) had anticipated. Their ambiguous nature and sectarian divisiveness weakened their credibility among the mass of factory workers, who despite their growing radicalization and desire for autonomy "still look[ed] to the unions for their economic security" in the absence of a credible alternative (ibid.).

The culturally enriching but politically problematic interaction of the New Left groups with the autonomous workers', students', countercultural youth, and women's social movements combined with repression and the unions' recuperation of factory struggles to cause their decline, including that of PO. This was to have dire consequences for the autonomous workers' assemblies, most of which were both integrated locally and coordinated nationally, if loosely, by PO. The process had begun as early as 1970, according to Gambino (1999):

> The unions had renounced what they could have done and the moderate governments had introduced a series of economic measures to regain the initiative. It was like an archipelago: some islands of resistance here and there, Porto Marghera, Pirelli, even Fiat, a few factories in Tuscany, Emilia-Romagna, Naples, and Messina. After the decision by the union confederations [in July 1970] to cancel the general strike, we felt we no longer had interlocutors or openings. We began to see them as accomplices of the Italian system. The trade unions of the PCI and PSI were uninterested in a profound change in the political situation.

## The Autonomous Workers' Assemblies

The formal dissolution of PO in 1973 and the establishment of the factory councils reimposed the question of organization on the autonomous movement both within and outside the factory. The compact nature of the 1968–69 students' and workers' movements had been due in no small measure to the influence of operaist intellectuals and political leaders. However, with the decision of the New Left groups to disband between 1973 and 1976, the organic links between movement and factory struggles also vanished or became intensely strained. How did the emerging but disarticulated movement of Autonomia seek to maintain these links, given the rapid social transformations and industrial restructuring society and the economy were undergoing?

The answer can be found to some extent in the autonomists' localist practices, which resulted in a diversity of sites for work-based struggle, by no means limited to the large industrial factory. In Turin, Italy's industrial capital, Autonomia activists were mainly based in Fiat and organized through the Political Coordinating Committee, but despite the centrality of the Fiat struggles to the development of operaist thought since the 1962 Piazza Statuto riots, elsewhere industrial workers were a minority within both Autonomia and the New Left groups. The only exception was in LC, which did not disband until 1976.

The main links between Autonomia and the autonomous workers' movement were to be found elsewhere. In Rome, the Volsci[18] organized among the city's dominant service sector, the "coordinating committee of the autonomous organisms of service workers" (*Rosso* 1975, 5), bringing together the Policlinic hospital workers, ENEL energy workers, rail and postal workers, RAI television journalists, and Al Italia air crew. In Milan, the remnants of the Gruppo Gramsci[19] and PO worked with the autonomous workers of Sit-Siemens, Alfa Romeo, and Pirelli, and later among the extensive network of post-Fordist small factories in the North known as the *indotto* (hinterland), coordinating the different assemblies through their CPO. In the Veneto region of northeastern Italy, Autonomia had a particularly strong presence among the petrochemical workers in the shape of the Assemblea Autonoma di Porto Marghera, formed in 1972 and dissolved in 1979 following the April 7 mass arrests (see note 23, this chapter). Sbrogio (2009, 73), a former autonomist participant and former political prisoner, describes how the foundation of this assemblea autonoma was based on the autonomous workers' movement's historic parallel struggles against the employers and the unions, the latter seen as the antiworker collaborators of the former, as well as the complex, entwined nature of their relationship with the local factory councils and, indeed, the unions linked to the CGIL:

> "Tuesday, March 6, 1973, at the meeting of the Porto Marghera Factory Council, the Autonomous Assembly succeeds in having approved, as a proposal within the contractual struggle, the payment of ENEL[20] electricity bills at 8 lira a kilowatt, the same as companies pay" (*Potere Operaio del Lunedì*,

---

18 Nickname of the Rome autonomists, taken from Via Volsci, in the historic working-class quarter of San Lorenzo, where their headquarters and Radio Onda Rossa, their transmitter, were situated.
19 A small but influential New Left group, thanks to the importance of its intellectuals including Romano Madera and the later internationally renowned sociologist Giovanni Arrighi, which contributed its journal, *Rosso—giornale dentro il movimento,* to Milanese and Northern Autonomia when it merged with PO in 1973 to form Autonomia Operaia Organizzata (Organized Workers' Autonomy) in Milan.
20 Ente Nazionale per l'Energia Elettrica (National Firm for Electrical Energy), the main supplier of electricity at that time.

no. 46, March 25, 1973); this refers to an initiative launched by the ENEL Political Committee in Rome and other autonomous workers' organisms, which they were trying to generalize nationally (Sbrogio 2009, 134).

Certainly, the relationship between Autonomia and the autonomous workers' movement was more problematic than it had been with the New Left groups, who had had a more rigidly Leninist belief in "workers' centrality" and the subordination of the struggles of other sectors of the working class to those at the point of production. This is partly explained by the sociocultural and intergenerational friction between the generally "guaranteed" Fordist "mass workers" and the "socialized workers" (often students involved in deregulated "black work") of the post-Fordist "diffused factory," who saw themselves even more exploited as flexible "non-guaranteed" workers. Here, an Autonomia activist from nearby Padua expresses his resentment at the instrumental nature of the relationship between the Veneto political collectives and the Porto Marghera autonomous workers:

> They used you, but if someone had a problem, they sent you home. People didn't eat, they were there every morning to hand out leaflets, do pickets, they really bust themselves, but the organizing was done by the Workers' Autonomous Assembly. The argument we made was that the organization had to be inclusive, that beyond the strategic argument the complexity was in the fact that we were all in this organization ... made up of students, workers, [that] it would be better if it called itself an inclusive organization and not one calling itself workers, even if autonomous (*Memoria* 1974).

The first autonomous workers' assemblies, of which the Porto Marghera assembly was one of the most important, were constituted in 1973 following the disbanding of PO, the absorption of the factory councils by the unions, and the crisis of the New Left groups, although Bobbio (1988) mentions the earlier creation, in 1971, of the similar Unitary Workers' Assemblies (UWA—*assemblee operaie unitarie*) by LC, PO, and other New Left factory militants at Fiat, Pirelli, and Alfa Romeo. The assemblies were created as organizations broad enough to organize all the "factory vanguards" and as a rival to the union-infiltrated factory councils. As well as militants from PO, they also contained members of LC and AO.

However, the experience of the UWA in particular and of the autonomous workers' assemblies in general was considered a failure by LC and AO, both of which had largely withdrawn from such organizations by 1973. With the dissolution of PO in the same year, the assemblies became the structural base for the new organization, Autonomia Operaia. The main force behind the assemblies was a complex network of worker-political activists formed by the struggles of the early 1970s, above all at Fiat in the 1972–73 cycles of strikes and occupations, which produced the unprecedented phenomenon known as the Workers' Party of Mirafiori (Negri 1979).

In Turin in March 1973 a group of mainly young, autonomously organized workers, some armed and masked with red bandanas, occupied Mirafiori and other Fiat factories for several days following the failure of an all-out strike, violently rejecting any kind of union-management negotiation. Through this occupation the "refusal of work had become a conscious movement" (Balestrini and Moroni, 1997, 435). During the action Mirafiori "took on the air of an impregnable fortress" (ibid.) and the security forces kept their distance. Faced with such a determined show of strength, management soon caved to all the workers' demands, accepting the imposition of egalitarian measures (ibid). However, the Workers' Party of Mirafiori did not spread nationally, either within the factories or in civil society, a reflection of the fragility of the autonomous workers' movement's loose network of localized organizations compared to the national bureaucracies of the unions and the institutional left.

Despite this peak and then relative setback, the assemblies' activities continued to link with those of the newly emerging "area of Autonomia," principally the Student Political Collectives (Colletivi Politici Studenteschi) and the autonomous collectives organized in the working-class districts of the metropolitan centers as part of a vast informal network of conflict in the neighborhoods, schools, and factories. However, the assemblies did not rely on these links for their contact with the outside world, producing their own publications such as *Senza Padroni* (Without Bosses) at Alfa Romeo, *Lavoro Zero* (Zero Work) at Porto Marghera, and *Mirafiori Rossa* (Red Mirafiori) at Fiat. While some of the assemblies, particularly at Alfa Romeo, survived until the 1990s, fusing with the Comitati di Base (rank and file—COBAS) autonomous service- and public-sector workers' movement of the late 1980s, most closed down as a result of the wave of repression and mass sackings conducted after 1979.

The assemblies failed to overcome internal sectarian divisions, particularly between Autonomia and LC; much of LC leaned increasingly toward the unions and the official left, with the idea of forming a "government of the lefts," while Autonomia adopted a much harder line. Nor were the assemblies sufficiently trusted—although their platform of demands often received more support among workers than the unions' did—or consolidated enough to replace the unions and the factory councils as the majority workers' organization. Consequently, the assemblies were left isolated and open to the accusations by the PCI and CGIL after 1978 of being fellow travelers of the Red Brigades and other armed organizations.

## Repression and Defeat of the Autonomous Workers' Movements

As the decade drew to a close, the autonomous workers' movement, both in the remaining large plants and the post-Fordist "diffused factory," found itself internally divided over tactics, and increasingly isolated and outmaneuvered by the revived unions and the intensifying speed of restructuring. The failure of the assemblies and the 1977 Movement[21] to coordinate and reinforce each other eliminated both currents as potentially majoritarian social forces, leaving them weakened and vulnerable to socioeconomic marginalization and political repression.

On December 2, 1977, the final rupture came between the unions and some of the factory vanguards attached to the remnants of the more moderate New Left groups on one side, and the assemblies on the other. A major national demonstration had been called in Rome by the FLM (Federazione dei Lavoratori Metalmecanici), the federation of metalworkers and historically the most militant union, in a final attempt to unite factory workers and the movements against the government's austerity policies. The Milanese "workers' left," particularly the autonomous workers of Alfa Romeo, proposed a national meeting on the same day to relaunch the now flagging 1977 Movement and the assemblies.

However, the movements were profoundly divided as to whether to participate in the FLM's march or express their repudiation of the unions' collaboration with restructuring through a separate autonomous march. On the day of the march, in an atmosphere of severe tension with thousands of heavily armed police on the streets, the FLM's stewards prevented any split from the march to the two separate autonomist meetings at the University of Rome, which thus failed to aggregate sufficient forces to make either a success. Meanwhile, two hundred thousand trade unionists marched through Rome, accentuating their strength in contrast to the weakness and isolation of both the autonomous workers' movement and the remnants of the 1977 Movement.

It was clearly the end of the "factory pact" that hitherto had guaranteed a militant working-class unity of sorts, however diverse and quarrelling. It

---

21 "The 1977 Movement was . . . a new and interesting movement because, firstly, it did not really have roots in previous movements. . . . It clearly had another social basis, different from both 1968 and 1973. It had a social composition based on youth who had broken with or rejected the political elites, including the elites of 1968, including therefore the groups of Lotta Continua or even of Autonomia. . . . So, it broke not only with the traditional communist movement, but also with 1968. It broke exactly with the vision of communism, while, at the end of the day, the workerists also thought of themselves as being the 'true communists.' The '77 Movement absolutely did not want to be 'truly communist'" (Cuninghame 2001, 96).

was also seen as a signal by the Confindustria (the umbrella organization representing the interests of Italian industrialists) that it had the full consent of the official workers' movement in launching a campaign of political expulsions from the large factories. In February 1978, following the fall of the government of national solidarity, which the PCI had supported, the union federations formally adopted what became known as the "EUR line," that of corporatist collaboration with government economic policy and the normalization of industrial relations that has since characterized Italian trade unionism.

The "Moro Affair" a few months later led to the isolation and criminalization of Autonomia Operaia and the more radical new social movements, although they had nothing to do with former DC prime minister Aldo Moro's kidnapping and murder by the Red Brigades.[22] By the end of the decade, the final battles against restructuring were fought with only a residual presence of the autonomist committees and assemblies in the factories, the majority of their militants having been sacked for political reasons or laid off. However, at the height of the 1977 Movement, the potential fusion of the autonomous youth, students', women's, and workers' movements had briefly seemed to promise a revival and revolutionary upturn in factory and workplace struggles.

Following the Moro Affair in 1978, the overall level of repression and fear intensified throughout civil society, causing demobilization and a mass withdrawal into private life on the one hand, and the increasing resort to armed, clandestine, organized violence on the other, leaving a vulnerable minority in open political activity. As political and democratic spaces closed down, a similar process occurred in the workplace. It became much easier for the unions and the official left to smear their opponents in the assemblies and the factory vanguards of the New Left as terrorists or fellow travelers.

Lists of suspected terrorists and sympathizers were drawn up by the unions and passed to management in the same way that the PCI called on the public to denounce anyone who even seemed to be a terrorist. The Red Brigades' response was to turn on local PCI and union activists in the fac-

---

22 Pietro Calogero, a judge linked to the PCI, arrested and charged Toni Negri and other intellectuals associated with Autonomia with terrorism and attempted subversion of the state on April 7, 1979. His theory was that Autonomia Operaia Organizzata (the Milanese branch of the autonomist movement) was the "brains" behind the Red Brigades, that the two organizations were one and the same, and that Negri and others in Autonomia were the "intellectual authors" of the kidnapping and murder of Aldo Moro, the former DC prime minister, in 1978. The accused proved that this theory was unfounded and an excuse for a witch hunt against the extraparliamentary left and, in particular, against Autonomia. After some initial ambivalence in the early 1970s, Autonomia generally denounced the Red Brigades as an anachronistic and counterproductive throwback to the Partisans of World War II.

tories, some of whom were killed or kneecapped. This fratricidal conflict, pitting worker against worker, finally destroyed what remained of the tenuous unity of the factory councils and played straight into the hands of management, who now felt secure enough to take on the most militant autonomous workers, sacking them for political reasons.

Fiat led the way, in late 1979 dismissing sixty-one of the most militant New Left and autonomist activists for "moral behavior not consistent with the well-being of the Company" (Red Notes 1981, 71). The unions reacted sluggishly given that some of the workers were accused of using violence during strikes and because they, like the PCI, were keen to see them expelled. With the initiative in hand, Fiat announced the redundancies of 14,500 workers in September 1980, "the biggest mass sacking in Italian history" (ibid.). A sense of profound outrage filled the working-class districts of Turin, fueling the desperate last stand of the Italian Fordist mass worker, a situation similar to the British miners' strike of 1984–85. However, the national unions were paralyzed by confusion; as well the PCI had recently ended the "Historic Compromise" pact, no longer useful to the elites, as a state of emergency with all-out repression and criminalization of the extraparliamentary left had taken its place.

The rest of the Italian manufacturing industry quickly followed suit, launching a wave of mass sackings and redundancies, including in 1982 a third of the workforce of Alfa Romeo, one of the bastions of the autonomous workers' assemblies. Post-Fordist deindustrialization and restructuring compounded the left's divisions, and a gathering atmosphere of social fear, brought about by the "diffuse guerrilla warfare" (Quadrelli 2008, 85) and draconian state repression known as the "Years of Lead," ended the hegemony of the mass worker as the central antagonist actor of the 1970s, and with it the Autonomia Operaia movement.

## Conclusions

The many struggles of Autonomia Operaia and the autonomous workers assemblies—for equality in pay and conditions for blue- and white-collar workers, for the elimination of pay differentials among blue-collar workers, for "less work and more money," for the direct democratization of labor relations and of the unions; and against restructuring, against the collaboration of the union bureaucracy, against the post-Fordist "diffused factory" and the informalization and flexibilization of labor, but above all against capitalist work as alienated activity—helped to change the nature of the Italian workplace and its institutions and made major contributions to the radical changes taking place throughout Italian society in the 1970s. Autonomia and the autonomous workers' assemblies were ultimately defeated by a combination of internal weaknesses and external political, economic, and historical forces, leaving behind an active but residual legacy (compared to their massification in the 1970s) in the form of the COBAS, the *centri sociali*,[23] and the "free radio" networks of the 1980s and 1990s, which transformed themselves after the 1999 "Battle in Seattle" WTO protests into core actors in the "alterglobalist," anticapitalist "movement of movements" (Cuninghame 2010).

One of the most important shifts since the 1970s has been the creation of a "society of non-work," one of whose most antagonistic subjects is the reconfiguring of the "socialized worker" as the "autonomous [self-employed] immaterial worker," central to the information and cyber economies (Virno and Hardt 1996; Hardt and Negri 2000, 2004, 2009). The refusal of work and of poverty now takes the form of "exodus" in all its varieties, including the mass migrations of economic and political refugees from the peripheries to the centers of the globalized economy, rather than mainly static resistance at the point of production.

## References

Assemblea Autonoma della Pirelli-Alfa Romeo and Comitato di Lotta della Sit Siemens. 1973. L'autonomia operaia e l'organizzazione (Milano febbraio 1973), discussion document, Milan. www.zzz.it/~ago/operai/autop.htm.

Balestrini, Nanni. 1971/2004. *Vogliamo Tutto.* Repr. Rome: Deriveapprodi.

Balestrini, Nanni and Primo Moroni. 1997. *L'orda d'oro: 1968–1977. La grande ondata rivoluzionaria e creativa, politica ed esistenziale.* Milan: Feltrinelli.

Bobbio, Luigi. 1979. *Lotta Continua—Storia di un'organizzazione rivoluzionaria.* Rome: Savelli.

Borgogno, R. 1997. Dai gruppi all'Autonomia. *Per il Sessantotto*, no. 11, 38–46.

Brodhead, F. 1984. Strategy, compromise and revolt: viewing the Italian workers' movement. *Radical America*, no. 5, 54.

Cantarow, E. 1973. Excerpts from a diary: women's liberation and workers' autonomy in Turin and Milan—Part II. *Liberation,* June, 16–25.

Cleaver, Harry. 2000. *Reading* Capital *politically.* Edinburgh: AK Press.

———. 1991. The inversion of class perspective in Marxian theory: From valorization to self-valorization. In *Essays in open Marxism*, vol. II, ed. Werner Bonefeld, Richard Gunn, and Kosmas Psychopedis, 106–144. London: Pluto Press.

23 Public buildings, such as disused schools or factories, often squatted (and sometimes conceded by the local government), taken over by groups of autonomists or anarchists (also by non-European immigrants and even football fans) to use as meeting plases and centers of cultural, social, and political activities, given the lack of provision of such facilities by local government. A social phenomenon that has since spread throughout Europe, North Africa, Japan, South Korea, and Argentina, it mushroomed in Italy in the 1990s, resulting in more than one hundred *centri sociali occupati/autogestiti* (squatted/self-managed social centers) throughout the major cities and towns.

Cuninghame, Patrick. 2001. For an analysis of Autonomia—an interview with Sergio Bologna. *Left History* 7(2): 89–102.

————. 2010. Autonomism as a global social movement. *WorkingUSA: The Journal of Labor and Society* 13 (December): 451–464.

Gambino, Ferruccio. 1999. Interview by author. Padua, Italy. June 1999.

Hardt, Michael and Antonio Negri. 2000. *Empire.* Cambridge, MA: Harvard University Press.

————. 2004. *Multitude: war and democracy in the age of empire.* New York: Penguin Press.

————. 2009. *Commonwealth.* Cambridge, MA: Belknap Press of Harvard University Press.

Hobsbawm, Eric. 1994. *Age of extremes: The short twentieth century, 1914–1991.* London: Michael Joseph.

Katsiaficas, George. 1997. *The subversion of politics: European autonomous social movements and the decolonization of everyday life.* Atlantic Highlands, NJ: Humanities Press.

Lumley, Robert. 1989. *States of emergency: Cultures of revolt in Italy from 1968 to 1978.* London: Verso Books.

*Memoria.* 1974. Liberiamo gli anni '70. *Memoria* 7, Padua. Excerpt of an interview with a former Autonomia militant. www.sherwood.it/anni70/crono.htm; no longer online.

Negri, Antonio. 1979. The workers' party of Mirafiori. In Red Notes/CSE Books 1979.

Pozzi, Paolo and R. Tommasini, eds. 1979. *Tony Negri: dall'operaio massa all'operaio sociale— intervista sull'operaismo.* Milan: Multhipla edizioni.

Quadrelli, Emilio. 2008. *Autonomia Operaia: scienza della politica e arte della guerra dal '68 ai movimenti globali.* Rimini: NdA Press.

Red Notes. 1981. *Italy 1980–81: After Marx, jail! The attempted destruction of a communist movement.* London: Red Notes.

Red Notes and CSE Books, eds. 1979. *Working-class autonomy and the crisis: Italian Marxist texts of the theory and practice of a class movement: 1964–79.* London: Red Notes/CSE Books.

*Rosso.* 1975. Il coordinamento degli organismi autonomi operai dei servizi. *Rosso,* no. 29, November.

Sacchetto, Devi and Gianni Sbrogio, eds. 2009. *Quando il potere é operaio.* Rome: Manifestolibri.

Sbrogio, Gianni. 2009. Il lungo percorso delle lotte operaie a Porto Marghera. In Sacchetto and Sbrogio 2009, 12–136.

Scavino, M. 1997. Operai nel labirinto. Le avanguardie di fabbrica e il movimento del '77. *Per Il Sessantotto,* no. 11 (December): 21–30.

Virno, Paolo and Michael Hardt, eds. 1996. *Radical thought in Italy: A potential politics.* Minneapolis: University of Minnesota Press.

Wright, Steve. 2002. *Storming heaven: Class composition and struggle in Italian autonomist Marxism.* London: Pluto Press.

# 18

# Recipe for Anarchy

## British Columbia's Telephone Workers' Occupation of 1981

**Elaine Bernard**

For five days in February 1981 telephone workers in Canada's westernmost province of British Columbia operated the phone exchanges province-wide under workers' control, and occupied the enterprise.[1] This action constituted one of the most innovative strikes in North America. The occupation resulted, for a brief period of time, in the operation of a privately owned utility under workers' control and allowed observers a glimpse at how things could be at the telephone company if the workers were in charge.

This radical action neither arose from the traditional strength of the labor movement and its power to stop production, nor was it an ambitious leap by a radical union. Rather, the union turned to the occupation because of its own relative weakness, which forced it to widen its support as well as to seek new allies and develop new tactics. The occupiers saw themselves as not only engaging in a labor dispute, but at a higher level, also protecting a public good (telecommunications) from mismanagement by its private sector monopoly owners—BC Telephone.

The occupation of BC Telephone was the direct product of a decade-long battle between workers and management on issues of technological change. The 1970s had heralded the computer age at the phone company, and the central concern of the workers facing this massive technological change was job security. Automation meant that fewer workers, with less training, could maintain and operate the telephone network. While the company argued that jobs would be secure because of the overall growth in the telecommunications and information field, the workers did not believe it. In the post–World War

---

1 This revised article is reprinted with permission of the publisher from *Workers, Capital, and the State in British Columbia: Selected Papers*, edited by Rennie Warburton and David Coburn © University of British Columbia Press, 1988. All rights reserved by the publisher.

II era, phone workers had experienced a massive technological change with the move from operator-handled calls to automatic dial. With this change, the workforce had grown while the new system was being installed, tested, and integrated. But this temporary growth was deceptive because once a majority of the exchanges had been changed over to the new dial system, the parallel manual system disappeared, and with it went hundreds of jobs.

## New Technology and Telephone Worker Labor Conflict

An additional concern with technological change was the continuing loss of collective bargaining power by the union. As early as 1969, when the union threatened to take their first strike action in fifty years, a company negotiator confided to the federal conciliation officer that the company did not fear a strike. Management was confident that it could maintain operations throughout a strike; it also knew that "no telephone union [had] ever won a strike," even though strikes in the industry lasted "on an average seventy days" (Department of Labour 1969). While the 1969 strike lasted more than a month, as predicted by management the company had sufficient supervisory staff, non–bargaining unit workers, and professional employees to provide a powerful strikebreaking force that maintained the network during the strike. The new wave of automation would make the job of strikebreaking even easier.

The decade preceding the 1981 occupation saw constant conflict between the union and company over the contracting out of work, changes in work methods and organization, the transfer of tasks from one component to another within the bargaining unit, attempts to transfer bargaining union work to non–bargaining unit personnel, reclassification of jobs, and the opening of self-service Phone Mart stores. All these issues were rooted in the workers' growing concern for job security and the weakening of their union. In their quest for job security, the workers found themselves fighting a defensive battle to preserve their jobs and their work, a battle that brought the union into conflict with the company's view of management rights. To the company, choices of equipment, the organization of labor in the workplace, and decisions on the nature of work not explicitly covered by the contract were the sole concern of management. It follows from such a view that changes in work and equipment, regardless of the consequences for labor, were the sole right of management (Bernard 1982).

## Employer Lockout

In the 1977 negotiations this conflict culminated in a three-month lockout. Using the restrained bargaining climate accompanying the federal government's wage- and price-control legislation, the company demanded the elimination of the restrictive contracting-out clause and the inclusion of a management rights clause in the new collective agreement. With the increased use of computers at BC Telephone, management wanted to rid itself of this restrictive clause in order to contract out repairs and maintenance of computers. However, the union was adamant about preserving the existing language, which assured that the union members would continue to service and be retrained in the use of new equipment, thereby constituting an essential component of the workforce's job security.

With the breakdown of negotiations in July 1977, the union took a successful strike vote. Recognizing the difficulty of applying pressure on the company through a full strike, the union opted for selective one-day walkouts. The company countered the union's strategy of rotating strikes with rotating lockouts. By the end of November 1977, the entire unionized workforce, approximately ten thousand workers, were on the streets, staying out until February 1978. The new collective agreement that settled this dispute included 1) the retention of most of the old wording to the contracting-out clause, 2) the addition of a special union-company contracting-out and technological change committee, and 3) a guarantee by the company that regular employees with two or more years' seniority would not lose their jobs as a result of technological change.

In spite of agreement on the new contract, the 1977–78 lockout ended with a great deal of bitterness. The usually routine signing of a back-to-work agreement prolonged the lockout for a week when, as a requirement for returning to work, the company demanded that each employee sign a statement guaranteeing no more job action and assuring his/her willingness to work alongside management personnel. Additionally, the company informed the union that they would call employees back to work at their discretion over a nine-day period. The union refused to accept these terms and the company remained adamant that the individual employee guarantees were a prerequisite to any return to work. The union decided to break the deadlock and force an end to the lockout by publicly announcing that all employees would be returning to work on Monday, February 13, whether a back-to-work agreement was signed or not. The prospect of thousands of workers returning to work and congregating outside BC Telephone buildings around the province brought sufficient pressure on the company that a nondiscriminatory return-to-work agreement acceptable to the union was signed (*Vancouver Province* 1978; 1980).

This dramatic ending to the 1977–78 lockout assured that the atmosphere at BC Telephone would remain tense, with most workers recognizing that the settlement was simply a pause before the next round in the continuing dispute. It was little more than a year later when the union and company began bargaining again, in the fall of 1979, on a contract that expired in January 1980. The union recognized that it was in for another long, hard battle and suspected that the company felt that the three-month lockout in 1977–78 had sapped the union's strength. From this position of weakness the union was driven to seek new tactics in order to apply pressure on the company for a settlement.

## Labor Militancy

The union again turned to a strategy of economic pressure through selective job action, though this time more carefully targeted. It also sought to rally public pressure to force the company to maintain and improve service and prevent a lockout of workers that might further reduce service. The key to the public campaign was the union's unprecedented intervention in the company's rate-increase hearings of the federal regulatory body, the Canadian Radio-Television Commission (CRTC).

In this remarkable set of hearings, which lasted a record forty-one days (the longest in the CRTC's history), the union opposed the company's rate-increase application on the grounds that any increase in cost to consumers should be contingent on an improvement in service. The union argued that the company's massive automation campaign was not designed to improve service to the public but rather to create an outlet for the sale of GTE (BC Telephone's parent company) equipment, with telephone subscribers in British Columbia footing the bill through higher rates. The union opposed the company's centralization plans, including the proposed office closures, which were estimated to eliminate 850 jobs from small communities around the province and millions of dollars from the local economies. Union witnesses testified that the company was reducing the quality of service to customers while at the same time driving up the rates of telephone service (CRTC 1980b; see also testimony in CRTC 1980a).

In aligning with consumers and community groups in opposition to the company's requested rate increase, the telephone workers played an invaluable role as expert witnesses. They were experts in the telecommunications industry, and the CRTC intervention helped consolidate this consciousness. As well, the hearings gave the union a public forum to argue that the company, not the workers, was responsible for inadequate service and high telephone rates. The union was taking the offensive by publicly challenging management's plan for the future of the telephone network. Workers had left the traditional industrial relations terrain of the wage and benefit package and were raising the issue of the company's use of new technology, demanding that the company justify its program.

## Worker Direct Action at BC Telephone

On the economic front, the union had started a "Super Service" campaign early in 1980, a form of work-to-rule in which workers followed company regulations to the letter, resulting in production sinking to all-time lows. With the company's rejection of a conciliation report, the union escalated its job action. Starting September 22, 1980, 530 craft workers in Special Services, one of the company's most lucrative sectors, reported to work but refused all assignments except emergency repair work. This targeted action was aimed at BC Telephone's moneymaking areas, including its major business accounts; it did not affect the vast majority of telephone subscribers.

The striking workers reported to work and then "sat-in" in the coffee rooms, garages, or spare rooms in the compound. There were no pickets because the purpose of the selective strike was to place economic pressure on the company while leaving the majority of employees on the job. As the striking workers were carrying on the battle for the whole union, they were paid 70 percent of their gross wage from the union's strike fund. To help fund the selective strike, the more than ten thousand employees remaining on the job were asked to contribute thirteen dollars a week to the strike fund.

Within weeks, the selective strike produced a significant backlog in construction and switchboard installations and repair. The company began sending out supervisors to replace the striking employees. The union responded by following the supervisors to the job sites with flying picket squads. As supervisors left the BC Telephone buildings, they were followed through the streets by union pickets. As a result of the union's flying squads, most companies with an organized workforce decided to wait until the end of the dispute rather than risk a picket and a shutdown of their job site.

In early November, the company obtained an injunction against the union's flying pickets, limiting picketing to two individuals per building entrance. At the beginning of December, the company was granted variance in the original injunction. The new wording of the court order allowed the company to expel the 530 sit-in strikers from company property throughout the province. It prohibited the union "from trespassing on any premises owned, leased or otherwise in the possession of the Plaintiff in the province of British Columbia by sitting in and refusing to leave such premises within ten minutes of being told by the Plaintiff to leave and not return until notified by the Plaintiff." With the expulsion from company property of the 530 strikers and the new wording of the injunction, the company appeared to be preparing for a lockout (BC Telephone 1980).

Early in 1981, negotiations started again with the aid of a federal mediator, but by the middle of the month they had once again broken off. A week later the company initiated a campaign of selective suspensions. Starting in mid-January, the company suspended a few hundred workers a week.

The union, having paid the original 530 strikers 70 percent of their gross wage, continued the policy for the additional workers put on the streets through the escalating suspensions.

The union's tactic of a selective strike had been calculated to soften the employer by shutting down some of BC Telephone's most lucrative services. But as the company was well aware, the selective strike also took a toll on the union, with the growing ranks of locked-out employees draining the union's dwindling strike fund, eventually leaving the union with no money and with all of its members locked out. As well, the company avoided the unfavorable publicity that would accompany a mass lockout by locking out only a few hundred workers at a time through suspensions for the duration of the dispute.

## Employer Intimidation of Workers

By the end of January 1981, close to one thousand workers were off the job. On January 29, the CRTC brought down its decision, granting the company its rate increase with the warning that a "minimum acceptable level of service quality" had to be reached by the end of 1981 or the commission would take "action appropriate to the response of the company" (CRTC 1981).

There was a general feeling among the workers that, now that the company had received all it had asked of the CRTC, a total lockout was imminent. The union's strategy, unchanged since September, was starting to falter in face of the company's selective lockouts. In closed sessions of convention in January, the union had brainstormed on various actions that could be taken in the face of a lockout, including a possible union occupation of BC Telephone buildings. The union's strike coordinator had asked local strike captains to discreetly poll their members to ascertain whether they would be willing to stay on the job in case of a company attempt at a full-scale lockout.

The occupation began on Tuesday, February 3, when about two dozen phone workers in Nanaimo and Duncan on Vancouver Island were suspended for "going slow." In response to the suspensions, which the workers interpreted as a prelude to a full lockout in Nanaimo, the switchmen gathered in the lunchroom of the company's Nanaimo headquarters on Fitzwilliam Street and occupied the telephone building. The occupiers secured the doors and posted groups of union members at the main entrance. The door committee asked for union cards and checked identification of personnel seeking admission into the building. Management personnel were allowed to remain in the building but were relegated to a suite of offices on the ground floor. And once they had left, they were not permitted reentrance into the building. Workers replaced all supervisors and the occupiers took over responsibility for continued staffing of the operating boards and maintaining the switching equipment. From late afternoon well into the evening, shop stewards phoned workers at home, setting up shift schedules to cover the boards twenty-four hours a day and to provide security staff for the buildings.

## Worker Resilience

By evening, reinforcements started to arrive with sleeping bags, snacks, and provisions for a long stay. The unionists vowed to stay in the buildings "until we get our contract." Defending their action, the occupiers explained, "If we leave, we feel the public will get inferior service from the supervisory personnel, who are not trained to operate the equipment properly." A local union official told reporters, "We're just your common or garden variety switchmen, and when people, ordinary people, get desperate enough to take a building over things are getting pretty desperate." In reply to the company's claim that the switchmen had not been producing, the union spokesperson explained, "When you've been sixteen months without a contract you're not exactly a star performer. . . . Morale had been very low and hasn't been getting any better." He charged that the company had been keeping "everyone in a state of turmoil and upset," with people becoming "more and more frustrated" (*Vancouver Sun* 1981a).

The occupation brought about a complete change in atmosphere in the Nanaimo telephone building. Grinning faces from people enjoying their jobs could be seen everywhere. A makeshift banner announcing "Under New Management, T.W.U." was hung from the microwave tower with smaller door signs proclaiming "B.C. Tel, Now 100% Canadian Owned." Operating boards were fully staffed, with experienced operators teaching clerical and craft workers the rudiments of operating. "It's almost been a carnival since we took over," commented an occupant. "People are glad to be free of supervisors." As word of the occupation spread, BC Telephone workers throughout the province called the Nanaimo office with messages of support and encouragement (*Vancouver Sun* 1981a; *Nanaimo Times* 1981).

In contrast to the jovial atmosphere in Nanaimo, there was increased tension in every other phone center in the province. Over two months before, the company had obtained an injunction that specifically prohibited sit-ins. While the union saw its action as a defensive move aimed at preventing a company lockout, few thought that the courts would side with the union. The union executive met all day Wednesday to discuss a course of action, and two union officers were sent to Nanaimo to view the occupation firsthand and take a report to the executive.

In the other telephone offices throughout the province, workers spent Wednesday discussing the Nanaimo action, asking themselves: If a request came from the union office for a province-wide occupation, would I participate? Nanaimo provided a valuable example. Newspaper articles and television news items from Nanaimo showed that the occupation was peaceful and the workers were enjoying themselves. Initial reaction of the public and press was not unfavorable. As well, the news reports clearly showed that the action was not a desperate act of an isolated minority. The occupiers in Nanaimo were as diverse a group of telephone workers as existed in any other center in the province. A union member in Nanaimo struck a common chord when he stated, "We're not playing snakes and ladders here. I've got a wife and kids. I need to get a decent living out of this company and I'm going to put my job on the line for it."

## Workers Escalate Occupations

On Thursday morning, February 5, the union extended the occupations throughout the province, calling telephone workers around the province with instructions to take over service. By noon, the occupations had swept British Columbia. The union president defended the workers' takeover, explaining that in response to "provocations" and a company "attempt to force a lockout" the workers had decided to "maintain the telephone service . . . staying on the job and providing basic telephone service." The union was careful in its statements to use defensive wording, referring to its action as "staffing the offices for essential services" (TWU 1981).

The occupied exchanges across the province were quickly transformed. Supervisors were asked either to leave the buildings or to remain in designated areas. Most management personnel opted to go home. Supervisors, police, or reporters wishing to inspect the buildings were granted entry and accompanied on their tours by union members. There were two main assignments in each building: securing entrances in order to restrict access to the buildings and ensure that the union stayed in control, and staffing the operating boards. Strike leaders in many areas stayed the full five days inside the buildings, but the vast majority of workers entered and left the buildings according to union-organized schedules.

The union executive set out general rules of conduct in the occupied buildings, including the provision that "there is to be no damage and no violence." The union's position in the face of a possible police attempt to expel the occupiers was to urge members to resist passively by sitting or lying down, forcing the police to remove each worker bodily. Workers held meetings in most occupied buildings and worked out shifts, assignments, and "occupation rules."

With the workers in control, the workplace regimentation demanded by the company was abandoned. Operators were no longer required to place a flag on the supervisor's desk when going to the washroom. Breaks were taken as required, and no one was reprimanded for taking too long with a caller. If workers found that calls were building up, they recruited more operator volunteers and trained them on the operating equipment. Operators varied their responses from the rigid mechanical replies demanded by the company; in some areas operators agreed to answer directory assistance inquiries with "T.W.U. directory assistance" or "BC Tel, under workers' control." Workers rotated their jobs, helping to alleviate the monotony. Many workers toured the buildings and were introduced to jobs and tasks they had heard about during their years with the telephone company but had never seen in practice. For many, it was the first time they had seen other areas in the buildings. In a number of buildings operator lounges and coffee rooms were transformed into child-care centers.

But the key difference was the atmosphere of cooperation and responsibility. Craft and clerical workers gained new respect for the operators and greater sympathy for the stress involved in that job. More than one craft worker abandoned operating after only a few hours, in disbelief that anyone could work under such conditions for seven hours a day. For the first time in many years, telephone workers began to feel proud of the work they did. They were still able to assert some control and authority, but it was limited because the pace and structure of work were dictated by the machinery. Most felt a tremendous relief from the feeling of being constantly monitored.

The five days during which the union occupied the telephone exchanges had an exciting quality to them. In most areas of the world, the seizure of the telephone exchanges by workers would constitute the first act of a revolution. While the media characterized the occupation as "anarchy," most saw it as a further escalation of a long-standing labor dispute (*Vancouver Province* 1981a). By seizing the telephone buildings the union had gone beyond the normal bounds of collective bargaining, but the union members felt that their inability to have any effect on the telephone company through traditional tactics made the occupation necessary and, indeed, justified.

A unique set of circumstances combined to allow the union to win public sympathy in this dispute. The drawn-out CRTC rate hearings had brought BC Telephone under public fire. In the highly publicized hearings, British Columbians were constantly reminded of the company's large profits and arrogant management. As the phone workers argued that the company's rate increase was not merited and criticized the company's quality of service, there was little public sympathy left for the company.

## Mass Support for Workers' Action

When the company refused to sign the conciliation report, it was widely condemned for deteriorating labor relations. The union's occupation was a peaceful and disciplined action, which saw the continuation of basic telephone service for the public. For many, it was a novelty, with subscribers able to chat with operators. By continuing to staff the operating services, the union was able to show the public, more clearly than any press statements could, its desire to maintain service. With the union in control the pressure was now on the company.

In addition to public attention and support, the dispute had been closely monitored by the province's union central, the BC Federation of Labour. The Federation's largest private-sector union and the International Woodworkers of America (IWA) had intervened along with the telephone workers to oppose the BC Telephone rate increase. With the province-wide takeover of telephone buildings, the Federation called a special meeting of affiliated staff and proposed a strategy of support for the telephone workers as well as three other groups of workers on strike at the same time. The Federation characterized the disputes as part of a wider campaign by the Employers Council of British Columbia to "stonewall" on collective bargaining, using courts, injunctions, and industrial inquiry commissions to drag out disputes and avoid bargaining. In response to this escalating offensive, the Federation announced that it would initiate an "escalating program of economic action" in support of the striking workers. The Federation president promised, "We will win these strikes using the full force of our militant tradition." The Federation president characterized this new stage in the dispute as an "industrial relations war on the employers of British Columbia" (BC Federation of Labour 1981a).

The following day, leaders of the BC Federation of Labour underlined their support of the occupation by touring the occupied William Farrell Building at 768 Seymour Street in Vancouver. The visit boosted the morale of the telephone workers by demonstrating the support of the Federation. Commenting on the significance of this tour, the *Vancouver Province* termed the action an endorsement of the TWU's takeover, warning that it constituted a "recipe for anarchy." "Now that the precedent of supporting a takeover of property has been set" asked the *Province*, "in the future might we not expect to see, for example, longshoremen taking over the wharves? Bus drivers seizing their buses? Tellers taking over banks? All could be equally justified" (1981a).

## Linking to Global Mass Actions

The occupation coincided with a fortuitous time in world events. Throughout the days of the occupation, the press carried stories on the occupation of factories and worksites in Poland by the trade union Solidarity. Most Western leaders were publicly defending the Polish workers and condemning the Polish government. This stance in effect gave legitimacy to occupations as a form of popular dissent.

The openness with which the TWU welcomed reporters into the occupied BC Telephone buildings made it clear that the workers felt they had nothing to hide and did not fear public scrutiny. The press tours also allowed the union to reject company allegations that damage was being done to equipment. As well, the occupiers had a chance to make their case to the press, explaining firsthand many of their long-standing grievances.

The vulnerability of the equipment in the buildings occupied by the union made it highly unlikely the police would risk a surprise expulsion or raid. In fact, as far as the police were concerned, until the courts presented them with a warrant, the occupation was part of a labor dispute and they had no plans to intervene. For its part, the union had guaranteed that no damage to equipment would take place. But the situation could change quickly with an attempted expulsion of the workers. While the union had asked workers passively to resist an expulsion attempt, in the heat of such a confrontation it would be difficult to predict the reaction of the workers or the police. As well, any action taking place in one part of the province could instantly be communicated to all other occupied centers as the workers were occupying the province's central communication network. In addition to British Columbia's intra-provincial telecommunications links, the occupiers handled telecommunications to Asia, Canada's west coast defense communications network, and national television and radio connections. Any attempt to isolate one exchange would require a complete communications shutdown for cities or even regions. To risk such a communications shutdown was unthinkable.

Before the extension of the occupation across the province, the company was in the process of seeking contempt charges against the union for the Nanaimo takeover. BC Telephone charged that the December 1980 injunction specifically prohibited sit-ins, and the mass occupation was in contempt of this injunction. A court date was set for the following Monday, February 9, and over the weekend the occupiers discussed the possible outcome of the court hearing on the contempt charges.

## Workers Face Legal Challenge and Court Orders

In its defense, the union argued that the occupation was provoked by the company's suspension of telephone workers in Duncan and Nanaimo. The union's lawyer outlined the peaceful nature of the sit-ins and noted that there had been no damage to company equipment. The occupation had in fact defused the mounting antagonisms at the telephone company. By implication, the interests of the public had been served by the continuation of the telephone service by the union. In an affidavit to the court, a union official from Nanaimo stated, "It is my opinion and the unanimous opinion of the executive of Local 3 [Nanaimo] of the Telecommunications Workers Union that we have averted a much more serious confrontation between the union and the Company" and that relations between the workers and lower management had improved as a result of the occupation (Supreme Court of British Columbia 1981).

The court rejected the union's argument, denouncing the union for setting itself as sole arbiter of "what is in the best interests of the public, the union members, and even the company." Finding the union guilty of criminal contempt, the judge charged that "a more blatant affront to the authority of this Court, the law and the basic principles of an ordered society would be difficult to imagine." The court ruled that the union would be fined an undetermined amount and that the fine would be increased for each day the union continued in the occupation (ibid.). The sentencing was suspended for two days, as the court awaited the union's response to the order that it evacuate the buildings.

## Workers and Union End Occupation

While the union had pledged to remain in the buildings until a contract was signed, the union leadership felt that with the court conviction they would eventually be forced out. The discussion turned to whether or not to follow through with the tactic of passive resistance. The union executive felt that the tactic would divide the union, with some members opting to remain in the buildings until carried out and others walking out on their own. The solidarity, cooperation, and general good feeling built up during the occupation would be lost if some workers left the buildings out of fear of arrest or physical intimidation. As well, the confrontation with police inherent in the tactic might lead to damage and violence, which, regardless of circumstances, would be blamed on the union. The union would lose the support it enjoyed to date.

A second tactic—defiance of the court order—was discussed, but the majority view was that this would lead to the smashing of the union. With the union convicted of criminal contempt, the TWU was no longer taking on just the phone company. Defiance of the court order meant the union had to contend with the police, the courts, and possibly the military—in short, the Canadian state.

Neither of these two alternatives was considered realistic, and so the union executive decided to order an end to the occupation. With the workers on the street and public sympathy behind the union, they reasoned, the dispute could still be won. In a communication sent to the occupied buildings, the union leadership commended the telephone workers for the occupation, stating, "We have provided the people of British Columbia with telephone service despite countless management provocations designed to lock us out." It described the court ruling as "granting the company the lockout which B.C. Tel had not been able to achieve on its own" and promised escalation in the form of a province-wide strike. The statement included instructions to be followed during the evacuation of the buildings. Anticipating that the company would accuse workers of sabotage, the union instructed local areas to arrange for tours of all occupied buildings; only after establishing that no telephone equipment or facility had been damaged were the workers to leave the company premises together in a disciplined, orderly march out (TWU 1981b).

Most of the buildings were vacated later Monday evening or early Tuesday morning. The one exception was 768 Seymour, BC Telephone's "nerve center." The tour of the twelve-floor building started at 9:00 a.m. on Tuesday and ended with a march out at noon. Trade unionists, largely construction workers from downtown Vancouver, left their job sites shortly before noon and gathered in front of the BC Telephone building in a massive show of solidarity. The demonstration filled the street and crowded into a four-story parking garage opposite the building. At noon, the telephone workers marched out of the building led by a unionist playing the bagpipes.

For the first few days of the all-out strike, TWU locals around the province sent flying pickets to shut down anything remotely connected to BC Telephone. The union leadership warned that the union was awaiting sentencing on conviction for contempt of a court injunction and that further violations of the injunction would leave the union in a precarious position. Local strike captains were told to restrict picketing to two workers per building entrance. The return to the streets after the five-day occupation left emotions running high.

## Outcome and Analysis of BC Telephone Workers' Occupation

With the end of the occupation, and in light of the national attention the dispute had garnered, the federal labor minister sent his senior mediator to end the dispute. Negotiations were started but broke off after six days when the company demanded that any settlement be contingent upon a further telephone rate hike. The demand shocked even the mediator, who claimed, "We have an agreement, but I can't cope with a situation where one party [BC Tel] puts a third party [CRTC] into the picture." Writing a rate increase into the collective agreement was, in the words of the mediator, "a new experience in any mediation I've been involved in." The federal labor minister called it "bizarre" and characterized the demand as "totally outside the field of labor relations . . . I am not aware in my experience of any occasion in history in which any utility company ever before thought to put such a clause in a collective agreement," he explained (*Vancouver Sun* 1981b).

The newspapers were also quick to condemn the company's proposal. The *Vancouver Sun* termed it "corporate blackmail," charging that "with one crude slash the company has cut its own credibility in this dispute." The *Province* termed the company's proposal "preposterous," stating that "no company can expect a guaranteed recovery of its costs and such a suggestion can come only from someone dwelling in Never-Never Land" (*Vancouver Province* 1981b, *Vancouver Sun* 1981c).

In response to the public outcry, the company agreed to reopen negotiations with a new mediator; on March 2 a tentative agreement was reached. But the dispute was far from over. During the course of the strike, supervisors had fired a total of twenty-four unionists for strike-related activities. The union regarded these firings as victimizations and contended that if it allowed the company to get away with these firings, "Every struck employer would simply fire strikers to weaken the union and break the strike" (Clark 1981).

The company argued that the fired employees had "abused their strike privilege," a statement that infuriated unionists, who felt that strike action was a right, not a privilege. BC Telephone proposed that the union seek reinstatement of the twenty-four through the grievance procedure. The company urged that the rest of the strikers return to work until the fate of the twenty-four was settled. This proposal was rejected by the union and, on March 6, talks broke off once again (*Vancouver Province* 1981c).

In the last week of February, the BC Federation of Labour announced that one-day general strikes were to be held in different regions of the province in an escalating campaign in support of the telephone workers. The Federation warned that the one-day actions might culminate in a province-wide general strike. Nanaimo, where the occupation had begun and a city noted for its strong labor traditions, was appropriately chosen as the center for the first strike (*Calgary Herald* 1981; BC Federation of Labour 1981b).

On Friday, March 6, Nanaimo was closed down for one day. Ferries, buses, pulp and paper operations, the wood mill, the wharves, grocery stores, construction sites, provincial government offices, liquor stores, federal government offices, post offices—every workplace with a union was closed from midnight Thursday to midnight Friday. The press condemned the solidarity action, but despite these criticisms the Federation announced that a second solidarity action would take place on March 20 in the East Kootenays, an important resource center for mining and forestry (*Vancouver Sun* 1981d).

On March 14, the union and company agreed to a back-to-work agreement. Subject to membership ratification of the contract, all employees were to return to work on March 23. The evening before the return to work, a sole arbitrator was to submit a binding interim decision on the twenty-four fired workers; he had the power to recommend suspension of any or all of them. Those suspended would report to work on the morning of March 23 but would leave immediately, although they would collect their full salary pending the final outcome of the arbitration (Hope 1981).[2] During the following week the union held ratification meetings around the province. On March 20, the contract was adopted and the following day the agreement was signed. The BC Federation of Labour postponed indefinitely its second one-day strike.

With the return to work of the telephone workers, the arbitrator, Allan Hope, brought down his interim decision that ten employees were to be temporarily suspended. A little over a week later, in his final report, he ordered full reinstatement of these suspended employees, arguing that the strike had been free of violence. With ten thousand workers on strike, he argued, "the mathematics of the dispute indicated that there were hundreds of confrontations daily between union members and supervisors." "I can say," he continued, "that there was not so much as a bloody nose in those hundreds of individual confrontations that took place." BC Telephone immediately announced that it would appeal the "binding decision" to the Supreme Court of British Columbia.[3] After a confrontation lasting 536 days, including a four-month selective strike, a seven-day occupation in Nanaimo, a five-day province-wide occupation of telephone exchanges, a one-day general strike in Nanaimo, the intervention of the federal labor minister, the provincial labor minister, the provincial leaders of the opposition, and half a dozen mediators, the telephone workers had concluded another collective agreement.

## Conclusion

The telephone workers' occupation was a remarkable action that moved well beyond the usual bounds of collective bargaining. Key to the dispute was the phone workers' decision to challenge management's right to manage the industry as it saw fit. And for a brief period of time, before the union bowed to the courts, there was the chance to envision how things might be if not only the phone workers ran the telephone company, but the longshoremen also took over the wharves, the bus drivers seized their buses, and

---

2 If the arbitrator decided to suspend or dismiss the employee(s), the union would have to reimburse the company for the employees' wages.
3 Hope's award only applied to twenty-three members. One of the fired employees, Mort Johnson, had brought a libel suit against BC Telephone when he was fired on charges of destroying company property. The company later apologized, explaining that it was a case of mistaken identity. On receipt of a written apology Johnson dropped the suit against the company.

the tellers took over the banks.

The telephone workers' intervention into the regulator rate hearings crystallized their new sense of entitlement and authority as they allied with other labor unions, the community, and consumer groups in the role of experts in the telecommunications industry. After close to a century of scientific management and de-skilling, the telephone workers recognized that they were still the basic producers and as such the experts on work in the industry. With each technological development and the accompanying radical restructuring of work, the workers recognized the urgent need for them to assert their voice and their concerns in the workplace, before it was too late.

The dilemma facing the telephone workers was that just as they began to recognize the need to assert more control over decision making in the workplace, they lost the industrial strength to win such major concessions from the company: they lost the ability to shut down production. In this respect, the experience of the telephone workers is not significantly different from what is happening to many organized workplaces in which workers have experienced a continual weakening of their strike weapon, either through the use of technology and the inclusion of non–bargaining unit professionals in the industry, through legislative circumscription of the right to strike, or through the role of the courts in curtailing strike activity. It is valuable to remember that the telephone workers' action came out of a position of weakness rather than strength. One suspects that, had the members not feared a lockout, trusted in the company's promise of job security, and felt they could exert sufficient pressure on the company through more traditional industrial actions, the occupation would not have occurred. Industrial peace will not necessarily be the outcome of the weakening of the industrial strength of unions through technological change and automation.

It is also instructive to note the speed at which the telephone workers' consciousness had changed from 1969 to 1981. Little more than a decade before the occupation, the telephone workers had been widely characterized within the labor movement as a "company union." In the 1969 strike, the union executive worried that they could not bring their members out on strike. By the time of the 1981 occupation, the union executive was seriously troubled that it could not persuade the workers to end the occupation.

## References

BC Federation of Labour. 1981a. Press release. February 7.

———. 1981b. *Labour News* 2, no. 1, March.

BC Telephone Company. 1980. *Bulletin* 23, no. 192, December 3.

Bernard, Elaine. 1982. *The long distance feeling: A history of the Telecommunication Workers Union*. Vancouver: New Star.

*Calgary Herald*. 1981. B.C. labour group planning rotating general walkouts. March 4.

Clark, Bill. 1981. Letter to the membership. March 5, 1981. UBC Library, Special Collections.

CRTC. 1980a. Rate hearings. Vancouver, September 30–December 4.

CRTC. 1980b. T.W.U. intervention to the CRTC hearings on B.C. Telephone Company's request for a rate increase. July 31. UBC Library, Special Collections.

CRTC. 1981. Telecom Decision CRTC, 81–3, British Columbia Telephone Company general increase in rate, January 29, 1981, 15–16. UBC Library, Special Collections.

Department of Labour. 1969. Letter from D. S. Tysoe to W. P. Kelly, director, Conciliation and Arbitration branch. May 26.

Hope, Allan. 1981. Arbitration award, B. C. Telephone and T. W. U. March 24, 25, 26, 27, 30.

*Nanaimo Times*. 1981. BC Tel sit-in sweeps province. February 5.

Supreme Court of British Columbia. 1981. Reason for Judgment, C804526. Vancouver, February 9.

*Vancouver Province*. 1978. Tel union can return but. . . . February 10.

———. 1980. Long, ruthless battle seen at B.C. Tel. September 24.

———. 1981a. Recipe for anarchy. February 10.

———. 1981b. Preposterous proposal. February 19.

———. 1981c. B.C. Telephone advertisement, March 8.

*Vancouver Sun*. 1981a. Desperate workers seize B.C. Tel office. February 4.

———. 1981b. Regan rips "bizarre" B.C. Tel. February 19.

———. 1981c. Corporate blackmail. February 20.

———. 1981d. Regional walkout brings island area to standstill. March 6.

TWU 1981a. Press release. February 5.

———. 1981b. Press release. February 9.

# VI

# Workers' Control, 1990–2010

# 19

# Workers' Control in India's Communist-Ruled State

Labor Struggles and Trade Unions in West Bengal

**Arup Kumar Sen**

In his projection of the communist society succeeding capitalism, Karl Marx drew on the writings of his predecessors—such as Saint-Simon, Charles Fourier, and Robert Owen—all of whom envisaged a postcapitalist society without the exploitation of human by human. Marx called this new community an "association" or "union" of "free individuals" based on a new mode of production—the "communist" or "associated mode of production" (see Chattopadhyay 2007, 247–58).

Vladimir I. Lenin filled an evident gap in Marx's theories by delineating the relationship of the party to the class it represents (McLellan 1983, 151–71). Lenin had a major difference on this issue with Rosa Luxemburg, who accused him of following the policy of "elimination of democracy" in the process of socialist construction in Russia: "Decree, dictatorial force of the factory overseer, draconian penalties, rule by terror. . . . It is rule by terror which demoralizes" (see Hudis and Anderson 2005, 306–07). It is ironic that in early 1921 Lenin himself characterized the Soviet Union as "a workers' state with bureaucratic distortion" (McLellan 1983).

The Italian Marxist theorist, Antonio Gramsci, identified the factory council as the site of workers' democracy. He argued that the "true process of proletarian revolution cannot be identified with the development and action of revolutionary organizations of a voluntary and contractual type, such as the political party or the trade unions" as these organizations are born on the terrain of bourgeois democracy and political liberty (1978, 378). The factory council, argued Gramsci, is the negation of industrial legality; it leads the working class toward the conquest of industrial power. The power of the council lies in the fact that it is comprised of workers; its formation thus coincides with the consciousness of the working class in pursuit of autonomous emancipation from capital, seeking to affirm its independence and self-directed initiative in the creation of its own history (ibid., 387–89).

Gramsci's discourse on workers' power is organically connected with his vision of socialist reconstruction in a postcapitalist society. But his theoretical insights are also relevant to understanding workers' initiatives of self-management within a capitalist system. Through presenting prominent examples of the practice, this chapter explores the possibilities and predicaments of workers' control as practiced in West Bengal, a democratic state in India ruled for many years by the Communist Party.

## A Cooperative of Tribal Workers

The Saongaon Tea and Allied Plantation Workers' Cooperative Ltd. comprised workers from the Sonali Tea Estate, located in the Jalpaiguri district in the northern region of West Bengal. The cooperative had about five hundred workers, half of whom were women. All the workers were tribals from the Chotanagpur region of Bihar—among India's most impoverished states—and most were descendants of rural residents brought to the tea-growing region as indentured labor (Bhowmik 1988, 2705).

In September 1973, due to the company's accumulated losses, management decided that it would no longer operate the plantation. The company's board of directors passed a resolution handing over the plantation and its liabilities to its workers. In September 1974 the workers formed a cooperative society, and the plantation showed a marked improvement under its management. By 1977 the annual production of the plantation had recorded the highest yield of green leaves in its history, concomitantly improving the conditions of the workers. All the development activities were carried out by the cooperative's income from the sale of green leaves. It received no loan, subsidy, or grant from any source (ibid., 2705).

The workers of the Sonali Tea Estate were inspired in their new venture by their union, Cha Bagan Workers' Union, and especially motivated by its general secretary, who took up the Sonali cause as his personal challenge and mission. One unique feature of the cooperative was that the plantation was operated exclusively by the workers without professional assistance; management was performed by the workers with guidance from the union. The cooperative decided to discard traditional methods of maintaining discipline, such as charge sheets, summons, etc. Persuasion, rather than coercion, was used to discipline erring workers. Meetings were held frequently in the labor lines to encourage the workers to understand that any harm done to the plantation would harm them as well (ibid., 2705–06). Remarkably, managers from nearby tea gardens visited Sonali to inquire whether the cooperative had disciplinary problems. They were reportedly astonished by the fact that the Sonali workers normally arrived at work between 6:00 and 6:30 a.m., whereas nearby gardens had difficulty ensuring their workers arrived by 7:00 a.m. (Sen 1986, M-77).

The success of the Sonali cooperative was short-lived because the former owners, upon seeing the success of the plantation, decided to stage a comeback. They filed a suit in Calcutta High Court challenging the validity of the cooperative. In July 1978, the cooperative had to hand over possession of the plantation to a court receiver. In the late 1980s, the cooperative was involved in litigation over the ownership of the plantation and its operations had been stayed by a court order (Bhowmik 1988, 2706).

## The Jute Industry Experience

Calcutta (now Kolkata), a once-vibrant industrial metropolis, fell into an economic downturn during the late 1960s, when the city witnessed the decline of several large-scale industries, including the closure of many engineering and jute manufacturing units. Almost thirty years into this depressing industrial scenario, a large number of workers' cooperatives were found to have survived for more than a decade. A survey conducted in 1989 identified more than twenty such cooperatives in medium-scale industries in Calcutta (Bhowmik 1995, 29).

The New Central Jute Mills (NCJM) of Calcutta, a large enterprise, started running as a workers' cooperative in 1989, subsequently increasing its turnover by 50 percent: from Rs. 56 crore in 1988–89 to Rs. 84 crore in 1991–1992, with an operating profit that year of Rs. 4.69 crore (Roy 1994, 2534).[1]

The NCJM had been owned by the Sahu Jain industrial family since the early 1950s. The company went through a financial crisis in the 1980s and workers faced lockout four times during 1982–87. The last lockout, in 1986–1987, had continued almost a year. Many workers faced starvation for days. Some workers returned to their native states of Bihar and Uttar Pradesh (UP), some committed suicide, and others turned to begging.

The workers' cooperative was formed in 1989 primarily to save jobs. The managing director (MD) of the company, together with the local government and local political leaders, held protracted discussions with the fourteen trade unions of different political persuasions representing workers in the company. Eventually, all the unions agreed to negotiate with the top management to discuss the possibility of reopening the company. After a

---

1 Note that 1 crore is equal to 10 million rupees. In 1989, the exchange rate was 16 Indian rupees to 1 U.S. dollar. As such, in 1989, 1 crore rupees was equivalent to US$625,000.

number of meetings, some unions expressed support for the idea of forming an industrial cooperative. All the unions collectively called a mass workers' meeting to gain the workers' support for forming a cooperative (Kandathil and Varman 2002).

Subsequently, an application was sent to the Board of Industrial and Financial Reconstruction (BIFR), a governmental agency authorized to assist legally and financially in the revival of dying industrial units. Ultimately, with the support of the West Bengal government, the NCJM was legally converted into a worker-owned cooperative. By the late 1990s the company employed approximately seven thousand workers, of which about 60 percent were migrants from the rural areas of Bihar and UP (ibid.).

A plant-level consultative committee (PLCC) was constituted in 1989 to ensure a "democratic decision making system" and to create "a sense of belonging and confidence among the employees in the functioning of the company." Yet the cooperative could not pay the full wages of the employees consistently. The trade unions tried to explain the financial difficulties to the workers; however, upon obtaining factual evidence that trade union representatives (TURs) and some staff members were provided travel allowances, paid leave for attending union meetings, and dearness allowances (DAs),[2] the workers did not believe the cooperative was deficient in funds. Moreover, the workers raised the complaint that unions nominated only "loyal" members to the PLCC, excluding shop-floor members who really understood the workers' problems. In response, many unions replaced their PLCC members with shop-floor representatives.

Thereafter, the workers' representatives took up the issue of payment frequently and vigorously. During the period 1994–96, the payment of wages and salaries was often delayed. But many of the workers belonging to the more powerful unions managed to get loans secretly from the employees' provident fund with the MD's approval, while such an opportunity was denied to others on account of the alleged poor financial health of the company. This contributed to tension between the workers and the unions. Subsequently, a strong workers' protest led to the manhandling of union officials and finally resulted in a factory-wide layoff. After nine months, the layoff was revoked in 1997 with the appointment of a new MD (ibid.).

The most spectacular assertion of workers' power took place in the Kanoria Jute Mill, located in the town of Phuleswar in the Howrah district. In response to a crisis in the state jute industry, the mill was taken over and run by the Mafatlal Group from 1987–91. In 1991, the Board of Industrial

---

2 The DA, comparable to a cost-of-living increase, is calculated on the basis of the cost-of-living index and added to the base salary.

and Financial Reconstruction (BIFR) found a new financier, Shiv Shankar Pasari, to run the mill, and he took over the reins the same year. Over the next two years, Pasari introduced various repressive measures, including taking a deduction from the workers' daily wages (*katouti*), paying workers by the voucher system, denying benefits like PF (provident fund), ESI (employees' state insurance), and so on, employing retired and retrenched workers at one-third the wages of regular workers without legal benefits, and denying payment to the regular workers. One of the veteran workers recounted that Pasari "unleashed a reign of terror" (Mukherjee 2001).

In May 1992, the Kanoria Jute Mill workers staged a "rail roko" demonstration—a disruption of train service—to take their demands public. During the action they made contact with a group of non-mainstream left workers who had worked with the legendary trade union leader Shankar Guha Niyogi.[3] In 1993, the group of political activists took the initiative in forming a radical union, the Kanoria Jute Sangrami Sramik Union (KJSSU), and a large number of the four thousand total jute mill workers gave the new union their support. On November 23, 1993, the mill workers started a tool-down strike demanding better treatment and DAs. Pasari retaliated and hung a lockout notice on November 26. On the same day the workers forced open the gates and captured the mill canteen. This unprecedented event initiated a ten-month occupation (ibid.).

The majority of the Kanoria workers hailed from neighboring villages, where they held a series of meetings to convince the local farmers of the sincerity of their struggle. Capturing the mill canteen and starting a community kitchen were just the first phase; with the help of local farmers, community kitchens were also opened in the villages. All over the country meetings were organized to win support among other workers, farmers, and democratic-minded persons and organizations. In the lengthy struggle that followed, the Kanoria leaders used tactics including "rail roko," road blockade, and hunger strike to motivate the workers and strengthen support for their cause (ibid.).

One of the top-ranking leaders of the Kanoria struggle, Kushal Debnath, described how the initial strike over DAs transformed into a workers' movement, fighting for the survival of the mill through a plan to establish a workers' cooperative. According to Debnath, the workers put forward four proposals:

> The promoter himself (Pasari) could run the mill himself after paying the workers what they were owed;

---

3 Shankar Guha Niyogi, a social philosopher and trade unionist, led a radical union of workers in Chattisgarh and was murdered in the early 1990s.

Any other individual owner could run the mill after paying the workers
what they were owed;

The government itself could run the mill;

If all the above-mentioned proposals failed, the workers would run the
mill by forming a cooperative of their own (2003).

On October 1, 1994, the mill reopened under Pasari's ownership after a
tripartite agreement was signed between the BIFR, the management, and
the Kanoria workers' unions. According to the agreement, the management
would pay the workers' wages and allowances as per the industry's stipula-
tions. Over the next six years, Pasari betrayed the agreement and there were
six closures. In 2000, due to flagging morale and differences within the
movement, the KJSSU split and a sizable number of the workers formed
the Sangrami Sramik Union (SSU), which enjoyed majority support. The
BIFR rejected a revival scheme proposed by Pasari, but also rejected KJSSU's
earlier proposal to run the mill as a workers' cooperative on the grounds that
the union no longer had majority support among the workers. The BIFR
opined that the mill "was not likely to become viable on a long term basis
and hence it was just, equitable, and in public interest that it was wound up,"
in other words, permanently closed down (see Mukherjee 2001).

The KJSSU went to the Appellant Authority for Industrial and Financial Reconstruction (AAIFR) to appeal the BIFR order. But the AAIFR
rejected the appeal and upheld the BIFR order for liquidation of the mill.
The union presented a writ petition before the Calcutta High Court to
challenge the BIFR and AAIFR orders, claiming that the reopening of the
mill would be possible with a proper revival package. After hearing all the
parties, the Calcutta High Court asked the BIFR to reconsider the matter
in June 2008. The case is still pending in court.

## State, Labor, and Worker Struggles

The state of West Bengal has been ruled for the past thirty-three years by
the Communist Party of India (Marxist)—CPI(M)—with the support of
some small left parties. Over the last three decades West Bengal has also
witnessed the closure of many of its industrial enterprises and the misery
of its workers. Biren Roy, a veteran trade union activist and leader of the
CITU (Central Indian Trade Union), criticized the CPI(M)-led Left Front
government for failing to take initiatives to support alternative means, such
as workers' cooperatives, of salvaging shuttered companies (Fernandes
1999). The historian of the Saongaon Workers' Cooperative, Sharit Kumar
Bhowmik, put forward a similar critique:

> One of the biggest disadvantages for the workers is that the government
> has remained totally indifferent to their plight. It could have helped save

this experiment by taking over the plantation under the provisions of the Tea [Amendment] Acts of 1976 and 1983 which empower the state government to take over a sick unit for a period of ten years, irrespective of legal problems. The plantation could then be handed over to the co-operative. Or else, it could have initiated negotiations with the litigants on behalf of the workers so as to reach some settlement. The indifference of the state government is undoubtedly causing a great deal of harm to the workers and to this unique experiment (1988, 2706).

The success of the workers' cooperative in the New Central Jute Mills is largely due to the fact that the multiple unions, with affiliations to diverse ideological federations, collaborated to promote the cooperative to protect the interest of the workers. This is a rare instance in West Bengal (Bhowmik 1995, 32).

The majority of the workers in currently functioning workers' cooperatives in West Bengal are members of the CPI(M)-backed, CITU-affiliated unions. However, the achievements of the workers in managing the production process have hardly been highlighted by the CITU at the national or state levels. The same is true of the AITUC, backed by the Communist Party of India (CPI), another constituent of the Left Front government. It should be mentioned here that the workers' cooperative at the Sonali Tea Estate was backed by the Cha Bagan Workers' Union, affiliated to the AITUC. The union's general secretary, who championed the Sonali cause, was disowned by the union, the central organization, and the party, which subsequently dissociated themselves from all such ventures. This testifies that the left trade union federations in India give little importance to workers' cooperatives (Bhowmik 1995, 32; Sen 1986, M-75).

The Kanoria mill workers' movement posed a direct challenge to the state and captains of industry. The various chambers of commerce and industry could not accept the audacity of the workers' encroaching on their "sacred" property rights. Their spokespersons criticized the workers' takeover of the mill premises as "illegal," "illogical," and "unusual." One commentator expressed early concern that the overall control of the capitalist class over the levers of socioeconomic machinery would create barriers to the procurement of the raw jute in the factory and sale of finished products in the market as a strategy to meet the challenge posed by the militant workers (*Economic & Political Weekly* 1994, 22). Renowned trade union activist A. K. Roy (1994) questioned the pro-capitalist bias of the Calcutta High Court judgment regarding the Kanoria mill:

> If an industry is techno-economically bankrupt, then that should be scrapped; if not it should be revived. If the employer fails and the government falters, the workers have the right to step in. The Calcutta High Court by permitting occupation but denying production has gone only halfway

while the Allahabad High Court in its historic judgment by Justice R S Dhawan on October 15, 1992 in the matter of Kripal Ispat, Gorakhpur, declared the workers' right of ownership of such units for which the Kanoria workers are fighting (2533).

The hostile behavior of the industrialists and the judiciary toward the Kanoria workers' militant struggle was to be expected. The CPI(M)–led Left Front government also displayed a hostile attitude toward the movement. One reason for this behavior is that the Kanoria workers supported a militant union and deserted all recognized trade unions, including those affiliated with the national CITU. Moreover, the West Bengal government concurrently developed "friendliness" agreements with private business leaders and multinationals to invite "capital." Clearly, while the workers were seeking to advance a more militant labor movement, the established labor unions were developing harmonious relations with capitalist interests. If, instead, the trade unions and the Communist Party had joined with the workers' insurgency and tangibly opposed foreign investments undermining wages and working conditions, a more cohesive and powerful workers' movement would have emerged (ibid.).

## In Search of a Theory

One can argue that it is merely utopian thinking to expect that working-class initiatives would be successful in a Communist-ruled state in India under the capitalist system. But Gramsci's conceptualization of counter-hegemonic struggle against capitalism demands that Communist parties provide leadership over working-class struggles. The experiments in workers' control in West Bengal received either hostile or apathetic responses from the Communist Party in power. This is not a unique case. The postrevolution history of the Soviet Union and the current history of China testify that Communist Party rule did not lead to workers' power and emancipation of the working class. Gramsci's conceptualization of the factory council and Rosa Luxemburg's debate with Lenin are still relevant in conceptualizing workers' power and control in the twenty-first century.

Gramsci expected that the working-class struggle would go beyond "industrial legality" through the factory council. In a country like India, the capitalist state will not tolerate such a militant struggle. But the formation of workers' cooperatives through legal struggle can ensure at a minimum the security of the livelihood of the workers in the capitalist system. In the late 1980s just such a legal battle was won by the workers of Kamani Tubes Ltd. in the state of Maharashtra (Srinivas 1993). It was a spectacular instance of workers' takeover of industry in India. And the militant union of the Kanoria workers is waging an ongoing, protracted legal battle for workers' control through the formation of a workers' cooperative. These working-class struggles in India should draw attention to the viability of legal struggle. At the same time, the experience of the New Central Jute Mills warns us that the hierarchical culture of the trade unions may persist within the workers' cooperative, with trade union representatives enjoying special privileges. In fact, the workers' cooperatives in India offer both possibilities and predicaments. Gramsci's astute critique of political parties and trade unions continues to be relevant to understanding labor politics in India.[4]

## References

Bhowmik, Sharit Kumar. 1988. Ideology and the cooperative movement. *Economic and Political Weekly*. December 17.

_____. 1995. Worker cooperatives. Seminar, May.

Chattopadhyay, Paresh. 2007. Towards a society of free and associated individuals: Communism. In *Anti-Capitalism: A Marxist introduction*, ed. Alfredo Saad-Filho. Indian edition. London: Pluto Press.

Debnath, Kushal. 2003. West Bengal: The neo-liberal offensive in industry and the workers' resistance. *Revolutionary Democracy*, April.

*Economic & Political Weekly* [Special Correspondent]. 1994. Kanoria jute workers' historic struggle. *Economic & Political Weekly*, January 1–8.

Fernandes, Leela. 1999. *Producing workers: The politics of gender, class, and culture in the Calcutta jute mills*. Indian edition. New Delhi: Vistaar Publications.

Gramsci, Antonio. 1978. The Turin workers' councils. In *Revolution and class struggle: A reader in Marxist politics*, ed. Robin Blackburn. Sussex, UK: Harvester Press.

Hudis, Peter and Kelvin B. Anderson, eds. 2005. *The Rosa Luxemburg reader*. Indian edition. New York: Monthly Review Press.

Kandathil, George Mathew and Rahul Varman. 2002. *Contradictions of workers' participation: Case study of a workers' owned jute mill*. Paper presented at the 11th Conference of the International Association for the Economics of Participation, Catholic University of Brussels, Belgium, July 2002.

McLellan, David. 1983. Politics. In *Marx: The first hundred years*, ed. D. McLellan. London: Fontana Paperbacks.

Mukherjee, Malay. 2001. A history of the struggle of the workers of Kanoria jute mills. *Indian Labour Journal*, August–September.

Roy, A. K. 1994. Kamani to Kanoria: Marxists and workers' co-operatives. *Economic & Political Weekly*, September 24.

Sen, Ratna. 1986. Experiment in workers' management: Sonali tea garden, 1973–1981. *Economic & Political Weekly*, August 30.

Srinivas, B. 1993. *Worker takeover in industry: The Kamani tubes experiment*. New Delhi: Sage Publications.

4 I have benefited from discussions with Debdas Banerjee in writing this article. Mausumi Bhattacharyya drew my attention to some materials unknown to me. The responsibility for the judgments expressed is, of course, mine.

# 20

# Argentinean Worker-Taken Factories
## Trajectories of Workers' Control under the Economic Crisis

**Marina Kabat**

The factory takeover movement that erupted in Argentina during the 2001 economic crisis gave rise to important debates. When the crisis that impelled the movement was ameliorated and capitalism seemed to have recovered its equilibrium, there was discussion as to whether it was possible for these factories—run by workers' councils—to continue to survive under workers' control, maintaining their socialized characteristics. Some authors considered it quite likely; furthermore, on the basis of these taken factories (*fabricas tomadas*), they believed it would be possible to construct a social economy that could coexist with the capitalistic economy. Quickly these expectations were contradicted by reality. With the recovery of the Argentinean national economy and the decline of the popular political movement, these worker-controlled factories were subdued by the dynamic of capitalism.

The factories experienced different processes. The workers' councils had to contend with technical obsolescence, debt, and the obligation to indemnify the former owners of the factories in order to survive capitalistic competition. Many worker-controlled firms couldn't survive. Others managed to persist but at the price of self-exploitation of the workers, who earned less than salaried employees in capitalistic firms. In some factories there was a return of capital command over production, for example, customers lending money to the firm. Many taken factories did not have the resources to obtain necessary production materials so they agreed to work with materials provided by the customers, who then paid only for labor. Yet the more competitive worker-controlled factories tended to evolve in a different direction. Some of them hired salaried workers, thereby reintroducing capitalistic relations within the factory.

This chapter analyzes the evolution of these two types of recovered factories—those more successful in capitalist terms and those less able to survive economic competition. The research examines the economic and political context in which they developed and focuses on paradigmatic cases such as Brukman, a textile factory in Buenos Aires, and Zanón, a ceramics factory in the south, studying their economic viability, their relationship with the state, and the new forms of work organization they promoted. The methodology is based on statistical analysis, historical research on Argentinean expropriated factories, and the trajectories of workers' control in changing periods of economic crisis, making use of empirical research, interviews with workers, and ethnographic methods and observations inside the plants.

It is our belief that taken factories and their workers' councils are one of the greatest accomplishments of the workers' movement. However, to overlook their limitations and contradictions will not help to preserve them. On the contrary, only an objective study of their characteristics and shortcomings will help remove present obstacles and develop their complete potential for the future.

One of their crippling limitations is the industrial form they must adopt to obtain legal status within capitalism; that is, the form of cooperative organizations. Many taken factories refused this solution, but it was the only option acceptable to the government. The taken factories were not born as cooperatives. On the contrary, they started as workers' councils; this was the case with the most important taken factories, including Zanón and Brukman. But under economic and political pressure as well as repression, these workers' councils decided to transform themselves into cooperatives.

◆

There is a political current with close ties to the government that has tried to redirect the taken-factories movement to make it more acceptable in capitalistic terms. This movement has rejected the tactic of occupation (although it too used this tactic at the beginning); it has privileged negotiation agreements and defends the cooperative model as the ultimate solution for workers. Workers orientated to this group usually form a cooperative as the first step. But these are not the cases analyzed here.

From our point of view it is important to distinguish between taken factories—those that have undergone an occupation process, implying direct action—and the rest of the so-called "recovered enterprises." Though the two groups share some characteristics, they have resulted from dissimilar experiences, with different internal organization and divergent political horizons. Furthermore, workers' councils play a much more important and active role in taken factories; in the majority of recovered firms councils have little to no presence. Thus the focus of this chapter is on taken factories; recovered firms are analyzed only for the purposes of comparison.

## Political Context of the Factory Takeover Movement

The popular manifestation known as the Argentinazo,[1] a working-class insurrection that took place amid the country's financial collapse of December 19–20, 2001, initiated a revolutionary process in which factory occupation played a prominent role. The factory takeover movement served as a catalyst for the popular mobilization that accompanied the Argentinazo but at the same time was one of its major beneficiaries—it would not have been able to sustain itself without the popular mobilization or the support of the organizations that led the process.

Likewise, the ceramic factory Zanón in the southern province of Neuquen would not have had the chance to resist seven eviction attempts without the aid of several political organizations, especially the unemployed movement.[2] The same happened in the Brukman textile workshop, located in the capital city of Buenos Aires. Brukman workers occupied the factory on December 18, 2001, only two days before the Argentinazo forced the president to resign. The Brukman occupation was supported by both the *piquetero*[3] and the assembly movements. The first eviction attempt took place the same day as the first meeting of all the popular assemblies from different neighborhoods. After the meeting of assemblies, four hundred people marched to the Brukman factory to defend the workers' occupation. The government organized a huge repressive force to expel the employees from the plant, but not even the manager could enter the factory. A massive and long-lasting encampment at the doors of the factory prevented his entrance and finally obtained expropriation of the firm. In another occupied factory, Grissinopoli, the neighbors installed a siren that could be turned on in the event of an attempt at eviction so they could go to help.

A third example among many concerns the printing plant Artes Gráficas Chilavert. When the workers decided to occupy the factory, taking

---

1 In the Argentinazo, December 19–20, 2001, an alliance of class fractions challenged the state and, through popular demonstrations and direct actions overthrew president Fernando de la Rúa, who intended to implement a neoliberal economic adjustment plan sponsored by multilateral lending agencies.

2 For further information see Pascucci 2009 and Kabat 2009.

3 The piquetero movement is comprised of workers who became unemployed and lived in poverty during the Argentine economic crisis and social turmoil that emerged in the 1990s and continue into the second decade of the twenty-first century. Piquetero activists have demanded food, health care, and social services and have developed a culture of popular struggle.

production into their own hands, police surrounded the plant and tried to disrupt the manufacturing process. But neighbors organized among themselves to convey supplies to the workers through the houses next to the factory. In fact, the first book run manufactured clandestinely by Chilavert under workers' control was delivered from the factory, in spite of the surrounding police force, through a hole in the wall separating the factory from a neighbor's house. This neighbor also helped distribute the books and collect resources for the workers.

These examples illustrate that the factory takeover movement was rooted in the larger class struggle. It helped create the clamor from which this movement was born and gave rise to the acts of solidarity and the campaigns that enabled its growth and survival. When this bigger political movement weakened, so did the factory takeover movement. The years between 2002 and 2009 witnessed an apparent retreat in the class struggle in Argentina, as a partial economic recovery and the effects of repression and co-optation resulted in a decline in the level of political activity and mobilization. However, this decline should be considered only relative because class struggle has not receded to the levels before the 2001 crisis and Argentinazo insurrection. The organizations built during this political process have not disappeared; they have even gained new sectors, especially among teachers, subway employees, and factory personnel. With the return of economic crisis from 2008 to 2010, the class struggle has escalated into skilled and professional labor markets that had been regarded as less vulnerable to a decline in wage rates and economic destabilization (for a more detailed description of the Argentinean class struggle see Sartelli 2007).

A parallel experience can be seen in the factory takeover movement: after 2002 there was a relative decline. Some taken factories could not survive in the competitive environment and closed their doors. Some evolved in a capitalistic manner, reintroducing wage labor within the firm. Many were co-opted by the government—in exchange for subsidies they abandoned political confrontation and removed their more radical elements. Others simply reduced their political activities—time for assemblies and political discussion in the workplace is naturally limited, and the number of demonstrations simply diminished. Some new takeovers arose during this period, but their expectations and willingness to face conflict were much lower. As confrontation was reduced, the overall number of occupations dropped markedly. There were 123 enterprises taken over between 2000 and 2004; during 2005–2008 there were only 23 (Palomino et al. 2005).

Nevertheless it can be considered a success that in these adverse conditions many taken factories managed to survive and maintained a degree of political activity, which, in certain cases, such as that of Zanón, remains of particular importance. The recurrence of the economic crisis will likely revitalize the factory takeover movement; as of 2009 new taken factories had appeared, giving rise to a fresh wave of solidarity campaigns. In this context, it is important to heed the lessons of the recent past, lessons that can be useful for workers everywhere, not only in Argentina.

Concentrated in metropolitan areas, the factory takeover movement has been particularly strong in the Buenos Aires province, especially in the districts surrounding the capital. Other provinces leading the process are the industrial centers of Córdoba and Santa Fe; also involved are the provinces of Neuquen, Entre Rios, Chaco, Jujuy, Rio Negro, Mendoza, and Tierra del Fuego.

The movement is mainly consolidated among undercapitalized secondary sector enterprises with few links to international markets. This is a consequence of the process of concentration and centralization of capital and the bankruptcy of many industrial firms. Behind the secondary sector come the service companies. Two examples from this sector are the Hotel Bauen in the center of Buenos Aires and the public transportation company Transportes del Oeste. The list also includes firms related to education and health services as well as commerce. Within the secondary sector, 26 percent of all taken factories are in the metallurgical industries, which include foundries, tube and foundation construction, and automotive parts manufacture. Food processing and preparation represents the next largest group within the secondary sector, comprising 25 percent of total cases. Within the food branch the taken factories are quite heterogeneous, ranging from meat processing plants with nearly five hundred workers, such as Yaguané, to several small enterprises, such as Grissinopoli, a bread products manufacturer, and SASETRU, a pasta manufacturer (Fontenla 2007).

## Constraints on Worker-Occupied Factories

Workers who take production into their own hands face several obstacles and constraints. The first consideration is the fact that the vast majority of workers' occupations take place in plants in which the capitalist firm has already gone bankrupt. According to Argentinean bankruptcy law, the workers that take control of the factory assume all its previous debts, a heavy inheritance for the workers' councils.

A second constraint relates to the legal form of the expropriation. Initially, the workers forming a cooperative obtain the temporary use of the factory for a period of two years. After that, they are forced to buy the firm from the capitalist. They are allowed to subtract the salaries and benefits owed them by their former employer; however, if the workers are successful in producing a profit, the original firm accrues this value. Consequently, in two years' time they will have to buy the company at a price much higher than it was when they took charge of the firm. For example, the meat processing plant Yaguané was valued at $3,250,000 in 1997, the year in which the workers took control. In 2004, when the expropriation was obtained, the firm's value had increased to $38,000,000. This process only applies to situations in which the expropriation is actually obtained, however; this is not the result for the majority of appropriated enterprises. An alternate type of resolution involves the rental of the plant, whether by a legal arrangement or by a direct arrangement with the capitalist owners. In many cases there is either no resolution or a provisional one.

When the creation of a cooperative has been preceded by an occupation process, expropriation has been achieved more frequently. According to research carried out in 2004, most taken factories had obtained an expropriation, while the firms without a takeover action achieved expropriation only in approximately a third of the cases (see Trinchero 2004). These findings are acknowledged even by those who regard conflict and occupation as being somehow negative for the recovery of the factories.

Workers have fought for better arrangements. The cooperative option, especially the expropriation agreement mentioned above, is not the most progressive solution and involves risks. One has already been described: workers must take responsibility for the company's debts and buy the factory from the capitalist owner who had driven it to bankruptcy in the first place. The debt burden, as well as the obligation to compensate the owner, threatens to financially choke the taken factories. Another risk involves the transformation of a worker's legal standing once the cooperative is in order. Legal rights of workers do not extend to the associates of a cooperative, and minimum wage, social welfare, and other benefits are lost with the legal confirmation of the cooperative. This is why in the more politically conscious factories the workers have battled for the nationalization of the firm under workers' control, as well as for expropriation without indemnification.

Nationalization, which has been more frequently achieved in taken factories in Venezuela than in Argentina, allows the workers to preserve their labor rights. The Argentine government was inflexible on this point; the INAES (National Institute of Cooperative Enterprise and Social Economy), a government institution created in 2000, insisted that cooperative organization was the only legal option for taken factories. In order to increase government control over cooperatives, in 2003 INAES announced Resolution #2037, establishing new regulations for cooperatives and increasing its own jurisdiction over them. In this context the workers were forced to accept the cooperative solution as the only way to prevent eviction and to achieve the legal stability necessary for production.

Brukman and Zanón, by all accounts the two most important taken factories, both originally rejected the creation of a cooperative. Repression and lack of economic support from the government finally forced them to accept the cooperative form, although the workers from both factories resisted for almost two years: 2001–2003 at Brukman and 2002–2004 at Zanón. The repression suffered by these workers and the negative results of their requests for nationalization under workers' control served as a test case and thus had deterrent effects on developments at other taken factories.

The women working in the old Brukman factory organized as a cooperative only following a series of disputes with the state. After the employers of the company abandoned the installations on December 18, 2001, the seamstresses occupied the factory and put the machines to work. In March 2002 they presented a proposal to the legislature of Buenos Aires requesting the nationalization of the firm under workers' control. The legislature started discussion of the project in July 2002.

The motivation for proposing the "cooperative" model initially was that, as one worker said, if nationalization failed, they "wouldn't have any salary or social security" (Heller 2005, 195). In early 2003 Brukman workers still defended the nationalization under workers' control. That year they laid out the following proposal:

> For a year and a half we have been proposing the factory statization under worker control. But we aren't intransigents, as the government says . . . we said that we were open to other legal forms. But we don't agree to accept a micro-entrepreneurship, destined to fail, as traditional party politicians have proposed to us, where we should end up carrying enormous debts on our workers' shoulders and where we should pay from our own pockets social security charges and pension. We are qualified workers, men and women. Politicians can't squash our workers' experience, which can be put at the service of the Argentinean community. Our factory can be part of the solution and not the problem as these Mrs. Politicians, who seem to live on another planet, think (Brukman Workers 2003).

Only after their eviction from the factory later that year, with ferocious repression against them and their supporters, did the Brukman workers finally accept the formation of a cooperative as a means of providing a positive exit to the conflict.

The Zanón ceramics workers were always aware of the dangers involved with the cooperative form. They reasoned that a self-governing management by the workers would not be possible with the cooperative form because it did not provide for the full organization and functioning of a democracy. They also contended that the military dictatorship–sanctioned cooperative law contradicted workers' democracy. Therefore, they considered the regulations controlling the union of ceramics workers—regulations drafted by Zanón and three other factories, the "Ceramics Code"—as well as the "Norms of Cohabitation of Zanón under Workers' Control," drawn up by the occupying workers, to be above the norms stipulated by the statute of the cooperative ("Norms" quoted in Tirachini 2004).

As with the Brukman workers, the Zanón workers presented a proposal for nationalization under workers' control. In this case it was a "proposal for transitory workers' management," presented with the support of the National University of Comahue and the University of Buenos Aires. In March 2002 production was started; approximately one month later, on April 8, the workers faced another attempt at eviction. By then some fifty thousand people had endorsed the nationalization process with their signatures.

In May 2004, after twenty-seven months of production managed by the workers, the FaSinPat cooperative was established—the acronym stands for "factory without a boss." The workers still view the constitution of the cooperative as a temporary measure, as they continue to demand nationalization under workers' control.

As mentioned, the formation of a cooperative also permits the reappearance of capitalist relations within the factory because the cooperative associates are allowed to contract wage labor. Some factories are in a worse financial situation from this vantage point because they are also a limited-liability company in which workers jointly own stock with outside investors. This is the situation with Yaguané, a meat processing plant, and Pauny, a rural machine factory. In the case of Pauny, a public limited company (PLC), the workers of the factory, who formed the Cooperative of Metallurgical Labor Las Varillas Ltd., hold only about a third of the stock's portfolio (Moreno 2009).

A third constraint that makes the cooperative option less favorable is the lack of capital to initiate production and the technological obsolescence of the taken factories. The lack of capital is a crucial problem in that it promotes dependency on suppliers or customers. In many cases the workers' council agrees to work with supplies provided by the customers, who then pay for the industrial processing. In the beginning, this allows factories to conserve labor and reestablish production. But it also reduces earnings, which are generally limited to the pay of the workforce, and creates dependency upon these clients. Consequently, for many workers of the taken factories, externalizing the raw-material aspect of the production chain is viewed as only an initial stage, during which they try to generate enough capital to become independent. In general, this approach to production has not disappeared, although its importance has diminished in some sectors. On average, the taken factories that improve their economic situation rely on production with supplies provided by the customers only 40–50 percent of the time. In many cases, the production using the customer's own material is carried out on request because the factories do not have enough capital to produce for stock.

Frequently a vicious cycle emerges in which a lack of capital impels workers to adopt certain kinds of productive strategies, which in turn perpetuate the shortage of capital. Thus the level of profit of the taken factories tends to be very low. Brukman, for instance, in 2004 worked partially with customers' supplies and partially with its own materials. But in 2008 they were working only with clients' supplies. Graciela, a Brukman worker interviewed in 2008, said:

> We've been struggling for six years and in fact instead of going up we're going down. I can tell you that everything is great, that we sell to everyone, but that's not true. At the end of the week you get two pesos. It is a political matter, but I believe that under capitalism cooperatives don't work.... We're fighting to be able to buy, but now it's all fazon work[3] ... the fazon work is like having a boss, and that gives you much anger, it produces much anxiety because you deliver the fazon work and they don't pay you or they give you a ninety-day post-dated check. They do as it pleases them most.[4]

Yet another problem with the cooperative model lies in the technological backwardness of the taken factories. On average, the machinery of the taken factories (not including printing industries) is forty years old. Most of the taken factories were constructed before 1970, and less than 15 percent of them were created after 1990 or had renovated their equipment during that time (see Trinchero 2004). In the case of the metallurgical firm IMPA, the machinery was more than fifty years old. According to an interview with the IMPA workers, new purchases after the workers took control did not redress the problems because they only filled gaps in the productive system rather than replacing defunct elements.

Many of the taken factories had also been deliberately emptied of equipment by their owners before the formal bankruptcy of the firm and the subsequent occupation by the workers. The workers' councils had to take an obsolete and dismantled factory and make it work again. In some instances, the holes left by the capitalist plundering had to be circumnavigated by outsourcing stages of the productive process. In these cases, "outsourcing" does not imply an economic advantage; workers opted for this only when there was no other choice. For example, as we were told in a 2009 interview, the

---

3 Fazon work refers to on-demand work for a customer who provides the raw materials and pays only for the labor.
4 All interviews quoted, except when mentioned to the contrary, come from the Oral Archive in the CEICS, Center of Study and Research in Social Sciences (Centro de Estudios en Ciencias Sociales, www.ceics.org.ar.) The interviews as well as the observations on which this chapter is based were conducted by researchers of the Labor Process Research Group from the CEICS, directed by Marina Kabat. Other scholars that participated in this group are Silvina Pascucci, Nicolas Villanova, and Florencia Moreno.

metallurgical cooperative Diogenes Taborda, which manufactured agricultural machines, needed a special metal beam that cost more than forty thousand dollars. They tried to offer another machine in exchange for the equipment, and they asked for state subsidies to buy it, but when neither of these attempts was successful, the workers had to outsource part of the productive process in order to continue manufacturing.

In other cases the lack of better equipment does not force the outsourcing, but it affects the competitive capability of the factory. In 2004 Brukman lost an export contract because of the low production capacity of their machines, a problem that persisted. In 2008 a worker said: "We need more machines, more technological ones, of course, but for that we need a larger budget." Then she listed the machines they needed, and most of them cost more than thirty thousand dollars. The prohibitively high cost of repair for the equipment presented another problem. Two Brukman workers are in charge of maintaining the machines, but they don't have the expertise to fix every problem that appears. As mentioned, the deficiency of the equipment is a legacy of the former capitalist owner. Prior to the takeover, for a brief period Brukman had an automatic cutting machine, but the firm did not complete the payments and had to give it back. When the workers took over the plant the cutting was again done by hand and continues to be done so today.

Taken factories in the printing industry have newer machines; however, technological advances have been extremely rapid in this sector, so even though equipment might not be particularly old, it is sometimes nevertheless technically obsolete. These accelerated technological advances are symptomatic of the deeper process of concentration and centralization that has affected this sector, leading many firms to bankruptcy. This is why there are so many taken factories among the printing industry: Chilavert, as mentioned, or more recently, INDUGRAF. These taken factories operate in a highly competitive sector and for this reason some have entered into agreements to make collective purchases in order to reduce costs. They have even created a cooperative network.

The scale of production is a problem that affects all taken factories. The majority are small factories, although the big meat-processing plants represent an exception to this general rule. The ceramics plant, Zanón, can be considered an exception too if analyzed from a national point of view. But it is still a relatively small factory in comparison to the world competition in its particular economic branch. The problem of scale is exacerbated by the meager use of the spatial capacity in these factories. In 2004 half the taken factories employed less than 50 percent of their installed capacity (see Trinchero 2004).

## Worker-Introduced Changes in the Labor Process

The practical demonstration that employers are not needed and that workers can take control of production by themselves has been the main transformation introduced by the taken factories. Not long ago each of these workers occupied an isolated place in production, obeyed orders from above, and had no chance to transmit their opinions, not even about their own specific jobs. Now they collectively decide about all aspects of production.

Another reform introduced in the taken factories relates to the earning structure. Many taken factories have decided to establish equal remunerations for all workers. But some have maintained previous differences. The meat-processing plant La Foresta, for example, maintains the earning disparities between craft workers and unskilled laborers, a decision made by the factory's general assembly. According to a 2009 interview, the highest-earning workers receive twice the income of the lowest-earning workers. These disparities may be related to the nature of a given job involving many different degrees of skill; this is the explanation offered by the workers themselves. However, other factories with the same characteristics, such as the Bragado meat-processing plant, have chosen an egalitarian remuneration system.

A comprehensive analysis of taken factories shows that the essential factor for the selection of an egalitarian income system versus a pay scale seems to be the development of political consciousness among the workers: an egalitarian income system is more frequently found in those taken factories that have faced important struggles, and is much less common among the factories that have not experienced any conflict. Seventy-one percent of recovered factories that were occupied by the workers have egalitarian incomes. In contrast, recovered factories with no history of occupation because they resulted from an arrangement with the capitalist owner have egalitarian incomes in only 31 percent of the cases.

A similar disparity manifests in the decision to contract wage labor. As a consequence of becoming members of a cooperative, workers no longer earn salaries but benefit as partners. For the factories with more serious economic problems, this can lead to self-exploitation of the workers, whose incomes can descend below minimum-wage levels even with longer working hours. In the more economically successful factories, in contrast, there is the temptation to improve incomes by hiring wage labor. This labor does not belong to the cooperative, does not have the right to participate in the assemblies, and is indeed exploited by the cooperative associates among whom earnings are distributed. In some factories, such as Cooperativa de trabajo La nueva Esperanza Ltda, the number of wageworkers is almost as high as the number of cooperative workers. In this case, according to a 2009 interview, there were sixteen members of the cooperative and fourteen contracted wageworkers.

In factories with a deeper political consciousness—the product of a major political struggle—no wage labor is contracted. They have instead enlarged production by adding more workers with the same status as the original cooperative members. For example, at Brukman only 32 out of 132 factory workers supported the entire struggle process and eventually founded the cooperative. When production increased they added more workers, who also became part of the cooperative with the same rights as the original members. The same happened at Zanón, where the new workers were unemployed individuals recruited from the piquetero movement that had supported the occupation of the factory.

A third important element introduced by workers' control is the change in the labor process. In these factories, the productive process[5] has not undergone important modifications; mechanized work has remained basically static and the same holds true for manual work. In some instances a certain task may have been mechanized, but because of the capital constraints mentioned above, this is not a common occurrence. The main changes in the labor process have, instead, been related to division of labor, including a tendency to eliminate the separation between manual and intellectual work, the appearance of new means of delegating tasks, and an increase in workers' versatility.

There have been important modifications regarding the distribution of tasks among workers. Research carried out with Zanón workers shows that the majority of workers (52 percent) have switched from their previous job assignments (Chirico et al. 2003). In the majority of taken factories, the number of workers that held on throughout the struggle and resisted until the formation of the cooperative is smaller than the workforce formerly employed by the capitalist firm. Thus when production begins again many tasks must be reassigned. Other factors also contribute. In order to increase productivity, for instance, workers have become more versatile. One Brukman worker said that prior to the factory occupation she only sewed pockets, but now, once finished with sewing, she performs other functions to finish a garment. In addition, the common experience of the struggle has reduced prior mistrust among workers, and what were formerly craft secrets are now shared openly with coworkers.

Necessity has forced others to develop new skills. Sergio from Brukman, who has committed to the maintenance of the machinery, has had to expand his knowledge in order to fix the various machines in the factory. He

---

5 We use the definition of Marx, who distinguishes "productive process" from "labor process." The former refers to all the technical stages in the production of a good, while "labor process" describes all the instances in which workers add value to the product. Thus the latter concept is much more focused on workers' activities. See Marx 1990.

also states that with the help of members of the engineering faculty of the University of Buenos Aires, "We redesigned the factory, we put all the machines on the same floor, in order to save energy and to be all together" (Vales and Hacher 2003). This also helped simplify the labor process.

In many cases, as with the taken factories in the printing industry, the administrative employees of the firm do not participate in the struggle. Therefore, when the workers reinitiate production, some of them must perform those administrative jobs.[6] Former manual workers confront the necessity of learning to manage the accounts and handle the legal and economic management of the firm. In this way the taken factories have made advances in the elimination of the division between manual and intellectual work. They also can be regarded as schools in which workers gain knowledge about the economic organization of society.

## Internal Organization of Workers

There is a great heterogeneity among taken factories; some go far beyond others in the collective decision-making process. Yet, guided by the cooperative form, and as such required to follow regulations as established in the law of cooperatives, they all share some patterns. The direction of the factory is the responsibility of the administrative council, comprised of a president, secretary, treasurer, and trustee, chosen at sectional meetings, which are held with differing frequencies depending on the cooperative. The assemblies can function on a weekly or monthly basis, but there are cases in which the general assembly gathers only once a year and its decision-making power is more formal than substantive. When the assembly meets more often the president has less power—the roles of the cooperative officers are different in each factory. As the general assemblies become more infrequent, the risk of their being reduced to ceremonial acts increases and the cooperative directors tend to make decisions without consulting the rest of the workers.

This has led to the emergence of internal conflicts. In Yaguané, for example, in April 2004 the assembly dismissed its president, Daniel Flores, a former workers' delegate. According to Hernán Ares from the new commission that leads the cooperative: "There was a period among his management that the meat-processing plant grew: we slaughtered, we exported, we asked for credits . . . . More than 6,000 heads of cattle were killed each week but the workers remained in the same very poor wage and working conditions we have always had, including dismissals" (Lavaca.org 2004).

---

6 The experience of the print workers is described by the workers themselves at Red Gráfica Cooperativa, www.redgraficacoop.com.ar/quienessomos.php.

Hotel Bauen workers interviewed by the CEICS in 2008 described a similar situation: between 2003 and 2005 the directorate of the cooperative had to be expelled because it intended to sell the firm to capitalist entrepreneurs. The workers rejected this attempt and reorganized the cooperative's structure in a more democratic way. Although in the two cases mentioned the workers managed to solve the problem, these examples illustrate the risks inherent in the cooperative form.

In some cases a more complex structure has developed. In the printing industry, the factory takeover process laid the foundation for the unification of different endeavors with the objective of making their production more profitable and competitive in the market. One example is the Cooperative Graphics Network (Red Gráfica Cooperativa), which started taking shape in July 2006 when seven cooperatives united to establish a common work agenda. After analyzing the potentialities of their integration, the network was constituted as a federation on July 5, 2007. The founding cooperatives were El Sol, Artes Gráficas Chilavert, Campichuelo, Cogtal, Patricios, Ferrograf, and Cooperativa de Gráficos Asociados Ltd. Two years later, in 2009, three other cooperatives formally joined the federation: Idelgraff, La Nueva Unión, and Punto Gráfico. Since 2010, the cooperatives Envases Flexibles Mataderos, Gráfica Loria, Impresiones Barracas, Montes de Oca, and Visión 7 were also incorporated into the federation.[7]

The network maintains a vertical organizational structure, made up of seven different labor sectors: production, commercialization, purchasing, communications, social action, training, technical assistance, and projects. Each of these sectors has two representatives from each cooperative in the network. These sector representatives are subject to input from a general operational coordination, represented by a member with two assistants, one administrative and the other commercial. Above this general coordination is the administration council, made up of three incumbent councillors and two substitutes. The president, secretary, and treasurer who make up the administration council are chosen by one member of each cooperative. In turn, the assembly of associates is the governmental organ of the federation. It is formed of an incumbent delegate and a substitute designated by each one of the cooperatives in the network.

When not part of a cooperative structure, the workers have had to establish an organization that allows them to take charge of production. The characteristics of production in each factory, the number of workers, and, again, their political development, determine different organizational forms.

---

7 See the history of the cooperative network at Red Gráfica Cooperativa, www.redgraficacoop.com.ar/quienessomos.php

Here the variation is much broader than that concerning the cooperative structure. It is therefore impossible to generalize, so the analysis focuses on the case of Zanón.

When the Zanón workers took over the factory and initiated production, certain internal problems emerged. In September 2002, in order to save the factory, the workers drafted and approved in a general assembly a form of internal statute entitled "The Norms of Cohabitation of Zanón under Workers' Control." The document laid out the foundations ruling the organizational dynamic. As mentioned earlier, the "Ceramics Code" and the "Norms" were considered valid beyond the cooperative structure.

In the months prior to the takeover in October 2001, the workers had begun to organize in incipient committees, an approach that continues to inform the running of the factory. For example, after the July 2000 death of Daniel Ferrás in a workshop accident the ceramics workers created a committee for hygiene and safety, the function of which was to supervise the labor safety of the plant workers. This committee continued to function under the workers' management. It is worth noting that there was a significant diminution in the number of accidents because of it. Likewise, during the crisis of the capitalist company, when workers' salaries were left in arrears by the employer, the workers created a sales committee in order to boost the liquidation of stocks and, consequently, the recovery of indebted salaries. A similar response can be observed in their creation of a press and circulation committee to publicize the conflict.

As Aiziczon (2006) has pointed out, all the activities of Zanón's production process are divided into fifty-six sectors, among which are the atomizers, press, lines, ovens, selections, paste laboratory, glazing laboratory, maintenance, stock and dispatch, purchases, sales, administration, security, press, and circulation. The workers from each of these sectors over the three shifts choose a coordinator, who is in charge of maintaining a "control form" of the productive process and compiling the day-to-day needs and problems. These coordinators are part of the council, which is the organ of management and production planning. This organ then proposes a general coordinator for the whole factory. Each council meeting is composed of the general coordinator, the coordinators from each sector, and three members of the internal commission or board of directors from the ceramics union. It is important to note that each of the coordinators is revocable by the general assembly. In effect, the organizational dynamic of the factory proposes the periodic rotation of these posts in order that everyone gets a chance at assuming the directive responsibilities.

The assembly is the workers' maximal organ of decision-making. On the shift level, the workers carry out weekly assemblies for each shift of an informative or decision-making character; and on the factory-wide level there are general assemblies. The former take place twice a week and are open. Generally, the list of issues to be discussed is displayed at the factory's entrance so as to inform the workers and, subsequently, the resolutions are voted on. A wide range of questions is discussed in such meetings, such as internal or disciplinary problems. If these problems arise repeatedly, the case is submitted to a coordinators' meeting and, if necessary, they are resolved in a general assembly. All the resolutions made by the coordinators of each sector are passed to the general assembly, which convenes once a month, where they are accepted or revoked.

## Final Reflections

The factory takeover movement in Argentina, as in all of Latin America, is a central component of the political process opened in these countries. Factory occupation and production under workers' control possess a highly propagandistic nature: they demonstrate to workers all around the globe their own power and potentiality while exposing the parasitic character of the capitalist class. Nothing can be clearer than the example of workers who restart production enterprises emptied and bankrupted by their former owners.

But only a socialist approach can enable these taken factories to fulfill their real destiny. The opposing option, leaving them to the influx of capitalist tendencies, would force them to evolve in either of two capitalist ways. In the successful version the factory would accumulate profit and resemble any other capitalist firm, with characteristics such as the employment of wage labor. Less successful factories would confront bankruptcy, self-exploitation, or hidden proletarianization under the real management of the clients providing supplies. If these two options have not fully developed in Argentina it is because the political movement that arose in the Argentinazo insurrection has not been defeated. Its persistence has helped to reinforce the taken factories' resistance under adverse circumstances.

The reprise of the economic crisis and the resurgence of the political movement have opened new horizons for the taken factories. In this context the workers urgently need to learn from these recent experiences and this chapter is intended as a modest contribution toward that goal.

## References

Aiziczon, Fernando. 2006. Teoría y práctica del Control Obrero: El caso de Cerámica Zanón, Neuquén, 2002–2005. *Revista Herramienta,* no. 31.

Brukman Workers. 2003. Propaganda text. www.lafogata.org/003arg/arg5/bruk_destino.htm.

Chirico, Domingo, et al. 2003. Caracterización socioeconómica de los obreros de Zanón. *Razón y Revolución*, no. 11 (Winter).

Fontenla, Eduardo, H. 2007. Cooperativas que recuperan empresas y fábricas en crisis. Licentiate thesis. Buenos Aires, Universidad Nacional de Lanus, February.

Heller, Pablo. 2002. Control obrero, cooperativas y fábricas ocupadas. *Razón y Revolución,* no. 10 (Spring).

_____. 2005. *Fábricas ocupadas. Argentina 2000–2004*. Buenos Aires: Rumbos.

Kabat, Marina. 2009. Unions and protest of the unemployed 1990s. In *International encyclopedia of revolution and protest*, ed. Immanuel Ness. Oxford: Wiley-Blackwell Publishers.

Lavaca.org. 2004. *La represión que nadie vio*. October 21. www.rebelión.org/noticia.php?id=6425.

Marx, Karl: 1990. *Capital. A critique of political economy*. London: Penguin and New Left Review.

Moreno, Florencia. 2009. Centro de Estudio e Investigación en Ciencias Sociales (CEICS): Potencialidades y debilidades de las fábricas ocupadas. Estudio de caso de Brukman, Pauny S.A., Frigorífico Bragado y Frigorífico La Foresta. Primer Congreso Nacional Sobre Protesta Social, Acción Colectiva y Movimientos Sociales. Buenos Aires, March 30–31.

Palomino, Héctor, Ivanna Bleynat, Silvia Garro, and Carla Giacomuzzi. 2005. *Empresas Recuperadas por sus trabajadores (2002–2008). El universo, la continuidad y los cambios en el movimiento*. Buenos Aires: University of Buenos Aires.

Pascucci, Silvina. 2009. Piquetero movement. In *International encyclopedia of revolution and protest*, ed. Immanuel Ness. Oxford: Wiley-Blackwell Publishers.

Sartelli, Eduardo. 2007. *Contra la cultura del trabajo, Una crítica marxista del sentido de la vida bajo la sociedad capitalista,* Buenos Aires: Razón y Revolución.

_____. 2007. *La plaza es nuestra. El Argentinazo a la luz de la lucha de la clase obrera en el siglo XX*. Buenos Aires: Razón y Revolución.

Tirachini, Blanca. 2004. Empresas recuperadas: recuperación del derecho al trabajo. *Revista del Instituto Interamericano de Derechos Humanos,* vol. 40.

Trinchero, ed. 2004. Las empresas recuperadas en la Argentina: Informe del Segundo Relevamiento del Programa Facultad Abierta, UBACyT de Urgencia Social F-701. SEUBE Facultad de Filosofia y Letras, University of Buenos Aires.

Trotsky, Leon. 2002. El control obrero de la producción. *Razón y Revolución,* no. 10 (Spring).

Vales, Laura and Sebastian Hacher. 2003. Brukman: La confección de un destino. LaFogata. www.lafogata.org/003arg/arg5/bruk_destino.htm.

# 21

## Workers' Control under Venezuela's Bolivarian Revolution

**Dario Azzellini**

When Hugo Chávez assumed the presidency in February 1999, Venezuela was undergoing an extended crisis. A flight of capital and a sustained period of deindustrialization had led, beginning in the early 1980s, to the closure of thousands of production sites. In accordance with a mandate from the majority of the population, the Chávez government embarked upon a series of economic and social transformations of the country, supported by broad movements from below. The new constitution of 1999 set forth the first measures directed toward this overall goal, defined initially as the establishment of a "humanistic and solidarity economy," through a process known as the Bolivarian Revolution. The proposed transformations include the diversification of production of the largely oil-dependent economy, the assumption of control over the secondary processing of Venezuela's own resources, and the democratization of the ownership and management of the means of production. Since early 2005 the Bolivarian Revolution has been viewed within a framework of socialist transformation, following Chávez's declaration that Venezuela would be pursuing a path toward "a socialism of the twenty-first century."

The following chapter appraises and analyzes different organizational efforts to democratize property and management of the means of production. The empirical studies focus on workers' experiences with co- and self-management in the state-owned aluminium smelter Alcasa and the nationalized valve factory Inveval. In light of their successes and failures, the research presents the different politics adopted by these institutions and looks at the debates within the workers' movement about the collective control of the means of production.

During its first years, the government renationalized core sectors of the oil industry and sought to boost national private industry with favorable loans and protectionist measures. The private sector accepted the assistance but opposed democratization or a transformation of the economy. The defeats of the opposition in 2002 and 2003, achieved mainly through self-mobilization from below, opened up the path for laws, measures, and social practices directed at a structural transformation of the economy. The government concentrated primarily on state-guided production and distribution and the promotion of cooperatives and comanagement models. In a simultaneous reaction from below, several factories that had closed down after the employers' strike of 2002–2003 were taken over by their workers.

The socialist directive adopted by the government in 2005 initiated the nationalization of key industries and unproductive factories, as well as the strengthening and expansion of the collective and state-owned sectors. The strategy for constructing an economy situated beyond a capitalist logic and democratizing economic cycles is based on the expansion and consolidation of a popular, social, and communal economy consisting of self-managed, state-promoted units. This approach is rooted in a theory of radical endogenous development: sustainable development based on Venezuela's own resources, collective management of the means of production, and a more active role of the state.

The economic sectors designated for strengthening by the state were identified as solidarity, social, popular, and communal—although these categories were not clearly delineated. Until 2004, the state concentrated on establishing small cooperatives; the efforts of different institutions were widely uncoordinated. A systematic program to create the base for an alternative economy was finally initiated in 2004 with the formation of the Ministry for Popular Economy (Minep)[1] (Díaz 2006, 163f). Subsequently the emphasis has been on building a "popular economy" and "communal economy" rooted in communities. The idea of communal production and consumption cycles is based on Istvan Mészáros's basic ideas for a transition to socialism presented in *Beyond Capital* (1995, 759–770). In the ensuing years several different forms of collective, comanagement, and self-management enterprise models have been introduced, supported, and advanced.

## Cooperatives

A cooperative culture was largely undeveloped in Venezuela prior to Chávez's first term. In 1998 only about eight hundred firms involving roughly twenty thousand members were officially registered, primarily in

---

1 In 2008, the organizational name was changed to the Ministry of Communal Economy (Minec), and in 2009 to the Ministry of Communes (Milco).

the finance and transport sectors (Melcher 2008).[2] The 1999 constitution administered new license and massive state assistance to cooperatives, which were considered significant to creating and sustaining social and economic balance (Díaz 2006, 160–163). In 2001 the process of creating cooperatives was greatly simplified: they were exempt from registration charges, and, if they qualified, gained preferential tax treatment and access to loans and state contracts. State institutions and enterprises contracting with the state are now required to have transparent contracting mechanisms that prioritize cooperatives. Funding is provided through newly founded public banks via micro-credit programs with low interest rates and greater flexibility in terms. The Ministry that supports the collective communal economy invested more than $1 billion in cooperatives from 2003 to 2008 (Sunacoop 2009).

These favorable conditions led to a boom in the formation of cooperatives. By December 2009, according to Sunacoop, the national cooperative supervisory institute, 274,000 cooperatives registered and about 27 percent (73,968) of those were certified, bringing the national cooperative membership to an estimated total of 2 million, although some people participated in more than one cooperative and also have a job (Baute 2009). In 2009, cooperatives produced around 2 percent of the GDP, but their rapid growth made it difficult to determine exact figures. Moreover, the accountancy of many cooperatives was poor and inspections by Sunacoop infrequent (Ellner 2008).

The initial idea that cooperatives would automatically "produce for the satisfaction of social needs" and that their internal solidarity based on collective property "would extend to their local communities, spontaneously" proved in error. Most cooperatives still followed the logic of capital; concentrating on the maximization of net revenue without supporting the surrounding communities, many failed to integrate new members in order to earn more, and some produced mainly for export instead of first satisfying internal needs (Piñeiro 2010).

Even the majority of the cooperatives created by the Misión Vuelvan Caras, a program for job and sociopolitical training aimed at the promotion of collective work structures, followed capitalist logic. Starting in 2005 more than one hundred endogenous development cores (*nudes*) were established for creating and training networks of cooperatives as cultivating grounds for an anticapitalist economy. The program did not fully achieve its basic goals: before being reconstituted at the end of 2007, Misión Vuelvan Caras trained

---

2 The total number varies among different sources between 762 (Melcher 2008), 800 (Díaz 2006, 151), and 877 (Piñeiro 2007). Sunacoop director Juan Carlos Baute estimated in a personal interview a total of 800–900 cooperatives for the year 1998.

around eight hundred thousand people and founded ten thousand cooperatives, but the original goal was 50 percent higher (Azzellini 2010b, 224). The
initial pursuit of community-based production achieved minimal success.

The stiffest obstacles to the successful functioning of cooperatives have
been the "capitalist" orientations of their members, the ineptitude of state officials, and a lack of knowledge among the workers of labor and administrative processes (Melcher 2008). Piñeiro established that the social cohesion
of these cooperatives is undermined by internal conflicts, caused mainly by
inexperience with regard to social relations and administrative tasks, and that
these conflicts are aggravated by the lack of collective supervision (2010).
The problem is in part due to the fact that most participants in the new cooperatives belong to marginalized sectors of society, have little or no nondo-
mestic work experience, and have relatively low levels of education. An
additional problem is that there is little coordination among cooperatives.

Nevertheless, many supporters of the Bolivarian process assume that in
the interim a solid cooperative sector will consolidate. Moreover, they emphasize the great value of the cooperative experience and, accordingly, do not
view these efforts as poor investments. The creation of many small companies, even if they are not fully in line with the cooperative philosophy, represents a certain "democratisation of capital" within the extremely monopolistic
and oligopolistic Venezuelan market (Ellner 2008). But the creation of cooperatives brings about its own contradictions. Work relations can be deregulated through cooperatives, and having many owners instead of one does
not preclude capitalist forms of functioning. The model has also pushed some
associates to embrace the logic of the employer—consequently, some workers
have criticized cooperative ownership, especially in companies with shared
ownership, such as state/worker-owned enterprises in which the workers run
their part as a cooperative.

## EPSs: Three Names, One Shortcut

In 2005, a new model was created that facilitated a new arrangement among
enterprises. The social production companies (EPSs) received government assistance and priority in state contracts. In exchange EPSs were required to in-
vest part of their profits in the communities, introduce a comanagement
schema in agreement with the workers, and support the creation of cooperatives in production chains. The form of property—state, private, or collective—
was not of concern. Some state-owned companies started creating chains of
suppliers that gave priority to cooperatives, but no general reorientation could
be forced and the promotion of social responsibility through material advantages did not prove successful on a larger scale. Many companies registered as
an EPS just to receive government aid (Díaz 2006, 157–158).

After the second half of 2007, no more official EPSs were founded, although the term was still used in a general sense for "socialist production companies" (Álvarez and Rodríguez 2007) and "social property companies." "Direct social property" refers to common property managed directly by the people, through workers' councils together with either Consejos Comunales (community councils), a nonrepresentational form of local self-organization established in late 2005, or the Comunas, the next level of local self-organization—each Comuna is comprised of several Consejos Comunales (for more details about the local council system see Azzellini 2010a).[3] Social property companies can be established by communities on their own or by institutions and then transferred in response to the need for stronger control of social property by the communities (Piñeiro 2010).

In 2007 the government started building two hundred "socialist factories," intended to become social property companies as well as socialist production companies (EPS factories).[4] The workers were selected by the local Consejos Comunales and the required professionals were sourced from state institutions. These socialist factories were urged to create nonmarket systems for the exchange of commodities. In September 2008, thirty-one EPS factories were in operation (fourteen milk, ten corn, four plastic construction materials, and three auto replacement parts) and by late 2009 the number had grown to an estimated seventy to eighty EPS factories (Piñeiro 2010). The aim was to gradually transfer the control of the plants to the workers and the communities, but most institutions have done little to organize this process.

Since 2008 the formation of social property enterprises has been promoted among the communities, with the intention that they would take over local services, such as the distribution of cooking gas[5] and local transportation, as well as the creation of local production. The core objective is re-communalization of formerly privatized public services, under direct and collective community control. The decision about the form and administration of the companies lies in the hands of the communities via the Consejos Comunales, which also determine the allocation of jobs in the community-managed companies. By the end of 2009, 271 direct social property enterprises had been founded by communities throughout Venezuela. Communities and the state have shared responsibility in 1,084 community-based social production units

---

3 These formations are in contrast to indirect social property, for example, strategic national industries that are managed by the state.

4 The "socialist factories" included the following plants: eighty-eight food processing; twelve chemical; forty-eight machine tools; eight electronics and computer/cell phones; ten plastic, tires, and glass; eight transport facilities; four construction; and three recycling industries. Most were built with the contribution of machines and expertise from Argentina, China, Iran, Russia, and Belarus (Azzellini 2009, 188).

5 Community-controlled reseller network for liquid gas.

(ABN 2009), a figure significantly more promising than previous collective production initiatives. As evidenced by the success of the Consejos Comunales, Venezuelans identify much more strongly with their community than with their workplace.

## Recovered Companies

In the course and aftermath of the employers' lockout of 2002–2003, workers took over several small and mid-sized factories in response to unpaid wages. At first the government relegated these cases to the labor courts but finally began authorizing expropriations in January 2005. Although the constitution had made expropriations possible as of 2000, through the end of 2006 there were few cases aside from those in the oil sector. In January 2005, the paper factory Venepal (now Invepal) was expropriated; then, in April 2005, the Constructora Nacional de Válvulas (CNV, now Inveval), which produces valves primarily for the oil industry. Both factories had been taken over by their workers in 2003 and needed investments and cash flow to restart production—the CNV was not producing, and Venepal produced only relatively small amounts of paper products for a short period of time. In July 2005, the government began to devote special attention to closed businesses; this change has since allowed for the expropriation of hundreds of companies.

A second wave of expropriations followed in 2009 and 2010, initiated by Venezuela's governmental consumer protection institute, INDEPABIS (Instituto para la Defensa de las Personas en el Acceso a los Bienes y Servicios), created to supervise prices and act against speculation on the prices of basic goods as well as to guarantee workers' rights. The INDEPABIS also promotes workers' councils in the expropriated enterprises. Since 2009, expropriations have taken place mainly in the food-processing sector, among oil-exploration enterprises, and among small private banks that had engaged in fraud.

In 2005 and 2006 the political climate was especially favorable to expropriations of shuttered or unproductive enterprises. After the Bolivarian process proved victorious over the 2002 coup d'état, the "entrepreneurs strike" of 2002–2003, and the referendum against Chávez in 2004, the opposition was on the defensive. The need to boost production and the factory takeovers coincided; the "recuperations from below" found an echo "from above." In July 2005, in a television appearance Chávez read a list of more than one thousand firms with wholly or partially reduced production and announced that 136 shuttered companies were under concrete consideration for expropriation (RNV 2005). Labor minister María Cristina Iglesias urged unions and former workers to "recover" the unproductive enterprises. The Bolivarian union umbrella organization, UNT, announced immediately that eight hundred closed plants would be occupied (Azzellini 2009, 174).

But only a small fraction of those plants were actually occupied. Even the total number of occupations, expropriations, and purchases by the state remained far below the proclaimed eight hundred, revealing a contradiction between the state's claim to be prioritizing processes from below and the real degree of workers' self-initiative. The workers did not have the strength to organize massive takeovers, nor did the state institutions show sufficient commitment to promoting and supporting the measures. For a long time Chávez seemed to be nearly the only government official supporting workers' takeovers (Cormenzana 2009b). In addition, the UNT failed to follow its own announced plan for company occupations. Even the leftist UNT current C-CURA, despite its central role in many occupations and labor disputes, failed to turn mass factory occupations into reality.[6] Without pressure from below, the president's initiative drowned in the bureaucratic apparatus.

Expropriations, in general, tend to be a consequence of popular pressure on state institutions through workers' occupations and mobilizations. These mobilizations are typically born out of defensive actions, usually in the interest of maintaining the workplace. Radicalization and deeper political reflection among the participants usually follow the takeover, but the recuperations and struggles for nationalization have rarely managed to start a regional dynamic (Lebowitz 2006).[7] Most factory seizures result from unproductive operation by the capitalist owners; thus, just a few of the occupied factories in Venezuela, such as the water tap and pipe factory INAF, have been able to produce under workers' control. INAF, like many other Venezuelan and Latin American worker-expropriated factories, has obsolete machinery and needs huge financial investments to perpetuate efficient production. In this capacity, state support is crucial, because apart from the private sector—which is so resistant to workers' control—the state is the only entity capable of making such investments. Without state support these factories have to compete on the terms of the capitalist market and adapt to its rules.

Expropriations have become more systematic since 2007, aiming to build productive chains and giving the government and communities control over

6 The Class Unity Revolutionary and Autonomous Current (C-CURA) was one of the biggest and most active currents in the UNT. It had a Trotskyist background. It split in 2007; the minority kept the name C-CURA and took stands against joining the PSUV and the constitutional reform, and the majority organized as Marea Socialista (Socialist Tide), joined the PSUV, and stated critical support for the government.

7 There have also been some exceptions. The best-known is the struggle of the steelworkers of Sidor (Siderúrgica de Orinoco) in 2007–2008 to achieve nationalization of the plant. Despite the negative attitude of the Bolivarian governor of the region the movement had strong local support and mobilized until Chávez ordered the nationalization of the company.

many aspects of food production and distribution in order to guarantee the food supply and challenge speculation. But the limited involvement of state institutions in preparing workers to take control over the production process contributes to growing conflicts between workers and those institutions. Some sites expropriated since 2009 through consumer protection, via INDEPABIS, have received more assistance. However, these notable exceptions have occurred mainly in situations in which the workers have shown confidence in taking control and managing the enterprises.

## Comanagement, Self-Management, and Workers' Control

*Cogestión* (comanagement) refers to workers' participation in the management of their companies. It was conceived by the rank and file in the state-owned electricity suppliers CADELA and CADAFE during the 2002–2003 entrepreneurs' strike, and was promoted in 2005–2006, mainly in state-owned and mixed-ownership enterprises. As no legal basis yet exists for comanagement, different models have been implemented. So-called strategic companies, such as the national oil company PdVSA, were excluded from the promotion of cogestión; according to official arguments, those companies can't be "left up" to the employees because of their importance. Supporters of workers' participation assert that the strategic importance is more likely an argument in favor of comanagement than against it. Indeed, during the entrepreneurs' strike, PdVSA was abandoned by management and put back into operation by the workers.

Through the government program Fábrica Adentro, created in 2005, private companies are given access to loans with low interest rates and government subsidies if the owners and employees agree on some form of comanagement. More than one thousand small and mid-sized companies have participated in the program, but workers' participation in decision-making structures has proven nonexistent and minority participation in the ownership tends to be the rule. Conflicts over the introduction of comanagement and its application have also arisen in the aforementioned expropriated paper and valve factories.

### Alcasa: The State-Owned Aluminum Smelter

Among the state-owned companies, Alcasa, Venezuela's second-largest aluminium smelter, was selected as a testing ground for comanagement. Located in Ciudad Guayana in the state of Bolívar, Alcasa is part of the state-owned industrial conglomerate CVG (seventeen companies, mainly heavy industries), and formally administered by the Ministry of Basic Industries and Mines (Mibam). In February 2005, at Chávez's proposal, Carlos Lanz was named director of Alcasa by the shareholders' meeting. He defined his goal as workers' control. Some fifteen days after Lanz assumed his role, each department head was replaced by three workers elected by a department assembly, sharing the job and earning the same wages as the workers. The factory assembly was established as the highest authority inside the plant, followed by roundtables of department spokespeople[8] and then by the heads of department. All the department heads and spokespeople were elected in assemblies and could be removed by them as well. The departments made decisions collectively from below about work organization and investments. But management and administration stayed largely the same.

The workers brought various training missions into Alcasa. An education center was set up inside the plant where workers organized sociopolitical training. Alcasa has also since become an EPS, establishing cooperatives for further processing of aluminium. The goal, besides the democratization of the plant, was to reestablish productivity and profitability. In the previous seventeen years, Alcasa had been driven to inefficiency and into huge debts as preparation for privatization.

In November 2005, a new executive board was elected by the shareholders' meeting. Three members came from the CVG, two were employees of Alcasa, and two were members of the organized local population—a professor from the Bolivarian University of Venezuela and an economist (Prensa Alcasa 2005). Through the innovations in the factory, production levels at Alcasa increased by 11 percent (Bruce 2005), and all accumulated debts in salaries and pensions to workers and former workers had been paid in full by 2006. In July 2006, Lanz presented himself for election in Alcasa and won 1,800 out of 1,920 workers' votes, confirming him as president of the company.

At the end of 2006, Alcasa and the plant's union signed a new collective agreement that included the constitution of factory councils (Prensa Alcasa 2007).[9] The newly founded department for cooperatives supported the consolidation of the cooperatives working within Alcasa, leading to the formation of twelve huge cooperatives. All the cooperative workers gained access to the same services inside the factory as the Alcasa workers, including access to the canteen, the internal transportation system, and leisure facilities. The cooperatives no longer had to engage in open competition with private companies seeking contracts, and the different Alcasa departments pledged to favor cooperatives—going so far as to sign agreements. The in-

8 One spokesperson for ten workers.
9 For further information about the transformation efforts at Alcasa under Carlos Lanz see Azzellini and Ressler 2006.

clusion of subcontracted workers and cooperative members as full workers of Alcasa was well planned and prepared. But the work was mainly the effort of the department of cooperatives. The overall sociopolitical education of the administration was neglected, which had drastic consequences.

### Defeat of Cogestión: Causes and Perspectives

When Lanz left Alcasa in May 2007, the whole cogestión process suffered a severe setback. The new president showed little interest in comanagement, and since no statutes had been established to keep the process as open as possible, the collective decisions of the departments were no longer respected. Active engagement among the workers dropped rapidly, and the councils were not constituted at all. Productivity dropped and Alcasa, once again, suffered enormous losses. Most of the employees no longer advocated cogestión or workers' councils.

How did the process collapse so quickly? One important reason for its failure derived from the interests at stake. Because of the importance of basic industry in the region, especially Alcasa and the steel mill Sidor, politicians and the factory administration had little incentive to strengthen the workers' participation in comanagement. Clientelistic networks in the CVG and regional politics worked against cogestión. The absent statutes made it quite easy. Those workers who were more involved in the process observed that leaving the administration and the management in place at Alcasa under cogestión had been an error. While Lanz was president they had offered passive resistance; as soon as he left, they resumed their corrupt practices.

After Lanz departed, the staff of Alcasa grew from 2,700 to 3,300, but just sixty were former cooperative members; the rest were mainly relatives, friends, or clients of the patronage networks in and around the factory. Truckloads of tons of precious aluminium—leftovers from the production process—were sold illegally and Alcasa once again started selling aluminium below the market price to generate immediate cash flow. In 2008, a new president of Alcasa was appointed, but he did not improve the situation, forcing the cooperatives to compete again for contracts and opposing the social projects undertaken by Alcasa workers in four communities, including school repairs financed by Alcasa's social fund. Nonetheless, the cogestión experience was not in vain. A worker explains:

> Just the fact that hundreds of workers participated actively in the process of transformation of Alcasa is very important. The fact that they spoke out in assemblies and discussed directly with the company's management, which never happened before in this plant, is also an important lesson.
>
> The roundtables did not work out and the dense bureaucracy led to the actual situation of the cogestión, it's somehow paralyzed . . . but with great experiences and progress The workers learned that it's possible to administrate

and control the whole production process by themselves. A great lesson!!!
And that while we were always told that is impossible (León 2009).

The struggle for workers' control continued. Those in favor maintained
their education center inside Alcasa, set up the "workers' control collective,"
and developed it into an important force. They participated in regional
grassroots coordination, supported the workers of the Sidor steel plant in
their struggle for nationalization, and offered advice concerning workers'
councils and cogestión.

The fact that the basic industries in Venezuela need modernization is clear.
The best option for maximizing both democracy and the viability of firms is
an efficient and transparent network of basic industries in transition to models
of workers' control. Although the revolutionary wing of the workers in the
CVG companies wanted democracy and workers' control, most workers did
not take any stand at all. But those favoring workers' control have an important
ally. In May 2009 Chávez participated in a weekend workshop with more than
three hundred workers from the iron, steel, and aluminium plants of the CVG,
including the workers from Alcasa. They discussed possible solutions to the
problems of the respective sectors and drew up nine strategic guidelines for
the restructuring and transformation of the CVG. Production control by the
workers was at the top of the list. Chávez authorized a ministerial commission
to develop a plan based on the guidelines drafted during the workshop.

The socialist plan "Guayana 2019" was born and approved by Chávez
in August 2009. He bypassed the regional governor, Rangel, and the Mibam
minister, Sanz, as both showed little enthusiasm for the measures. As the
title indicates, the restructuring is a long-term plan. Factory councils were
not decreed by Chávez, a fact appreciated by the workers since councils
need to be created by the workers' own efforts; otherwise they have little or
no chance of success (Trabajadores de CVG/Alcasa 2009).

After months of inaction, in May 2010, Chávez nominated workers from
each of the seventeen CVG factories to serve as their respective directors—
all of whom were also chosen by the workers who had participated in the
workshops and discussions. Elio Sayago, an environmental engineer and activist for workers' control, was named president of Alcasa and the next round
in the struggle for workers' control commenced. Immediately conflicts arose
in the factory, with the corrupt unions striking in an effort to sabotage the
workers' control. Some issues were resolved quickly by calling for an open
assembly of all the workers of the departments involved, but others have persisted; it remains unclear whether the establishment of workers' control and
the restructuring of the basic industries will be achieved. However, it is clear
that Elio Sayago and the plan for restructuring Alcasa and implementing
workers' control have the support of the vast majority of workers. Early on
the morning of November 9, 2010, a scant two dozen corrupt union leaders

entered the factory before the first shift, chained the gates, and attempted to "take over" the presidency of the factory as in a coup d'etat—but an estimated six hundred workers from the first shift accompanied Sayago into the factory to make it perfectly evident who has their support (Marea Socialista 2010).

### Inveval: The "Reconquered" Factory

In April 2005 CNV (now Inveval), located in the state of Miranda, near Caracas, was expropriated by presidential decree. As mentioned, the factory produced valves for the oil industry and was owned by former PdVSA director and opposition leader Andrés Sosa Pietri. Shut down during the entrepreneurs' strike of 2002–2003, the plant was then due to be reopened, but only with severe wage cuts and the elimination of compensation for dismissed workers. The workers refused to accept the terms and sixty-three of them occupied the factory, demanding payment. The Ministry of Labor ordered that the workers be rehired and withheld wages paid, but the owner did not adhere to that decision and the factory was finally expropriated (Azzellini 2007, 51–53; Cormenzana 2009a, 27–43).

### From Expropriation to Comanagement

The difficulties encountered by Inveval's workers' in consolidating self-management in the factory revealed the emergence of class struggle within the capitalist economy as well as state enterprises and institutions. Encouraged by Chávez's official promotion of expropriation, the workers favored a worker-controlled enterprise. While they sought to define such a model, the bureaucracy of the state ministries was busy seeking to prevent the initiative. The ministries—the Minep and later the Milco—failed to meet the requirements for organizing support for the factory in order to put it to work again. It is not clear if this happened by intent or due to a lack of information or experience—the ministries either saw a factory under workers' control as undermining their authority or they were following traditional capitalist guidelines. The tension started with the fact that while Inveval was expropriated, Acerven, Inveval's foundry—which was located in a different city—was not.

The Inveval workers rejected the Minep proposal for comanagement. Instead of a workers' majority in the management and a worker as president, as requested and as promised by Chávez, the ministry proposed that the directors would be appointed by the state. After tough negotiations and eight different proposals rejected by one side or the other, in August 2005 a compromise comanagement agreement was signed. Inveval became a stock company with 51 percent state ownership and 49 percent employee ownership in a joint cooperative. But the workers' assembly would elect three out of five executive board members, including the president, and the ministry would appoint the remaining two. Ultimately, the ministry did not even send representatives to the board.

Inveval finally began operating again in mid-2006 with equal salaries for all. Before reopening and resuming operation, the plant had been renovated by the workers with materials received from the ministry. However, due to the lack of foundry facilities, the sole task of the reopened company was the maintenance and repair of industrial valves. Attempts to produce valves in other foundries on behalf of Inveval were not very successful: the private entrepreneurs presented a united front and refused production or delivered deficient parts.

All decisions that affected the factory were taken up in the weekly cooperative assembly. But because the state was the majority stockholder, all important decisions had to be approved by the ministry. The assembly decided from the beginning on a wage increase and a seven-hour workday. From 4:00 p.m. onward, various training programs took place in the plant. Overall, thirty-seven of sixty-three employees participated in educational programs. Some workers took reading and writing lessons or finished primary school, others received the equivalent of a high school education, and some even attended evening university courses. Courses in sociopolitical, technical, administrative, and productive training were also offered. The programs were partly self-organized and partly presented by the personnel of the state work-training institution, INCES. The training programs aimed to help abolish the social division of labor. From 2006 on, only the president, members of the board, coordinators of the production sections, and administration of the factory had defined tasks; all other workers assumed a range of tasks that conformed to their abilities and level of knowledge.

### From Cooperative to Socialist Factory

For nearly two years following the comanagement accord, the workers tried to manage Inveval on their own without being guided by capitalist logic. But ultimately the workers concluded that their aim was not feasible. Separation of the labor and decision-making arenas contributed to worker apathy and isolation of the board of directors. The legal framework made direct administration by all the workers impossible. As part owners, the workers were also pushed toward assuming capitalist logic: the cooperative did not just own a share of the factory but also its debt. The workers complained that they were drawn into the cycle of living to work and pay the debt. "The cooperative feeds capitalism because it's created as part of the capitalist system and that's what we don't want. . . . We didn't kick out one capitalist to create 60 new ones" (Gonzalez 2008).

In January 2007, when Chávez publically called for strengthening the revolution through workers' councils, the Inveval workers did not hesitate, organizing an assembly and immediately electing a factory council with thirty-two members, ending the cooperative activities, and introducing a new organization model for the factory. The assembly of all the workers was established as the highest decision-making organ. It meets once a month and on specific occasions. The elected council, composed of spokespeople from each department and other workers, follows next in the hierarchy. It meets once a week and discusses the points evaluated previously only by the board of directors. The council has created several commissions: sociopolitical matters, finances and administration, accountability and follow-up, discipline, technical aspects, and services. Each commission has to bring back reports to the council. Any position is revocable by the workers' assembly.

Inveval also adopted a new ownership model and is now fully socially owned. As of mid-2008, the cooperative was officially dissolved; the workers are no longer stockholders of Inveval, but directly employed by Inveval. The Inveval workers have successfully transformed comanagement into workers' control. Meanwhile, the workers researched the possibility of purchasing or forcing the expropriation of various foundries, as well as the possibility of the money-less transfer of commodities. Problems with the ministries continue with respect to delays in the payment of approved finances. The state-owned oil industry, PdVSA, even tried to sever its agreements with Inveval (Cormenzana 2009a, 203–204). However, against these odds of institutional and private economic resistance, the workers' determination, organization, and political training have made it possible for them to continue managing a factory under workers' control. Despite the fact that the institutions did not follow repeated calls for expropriation, not even Chávez's mid-2008 order, on May 4, 2010, the National Assembly finally declared the foundry Acerven to be of public interest, a condition for expropriation (Aporrea.org 2010).

## From Comanagement to Councils

As early as 2006, comanagement experiences led the most politically active workers to reject the models that turned them into owners. Within a year, Chávez identified workers' councils as a path for workers to follow. Nevertheless, after the failures of comanagement experiences, most institutions focused more on efficient state management than on workers' control. In a personal interview in early 2010, the vice minister of work, Elio Colmenares, defined workers' control as the control by the workers of the administrative bureaucracy in order to guarantee the realization of the state's policies, which are supposed to be generated by a common interest and for a common benefit.

Colmenares's view, which resembles aspects of failed "state socialism," represents a major line of thinking within the Ministry of Work. But the position is not shared by the entire government; different approaches to management exist and the situation is constantly subject to change. This disparity is due in part to the fact that contradictions and class struggle are pervasive within the institutions themselves. Publicly, Chávez and others in the government speak freely about workers' control, encouraging the takeover of factories mismanaged by private owners. The expropriations show that there is political will for structural changes. Upon nationalization, however, the institutions leave little space for workers' initiatives and tend toward maintaining control of management and production. The absence of a defined government policy on workers' control and expropriation leads many workers to see nationalization mainly as a job guarantee, without considering collective management.

Meanwhile, politically active workers are mostly in favor of models that transform the companies into state or social property, managed entirely by the employees and the communities (Lebowitz 2006). This approach is also supported by the CST (Consejos Socialistas de Trabajadores—socialist workers' councils), the largest forum of existing workers' councils and initiatives (CST 2009). Their debates about workers' control, self-management, and co-management invoke Marx, Gramsci, Trotsky, and Pannekoek and the historical tradition of council communism (Giordani 2009; 2007). The experiences of workers' self-management in Yugoslavia and Argentina are also referenced.

In a document drafted during a national workshop of the CST, co-gestión was criticized as being inappropriate for the construction of socialism: The document concluded, erroneously, that it is the property of the means of production—the capital—that generates the right to participate in decision making. Whereas in socialist theory it is the labor in any of its forms—material or intellectual, simple or complex, recognized as the origin of the social wealth—that generates the right to participate in the management of the companies. "If the company shares are private property of some workers and/or capitalists, they can't be also the property of other workers, neither of the communities, nor of the people as a whole. As a consequence neither the surplus produced in the process of production can be property of all people. . . . With the shareholder property the workers are objectively transformed into new capitalists" (MinTrab 2008, 13–14).

Instead, the CST proposed a council-based model of multiple and mixed management, with councils of workers, communities, resource production nodes, and—for large companies—the involvement of the state (MinTrab 2008).

Currently the plants with workers' councils are still the exception. The first council in Venezuela was created at the end of 2006 in Sanitarios Maracay and lasted nine months until the workers were evicted. Next, councils were introduced at INAF, the water tap and pipe factory taken over in 2006 by workers who had initially founded a cooperative. A similar development occurred the same year in Maracay at the Gotcha textile factory, likewise taken over by workers. The workers of Inveval introduced workers' councils in early 2007. Other factories, mostly taken over by workers during conflicts, also introduced councils. The search for an anticapitalist perspective in factory organization continues to lead workers to the council model.

## Search for a Socialist Economy

During its first ten years, the Venezuelan transformation process achieved relative sovereignty within the framework of capitalism. It improved the social situation, broadened political and economic participation, and followed a different model of development. The productivity of the national market has grown and diversification of the economy has begun. In the private sector, democratization of the ownership structure within capitalist parameters has been initiated. The development of hundreds of thousands of new small and mid-sized businesses, as well as the state ownership of food production, have made it possible to break the monopolistic and oligopolistic controls of the Venezuelan market. And after a good deal of trial and error, "direct social property" has become the property model officially supported by the government and preferred by the workers.

The transformation and democratization of the economy has proved the most difficult. The administration of most companies is neither under workers' nor community control. Surrounded by a capitalist system and logic, it has been extremely challenging to establish collective production processes. Questions over the distribution of work and the resulting gains are particularly conflictive. However, where workers have succeeded in gaining control of their workplace, it can be observed that they have usually developed solidarity ties with surrounding communities, abolished hierarchical structures, made themselves accountable to the workers' assembly, and in most cases introduced equal salaries and increased the number of employed workers.

Workers' councils seem to be the best solution and are growing in number. But it still cannot be said whether the councils will continue to expand or models of state administration will impose themselves. The fact that the councils are not organized from above could make continued organic growth possible. Struggle with the bureaucracy is inevitable, but workers' councils have the advantage of "being right," as far as the normative orientation is concerned. Historically, councils have emerged at the outset of revolutionary unrest and have later been displaced by a bureaucratic work command. Perhaps the process of establishing councils will prove more successful if it allows time for discussions, organizing, self-education, and practice.

The parallel existence of different socioeconomic structures and experimentation with different enterprise models has run at a high cost for the government, and the private appropriation of public resources by clientelistic networks has made an internal economic transformation much more difficult. As Chávez has acknowledged several times, the most reliable instrument against corruption is workers' control, which is also the reason for its many detractors. In the end, it can be stated that a variety of different measures to promote structural economic changes have been put to work in Venezuela, as well as the democratization of property and management of the means of production. Some initiatives aspire to abolish the division between manual and intellectual work and to overcome capitalist relations. Others simply aim for a democratization of capitalist relations. Despite all the problems and errors, an astounding variety of cooperatives, EPSs, and other alternative company models have arisen over the past decade. The search for an alternative economy is thus firmly on the agenda.

Proposals such as that of the valve factory Inveval, seeking to transfer commodities without money, on the basis of need, show a strong will to overcome capitalist relations, even if it is still unclear how this could be put into practice. The official normative orientation for socialist factories is that the production of goods should shift from the demands of a capitalist market. Production should serve to fulfill social needs and be transferred to the consumers without financial interests at the forefront. These debates are very important, even if most people today ascribe to capitalist economic categories a universal and transhistorical validity. But these categories are integral to capitalism in particular. Social structures are only valid for, and inside of, human social relations. As such, capitalist categories simply represent the structure of rules in capitalist societies into which humans have historically entered (Agnoli 1999). So the search for alternatives should not be confined to the realm of the existing.

## References

Agnoli, Johannes. 1999. Subversive Theorie: Die Sache selbst und ihre Geschichte. In *Gesammelte Werke*, vol. 3, 2nd ed. Freiburg: Cairá.

Álvarez, Victor R. and Davgla A. Rodríguez. 2007. *Guía teórico-práctica para la creación de EPS. Empresas de Producción Socialista*, Barquisimeto, Venezuela: CVG Venalum.

ABN (Agencia Bolivariana de Noticias). 2009. Los Consejos Comunales deberán funcionar como bujías de la economía socialista. December 30. www.rebelion.org/noticia.php?id=98094.

Aporrea.org. 2010. Declaran de utilidad pública e interés social los bienes de ACERVEN. Aporrea.org. May 4. www.aporrea.org/endogeno/n156623.html.

Azzellini, Dario. 2007. Von den Mühen der Ebene: Solidarische Ökonomie, kollektive Eigentumsformen, Enteignungen und Arbeitermit—und Selbstverwaltung. In *Revolution als Prozess: Selbstorganisierung und Partizipation in Venezuela*, ed. Andrej Holm, 38–57. Hamburg: VSA-Verlag.

_____ 2009. Venezuela's solidarity economy: Collective ownership, expropriation, and workers self-management. *WorkingUSA: The Journal of Labor and Society* 12/2 (June): 171–191.

_____ 2010a. Constituent power in motion: Ten years of transformation in Venezuela. *Socialism and Democracy*, 24 (2): 8-30.

_____ 2010b. *Partizipation, Arbeiterkontrolle und die Commune: Bewegungen und soziale Transformation am Beispiel Venezuela*. Hamburg: VSA.

Azzellini, Dario and Oliver Ressler. 2006. *5 Fábricas. Control Obrero en Venezuela* (film). Caracas/Berlin/Vienna.

Baute, Juan Carlos. 2009. Las cooperativas no desaparecerán. *Últimas Noticias*. June 17. www.aporrea.org/poderpopular/n136615.html.

Bruce, Ian. 2005. Venezuela promueve la cogestión. *BBC News*. August 19. http://news.bbc.co.uk/hi/spanish/business/newsid_4167000/4167054.stm.

Cormenzana, Pablo. 2009a. *La batalla de Inveval. La lucha por el control obrero en Venezuela*. Madrid: Fundación Federico Engels.

_____ . 2009b. Inveval: a 4 años de su creación, el control obrero está más vigente que nunca. Aporrea.org. April 28. www.aporrea.org/poderpopular/a76854.html.

CST (Consejos Socialistas de Trabajadoras y Trabajadores de Venezuela). 2009. *I Encuentro Nacional de Consejos Socialistas de Trabajadoras y Trabajadores de Venezuela*. June 27. Caracas: CST.

Díaz Rangel, Eleazar. 2006. *Todo Chávez. De Sabaneta als socialismo del siglo XXI*. Caracas: Planeta.

Ellner, Steve. 2008. Las tensiones entre la base y la dirigencia en las filas del chavismo. *Revista Venezolana de Economía y Ciencias Sociales* 14 (1): 49–64. Caracas: UCV.

Giordani C., Jorge A. 2009. *Gramsci, Italia y Venezuela*. Valencia: Vadell Hermanos Editores.

Lanz Rodríguez, Carlos. 2007. *Consejo de Fábrica y Construcción Socialista. Antecedentes teóricos e históricos de un debate inconcluso*. Guayana, Venezuela: Mibam/CVG Alcasa.

Lebowitz, Michael. 2006. *Build it now: Socialism for the 21ˢᵗ century*. New York: Monthly Review Press.

Marea Socialista. 2010. En CVG ALCASA, Trabajadores derrotan golpe de Estado orquestado por la FBT (Movimiento 21). November 10. www.aporrea.org/endogeno/n169305.html.

Melcher, Dorotea. 2008. Cooperativismo en Venezuela: Teoría y praxis. *Revista Venezolana de Economía y Ciencias Sociales* 14 (1): 95–106. Caracas: UCV.

Mészáros, Istvan. 1995. *Beyond capital: Towards a theory of transition*. London: Merlin Press.

MinTrab [Ministerio del Poder Popular para el Trabajo y Seguridad Social], ed. 2008. *La gestión socialista de la economía y las empresas. Propuesta de trabajadores (as) al pueblo y gobierno de la República Bolivariana de Venezuela. Conclusiones del tercer seminario nacional sobre formación y gestión socialista. Valencia. April 18–19*. Caracas: MinTrab.

Piñeiro Harnecker, Camila. 2010. Venezuelan cooperatives: Practice and challenges. Unpublished paper, 28th ILPC, March 15–17, Rutgers University.

Prensa Alcasa. 2005. Designada nueva Junta Directiva de Alcasa que tendrá por objetivo impulsar proceso cogestionario. November 24. www.aporrea.org/endogeno/n69123.html.

_____ . 2007. Alcasa propone activar el poder constituyente para construir Consejos de Fábrica. February 20. www.aporrea.org/endogeno/n90891.html.

RNV. 2005. Expropiaciones de empresas cerradas anuncia Presidente Chávez. RNV. July 18. www.rnv.gov.ve/noticias/index.php?act=ST&f=2&t=20185.

Sunacoop. 2009. Entrevista a Juan Carlos Baute/Presidente de Sunacoop. January 16. www.sunacoop.gob.ve/noticias_detalle.php?id=1361.

Trabajadores de CVG/Alcasa. 2009. Control Obrero. Publicación de trabajadores de CVG/Alcasa. September 16. www.aporrea.org/endogeno/a86731.html.

Interviews

Colmenares, Elio. 2010. Interview by Maurizio Atzeri and Dario Azzellini. Caracas, January.

Gonzalez, Julio. 2008. Interview by author.[Inveval worker].

León, Osvaldo. 2009. Interview by author [Alcasa worker].

# 22

# Brazilian Recovered Factories
## The Constraints of Workers' Control

**Maurício Sardá de Faria and Henrique T. Novaes**

*Translated by Patricia Aguiar Ramos*

This chapter discusses the phenomenon of Brazilian recovered factories (RFs), companies undergoing a bankruptcy process that were taken over, modified, and run by their employees.

The first section places the RFs in perspective by presenting a short history of the struggles for self-management, while the second section provides a better understanding of the Latin American historical context that led to their creation. The third section explores the unions' role in the factory-recovery process, and the fourth section offers a few statistics on the number of factories, the workers, areas of function, and so on. The fifth section briefly examines the RFs, highlighting the contradictions, limitations, and possibilities they offer for the development of the Brazilian working class's organization of practices and autonomous social relations, and two particular cases are examined (Cooperminas and Catende Harmonia Project). The sixth section analyzes the "factories in deadlock," companies inclined toward nationalization under workers' control but lacking state support. The final section observes the RFs at a crossroads: although the RFs utilize elements that lead to a superior form of production via self-management and the collective possession of the means of production, they are in some respects experiencing a period of decline.

We also analyze the limits imposed by the market, the defensive historical context, the RFs workers' world vision, the Brazilian left-wing theoretical crisis, and the absence of more profound worker struggles that could lead to a "society beyond capital" (Mészáros 2002). The chapter concludes with some final considerations.

## History of the Social Struggles for Autonomy

Workers' self-management initiatives and struggles for control over the production of the means of life have been documented for at least two centuries.

The principle of association assumed a dual function that only later was separated: the organization of the production of the means of life and collective resistance through social relations of production. When solidarity, the driving force for collectivism, was present, the self-organization process was actualized in a perpetual cycle. The self-management of their struggles showed workers the inseparable need for the self-management of both production and "social life" (Tragtenberg, 1986).

Either in the context of revolutionary outbreak or the intensification of class conflict, workers have practiced the strategy of bringing together the two different sides of the associative principle: resistance and the production of the means of life. When faced with the flight of employers or the removal of authority, workers have recognized the need to take the production of the means of life into their own hands. It is important to note that in Brazil, since the sixteenth century, there have been countless popular struggles that together constitute—consciously or unconsciously—the framework for the resistance in both the city and countryside. The Palmares Quilombo may be the remotest and yet the most significant experience from the post-Columbian period.[1]

With the emergence of the peasant leagues, the rise of the urban working-class struggles, and the "base reforms" introduced by João Goulart (1962–64) in the 1960s, the rising tide of struggle led some historians to believe that Brazil—as well as the whole of Latin America—was marching toward socialism. With Brazil's civil-military dictatorship (1964–1985), however, there was a rupture between working-class and peasant struggles that undermined all workers.

By the late 1970s, however, the defeat of the military regime led to the emergence of new social movements such as "new unionism," the Landless Workers' Movement, the Movement of Dam-Affected People, struggles for adequate housing, and others. In the 1990s, the solidarity economy began its ascent as well.[2]

In the context of these new social movements, the RFs and factories seeking nationalization can be viewed as part of an attempt to find conti-

---

1 One should not forget that before the arrival of Columbus, extremely complex societies existed in Latin America that could also be considered "self-managed." These societies influenced Marx and Engels's thoughts about communism. For some post-Columbian examples, see Péret 1999 and Lugon 1949.

2 The solidarity economy in Latin America, in spite of some connections to "third sector" theories and practices, is more politicized than in Europe. Cruz (2006) defines the solidarity economy as "the set of economic associative initiatives that a) labour, b) the property of means of operation (production, consumption, credit, etc.), c) the economic results, d) knowledge about their operation, e) the power to decide on matters relating to it are shared by all those who participate directly, looking for relations of equality and solidarity among its participants" (69).

nuity with the earlier class struggle, in the wider framework of the Brazilian struggles of the 1960s, which were interrupted by the military dictatorship and finally gained traction again in the 1980s and 1990s.

It is conceivable that the experience of the RFs, among many others, represents the recovery of territory in the class struggle, the significance of which was underestimated in the twentieth century: the cooperative production of the means of life. Within this dimension—which involves the organization of the working process and established decision-making mechanisms, as well as forms of control and management of the productive units—self-management reveals itself to be essential.

## The Latin American Historical Context

The Brazilian experiences with the solidarity economy, from the 1990s on, conquered some ground for the Latin American social movements, albeit in a defensive context. President Fernando Henrique Cardoso (1995–January 2003) deepened neoliberal capitalist voracity and its inherent financialization of the economy (Chesnais 1994, 2004), opening of commercial space, low growth, and productive restructuring processes (Toyotism). In the mid-1980s, Brazil lived through the "transition without ruptures" of the civil-military dictatorship and state reforms, which led to the reduction of certain social functions of the state, offensive actions against social and working rights, privatizations, and denationalizations. As a consequence, unemployment and structural subemployment were significantly increased.

From this standpoint, the RF phenomenon—which, in the 1980s, had been no more than a series of isolated experiences—was reignited with the crisis in production, especially within family-managed firms. In the 1990s, instances of factory takeovers increased significantly, with the number of such cases leveling off by the beginning of the twenty-first century.

The RFs might be, in one sense, a unique social phenomenon rooted in the previous experiences of the Latin American working-class and labor movement, wherein the traditional unions were unable to overcome the hegemony of financial capital and their struggles for contracts were largely thwarted. Self-management experiences have achieved a significant amount of social space since then, including the creation in 2003 of the SENAES (National Secretariat of Solidarity Economy) in the Ministry of Labor and Employment of Lula's government.[3]

---

3 Quantitatively speaking, the mapping of the solidarity economical companies by SENAES together with the Solidarity Economy Brazilian Forum found about one hundred fifty recovered companies out of the twenty-two thousand companies registered (SENAES 2005). To access the mapping data, visit Portal do Trabalho e Emprego, www.mte.gov.br/ecosolidaria/sies.asp.

In another sense, the RFs are the product of an anticapitalist "storm" in Latin America involving a wide range of popular rebellions: the struggles against the privatization of water, electricity, gas, and oil (primarily in Bolivia, Ecuador, and Venezuela); the *piqueteros* interdicting streets and highways to block the flow of commodities and traffic in Argentina; the Landless Workers' Movement's struggles against landlordism; the struggles against "minimum state" policies; and other movements against the privatization of national companies throughout Latin America.

### The Unions

Since the first self-managed enterprises emerged, the increase in their number has been followed by a modest opening of the unions to cooperativism and similar ideas. The union is usually the first institution workers call upon to step in as a legal representative, for instance, when a factory goes bankrupt. In such cases more and more workers were motivated to pursue self-management and comanagement experiences, as suggested by the unions.

This new approach was evident in the support unions gave to the creation of institutions specifically to promote the solidarity economy and self-management. In 1994, for example, the ANTEAG (National Association of Workers of Self-Managed and Stock Participation Companies) was established through a collaborative project initiated in 1991 between the shoe company Markeli, located in Franca (state of São Paulo), and the local unions. Among the recovered companies associated with ANTEAG are Catende Harmonia, Cooperminas, and fourteen others. RFs have more or less similar patterns of transformation, described in the section "Statistics and Generalizations." Catende Harmonia and Cooperminas are atypical in their size and longevity. The largest Brazilian union, CUT (Unified Workers Central) from the first moment supported the recovery of companies and also participated in the discussion around alternative job creation strategies. The first instances of this wave of self-management started to emerge in association with unions organized by CUT, in response to company closures. Workers needed a precise set of tactics for dealing with these situations. The most common union practice was, and still is, negotiating to guarantee that all workers receive their compensation, as well as trying to hold employers accountable to labor law and workers' rights. Until this period, union intervention in management represented a taboo to the union movement. It implied a redefinition of the division between employers and managers—those who make decisions about the productive units—and the unions—those who negotiate the hours of work and the workforce's value—and was seen as leading to a third type of unionism, beyond the "conciliation or countercharge" duality.

Faced with high rates of unemployment in Brazil's most important industrial belt, the ABC Paulista's Metallurgical Union (the greater São Paulo branch, which encompasses major cities including Santo André, São Bernardo do Campo, Diadema, and São Caetano) decided to support the creation of cooperatives in the area in order to retain the jobs of its members. In its second congress, in 1996, the union committed itself to the propagation of self-managed enterprises and cooperatives as alternative ways of creating jobs, thereby initiating historical changes in its relationship with its members—such as the understanding that the right to unionization also applied to the cooperative members in the metallurgical field (Oda 2001). Another significant development was the foundation of a partnership among the metallurgical union, the Lega delle Cooperative (Italy's largest cooperative federation), and three more large Italian union units, mainly from the Emilia Romagna region, in order to exchange information as well as to visit and observe practices.

In 1999, CUT created the ADS (Solidarity Development Agency). The ADS aims to provide credit and technical assistance for groups wishing to set up cooperatives. To do so, CUT signed an agreement with Sebrae, a public institution devoted to promoting entrepreneurship. The same year, the metallurgical cooperatives joined forces—with the union's help—to create UNISOL (Cooperatives Union and Solidarity). Initially active only in the state of São Paulo, UNISOL's mission was to organize and represent these constituents as well as to fight the "coopercats"—those who tried to use the cooperatives to damage labor relations—and to encourage the creation of genuine and authentic cooperatives. Soon UNISOL grew and spread nationally, leading to the creation of UNISOL Brazil, an institution that today includes about 280 cooperatives and affiliated associations, of which twenty-five are RFs. Although representing less than 10 percent of the total cooperatives affiliated with UNISOL, the recovered companies generate 75 percent of the total annual financial movement, about R$1 billion (US$535 million).

## Statistics and Overview

The RFs have been the subject of a great deal of research and statistical analysis. The main data comes from the SIES (Solidarity Economy Information System) and reveals that at least seventy solidarity economy enterprises can actually be categorized either as RFs or as second-degree organizations from recovered companies (SENAES 2007). A previous study (Faria 2005) found 65 such experiences involving 12,070 workers, including 4,000 from Catende Harmonia alone.[4]

---

4 SIES data is not very accurate regarding the RFs. It is known, though, that only forty-one enterprises are supported by representative bodies, sixteen by ANTEAG and twenty-five by UNISOL. The numbers cited in this chapter reflect a reduction made in response to the data collected about the main reason for the enterprise's creation.

The SIES data puts the total estimate of workers in these companies slightly lower, at ten thousand workers, most of whom are men. Their predominant legal form is the cooperative, and regional distribution finds most in the south or southeast of Brazil—the most industrialized areas of the country—and mainly in urban areas. The main economic sector is composed of industries (metallurgy, textile, shoe, glass and crystal, and ceramic), as well as mineral extraction and services.

Beyond quantification, field research carried out in 2005 with twenty-eight RF experiences in Brazil identified a self-management typology based on standards related to management, market, credit, technology, institutional forms of participation, and property (Tauile et al. 2005). Seven distinct types emerged, ranging from "socially desirable"—as in the case of self-managed workers—to "socially unacceptable," the "coop-ercats," or outsourced organizations. Research (Vieitez and Dal Ri 2001; Faria 2005; Novaes 2007; Henriques 2007) demonstrates the heterogeneous and contradictory nature of the cases under study and establishes a general portrait of the Brazilian experiences through the end of the 1990s, as detailed below:

a) Almost all RF experiences are the result of the recovery of a family business—bankruptcy or pre-bankruptcy; in many cases it is the result of an unsuccessful family succession process. It is not rare to find factories created in the early twentieth century that have machines more than fifty years old.

b) Usually these companies already carry a bulky passive labor force with them, and it is common for their workers to live through long periods of salary delay and denial of working and social rights that can last for months or even years.

c) When the closure of a production site cannot be avoided, workers organize to claim their rights. But when the owner withdraws, in some cases a new initiative emerges to keep the factory running.

d) In many cases, the union assumes the lead role in workers' organization, in the presentation and discussion of the possible ways to keep the company open, and in negotiation with the former owners, the public, and private bodies for financial support. Sometimes the union becomes co-responsible for managing these companies under workers' control.

e) It might occur that workers waive their working rights and contractual dismissal money in exchange for the companies' collective ownership of the means of production.

f) In most cases, they have opted for the cooperative form of organization, since previously there was no legal framework recognizing this specific, recent phenomenon in Brazil. Now it is possible for workers also to self-organize as limited companies or corporations.

g) Use of the term "self-management" is common, as it refers both to changes in the companies' form of ownership, and to the democratic/cooperative features of the organization and management. The experiences documented in Brazil usually maintained the prior division of work, with the main changes occurring in the division of salary, the distribution of surplus money, and the factory's decision-making process, which usually takes place through assemblies of all the workers.

h) In spite of identifiable changes in the division of remuneration, there are not many Brazilian experiences that opted for an egalitarian share. In Argentina, in contrast, the research coordinated by Ruggeri (2005) verified that 44 percent of the Argentinean factories chose remuneration equality.

i) The new self-management situation influences workers' motivation, at least for a certain period of time, and makes them more willing to perform their jobs with care and commitment.

j) In the RFs, the competitive strategy may include mechanisms such as the extension of unpaid working hours or even flexing the wage to respond to market changes. In other words, in the eventual impossibility of an investment in new technologies or a renovation of the existing technology, these companies may resort to specific mechanisms to make their economic processes happen.

k) There is a low level of "politicization" on the part of the workers regarding the need to unify the struggles of the working class with the construction of a society "beyond capital" (Mészáros 2002); this is more common among the leadership of factories that aim toward nationalization.

The following section presents a more detailed account of some of these Brazilian experiences in order to provide a better understanding of the potential, the contradictions, and the limits of the RF self-management processes.

## Special Cases: Cooperminas and the Catende Harmonia Project

Two cases serve to illustrate the potential and success of RFs in Brazil. The first is CBCA, known today as Cooperminas (located in Criciúma, state of Santa Catarina, in southern Brazil), whose struggle began in the mid-1980s and probably stands as the oldest of the RF experiences. The second is the

Catende Harmonia Project, which started in the 1990s and is surely the largest and most complex process of recovery of a bankrupted company in Brazil.

The original CBCA (Brazilian Coal Company of Araranguá) was founded in 1917 to extract coal in the city of Criciúma in Santa Catarina. Although it was one of the first RFs, the company's acquisition process is similar to almost all other cases in Brazil. In 1987, having had their salaries delayed for several months, the workers launched an active struggle to recover their working rights. CBCA then closed its doors. The workers organized to defend their jobs, initially requesting that the mine be nationalized. In the process, workers agreed to have the company reopen, with the Criciúma's Miners' Union as an assignee in bankruptcy. The company functioned in this way for ten years, until in 1997 an agreement was made between the workers and the former owners that led to the creation of Cooperminas.

Three aspects of this experience must be highlighted. First, during the initial recovery period, the workers had to struggle intensely to keep the mine under their control and avoid the auction of the property to pay its creditors. In one action, with the national press present, workers arrived at the mine with dynamite strapped to their own bodies to block the removal of equipment from the mine. The second aspect relates to the working conditions of the mine. Visits underground in 1992 and again in 2005 showed the vast improvements the CBCA miners had achieved in their working conditions. Ventilation, lighting, and safety improved, and new equipment had been acquired to reduce pollution in the mine's interior. The third aspect concerns the market. The mining cooperative has, as do the other miners in the region do, a coal share with a guaranteed purchase by the thermoelectric mills, which allows for a certain level of stability and makes long-term projection possible.

At the outset of the mine's self-management process, workers created new institutions with dual political and management features. The mine commission was elected by workers from each shift and was responsible for both political and strategic decisions, as well as contributing to the organization of the working process. The assemblies were massive and almost all the 1,200 miners participated. On occasion the general assembly substituted for the cooperative president; as well, in some instances the mine commission's members' mandates were revoked. As time passed, most of these collective decision-making entities were institutionally co-opted and functioned more as a top-down transmission belt.

This bureaucratic form of the participation in the mine engendered, foremost, passivity among the workers. The democratic differentiation of the cooperative process led to the emergence of a kind of a cooperative corporatism, causing the company to become more and more self-isolated. The lack of involvement on the part of Cooperminas miners in other labor struggles in the area and in the larger RF movement that followed in its footsteps is an indication of the workers' inactivity and the consolidation of bureaucratic processes.

The miners from Criciúma have a privileged situation with regard to the production flow—they sell their entire output to a large corporation in a guaranteed market. This arrangement has not resulted in better conditions for the company's progress toward self-management, however. On the contrary; given that the process has been ongoing for almost twenty-five years and the miners have an early retirement (after fifteen years), many of those who fought for the company have already retired, creating a division between the "new" and the "old" employees. The lack of a systematic process to promote self-management, as well as a lack of emphasis on their own company's history and struggles, has fostered an atmosphere of apathy toward the democratic processes that need workers' participation. Attendance at workers' assemblies is very low and the meetings are viewed as bureaucratic rituals. The mine commissions, over the course of time, have turned into spaces to legitimate the decisions made by the company's "technicians" and "managers." The function of the commissions, these days, seems mainly to be one of defusing internal conflicts and solving issues about the transference of the company's management.

The Catende Harmonia Project revolves around a sugar mill conglomerate created in 1892 out of the former Milagre da Conceição mill, built in 1829, and consists of forty-eight individual mills spread along twenty-six thousand hectares in Pernambuco's Zona da Mata Sul, covering five cities: Catende, Jaqueira, Palmares, Água Preta, and Xexéu. The sugar mill passed from owner to owner until the 1950s, when, under the control of "the lieutenant," Colonel Antônio Ferreira da Costa, it became the largest sugar mill in Latin America. Under "the lieutenant's" management, a railroad was built to transport the products, a hydroelectric plant constructed to ensure the energy supply, and the country's first anhydrous alcohol distillery was built as well.

By the end of the 1980s the mill was in crisis due to the closing of the IAA (Alcohol and Sugar Institute). The situation worsened in 1993, which saw 2,300 workers fired. This mass dismissal incited a struggle, with workers who lived in company houses on mill land refusing to leave their homes unless they got their working rights. The rural unions, supported by Contag (National Confederation of Agricultural Workers), CUT, and CPT (Pastoral Land Commission, the bishops of the Catholic Church), encouraged the struggle. In 1995, the company declared bankruptcy. The workers took over and started the Catende Harmonia Project. The company's debts were up to R$1.2 billion (US$ 642 million)—Bank of Brasil is the greatest creditor, with

R$480 million. The property is worth R$67 million (US$36 million), and the labor liabilities are worth R$62 million (US$33 million). In 1998, workers created one organization, the Agrícola Harmonia Company, to receive the former Catende Mill's property. In 2002, a group of peasants and land workers created a production cooperative, the Family Agriculturists Harmonia Cooperative. They were funded by creditors of the former company who live on the mill's lands. Overall, between agriculture and industry, the project involves about four thousand families, or about twenty thousand people. In addition to the forty-eight mills and the main sugar mill the property also includes the aforementioned hydroelectric plant, a pottery workshop, a carpentry workshop, a hospital, seven irrigation dams and channels, one vehicle fleet (tractors, trucks, etc.), and several "mansions," one of which was converted into an educational center.[5] In the first seven years of the project, the illiteracy rate among its members dropped from 82 percent to 16.7 percent.[6]

In contrast to the other sugar mills in the area, Catende Harmonia, from the start, could count on great involvement from its workers. After the struggle against layoffs and the company's bankruptcy, the workers began to construct the organization of Catende Harmonia.[7] The management structure was complex. The assignee in bankruptcy was nominated by a judge but chosen in a meeting of more than three thousand workers. The Catende Harmonia Management Council, about 120 workers in total, was composed of delegates from all forty-eight mills, including delegates from five rural units and delegates of the mill workers' council. Its function was to meet with the consultants and overseers on the executive committee and to lead the project. The collective deliberation process, when involving an important issue, usually went through debates in the mills and discussions in the management council until reaching the general assembly. This decision-making process ultimately required great effort, not least due to the precarious modes of communication (even today they use a radio to organize the mill's assemblies) and the vast costs involved in the transportation of four thousand producers.

There were also women's and youth associations. Many advisory institutions operated alongside the workers' organizations in the diversification

---

5 During the period of enslavement, masters lived at the mansions and enslaved people lived in shanties.

6 For a more in-depth view of sugarcane in the northeast of Brazil, we suggest the works of José Lins do Rego. Rego was a novelist of Brazil's Northeastern school, best known for his five-volume *Sugar Cane Cycle*. His books have been translated into multiple languages. See, for example, *Plantation Boy* (*Menino de engeho*, 1932).

7 After numerous legal battles, the workers "received" the twenty-six thousand hectares of land, but the sugar mill itself was not included and remained in bankruptcy.

of the agricultural production through polyculture. Workers even created the Harmonia Cooperative, which has as its main objective the organization of rural workers. In spite of the efforts toward workers' democratic organizing in Catende Harmonia, financial problems and the resulting inability to guarantee the continued existence of the plantation, the harvest, and the milling have been a major obstacle to the consolidation of a new political culture. This has led to setbacks in the organization of the rural workers and in their relations to the mill workers. It is important to recall that the previous mill owners encouraged the separation between field workers and plant workers, or between "field" and "city." This division was historically maintained by mill owners to avoid connections between the plant workers and peasants. With self-management in Catende Harmonia the division has lessened, as the management council includes representatives of both groups, but this new organizational form could not totally breach this separation.

The cooperative project also experienced resistance from some workers, largely due to previous use of the cooperative form to deteriorate labor relations and exploit workers from the northeast of Brazil. Even today the cooperative alternative is viewed with suspicion by a segment of workers in the project.[8] Nevertheless, the mechanisms and forms of participation exercised in Catende Harmonia have brought dramatic changes to the area and represent a great contrast to the other sugar-alcohol operations of the Brazilian northeast, many of which still show evidence of forced or even enslaved labor.

For what it has accomplished in terms of changes in the work relations and political culture, the Catende Harmonia Project goes beyond the mere recovery of a bankrupted company. It has brought an alternative form of economic, social, cultural, and political development to the state of Pernambuco's countryside. However, it is important to note that this project is qualitatively different from other RF experiences, especially regarding the agrarian reform's settlement projects, the result of maintaining the mill's land and facilities as social property belonging to all the project's participants. Thus, in the countryside, family agriculture and sugarcane crops cohabit on common land.

Finally, the conversion of production must be mentioned as part of the search for social technologies suitable to the self-management process. Catende Harmonia and the agrarian reform's settlement cooperative have initiated production diversification in the development of new products. One

---

8 Under the mill's former owner, at workers' "cooperatives" or sheds—essentially small grocery stores—workers were practically obliged to buy products that were overpriced and of bad quality. This arrangement is similar to the "truck system." To learn more about what "cooperative" means to mill workers, see Julião (1962 and 1972).

initiative is a small alcohol distillery for the agrarian reform's settlements and family farming communities. Another is the construction of small biodiesel engines, aiming at the rural communities' energy independence. These might be the first steps toward linking the solidarity economy businesses into an independent economic system, organized under criteria and principles of efficiency. Yet there is still a long way to go before the RFs are interlinked in a system that includes the self-management initiatives of other countries.

## Factories in Deadlock: The Quest for Nationalization

The three factories (Cipla, Flaskô, and Interfibras) that requested nationalization under workers' control did not receive a positive response from the government and had a difficult time existing. In these specific cases, the preference for "nationalization under workers' control" functions as a criticism of the cooperative form, which attempts to survive in the capitalist system. The precarious legal status of these companies and the lack of government support for their nationalization proposals have left these workers and their factories vulnerable to legal attacks, apart from the many difficulties they already had accessing credit and organizing workers' actions.

Notwithstanding the ideological component of the nationalization claim, the financial argument is also present. Nationalization is seen as a guarantee of advantageous energy supply from the state and of wage security in times of crisis. However, even when the struggle is for "nationalization under workers' control," the workers from these factories seem to underestimate the nature of the capitalist state, especially an authoritarian Latin American state that does not recognize self-managed companies. In addition, there is a great risk of bureaucratization, as evidenced by companies embraced by the state in the 1950s.

In these cases, the historical and theoretical mistake of seeking workers' emancipation solely through possessing the means of production is repeated, leaving the workers exploited by the state instead of by private employers. It is a very complicated scenario without many concomitant transformations: if the cooperatives and associations formed from RFs are deteriorating for having to compete in the capitalist system, the factories in deadlock have to face two terrible possibilities: the high probability of bureaucratization, embodying all the characteristics of the Latin American state (if they are indeed embraced by the state), or dissolution if they do not come up with a plan soon enough. In these cases, since the workers do not consider the creation of a cooperative to be a possible solution, the inability to secure financing, among other issues, will inevitably result in liquidation.

Perhaps the region's most fascinating case is the FaSinPat ("factory without a boss") cooperative at the ceramics factory Zanón in Argentina, which had aimed at nationalization but whose request wasn't accepted by the Kirchner government. The Zanón workers decided to confront the capitalist state and, at the same time, established new alliances with certain state entities (public universities, technical advice institutes, congressmen, and others), as well as other workers. They have recovered their formerly bureaucratized union and implemented the rotation of strategic functions, evoking the orientations of the 1969 Cordobazo such as class consciousness, the unification of class struggles, the importance of self-management, and overcoming Taylorist work practices (Aiziczon 2009; Novaes 2009; see also ch. 20 of this volume for an in-depth examination of the Zanón experience).

## Recovered Factories at a Crossroads

Although inserted into the commodity production system and therefore tending to reproduce the inherited work relations, the RFs have been capable of achieving some changes in the work process, mostly in the following categories: a) "software": cultural changes related to salary and surplus allocation: more egalitarian "compensation" (formerly salaries), more egalitarian or proportional disbursement (leftovers distributed at the end of the year), factories' partial accommodation of workers' interests (better working conditions), and knowledge appropriation regarding the productive process without changes in the division of labor; b) "orgware": knowledge appropriation of the productive process with changes in the division of labor; and c) "hardware": changes related to machinery acquisition, to adaptations, and to revitalization.

However, the RFs face countless obstacles, including the following: a) an extremely unfavorable, defensive context that stifles the growth of self-management in the aim of preventing the "contamination" of other workers in favor of the creation of a society "beyond capital"; b) a hostile environment—the market—that strangles the RFs' development; c) internal organizational problems, such as the absence of rotations, the bureaucratization of strategic decisions, and so on; d) the left-wing theoretical crisis (including how to view the RFs), leading to theoretical "patches," a mix of capitalist ideas and small reform pinches; e) difficulties accessing public policies; and f) the economic isolation between self-managed enterprises. As for this last item, the Portuguese Revolution of 1975–76 and Poland in the early 1980s created a "market of solidarity" and networks among self-managed enterprises, so there are precedents.

From an ideological point of view and in light of the left-wing theoretical crisis, it may be asserted that the RFs are far from being strong social movements or from crafting new and powerful alliances with other social movements. While aware of the resistance and constraints they face, they haven't yet written an anticapitalist manifesto.[9] In many cases, the members of the administrative bureaucracy, more and more entrenched in their strategic jobs, are content just to know how to operate the factory. Have they become the new bosses?

Despite the challenges and degeneration, however, there is no doubt that the very existence of numerous RFs (at least seventy in Brazil and two hundred in Argentina) represents an achievement that must be preserved and observed closely by workers. They might serve as an inspiration to dynamic capitalist sectors, which so far have been immune to self-management practices in their working processes.

In a country like Brazil, where the bourgeoisie has never been inclined to hand over anything at all, occupation experiences and the collective possession of the means of production of companies such as Catende Mill, CBCA, Uniforja, Fogões Geral, Cipla, Interfibras, and others cannot be ignored. It is also impossible to be indifferent after entering a factory like the former Botões Diamantina, now Cooperbotões, in Curitiba's industrial belt (in the state of Paraná, southern Brazil), and watching the factory workers handling all different matters themselves, with the CUT flag hanging in the conference room. At Cipla, one of the factories in deadlock, a new conference room was named the Ferreirinha room, in honor of an old metallurgical militant born close by.

Self-management is understood in this essay as a militant utopia, an organizational project that identifies the production process of the means of life as the key to transforming the society as a whole. Self-management—when necessary, combined with representative practices—aims to extend forms of pure democracy inside the company. It also demands that the fragmented and inferior condition of workers in the process of production be overcome. It means transcending, even if partially, their alienation and overcoming their economic exploitation and political oppression. The fragmentation of work activities is replaced by collective work and by workers' rotation in various types of jobs, so all participants get to know the steps of the productive process and are able to empathize with their fellow workers. An additional hope is that workers in self-managed companies would permit the rotation of tasks within the factory, as no one should be doomed to carry out only one kind of job for the rest of their lives.

---

9 Despite the fact that the entities representing the RFs have written chapters, organized books, and more, showing us their social projects, it is inaccurate to state that there is an anticapitalist theory to them. Even so, the differences between ANTEAG and UNISOL must be recognized. ANTEAG is older (1994), has a smaller structure, and organizes about sixteen RFs. UNISOL is newer, belongs to CUT—Brazil's largest union—and organizes about twenty-five RFs and some popular cooperatives created in the 2000s. To learn more about the differences between ANTEAG and UNISOL see Cruz 2006.

Ideally, in self-management, wage differences are abolished or, if they are continued, are decided among all the workers. The workers' previously inferior status is overcome by their participation in decisions about the company and its relation to society—including why, what, how much, and in what manner a certain product will be produced.

Self-management does not indicate the absence of discipline, although disciplinary guidelines and standards are decided collectively. Both standards and constitutions that govern the company's internal relations are not defined in advance, instead they are established according to the practical relations among the company's divisions, and participants must be open to following the changes in these relations.

In the internal sphere of work structure, self-management aims to reduce hierarchical stratification and achieve a leveling of relations. Self-managed factories must be open to cooperating with other social movements, especially those that also intend to take charge of their means of production. Thus the RFs may be a sort of "seismograph" charting the possibilities of overcoming the alienation of labor,[10] reuniting *homo faber* and *homo sapiens* (Gramsci 1977) in service of the decommodification of the society, building a class-free society with no state, and with an "associated producers' global control of the working process" (Mészáros 2002). In other words, the RFs foreshadow and present potential elements of what could be a superior form of production. In the meantime, such isolated cases have not been successful in overcoming the commoditized production system, a development that would require the unification of social movement struggles. Unfortunately, there is insufficient space to discuss this subject in the present chapter.

## Conclusion

The cooperatives and associations of production described here are practical experiences of workers' self-organization, aiming to the "positive transcendence of labour's self-alienation" (Mészáros 2002). Yet one might also conclude, from historical experience, that if the cooperatives and workers' associations isolate themselves from other social struggles, they will disappear or endure only painfully.

Rosa Luxemburg identified workers' cooperatives as hybrid forms, as they embody characteristics of conventional companies along with other features more typical of an emancipatory project. Alternatively, since hybrid beings cannot reproduce themselves and consequently neither can they

---

10 Alienation is understood as the loss of control over the products of one's labor, over the working process, over oneself and over human civilization (Marx 1982; Mészáros 2002; Antunes 2005).

flourish, perhaps the designation "amphibian" is preferable, as it describes a creature that lives in two different environments depending on its life stage. In that sense, the cooperatives of resistance, and among them some RFs, represent "nymph-stage amphibians" that will either flourish or decline depending on the historical process in which they evolve.

Last, it must be stated that the observation of the RFs and the factories in deadlock does not admit a binary analysis; the observation must document both the progress and the setbacks occurring in the factories' spheres, as well as noting the possible transformations of the phenomenon. However, it is important to recognize that, although the transformation of the form of ownership of the means of production might be significant, it has not yet overcome the exploitation and class oppression inherent to the capitalist productive social relations.

## References

Aiziczon, Fernando. 2009. *Zanón—una experiencia de lucha obrera.* Buenos Aires: Herramienta.

ANTEAG. 2004. *Autogestão em Avaliação—Ibase/Anteag.* São Paulo: Gráfica Yangraf.

Antunes, Ricardo. 2005. *O caracol e sua concha—ensaios sobre a nova morfologia do trabalho.* São Paulo: Boitempo Editorial.

_____., ed. 2007. *Riqueza e Miséria do Trabalho no Brasil.* São Paulo: Boitempo Editorial.

Bernardo, João. 1986. A autonomia das lutas operárias. In *Organização, trabalho e tecnologia,* ed. Lúcia O. Bruno and Cleusa Saccardo. São Paulo: Atlas.

_____. 2000. *Transnacionalização do capital e fragmentação dos trabalhadores—ainda há lugar para os sindicatos?* São Paulo: Boitempo Editorial.

_____. 2004. *Democracia totalitária: teoria e prática da empresa soberana.* São Paulo: Cortez.

Bertullo, Jorge Milton Silveira, Gabriel Ilveira, and Diego Castro. 2003. *El cooperativismo en Uruguay.* Montevideo: Unidad de Estudios Cooperativos, Universidad de la República.

Bruhat, Jean. 1952. *Histoire du mouvemente ouvrier français. Tome I—Des orígenes a la revolte des canuts.* Paris: Éditions Sociales.

Bruno, Lúcia O. 1986. *O que é autonomia operária?* São Paulo: Brasiliense.

Chesnais, François. 1994. *La Mondialisation du capital.* Paris: Syros.

Chesnais, François, ed. 2004. *La finance mondialisée. Racines sociales et politiques, configuration, conséquences.* Paris: Ed. La Découverte.

Cruz, Antônio. 2006. *A diferença da igualdade. A dinâmica econômica da economia solidária em quatro cidades do Mercosul.* Tese (Doutorado em Economia). Unicamp, Campinas.

Dagnino, Renato. 2008. *Neutralidade da ciência e determinismo tecnológico.* Campinas: Editora da Unicamp.

Faria, M. S. 1992. *Massa falida CBCA: proposta de leitura weberiana numa experiência de gestão operária.* Monografia de conclusão de curso de graduação em Administração. Florianópolis, UFSC.

_____. 1997. " . . . Se a coisa é por aí, que autogestão é essa . . . ?" *Um estudo da experiência "autogestionária" dos trabalhadores da Makerli Calçados.* Dissertação (Mestrado em Administração). Universidade Federal de Santa Catarina, Florianópolis.

_____. 2005. *Autogestão, Cooperativa, Economia Solidária: avatares do trabalho e do capital.*

Tese de doutorado. Florianópolis, UFSC, Sociologia Política, 2005.

Faria, M. S., R. Dagnino, and H. T. Novaes. 2008. Do fetichismo da organização e da tecnologia ao mimetismo tecnológico: os labirintos das fábricas recuperadas. *Review Katalysis*, May–June.

Gramsci, Antonio. 1977. *Selections from political writings*. London: Lawrence and Wishart.

Henriques, Flavio C. 2007. *Assessoria a empreendimentos de autogestão*. M.Sc. Universidade Federal do Rio de Janeiro, Instituto Alberto Luiz Coimbra de Pós-Graduação e Pesquisa em Engenharia. COPPE/UFRJ, Rio de Janeiro.

Holzmann, Lorena. 2001. *Operários sem patrão. Gestão cooperativa e dilemas da democracia.* São Carlos: Editora da UFS Car.

Julião, Francisco. 1962. *Que são as Ligas Camponesas?* Rio de Janeiro: Civilização Brasileira.

_____. 1972. *Cambao—the Yoke.* London: Penguin Books.

Kleiman, Fernando. 2008. *Lições de Catende—a construção de uma autogestão em Pernambuco.* São Paulo: Annablume.

Lebowitz, Michael A. 2005. Constructing co-management in Venezuela: contradictions along the path. *MRZine*, January 24. [Transcript of speech given in Caracas, Unión Nacional de Trabajadores, Encuentro Nacional de trabajadores hacia la recuperación de empresas.] http://mrzine.monthlyreview.org/lebowitz241005.html.

Lugon, Clovis. 1949. *La republique communiste chretienne des Guaranis (1610—1768).* Paris: Les Editions Ouvrieres.

_____. 2009. *A República Guarani.* São Paulo: Expressão Popular.

Luxemburg, Rosa. 1999. *Reforma ou revolução?* São Paulo: Expressão Popular.

Marx, Karl. 1987. *Manuscritos econômico-filosóficos e outros textos escolhidos.* São Paulo: Nova Cultural (Os Pensadores).

_____. 1988. *O capital: crítica da economia política*, vol. 1. São Paulo: Nova Cultural.

Meister, Albert. 1972. Quelques aspects historiques de l'associationnisme en France. In *Vers uni sociologie des associations*, ed. Albert Meister, 49–108. Paris: Les Editions Ouvrières.

Mészáros, István. 2002. *Para além do capital.* Campinas: Boitempo Editorial/Editora da Unicamp.

Moissonier, Maurice. 1988. *Les canuts: "Vivre en travaillant ou mourir en combattant."* Paris: Messidor/Éditions Sociales.

Nascimento, Cláudio. 2005. Do "Beco dos Sapos" aos canaviais de Catende. (Os "ciclos longos" das lutas autogestionárias). SENAES, April. www.mte.senaes.gov.br.

Novaes, Henrique T. 2007a. De tsunami a marola: uma breve história das fábricas recuperadas na América Latina. *Revista Lutas & Resistências*, no. 2: 84-97, Londrina.

_____. 2007b. *O Fetiche da Tecnologia—a experiência das Fábricas Recuperadas.* São Paulo: Expressão Popular-FAPESP.

_____. 2009. Renascendo das Cinzas? A relação das universidades argentinas com a "fábrica sem patrões" Zanón. Caracas, IV Encuentro de Jóvenes Investigadores, April.

_____. 2009. De Neuquén para o mundo—uma breve história dos bravos lutadores da FaSinPat Zanón. Passa Palavra. December 4. http://passapalavra.info/?p=15791.

Oda, N. T. 2001. Gestão e trabalho em cooperativas de produção: dilemas e alternativas à participação. Dissertação (Mestrado em Engenharia)—Universidade de São Paulo (USP), Escola Politécnica, São Paulo.

Péret, Benjamin. 1999. *La commune des Palmares—que fut le quilombo des Palmares ?* Paris: Editeur Syllepse.

Rude, Fernand. 1982. *Les revoltes des canuts (Novembre 1831–Avril 1834).* Paris: François Maspero.

Ruggeri, Andres, ed. 2009. *Las empresas recuperadas—autogestion obrera en Argentina y America Latina.* Buenos Aires: Editorial de la Facultad de Filosofia y Letras (Universidad de Buenos Aires).

SENAES. 2007. Mapping data. www.mte.gov.br/ecosolidaria/sies.asp.

Singer, Paul. 2002. A recente ressurreição da Economia Solidária. In *Produzir para viver, os ca-*

*minhos da produção não capitalista*, ed. B. Sousa Santos, 81–129. Rio de Janeiro: Civilização Brasileira.

Storch, S. 1985. Discussão da Participação dos Trabalhadores na Empresa. In *Processo e Relações de Trabalho no Brasil*, ed. Fleury, M. T. and R. M. Fischer. São Paulo: Ed. Atlas.

Tauile, José et al. 2005. Empreendimentos Autogestionários Provenientes de Massa Falida. Brasília: MTE/ IPEA/ANPEC/SENAES.

Tiriba, Lia. 2001. *Economia Popular e Cultura do Trabalho*. Ijuí: Ed. Unijuí.

Tragtenberg, Mauricio. 1986. *Reflexões sobre socialismo*. São Paulo: Moderna.

Vieitez, C. G. and N. Dal Ri. 2001. *Trabalho associado*. Rio de Janeiro: DP&A.

# Editor Biographies

© Tabore Rector

### Immanuel Ness

Immanuel Ness's research focuses on worker resistance and social movements, proletarianization, syndicalism, and migration. He recently completed *Guest Workers, Corporate Despotism and Labor Resistance* (University of Illinois Press, 2011). He is also working on a manuscript focusing on syndicalism and new forms of worker representation. His work includes *Immigrants, Unions, and the U.S. Labor Market* (Temple University Press) and *Trade Unions and the Betrayal of the Unemployed* (Garland, 1998). Ness has lectured throughout the world (Asia, Europe, North and South America) and at numerous academic conferences on low-wage worker organizing and immigrants. He is editor of the quarterly journal, *WorkingUSA: The Journal of Labor and Society*, published by Wiley-Blackwell Publishing. In 2005, his four-volume work *Encyclopedia of American Social Movements* was awarded Outstanding Reference Source by the Reference and User Services Association of the American Library Association. The work was selected as best reference for 2005 by *Library Journal*. He has received awards for his other reference works, including *Encyclopedia of Third Parties in America*. In 2009, he published the critically acclaimed, eight-volume, four-thousand-page *International Encyclopedia of Revolution and Protest: 1500 to Present*.

© Belinda Hernández

# Dario Azzellini

Dario Azzellini is a political scientist and lecturer at Johannes Kepler University in Linz, Austria, and a writer and documentary film director based in Berlin and Caracas. He holds a PhD in political sciences from the Goethe University in Frankfurt, Germany, and is finishing a PhD in sociology at the BUAP in Puebla, Mexico. His research and writing focus on social and revolutionary militancy, migration and racism, people's power and self-administration, workers' control, and Latin America. He served as associate editor for the *International Encyclopedia of Revolution and Protest: 1500 to the Present*, published by Wiley-Blackwell in 2009, and was primary editor for the sections on Latin America, the Spanish Caribbean, and the New Left in Italy. He serves as associate editor for *WorkingUSA: The Journal of Labor and Society* and for *Cuadernos de Marte,* an academic publication about war sociology published by the University of Buenos Aires. He has published several books, essays, and peer review articles, and has produced documentaries about social movements, privatization of military services, and migration and racism, covering Italy, Mexico, Nicaragua, Colombia, and Venezuela. Among his works is *The Business of War* (Assoziation A, 2002), a book about the privatization of military services, translated and published in Germany, Argentina, Bolivia, France, Indonesia, Italy, Spain, and Venezuela. Azzellini has been invited to speak at conferences in Europe, North America, South America, and Asia.

# Author Biographies

### Elaine Bernard

Elaine Bernard is the executive director of the Labor and Worklife Program and the Harvard Trade Union Program at Harvard Law School. Born and raised in Canada, Bernard has a BA from the University of Alberta, an MA from the University of British Columbia, and a PhD from Simon Fraser University. Her current research and teaching interests are in the areas of international comparative labor movements, union leadership, and governance, and the role of unions in promoting civil society, democracy, and economic growth.

### Alberto Bonnet

Alberto Bonnet holds a doctorate of social sciences from the BUAP (Mexico) and magister in economy and licentiate in philosophy from the University of Buenos Aires (Argentina). He is regularly an instructor and researcher at the UBA and at the University of Quilmes. These days his main interests include, on one hand, certain problems linked with the analysis of accumulation, domination, and social struggle in contemporary Argentina; and, on the other hand, more theoretical problems linked with the capitalist state and the class struggle. The author of several books and articles, he is currently completing an essay, "The Constellation of the Red Stars," on Marxism and workers' councils.

### Sheila Cohen

Sheila Cohen has been a trade union activist, educator, researcher, and writer for many years. From 1990 to 1995 she edited and distributed the rank-and-file trade union paper *Trade Union News* and organized a number of conferences and day schools with trade union activists. In 2006, her book *Ramparts of Resistance: Why Workers Lost Their Power, and How to Get It Back* was published by Pluto Press, and she has also produced a series of pamphlets and articles on the nature of work and trade unionism. She has been involved with the National Shop Stewards' Network and is employed with the Work and Employment Research Unit (WERU) at the University of Hertfordshire, UK.

## Patrick Cuninghame

Patrick Cuninghame is a lecturer in sociology and politics at the Universidad Autonoma Metropolitana in Mexico City. He is a member of the editorial board of *Argumentos* and *Societies without Borders* and an ISA-RC30 (Sociology of Work) executive committee member. He received a PhD in sociology from Middlesex University, London, in 2002 with a thesis on the Autonomia Operaia (Workers' Autonomy) movement in Italy in the 1970s. He was a member of the editorial committees of *Capital & Class* and *London Notes*, and has published articles in various languages on autonomous social movements in Britain, Italy, Mexico, and Latin America.

## Pietro Di Paola

Pietro Di Paola is a lecturer in history at the University of Lincoln (UK). His research interests include the history of anarchism, political diaspora, and contemporary social movements. In 1997 he graduated from the University of Venice with a thesis analyzing the experience of working-class autonomy in a factory in the industrial area of Porto Marghera (Venice) between 1969 and 1980. He obtained his PhD at Goldsmiths College, University of London, in 2004 with the dissertation *Italian Anarchists in London, 1870–1914*. His publications include *Breve storia dell'anarchia* (Rome: Carocci), "Il Biennio Rosso" in *The International Encyclopedia of Revolution and Protest*, edited by Immanuel Ness (Wiley-Blackwell Publishing, 2009); Rudolf Rocker, *Sindrome da filo spinato. Rapporto di un tedesco internato a Londra (1914–1918)*, edited by Pietro Di Paola (Caserta: Spartaco, 2006); Errico Malatesta, *Autobiografia mai scritta*, edited by Piero Brunello and Pietro Di Paola (Caserta: Spartaco, 2003); "Gli anarchici tra le due guerre" in *Guerre, anteguerra, dopoguerra. Il fascismo e la seconda guerra mondiale*, vol. II, edited by M. Isnenghi (Turin: UTET, 2008).

## Andy Durgan

Andy Durgan lives and works in Barcelona. He has published in various languages on different aspects of Spanish history, in particular relating to the civil war, its origins, and the labor movement. These include *B. O. C. 1930–1936: El Bloque Obrero y Campesino* (Barcelona: Laertes, 1996) and *The Spanish Civil War* (Basingstoke: Palgrave, 2007). He was historical advisor for the award-winning Ken Loach film *Land and Freedom* (1996) and a founding member of the Fundació Andreu Nin.

## Donny Gluckstein

Donny Gluckstein's previous books include *The Paris Commune: A Revolution in Democracy* (2006), *The Nazis, Capitalism and the Working Class* (1999), *The Tragedy of Bukharin* (1994), and *The Western Soviets: Workers' Councils versus Parliament, 1915–1920* (1985). He is the coauthor, with Tony Cliff, of *The Labour Party: A Marxist History* (1988) and *Marxism and Trade Union Struggle: The General Strike of 1926* (1986). Donny lectures in history in Edinburgh, Scotland. He is a trade union activist and member of his union's national executive. He is also a long-standing member of the Socialist Workers' Party (UK).

## Ralf Hoffrogge

Ralf Hoffrogge was born in northern Germany in 1980. He studied history, psychology, and political science at the Freie Universität Berlin. His studies focused on political economy, Marxist theory, and the history of social movements, especially the German students' movement in the former West Germany as well as German labor history; a second focus was the history of fascism and the Holocaust. For the academic year 2005–2006 he was granted a Fulbright and studied for two semesters at Washington University in St. Louis, Missouri. During his time at the Freie Universität, Hoffrogge was a student activist and organized campaigns against the privatization of the German educational system and published historical and political articles on educational issues. He was also elected to the student parliament at the university and served as vice chairman of the FU student council (AStA). In 2008 Hoffrogge finished his masters degree and his thesis was published as a monograph entitled *Richard Müller—Der Mann hinter der Novemberrevolution* (Richard Müller—the Man behind the German Revolution). Since 2009 Hoffrogge has been a PhD candidate at the University of Potsdam. He has received a scholarship from the Rosa Luxemburg Foundation to support his doctoral work. His PhD thesis will focus on the biography of Werner Scholem (1895–1940), a German-Jewish Communist active in the 1920s, who was one of the few German Communist officials to oppose the politics of Stalin as early as 1925.

## Marina Kabat

Marina Kabat holds a PhD in history and is a specialist in labor studies. A graduate of the University of Buenos Aires, Kabat serves as a researcher at the National Council of Scientific and Technical Research (CONICET), which conducts studies of industry, the organization of work, and labor conflicts from historical and contemporary contexts. She coordinates the CEICS (Center for Studies in Social Sciences), a leading social science research group in Argentina. Kabat is editor of *Razón y Revolución*, a Marxist journal. She is also the author of *Labour Process and Working Class in the Footwear Industry, 1880–1940* (Ediciones RyR, 2005) and has published numerous articles, including "Changes in the Work Organization of the Argentinean Footwear Industry" and "The Relative Surplus Population: An Obscure Marxist Conception of the Working Class." Kabat teaches at the University of Buenos Aires and has developed extensive outreach, focusing on training for teachers engaged in labor activism.

## Zbigniew Marcin Kowalewski

Zbigniew Marcin Kowalewski is a former researcher in the Polish Academy of Sciences; he is currently the assistant editor in chief of the Polish edition of *Le Monde Diplomatique*; an independent researcher in history, theories and strategies of labor, national liberation and revolutionary movements; and a militant of the workers' movement. In 1980–81 he was a regional leader of the trade union Solidarity in a large industrial center and a national leader of the movement for workers' self-management. He has spoken and written extensively about this experience, including a book, *Rendez-nous nos usines! Solidarnosc dans le combat pour l'autogestion ouvrière* (La Brèche: Paris, 1985); and an interview (C. Phelps, "Solidarnosc in Lodz: An Interview with Zbigniew Marcin Kowalewski"), which appeared in *International Labor and Working-Class History* (no. 73, Spring 2008).

## David Mandel

David Mandel teaches political science at the Université du Québec à Montréal, where he specializes in the Soviet Union and its successor states. His main research interest has been that region's working class, its history, and its contemporary situation. He is a longtime union and left political activist in Canada, as well as in Russia and Ukraine, where he cofounded the School for Worker Democracy. Among his publications on workers are *Labour After Communism: Autoworkers and Their Unions in Russia, Ukraine and Belarus* (Montreal: Black Rose Books, 2004); *Rabotyagi: Perestroika and After, the View from Below* (New York: Monthly Review Press, 1993); *Perestroika and Soviet Society: Rebirth of the Soviet Labour Movement* (Montreal: Black Rose Books, 1991); *The Petrograd Workers and the Soviet Seizure of Power* (London: Macmillan Press, 1984); *The Petrograd Workers and the Fall of the Old Regime* (London: Macmillan Press, 1983).

## Goran Music

Goran Music studied international trade in the economics faculty at the University of Belgrade, where he was active in various grassroots initiatives for labor and student rights. In 2007 he defended a double MA thesis in global history at the University of Vienna and University of Leipzig on the comparative analysis of the 1968 movements in Belgrade and Mexico City. He is currently researching the Yugoslav labor movement in the decade preceding the breakup of the country as part of the PhD program at the European University Institute in Florence, and collaborating on a project tracing the development of hip-hop culture in Serbia.

## Henrique T. Novaes

Henrique T. Novaes graduated in economic science at São Paulo State University (UNESP). He earned his masters degree at the State University of Campinas (Unicamp) in Brazil, where he conducted research on Latin American recovered factories and the history of workers' self-management of factories and of agrarian class struggles. He is currently completing his PhD program at Unicamp, where his dissertation examines the relationship between the university and Latin American social movements. Novaes is author of the book *The Fetish of Technology: the Experience of Recovered Factories* (Expressão Popular-FAPESP, 2007).

## Peter Robinson

Peter Robinson was an active socialist in Britain building support for the Portuguese Revolution. He traveled to Portugal in the summer of 1975 and worked as a political organizer in Lisbon with revolutionary left and workers' organizations from October 1975 to June 1976. He returned to Portugal in the late 1970s and mid-1980s to conduct research, especially through interviewing activists. He holds an M Phil from the Centre for Sociology and Social University, Open University. He is author of "Portugal 1974–75: The Forgotten Dream," *Socialist History Society,* Occasional Papers, no. 9, and "Portugal 1974–75," in *Revolutionary Rehearsals,* edited by Colin Baker.

# Maurício Sardá de Faria

Maurício Sardá de Faria is a professor of sociology at Federal University of Pariba in Brazil and holds a PhD in political sociology from the Federal University of Santa Catarina, where he studied labor and work. He is the director of the National Secretariat of Solidarity Economy (SENAES) at the Ministry of Labour and Employment of Brazil.

# Gabriela Scodeller

Gabriela Scodeller received a PhD in history from the National University of La Plata, Argentina. She carried out research at the Gino Germani Institute of the University of Buenos Aires. She teaches at the National University of Cuyo, Mendoza, specializing in the history of the Argentine labor movement. Scodeller's work currently focuses on workers' consciousness and intra-class struggles as a constituting element in the processes of class formation. Her recent publications include "Praxis and the Workers' Movement," *Revista Utopía y Praxis Latinoamericana*; "Labour Struggles in Argentinas' Recent History: A Standpoint," *A Contracorriente*; and "Workers' Consciousness: Notes for a Historical Approach," *Revista Austral de Ciencias Sociales*.

# Arup Kumar Sen

Arup Kumar Sen is assistant professor in the Department of Commerce, Serampore College, West Bengal, India. He completed his PhD in the Department of Business Management at the University of Calcutta. His special area of research interest is labor history; his PhD topic was "A Study of Labour Management Relations in Select Industries in Eastern and Western India: 1918–39." Dr. Sen is a regular contributor to the Indian left publication *Economic & Political Weekly* as well as to *Mainstream*. His current research and writing focus on land acquisition, the deterioration of peasant life (de-peasantization), and the growth of state violence in the Indian state of West Bengal.

# Samuel J. Southgate

Samuel J. Southgate is a PhD candidate in political science at Yale University. He recently completed a masters degree with distinction in Middle Eastern studies at the School of Oriental and African Studies, London, where he wrote his dissertation on the relationship between nationalist and Islamist movements and ideologies in Algeria, Lebanon, and Palestine. His research interests include North African history, social movements and contentious politics, Islamism, and theories of nationalism. Southgate was a journalist in the UK and a branch officer of the National Union of Journalists.

## Jafar Suryomenggolo

Jafar Suryomenggolo is a research fellow at the Center for Southeast Asian Studies, Kyoto University, Japan. His doctoral thesis examines the history of the Indonesian labor movement during the revolution. His publications include "Labour Law without 'Rights' in Indonesia: The Making of Un-dang-Undang Kerdja 1948," *International Journal of Comparative Labour Law and Industrial Relations* 25, no. 4 (2009); "Early Years of Serikat Buruh Kereta Api (Railway Workers Union): Formation and Orientation," *Tounan Ajia Kenkyu* 45, no. 4 (2008); and "Labour, Politics and the Law: A Legal-Political Analysis of Labour Law Reform Program," *Labour and Management in Development* 9 (2008).

## Alan Tuckman

Dr. Alan Tuckman is a senior lecturer in human resource management at Nottingham Trent University. His research focuses on work, employment, and society, including the construction, chemical, and automobile industries, and most recently within a call center. His work includes the analysis of factory occupations, strikes, and sociology of organizations, time studies, working-class agency, and working-class consciousness. He is author of: "Defying Extinction? The Revival of the Strike in UK Employment Relations," *WorkingUSA: The Journal of Labor and Society*, September 2010.

## Victor Wallis

Victor Wallis teaches in the liberal arts department at the Berklee College of Music and is the managing editor of *Socialism and Democracy*. He previously taught political science for many years at Indiana University-Purdue University at Indianapolis. He first encountered worker-control issues in the context of the aborted Chilean revolution of 1970–73. His articles—encompassing an array of subjects including ecology, political strategies, the U.S. left, and Latin American revolutionary film—have appeared in *Monthly Review, Capitalism Nature Socialism, New Political Science, Socialism and Democracy, Jump Cut, Organization & Environment,* and the *Historisch-Kritisches Wörterbuch des Marxismus;* his writings on ecological socialism have been translated into nine languages.

# Index

# Also from Haymarket Books

### Class Struggle and Resistance in Africa

Edited by Leo Zeilig • "This fascinating book fills a vacuum that has weakened the believers in Marxist resistance in Africa," writes Joseph Iranola Akinlaja, general secretary of the National Union of Petroleum and Natural Gas Workers, Nigeria. This collection of essays and interviews studies class struggle and social empowerment on the African continent. ISBN: 978-1-931859-68-4

### Fields of Resistance: The Struggle of Florida's Farmworkers for Justice

Silvia Giagnoni • In Immokalee, Florida, the tomato capital of the world, farmworkers organized themselves into the Coalition of Immokalee Workers and launched a nationwide campaign that forced McDonald's, Burger King, and Taco Bell to recognize their demands for workers' rights. ISBN: 978-1-60846-093-9

### The Labor Wars: From the Molly Maguires to the Sit-Downs

Sidney Lens • The rise of the American labor movement was characterized by bloody and revolutionary battles. From the first famous martyrs, the Molly Maguires in the Pennsylvania coalfields in the nineteenth century, to the crucial workers' victory of the 1930s in the sit-down strikes against General Motors, it has a history of pitched battles that frequently erupted into open warfare. ISBN: 978-1-931859-70-7

### The Lean Years and The Turbulent Years
### Histories of the American Worker, 1920–1941

Irving Bernstein, introduction by Frances Fox Piven • This two-volume history compiles a meticulous study of the lives and struggles of workers from the "roaring" twenties to the Great Depression of the thirties. Bernstein's account relates both the trajectory from industrialization to mass strike waves for industrial unionism and the ingredients for the shifting consciousness that made millions fight back. *Lean Years* ISBN: 978-1-60846-063-2; *Turbulent Years* ISBN: 978-1-60846-064-9

### Live Working or Die Fighting: How the Working Class Went Global

Paul Mason • The stories in this book come to life through the voices of remarkable individuals: child laborers in Dickensian England, visionary women on Parisian barricades, gun-toting railway strikers in America's Wild West, and beer-swilling German metalworkers who tried to stop the First World War. It is a story of urban slums, self-help cooperatives, choirs and brass bands, free love, and self-education by candlelight. *Live Working or Die Fighting* celebrates a common history of defiance, idealism, and self-sacrifice, one as alive and active today as it was two hundred years ago. It is a unique and inspirational book. ISBN: 978-1-60846-070-0

### The Paris Commune: A Revolution in Democracy

Donny Gluckstein • When Parisian workers established the world's first workers' democracy, there were no blueprints for the society they might build. This detailed study examines their brief experiment in collective social, economic, and political equality, with attention to the historic problems of the commune, critical debates over its implications, and the lingering inspiration of the glimpse of a better world its history provides. ISBN: 978-1-60846-118-9

### The Political Economy of Racism

Melvin Leiman • "An intense and compact resource for understanding how the political economy of racism evolved in the United States" (*Science & Society*). Racism is about more than individual prejudice. And it is hardly the relic of a past era. This scholarly, readable, and provocative book shows how the persistence of racism in America relies on the changing interests of those who hold the real power in society and use every possible means to hold onto it. ISBN: 978-1-60846-066-3

### Revolution in Seattle: A Memoir

Harvey O'Connor • Celebrated labor journalist Harvey O'Connor captures the courage and defiance of workers on the march against the carnage of the First World War and the dramatic inequality that marked the era. In particular, O'Connor's remembrances of the Seattle General Strike of 1919—the first in the nation—showcase his abiding faith in the potential of working people to transform society, and illuminate the vibrancy and militancy of the early American labor movement. ISBN: 978-1-931859-74-5

### Sin Patrón: Stories from Argentina's Worker-Run Factories

lavaca collective, foreword by Naomi Klein and Avi Lewis • The worker-run factories of Argentina offer an inspirational example of a struggle for social change that has achieved a real victory against corporate globalization. *Sin Patrón* lets the workers themselves tell their stories. ISBN: 978-1-931859-43-1

### Subterranean Fire: A History
### of Working-Class Radicalism in the United States

Sharon Smith • Workers in the United States have a rich tradition of fighting back and achieving gains previously thought unthinkable, from the weekend to health care to the right to even form a union. Smith shows how a return to the fighting traditions of US labor history, with their emphasis on rank-and-file strategies for change, can turn around the modern labor movement. ISBN: 978-1-931859-23-3

## About Haymarket Books

Haymarket Books is a nonprofit, progressive book distributor and publisher, a project of the Center for Economic Research and Social Change. We believe that activists need to take ideas, history, and politics into the many struggles for social justice today. Learning the lessons of past victories, as well as defeats, can arm a new generation of fighters for a better world. As Karl Marx said, "The philosophers have merely interpreted the world; the point, however, is to change it."

We take inspiration and courage from our namesakes, the Haymarket Martyrs, who gave their lives fighting for a better world. Their 1886 struggle for the eight-hour day, which gave us May Day, the international workers' holiday, reminds workers around the world that ordinary people can organize and struggle for their own liberation. These struggles continue today across the globe—struggles against oppression, exploitation, hunger, and poverty.

It was August Spies, one of the Martyrs targeted for being an immigrant and an anarchist, who predicted the battles being fought to this day. "If you think that by hanging us you can stamp out the labor movement," Spies told the judge, "then hang us. Here you will tread upon a spark, but here, and there, and behind you, and in front of you, and everywhere, the flames will blaze up. It is a subterranean fire. You cannot put it out. The ground is on fire upon which you stand."

We could not succeed in our publishing efforts without the generous financial support of our readers. Many people contribute to our project through the Haymarket Sustainers program, where donors receive free books in return for their monetary support. If you would like to be a part of this program, please contact us at info@haymarketbooks.org.

Order these titles and more online at www.haymarketbooks.org or call 773-583-7884.